PEARSON   ALWAYS LEARNING

D0222885

Anthony Falikowski
Sheridan College Institute of Technology and Advanced Learning

Mastering Human Relations

Fifth Edition

Taken from:
Mastering Human Relations, Fourth Edition
by Anthony Falikowski

Cover Art: Courtesy of Laughing Stock/Corbis Images.

Taken from:

Mastering Human Relations, Fourth Edition
by Anthony Falikowski
Copyright © 2007, 2002, 1999, 1996 by Pearson Education, Inc.
Published by Pearson Canada
Toronto, Ontario

Pearson Learning Solutions, 501 Boylston Street, Suite 900, Boston, MA 02116
A Pearson Education Company
www.pearsoned.com

Printed in the United States of America

1 2 3 4 5 6 7 8 9 10 V011 17 16 15 14 13 12

000200010271286296

LF/CK

ISBN 10: 1-256-83911-6
ISBN 13: 978-1-256-83911-8

Dedicated with love to Michael, Heather, Michelle and Pamela, those who have given me joy and pleasure beyond measure!

About the Author

Dr. Anthony Falikowski, better known to his students as Tony, is an internationally published author and professor at Sheridan College Institute of Technology and Advanced Learning in Oakville, Ontario. A graduate of the University of Toronto, he has taught courses in psychology, philosophy, and human relations for over three decades. Tony is Reality Therapy Certified, a certified philosophical practitioner, and a qualified MBTI personality type analyst, having conducted behavioural training and development workshops for schools and organizations in both Canada and the United States. In addition to also holding a certificate in Enneagram Psychology studies from Loyola University in Chicago, he has been listed in *Who's Who in the Humanities* and in *Profiles in Business and Management: An International Directory of Scholars and Their Research*, published by the Harvard Business School.

For fun, Tony enjoys biking, hockey, travelling, music, the outdoors, playing guitar, watching comedy shows, and dining out with family.

Part I   Personal Dimensions of Human Relations Mastery ... 2

Chapter 1   Starting with Self and Person Perception ... 2

Chapter 2   Understanding and Communicating with Different Personality Types ... 44

Chapter 3   Morals, Manners, and Attitude Adjustments for Effective Human Relations ... 82

Chapter 4   Psycho-Logical Defensiveness: Unconscious and Irrational Factors in Interpersonal Communication ... 120

Chapter 5   Motivation and Emotion in Human Relations ... 172

Chapter 6   Stress and Lifestyle Management: Good News for Jitterbugs and Adrenalin Junkies ... 228

Chapter 7   Cultivating Character, Meaning and Purpose in Life ... 268

Part II   Social and Interpersonal Dimensions of Human Relations Mastery ... 316

Chapter 8   Games People Play: Better Relationships Through Transactional Analysis ... 316

Chapter 9   Gender, Culture and Nonverbal Cues in Communication ... 358

Chapter 10   How to Resolve Conflicts ... 412

Chapter 11   Leadership Skills Development ... 444

Appendix
Progress Check Answers ... 475
Index ... 487

Preface and Introduction to the Fifth Edition ... xiii
Acknowledgements ... xxiv

Part I Personal Dimensions of Human Relations Mastery ... 2

Chapter 1 Starting with Self and Person Perception ... 2

The Self ... 4
Self-Diagnostic 1.1
What's My Self-Concept? ... 5

Application Exercise 1.1
Be the Star That You Are ... 13

Perception ... 20
Application Exercise 1.2
May I Have the First Section, Please? ... 25

Perceptual Errors ... 27
How to Reduce Errors in Perception ... 33
Perceptual Influences on Interpersonal Attraction ... 34
Study Guide ... 37
Key Terms ... 37
Progress Check 1.1 ... 37
Summary ... 39
Related Readings ... 43

Chapter 2 Understanding and Communicating with Different Personality Types ... 44

Who Am I? ... 46
Self Diagnostic 2.1
Pinpointing My Personality Preferences ... 48

Personality Types: Recognizable Patterns of Diversity ... 51
Reflection Poem
Please Understand Me ... 53

Application Exercise 2.1
Working in Your Wrong Hand ... 57

Type Classifications ... 69
Application Exercise 2.2
Classroom Chemistry ... 71

Application Exercise 2.3
TV Types Have Different Stripes ... 73

Guidelines for the Proper Application of Psychological Type ... 74

Contents

Study Guide ... 77
Key Terms ... 77
Progress Check 2.1 ... 77
Summary ... 79
Related Readings ... 80

Chapter 3 **Morals, Manners, and Attitude Adjustments for Effective Human Relations ... 82**

Self Diagnostic 3.1
How Assertive Am I? ... 84

Character Is Destiny ... 84
Attitude Adjustments for Effective Human Relations ... 86
Morals and Virtues for Character Development and Interpersonal Communications ... 96
Mind your Manners ... 106
Application Exercise 3.1
Tacky Use of Technology ... 109

Study Guide ... 114
Key Terms ... 114
Progress Check 3.1 ... 114
Summary ... 117
Related Readings ... 119

Chapter 4 **Psycho-Logical Defensiveness:**
Unconscious and Irrational Factors in Interpersonal Communication ... 120

"Psycho-Logical" Defensiveness Can Be Offensive to Others ... 122
Self Diagnostic 4.1
How Defensive Am I? ... 122

Unconscious and Irrational Defensiveness ... 124
Application Exercise 4.1
Dream Work ... 127

PSYCHO-logical Defence Mechanisms ... 127
Reflection Poem
A Poison Tree ... 136

Defence Mechanisms in Summary ... 145
Application Exercise 4.2
Name the Defence Mechanism ... 146

Application Exercise 4.3
Dealing with Defensiveness ... 147

Thinking Straight Can Help You Relate ... 148
Self Diagnostic 4.2
How Reasonable Am I? ... 149

Fallacies and Psycho-LOGICAL Defensiveness ... 149

Application Exercise 4.4
Identify the Fallacy ... 162

Study Guide ... 164
Key Terms ... 164
Progress Check 4.1 ... 164
Summary ... 166
Related Readings ... 170

Chapter 5 | **Motivation and Emotion in Human Relations** ... 172

Motivational Mysteries ... 174
The Nature of Motivation ... 175
Theories of Motivation: What Makes Me Tick? ... 177
Self Diagnostic 5.1
Internal Control Index ... 178

Application Exercise 5.1
Picture, Picture in the Book ... 192

Application Exercise 5.2
The TBWA—Total Behaviour and Wants Analysis ... 200

Emotions and Emotional Intelligence ... 204
Study Guide ... 222
Key Terms ... 222
Progress Check 5.1 ... 223
Summary ... 225
Related Readings ... 226

Chapter 6 | **Stress and Lifestyle Management:**
Good News for Jitterbugs and Adrenalin Junkies ... 228

Stressed Out About School? ... 230
The Nature of Stress ... 230
Understanding Stress in Terms of Stressors ... 231
Stress As a Response: General Adaptation Syndrome (GAS) ... 236
Showcase Profile
Hans Selye ... 237

Self Diagnostic 6.1
Stress...Let Me Sum It Up! ... 240

Distress Versus Eustress ... 242
Stress as an Interaction ... 243
Ways to Cope with Stress: Effective and Ineffective Strategies ... 246
Self Diagnostic 6.2
How Is My Current Thinking Contributing to My Personal Stress? ... 255

Application Exercise 6.1
Practice in Cognitive Coping ... 257

Application Exercise 6.2
Achieving Calm Through Focused Attention ... 259

Study Guide ... 263
Key Terms ... 263

Contents

Progress Check 6.1 ... 263
Summary ... 265
Related Readings ... 267

Chapter 7 **Cultivating Character, Meaning and Purpose in Life** ... 268

The Self and Self-Transcendence ... 270
The Enneagram: A Path to Personal Liberation ... 272
Self Diagnostic 7.1
What's My Enneagram Type? ... 275

Application Exercise 7.1
Self-Expressions ... 288

Life...and May I Ask, What's the Meaning of This? ... 290
The Heroic Journey: Living Based on Archetypal Psychology ... 297
Self Diagnostic 7.2
What Kind of Hero Are You, Anyway? ... 302

Application Exercise 7.2
My Life Story Is a Heroic Myth ... 307

Study Guide ... 310
Key Terms ... 310
Progress Check 7.1 ... 310
Summary ... 312
Related Readings ... 314

Part II **Social and Interpersonal Dimensions of Human Relations Mastery** ... 316

Chapter 8 **Games People Play:**
Better Relationships Through Transactional Analysis ... 316

Transactional Analysis ... 318
Showcase Profile
Eric Berne ... 319

Self Diagnostic 8.1
What's My Dominant Ego State? ... 319

Showcase Profile
Wilder Graves Penfield ... 324

Application Exercise 8.1
Exploring Your Ego States ... 329

Types of Transactions ... 330
Strokes ... 335
Life Positions ... 337
Games ... 340
Roles Played in Psychological Games ... 346
How to Break Up Psychological Games ... 347
Application Exercise 8.2
Ego States and the Effective Memorandum ... 349

Application Exercise 8.3
Events and Ego-State Reactions ... 350

Study Guide ... 352
Key Terms ... 352
Progress Check 8.1 ... 352
Summary ... 355
Related Readings ... 356

Chapter 9 **Gender, Culture and Nonverbal Cues in Communication** ... 358

Reflection Poem
Coming and Going ... 360

Gender Communications: He Said, She Said ... 361
Application Exercise 9.1
Dad or Joe: Who Should Go? ... 362

Culture and Communication: Inside Looking Out, Outside Looking In ... 369
Point of View
Art of Communication Is as Varied as the World's Culture ... 378

Nonverbal Communication: You Don't Say! ... 379
Application Exercise 9.2
Don't Talk to Me! ... 381

Application Exercise 9.3
Clothes Talk ... 389

Self Diagnostic 9.1
How Tactile Are You? ... 403

Study Guide ... 405
Key Terms ... 405
Progress Check 9.1 ... 405
Summary ... 408
Related Readings ... 410

Chapter 10 **How to Resolve Conflicts** ... 412

The Experience of Conflict ... 414
The Nature of Conflict ... 414
Reflection Poem
The Six Men of Indostan ... 415

Types of Conflict ... 417
Reflection Poem
Conflict Resolutions for Life ... 419

Benefits of Conflict ... 420
Psychological Orientations to Conflict ... 421
Application Exercise 10.1
My Personal Experience of Conflict ... 426

Conflict Management Styles ... 426
Self Diagnostic 10.1
What's My Conflict Management Style? ... 428

Application Exercise 10.2
Pick the Most Appropriate Conflict Resolution Style ... 433

Win-Win Conflict Resolutions ... 433
Symptoms of Inner Peace ... 437
Application Exercise 10.3
Type Tips for Conflict Resolutions ... 437

Study Guide ... 440
Key Terms ... 440
Progress Check 10.1 ... 440
Summary ... 442
Related Readings ... 443

Chapter 11   Leadership Skills Development ... 444

Life and Leadership ... 446
Application Exercise 11.1
Take Me to Your Leader ... 448

Approaches to Leadership ... 450
Application Exercise 11.2
Boss-Behaviour Analysis ... 453

Application Exercise 11.3
Following the Leader at Camp Athabasca ... 458

Self Diagnostic 11.1
Assessing Your Leadership Temperament ... 460

Study Guide ... 470
Key Terms ... 470
Progress Check 11.1 ... 470
Summary ... 472
Related Readings ... 474

Appendix Progress Check Answers ... 475
References ... 480
Index ... 487
Photo Credits ... 496

Preface and Introduction to the Fifth Edition

Personal growth without interpersonal communication is empty,
Interpersonal communication without personal growth is blind.

The first edition of *Mastering Human Relations* was initially written to facilitate the personal growth of students while at the same time helping them develop many of the "people skills" that are so important to anyone's success in life. I came to understand from letters and personal contacts that employers were increasingly demanding that post-secondary institutions produce graduates with good oral and interpersonal communication skills. I appreciated the fact that specialized knowledge and practical skills training alone—though surely important for career advancement—were not sufficient to enable individuals to maximize their potential or vocational dreams. Employers typically seek mature, responsible and well-adjusted people who are confident, enthusiastic, friendly, motivated, and socially polished. Much to the chagrin of some highly intelligent and skilled individuals, landing a job is sometimes more about self-presentation and the ability to communicate well and get along with others in teams than it is about qualifications and expert knowledge. Many times I've witnessed candidates with fewer credentials get chosen for jobs over more highly qualified individuals primarily because the former were better able to work with people and because, therefore, they displayed greater leadership potential. It was with this in mind that the first edition of *Mastering Human Relations* was written.

In the years that have passed since the book was first released, I have been immensely gratified by all those who have read it and told me that they have greatly enjoyed it and personally benefited by its use. Inspired by this, I have already written second, third, and fourth editions that were well received. In this, the Fifth Edition, I include a new chapter entitled: "Morals, Manners, and Attitude Adjustments for Effective Human Relations." Students will learn how matters of ethics and etiquette are essential to getting along with others and functioning in a professional and responsible way. I have also combined previous Chapters Two and Three to produce a more efficient treatment of psychological type and its impact on communication dynamics.

To help develop the "people skills" so important to students' futures, we will be examining in this text a number of psycho-social variables that influence the process of interpersonal communication. If you look at the figure entitled, "Communication Dynamics," you'll see a number of significant factors labelled within what has by now become a familiar model of communication. The standard model includes the following elements: sender, receiver, message, channel, noise, encoding and decoding. In this book, we will flesh out each one of these basic elements in some detail. For example, rather than discuss sender-receiver transactions in a purely abstract fashion, we will explore how personality type, individual motivation, temperament, ego-states, gender, and self-concept all influence the functions of encoding and decoding messages. Senders and receivers are not abstract entities, but real persons influenced by psychodynamic processes that must be understood if the process of communication is to be properly understood. In fleshing out the communication model, we will also see how messages can be sent by different channels and how they can be expressed in a variety of modes—verbal, non-verbal, surface and ulterior—depending on the intentions and behavioural cues exhibited by the communicator. "Noise," too, will be one of our concerns. Interpersonal communication often gets bogged down not only by environmental factors (e.g., heat, loud construction work) but also by psychological interference. In this text we will see how things such as conflict, stress, irrationality, defensiveness and psychological game-playing all get in the way of productive dialogue.

Though this text tends to focus more on the psychology of interpersonal relations, we will not forget how cultural and organizational factors impact on communication dynamics as well. For instance, we learn how ethnic, linguistic and organizational variables such as leadership influence the nature and purpose of communication, and how human relations are affected by them.

In this revision, the organization of the text is divided into two main parts. Part 1, which comprises seven chapters in total, is entitled: *"Personal Dimensions of Human Relations Mastery."* As the title suggests, the first part deals with matters pertaining to the individual and their impact on the communication process. In Chapter 1 we begin with the self and person perception. Where better to start our journey to human relations mastery than with oneself and one's perception of the world and others. Chapter 1 invites students to look at themselves, explore their self-concepts, reflect on matters of self-esteem, and determine whether, when, and/or how much self-disclosure is appropriate. Students are also asked to investigate matters of person perception and how personal factors can influence how others are seen. Previous users of the book will notice the inclusion of a new self-diagnostic in Chapter 1 entitled "What's My Self-Concept?". Not only will this tool enable students to gain in self-knowledge, but it will also prove useful in enhancing their self-esteem.

Still on the subject of the self, and given the current era of electronic communications, the Fifth Edition now includes a new section on "Self-Presentation and Your On-Line Persona." Students learn about impression management not only in real-life person-to-person communications, but also as it relates to how one presents oneself and is perceived by others on the Internet. Suggestions are offered as to how one might manage a favourable impression through such things as homepages, email addresses, and *emoticons*. Another exciting new element in Chapter 1 deals with perceptual influences on interpersonal attraction. The information presented here should help students

Communication Dynamics

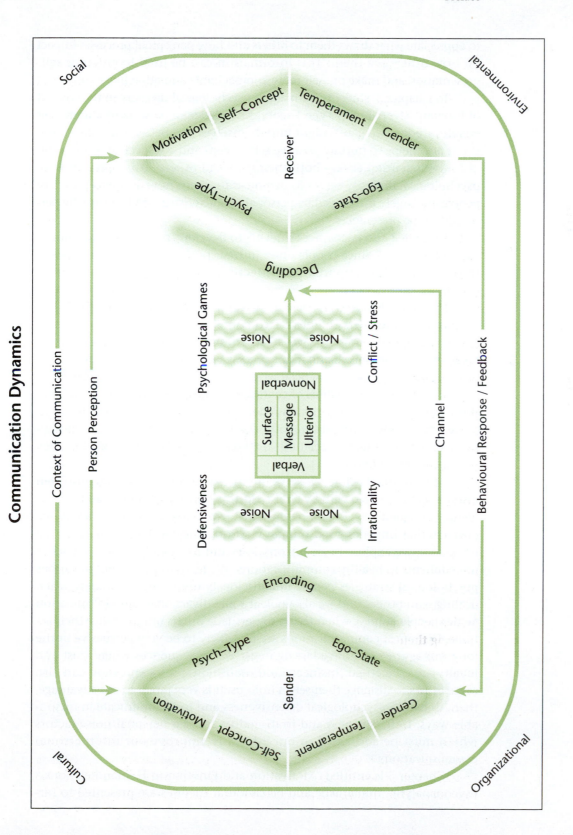

to appreciate what draws them to others and how perceptual processes impact on how others see them. This information can be used to enhance self-presentation and make oneself more approachable and attractive to others.

In Chapter 2, students learn about psychological diversity in the context of Jungian, Myers-Briggs Type Theory. Knowledge of personality differences enables students to gain insight into themselves and better understand others. It also helps to nurture positive self-esteem and a respectful recognition of individual uniqueness—both their own and others'. An appreciation of psychological diversity serves to demonstrate again how our perceptions of people are largely influenced by personal characteristics—in this case, by personality type preferences.

Chapter 2 also encourages students to develop "psych-smart communication strategies." Since people differ in their outlooks, attitudes and orientations to life, it is important for effective communicators to alter their communications to suit the preferences of others. What is said and how messages should be delivered can be modified as a function of psychological type. Attention to type offers an unexpected bonus: A concentrated focus on constructing and delivering messages to accommodate the preferences of others takes attention off oneself and in the process promotes greater self-confidence, surely something that is beneficial when trying to master human relations.

Chapter 3 brings matters of character, etiquette, morals, and values into the discussion. Mastering human relations requires a certain amount of finesse, virtue, and personal integrity. Discussions of such things are not always addressed in human relations textbooks, though they should be. They will be addressed here.

As mentioned before, effective interpersonal communications are often disrupted or interfered with by "noise" factors. The idea of noise can be taken literally or figuratively. Regarding the latter, psychological defensiveness is one obstacle that impedes good human relations and productive dialogue. In Chapter 4, we explore those unconscious and irrational factors that act as impediments to healthy communications. We learn to put names to various psychological strategies people unconsciously use to reduce anxiety when dealing with others, and we also look at some diversionary and intimidation tactics people employ when trying to persuade others or rationalize their actions. Dishonest communications are not likely to be very persuasive in the long run as they can have lasting negative consequences where trust and loyalty are concerned. Insincere and inauthentic self-expression can also cause others to distance themselves from us. It is very much to our advantage, then, to reduce psychological defensiveness and to communicate in reasonable ways. Defensiveness and irrationality are two personal noise factors which must be addressed in our efforts to improve our interpersonal communications.

Chapter 5 is entitled "Motivation and Emotion in Human Relations." Psychoanalytic, humanistic and behavioural theories are presented to further our understanding of what makes us tick and influences others to do what they do. William Glasser's Choice Theory of Motivation is called upon to help us take more effective control of our lives. If we feel our lives are out of control or that we are powerless to get what we want or need, despair may cloud our outlook and hence negatively affect self-presentation, not to mention how well we get along with others. This chapter serves to reinforce the built-in assumption in Part 1 that we cannot master human relations if we find ourselves dysfunctional at a personal level. We must feel in control or at least expect that much of our future is a product of personal choice and self-determination.

This chapter also includes Daniel Goleman's work on emotional intelligence to help students develop those emotional competencies which are essential to leading a successful life, both personally and professionally. Underscoring a point already made in this Preface and Introduction, Goleman claims that emotional intelligence is frequently far more important than credentials, IQ or technical skills when it comes to succeeding in business, education, organizational administration and so forth. To the extent this is true, it will be well worth our while to explore the nature and complexity of emotional intelligence, or EQ as it's now called.

In Chapter 6 we use our preceding discussion of emotion as a convenient segue to move on to matters of stress and lifestyle management. Very related to emotional well-being, stress is something which can be considered another one of those noise factors that can seriously interfere with interpersonal communications. If people are "stressed-out" or preoccupied with worry, they are not likely to be functioning at their best; nor are they likely to be paying much attention to your concerns given their own self-preoccupations. Attention may be impaired, and hence the ability to listen with empathy and understanding. How many times have you refused to listen to other people's problems when you have thought that your own were more pressing or significant? Worried and fearful for yourself, how often have you discounted the legitimate concerns of others? I think it's safe to say that the more stressed and preoccupied one is about one's own life, the less patient and understanding one is likely to be toward others. By reducing stress you can open yourself up to others, listen more attentively, understand more compassionately, and relate more humanely. Doing all of this will further help you to master human relations. For purposes of learning how to reduce stress, numerous strategies for lifestyle management will be offered.

Chapter 7 concludes Part 1 of *Mastering Human Relations*. It deals with matters of character, meaning and purpose in life. This section of the book takes existential, moral and spiritual matters seriously. Spirituality is something which is important whether or not one is religious. If you're someone who is a practising member of a faith tradition, you no doubt define your spirituality in the context of your religious belief system. If you're not religious in any kind of traditional sense, you may still be confronted with questions of meaning, personal identity, your place in the universe, the ultimate value of life, or destiny, for example. You may be asking yourself, what's worth pursuing? Is there anything worth living and dying for? Is it better to see the world in this way or that? Should I be fair with people if that means that I'll diminish my profits? Such questions, though troubling in themselves, are ever present in everyone's life at either a conscious or an unconscious level. The answers we arrive at condition our interactions with others and determine the directions our lives will take. Whether or not an individual sees meaning and purpose is life is surely to affect that person's state of mind, motivational levels, enthusiasm, commitment, respect for others, treatment of the environment, willingness to cooperate and so forth. Spirituality should not simply be regarded as an afterthought to human relations development, but a central feature. To ignore its role is to complete only two-thirds of the job at hand. Mind and body get covered, but at the expense of the human soul. The story of Goethe's *Faust* reveals what happens when we sell our souls for other purely material and worldly concerns. The result is not a happy one!

Chapter 8 begins Part 2: *Social and Interpersonal Dimensions of Human Relations Mastery.* This chapter begins to explore person-to-person communications in terms of ego-state transactions. In this analysis we learn how people often play games that belie their overt communications. Surface communications are often accompanied by hidden or latent messages and ulterior motives. The theory of transactional analysis comes in handy here to illustrate how many of us "play games" when communicating with others. These games can undermine candid and productive communications by means of deception and inauthenticity. People may not always say what they mean or mean what they say in efforts to get what they want or feel better about themselves. As part of all this game-playing, some individuals may unconsciously or even consciously assume roles like "victim" or "persecutor" or "rescuer," which again helps them to feel better or get what they want. It doesn't take much imagination to appreciate how all this game-playing, victimization, persecution and inauthenticity interferes with effective interpersonal communications. By exposing games and learning about them, we can reduce psychological dishonesty in our own lives and work toward more effective interpersonal communications with others.

Chapter 9 addresses matters of gender, culture and non-verbal cues in interpersonal communication. It will be interesting to discover how men and women differ in their thinking and intentions when it comes to things like sharing stories and resolving conflicts. Gaining insight into the moral psychology of both men and women and learning how their different communication patterns are reflected in speech can offer tremendous benefits. Developing greater gender sensitivity can help us to empathize and understand the perspective of "the other sex" a little better than we currently do. In addition, by learning more about cultural influences on communication, we can deal with ethnic and racial diversity in a more successful fashion and without unintentionally offending people. Chapter 9 also includes a section on non-verbal communication. Things like choice of colour in clothing, use of personal space, and physical stature all have their roles in interpersonal communication. Knowing what those roles are, how they influence person perception, and how they impact on social interactions is clearly important for our purposes here.

Chapter 10 recognizes and accepts the fact that conflict is an inevitable part of human interaction. People simply do not always get along and often engage in heated disputes with each other, whether they occur in personal or professional life. It is extremely important, then, to develop conflict resolution skills, the primary goal in this section of the book. The nature and types of conflict are explored before looking at potential benefits of conflict, alternative psychological orientations toward it, and various conflict resolution strategies that can be used to effectively deal with it.

Chapter 11 completes our efforts in this human relations journey by aiding students in the development of their leadership skills. Various theories of leadership are presented along with application exercises designed to help them put theory into practice. It is important to develop leadership skills insofar as virtually everybody will have to assume leadership roles at some time in their lives. To be a good leader, whether at home, at work or in the community, one must know how to deal with subordinates or those put under one's charge. It's often the case that getting the best out of other people is beneficial to one's own aspirations and goals. Knowing how to persuade people to do what they otherwise wouldn't do, and doing so in a way which furthers everyone's happiness and nurtures mutual respect, is an extremely valuable life skill.

Special Features of Mastering Human Relations

Built-In Study Guide This text provides students with a built-in study guide to enhance academic performance. No additional workbook needs to be purchased. This guide is intended as an optional aid, not as a required tool. Certain instructors may wish to integrate some or all of the elements of the guide into their lesson plans as a way of complementing their teaching. Others may wish to have students use the guide primarily for independent study outside the classroom. Many aspects of the guide are suitable for workshops and tutorials. Regardless of how it's used, the guide offers many individual and group learning opportunities.

SQ3R Method of Learning:

The built-in student study guide is based on the SQ3R method of learning. SQ3R stands for **S**urvey, **Q**uestion, **R**ead, **R**ecite and **R**eview. Chapters are organized so that students can

- Survey the content to be covered
- Use focus Questions to direct their attention
- Read the material presented
- Recite and Review what was covered for self-testing.

For more details on the SQ3R System, please read my Message to Students.

Creative Enhancements Poems, comics, quotations, figures, tables, showcase profiles, photos and song lyrics are scattered throughout the text to make it more interesting and visually appealing for students. Sometimes simple quotations or comics can capture the essence of points made. At other times, they accent in an indirect and creative way what may otherwise be plainly expressed in theoretical, academic terminology.

Self-Diagnostics Along with interpersonal effectiveness, this book stresses personal growth. To this end, opportunities are provided throughout the text for students to do self-assessments on such topics as personality type and communication style. Interestingly enough, self-assessments can facilitate understanding and appreciation of others. For example, by appreciating our own uniqueness, we can learn to understand and appreciate the uniqueness of others. Note that self-diagnostics are used in this book as thought-provokers, ones that encourage positive self-consciousness on the part of students. Don't see them as providing anything final or conclusive. Self-diagnostics simply provide opportunities for initial self-reflection.

Application Exercises Application Exercises are included in this text to promote mastery of chapter material. Some of these exercises can be done individually, while others are designed to be done in groups. The Application Exercises of each chapter facilitate active learning and participation. Since it is possible to know a lot about human relations and still be terrible with people, it is important that students practise social interactions using the concepts covered. There's nothing as practical as a good theory as long as the theory gets applied, and that's what happens here!

Related Readings For students and faculty wishing to do further research on topics covered in any one chapter, related readings are listed.

Supplements

Mastering Human Relations Instructor's Resource Website: (*http://www
.pearsoncustom.com/can/humanrelations_ir*) includes the following instructor
supplements:

Instructor's Manual:
- This manual includes a sample course outline, lecture and discussion suggestions, and additional Application Exercises. The Instructor's Manual helps take much of the sting out of adopting a new textbook by having as much prepared for you as possible. The objective is to make Mastering Human Relations user-friendly for teachers, while at the same time interesting and useful for students.

Pearson Testbank:
- Multiple-choice, fill-in-the-blank, short-answer, and true/false questions are provided. The questions are graded at three levels of difficulty and relevant chapter and textbook pages are cited along with the correct answer for each question.

PowerPoint Presentations:
- This instructor's resource contains a variety of material for classroom use, including additional notes and activities for students.

Please go to *http://www.pearsoncustom.com/can/humanrelations_ir* to download these resources. Please contact your local sales representative for details and access.

Message to Students

Mastering Human Relations is a textbook written with you, the student, in mind. It aims to promote personal growth and social skills development. I think you will find much in this book that is interesting, practical and fun. I hope you enjoy all of the comics, poems, song lyrics, visuals and other creative enhancements that are included to make the book not only relevant and insightful, but stimulating as well. On a personal note, I especially enjoyed including the quotations that are sprinkled throughout. For me, they are inspirational and thought provoking. I hope they are for you too!

Designed for your personal use, *Mastering Human Relations* includes a built-in student Study Guide. This guide is based on the SQ3R system of learning. SQ3R is an acronym that stands for survey, question, read, recite and review. If you follow this system, you're more likely to successfully complete your course and master human relations in the process.

Step 1: Survey the Content to be Covered

Each of the chapters in Mastering Human Relations begins with an Overview. By simply glancing at the headings, you can survey ("S") the material you will be expected to master. Make sure, as well, to look over the Learning Outcomes. They have been explicitly stated here to make the overview and survey process easier. By perusing the outcomes at the outset, you can discover what you will be expected to know or to do by unit end. To promote mastery of content and skills, outcomes are numbered and placed where they are addressed. After completing a chapter, you should review the list of Learning Outcomes to ensure that you have assimilated the important information and have developed the skills marked for mastery. If not, you can go back and re-address the appropriate sections of the chapter.

Step 2: Direct your Reading Attention by Referring to the Focus Questions

Each chapter of this book contains Focus Questions, which make up the "Q" portion of the SQ3R methodology. You should examine the questions before actually reading the material contained in the chapter. The questions enable you to focus your attention while reading so that you know what is important. Your instructor may wish to use these questions for classroom discussion purposes. They can be helpful for your own personal reflections as well, as you get to know yourself better through the use of this text. By concentrating on the answers to the Focus Questions while you read, you will be better prepared for discussions, whether they take place in regular classes or in tutorials.

Step 3: Read the Chapter

Once you have an idea of what is in the chapter and what to look for, go ahead and read. I caution you to be patient. Reading theory is not like reading the newspaper or the comic strips. Don't be surprised if you find yourself going over the same paragraph more than once in order to understand what was stated. You are being introduced to a new subject of study with its own jargon and specialized vocabulary. What I would suggest you do while completing the first reading is highlight the important points. During your second reading, paraphrase the material you've highlighted, making sure you understand the notes you're taking. Just before writing your test on each unit, read the chapter a third time and memorize your notes on the information you now understand. Simply reading the text once or twice, the night before a test, and without notes and understanding, is not likely to result in success.

To assist you in your readings, I've boldfaced key terms and provided a running marginal glossary. I don't wish to leave you guessing what's important. A list of Key Terms is also found just before the Progress Check of each chapter. Make sure you are familiar with each term in the list; also make sure you understand each term and, where appropriate, are able to define it.

Step 4: Recite and Review

After reading the chapter, you should start the recitation and review process by doing the Progress Check. Your mastery of the content is reflected in your ability to correctly answer questions contained in the check. Your responses to each of the Progress Checks can be verified for correctness by referring to the Appendix at the end of the book. (No cheating, remember!)

Step 5: Review the Summaries

Chapter end summaries also serve to comprise the recitation and review component of the SQ3R methodology. You may examine them before and/or after doing the Progress Checks to consolidate learning and to make sure that outcomes have been achieved. Reviewing the summaries is definitely something you should do at test time to maximize your chances for success. Good Luck!

Acknowledgements

Numerous reviewers have helped me over the years with the gradual development of this book. William Glasser, the founder of Reality Therapy; Don Riso, the internationally known expert on enneagram transformational psychology; and Carol Pearson, author of *Awakening the Heroes Within: Twelve Archetypes to Help Us Find Ourselves and Transform the World*, are three individuals with whom I've studied and who were gracious enough to read and provide feedback on earlier, preliminary drafts of this work. I thank them for their efforts and good counsel and hope you enjoy their ideas as I've presented them to you in this text. Other reviewers I wish to thank are: Gary Anderson, Camosun College; Jeffrey Arbus, Sault College; Sue Bell, Georgian College; Bev Brown, Niagara College; Bill Gapen, George Brown College; Tom Hanrahan, Canadore College; Harry Havey, Red River Community College; Dalton Kehoe, York University; Kathy Kennedy, St. Lawrence College; Paul Koziey, University of Alberta; R. Douglas Markle, Fanshawe College; Paul Miskin, George Brown College; Norm Naisbitt, Fanshawe College; Sara Pawson, Kwantlen College; Marilyn Sorensen, Medicine Hat College; Sheila Trask, College of the North Atlantic.

I would also like to thank the editorial staff at Pearson Education and Pearson Learning Solutions, especially Gilaine Waterbury and Liz Faerm, who helped to make this fifth edition possible.

In closing, I would also like to acknowledge the important contribution my many students have made indirectly. Through them, I have learned what works and what doesn't. I have also seen their interest and enthusiastic responses to the material presented, giving me confidence that I'm on the right track and that the book makes a valuable contribution to the development of their interpersonal skills. Also, by trying to teach students what I should learn myself, they have helped me to grow in humility, appreciation and understanding—valuable gifts for anyone. Thank you to all!

Oh, that God the gift would give us to see ourselves as others see us.

~Robert Burns

Starting with Self and Person Perception

1

Chapter Overview

The Self
- Self-Concept
- Self-Diagnostic 1.1 What's My Self-Concept?
- Self-Awareness
- Self-Disclosure
- Self-Esteem

Application Exercise 1.1 Be the Star That You Are
- Self-Presentation and Your Online Persona

Perception
- The Construction of Personal and Social Reality
- Selecting
- Organizing

Application Exercise 1.2: May I Have the First Section, Please?
- Interpreting
- How I See the World Is My Responsibility

Perceptual Errors
- Stereotyping
- Self-Fulfilling Prophecy
- Halo Effect
- Attribution Errors
- Proximity
- Role Definition

How to Reduce Errors in Perception

Perceptual Influences on Interpersonal Attraction

Study Guide
• Key Terms
• Progress Check 1.1

• Summary
• Related Readings

Learning Outcomes

After successfully completing this chapter, you will be able to

(1.1) Explain what's meant by self-concept
(1.2) Increase self-awareness while displaying appropriate self-disclosure
(1.3) Define and enhance personal self-esteem
(1.4) Provide alternative explanations of perception
(1.5) Explain how personal and social reality is "constructed"
(1.6) Demonstrate selective perception to yourself
(1.7) Understand how perception can be a matter of personal responsibility
(1.8) Describe a number of common perceptual errors
(1.9) Reduce errors in your perceptions of people and situations

Focus Questions

1. What is meant by self-concept?
2. Why are people reluctant to tell others about themselves?
3. What are some of the 'shoulds' and 'shouldn'ts' concerning self-disclosure?
4. What are some of the factors influencing self-esteem?
5. How does self-esteem influence interpersonal communications?
6. How can self-esteem be enhanced?
7. How does perception work?
8. What does it mean to suggest that personal and interpersonal reality are "constructed"?
9. What is meant by the concept of perceptual filter?
10. How can person perceptions be mistaken?
11. What can be done to correct person perceptions?

(1.1) ····· # The Self

Self-Concept

self

An important factor in inter-personal relationships. Your beliefs, attitudes, values, feelings, preferences and dispositions, both known and unknown, combine to make you who you are.

self-concept

In general terms, self-concept refers to the overall way you see and understand yourself. It includes all of your self-re-ferring beliefs and attitudes, as well as all of your recog-nized values, feelings, prefer-ences and dispositions.

In all communication the most important part is the self. Who you are and how you see yourself in-fluences the way you re-spond to others.
~Joseph A. DeVito

… how we summarize in-formation about other people is bound up with our own view of self.
~N.A. Kuiper and T.B. Rogers

…for the love of one's neighbour is not possible without love of one's self.
~Herman Hesse

4

Writers, poets and psychologists have for a very long time recognized the importance of the **self** to interpersonal relations. People with a poor self-con-cept, for example, can be their own worst enemy when trying to establish healthy and happy communications with others. They may fall prey to un-wanted self-fulfilling prophecies. People who think of themselves as unat-tractive or undesirable, for instance, may dress and act accordingly. They may avoid others, allow personal hygiene to slip and present themselves in unpleasant ways, thereby causing others to respond to them negatively. This negative response can subsequently reinforce the initial poor self-concept in a kind of downward spiralling effect. Conversely, people with positive self-con-cepts may expect the best, display optimism, and elicit support from others. The resulting spiral here is positive and upward.

In general terms, the notion of **self-concept** refers to the overall way you perceive yourself. It includes all of your self-referring beliefs and atti-tudes, as well as all of your personally recognized values, feelings, preferences and dispositions. In combination, such things constitute who you are. The self can, in principle, be conceptualized in many different ways. Some say there is not just one self, but many selves. It is possible, for instance, to talk about your private self, your social self, your work self, your leisure self, your serious self, your ideal self or your physical self. Your personal self-concept depends on what you choose to pay attention to. Of course, there are external fac-tors influencing the formation of anyone's self-concept. In early develop-ment, parents, teachers and significant others function as mirrors to the self. What they say or tell us about ourselves, how they respond to our actions, and what opportunities they provide us influence the development of self-concept. Children who were repeatedly told that they were a "mistake," for example, may struggle to develop a positive self-concept. They may try to become peo-ple they're not or experience debilitating insecurity. They may feel negative emotions and begin to see themselves as undesirable or unloved by others. Fortunately, self-concepts are not static (Atwater, 1999). They change with time and experience. Thus, it's possible to build positive self-concepts, even if neg-ative ones were initially formed. To learn more about your self perceptions complete Self-Diagnostic 1.1 "What's My Self-Concept?"

The significance of self to interpersonal relations can be illustrated by the fact that what you reveal about yourself affects how others respond to you. If you tell people little or nothing about yourself, you remain a mystery to them. Not knowing who you are, they may not see the real you, but only a projection of their own fears and insecurities. Furthermore, if you do not share some part of yourself with others, they may also be reluctant to tell you about them-selves, thereby creating cold and distant communications. A refusal to open up could even lead to hostility and mistrust. History teaches us that people

Self
Diagnostic
1.1

What's My Self-Concept?

1.1

Part One

Aim: In this self-diagnostic, you are provided with a rating scale for measuring your self-concept (Rathus and Nevid, 1995: 77). This instrument will help you to form an impression or concept of yourself based on a listing of personal traits.

Fair	—:	—:	—:	—:	—:	—:	—	Unfair
	1	2	3	4	5	6	7	
Independent	—:	—:	—:	—:	—:	—:	—	Dependent
	1	2	3	4	5	6	7	
Religious	—:	—:	—:	—:	—:	—:	—	Irreligious
	1	2	3	4	5	6	7	
Selfish	—:	—:	—:	—:	—:	—:	—	Unselfish
	1	2	3	4	5	6	7	
Self-confident	—:	—:	—:	—:	—:	—:	—	Lacking confidence
	1	2	3	4	5	6	7	
Competent	—:	—:	—:	—:	—:	—:	—	Incompetent
	1	2	3	4	5	6	7	
Important	—:	—:	—:	—:	—:	—:	—	Unimportant
	1	2	3	4	5	6	7	
Attractive	—:	—:	—:	—:	—:	—:	—	Unattractive
	1	2	3	4	5	6	7	
Educated	—:	—:	—:	—:	—:	—:	—	Uneducated
	1	2	3	4	5	6	7	
Sociable	—:	—:	—:	—:	—:	—:	—	Unsociable
	1	2	3	4	5	6	7	
Kind	—:	—:	—:	—:	—:	—:	—	Cruel
	1	2	3	4	5	6	7	
Wise	—:	—:	—:	—:	—:	—:	—	Foolish
	1	2	3	4	5	6	7	
Graceful	—:	—:	—:	—:	—:	—:	—	Awkward
	1	2	3	4	5	6	7	
Intelligent	—:	—:	—:	—:	—:	—:	—	Unintelligent
	1	2	3	4	5	6	7	
Artistic	—:	—:	—:	—:	—:	—:	—	Inartistic
	1	2	3	4	5	6	7	
Tall	—:	—:	—:	—:	—:	—:	—	Short
	1	2	3	4	5	6	7	
Obese	—:	—:	—:	—:	—:	—:	—	Skinny
	1	2	3	4	5	6	7	

Instructions: Imagine that your personal traits can be identified using bipolar dimensions like those provided below. Place an "X" in one of the seven spaces for each bipolar dimension. For example, with respect to being fair (the first dimension), what would you fill in? In terms of fairness are you...

1 = extremely fair
2 = rather fair
3 = somewhat fair
4 = equally fair and unfair; or not sure

5 = somewhat unfair
6 = rather unfair
7 = extremely unfair

Part Two

Aim: To explore your level of self-esteem

Instructions: Self-esteem often hinges on the congruence between our self-concept and our ideal self, the self we would like to be or think we ought to be. With this in mind, go back to the bipolar list of traits, only this time place a check in the spaces which indicate where you think you ought or would like to be for each of the dimensions. Compare your Xs and check-marks. Are they relatively close together, identical, or distantly separated? Think about the results. Record your observations, thoughts and feelings as you do the comparison. What do your results suggest?

Based on Spencer A. Rathus & Jeffrey Nevid (1995), *Adjustment & Growth: The Challenges of Life*, 6/e. Fort Worth, TX: Harcourt Brace Publishers.

5

frequently become suspicious of individuals and things they don't understand. They tend to attack the unknown as a kind of psychological defence against anxiety. Thus, if you wish to make your interpersonal relations warmer, you might need to engage in more self-disclosure. Of course, self-disclosure hinges largely on self-awareness. You can't consciously disclose what you don't know about yourself. Without self-awareness you may also end up unintentionally disclosing things about yourself that you wish you hadn't. In what follows, we will look a little more closely at self-awareness and self-disclosure as they pertain to human relations. We'll look at ways to increase self-awareness and provide some guidelines to help us distinguish between appropriate and inappropriate self-disclosure. We'll also consider the issue of self-esteem.

(1.2) Self-Awareness

Joseph Luft and Harry Ingham (1984) have provided us with one explanation of **self-awareness**. Together they created a theoretical device called the Johari Window, a label that combines their first names. This device divides the self into four areas. Each captures aspects of the self, reflecting levels of awareness and disclosure. When all of these areas are considered together, a four-part grid results. See Figure 1.1 on page 8.

The Open Self In the **open self** quadrant are things about your self that are known both by you and others. For example, you're clearly aware of your name, gender, skin colour and the college or university you attend. So too are others. You also know what your favourite sports teams are, as well as your preferred musical artists. You can choose to share this kind of information with others. If you do, such information becomes part of your open self. Generally speaking, whatever attitudes, feelings, ideas, desires, motivations and so on that you regard as yours and that you display publicly belong to your open self.

The size of the open self can vary. Depending on the time and place, we may open up to others or perhaps choose to remain tight-lipped (Johnson, 1990: 36–37). As mentioned earlier, if people are to build deep and meaningful relationships, they must be prepared to share themselves with others. If we don't let others get to know us, communication becomes very difficult.

Psychological type may have an influence here. If researchers on type are correct, introverts will probably share less about themselves compared to extraverts (see Chapter Two). To the extent this is true, introverts may be somewhat more challenged in the realm of interpersonal communications. Joseph Luft (1984) claims that the smaller the open self quadrant, the poorer the communication.

The Blind Self When it comes to self-awareness, there are things that others can see in us but we cannot see in ourselves. This is our **blind self**. For example, you may display certain quirky peculiarities without knowing it; others may notice right away. Perhaps you play with your hair when conversing or become very polite as a defensive reaction to anger. If you don't recognize these things about yourself, they belong to your blind self. It is important that you discover as much as you can about the blind self. By increasing self-awareness in this area you will be better able to manage the impressions you make on others. Other people's reactions to you will also become more understandable. When people react to aspects of your personality that you're unaware of, their

---

self-awareness
The extent to which you know and understand yourself. Luft and Ingham provided one explanation of self-awareness, envisioning a theoretical four-part grid (the Johari Window) dividing the self into four areas (open self, blind self, hidden self and unknown self), each capturing the aspects of the self, reflecting levels of awareness and disclosure.

open self
The part of the self which you know and which you choose to share with others.

If a man wants to be of the greatest possible value to his fellow creatures let him begin the long, solitary task of perfecting himself.
~Robertson Davies

Perception is a selective process and the picture we have of ourselves is a vital factor in determining the richness and variety of the perceptions selected.
~Don Hamachek

blind self
The part of our self that others can see but that we cannot see ourselves.

behaviour may seem strange. When you know what you do and say, how you appear and what impressions you make, others' reactions can become not only more comprehensible but sometimes even predictable (Weaver, 1996).

The Unknown Self The **unknown self** is the part of you that neither you nor others know. Much of what makes up the unknown self is buried in the unconscious (DeVito, 1998). To gain greater awareness of the unknown self, you could avail yourself of certain psychotherapeutic techniques like dream analysis or hypnosis, or you could engage in further self-exploration with trusted family members, friends or loved ones. It is important to gain insight into your unknown self, for if you don't, your untapped resources will go unused. Your full potential will never be actualized and you will not become the person you could be (Weaver, 1996). Through interactions with others, you can discover more about yourself and reduce this portion of your self.

unknown self
The part of you that neither you nor others know. It is important to gain insight into the unknown self (much of which is buried in the unconscious) to actualize your full potential.

The Hidden Self The **hidden self** is the part over which you have complete control. There are things about yourself that you know, but you choose not to share with others (e.g., your finances or previous relationships). The hidden self is personal and private and never needs to be disclosed. All of us establish personal boundaries that we use to protect our innermost selves. What we choose to share and withhold from others is a matter of self-disclosure.

hidden self
The part of you that you have no wish to share with others.

It is worth noting that the four areas of the self are interdependent. Changes in one area affect other areas. For example, when you expand your open self by being more self-disclosing, you reduce the size of the hidden self. As you encourage others to be self-disclosing about what was once hidden but now is open for them, and as you allow them to be honest with you, your blind self also diminishes (Johnson, 1999). Let's say, for instance, that you express a radical political viewpoint that startles a listener. The reaction may come from the fact that the listener has always perceived you as a staunch conservative and has treated you accordingly. By communicating your radical politics openly, you may find yourself revealing things that were always hidden, or at least previously unexpressed. Now that the listener has shared his surprise with you, you realize what impression(s) you have unwittingly made on others in the past. The impressions you made were part of your blind self. You didn't know how you appeared. Now that it has been revealed and shared with you, the impression you make becomes a part of your open self. See Figure 1.2 on page 10 for a representation of the four selves.

How to Increase Self-Awareness

Adopt the perspective of others Try to see yourself through the eyes of your friends and acquaintances.

Create a list of your attitudinal, behavioural and perceptual tendencies How do you generally orient to people? What do you look for when perceiving them? How do you act as a result?

Pay close attention to others with whom you interact They serve as a kind of

7

By letting you know me, I allow you to like me. By disclosing myself to you, I create the potential for trust, caring, commitment, growth, self-understanding and friendship.
~David Johnson

Figure 1.1

The Johari Window

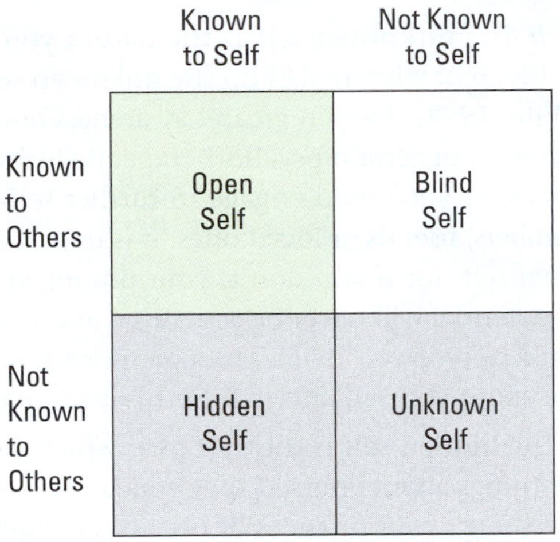

	Known to Self	Not Known to Self
Known to Others	Open Self	Blind Self
Not Known to Others	Hidden Self	Unknown Self

Source: From *Group Processes: An Introduction to Group Dynamics* by Joseph Luft, by permission of Mayfield Publishing Company. Copyright 1984 by Joseph Luft.

mirror to the self. Look for any verbal and nonverbal clues that might provide new insights into yourself. Remember the advice given to us by the German poet Goethe, who suggested that if we wish to learn more about ourselves, we should look at others.

Increase openness to others The size of your blind self can be reduced if you allow others to know you better and respond to you. Through witnessing others' reactions to you and carefully listening to their responses, you can learn things about yourself that you didn't know. As others disclose their feelings and their perception of you, you increase your self-awareness.

Self-Disclosure

self-disclosure
The act of revealing new information about yourself to others. It may be intentional or unintentional (i.e. communicated through verbal cues or body language). What is revealed may be significant or relatively unimportant. Ideally, self-disclosure should be, as much as possible, a matter of conscious and deliberate choice.

As we just learned in the preceding discussion, the various panes of the Johari Window can vary in size depending on people's self-awareness and willingness to share themselves with others. In this part of the chapter we will examine a little more closely the nature of self-disclosure, its risks and benefits, as well as a few guidelines for its use. If you are going to increase the size of your open self and reduce the dimensions of your hidden, blind and unknown selves, in hopes of improving interpersonal relations, you should proceed carefully with an informed understanding.

Self-disclosure involves the intentional act of revealing information about yourself to others. This information represents something new, not previously known. The information relayed in self-disclosure may be either important or insignificant. You may choose to disclose something highly personal, or something rather trivial such as your preference in candy bars. One could argue that some self-disclosure is unconscious and, hence, unintentional. Nonverbal cues may, for instance, reveal your true feelings and falsify what you actually say to others. In this case, others may learn more about you through your body language and tone of voice than through what you say. Inadvertent slips of the tongue, as well, may uncover hidden desires that you've been trying to conceal from others (DeVito, 1997). By increasing self-awareness and by making the open self larger, the blind, hidden and unknown selves—which give rise to unconscious or unwanted self-disclosure—can be reduced. Ideally, self-disclosure should be a matter of conscious and deliberate choice. Remember, by increasing self-awareness, unwanted self-disclosure can be minimized, so let us focus our attention on purposeful self-revelation.

Self-disclosure is not some kind of emotional dumping or process of laying blame. Nor is it about brutally insensitive honesty or indiscriminate frankness. Self-disclosure refers to sharing parts of yourself with others in ways that respect their rights and sensitivities. Proper self-disclosure takes into account the impact it is likely to have on others. It is not surprising that people are often afraid to engage in self-disclosure. When you choose to tell others about yourself, "you expose yourself not only to a lover's balm, but also to a hater's bombs! When he knows you, he knows just where to plant them for maximum effect" (Jourard, 1971: 5). To put it more plainly, what you give away about yourself today may be used against you tomorrow. Fear of this possibility prevents many from self-disclosing. Also, people are afraid of rejection (Weaver, 1996). If we lay down our social masks and allow people to see us as we really are, they may not accept us. They may not give us the support or kind of reaction we were hoping for. What then? We may also avoid self-disclosure if we fear hurting others. Perhaps our true feelings and thoughts would emotionally wound the people we care about. Instead of being honest and forthright, then, we may choose to remain private. Last, we may opt against self-disclosure because we do not wish to project an unwanted image. If I tell you about myself, you may begin to paint a picture of me that I don't like. In this case, little or no significant self-disclosure would be forthcoming.

Notwithstanding the risks, self-disclosure does have many potential benefits. When you choose to share things about yourself with others, you open the door for others to do the same. When mutual self-disclosure takes place, people get to know and understand one another better. The scene is thus set for closeness and greater intimacy. Without self-disclosure it would be difficult, if not impossible, to establish and maintain friendships. Liking someone and being liked entails interactive caring and sharing. It is difficult to help a friend, empathize with that person or share useful feedback if that

Figure 1.2

Variations of the Johari Window

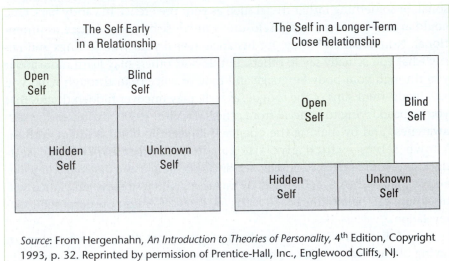

Source: From Hergenhahn, *An Introduction to Theories of Personality*, 4th Edition, Copyright 1993, p. 32. Reprinted by permission of Prentice-Hall, Inc., Englewood Cliffs, NJ.

person refuses to self-disclose. Likewise, how can anyone help you or respond appropriately if you are hiding your true self? By sharing ourselves with others, we afford them an opportunity to respond to us. We discover much about ourselves by noticing how others react to us. As we reduce the size of our blind self, we grow in self-awareness and assume greater control of our lives.

Finally, researchers have found some interesting correlations between self-disclosure and personal well-being. For instance, people who display good mental health typically exhibit high disclosure to a few significant others and medium disclosure to others in a social environment (Cozby, 1973). Also, people who self-disclose have been found to have more effective immune systems than those who do not (Pennebacker, 1991). They seem to be able to ward off illnesses more effectively. If you want to be healthier and happier, you might consider the importance of self-disclosure.

Guidelines for Self-Disclosure By emphasizing the benefits of self-disclosure to personal well-being and interpersonal relations, I do not suggest that you should go out and spill your guts to every stranger on the street. Self-disclosure is something you ought to think about seriously, and when you decide to disclose, you should proceed with caution. Some helpful guidelines for self-disclosing are provided below. See Table 1.1 on page 15 for tips on listening and responding to other people's self-disclosures.

Examine and evaluate your intentions Before you begin disclosing your feelings, thoughts, values, habitual behaviours or your past, ask yourself this question: "What's motivating me?" Are you self-disclosing to enhance a

Appropriate self-disclosure forms a solid basis for friendship and intimate relations.

relationship? Or are you telling someone about some "good dirt" in your past that will likely cause hurt to a third party? When self-disclosures have hurtful intentions, they are probably best avoided, especially when relationships are valued and considered worth cultivating.

Think about the appropriate amount of self-disclosure Researchers have suggested that "relational satisfaction" is likely to be greater at moderate levels of disclosure (Gilbert, 1976). It's not necessarily the case that ever-increasing self-disclosure leads to ever more intimate and stronger relationships. This idea is only true when both people in a relationship have healthy self-concepts, when both are prepared to take risks, and when each displays unconditional positive regard toward the other. When these things are lacking there is a "curvilinear relationship" between self-disclosure and relational satisfaction. Thus, there can be too much, as well as too little, self-disclosure between people. As a general rule of thumb, self-disclose in moderation.

Pick your spots Don't self-disclose indiscriminately. Make sure the disclosure occurs at the right time, at the right place and with the right person. Try to avoid making intimate self-disclosures with strangers. Ask if the self-disclosure you are about to make naturally flows out of the situation or relationship. Bringing up your personal ambitions at a funeral is not likely to be appropriate.

Pay attention to others' self-disclosures After self-disclosing, allow your listener time to reciprocate with his own disclosures. If there is no reciprocation, you may be getting the message that your disclosures are not wanted or appreciated. Self-disclosure is a two-way street. Clues about what you should disclose can be gained by carefully paying attention to others.

Be prepared to live with what you reveal about yourself Disclose only things about yourself that you are prepared to have others know. Self-disclosures cannot be erased from the minds of others. Once you reveal facts about yourself, they are public knowledge. While self-disclosure requires a certain amount of risk, it should not be based on unwise or imprudent judgments.

1.3 Self-Esteem

We learned earlier that self-concept is the cognitive part of self-perception. As individuals, we all have perceptions of ourselves that we can describe. Someone could say, "I'm short," "I'm tall," "I'm a Chinese-Canadian," or "I'm Protestant." In all of these purely descriptive statements, notice the neutrality. Being short or tall is not presented as either good or bad. Presenting oneself as a Protestant or a Chinese-Canadian is regarded neither as praiseworthy nor blameworthy. Descriptive labels do exactly what they are designed to do, that is, describe.

1.7

self-esteem
The result of the value judgments one makes about oneself. Ultimately, self-esteem is a matter of personal responsibility: while cultural ideals and group norms have an impact on self-esteem, nobody can make you feel unhappy or insecure about yourself without your permission.

With **self-esteem**, however, an emotional or affective component is added to self-perception (Hamachek, 1997). Not only do we have different perceptions of ourselves, but we also make value judgments based on those perceptions. Seeing yourself as short is one thing; liking what you see is another. Perhaps you dislike your height. Maybe you wish you were taller. Maybe you think of yourself as a "shrimp." If so, you may experience some negative feelings every time you consider your physical stature. Take note here that greater height, in itself, is neither good nor bad. An Asian student in one of my classes once told me how tall people are shunned in his culture. Apparently, in some regions of Japan, they are regarded as untrustworthy. They stand out as unacceptably different. However, height in North American culture is something cherished. Many men wish they were tall, dark and handsome, while a good number of women complain they are too short and believe that clothes always look better on taller, slimmer people. Of course, the value judgments made on self-perceptions are ultimately a matter of personal responsibility. Nobody can make you feel unhappy or insecure about yourself without your permission. This is not to say that cultural ideals and group norms have no impact on self-esteem; they do if you let them. Maintaining self-esteem in the face of societal standards and social values is not always easy.

A few inspirational words from e.e. cummings might be in order here.

To be nobody but yourself—in a world which is doing its best, night and day, to make you everybody else—means to fight the hardest battle which any human being can fight, and never stop fighting.

It's worth underscoring here the fact that self-esteem does not equal egoism (Reece and Brandt, 2000). Having self-esteem is not about glorifying yourself at the expense of others. It also does not involve any attempt to diminish others or denigrate them for purposes of personal elevation. If you ever see people appearing arrogant and boastful, or if you witness them overestimating themselves in public, you're probably observing inadequate self-esteem in action. It's almost folk wisdom now to say that people who brag and put others down are trying to make themselves feel better. Be careful then to distinguish between healthy self-esteem (self-respect) and the insecure egotistical personality. Bragging for purposes of a "put down" certainly doesn't help others to feel better about themselves and, in the long run, it probably doesn't help you either.

A person's level of self-esteem is influenced by a number of factors. As suggested above, cultural ideals and social comparisons play a role. People trying to achieve a sense of self often look to others to see how they measure up. We compare grades to see how smart we are. We compare salaries to see how successful we are. We compare clothes to see how fashionable we are. Social comparison allows us to place ourselves somewhere in the social pecking order. Many people feel a need to see themselves in relation to others and make self-evaluative judgments on that basis, saying things like, "Compared to that guy, I'm not so bad." In this case, social comparison helps the person feel better about herself.

Be the Star That You Are

application
exercise

1.1

1.4 The objective of this exercise is to facilitate self-disclosure in a small group. To respond to each of the questions below, first copy the star (Figure 1.3) on a large piece of paper and then draw a picture in the appropriate corresponding part. Don't worry about your artistic talent. What is more important is what you choose to say about each illustration. Once your pictures are finished, join a small group (three to five people) to share information about yourself. Have others in the group respond to your self-disclosures. See what you learn from their reactions.

Questions

1. What is the most important value or belief in your life?

2. What is the best thing you've ever done or had happen to you?

3. What was the happiest moment in your life?

4. What activity do you like?

5. If you could be described in one word, what would it be?

6. What would you like others to know about you?

Figure 1.3
Be the Star That You Are

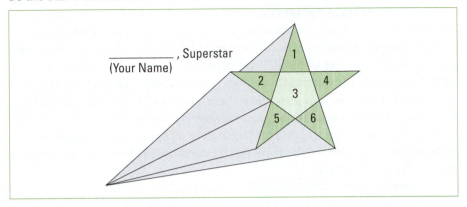

Self-esteem is also influenced by personal aspirations (Hamachek, 1997). If we continually set unrealistic goals for ourselves and fail in their pursuit, for instance, we will probably develop low self-esteem and consider ourselves as "losers." By contrast, if we set attainable goals and achieve them, we're likely to feel better about ourselves. Another factor influencing self-esteem is feedback from others. What people say about us and how they respond to us can obviously have an impact on self-concept and self-esteem. If others are constantly praising our good efforts and congratulating us on our accomplishments, we may begin to see ourselves as successful and feel good about that. Childhood upbringing also influences self-esteem. Researchers have observed that children who are brought up in a permissive environment tend to develop lower self-esteem than children who are raised in a firmer and more demanding home (Reece and Brandt, 2000). In the latter case, expectations are high, discipline is more consistent and greater parental involvement in the lives of children is evident. In short, our current level of self-esteem has probably been influenced, in part at least, by our childhood experiences.

It's possible that self-esteem is also affected by gender and sex-role definitions (Monteiro, 1978). One report included in the *New York Times* cites a study of female undergraduates at six prestigious colleges in the northeast region of the United States. Researchers found that women generally displayed lower self-esteem and lower aspirations than men, even though their grades were roughly equivalent. Given that all people in the study were about the same in terms of academic success, the possibility that gender expectations and cultural views negatively affect women is quite real.

Clearly, self-esteem is very important to human relations. See Table 1.2 for a summary of the effects of high and low self-esteem on interpersonal communication. This material is based on the work of Brooks and Emmert (1976).

Table 1.1

Listening and Responding to Other People's Self-Disclosures

1. **Pay close attention** There's a difference between hearing and listening. It's possible to be miles away in thought while someone is speaking. Concentrate on what is said. Be present in mind as well as body.
   If necessary, offer to change locations to reduce external noise and interference. Don't just hear what is said, but really listen. Sometimes it's as important to hear what isn't said as what is.

2. **Suspend judgment** A critical attitude is not likely to encourage others' self-disclosures. Try to suspend judgment whenever people tell you about themselves. If you tend to be judgmental, others will probably become defensive and less likely to share personal information. You can facilitate openness by acceptance. You don't have to like everything that is self-disclosed; on the other hand, though, you don't always have to blame, condemn and judge. Ask yourself whether you would be more or less likely to self-disclose to those who pronounce judgment on you.

3. **Reflect back to the speaker what is said** By paraphrasing what others self-disclose you can show personal interest and your level of understanding. If an individual perceives you as empathic and truly interested, self-disclosures are more likely to occur.

4. **Remember other people's self-disclosures** If you easily forget self-disclosed information that is considered important and divulged at some risk on the part of the other, you may indirectly communicate the message that you don't care. Besides hurting the other person emotionally, it can create psychological distance and lessen the chance for further self-disclosures.

5. **Listen with honesty and integrity** Don't try to fool people that you're interested in them when all you really want is someone's "good dirt" to spread around. This action surely constitutes some sort of personal violation. Know why you are choosing to listen. Don't abuse the confidence of others. Respect their right to privacy.

6. **Reassure and support** Help people feel that they have made the right choice by self-disclosing. Support them as individuals and reassure them that what has been told to you has been received in confidence and with sincere efforts to understand and appreciate. This reassurance can be communicated directly with words or indirectly through nonverbal cues (e.g., eye contact or touch).

7. **Reciprocate with appropriate self-disclosures of your own** When someone self-discloses, that person often takes a psychological risk. A certain amount of trust may be placed in you. By responding with your own appropriate self-disclosures, you can begin to build a relationship of mutual trust (see the guidelines for self-disclosure earlier in the chapter).

15

Given the significant effects of self-esteem on interpersonal relations, it's important that we try to enhance it in ourselves if we wish to be more effective with people and happier about ourselves. Here are a few suggestions made by writers in the field of human relations to help you enhance your self-esteem (see DeVito, 1998; Napoli, Kilbride and Tebbs, 1992).

How to Enhance Self-Esteem

Engage in positive self-talk We all carry on inner dialogues by talking to ourselves in our minds. The next time you do, experiment with some self-affirmations. Say good things about yourself. Remind yourself of your past achievements and personal victories. Think about your strengths and positive qualities. Discuss future possibilities; don't talk about your weaknesses and limitations.

Surround yourself with supportive people I once heard a famous motivational speaker talk about his successful career. He claimed that part of his success was due to the fact that he chose to hang around with only those people who were positive and supportive. Such people nourished and energized his soul. He made the point that it is hard to feel good about yourself and to accomplish things if others around you are always finding fault with you or discouraging your efforts.

Set realistic goals for yourself If you seek unattainable goals, you're setting yourself up for failure and all the disappointment and ill feelings that ac-

Table 1.2

Some Effects of Self-Esteem on Interpersonal Communication

Low Self-Esteem People with low self-esteem	High Self-Esteem People with high self-esteem
• Are overly sensitive to criticism; they must be handled with care	• Regard themselves as others' equals
• Overreact to praise; they make too much out of little comments of support and encouragement	• Feel confident about handling problems or situations as they arise; they welcome challenge
• Display hypercritical attitudes; they frequently complain, criticize and find fault	• Accept praise without embarrassment or self-indulgence
• Respond pessimistically to competitive situations	• Acknowledge and accept all aspects of the self (good as well as not good)
	• Seek improvement; they accept responsibility for themselves; they openly receive suggestions and criticisms

company it. Be sure to go after the achievable. One success will build upon the next until success will become a way of life and a part of your self-concept.

Disregard counterproductive irrational beliefs If you believe, for example, that you must always please everyone all of the time, you're likely to drive yourself crazy. Don't get down on yourself. It's simply unreasonable to think you can always satisfy everybody. If you continue thinking and believing irrational thoughts (e.g., one broken date means nobody loves you), you will undermine your own self-esteem.

Change your presentation of self Try to communicate more positively about yourself to others. If you value and appreciate yourself, you will influence others to value and appreciate you as well. People who present themselves as energetic, enthusiastic, interesting and fun-loving, for example, will probably elicit different responses from people who present themselves as listless, apathetic and bored. Whom would you prefer to be with?

Self-Presentation and Your Online Persona

With the growing influence of digital and computer technology on everyday life, people no longer always need to conduct their business affairs or even their social transactions in conventional ways. Some are even hesitant to do so. For example, in an era of efficiency and instant gratification, many are reluctant to communicate by letter because "snail-mail" is considered so painfully slow. Phone calls may be an improvement, but then we often find ourselves on hold or playing telephone tag in our efforts to contact the person or persons with whom we wish to speak. As for face-to-face meetings, they may be inconvenient or virtually impossible given the hectic schedules by which so many of us live. As an alternative, more and more people are turning to the Internet as a quicker, more efficient mode of communication. Some write hundreds of text messages on their cell phones every day. Others rely more on social networking services. Communications may start online, but later migrate to other environments—think about online dating services, for instance. Others, however, never stray from the Net with even a phone call. In this case, one's online persona is all the other person gets to "see" of you. Likewise, what you know about your email or chat-line partner is conditioned by the online persona presented by that individual. In view of the fact that so much can often hinge on first impressions, it's important that your online persona makes a positive statement and that you don't inadvertently communicate inaccurate, misleading or unflattering messages about yourself. Let's now examine some features of electronic communications and learn how we can take steps to manage the impressions we make.[1]

---

[1] The information which follows is largely drawn from Patricia Wallace's book, *The Psychology of the Internet*, Cambridge, UK: Cambridge University Press, 1999.

Warm and Cold Impressions Classic research has shown that we all have a tendency to leap to conclusions about others with blinding speed, though we often have few cues upon which to base those conclusions (Solomon Asch, 1946). For instance, if we initially come across as "warm," the general impression we make will be more favourable; conversely, if we appear "cold," the first impression we make will be less favourable. As Patricia Wallace (1999, p.15) puts it: "*Warm* and *cold* say a great deal about our dispositions and influence how others will react to us in social settings. They are heavily weighted central traits when people are forming a first impression. You may be considered brilliant and industrious, but these will pale next to your warmth or coldness."

The idea that perceived warmth and coldness plays an important role in establishing first impressions may not concern you much—that is, if you consider yourself to be a person who exudes warmth to begin with. A problem arises, however, because the Internet is a "chilly" medium by its very nature. Early research in socio-emotional expressions online suggests that we all seem a little cooler, more task-oriented and irascible than we might actually be in person (Hiltz and Turoff, 1978). In a group context, face-to-face groups express more agreement with one another in comparison with computer-mediated groups. In the latter case, such groups are more likely to express disagreement and make fewer remarks that might relieve a tense situation (Fuller, 1996). So, in fact, "We don't just *appear* a little cooler, testier, and disagreeable because of the limitations of the medium. Online, we appear to be less inclined to *perform* those little civilities common to social interactions. Predictably, people react to our cooler, more task-oriented impressions and respond in kind" (Wallace, 1999: 17).

To give greater warmth to your online communications, whether in groups or pairs, it would be useful to express more agreement as a way of releasing tension. Another strategy is to soften typed verbal disagreements with expressions like, "Let me think…I'm not quite sure I agree with that." Contrast this softer response with the harder variation: "I think you're dead wrong, period!" Even if your emotional intelligence quotient is high (see Chapter 5), be aware that your affective sensitivities may be a little less acute online.

Another strategy to add warmth to online communications, especially in the context of informal messaging between friends, is to use **emoticons**. These are playful combinations of punctuation marks designed to show facial expressions (Wallace, 1999). They serve as graphic accents to enhance the socio-emotional content of the intended message (Witmer and Katzman, 1997). Imagine lying on your side or looking sideways to better see a smile :-), a frown :-(, a wink ;), and an extended tongue :P.

Our online communications can be further warmed through the use of **linguistic softeners**. Such things add an element of hesitation or uncertainty. They can be beneficial when we don't wish to be too abrupt or sound too dogmatic in the presentation of our personal views. In face-to-face com-

emoticons
Playful punctuation marks used for socio-emotional enhancement of electronic messages.

linguistic softeners
Language designed to make email messages sound less decisive and bold.

munications, we can raise our vocal pitch at the end of a sentence so that even disagreements come across more like questions. Filler words such as "y'know" and "like" have the effect of making any utterance sound less decisive and bold. Abbreviations have also come to be used to reduce the brusqueness of typical messages. Examples include the following: IMHO (in my humble opinion), BTW (by the way) and FWIW (for what it's worth).

Email Addresses Vital to your online first impression are your **email addresses**. They may convey information about your character, interests, values, occupation, affiliations or taste, and so on. Patricia Wallace provides us with the following hypothetical examples.

> **tufdude888@aol.com**   **foxylady@flash.net**
> **jtravis@vs2.harvard.edu**   **rgoldman6@microsoft.com**

email addresses
Electronic addresses on the Internet.

As she suggests, we might be tempted to question *tufdude*'s objectivity about women, or be more inclined to listen to *rgoldman*'s views on the future of the Internet than *foxylady*'s. You might also make some assumptions about the intelligence or position of *jtravis* given that the domain name to the right of the "@" symbol indicates some affiliation with Harvard University, a highly prestigious academic institution. While it's not always possible to choose your domain name, it is important to take into account what impression is made by the rest of the email address. Could *foxylady*, for instance, be jeopardizing her chances of becoming a fundraising officer for a local religiously-based charity? What first impression has *foxylady* likely left and is this one to her advantage? As the TV commercial reminds us, "You never get a second chance to make a first impression." It's important therefore to make the one we want, in part through our electronic communications.

Homepage Construction As a way of creating a favourable impression online, many have opted to **construct homepages**. This is often the case with college and university instructors, for example, who either teach distance education courses and are forced to introduce themselves electronically, or simply wish to humanize themselves to their in-class students by self-disclosing personal information in a creative and non-threatening fashion. A homepage is like a billboard or yellow pages advertisement. It constitutes a cost-effective way to create an impression, polish your online persona and reveal something about yourself. With a small amount of effort, one can produce a finely crafted self-presentation for the whole world to see (Wallace, 1999).

homepage construction
A useful method for creating an online persona and favourable first impression.

An advantage of using the homepage is that we can display our ideal selves. We can retouch photos, present our creative works and list our achievements to establish expertise and credibility. We can also add weblinks to our favourite sites on the Internet, thereby disclosing our diverse interests and cosmopolitan tastes. With homepages, we are able to present a composite picture of ourselves. We can make a personal statement of identity and show others what we stand for and what is deemed important to us. Commercial software programs currently exist to help facilitate homepage construction.

Workshops and seminars are often offered and designed to do the same. You might wish to check out these possibilities. Good luck ! :-)

Social Networking Of course, many if not most young people today are tech-savvy. The personal Facebook page, which includes photos of oneself and lists friends, interests, hobbies and political views etc., is the private individual's equivalent to the corporate home page. New contacts can be made through common friends. People who were previously unacquainted can introduce themselves and share common interests. People's comings and goings or new developments in their lives can be easily monitored. For safety's sake, security filters can restrict who gets access to the information posted; nonetheless, it is wise not to include any pictures and information that may come back to jeopardize the achievement of your future goals. More and more employers check out job applicants' Facebook pages to see what individuals are like in their private lives. What they find is thought to reflect much about the applicant's character and personality. What does your social networking page say about you?

Perception

Because their hearts are pure, the innocent defend true perception instead of defending themselves against it.

~A Course in Miracles

perception
The means through which we become aware of our physical and social surroundings. We gather information, experience people, give meaning to situations, attribute motives and intentions to individuals, form impressions and learn about ourselves and the world.

(1.4)

empiricists
Theorists who believe all knowledge derives from experience.

Developing an understanding of **perception** is important to mastering human relations. Perception and interpersonal communication are so intimately related that it is virtually impossible to understand one without the other. By means of perception, we become aware of our physical and social surroundings. We gather information, experience people, give meaning to situations, attribute motives and intentions to individuals, form impressions and learn about ourselves and others in the world. The window of perception enables us to see inside while looking out.

For centuries, philosophers have argued over the nature of perception in their quest for knowledge. **Empiricists**, like John Locke, have claimed that the mind is like a blank slate. For him, the mind perceives only that which experience presents. In his view, all knowledge is a product of experience and derived from it. In psychological terms, this theory means that people are essentially passive organisms and serve as stimulus receptors. Experience simply imprints itself on the mind. Perception is thus a reflection of external reality. For the empiricist, people, situations and events are "out there," so to speak, separate from the person perceiving them. External reality possesses a kind of independent status. Perhaps you have always been an empiricist without knowing it. If you have ever said things like "Seeing is believing" or "I know, I saw it with my own two eyes," you have probably made empiricist assumptions about perception.

According to **rationalist thinkers**, reason, not experience is the ultimate source of all knowledge. For them, experience is something that can be deceiving. Even though the saying is "Seeing is believing," surely you have been deceived before by what you have seen. Optical illusions cause people to arrive at false conclusions. Circumstantial evidence can sometimes convict innocent people. Things are not always as they appear. In short, experience cannot provide absolute certainty. What is true today may be false tomorrow; what looks true from here may look false from there. If you are a rationalist, you may distrust your sensory experience, seeking to find greater assurance through reasoning and thought processes.

Finally, if you adopt the **interactionist theory of knowledge** of philosopher Immanuel Kant or psychologist Jean Piaget, you grant both reason and experience a place in the formation of knowledge. You recognize how the contents of experience (sensory data) are poured into the forms of rational understanding provided by the mind to produce knowledge and our perceptions of the world. This point will be explained momentarily. For purposes of the discussion that follows, you should know that we will be adopting an interactionist perspective.

The Construction of Personal and Social Reality

1.5

When you understand perception in interactive terms, it becomes clear that how we see ourselves and others is more than a simple matter of passively receiving external stimuli. The perception of self and others is an active process. The experience of reality is a **construction**, not a recording. To illustrate how your mind actively constructs reality and gives meaning to it, let's look at Figures 1.4 and 1.5. Ask yourself what you see.

Do you see a triangle in Figure 1.4? If so, your mind actively linked the three dots together. Perhaps you saw the "therefore" symbol from logic and mathematics. Sensory experience provided the raw data or contents of this

rationalist thinkers
People for whom reason, not experience, is the ultimate source of all knowledge. Rationalists may distrust their sensory experiences, and seek to find greater assurance through reasoning and thought processes.

interactionist theory of knowledge
The idea that knowledge entails a construction involving both reason and experience.

What you see is what you get.
~Anonymous

The essence of genius is to know what to overlook.
~William James

construction
The term used to describe our experience of reality. The mind actively constructs reality and gives meaning to it.

Figure 1.4

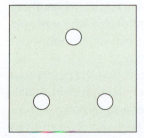

Figure 1.5

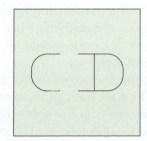

21

The world we see merely reflects our internal frame of reference—the dominant ideas, wishes and emotions in our minds. "Projection makes perception."...If we are using perception to justify our own mistakes—our anger, our impulses to attack, our lack of love in whatever form it may take—we will see a world of evil, destruction, malice, envy and despair. All this we must learn to forgive, not because we are being "good" and "charitable" but because what we are seeing is not true.
~A Course in Miracles

categories
Concepts or mental structures that give form to the contents of experience. They organize incoming information in ways we can assimilate or make sense of.

Perceiving something clearly and distinctly is essentially a matter of perceiving certain logical relationships.
~Harry G. Frankfurt

While all our knowledge begins with experience, it does not follow that it all arises out of experience.
~Immanuel Kant

perception, while your mind provided the form of understanding. What you probably did not see is what I actually intended to draw. What you "should" have seen are three unrelated dots—what I in fact presented to you.

What do you see in Figure 1.5? Nothing? A shoe? Perhaps you saw the letters C and D. If so, ask yourself now what they mean. If you come from a computer background, the letters may mean "change directory." If you know something about fashion, they may stand for the designer Christian Dior. If you are a music enthusiast, they could mean "compact disc." However, if you just saw the comedy *Roxanne*, you might conclude that CD refers to the nickname of the firechief Steve Martin plays in the film. From these examples you can better appreciate the notion that we are not completely external and independent of reality. We actually do something to incoming sensory information in order to make sense of the world. The next time you see somebody or perceive a situation in a certain way, remember that your mind has played a part in the construction of the experience.

The active process of perception involves the application of **categories**. Think of a category as a concept, schema or mental structure. The categories of the mind give form to the contents of experience. They organize incoming information in ways we can assimilate or make sense of. Sometimes the demands of external reality force us to change our ways of thinking. Forms of understanding must therefore be significantly altered to accommodate novel situations to make sense of the world. To help demonstrate how mental forms give structure to experience, look at the four frames in Figure 1.6, each containing what at first glance appear to be random shapes. What do you see? (Don't read on until you've looked at the frames.)

As you looked at the frames, did you notice how your "mind's eye" kept trying to arrange and rearrange the shapes in each frame to "fit" some idea or concept of what it might be? Your mind spontaneously tried to assimilate the sensory data into pre-existing forms. Perhaps you were readily able to see the objects contained in each frame, perhaps not. Now, let me give you perceptual categories that you can use in each frame in order to make sense of it. In Frame A, look for a person on a bicycle. In Frame B, look for a teapot. In Frame C, you will find three shoes, while in Frame D, there is a water faucet. I suspect now that you have been given the forms, you will begin to mentally arrange the sensory data to see what is there. Imagine, however, that you lived in a culture where running tap water did not exist, where there were no such things as bicycles, where tea was unheard of and where people walked barefoot. In that culture, would anyone "see" a bicycle, teapot, shoes or a faucet? Certainly not.

Another important aspect of reality construction is that the perceptual categories we use to make sense of the world are largely a product of socialization. Some categories—such as space, time, number and causality—seem to be innate or biologically preprogrammed, but most are handed down to us

Figure 1.6
What Do You See?

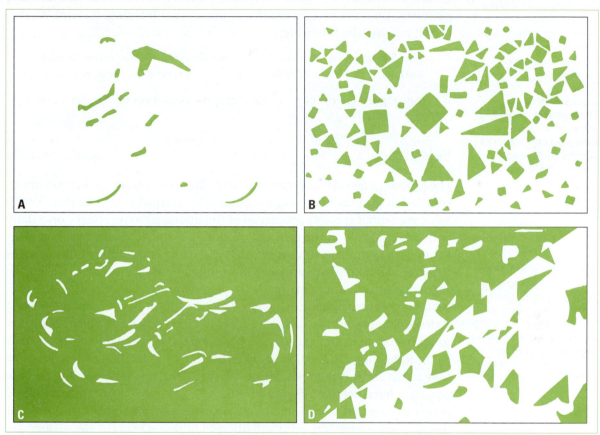

by our family, culture, friends and social institutions. In some ways we see what we are conditioned to see.

Perceptual categories that organize social experience are not static. They develop and change as we grow. Furthermore, no two people have identical sets of perceptual categories. Different people, circumstances and experiences in our lives create alternative ways of looking at the world. What we in fact perceive is greatly influenced by our values, needs, goals, preferences, interests, beliefs, attitudes, expectations, wants, language and education. It is unlikely, therefore, that any two people will ever see life in exactly the same way. For example, if you have been encouraged to become an aspiring businessperson, you may see the chief executive officer of the corporation for which you work as highly admirable and successful. However, a student with communist leanings may see the same CEO as an exploitative economic opportunist. An education in Marxism can filter perceptions very differently as

All ideas come from sensations or reflection—Let us then suppose the mind to be, as we say, white paper, void of all characters, without any ideas—How comes it to be furnished?...Whence has it all the materials of reason and knowledge? To this I answer, in one word, from experience. In that all knowledge is founded; and from that it ultimately derives itself.
~John Locke

23

...no form of knowledge, not even perceptual knowledge, constitutes a simple copy of reality, because it always includes a process of assimilation to previous structures.
~Jean Piaget

perceptual filtering
The process of channelling sensory data through our perceptual categories. Our filtering system determines how we view the world.

compared with an education in business. Clearly, then, things such as acquired knowledge and personal value systems can influence how anyone perceives. Commenting on the role of **perceptual filtering**, Richard Weaver (1993: 76) says the following:

> *Our filtering system determines how we view the world. The world exists for us as we perceive it. We cannot "tell it like it is"; we can only tell it like we perceive it.*

See Figure 1.7 on page 31 for a graphic depiction of Weaver's point.

Selecting

selecting
A part of the process of perception in which our minds limit the quantity of stimuli to which we attribute meaning. We tend to choose sensory data or communication messages we agree with and which are most meaningful to us.

The process of perceptual construction involves not only an application of categories but also selection, organization and interpretation (Weaver, 1996). Since we cannot possibly process all of the information we receive on a daily basis, our minds limit the quantity of stimuli to which we attribute meaning. In **selecting**, we tend to choose sensory data or communication messages we agree with and which are most meaningful to us. For instance, we tend to register positive comments made by people we like and negative or unacceptable comments made by people we don't like or don't support. The rest go largely unnoticed. Also, what we select to perceive will be influenced by personal history and past experience. If we were always taught to believe that being industrious is good, we may notice how hardworking someone is or how much effort is put forth on the playing field. If good grooming and appearance have been reinforced in our lives, we may pay attention to how people dress and style their hair. You can experience first-hand the process of selective perception by paying attention to how you read the newspaper. Do the experiential exercise which follows.

Organizing

organizing
The process of perception that includes enlarging, simplifying and closing.

enlarging
Putting words into a larger context so that they can be understood better.

simplifying
A way to organize perception, by attempting to reduce the amount and complexity of the information we receive.

As mentioned, active perception involves **organizing** information. One way to organize incoming data is "to put the words we hear into a larger context so that we can understand them better" (Weaver, 1993: 81). This aspect of organization is called **enlarging**. When we enlarge, we actually look for a frame of reference to help to make sense of the received message. For example, to make sense of an ambiguous comment (one having more than one possible meaning) we might enlarge it by looking at the speaker's nonverbal communication. We might relate it to what the person said earlier, what happened before, or what the speaker's mood was when the comment was made.

A second way to organize perception is by means of **simplifying**. For example, as you read this section of the text on perception, your mind is probably trying to order the incoming data so that the essential information can be recalled later on for testing purposes. You may take notes using headings or use point form to condense large amounts of material. In my college lectures I often summarize paragraphs of books by trying to capture in a nutshell what the author is trying to communicate. I try to say, in one sentence, what may be expressed in half a page. In this case I share the products of my own simplifying with students. This is hard for me, I might add, for I usually find it easier to say in a paragraph what could be said in a simple sentence.

Closing is a third aspect of perceptual organization. When we perceptually "close," we try to fill in the gaps between pieces of information (Weaver, 1996). If you saw a triangle in the three random dots illustrated in Figure 1.4, you can appreciate how you connected them to form one unified whole. Spontaneously, your mind took fragmented bits of information and imposed closure. Other examples of closure include finishing someone else's sentence or filling in the missing parts of a conversation when only fragments of it can be overheard due to external noise.

closing
A way to organize perceptions by filling the gaps between pieces of information.

May I Have the First Section, Please?

application
exercise
1.2

Instructions: Pick up a copy of the newspaper. Start reading and leafing through it as you normally would. If a newspaper is not readily available, recall your usual way of going through it. Answer the questions below. Discuss your answers with others in the class.

1.6

Which section of the newspaper did you turn to first? Why?

In what order did you read the remaining sections of the newspaper? Is this an order you often choose? Does this suggest anything about your interests and priorities?

Were there any sections or articles you opted not to read? What parts of the paper did you ignore purposely or unwittingly? What didn't you look at?

Have you started reading sections or articles of the newspaper recently that you used to ignore? Are you now ignoring sections that you once read? If so, what does this shift tell you about yourself? What changes in your life have taken place to influence your selection of information in the paper?

For thought: This exercise was developed to help you better understand the process of selective perception. When "reading" people and situations, what do you tend to notice first? What goes overlooked? If you don't see everything about a person or situation, then what exactly do you see? Do you notice things about people now that you never did before? What do your perceptions of others tell you about yourself?

25

Differing interpretations of art clearly show how individual perception is an active process of construction.

Why say in a few words
that which could be said
in many?
~*Tonee Balonee*

Simplicity is very difficult
for twisted minds.
~*A Course in Miracles*

Interpreting

interpreting
A part of the process of perception in which we give meaning to information, evaluate it and arrive at conclusions about it. Essentially, it involves identification and evaluation.

In addition to selecting and organizing information, the process of perception also involves **interpreting** it. When we interpret, we give meaning to information, evaluate it, and arrive at conclusions about it. We can then respond appropriately and better predict future events (Weaver, 1993). Interpretation involves identification and evaluation. A bump in the night, for example, may be somewhat frightening until it is identified as the banging water pipes in the basement. Once the noise is identified, it is spontaneously evaluated. The first question, "What's that noise?" is followed by the second, "Is it dangerous?" When we evaluate sensory information, we call upon all our knowledge and previous experience. Of course, sometimes our interpretations are erroneous. We may mislabel the noise, for instance, identifying it as something it is not. The bump may have been a burglar. We may also incorrectly evaluate the danger factor. We could conclude that the situation does not need our immediate attention when it really does. While errors can be made on both counts, sensory identification is usually fairly reliable, whereas interpretation is open to greater question (Weaver, 1996).

1.7 ····· ## How I See the World Is My Responsibility

When perception is understood as an active process of construction, the notion that we are largely responsible for what we see becomes intuitively clear. While it is true that our parents, teachers and other cultural influences helped to form our current perceptions, as adults we can constantly make changes. We can add to our list of perceptual categories through learning, experience and rational choice. We can also modify or reject categories we were raised with. For example, we can choose to see people as morally equal, not unequal, because of differences in skin colour. If we have unconsciously ignored certain kinds of sensory information in the past, we can now choose to pay attention. If we have defensively blocked out undesirable messages before, we can now opt to listen and perhaps learn from our adversaries. When planning to experience things in the future, we can decide what to look for and even prepare for experiential opportunities. Before visiting an art gallery, for instance, we could read art history books and stock up on artistic categories that will help us to appreciate the artwork on view. Whether we see a painting as a good example of French Impressionism or as a nice accent piece for our living room depends on us. Instead of concluding that "What you see is what you get," perhaps we ought to say, "What I see depends on me."

In the context of human relations development, the perception of "self" and "others" is vitally important. If we don't like what we see in ourselves, this will affect our self-esteem, our world-view, and the ways in which we communicate and respond to others. Similarly, how we see other people may determine whether we approach them, talk to them, avoid them, criticize them, trust them or ignore them. Social perception may have us attribute causes to people's behaviour, label them in certain ways or read things into their intentions and motivations. Whether we look at ourselves or at others, it is important to know the factors that influence our perception. Let us now turn to some common **perceptual errors** that distort our person perceptions and influence our interactions with others.

perceptual errors
Errors of perception that distort our vision and influence our interactions with others. Examples include: stereotyping, self-fulfilling prophecies, the halo effect, errors in attribution, proximity and role definition.

1. 8 ····· # Perceptual Errors

Stereotyping

Existentialist philosophers have argued that individuals are as unique as their fingerprints. They support this argument with the fact that never before in the history of humanity has there been another you and never for all eternity will there be another you. Individual uniqueness is universal. Not only are we different, but so too is everyone else. In view of this individual uniqueness, a

What I See Depends on Me

Source: "The Investigation" © John Jonik, *Psychology Today*, 1984

stereotyping
A perceptual error in which we lump different individuals together by wrongly attributing to them common characteristics.

selectivity
A process in perception that perpetuates stereotypes. When we have a stereotype, we often unconsciously but actively look for things in others that confirm it, and disregard perceptions that are inconsistent with our stereotype.

perceptual mistake we sometimes make is lumping different individuals together and wrongly attributing to them common characteristics. This perceptual error is better known as **stereotyping**.

The tendency toward stereotyping exists in the minds of many perceivers and leads us to make incorrect judgments about people, most of whom are strangers to us. For instance, we may assume that all foreign college students from Asia excel in computer science, every Quebecker is a separatist, all men lack feeling, all feminists are man-haters, or all Canadians play hockey and drink beer. How would you feel having your individual uniqueness so easily dismissed by someone else pigeon-holing you into some kind of racial, ethnic, linguistic, national or gender stereotype? Chances are pretty good that you would feel violated, angry or hurt. Misrepresentations, arising out of stereotyping, can lead to negative feelings, which can damage interpersonal relationships.

Notwithstanding the fact that stereotyping distorts the truth about individuals and thereby causes inaccuracy in social perception, it persists. One reason is that stereotyping is functional (Weaver, 1996; Weiten, Lloyd and Lashley, 1999). This process helps us to simplify the complex information we receive about others in the external world. We may not have the capacity, patience, interest or desire to learn about the uniqueness of all those whom we encounter. Instead, we may reduce people to stereotypes in order to simplify matters. However, what we gain in (over)simplification, we lose in accuracy.

The process of **selectivity** in perception also perpetuates stereotypes. When we have a stereotype, we often unconsciously but actively look for things in others that confirm it. If you stereotype all Lutonians (a fictitious race of people created by the late comedian John Candy) as stupid, for instance, you might not hear the intelligent things they say. As singer-songwriter Paul Simon put it, "A man hears what he wants to hear and disregards the rest." Perceptions that are inconsistent with any stereotypes may be ignored, easily forgotten or denied. An intelligent comment by a Lutonian could thus be discounted as mere "book learning" or dismissed as a repetition of what someone else said before. Intelligent comments will not be received and accepted at face value.

Self-Fulfilling Prophecy

The **self-fulfilling prophecy** is another perceptual process that influences social interaction. It occurs when you make a prediction about something or somebody that comes true, mainly because you made the prediction and behaved as if it were true. If you enter a room thinking the people there won't like you, you may act coldly and aggressively toward them. If you do, they may respond to you in unfriendly ways. What you end up seeing are people who don't behave nicely toward you, just as you expected. What you may not see is that you actually helped cause the unfriendliness.

Self-fulfilling prophecies can work positively as well. In one classic psychological study, teachers were told that certain pupils in their classes were late bloomers, but they were expected to do exceptionally well. In truth, children's names were drawn at random by the researchers. The results of the study indicated that selected students did in fact perform at higher academic levels compared with the students who were not named as ones possessing exceptional abilities. Given the randomness of the selection procedure, the teachers' expectations probably generated special attention to the selected students, thereby naturally affecting their performance. This widely known example of the self-fulfilling prophecy is referred to as the **Pygmalion effect.** (Rosenthal and Jacobson, 1968).

Halo Effect

The process of selective perception can sometimes lead to what's called the **halo effect**. The halo effect occurs when people form a general impression of an individual based on a single characteristic, or a limited number of characteristics attributed to that individual. For example, if you believe that a person possesses several positive qualities, you may conclude that the individual possesses certain other positive qualities. Your perception of other people may thus be filtered by an "implicit personality theory" of which you may not even be conscious (DeVito, 1998). On this note, DeVito asks how we would complete the following sentences.

John is energetic, eager and (intelligent, unintelligent). May is bold, defiant and (extraverted, introverted). Joe is bright, lively and (thin, fat). Jane is attractive, intelligent and (believable, unbelievable).

As DeVito points out, some choices seem right, others wrong, depending on our implicit personality theory. "Most people's rules tell them that a person who is energetic and eager is also intelligent. Of course, there is no logical reason an unintelligent person could not be energetic and eager" (DeVito, 1993: 49). Given this notion, you may see qualities in people that are not there. You may also ignore or distort qualities and characteristics in people that

self-fulfilling prophecy
A process that influences perception and social interaction. It occurs when you make a prediction about something or somebody that comes true, mainly because you made the prediction and behaved as if it were true.

Pygmalion effect
A tendency to attribute positive characteristics to, or hold positive expectations of, persons about whom (groundless) positive information has been provided.

halo effect
A general impression of a person based on one or two characteristics.

29

do not conform to your implicit personality theory. Before you look at very many more people, it is worth reconsidering your psychological assumptions about them. You may be witnessing your assumptions, not necessarily what is true about them. Be careful, as well, not to fall victim to the **reverse halo effect**. The presence of a few negative qualities does not mean that more are lurking. A selfish, egotistical person needn't be dishonest or emotionally abusive to others. Finally, do not jump to conclusions about people based on what you observe. Two people can do the same thing for very different reasons. Two storekeepers can return the correct change to a young customer, one because of fear that dishonesty may hurt business in the long run (an act of self-interest), the other because treating all people honestly is simply the right and virtuous thing to do (an act of morality). The storekeeper's intentions are thus more significant than the observed actions themselves. Again, maybe the saying "Seeing is believing" should be amended this time to something like "Given what I see, what should I believe?" This brings us to another kind of perceptual error.

Attribution Errors

In the storekeeper example, we learned that the same behaviour can be attributed to different intentions and motivations. This idea is important to note, for sometimes our attributions are incorrect. To better appreciate the nature of **attribution errors**, it is helpful to explain the kinds of attributions that we can make. When we observe someone's behaviour, it is possible to attribute to it either internal or external causes. Perhaps the person's bad mood (internal cause) led to explosive behaviour. Or maybe the individual barked at us because of something that happened at work that day (external cause). The internal–external dimension of attribution thus locates the source of behaviour as inside or outside. Internal attributions "ascribe the causes of behaviour to personal dispositions, traits, abilities, and feelings" (Weiten, Lloyd and Lashley, 1999). External attributions ascribe the causes of people's behaviour to situational factors. Environmental demands, constraints and events may give rise to certain behaviour.

A second dimension relevant to attribution is stability. Some causes of behaviour (internal or external) are temporary or unstable (e.g., a weakened physical condition brought on by the flu). Others may be stable or permanent (e.g., one's temperament or the demands of a job). Understanding attribution in terms of the two dimensions just mentioned allows us to form a four-part grid. See Figure 1.8.

It is important to note that we often predictably make certain types of attributional errors when interpreting, evaluating or trying to understand people's behaviour, including our own. One good way of understanding these errors is in terms of **actor–observer differences** (Weiten, Lloyd and Lashley, 1999).

reverse halo effect
A perceptual error which occurs when people form a negative general impression of an individual based on a single negative characteristic, or a limited number of negative characteristics, attributed to that individual.

attribution errors
Perceptual errors made when we mistakenly attribute behaviour (our own, or someone else's) to a particular internal or external cause. We may also make an attribution error when we fail to distinguish between unstable and stable causes. Finally, identified actor–observer differences contribute to errors in attribution.

actor–observer differences
A factor contributing to perceptual errors, depending on whether one is the agent of the action or the spectator of it.

30

Figure 1.7
Appearance Versus Reality

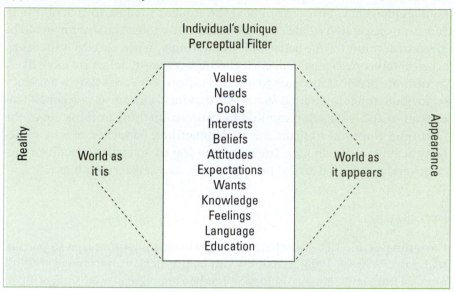

In any behavioural situation, the actor performs and the observer looks on. Research indicates that actors and observers see situations differently (Jones and Nisbett, 1971). As a result, we can find very interesting and different explanations for things like failure and success. A student who fails an exam, for instance, may find fault with the test measure, the noise in the room during the testing or the fact that unforeseen circumstances prevented her from properly studying. As observers, we and the instructor may attribute the

Figure 1.8
Type of Attributions

	Unstable	Stable
Internal	Internal–Unstable Cause	Internal–Stable Cause
External	External–Unstable Cause	External–Stable Cause

student's failure to poor study skills, lack of intelligence or irresponsibility. If the student was indeed prevented from studying for an exam because of a family emergency, but we attributed the student's failure to lack of intelligence, misperception would certainly occur. The wrong explanation would be given to account for the behaviour. Interestingly, when success is the issue, actor–observer perceptual tendencies become reversed. Actors are more likely to attribute personal successes to internal factors. Observers have a tendency to attribute them to external factors, such as luck. Of course, perceptual tendencies in either direction can lead to error—something to think about the next time you want to figure out why something happened or why somebody acted in a certain way. The next time you try to explain your own successes and failures, be careful not to fall prey to a **self-serving bias**.

Proximity

Proximity is another important factor that can sometimes lead to perceptual error (Weaver, 1996). Proximity can be physical or psychological. With physical proximity, distance influences our perception of people. Someone perceived as attractive from a distance may be seen as less attractive up close. Skin blemishes and other facial features that were unnoticeable from afar may become prominent when near. In this case, vision corrected by closer proximity could turn initial attraction into disinterest or repulsion.

Psychological proximity deals with similarity of attitude. We tend to evaluate people who display attitudes similar to our own more positively than we do people whose attitudes are dissimilar to ours. For instance, when students and teachers are attitudinally similar, teachers get higher scores when rated on things like open-mindedness, personal attractiveness and teaching skills. When teachers' attitudes are largely dissimilar, their ratings are lower (Good and Good, 1973, cited in Weaver, 1996). Of course, something like a person's open-mindedness does not hinge on other people's attitudes; only the perception of it does. The next time you evaluate another person's performance, it might be useful to take your attitudinal similarities and dissimilarities into account. Maybe what is required is not a change in someone else's behaviour but an attitude adjustment on your part.

Psychological proximity refers not only to attitude but to our readiness or predisposition to respond in certain ways. A photographer watching a movie might notice the lighting and camera angles used in filming; an actress might be more inclined to focus on the timing and physical movements of the performers; an economist might fixate on the cost of background scenery, the special effects and props. The point is that people bring their own experiences and mindset to any event or situation. Different individuals are psychologically closer to different aspects of what is perceived. Most people's psychological mindset can influence perception as much as, if not more than, the actual facts of the event witnessed (Weaver, 1996). To the extent that

self-serving bias
The tendencies among actors and observers to see situations differently. For instance, in the case of a personal success, the actor is likely to ascribe this success to internal factors, whereas the observer is likely to attribute another's success to external factors. In the case of personal failures, the reverse is true. Such tendencies in either direction can lead to error.

proximity
A factor that can sometimes lead to perceptual error. Proximity can be either physical or psychological. In the case of physical proximity, distance influences our perception of people (someone perceived as attractive from a distance may be seen as less attractive up close). Psychological proximity deals with similarity of attitude. We tend to evaluate people who display attitudes similar to our own more positively than we do people whose attitudes are dissimilar to ours.

this is true, perceptions can become distorted in one direction or another. Given our current mindset, we may attribute undue importance to certain variables when describing or explaining people, situations and events when, in fact, others are more significant.

Role Definition

In society, we all play **roles**. Your role, as you read this book, is that of a student. At your full- or part-time job, your role is worker. At home, your role may be that of brother, sister, mother or father. In fact, there are many types of roles: family, gender, occupational and so on. The roles that we play affect our personal needs, our attitudes and expectations, our beliefs and the perspective we take when perceiving people and situations. For instance, if we live by traditional gender roles (e.g., those accepted by the arch-conservative Archie Bunker in the classic sitcom *All in the Family*), the same behaviour exhibited by males and females will be perceived differently. An aggressive male may be seen as self-willed and determined. An aggressive female may be perceived as domineering and bitchy. In both cases, the behaviour is the same, but when it is observed and filtered through the lenses of traditional role definition, it is perceived positively in the case of the male and negatively in the case of the female. Roles, then, influence our perceptions and, as the example above illustrates, can often lead to bias and inconsistent evaluation.

Oprah Winfrey, a powerful billionaire and business executive, shatters any stereotypes of African American women.

Courtesy of Mike Nelson/Corbis Images.

roles
The many parts we play in society. There are many types of roles: family, gender, occupational and so on. The roles we play affect our personal needs, our attitudes and expectations, our beliefs and the perspective we take when perceiving people and situations.

   As we have seen, perceptual errors are numerous. They result from stereotyping, self-fulfilling prophecies, halo effects, attribution errors, proximity and role definition. Remember as well that perception is largely a matter of personal responsibility. Richard Weaver (1996) has made a number of useful recommendations for minimizing your own perceptual errors. An abbreviated paraphrased list of them follows.

1. 9 ⋯⋯

How to Reduce Errors in Perception

Avoid hasty conclusions Don't overgeneralize. Base conclusions on strong evidence and repeated observations. Maintain a healthy balance between openness and skepticism. Expand your perceptual frame of reference by broadening your personal experience. Encourage communication to gain new evidence and to form new impressions. Guard against selective perception. Don't overlook contradictory information.

Allow yourself more time Develop more accurate perceptions of people by spending more time with them and getting closer to them. Erroneous initial

All the world's a stage,
And all the men and
women merely players.
~*Shakespeare, As You Like
It, Act 2, Scene 7*

impressions may change to more accurate ones with time. Temporarily suspend judgment. Show patience. Give your mind time to analyze and sift through relevant information before making judgments.

Make yourself available Be present for others both in mind and body. When you are with others, try to see things from their vantage point. Communicate in sincere and meaningful ways. Go beyond superficial niceties. Be open and honest. Attempt to connect and empathize. Show your reactions and participate in others' reactions.

Commit yourself Consciously decide to seek out as much information as possible before making a judgment or forming an opinion. More information will probably lead to less perceptual distortion. Develop your knowledge and expand your range of experience. One-sided people do not experience life fully.

Create the proper climate Try to create a climate conducive to communication, one in which self-disclosure is likely to occur. Develop mutual trust to allow for the exchange of honest messages. Make an effort not to manipulate others, dominate them or run their lives. Avoid pretense, defence and deception.

Make adjustments when necessary Since people and situations change, be flexible and prepared to change your perception. Also, develop perceptual sensitivity. Recognize that your own perceptions will change as your interests and experiences change. Today's perception may not be accurate if based on yesterday's attitudes.

Perceptual Influences on Interpersonal Attraction

Centuries ago, the ancient philosopher Aristotle declared human beings to be the "social animal." More recent empirical evidence seems to suggest we all have a need to belong (Baumeister and Leary, 1995). We want to connect with others and, in some cases, transform these connections into intimate and enduring relationships. Quite likely, our desire to form mutual attachments had early survival value for our ancestors. The more help there was, the easier it was to build shelters and hunt for food. Also, the likelihood of survival for a new-born infant could be significantly enhanced by the nurturing of two bonded parents who stayed together and supported each other. Today, when basic survival is not primarily at issue, finding a caring and supportive partner in whom we can confide helps us to feel accepted and prized as we are (Myers and Spencer, 2004). It's no fluke that people spend billions of dollars on such things as cosmetics, clothes, and diets to make themselves appear more desirable or attractive to others. We all long for acceptance and love and we fear the possibility of being ostracized. Even in our cyber-relations on the Internet, we can often feel hurt by being ignored in chat rooms or by having our emails go unanswered. Feeling left out we experience anxiety, paranoia, or perhaps some kind of general malaise manifesting itself in a kind of fragility of spirit (Williams and Zadro, 2001). We may feel like non-persons.

There are several key factors that influence **interpersonal attraction**: **proximity**, **physical attractiveness**, and **similarity** (Myers and Spencer, 2004). Notwithstanding the fact that proximity is something often giving rise to perceptual errors, as already discussed, it nonetheless still kindles liking. Interestingly, most people are likely to marry someone who lives in the same neighbourhood, works with the same employer or sits in the same classroom (Burr, 1973). Next time you're in the classroom, lecture hall or tutorial session, look around. You may be looking at your future spouse!

Proximity, better understood, is not so much about geographical distance, but **functional distance**, that is, how often people's paths cross. Even if people come from different neighbourhoods, they may still share the same entrances, parking lots and recreation areas. One study has found that randomly assigned university roommates are more likely to become good friends as opposed to enemies (Newcomb, 1961). Of course, frequent interactions cannot help but occur in such close quarters. They enable roommates to explore their similarities, to tune into one another, and to perceive themselves as a social unit (Arkin, Appleman and Burger, 1980). What we learn from proximity, whether geographic or functional, is that there exists a **repeated exposure effect**. Contrary to the old adage, familiarity does *not* usually breed contempt. Rather, it tends to breed fondness (Bornstein, 1989). Studies have shown that novel stimuli tend to be liked more and rated more positively after the rater has been repeatedly exposed to them. This insight is exploited in advertising. During election campaigns, the candidate with the most media exposure usually wins (McCullough and Ostrom, 1974). Political strategists who understand the repeated-exposure effect often replace reasoned argument with brief ads that drive home the candidate's name and sound bite message. So too do advertisers use repetition to increase sales for a product toward which consumers have no strong feelings (McCollough and Ostrom, ibid.).

In addition to proximity, physical attractiveness has also been found to be important when it comes to attraction or when considering someone as a dating or marriage partner. It's been discovered that physical attractiveness also influences prospective employers during job interviews (Mack and Rainey, 1990). The more attractive candidate for a job is more likely to be hired. Again, at the risk of dispelling some more age-old wisdom, it's not entirely true that "Beauty is in the eye of the beholder." There are indeed some widespread standards for physical attraction. For instance, tallness is regarded as an asset for men, though college women prefer dates who are average in height. By contrast, tall women tend to be viewed less positively by men (Sheppard and Strathman, 1989).

Both genders in current Western culture seem to prefer slenderness and find it more engaging (Franzoi and Herzog, 1987). Women display a preference for men with a V-taper to their physique (Horvath, 1981). They also prefer men to be slimmer than most men assume.

interpersonal attraction
A felt connection between persons.

proximity
Physical or functional distance between people.

physical attractiveness
Bodily features which attract one to another.

similarity
Commonality with respect to interests, attitudes and values.

functional distance
Proximity based on common use of space.

repeated exposure effect
The tendency to respond more favourably to stimuli that are repeatedly presented.

When it comes to physical characteristics such as height and, to some extent, body type, we are greatly impacted by genetics, hormones, and metabolism. There are some things you can do, however, to influence others' perceptions of your physical attractiveness. To begin with, you can smile more. Men and women are both perceived as more attractive when they are smiling (Reis et al., 1990). It's very much in your interest, then, to put on a happy face when meeting people or looking for a date. Findings also suggest that women prefer men who are outgoing and self-expressive. So, if you're a man, act accordingly if you wish to attract female attention. On the flipside, men responded negatively to women displaying behavioural patterns which women found attractive in men (Riggio and Woll, 1984). Thus, if you are a very outgoing or extremely self-expressive woman, take note that men will find you less physically attractive by virtue of your behaviour.

Finally, it you wish to enhance your physical attractiveness, you should also take **dominance** into account. College women find college men who display more dominance as more attractive. Given current social stereotypes, it's not too surprising perhaps that women who showed dominance were *not* rated as more attractive by men. Apparently, men still prefer women to be demure, though this may change in the future with evolving sex-roles in society.

dominance
The characteristic allowing one to have rule or sway over others.

A third key factor determining interpersonal attraction involves similarity. Here's an adage that does get confirmed for a change by empirical evidence: "Birds of a feather *do* flock together." This fact is illustrated by a finding which showed that roommate friendships at college flourished over a six-month period when roommates shared values and personality traits. They flourished even more when they *perceived* their roommates as similar. In this instance, perception meant more than reality (Lee and Bond, 1996).

In view of the impact of similarity, it shouldn't be too surprising that people who do not share our attitudes, values, and beliefs are often judged in a negative fashion. Dissimilarity breeds dislike. Actually, the idea that "opposites attract," say in dating or mating, has never been reliably demonstrated, with the single exception of sex (Buss, 1985). Average-looking people may be made to feel homely when in the company of beautiful people. Or, if you're someone prone to feeling moody and blue, you might find another's bubbly personality to be particularly annoying.

In conclusion to this chapter, allow me to repeat how person perception is a constructive process, one which is largely a product of selection, organization, and interpretation. The lesson learned is that not everybody sees the world or other people in the same way. In the next chapter, we will build on this insight by examining the notion of "psychological type," and how individual diversity can be understood in terms of it. By exploring type you can better understand yourself and others. What gets selected and organized in perception and how what's selected is interpreted and evaluated are both largely a function of type. People of different psychological types tend to perceive reality differently in fairly consistent and predictable ways. Let's see how.

Study Guide

Key Terms

self (4)
self-concept (4)
self-awareness (6)
open self (6)
blind self (6)
unknown self (7)
hidden self (7)
self-disclosure (8)
self-esteem (12)
emoticons (18)
linguistic softeners (18)
email addresses (19)
homepage construction (19)
perception (20)
empiricists (20)
rationalist thinkers (21)

interactionist theory of knowledge (21)
construction (21)
categories (22)
perceptual filtering (24)
selecting (24)
organizing (24)
enlarging (24)
simplifying (24)
closing (25)
interpreting (26)
perceptual errors (27)
stereotyping (28)
selectivity (28)
self-fulfilling prophecy (29)
Pygmalion effect (29)
halo effect (29)

reverse halo effect (30)
attribution errors (30)
actor–observer differences (30)
self-serving bias (32)
proximity (32)
roles (33)
interpersonal attraction (35)
proximity (35)
physical attractiveness (35)
similarity (35)
functional distance (35)
repeated exposure effect (35)
dominance (36)

Fill-in-the-Blank Questions

Instructions: Fill in each blank with the appropriate response from the list below.

Progress Check 1.1

interactionist
active
perceptual filters
halo effect
responsibility
attribution errors
emoticons
warm
halo effect
self-concept
open self
perception
empiricists
repeated

exposure effect
static
self-esteem
self-disclosure
self-talk
personal responsibility
self-awareness
social comparison
stereotyping
selective
interpretation
proximity
smiling

1. People who are able to make an initial _____ impression will be seen more favourably.

2. _____ are playful combinations of punctuation marks which show facial expressions.

3. _____, whether functional or physical, often contributes to interpersonal attraction.

4. During elections, political campaigners try to give their candidates the most media exposure to take advantage of the _____.

5. _____ more often can enhance anyone's attractiveness.

6. The process of perceptual construction involves selection, organization and _____.

7. The way I choose to see the world is my _____.

8. Whenever people wrongly lump others together and attribute to them common characteristics that they don't possess, they are guilty of _____.

9. When we meet somebody, we don't perceive everything about that person; we are _____ in our perception.

10. Forming a general impression of someone based on a single characteristic gives rise to the _____.

11. An effort to locate the source of behaviours as internal or external can sometimes lead to _____.

12. _____ refers to the overall way you see and understand yourself.

13. Self-concepts are not _____.

14. Self-disclosure hinges on _____.

15. The _____ is that part of yourself known by you and shared with others.

16. _____ is the act of revealing information about yourself to others.

17. The positive or negative evaluations we make about our self-concepts contribute to our _____.

18. The value judgments you make about yourself are a matter of _____.

19. Self-esteem can be affected by _____.

20. People can raise their self-esteem through the use of affirmations or positive _____.

True/False Questions

Instructions: Circle the appropriate letter next to each statement.

T F   1. Psychological perception is irrelevant to social relations.

T F   2. Rationalists believe that "what you see is what you get." Knowledge is based on experience.

T F   3. The figure made up of three dots has only one correct meaning.

T F   4. According to the interactionist viewpoint, perception is an active process.

T F   5. The filtering system of perception filters out erroneous messages to give us a truer picture of reality.

T F   6. The mind has a natural tendency to impose closure on incoming stimuli to make sense of the world.

T F   7. You can exercise considerable responsibility when it comes to how you choose to see life.

T F   8. The halo effect causes us to see "bad" people as "good" people.

T F   9. When we attribute behaviour to causal factors that are lasting or ongoing, we can say that the causes are stable.

T F 10. Students who fail an exam are likely to attribute their failure to external causes.

T F 11. Proximity, as a factor in perception, can be either physical or psychological.

T F 12. The notion of self-concept includes all of your self-referring values, beliefs, attitudes and feelings.

T F 13. There is only one self.

T F 14. The self-concept is static.

T F 15. Self-disclosure always improves relationships.

T F 16. The hidden self contains information about yourself that is buried in the unconscious.

T F 17. Introverts are likely to find self-disclosure more difficult than are extraverts.

T F 18. The Johari Window is a theoretical device used to explain the mechanisms of perception.

T F 19. People who rarely self-disclose have less effective immune systems compared to those who self-disclose more frequently.

T F 20. Egotism is another word for self-esteem.

Summary

1. How is perception important to human relations?
   • they are intimately related
   • through perception we gain awareness, experience people, attribute causes, give meaning and form impressions of others

2. How is perception an (inter)active process?

- perception involves construction (i.e., application of categories, assimilation to previous structures of understanding, accommodation)
- perception is a filtering process
- it involves selecting, organizing and interpreting

3. What are some common perceptual errors?

- stereotyping: lumping individuals together and attributing to them common characteristics
- self-fulfilling prophecy: seeing what one expects to see as a result of one's behaviour or expectations
- halo effect: taking one characteristic (either positive or negative) and perceiving others as related, when in fact they're not
- attributional errors: making mistakes when attributing causes or sources of behaviour
- proximity (physical or psychological): misperceiving because of distance. Evaluations may be biased in favour of those who display similar attributes to our own.
- roles: playing roles skews our perceptions

4. How can errors in perception be reduced?

- avoid hasty conclusions
- allow yourself more time
- make yourself available
- commit yourself to situations
- create the proper climate
- make adjustments when necessary

5. What is self-concept?

- the overall way you see and understand yourself
- all of your self-referring beliefs and attitudes, as well as your values, feelings, behavioural dispositions and preferences
- it is multi-faceted (e.g., there is your work self, your ideal self and your serious self)

6. What is the importance of self-concept to human relations?

- what you know about yourself, how you feel about yourself and what you reveal about yourself to others affects others' reactions to you

7. What are the four "panes" of the Johari Window?

- open self: known by yourself and others
- hidden self: known by yourself, not revealed to others
- blind self: known by others, not recognized in yourself
- unknown self: not known by yourself or others

8. How can self-awareness be increased?

   - adopt the perspective of others
   - create a list of your attitudes, behaviours and tendencies
   - pay close attention to how others react to you
   - increase openness to others to reduce the size of your blind self

9. What is self-disclosure?

   - the intentional act of revealing information about yourself to others
   - not about laying blame or emotional dumping
   - sharing parts of yourself with others in a way that respects them

10. Why are people reluctant to self-disclose?

    - fear that self-disclosure may be used against the self-discloser
    - fear of rejection
    - fear of others' reactions
    - fear of hurting others
    - fear of projecting an unwanted image

11. Why is self-disclosure important to social relationships?

    - mutual self-disclosure paves the way for friendship and intimacy
    - it allows for caring, sharing and empathy
    - it offers others an opportunity to respond to us
    - it enhances personal well-being, improves effectiveness of immune system and supports good mental health

12. What are some guidelines for appropriate self-disclosure?

    - examine and evaluate your intentions
    - think about the appropriate amount of self-disclosure
    - pick your spots for self-disclosure
    - pay attention to others' self-disclosure
    - be prepared to live with what you reveal about yourself

13. What is self-esteem?

    - the value judgment we make on our self-concept
    - a self-referring feeling
    - not self-glorification, arrogance, boastfulness or egoism
    - healthy self-respect

14. What are some factors influencing self-esteem?

    - social comparison
    - personal aspirations
    - feedback from others
    - childhood upbringing
    - gender and sex-role definitions

15. What are some effects of self-esteem on interpersonal relations?

Low self-esteem makes people

- overly sensitive to criticism
- overreact to praise
- adopt hypercritical attitudes
- respond pessimistically
- avoid competitive challenges

High self-esteem makes people

- treat other people as equals
- welcome challenges
- accept praise without embarrassment
- become more self-accepting
- desire to improve themselves
- accept personal responsibility

16. How can you enhance your self-esteem?

- engage in positive self-talk
- surround yourself with supportive people
- set realistic goals for yourself
- discard irrational beliefs
- change your self-presentation

Related Readings

Branden, Nathaniel (2000). *The Psychology of Self-Esteem*. New York: Bantam.

—————— (1988). *How to Raise Your Self-Esteem*. New York: Bantam.

Napoli, Vince, James L. Kilbride and Donald E. Tebbs (1992). *Adjustment and Growth in a Changing World*. 4th edition. St. Paul, MN: West Publishing Co.

Piaget, Jean (1969). *The Mechanisms of Perception*. London: Routledge.

Satir, Virginia (1988). *The New Peoplemaking*. Mountainview, CA: Science & Behavior Books Inc.

There's only one corner of the universe you can be certain of improving, and that's your own self.
~Aldous Huxley

Understanding and Communicating with Different Personality Types

2

Chapter Overview

Who Am I?
- Benefits of Self-Knowledge
- Self-Diagnostic 2.1 Pinpointing My Personality Preferences

Personality Types: Recognizable Patterns of Diversity
- Energy Source: Extraversion Versus Introversion
- Information Gathering: Sensing Versus Intuition

Application Exercise 2.1 Working in Your Wrong Hand

- Decision Making: Thinking Versus Feeling
- Orientation to the Outer World: Judging Versus Perceiving

Type Classifications

Application Exercise 2.2 Classroom Chemistry

Application Exercise 2.3 TV Types Have Different Stripes

Guidelines for the Proper Application of Psychological Type

Study Guide

- Key Terms
- Progress Check 2.1

- Summary
- Related Readings

Learning Outcomes

After successfully completing this chapter, you will be able to

2.1 List the benefits of self-understanding

2.2 Form a hypothesis about your personality type

2.3 Understand psychological diversity in terms of four bipolar scales

2.4 Explain the differences between extraversion and introversion

2.5 Appreciate how sensors and intuitives gather information differently

2.6 Elaborate on how thinkers and feelers differ in their preferred ways of making decisions

2.7 Explain how judging and perceiving types orient to the external world

2.8 Communicate better with people informed by an understanding of psychological type differences.

Focus Questions

1. Isn't it silly to ask, "Who am I?" What practical purpose could be served by finding an answer to this vague, disturbing question?

2. What makes me unique? What commonalities do I share with others?

3. What are the four scales explaining personality functioning according to Jungian psychology, as developed by Katharine Briggs and Isabel Briggs Myers?

4. What energizes people?

5. To what do people pay attention? How do some people perceive the world differently from others?

6. What are the two decision-making processes people use? How is one different from the other?

7. What are the two basic orientations to life people can adopt?

8. What four general categories can be used to summarize all 16 personality types?

Socrates understood the importance of self-knowledge to personal growth and social functioning.

self-knowledge
An understanding of who you are and how your personality works for you.

personality
The combination of one's unique behaviours, thoughts and feelings.

Know thyself.
~Socrates

2.1 ····· Who Am I?

In today's highly competitive, fast-moving world there is often little time or inclination to reflect and ask the question, "Who am I?" For many people, this question is simply too abstract or impractical to be taken seriously. Some may regard it as an exercise in navel-gazing; others may see the question as something more appropriately asked by philosophers, poets and dreamers. Most people are simply too busy trying to survive and earn a living to be concerned about matters of personal identity.

Benefits of Self-Knowledge

As a challenge to practical-minded "survivalists," let me suggest that the road to personal growth and interpersonal effectiveness begins with **self-knowledge**. After all, if you wish to maximize your potential, you must know what that potential is. If you want to work on problems or limitations imposed by your **personality**, you must recognize them in yourself. Furthermore, if you want to get along better with other people, you must understand how personalities differ, how one might impact on the other, and how each is perceived by the other. Without self-knowledge, your journey to human relations mastery will begin in darkness. Your direction will be uncertain and your destination unclear.

Self-knowledge has another practical aspect. To understand others, you need first to examine yourself. Once you begin to appreciate the mechanisms of personality and how they operate in your own life, you will start to observe some of the universals of human behaviour. You will see how others are much like yourself, discovering, for example, that your fears and insecurities are shared by other people. You may learn that the irritations and emotional conflicts you experience are quite similar to those experienced by people with whom you interact on a daily basis. On the other hand, as you discover some of the differences and unique qualities that set you apart from everyone else, you may then begin to appreciate the uniqueness of others. As you develop self-confidence and respect for yourself, trust and respect for others will naturally grow. This point underscores the spiritual insight that you can't love others until you love yourself. Once you begin reducing fear and insecurity and increasing respect and trust, your need to withdraw from others or to behave aggressively toward them will be reduced. Your interpersonal relationships will surely improve. In short, self-knowledge has a social payoff.

Studying how your personality functions can also present a range of possibilities that you may never have considered. Maybe you've always wanted to become a better person but have never known exactly how to do it. By studying your personality, you can discover alternative behavioural paths toward personal growth and development. Perhaps you're at your wits' end when it comes to coping and getting along with "difficult" people in your life. A study of personality can sometimes help you to understand why such people present challenges for you, and you can begin to see these individuals from a different perspective. You can start to explore alternative and useful ways of handling the people you may have given up on.

Understanding your personality can also help you to feel better about yourself. There is little worse than being down emotionally, but not knowing why. Maybe you're unaware of the things going on inside yourself that are contributing to your bad feelings. A better understanding of personality can uncover things about yourself that you have never consciously realized, thereby enabling you to take more effective control of your life. It can free you from debilitating negative emotions, and it can open the door to new and positive experiences. Self-knowledge can help you to establish organized plans for your career and life in general. It can give you a framework for decision making and action by helping you to live and work more productively.

Since the turn of the twentieth century, many different theories of personality have emerged. Two important ones have been the psychoanalytic and humanistic explanations. People such as Sigmund Freud (psychoanalytic) and Abraham Maslow (humanistic) have offered their own accounts of human personality functioning. Another account that has received widespread attention is an offshoot of Carl Jung's analytical theory of personality types. A mother-daughter team of Katharine Briggs and Isabel Briggs Myers has taken the original insights of Jung, added to them, and developed for practical use the **Myers-Briggs Type Indicator (MBTI®)**, an instrument used to help people identify their personality preferences. This instrument has been used by millions of people throughout the world for human resource development, team building and problem solving, as well as for personal counselling, therapy and education. The MBTI® is a restricted psychological assessment tool that can only be used by trained and qualified personnel.

For our purposes here, I have created my own personality self-diagnostic that is different from the MBTI® in terms of wording and format but is theoretically consistent with its ideas and assumptions. It can help you to start thinking about your personality preferences using concepts and insights discussed by Jung, Myers and Briggs. While my informal self-diagnostic obviously will not be as reliable and valid as the highly researched MBTI®, it can nonetheless help you form an initial hypothesis about your **psychological type**, the way you perceive, draw energy, make decisions and orient toward the world. Most people who have completed both the MBTI® and my self-diagnostic have tended to arrive at similar results. My self-diagnostic can therefore serve as a valuable tool for preliminary self-reflection. For those who are seriously interested in verifying their personality type, I would strongly suggest taking the MBTI with a qualified counsellor at your college

No man should part with his own individuality and become that of another. ~Channing

Myers-Briggs Type Indicator (MBTI®)
An instrument that is used to help people identify their personality preferences. Building on the original insights of Carl Jung's analytical theory of personality types, Briggs and Myers developed the four bipolar psychological scales to account for differences in people's perceptual and decision-making functions.

psychological type
The manner in which one perceives, draws energy, makes decisions and orients toward the world.

47

or university. Ideally, your instructor would be in a position to have it administered to you in class. Let us now establish our initial working hypothesis by completing Self-Diagnostic 2.1, Pinpointing My Personality Preferences.

Self Diagnostic

2.1 Pinpointing My Personality Preferences

2.2 This self-diagnostic tool can be used to further self-understanding. Note, however, that you're actually far too complex to "figure out" in one paper-and-pencil measure. Your results on this self-diagnostic can only serve, therefore, as a departure point for further self-exploration. See your results as a working hypothesis of who you are with respect to your preferences and inclinations.

Instructions: Below are pairs of statements listed under lettered columns. Compare the statements in each pair and circle the letter beside the one that most accurately describes your preferences, behaviours or mental habits. Be sure to circle one—and only one—letter in each pair. Some decisions may be difficult, especially when you like both statements. Simply pick the one for which you have the slightest preference. As well, choose the answer that feels right for you. Don't answer as you or others think you "should." Simply imagine yourself to be in a comfortable spot and answer the questions in a relaxed frame of mind. It's important to be accurate and honest. This is not your work self or student self answering; it is your "real" self, the deepest expression of who you are.

Circle the statement of each pair below that describes you most accurately, E or I.

E		I	
(E)	I like fast living.	(I)	I like quiet time and space to contemplate my affairs.
(E)	I like the world outside.	(I)	I like the inner world.
(E)	I like people and things.	(I)	I like ideas, thoughts and meanings.
(E)	I like to be talkative and outgoing.	(I)	I like to be quiet and reserved.
(E)	I like to be sociable with many.	I	I like to be introspective with few.
(E)	I like to be energized by activity.	(I)	I like to be energized by depth and intimacy.
(E)	I like to seek out new experiences.	I	I tend to avoid new experiences.
7	TOTAL	5	TOTAL	(12)

Add the number of both E and I statements circled. Place the letter with the highest total in the appropriate space below.

When it comes to E or I preferences, I tend to select E more.

Circle the statement of each pair below that describes you most accurately, S or N.

S

N

(S) I tend to be practical.

(N) I tend to be idealistic.

(S) I like the concrete.

N I like the abstract.

(S) I choose to use my eyes and ears and other senses to find out what's happening.

(N) I choose to use my imagination to come up with new possibilities and novel ways of doing things.

S I tend to be physically competitive.

(N) I tend to be intellectually competitive.

(S) I prefer to be results oriented.

(N) I prefer to be idea oriented.

(S) I like to look at the facts.

N I like symbols, concepts and meanings.

(S) I enjoy using skills I've already learned.

(N) I enjoy using new skills more than practising old ones.

6 TOTAL

6 TOTAL

Add the number of both S and N statements circled. Place the letter with the highest total in the appropriate space below.

When it comes to S or N preferences, I tend to select _____ more.

Circle the statement of each pair below that describes you most accurately, T or F.

T

F

(T) I like to make decisions based on logic.

(F) I like to make decisions based on feelings and values even if illogical.

(T) I tend to notice ineffective reasoning.

(F) I tend to notice when people need support.

(T) I prefer truthfulness over tact.

(F) I prefer tactfulness over truth.

(T) I decide more with my head.

(F) I decide more with my heart.

(T) I tend to focus on objective and universal principles.

(F) I tend to focus on subjective and personal motives.

(T) I like to deal with people firmly, when required.

(F) I like to deal with people compassionately, when required.

(T) I give more attention to ideas or things.

(F) I give more attention to human relationships.

___ TOTAL

___ TOTAL

Add the number of both T and F statements circled. Place the letter with the highest total in the appropriate space below.

When it comes to T or F preferences, I tend to select _____ more.

Circle the statement of each pair below that describes you most accurately, J or P.

J		P	
(J)	I like closure, a sense of being finished.	P	I like to hang loose and stay open to new things.
(J)	I prefer advance notice.	P	I prefer spontaneous challenges.
(J)	I am task oriented.	P	I am process oriented.
(J)	I like to plan and decide.	P	I like to adapt and change.
(J)	I sometimes jump to conclusions prematurely.	P	I tend to postpone decisions and procrastinate.
(J)	I like to make things come out as they should.	P	I like to deal with unexpected and unplanned happenings.
(J)	I like to finish one thing before starting another.	P	I like to do several things at the same time, though I have trouble finishing them.
___	TOTAL	___	TOTAL

Add the number of both J and P statements circled. Place the letter with the highest total in the appropriate space below.

When it comes to J or P preferences, I tend to select _____ more.

Summary of Results

Under each set of paired statements you indicated your preference. Now place the letters of your four preferences below. The four letters taken together represent your personality type according to this self-diagnostic (e.g., ENTJ or ISFP).

_____ _____ _____ _____ (My personality type preferences)

   E or I   S or N   T or F   J or P

Explanation of Results

The self-diagnostic you just completed is an informal assessment tool based on the personality theory initially put forward by Carl Gustav Jung, later refined and developed by Katharine Briggs and Isabel Briggs Myers. According to Jung, Myers and Briggs, people's behaviour is not completely random. Personality types reflect patterns in the ways people perceive and make judgments about the world. You may be extraverted or introverted (E or I), sensing or iNtuiting (S or N), thinking or feeling (T or F), and judging or perceiving (J or P). Your results, then, serve as a summary statement about your perceptual and decision-making mental processes. The rest of this chapter explains these preferences, thereby debriefing your results. For now, you may wish to glance at the summary description of your own type that follows as well as the other possibilities. Each type has its preferred energy source, its preferred way of gathering information and making judgments about it, as well as its particular orientation to the external world.

Summary Chart of Your Personality Preferences

Personality Type	Energy Source	Information Gathered	Decides with	Orientation to Outer World
ENTJ	External	Intuitively	Head	Judging
ENTP	External	Intuitively	Head	Perceiving
ENFJ	External	Intuitively	Heart	Judging
ENFP	External	Intuitively	Heart	Perceiving
ESFJ	External	Sensorily	Heart	Judging
ESFP	External	Sensorily	Heart	Perceiving
ESTJ	External	Sensorily	Head	Judging
ESTP	External	Sensorily	Head	Perceiving
INTP	Internal	Intuitively	Head	Perceiving
INTJ	Internal	Intuitively	Head	Judging
INFP	Internal	Intuitively	Heart	Perceiving
INFJ	Internal	Intuitively	Heart	Judging
ISFP	Internal	Sensorily	Heart	Perceiving
ISFJ	Internal	Sensorily	Heart	Judging
ISTP	Internal	Sensorily	Head	Perceiving
ISTJ	Internal	Sensorily	Head	Judging

(2.3) ····· # Personality Types: Recognizable Patterns of Diversity

According to Carl Jung, **human diversity** is not a completely random matter. At a psychological level, differences we see in people can be understood in terms of recognizable patterns. These patterns can be observed in the way people use their minds, particularly in the way they perceive the world and make judgments about it. **Perceptual mental processes** determine what we see or attend to in a situation. The **judgment function** influences how we make decisions about what we perceive. Jung also believed that differences in people can be understood in terms of **psychological attitude**. Attitude, in this context, refers to the energizing sources in life. Some individuals tend

human diversity
According to Carl Jung, this is not a completely random matter. Instead, on a psychological level, the many differences we see in people can be understood in terms of recognizable patterns.

perceptual mental processes
These processes determine what we see or attend to in a situation.

51

judgment function
This influences how we make decisions about what we perceive, according to Jung.

psychological attitude
Attitude, in this context, refers to the energizing sources in life. Some individuals tend to focus their lives externally, while others tend to be more focused on the inner world of ideas.

external orientation
The psychological stance adopted toward people, situations and events in the outer world.

to focus their lives externally, while others tend to be more focused on the inner world of ideas.

As I mentioned earlier, Katharine Briggs and Isabel Briggs Myers made some minor modifications to Jung's work and elaborated upon it. They added to Jung's conception of type the idea of **external orientation**, the psychological stance we adopt toward people, situations and events in the outer world. In what follows, you will find more detailed explanations of the orientations, attitudes, functions and mental processes that combine to establish type and type differences. The explanations will help you to better understand the results of Self-Diagnostic 2.1. They will also help you to appreciate for later purposes the usefulness and practical applications of psychological type for personal growth and interpersonal communication. See the four psychological preference scales in Table 2.1, which depict how the 16 personality types can be formed.

Table 2.1

The Four Psychological Preference Scales

Extraversion	or	Introversion
Sensing	or	iNtuition
Thinking	or	Feeling
Judging	or	Perceiving

Combining Preferences Leads to 16 Possible Personality Types

ISTJ	ISTP	ESTP	ESTJ
ISFJ	ISFP	ESFP	ESFJ
INFJ	INFP	ENFP	ENFJ
INTJ	INTP	ENTP	ENTJ

You're only Jung once, but that's nothing to be a Freud about.
~Anonymous

Nothing is more wondrous than human beings when they begin to discover themselves.
~Chinese Proverb

Energy Source: Extraversion Versus Introversion

Do You Have an Introverted or Extraverted Attitude?

Introvert to extravert: *"Pardon me for speaking while you were interrupting."*

Extravert to introvert: *"Do you have any other speeds besides slow and stop?"*

Probably by this time in your life you've referred to someone you know as being either introverted or extraverted. You likely have some intuitive notion of what these terms mean; however, you may not know that their technical psychological definition originates with the work of Carl Jung. According to Jung's analytical psychology, people differ with respect to the attitudes they adopt toward life. These attitudes are not something good or bad. Rather,

52

2.4

think of them as psychological postures or predispositions. Attitudes are characterized by what people find energizing. For instance, when you walk into a room full of people, are you predisposed to feel excited, or is it more likely that you'll feel drained?

Carl Gustav Jung was the founder of analytical psychology.

reflection poem

Please Understand Me

If I do not want what you want, please try not to tell me that my want is wrong.

Or if I believe other than you, at least pause before you correct my view.

Or if my emotion is less than yours, or more, given the same circumstances, try not to ask me to feel more strongly or weakly.

Or yet if I act, or fail to act, in the manner of your design for action, let me be.

I do not, for the moment at least, ask you to understand me. That will come only when you are willing to give up changing me into a copy of you.

~David Keirsey

Source: Reprinted by permission of the Board of Prometheus -Nemesis Book Co.

53

extraverts
Individuals who get their essential stimulation from the environment. They generally enjoy being sociable, expressive and involved in external matters.

introverts
Individuals who prefer to deal with the inner world of ideas. They are energized by concepts and inner reflections.

Having gifts that differ according to the grace given us, let us use them....
~Romans 12:6

Your response here reveals much about your attitude. Some people like to mingle and interact with many (**extraverts**), while others prefer to speak with one or two people at a time (**introverts**). (By the way, the correct spelling of extravert is "extrovert." However, Carl Jung's misspelling of the term has now become the convention for type theorists. It continues to be a source of irritation for spelling-bee champions!)

Introverts—Life's Private "I"s Attitudinal differences between introverts and extraverts are apparent when you look at the focus of their attention. Extraverts are more likely to focus their perceptions and judgments outwardly. The external world is their preoccupation. Introverts, by contrast, prefer to deal with the inner world of ideas; they are energized by concepts and inner reflections. This kind of individual (maybe you) would rather listen than talk. Intense and loud discussions are likely to be draining experiences. In order to "recharge," the introvert needs to be alone. Private time is important. "Alone, but not lonely" is a phrase that the introvert understands well.

If you are an introvert, chances are pretty good that sometime in your life you've felt underestimated. While I'm sure this happens to virtually everybody, this experience is more likely with introverts. The reason is that extraverts tend to outnumber introverts in the general population. Given the private nature of introverts, along with their smaller number, it's not surprising that many of the values and preferences of the extravert dominate North American culture. Of course, many introverts learn to play the extraverted game of life very well. They become excellent at public relations and quite efficient in dealing with external matters. The problem is that they often feel drained, not energized, by becoming good at what they least prefer. (To appreciate why, do Application Exercise 2.1, Working in Your Wrong Hand.)

Extraverts—Life's Party Types As you might guess, the extravert loves what the introvert least prefers. Extraverted types tend to be energized by people and action, their orientation being outward. They enjoy being sociable, expressive and involved in external affairs. Extraverts get their essential stimulation from the environment. As strong as the introvert's needs may be for privacy, so strong may be the extravert's need for social contact. In contrast to the introvert, whose thoughts and reflections give depth to life, the extravert prefers breadth. (Do you complain about courses that are too superficial—an introvert's comment—or ones that are too narrowly focused and hence boring—an extravert's comment?)

By natural inclination, extraverts tend to act before thinking, whereas introverts reflect and then (maybe) act. Extraverts tend to think out loud. Introverts think to themselves. I suppose Alice in Wonderland exposed her extraverted preferences when she said at one point that she couldn't tell what she was thinking until she heard what she said. Like the proverbial extravert, she was "thinking out loud."

Table 2.2

Key Descriptors—Sources of Energy

Introverts (I)	Extraverts (E)
Focus on inner world	Focus on outer world
Depth	Breadth
Private	Social
Reserved	Outgoing
Think before acting	Act before thinking
Reflective	Active

Where does your preference fall?

Introversion   *Extraversion*

High	Moderate	Low	Low	Moderate	High

Take note: We all display introverted and extraverted tendencies but usually prefer one over the other.

At this juncture, it is very important for you to note that we all display introverted and extraverted tendencies at different times; it's just that one is usually preferred and better developed. Nobody is entirely introverted or extraverted. We all show signs of both but are energized by one. Table 2.2 shows common preferred tendencies for introverts and extraverts. Also, find below some helpful hints that both introverts and extraverts can use in efforts to improve their communications with those of the opposite type.

2.8 Helpful Hints for Improving Communication

Tips for Introverts (Communicating with Extraverts)

- **Look alive** Some extraverts are frustrated by the speed at which introverts tend to respond. Try to be quicker in your responses and more spontaneous. Display a more lively, upbeat attitude.

- **Be expressive** For extraverts, you are part of the external world. Since they feed off your energy, make an attempt to show interest, emotion and involvement. Keep in mind that there's nothing wrong with enthusiasm. Just because you don't always show your feelings doesn't mean you don't have them or shouldn't express them.

- **Initiate contact** Rather than waiting for people to start conversations with you, you could start conversations yourself. Don't always leave it up to extraverts to get things going socially.

55

- **Provide feedback** Save others the guesswork of trying to figure out what you're silently thinking. Publicly state what's on your mind. Provide information on where you stand on particular issues. After all, "Nobody can appreciate your music if they can't hear the tune you're playing."

- **Change your nonverbal communication** If you're strongly introverted, you probably look very serious to others. Try to look more relaxed and try to smile more. Assume inviting physical postures. Appear open. Don't withdraw.

- **Practise "non-productive" conversation** Learn to appreciate the value of social interaction for its own sake. Chit-chatting can be fun. The quality of ideas exchanged needn't always be a priority. Spending time in "idle conversation" has worth. It builds morale and positive relations.

Tips for Extraverts (Communicating with Introverts)

- **Respect privacy** If you're highly extraverted, you may not mind living your life as an open book to others. You may think that you have nothing to hide, feeling comfortable with a lot of self-disclosure. Understand that introverts generally have a greater need for privacy. Try, therefore, not to invade their private psychological territory. Don't ask them embarrassing questions or put introverts on the psychological hot seat.

- **Take time to listen** Introverts tend to be less spontaneous than extraverts. Their response time is also slower. Make an effort to allow introverts time to reflect before acting or responding to you. Do not make surprise demands on introverts for quick or immediate responses. Such demands are not usually welcome.

- **Foster trust** Make sure you guard as secret what you've been told by introverts in confidence. The sphere of private information is probably larger for the introvert than it is for you, the extravert. Be sure not to make public what others consider private.

- **Don't overpower** Introverts may sometimes perceive your enthusiasm and energy as frivolous. Your excitement may not be appreciated. You may wish to think about toning down your efforts, in order not to overwhelm others. They may not be impressed by your strident nature or extravagant expressions.

- **Don't judge** Be careful not to evaluate the more methodical and quieter introvert as less able and more dull. Preferences of one type should not be used as a standard of evaluation for other types. All preferences have their advantages.

2.5 ..... ## Information Gathering: Sensing Versus Intuition

What Do You Pay Attention to When You Gather Information? Not all people experience and gather information about the world in the same way. How we take in information is determined by the psychological functions of sensing and intuition. We all use both functions in our lives, but again, we typically display a preference for one, and feel more confident about it.

Sensors—The Realists

Sensors, or sensing type individuals, can be fairly described as life's realists. Think of them as no-nonsense, "meat and potatoes" people. Sensing types pay a great deal of attention to information that is received through sensory channels. For them, seeing is believing.

Sensing types tend to focus on the here and now. They enjoy and experience what is currently happening, and focus less on what might be or could be. Their present orientation causes them to concentrate on the facts and details of situations, people and events. Their greatest trust is placed in first-hand experience.

sensors
Sensing type individuals pay a great deal of attention to information that is received through sensory channels and focus on the present. They like set procedures and established routines.

Working in Your Wrong Hand

application
exercise
2.1

2.5 ..... This exercise, or some variation of it, is often used in workshops designed to help people appreciate the difficulties that arise when trying to operate with opposite or lesser preferred psychological functions.

Instructions: Write your name, address and telephone number on a piece of paper with your "wrong" hand. If you're right-handed, use your left hand. If you're left-handed, use your right hand.

For discussion: After finishing this task, evaluate your work. Is it better or worse than what you could have done with your preferred hand? How did you feel working with your "wrong" hand? What would be the effect on you if you were forced to operate all day long using your less-preferred hand? What generalizations could you possibly make about people's behaviour using this experiential exercise?

Introverts: Recall a time when you were required to function as an extravert. Where were you? What did you have to do? How did you feel? What did you think? How did you experience this situation?

Extraverts: Recall a time when you were required to function as an introvert. Where were you? What did you have to do? How did you feel? What did you think? How did you experience this situation?

We see things not as they are—but as we are.
~Ken Keyes, Jr.

A noticeable characteristic of sensing types is their preference for set procedures and established routines. Deviations and unexpected changes to usual ways of doing things may not be welcomed. Sensing types also enjoy looking at things in terms of their component parts and pieces. They like things to be definite and measurable. Anything fuzzy and open-ended is not terribly appreciated. You can also notice that sensors have a sequential approach to life. They prefer to start at the beginning of things and methodically complete them, one step at a time. Sensors are at their best when allowed to work at things "hands on." The next time you meet a no-nonsense, concrete realist who's particularly interested in the facts and practical details, you're probably facing a sensor.

Intuitives—The Innovators

intuitives
Intuitives downplay sensory-based information and opt for intuitive hunches. They like exploring alternatives and change. They have a future orientation.

Intuitives are unlike sensors insofar as they prefer to process information by way of a "sixth sense." They may downplay sensory-based information and opt for intuitive hunches. In contrast to sensing types who prefer a routine, intuitives like exploring alternatives and change. For them, variety is the spice of life. This need for variety and change may make intuitives appear fickle or sometimes impractical, but this need is probably more reflective of their future orientation. Intuitives are possibility thinkers and frequently anticipate what might be or what could be. Intuitives crave opportunities to be inventive because doing things in accepted routine ways is boring or somehow limiting. Intuitives also don't seem to mind jumping in anywhere when

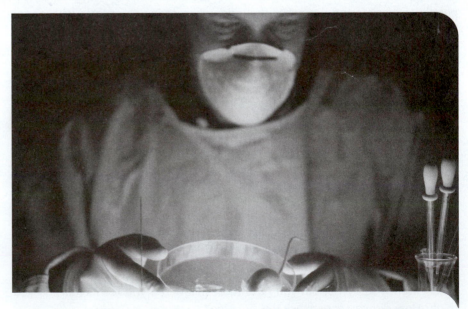

Scientists often use their sensing functions to formulate conclusions about minute and intricate processes.

Table 2.3

Key Descriptors—Information Gathering

Sensors (S)	Intuitives (N)
Perspire	Inspire
Focus on present	Focus on future
Like routine	Choose variety
Enjoy	Anticipate
Conserve	Change
Stress facts	Stress innovations
Take sequential approach	Take random approach
Look for details	Look for patterns
Practical	Imaginative
Follow directions	Pursue hunches

Albert Einstein's intuitive ideas have helped to change our understanding of the physical world.

Your imagination is your preview of life's coming attractions.
~Albert Einstein

Where does your preference fall?

Sensing   *Intuitive*

| High | Moderate | Low | Low | Moderate | High |

Take note: We all use sensing and intuitive processes, but usually prefer one over the other.

tasks must be done. For them, "intuitive leaps" are commonly made of "sequential steps." In this vein, intuitives like to look for patterns, relationships and overall designs rather than concentrate on the pieces and parts which make up the whole. The whole is the first object of attention.

Table 2.3 summarizes some of the key information gathering preferences of sensors and intuitives.

See below for help on how to communicate better with those of your opposite type.

Helpful Hints for Improving Communications

Tips for Sensors (Communicating with Intuitives)

- **Don't overgeneralize or state absolutes** Personal experience may give sensing realists confidence in their opinions and conclusions, but it does not guarantee necessary truth. You can be quite certain and confident but still be wrong. Understand that factual information is always incomplete and that your concrete experience is the experience of one. Not everybody experiences life the same way you do. Furthermore, experience cannot guarantee that something has been learned. "Experience is a great teacher; unfortunately not everybody understands the lesson."

- **Allow time for considering possibilities** Sensors prefer realism. The result is that you focus more on what "is" and less on what "could be." It's important not to limit your options with a limited imagination. Show greater tolerance toward idealistic thinking and intuitives who may have what you consider to be an unrealistic future orientation. Possibility thinking has real(istic) advantages.

- **Broaden your perspective** Try to display greater tolerance for broader-based conceptual thinking. Overreliance on facts and figures may get in the way of being productive or achieving longer-term goals. Preoccupation with details could lead intuitives to perceive you as petty.

- **Look for meanings and relationships** When communicating with intuitives, understand that they are less concerned with what the facts are and more concerned with what they mean. Expressing factual information outside of any meaningful context will be less effective with intuitives. For intuitives, facts need to be interpreted and related to something. Allow time for this interpretation. Put your communication in a more general context.

- **Find new ways of expressing information** Intuitives appreciate novelty, unusual modes of expression and challenges. Straightforward, matter-of-fact presentations could be experienced as boring and uninteresting. Try to perk up your communication with some delightful differences. Instead of merely informing intuitives, you could try to "inspire" them. Dispirited communications are less enjoyed.

Tips for Intuitives (Communicating with Sensors)

- **Focus on the here and now** You will make much more sense to the sensor if you adopt a present-time orientation. Talk about future scenarios and long-term possibilities may be regarded as "intellectual masturbation" by hard-core realists concerned about today's problems. Such talk may be pleasurable for you, but for the sensor, it is probably unproductive.

- **Base your opinions and suggestions on factual information** You can gain the confidence of sensors by keeping both feet on the ground. Try to relate your opinions and suggestions to facts, figures, surveys and empirical evidence. Your gut-level intuitions may carry little persuasive weight for the sensing realist.

- **Be more direct in your communication** If you wish to communicate more effectively with practical, matter-of-fact kinds of people, try to speak more directly. Metaphors and analogies may sound poetic to you, but they may serve as obstructions to individuals who prefer to be economical in their language. Why say in many words what can be said in few? Why say indirectly what can be said directly? Be a "word economist." Save words and enjoy the dividends!

- **Appear more level-headed and businesslike** Your natural enthusiasm, idealism, genius and inspiration as an intuitive can sometimes be perceived as "flaky" by the sensor. For the sensor, your enthusiasm should be based on substance, your idealism tempered by practicality, your genius founded on hard work, and your inspiration led by discipline. Without a realistic basis to support your insightful and long-term propositions, you could be seen as flighty. It's hard to put confidence in people whose heads seem to be in the clouds.

- **Respect traditional ways of doing things** Remember that the old ways of doing things are not always the wrong ways. For many, past procedures, rules and regulations offer stability and direction. They are not regarded as outdated or boring. Appreciate the sensor's preference for established, systematic approaches. Routine may make you restless, but it is reassuring to many sensors.

Quotations that might appeal to the Thinker:
"We are what we think; all that we are arises from our thoughts. With our thoughts we make the world."
~Buddha

Feeler: "The young man who has not wept is a savage, and the old man who will not laugh is a fool."
~Confucius

thinkers
People who take a logical approach to life. Thinkers tend to consider carefully the consequences of actions in an unbiased, impersonal way.

The way to a thinker's heart is through his mind.
~Tonee Balonee

2.6 Decision Making: Thinking Versus Feeling

Do You Prefer to Decide with Your Head or Your Heart? While our perceptions are obtained through sensing-intuiting channels, the thinking-feeling dimension of personality explains how we make decisions about what we see. As with attitudes and perceptual functions, people differ in ways explainable by a bipolar scale. Though we all use both thinking and feeling as a basis of decision making at different times in our lives, we generally prefer one over the other. The results of your self-diagnostic should begin to give you insights as to whether you're a thinking type or feeling type.

Thinkers—Life's Logicians People with thinking preferences take a logical, rational approach to life. Careful consideration is usually given to reasons, which are used to justify actions. **Thinkers** tend to consider the consequences of actions in an unbiased, impersonal way. Decisions are

Rodin's "The Thinker" captures the thoughtfulness of the T-type individual.

61

taken objectively and based on truth or probabilistic calculations. Thinking types desire to make firm decisions based on detached and impartial judgments. Thinkers thus tend to have an intellectual orientation to life. They can appear at times to be very "cerebral." They place great confidence in their mental and cognitive processes. When values and emotions play a part in their decision making, they are usually used to support logical conclusions. Given this, thinkers frequently choose to be truthful rather than tactful. They are sometimes less sensitive to people and more likely to be aware of rational considerations. They are most inclined to choose their heads over their hearts in most instances. Thinkers often consider it a greater compliment to be regarded as fair than as likeable or compassionate.

feelers
Individuals who make decisions based on their emotions and personal values.

Feelers—Life's Lovers People with feeling preferences tend to make decisions based on their emotions and personal values. When logic and reason come into play, they are typically employed to support values-oriented conclusions. We find, then, that **feelers** are more "people-people," and that they're less likely to be regarded as detached and aloof, which is sometimes the case with objective-minded thinkers. Feeling types pick heart over head, preferring tact over truth. When hard decisions must be made, they are more likely to be compassionate than firm. They are not likely to stick to rules and impersonal principles at any cost. On this score, feeling types can be described as humane and personally involved. It's not that there's something wrong with the desire to be just and objectively fair, but for the feeler, subjective considerations and personal values assume a greater importance.

Feeling types often base their decisions on emotion, which overrides what logic and reason dictate.

Feelers and thinkers usually make decisions according to their type's preferences, some of which are listed in Table 2.4.

Find below some more ways to improve your interpersonal communications with others, especially those who do not share your psychological type preferences.

2.8 Helpful Hints for Improving Communications

Tips for Thinkers (Communicating with Feelers)

- **Make communications personally relevant and meaningful** If you're a thinking-type person, you should consider making your

Table 2.4

Key Descriptors—Ways of Making Decisions

Thinkers (T)	Feelers (F)
Objective	Subjective
Impersonal	Personal
Rational	Emotional
Head	Heart
Truthful	Tactful
Logical	Values-oriented
Firm	Compassionate
Just	Humane
Critical	Appreciative

Where does your preference fall?

Thinking   *Feeling*

High	Moderate	Low	Low	Moderate	High

Take note: We all display thinking and feeling processes but prefer one over the other.

ideas more personally relevant and meaningful to the receivers of your messages. A theory or idea may be exciting to you and others sharing your preferences, but it can be boring, useless and irrelevant for people of the opposite type.

- **Be more appreciative of others' comments** Thinking-type individuals are likely to consider their rationality and objectivity as virtues, and in many ways they are. The problem with cool objectivity, however, is that it can be perceived as callousness. Having an intellectual evaluation and analysis for just about everything could get the thinking type labelled a terminal critic or someone who argues simply for the sake of argument, regardless of the issue or effects on people's emotions. Before attacking points made by others, take time to understand and appreciate what they mean. Paraphrase others' comments. Explore what they think and feel. Then, go on to express your point of view. Take time to really hear what is said.

- **Expand your communication messages** As a thinking-type person you may take great pride in the clarity, precision and conciseness of

63

your communications with others. However, a terse manner of expression is sometimes perceived as unfriendly and cold. If talking to you is like talking to a computer, you may wish to consider expanding your monosyllabic responses when answering others' questions. Perhaps you could elaborate on what you mean.

- **Make room for the nonrational and paradoxical** A helpful suggestion for you, the thinker, is to believe less that "life is a problem to be solved." See it more as a "mystery to be lived." Accept the proposition that not everything in life has a rational explanation or logical justification. Logic may be limited by whatever is mystical, ironic or paradoxical in life. Religious beliefs, for instance, may not be based on logic, but on faith. Such beliefs may lie beyond the domain of rational thought. Don't take rationality as the sole standard of truth.

Tips for Feelers (Communicating with Thinkers)

- **Get to the point** While other feelers like yourself may appreciate time-consuming communication, thinkers will probably not. Try to incorporate brevity in your messages to thinkers. Attempting to make friendly small talk could be perceived as a waste of time.

- **Be more objective** Try to reduce your naturally subjective orientation when communicating with thinkers. Your personal values and feelings may not be appreciated or regarded as very important to the subject at hand. The thinker is more impersonal and objective than you are. If you would have others listen and be persuaded, you must speak their language.

- **See both sides** There is absolutely nothing wrong with appreciating others. However, if personal likes and feelings get in the way of seeing flaws and difficulties, then problems can arise. Practise evaluating the pros and cons of different ideas, situations and alternatives.

- **Focus on content** If you're a high-level feeling type, process is probably more important to you than content. Chances are that you like experiential exercises and activities because of the personal involvement required. Remember that such process-oriented activities are less preferred by thinking types. In fact, some thinking types may greatly dislike "touchy-feely" communications. Be careful not to irritate or offend, especially in the case of introverted thinkers. Your personal approach may be perceived as a violation of privacy and inappropriate to the content being discussed.

2.7 Orientation to the Outer World: Judging Versus Perceiving

What's Your Preferred Way of Approaching External Reality? By now you have learned something about what energizes you, what you pay attention to when gathering information, and how you go about making decisions. However, it is also insightful for you to consider your psychological orientation to people, places and events in the external world. What is your preferred **lifestyle orientation**?

By the notion of lifestyle orientation, I'm not referring to your tastes in fashion or to your material possessions. Rather, the phrase refers to the psychological stance you assume vis-à-vis the world. Some of us tend to be judging types, while others are perceiving types. Be careful not to confuse judging with judgmental or perceiving with perceptive. No character evaluations are intended. It's just that people differ in their general approach to life. Neither approach is better or worse than the other.

The judging–perceiving distinction points to how we relate to external reality. Some of us are decision makers; others are more comfortable as information gatherers.

Judgers—Life's Organizers If you love making lists of things to do or if you like to use the expression "A place for everything and everything in its place," I would venture to guess that you are probably a judging type of person. **Judgers** create highly structured environments for themselves. Most activities are planned. For them, there may be a time and place for fun as well as an appropriate way to have it. For example, have you ever been to a party where there wasn't a moment of free time and where everything was organized and planned by the host? If so, you simply couldn't do what you wanted since the party organizer had decided in advance what should be done and when.

Not only are judging types well-organized and highly structured in their approach to life, they are also decisive. Judgers need closure and therefore enjoy making decisions about what ought or ought not to be done in a given situation. Once plans or schedules are established, strong judgers like to follow them closely. This decisiveness gives judgers a sense of order and control. Once the target is fixed and the course is set, judgers enjoy taking action to achieve their goal.

If you are a judging type, you use either thinking (T) or feeling (F) as a preferred way of dealing with the external world. Your life may be organized in terms of impersonal considerations (e.g., time schedules and budgets) or in terms of interpersonal dealings (e.g., values and feelings). You can be decisive either with your head or your heart. Both are rational (i.e., reasonable) ways of making decisions. The judging type prefers one over the other.

lifestyle orientation
The individual's psychological orientation to people, places and events in the external world.

judgers
Individuals who are well organized and highly structured in their approach to life. They also like to be definite and deliberate.

65

perceivers
Individuals who enjoy gathering information and adopt a rather tentative attitude toward life. In contrast to judgers who love to plan, schedule, organize and list, perceivers prefer to live spontaneously.

Perceivers—Mellow Fellows and Females People who display a strong preference for perceiving live noticeably different lifestyles compared to their judging cousins. In contrast to judgers who love to plan, schedule, organize and list, **perceivers** prefer to live spontaneously. Last-minute changes to schedules, for example, may not be seen as problems but rather as opportunities for new possibilities. Change is less of an enemy and more of a friend insofar as the perceiving person possesses the natural inclination to remain open to the unforeseen.

If you display a strong preference for perceiving, chances are pretty good that you feel uncomfortable when forced to arrive at quick conclusions. If you're typical of this type, you prefer to adopt a tentative approach to life. Your conclusions will sound less like categorical judgments and more like testable hypotheses. You may feel a constant urge to learn more or gather additional information before making any final conclusions. In fact, the act of gathering information is probably a great source of pleasure for you. (Do you find researching a paper is more fun than writing it?)

Perceivers are distinguished by the tolerance and adaptability that they display. They are less likely to use words like "should" and "ought" when it comes to other people's lives. "Live and let live" is a saying that the perceiving person might use as a personal guideline. Perceptives tend to go with the flow of life and just let things happen.

To learn all kinds of things, one must relate to all types of people.
~Anonymous

If you are a perceiver, either sensing or intuition is your preferred way of dealing with the external world. An ESFP, for instance, relies most heavily on sensing, while, by contrast, an ESFJ is most reliant on feeling. Remember, sensing and intuition are perceiving functions, whereas thinking and feeling are decision-making processes. The last letter of your type (i.e., J or P) indicates whether you prefer perceptual processes (S or N) or decision-making processes (T or F) in your dealings with the external world. "J" points to T or F preferences. "P" points to S or N preferences.

Judgers and perceivers approach external reality quite differently, as can be seen from the descriptors listed in Table 2.5.

Here are some final hints for how judgers and perceivers can improve communications with each other.

2.8 ····· Helpful Hints for Improving Communications

Tips for Judgers (Communicating with Perceivers)

- **Open up to the unexpected** Disruptions to your schedule need not necessarily be upsetting. Begin to see them as occasions to "stop and smell the roses." Some interruptions may even provide you with information and insights that can be used to reconsider your plans. Don't make other people who cause unexpected changes feel unwanted.

Table 2.5

Key Descriptors—Orientation to the Outer World

Judging (J)	Perceiving (P)
Structured	Flexible
Scheduled	Spontaneous
Ordered	Adaptive
Planned	Responsive to a variety of situations
Decisive	Wait-and-see attitude
Deliberate	Tendency to keep collecting new information
Definite	Tentative
Fixed	Flexible
Enjoy finishing	Enjoy starting

Where does your preference fall?

Judging   *Perceiving*

High   Moderate   Low   Low   Moderate   High

Take note: We all display judging and perceiving processes but prefer one over the other.

- **Build flexibility into your lifestyle** When organizing yourself, make sure you allow for "downtime." Make unforeseen circumstances foreseeable. In other words, expect the unexpected. Being psychologically prepared can help to reduce stress and frustration. Stressed and frustrated people are not usually pleasant to communicate with. Do everyone, including yourself, a favour, and "go with the flow."

- **Don't jump to conclusions** As a judger, your preference is to close matters as soon as possible. Note that your desire for closure may cause you to make decisions prematurely. Evaluations you make of people, situations and events may therefore be unjustified or ill-informed. If your stated conclusions are to be sound, they should be based on carefully considered information.

- **Listen to the other side** Counter-evidence to your own thinking may be uncomfortable to accept. Be careful not to repress or deny that which contradicts your personal beliefs, values, principles or ideas. Effective communication necessitates that you listen well, respect the viewpoints of others, and respond intelligently and sensitively to ideas contrary to your own.

- **Harness your need for control** Most J-types love to feel in control of situations. Plans, schedules, time frames and strategies of action provide a sense of personal power. While this may be good, caution yourself not to become overpowering. If you are controlled psychologically by your need to control, then you may become offensive to others. Most people do not like to feel dominated by others. If you wish to improve your communications as a judger, you may plan to relinquish some control and thereby "empower" others. Try this action as an experiment and witness how others begin to respond to you. If things get done and done well, but not according to your plans and schedules, what does it matter? Try not to communicate judgmentally with those having other styles of doing things.

Tips for Perceivers (Communicating with Judgers)

- **Be less vague** As a perceiver, you probably like to keep your options open. Perhaps you tend to make your decisions at the very last moment. Understand that, for judgers, this tendency of yours is a bit like "holding out." For judgers, the constant weighing of possibilities can represent vagueness or lack of preparation on your part. They may not be able to determine where you stand on particular issues. They have a greater need for quick confirmation. Tell judgers explicitly what considerations you are taking into account and what issues you need to resolve before coming to your final conclusions. If you can clearly articulate reasons for your present indecision or inaction, then at least you provide the organized J-type with an explanation for what's holding you up. This information will likely be appreciated.

- **Be more decisive** This tip is related to the one before. As a perceiver, you have a natural tendency to gather as much information as you can. Make sure that this information-gathering process does not get in the way of making necessary and timely decisions. Tentativeness about making decisions may be perceived as insecurity or incompetence. It will be difficult for you to persuade others and to sell your ideas if you cannot gain their confidence.

- **Watch your use of "yeah, but"** Since you are keenly aware of contingencies, possibilities and alternatives, you can no doubt frequently offer "yeah, but" objections, as I call them, to almost any proposal or suggestion. Don't let your "yeah, but" get in the way of productive dialogue. Ensure that your concerns are real. Always protesting on the basis of highly improbable scenarios, for example, will lead others to take your comments less seriously.

- **Ensure your communications are on time** J-types like to operate according to schedule. While delivering a memo a day late may mean little for you, it may mean a lot for the person who requested the memo. It is helpful, therefore, if you plan ahead for your pondering and procrastination. Having things well thought out in advance and allowing yourself lots of time for a consideration of possibilities will enable you to be more prepared and decisive. For example, at meetings you won't need to scramble and squirm at the last moment about where you stand on particular issues or policies. Appearing unclear and unprepared is not in your best interest, especially if you wish to be heard and respected for your point of view.

Type Classifications

In total there are 16 personality types, which are grouped into four categories. Find the four-letter combination that summarizes your personality preferences. What type are you?

Sensing-Thinking Types	Sensing-Feeling Types
ISTJ	ISFJ
ISTP	ISFP
ESTP	ESFP
ESTJ	ESFJ

Intuitive-Feeling Types	Intuitive-Thinking Types
INFJ	INTJ
INFP	INTP
ENFP	ENTP
ENFJ	ENTJ

My preferences indicate that I am probably a(n) _____ type.

Table 2.6

Summary of Type Characteristics

Sensing–Thinking People	**Sensing–Feeling People**
Focus on facts and details	Open to impulse and spontaneous acts
Speak and write directly to the point	Do what feels good
Adapt easily to established procedures and guidelines	Sensitive to others' feelings
Concerned with efficiency and utility	Decisions made according to personal likes and dislikes
Goal or task oriented	Prefer to learn through human interaction and personal experience
Emphasize accuracy	Enjoy activities involving emotional expression
Approach tasks sequentially	Persuasive through personal interaction
Focus on the present	Keen observers of human nature Interested in people

Intuitive–Feeling People	**Intuitive–Thinking People**
Open to the unconventional	Need time to plan and consider consequences of an action
See facts and details as part of the larger picture	Like to organize and synthesize information
Express themselves in new and unusual ways	Focus on impersonal considerations
Adapt to new circumstances	Decisions based on evidence and logical thinking
Process oriented	Prefer to learn vicariously through books and symbolic forms
Highly interested in beauty, symmetry and form	Enjoy logical thinking activities
Enjoy exploratory activities	Persuasive intellectually
Focus on the future	Store huge amounts of knowledge and information
	Interested in ideas, theories and concepts

Classroom Chemistry

2.5

No two college or university classes are alike. However, to explain why this is the case is a challenge. Instructors are sometimes amazed how a single lesson plan and delivery method can work wonderfully well in one section of a course and bomb in another. As a student, you may also wonder about the quiet and impersonal nature of your introductory psychology class, especially when you compare it to the noisy and emotionally charged nature of the psychological counselling class taught by the same instructor. Course content and class size might have some influence on atmosphere, but then again, the differences may have something to do with the psychological makeup of the students. The different makeup of each course section could affect the "chemistry of the classroom."

Instructions: On the blackboard or flip chart, draw a type table similar to the one illustrated below. You could also draw the table on a transparency sheet for overhead projection. Decide whether you wish to keep a permanent record for yourself.

ISTJ	ISFJ	INFJ	INTJ
ISTP	ISFP	INFP	INTP
ESTP	ESFP	ENFP	ENTP
ESTJ	ESFJ	ENFJ	ENTJ

Invite students to put their names (or check-marks) in the appropriate boxes as indicated by their psychological type. No student should be forced to do this and no reasons for refusal need to be given. Respect everyone's privacy. In case there is some insecurity about making any self-revelations, remember, no type is any better or worse than any other. After completing the type table, answer the following questions. (This may be done in small groups or all together as a class.)

Introversion Versus Extraversion

1. How many introverts are in the class?
2. How many extraverts are in the class?

Letter of higher frequency _____ (I or E)

Discussion: Given what you know about introverted and extraverted preferences, what predictions about the class would seem reasonable? For example, will large or small group discussions flow more easily? Will class participation come readily? How could the introverted–extraverted chemistry of the classroom contribute to everyone's benefit? How could it pose challenges?

Sensing Versus Intuition

1. How many sensing types are in the class?
2. How many intuitive types are in the class?

Letter of higher frequency _____ (S or N)

Discussion: Given what you know about sensing and intuiting preferences, what predictions about the class would be reasonable? Will the class be conducted in a routine way or will members opt for variety? Will people be more likely to perform in a step-by-step fashion or will they be more likely to jump in wherever they feel comfortable?

Thinking Versus Feeling

1. How many thinking types are in the class?
2. How many feeling types are in the class?

Letter of higher frequency _____ (T or F)

Discussion: Given what you know about thinking and feeling preferences, what predictions about the class would seem reasonable? For example, will the group tend to be concerned with personal values or objective and emotionally detached considerations?

Judging Versus Perceiving

1. How many judging types are in the class?
2. How many perceiving types are in the class?

Letter of higher frequency _____ (J or P)

Discussion: Given what you know about judging and perceiving preferences, what predictions about the class would seem reasonable? For example, will it be necessary for most students to function according to a strict timetable or will it be relatively easy to deviate from the lesson plans?

What are the four dominant preferences of your class? Is there anyone who is the "pure" classroom type—the one whose personality captures all the dominant preferences of the class?

_____ _____ _____ _____

  I or E   S or N   T or F   J or P

What are the class frequencies of

STs	Sensing-Thinking Types	_____	?
SFs	Sensing-Feeling Types	_____	?
NFs	ntuitive-Feeling Types	_____	?
NTs	Intuitive-Thinking Types	_____	?

Discussion: Given the chemistry of your class, what might be its strengths? What challenges might you anticipate? Who is likely to fit in most easily? What can be done to make others feel comfortable?

TV Types Have Different Stripes

application exercise
2.3

2.5

Now that you understand the basics of psychological type, it's time to apply your knowledge. Of course, there's nothing wrong in having a little bit of fun at the same time!

Instructions: Form small groups. Select a secretary and spokesperson for your group. Discuss the psychological profiles of the TV personalities and characters listed below. Place each name in the appropriate box labelled according to psychological preferences. If you need help, refer to the Summary of Type Characteristics. For a variation of this activity, change any of the TV characters or personalities to suit the viewing tastes of the class.

Caution: Your group may choose to focus on particular features of the TV character or personality not emphasized by other groups. If your group's placements are different from those of other groups, use these differences as a basis for class discussion. In the end, the placement is less important than the rationale behind it.

TV Personalities/Characters

Dr. Phil	Matt Damon	Jon Stewart
Nicolas Cage	Conan O'Brien	Oprah Winfrey
Carrie Bradshaw	Johnny Depp	Reese Witherspoon
Elizabeth Corday	Homer Simpson	Brad Pitt

ST	SF
NF	**NT**

Guidelines for the Proper Application of Psychological Type

As we have learned in this chapter, an application of psychological type theory is useful to facilitate personal growth and understanding of others. This is not to suggest, however, that psychological type applications are without risks or potential problems. If you choose to incorporate an understanding of type theory into future dealings with people or as a vehicle for personal or professional development, a number of recommendations should be kept in mind so that abuses do not occur. They are listed and briefly discussed as follows.

1. Do not pigeonhole Understandably, there is a certain amount of excitement which comes from identifying one's personality type, whether the discovery is based on the more valid and reliable Myers-Briggs Type Indicator or a more informal instrument like the one provided in this text. It's important not to be swept away by the excitement of discovery, however. Remember to see your revealed type as a working hypothesis—a starting point for further exploration. One paper-and-pencil measure done in the context of a class is probably not sufficient to determine your personality preferences with confidence. Human beings are complex creatures and so it's unlikely that discovering the "essence" of one's psychological type can be so easily uncovered, at least with certainty, with only one completed questionnaire in hand.

Just as you don't wish to prematurely slot yourself into some inappropriate category, make sure you don't pigeonhole someone else in the same way. Unless you are psychic, you can't read other people's minds and so cannot always tell what emotions, intentions, beliefs or attitudes underlie their overt behaviour, verbal utterances or other non-verbal cues. There can often be a lot of uncertainty and ambiguity about how another's behaviour should be interpreted. Trying to bend, re-shape, or twist someone's behaviour in your mind so that it conforms to your preconceived notions of that person's type is to do some sort of existential violence to the individual. There is a danger, then, in misidentification; there is also a danger of significant misperception leading to misinterpretation and misunderstanding both in regard to oneself and others. In your own case, you may just see what you want to see and disregard the rest. The danger here stems from a kind of psychological blindness.

2. Take type seriously As already intimated, it can surely be fun to learn about yourself as well as about the differences and similarities between yourself and others. Given the dangers just mentioned, though, be careful not to transform psychological type assessment tools into parlour games or activities "good-for-laugh," as we say. Gaining greater self-knowledge is something that has been advocated by philosophers and other great thinkers since ancient times. Trying to know yourself is not the same as playing the board game *Trivial Pursuit*. There is nothing trivial about self-discovery. Also, be careful not to be too casual about developing insights into the workings of other personality types. Something you've learned about introverts in general may not apply to a particular introverted friend, for example. Seriously discussing how or what is the case with that person can be illuminating. You could learn more about the individual and thereby develop a deeper appreciation of that person. Or, with the knowledge you glean from that individual, you could enrich your understanding regarding the intricacies of psychological type. In either case, you need to pay close and sober attention to personality dynamics.

3. Acknowledge that all types are equally valuable: On occasion, people are tempted to "cheat" on personality measures like the Myers-Briggs Type Indicator or its derivatives like my own. The reason for this may be because, in the mind of the person completing the questionnaire, some tendencies or predispositions are perceived as more desirable than others. For many people, the more desirable personality characteristics are those so deemed by the society in which they live. On the contemporary North American scene, for example, where business values tend to dominate, personality preferences like extraversion, adaptability, and practicality are often seen as more desirable than their opposites of introversion, inflexibility, and out-of-reach high-minded idealism. Thus, if you perceive yourself as a shy, withdrawn introvert with an idealistic, impractical bent, say, you may not see your personality type as equally valuable. Embarrassed about yourself, you may wish you were someone else—hence, the temptation to cheat or lie. Believing that some characteristics are better than others, you may perceive other personality types as better in comparison with your own. First of all, such evaluative judgment is inappropriate, resulting from a misunderstanding of type theory. Second, this misunderstanding is likely to cause unnecessary insecurity and lower self-esteem. A further caution: if you happen to display preferences considered more desirable in this particular society at this particular time, you may wrongly feel superior. We all have gifts that differ and we should cherish those gifts without arrogance.

4. Don't confuse strong preference with ability Proper humility regarding one's type can be developed if one recognizes that a strong preference does not necessarily imply excellence or ability. Take the socially desirable tendency of extraversion. It may be that you come out as "highly extraverted" on the MBTI®. Does this necessarily mean you are somehow blessed by nature or destined for greater things? Maybe, or maybe not. Perhaps you are so extraverted that you are regarded as an obnoxious loudmouth whose friendliness is over the top, and consequently intrusive and unwelcomed. In this scenario, your strong preference for something highly valued in the business world or the world of work turns out to be a liability for you personally. By contrast, a normally shy and withdrawn introvert can learn, even if reluctantly, to "extravert" and develop superior human relations skills. "Schmoozing" may not be this individual's first preference, but this doesn't mean it's a skill that's out of reach. People can, in principle, develop skills and abilities related to their lesser psychological preferences better than those of people who consider those same preferences as their highest.

5. Describe type preferences in non-judgmental terms No type or psychological preference is good or bad in itself and, as we've learned, even so-called "desirable" tendencies can turn out to be liabilities in particular cases if not properly expressed. Furthermore, no type is healthier or more dysfunctional than any other. All types can flourish and enjoy psychological well-being; so too can all types experience difficulties and obstacles to personal growth and development. The point is that psychological type measurements like the MBTI® are not designed to identify psychological disorders. Thus, normative judgments pertaining to which types are better or worse, healthier or unhealthier are inappropriate and should be avoided.

6. Don't discriminate on the basis of type Finally, given that "type preference" and "ability" are different, and that the former is no guarantee of the latter, we should never counsel or steer a person away from a particular career, relationship or activity solely on the basis of type information. Type does not explain everything necessary for success; it tells us nothing about competence and maturity, for instance—two things that are essential in many endeavours and undertakings. To deny someone a job because of a psychological type preference smacks of a new form of discrimination: "psychism," or "typism," or something to that effect. Certainly, psychological preferences should not serve as a basis for diminishing the life prospects of some to the advantage of others. This would constitute an unethical application of type theory.

Study Guide

Key Terms

self-knowledge (46)
personality (46)
Myers-Briggs Type
   Indicator (MBTI®)
   (47)
psychological type (47)
human diversity (51)

perceptual mental
   processes (51)
judgment function (51)
psychological attitude
   (51)
external orientation (52)
extraverts (54)
introverts (54)

sensors (57)
intuitives (58)
thinkers (61)
feelers (62)
lifestyle orientation (62)
judgers (63)
perceivers (66)

Fill-in-the-Blank Questions

Progress Check 2.1

Instructions: Fill in each blank with the appropriate answer from the list below.

intuitive-feeling
thinking
processes
bipolar
feeling
realists
outer
decision making
life orientation
perceptive

patterns
now
innovators
others
_____ (your type)
inner
analytical
future
judging
Jung

1. Self-understanding can help you to understand _____.

2. According to Self-Diagnostic 1.1, my personality type is _____.

3. Extraverts get their energy from the _____ world.

4. Introverts get their energy from the _____ world.

5. According to Myers and Briggs, there are four _____ scales that can be used to understand psychological type.

6. The Myers-Briggs Type Indicator is based on Carl Jung's _____ psychology.

7. Sensing and intuition are perceptual _____.

8. Sensing types tend to be _____.

9. Intuitive types tend to be _____.

10. Sensing types focus on the _____.

11. Intuitive types focus on the _____.

12. People who adopt a highly rational or logical approach to life are probably _____ types.

13. People who prefer to make decisions in personal and value-oriented ways are _____ types.

14. Thinking and feeling are both _____ functions.

15. Judging and perceiving reflect our _____.

16. If you love to plan, organize, make lists and get things finished, then you're probably a _____ type.

17. If you prefer a tentative approach to life and often feel a need to gather more information, then you're probably a _____ type.

18. The mirror opposite of the sensing–thinking type is the _____ type.

19. While individuals are unique, there still are recognizable _____ of perception and decision making that we share with others.

20. If you're worried about being too _____, that's nothing to be a Freud about.

True/False Questions

Instructions: Circle the appropriate letter next to each statement.

T F   1. Learning about your own personality can help you to understand others.

T F   2. There are no patterns or recognizable mental habits in people's perceptual and decision-making functions.

T F   3. According to type theory, having an attitude refers to a character flaw.

T F   4. An ENFP is someone displaying extraverted, intuitive, thinking and perceiving preferences.

T F   5. An ST prefers sensing–thinking functions.

T F   6. Psychological type is made up of four bipolar scales.

T F   7. Introverts are necessarily lonely people.

T F   8. Extraverts are always good with people.

T F   9. Sensing types have an innate sense of innovation and future possibilities.

T F 10. Intuitive types like to look for meanings and relationships.

T F 11. Thinking types don't have feelings.

T F 12. Feeling types can't think logically.

T F 13. Judging types are necessarily judgmental toward others.

T F 14. Perceptive types can never make decisions on time.

T F 15. Type talk is terrific.

Summary

1. Why is self-knowledge important?
   - it maximizes your potential
   - it develops your strengths
   - it works on your weaknesses
   - it increases self-awareness
   - it builds self-confidence
   - it helps you live more productively

2. How can self-knowledge help you socially?
   - discovering your personal uniqueness can help you to appreciate the uniqueness of others
   - your respect for others can increase
   - your defensiveness can be reduced by honouring yourself, thereby improving communications with others

3. What are the basic components of personality functioning according to Jung, Myers and Briggs?
   - attitudes: how you're energized
   - perceptual processes: how you take in information
   - decision-making functions: how you make judgments on what you perceive
   - life orientations: how you deal with the external world

4. What are the two basic attitudes?
   - extraversion: outer world, breadth, active, sociable
   - introversion: inner world, depth, reflective, private

5. What are the two basic perceptual processes?
   - sensing: present, routine, factual, details, practical
   - intuiting: future, variety, innovative, larger picture, imaginative

6. What are the two basic decision-making functions?
   - thinking: objective, rational, impersonal, head, firm, just
   - feeling: subjective, emotive, personal, heart, compassionate, humane

7. What are the two basic life orientations?
   - judging: structured, planned, decisive, ordered, scheduled
   - perceiving: flexible, responsive, tentative, adaptive, spontaneous

8. What four categories can be used to capture all 16 types?
   - sensing-thinking types
   - intuitive-feeling types
   - sensing-feeling types
   - intuitive-thinking types

Related Readings

Barr, Lee and Norma Barr (1989). *The Leadership Equation: Leadership Management and the Myers-Briggs*. Austin, TX: Eakin Press.

Briggs Myers, Isabel (1995). *Gifts Differing*, 10th Anniversary Edition. Palo Alto, CA: Consulting Psychologists Press, Inc.

Hirsh, Sandra and Jean Kummerow (1989). *Lifetypes*. New York: Warner Books.

Kroeger, Otto and Janet Thuesen (1993). *Type Talk at Work*. New York: Delacorte Press.

Malone, Peter and Dik Browne (2000). *Let A Viking Do It—Hagar and Family Illustrate the Myers-Briggs Type Indicator*. Available through Career/Lifeskills Resources, Concord, Ontario.

> Character cannot be developed in ease and quiet. Only through experience of trial and suffering can the soul be strengthened, vision cleared, ambition inspired, and success achieved.
> *~Helen Keller*

Courtesy of Library of Congress.

Morals, Manners, and Attitude Adjustments for Effective Human Relations

3

Chapter Overview

Character Is Destiny

Attitude Adjustments for Effective Human Relations

- Reduce egocentrism and try to be more objective
- Don't be so psychologically defensive
- Try not to be so much of a perfectionist
- Eliminate insincerity and deceit
- Be more rationally level-headed and tone down the histrionics
- Watch out for group think and conformity
- Adopt an attitude of healthy skepticism

- Eliminate aggressive arrogance
- Act on the principle of charity

Moral Principles and Virtues for Character Development and Interpersonal Communications

- Respect for Persons
- The Reciprocity Principle
- Integrity
- Responsibility
- Truthfulness
- Fairness
- Moderation
- Courage
- Prudence

Basic Manners

- Etiquette and electronics
- Punctuality
- Politeness and right speech
- Sensitivity to diversity
- Appearance
- Bragging and name dropping

Study Guide

- Key Terms
- Progress Check 3.1
- Summary
- Related Readings

Learning Outcomes

After successfully completing this chapter, you will be able to

(3.1) Appreciate the importance of human character in mastering human relations

(3.2) Identify those attitude adjustments necessary for effective communications

(3.3) Recognize and explain how morals play an important role in interpersonal relations

(3.4) Display better manners in public and in your dealings with others

(3.5) Reflect on personal weaknesses and things needing improvement as far as attitudes, morals, and manners are concerned

(3.6) Determine your general level of assertiveness

Focus Questions

1. What could it mean to say that character is destiny?
2. Are there any practical benefits to character development?
3. What are some attitudes worth developing?
4. What are some attitudes worth eliminating?
5. What moral principles and value considerations are relevant to interpersonal communications?
6. What are some bad manners we should try to dispense with?
7. What are some good manners worth cultivating?

Self Diagnostic 3.1

How Assertive Am I?

Instructions: Included below is a series of statements. Indicate your level of agreement with each using the scale provided.

1 = Completely and utterly unlike me
2 = Not usually like me
3 = Somewhat like me
4 = Frequently like me
5 = Almost always like me

_____ 1. I don't hide my feelings and express them openly and honesty.

_____ 2. I stand up for myself more than others typically do.

_____ 3. I let others know when I accomplish something significant.

_____ 4. I've rarely missed good opportunities because of my shyness.

_____ 5. I'm not reluctant to haggle with people about pricing, trying to get a better deal.

_____ 6. I will send back food or drink in a restaurant when such things are not to my liking.

_____ 7. I have no problem standing up to authorities or otherwise important people when I think they're wrong.

_____ 8. I'm quite prepared to offend others or hurt people's feelings if necessary to be fair or to do the right thing.

_____ 9. I like to be out there meeting and enjoying people.

_____ 10. I say what's on my mind and can even get somewhat explosive in public.

Scoring: Each one of the statements above reflects assertive behavior. The higher your score, the more assertive you likely are. The lowest score possible is 10. The highest possible score is 50.

Assertiveness: _Dorland's Medical Dictionary_ defines assertiveness as: _a form of behaviour characterized by a confident declaration or affirmation of a statement without need of proof; this affirms the person's rights or point of view without either aggressively threatening the rights of another (assuming a position of dominance) or submissively permitting another to ignore or deny one's rights or point of view._

Reflect on how assertive you are by comparing your score with those interpretive scores offered below. Do you need to become more or less assertive? What specifically do you need to do?

Scoring Key

10–20 = Not very assertive at all
21–39 = Occasionally assertive
40–50 = Often or almost always assertive

3.1 Character Is Destiny

character
Reflected by one's words and deeds; the moral side of personality.

The ancient philosopher Heraclitus claimed that, **"Character is destiny."** This simple assertion contains a very profound insight, which if understood and acted upon, could change the very direction and quality of your life. What Heraclitus is putting forth is that the kind of person you choose to become through your thoughts, words and deeds will directly impact on what your future turns out to be. You're not simply a victim of fate, but in many ways the architect of how things unfold for you. Even when it comes to things over which you seemingly have little or no control like illness and unemployment, say, you are still in control of your reactions. They tell others much about you. Do you whine or put on a brave face? Are you defeated or do you see your misfortune as an opportunity for heroism? Whatever the case, you are always master of how you choose to respond. You can think what you like and what you think will no doubt impact on how you feel. In difficult times, do your responses reflect strength of character or weak moral fiber? Are you a fighter or a wimp? Will people be impressed or unimpressed by what you say and do? Will they be drawn toward you or repulsed?

Of course, in the end you can't control other people's perceptions or what others think of you; nonetheless, what you say and do can strongly influence them, and what you say and do is certainly a matter of free will. By your words and actions, you set yourself as an example to the world; by them you reflect your character and broadcast the kind of person you are. You make lasting impressions on those with whom you interact on a daily basis. Seeing things in this light, it's useful to ask yourself: *"Is my character likely to open or close doors of opportunity?"* *"Will people be favourably predisposed or disgusted by how I present myself?"* *"Do I bring out the best or worst in others?"* A little bit of *character chiropractic* may be in order to realign yourself in ways that best serve your interests.

Individual character is reflected not only by our words and deeds, but also by the choices we make, choices that determine real-life practical outcomes whether they occur in personal, professional or informal social interactions. Common experience supports this view. Take, for example, individuals who choose to be abrasive and cynical. If those traits show up at a job interview, it's probably less likely that those individuals will be selected for available positions. Bosses usually wish to foster good organizational climates for those working under them. Hiring people who rub others the wrong way usually isn't good for productivity or morale.

So, if you choose to display elements of abrasiveness or cynicism in your psychological disposition, don't be surprised if you find it more difficult than most to land a job or establish a relationship with someone to whom you're attracted. Your prickly personality may be off-putting to others. Choose to put on a friendly face and remove the prickliness and you are likely to be pleasantly surprised by the results. Of course, feigned friendliness is not what I'm suggesting here; insincerity is not a trait worth developing. Rather, the friendliness should authentically reflect the feelings and character of the one displaying it.

In this chapter, we'll be looking at **morals, manners, and attitude adjustments** as they relate to personal **character development**. Examining matters of morality in this light can help us all find guidance for how we "ought" to behave as well as about how we should treat others and what

character development
Requires proper morals, manners, and attitude adjustments.

Out of the confusion of a crumbling society, will emerge individuals who are touched by higher guidance. These will inevitably flow together with others of like inspiration, and a new quality of society will begin to form. This is the true adventure of our time.
~Sir George Trevelyan

ethical considerations we should take into account in our dealings with them. As for manners, while proper etiquette seems to have taken a beating in recent years—insofar as in-your-face offensive nastiness and vulgarity rear their ugly heads more and more—there's little denying that common decency and decorum are still basic requirements for those occupying the upper echelons of any reputable company, institution or organization. Manners still have a place. With respect to attitudes, certain destructive psychological orientations and predispositions need to be eliminated, while other more positive ones need to be nurtured.

Attitude Adjustments for Effective Human Relations

Before getting to the morals and manners part of this discussion, it's helpful first to identify a number of attitudinal obstacles that need to be overcome. Let's just say the psychological soil must be prepared before we try to plant any positive behavioural habits or nurture any characterological traits. The weeds must be removed, as it were, so as not to choke off that which needs to flourish and grow. The psychological ground for growth needs to be prepared.

3.2

Attitude Adjustment One—Try to Reduce Egocentrism and Be More Objective
There are individuals in the world that cannot imagine how things look from other people's points of view. This psychological stance can be described as **cognitive egocentricism** (Piaget, 1954). With egocentrism, individuals do not de-centre from their own perspective, but see everything from a personal standpoint.

cognitive egocentrism
The inability to see things from another's point of view.

While it's quite natural to see reality from one's own perspective,—it would be hard not to—it's egocentric (or egoistic) to see things *only* in terms of one's own personal likes and dislikes, or solely from the vantage point of one's own interests, values, beliefs, and so on. Very young children, like egocentric adults, do not see the through the eyes of others. With children, this is due to psychological immaturity and cognitive underdevelopment. A young child who worries that mommy and daddy's divorce was caused by their own unwillingness to go to bed on time shows how cognitively immature people can see themselves as the centre of the universe and how they believe that everything that happens, happens because of them. In young children, such egocentrism is forgivable. It's even sadly endearing at times.

With older adults, however, egocentrism likely stems not so much from cognitive underdevelopment, but more from emotional insensitivity, selfishness, lack of care, or out of psychological defensiveness. It's not that extracting oneself from one's cognitively egocentric perspective is psychologically or developmentally impossible; rather, what looks like an inability to see things from alternative perspectives frequently results because some adults just can't be bothered about others. People, who are not willing to see reality from the standpoint of others, might rightly be described as **self-centred**. Not caring about others, they lack empathy. There's little desire to appreciate others or see the world through others' eyes.

Sadly, there are individuals who simply don't care or can't be bothered to know how things look to you and me or how others might interpret the same situation. . . . *That's their problem!* The thinking goes something like this: *The way I see things is the way they are.* Or, *the way you see things is wrong,* or possibly, *I don't care how you see the world; I'm right! Besides, you're not important to me anyway!* Of course, having a rational discussion with a self-centred, cognitively egocentric person is going to be problematic since nothing you say is really going to matter to that person. Your own views are not going to be taken seriously; they're more likely to be dismissed as irrelevant.

It doesn't take the psychological genius of Sigmund Freud to see how egocentrism can be regarded as selfish and immature. Most people like to be listened to and understood. They like their rights and interests to be acknowledged. To have others overlook us, ignore or de-value what's important to us is surely to create psychological distance. No doubt an egoistic orientation is a major contributing factor to conflict. Uncaring, insensitive individuals are likely to step on the toes of others, as it were, and balk at any suggestion that some sort of wrongdoing was committed.

As just intimated, people who don't care about us or bother to notice what's important to us can often trample over our interests. Choosing to alienate others and create interpersonal discord are *not* productive ways to improve one's human relations skills. Whatever perverse satisfaction might be gained by stomping on others' rights or by uncaringly dismissing others in a huff of confident egoistic superiority is far outweighed by the lasting impressions left on others—others who incidentally may later have an important influence on decisions made with respect to our own futures. Our success may hinge on the decisions of future bosses whom we have uncaringly dismissed in the past. . . . Not so good. This is especially so if our former colleagues, now bosses, have a good memory and hold grudges! There's a saying here that's relevant perhaps: *Don't burn your bridges.* Perhaps we should add: *Don't refuse to build your bridges!* Making and keeping friendly connections with people is at a bare minimum a very prudent thing to do. No doubt, it's good for other less utilitarian reasons as well.

Closely related to egocentrism is the idea of **self-serving bias**, something already discussed in Chapter One. An egocentric person seemingly can't help but put a positive spin on things so that they reflect best on that person. If one gets fired at work, it's because the economy is bad. If one does well on a test, it's because one is a genius. A low or failing grade simply means the test was unfair or the marker is was too hard in his or her assessment. Apparently, nothing negative is the fault or responsibility of egoistic self-serving individuals.

self-centred
Lacking care and empathy for others.

self-serving bias
Undeservedly attributing positives to oneself and negatives to others or external factors.

87

The fact, however, is that sometimes people's own behaviour *is* the cause of their losses, failures and disappointments. Much to the egoist's surprise, a failing grade may not be the fault of the professor, but the egoist's responsibility. Maybe the individual did not study properly or enough. Blaming others for one's own failures is a behavioural default position for the egocentric, self-serving person. Taking such a position is not likely to endear one to others. It is not recommended, certainly not if you wish to live a life of rationally enlightened self-interest—something to be contrasted with egoistic self-centredness.

By reducing egocentrism, not only do we create the conditions for fostering more empathy, we also make **objectivity** possible. Objectivity allows us to see situations from a variety of perspectives besides our own (John Rawls, 1971). This objectivity may not lead us to feel everyone's pain, as it were, in some kind of empathetic share-fest, but at least it makes it possible for us to understand and appreciate how things looks from alternative points of view. Of course, objectivity is necessary when it comes to making fair, rational, and informed judgments.

objectivity
The ability to see situations from a variety of perspectives.

Objectivity is the antithesis of a narrow self-serving bias as found with egocentrism. It is what allows one to arrive at negative conclusions and evaluations even when they apply to one's self. It takes objectivity to see in oneself what one doesn't like or would prefer not to admit is true. Seeing things objectively means getting outside of one's own mind space and seeing oneself and one's situation as impersonal others might—Simply put: To see ourselves as others see us. This can be a scary thing to do sometimes, but it shows maturity, rationality and courage. Choosing to make self-adjustments in light of objective data or external evaluation requires strength of character.

(3.2) ⋯⋯ *Attitude Adjustment Two—Reduce Fear and Psychological Defensiveness* The next chapter will be devoted to exploring psychological defensiveness in detail. Nonetheless, it's worthwhile to say a few things about this disruptive factor here.

defensiveness
A psychological stance in response to fear sure to disrupt harmonious relations with others.

Defensiveness is a psychological stance that is sure to disrupt harmonious relations with others. When one is defensive, there is typically some sort of fear or underlying anxiety, which may or may not be consciously recognized by the individual exhibiting it. Such fear and anxiety can contaminate interpersonal communications, not to mention leave the fearful and anxious person too psychologically disturbed to view situations in an accurately objective fashion. What is seen, as a result, may be little more a projection of the person's insecurities; not a true picture of how things actually are. For example, one person may resent the ambitions of another. That other may be attacked for being vain and selfish. While this could be true, it might also be the case here that the person is threatened and hence fearful of the competition presented. The attribution of selfish vanity to another could simply be a **projection** of the lower self-esteem possessed by the fearful and anxious individual. So, the next time you're about to criticize the motivations and actions of

projection
A defense mechanism used to reduce anxiety.

others, it may be worthwhile to stop and ask yourself whether, and to what extent, your criticisms are merely a reflection of your own insecurities. Not only are other people insecure and defensive, so are we!

3.2 *Attitude Adjustment Three—Don't Be So Much of a Perfectionist* Not too many people would argue with the idea that it's best to get things right or to do things correctly. It goes without saying that a right answer is better than a wrong answer or that it's better to do things properly, rather than improperly. Nevertheless, there's a difference between valuing correctness or perfection and presenting oneself as a **perfectionist**. Perfectionism leads to nit-picking and to giving heightened importance often to trivial matters (Riso, 1987). Perfectionists are often a pain to be around. They bug other people and cause irritation in them. Sadly, perfectionists can sometimes consider their perfectionism as a sign of their superiority. In other words, the very thing they prize is exactly the problem. Not so perfect!

A perfectionist is more likely to find fault with the efforts of others, than to highlight the valuable contributions others make. When people do their jobs, little or no praise may be given. Why should it be deserved? It's only right that the person should do their job properly. However, when mistakes are made, perfectionist response is typically swift and criticism often loud and severe, usually out of proportion with the nature of those mistakes.

Clearly, it's true that we shouldn't promote mistake making and that we should encourage responsible behaviour; it's just that the perfectionist takes all of this a little too far. There's too much delight in pointing out others' mistakes or there's a little too much intensity and too much urgency in the perfectionist's reactions to error; let's say the emotional response is out of proportion with what's at issue. The insistence to make things "right", the nit-picking, and the implicit suggestion often made that others are willing to let imperfections slide that should not be permitted, all make the perfectionist a pain in the hind side of others. Turning others off is no way to get ahead in any facet of your life.

Of course, nobody likes others coming down hard on them. People are often embarrassed by the mistakes they make. They don't wish them to be brought to another's attention or to be broadcast publically. The harshly critical perfectionist is likely to promote psychological distance and alienation from the person who becomes the recipient of his or her judgmental scorn.

It's nearly impossible for us to get emotionally close to people if we're always criticizing their performance, finding fault with them, or looking for mistakes in their efforts. It's best advised, then, to find the good first and then to encourage improvement in a sensitive and tactful way. Bombastic condemnation is no way to go. By the way, it might be advisable not to offer your "improvements," especially if you don't occupy an appropriate position of authority and/or your suggested improvements are not solicited. It's sometimes best to keep our noses out of other people's business.

perfectionist
One who nitpicks and gives heightened importance to trivial matters.

3.2 ·····

insincerity
Lack of genuine emotional expression.

deceit
A form of lying or dishonesty.

This above all: to thine
own self be true,
And it must follow, as the
night the day,
Thou canst not then be
false to any man.
~*Shakespeare, Hamlet Act 1,
scene 3, 78–82*

Attitude Adjustment Four—Eliminate Insincerity and Deceit To avoid criticism and allay fears of alienation, some people become people-pleasers. The hope is that if one does likeable things, one will be liked. It's understandably more difficult to criticize those who are nice to us. Ambivalence grows when we want to find fault with those to whom we owe favours. There are those who know this and, in a psychologically defensive maneuver, try to ingratiate themselves to us. In addition to doing us favours, the same individuals might pay us excessive compliments or express superfluous generosity for which we almost feel guilty—the hidden intent.

Now, to the extent we show generosity, likeability, or service to others simply to alleviate our fears and get what we want, to the same extent we're being insincere and deceitful. We should not only want to do the right things; we should want to do them for the right reasons. Surprisingly perhaps, attitudes like generosity or friendliness are, in themselves, not necessary good—especially if there are ulterior motives at play. There must be honest and honourable intent behind our generosity and friendliness, not to mention our other actions and words. To be found out, for example, that our positive well wishes and contributions are nothing more than a manipulative ploy is certainly to undermine effective human relations. If people no longer can trust our smile, our favourable comments or our generous actions, then we have done serious damage to our credibility and ourselves. Contrary to what's glibly advised in some business environments, you don't have it made once you're able to fake sincerity. Eventually you'll be found out much to your personal detriment. It's in your own best interest to be honest with others and true to yourself.

3.2 ·····

histrionics
Exaggerated and often inappropriate emotional displays.

Attitude Adjustment Five—Be More Rationally Levelheaded and Tone Down the Histrionics Humans are emotion filled creatures and it's only normal to express emotions. Such expression communicates to others how we feel; by expressing our feelings, we can often get what we want. Sometimes our emotional outbursts surprisingly reveal how we feel to ourselves. Prior to our own outbursts, we may not have known exactly how we really felt.

There are beautiful emotional expressions like love and care or jubilation and gratitude and other negative ones like hatred and bitterness stemming from destructive intentions such as revenge. It goes without saying, perhaps, that it's better to express positive emotions than negative ones. This is not to suggest that bad feelings should always be repressed. Sometimes we need to express our negative feelings for purposes of catharsis or maybe to let someone else know how disturbed we are. How can anyone respond to our frustrations if they don't know we're frustrated? Furthermore, repressing emotions can have devastating effects, as we shall learn in the next chapter. Not acknowledging our feelings either to ourselves or to others leaves us out of touch with ourselves and what's really going on inside of us.

While expressing emotions is necessary to good psychological health, a problem arises, however, if we are frequently prone to over express our emotions in public. For instance, it's difficult to speak with someone bursting at the seams with fury and rage. There may be good reasons for the upset, but an explosive emotional tone typically makes it more difficult to deal with those reasons. In a defensive posture resulting from another person's ranting attack, those on the receiving end of the rant could respond with their own expressions of anger. As some would recommend: *Fight fire with fire.* Witnessing two fire-breathing dragons attacking each other is not really pretty to watch, however. It's generally better to de-escalate tensions than to contribute to them. A calmer, more stable and controlled emotional tone in human communications is more likely to lead to productive interactions with others. Be sure to remember, though, that our own emotionally elevated tirades are just as annoying to others as their tirades are to us. To invert a common expression, let me say: *What's* bad *for the goose is also* bad *for the gander.*

With our emotions in control, we're better able to listen to the voice of reason. We can better listen with understanding to what others have to say. We can more objectively assess the claims they make and weigh the evidence they provide. When emotionally balanced and in rational control, we can also then see our own position more objectively, appreciating what others think about us. Objectivity and rationality go hand in hand.

A note of caution is in order here. As we've already learned in this book, some people are more extraverted than introverted, more feeling than thinking. For such people, public displays of emotion come more spontaneously; feelings are gladly and willingly shared with others. Some people, though, are more introverted and thinking in psychological orientation. They may be more reluctant to share their feelings; in fact, they may view public expressions of emotion as inappropriate in professional or work-related settings. In this regard, it is useful to monitor the level of ease in emotional expression in others. Unwelcomed probing into someone else's feelings may be taken as an inappropriate incursion into their emotional territory. Be careful not to engage in any emotional trespassing!

3.2 *Attitude Adjustment Six—Watch Out for Groupthink and Conformity* As social animals, most people crave a sense of belonging or togetherness. We find comfort and security in numbers. We like to be around others for fun. Groups give us power and influence that we wouldn't otherwise have as isolated individuals. So whether for love, fun, belonging, security or power, we seek out others. Many of us couldn't imagine what it would be like to live without other people. As the philosopher Aristotle once said about the social nature of Man: *He who is unable to live in society, or who has no need because he is sufficient for himself, must be either a beast or a god.*

He who is unable to live in society, or who has no need because he is sufficient for himself, must be either a beast or a god.
~Aristotle

groupthink
Going along with the crowd.

91

Assuming you're neither beast nor god, you probably have social needs like most people. There's nothing wrong with that. The problem, however, arises when we allow our need for social affiliation to cloud our judgments or influence our actions in detrimental ways. We may end up doing morally questionable things or engage in illegal acts in a group that we wouldn't do as individuals. We might tell a racist joke at someone else's expense to make our friends laugh and maintain our popularity. As a recent beer commercial recommends we do, we might say: "I'm in!" (As opposed to "I'm out!"), when deciding to party all night long and thereby show up late for work the next day. This may sound like naughty fun, but try to explain the irresponsible behaviour to your boss. I don't think the boss will be as amused as you are. Behave this way more than once or twice and you may find yourself on the unemployment line. In this case you could say to yourself: "I'm out!"—not fun for reasons other than those given in the commercial.

The point to be made here is that proper judgment needs to be exercised when going along with friends. Wisdom is rare. If everybody is choosing to do something, maybe it's not the most prudent thing for you to do. Numbers guarantee little. Majorities have been wrong in the past; they'll continue to be wrong in the future. What's needed is greater independent thought on your part. What your friends are doing or suggesting may or may not be advisable. It's up to you to make the rational informed choice and not to be swayed by some kind of **bandwagon effect**. If everyone's about to jump off the cliff, so to speak, there's no need for you to hurt yourself and do the same. In most extreme cases of groupthink, we have cult leaders commanding their followers to commit mass suicide or perform other morally questionable behaviours. Being your own person sometimes means swimming upstream against the crowd. Sometimes it means saying no to those who claim to know better. The aim here is not for you to become a rebel without a cause or to become a naysayer simply for the purpose of being contrary.

When you choose to be different or oppositional, you need to have good rational justifications. So too, is the case when you choose to go along with the crowd. Providing good rational justifications is what intelligent critically minded independence should enable you to do. Whether or not you should sometimes compromise and go along with others at your own expense is a discretionary matter left for you to decide. Whether or not you should object or fight back is your choice as well. As they say, you need to pick your battles. Little is accomplished always being at odds with others. **Mindless conformity** is what results when one always complies with the wishes of others, no matter what.

Attitude Adjustment Seven—Adopt an Attitude of Healthy Skepticism As just suggested, mindlessly going along with the crowd is not always advised. Conversely, mindlessly rejecting majority opinion is not to be advised either. If our basic tendency is to reject commonly held positions in a reflex fash-

bandwagon effect
Conforming in order to be popular or to fit in.

92

mindless conformity
Complying with the wishes of others, no matter what.

3.2

healthy skepticism
Thinking carefully and suspending judgment before all the evidence is in.

ion or to distrust and automatically question the motives of authorities, then we are most likely just being cynical. Being suspicious or distrustful for no good reason is irrational. Using isolated breaches of trust, for instance, on the part of some to make sweeping generalizations about human nature or about all other authorities, groups and/or institutions is unjustified. Always doubting the intentions of others might even get you dubbed a conspiracy theorist! This is not something you would want to include on your résumé!

By contrast to the cynic that summarily dismisses others or their claims out of suspicion and distrust, the healthy skeptic often suspends judgment and displays intellectual caution. The skeptic understands and appreciates the limitations of knowledge while at the same time demanding that the evidence and research be provided in support of any assertions that are made. Empirical claims need to be tested and verified. Moral positions must be justifiable and fair. When all the evidence is not in, it may be more appropriate to suspend judgment than jump to hasty conclusions. When new evidence presents itself, it may be necessary to change positions and question previously held beliefs. The healthy skeptic goes to where the evidence and research lead.

The skeptic's systematic doubting can be used as a method, not to cynically dismiss the intentions of others, but to establish the objective facts. Though asking questions can sometimes slow us down, doing so can usually help us to arrive at better conclusions and more effective decisions in practical or work related contexts. Having a bunch of "yes-men" and "yes-women" around just adds to **groupthink** and **peer pressure**; those who merely go along for the ride don't contribute much to intelligent investigation and debate. Having a healthy skeptic around is bound to keep everybody honest. **Healthy skepticism** is related to positive critical thinking, the sort that can identify the strengths and weaknesses in any variety of proposals, recommendations or courses of action, for example.

3.2 | *Attitude Adjustment Eight—Eliminate Aggressive Arrogance* Nobody likes a know-it-all, especially when the know-it-all is prepared to ram his or her version of the truth down your throat. Standing up for what you believe shows principled courage. Refusing to budge because you're a dogmatic bigot is quite another thing. Imposing a limited or distorted version of the truth on others is simply wrong.

aggressive arrogance
Presenting your version of the truth in a forceful or assertive manner, believing you know better.

In today's complex and diverse world, it's dangerous to assume that anyone has a monopoly on the truth, whether moral, cultural, social, religious, political or historical, for instance. Globalization, multiculturalism, and the need to communicate across borders and continents have created conditions, which make it less and less possible to smugly sit back and believe that our ways are always the best ways. As many Americans are now coming to realize, what's good for America is not necessarily what's best for the world in the same way that what's best for New York City is not necessary the

93

best for the rest of the country. Were a New Yorker or an American to claim the opposite, this might be seen by some as the height of arrogance.

The arrogance referred to here is the social equivalent to egocentric thinking. The difference is that the thinking is not self-centred, but more or less group centred; that is to say "**socio-centric**," "**religio-centric**," or "**ethno-centric**." One simply takes one's society, religion, culture or ethnicity and considers it superior or better is some fashion. The presumed superiority may be unwittingly assumed and just taken for granted as an unquestioned truth. Again, to take an American example, for a U.S. citizen to claim that the Muslim Hijab should be banned and that women who wear it are mindlessly exploited is to make a couple of questionable claims. Some citizens, born and raised in the U.S. actually choose to wear the Hijab; they're not necessarily forced to. In fact, as converts to Islam they may wear the religious garb in opposition to their parents who may fear discrimination against their daughters by racists and bigots in the society. In this case there's no exploitation and no mindlessness. Rather, there is heartfelt conviction and conscious choice.

With respect to banning religious dress or symbols, could you imagine any U.S. State banning the wearing of the cross in public? There would likely be an outcry by faithful Christians wishing to symbolically express their religious commitments in public. While not caring about others reflects a type of ego-centric selfishness, not respecting the practices of other religions, cultures, and societies reflects a kind of religio-centrism, ethno-centrism or socio-centrism, things that indicate insensitivity and ignorance. Such things serve as the basis for discriminatory attitudes and the horrific behaviours that flow from them.

Interestingly enough, insensitive ignorance often presents itself publically as a type of **aggressive arrogance**. Those who "know better" or have a superior knowledge based on their own group's values and beliefs are often prepared to fight for what they believe in, even if that means persecuting others, discriminating against them, looking down on them, or treating them unfairly. Adopting such negative attitudes and behaviours is not advised in today's multicultural, pluralistic and diverse world.

Discriminatory attitudes, based on ignorance and insensitivity, are not productive. You don't have to agree with people of all faiths, or of no faith, but you should respect their rights, show tolerance, and respect for them in order to minimize conflict and promote harmonious interpersonal communications. As society becomes less and less homogeneous with respect to values and outlooks, respect and tolerance will cease to be seen as merely nice discretionary things, but will come to be regarded as absolutely required things if civil unrest is to be avoided.

3.2 ⋯⋯ *Attitude Adjustment Nine—Adopt the Principle of Charity* When communicating with people, especially about controversial topics, things can often get heated. When they do, we might be inclined to take what someone has said out of context. We might also wish to take any ambiguous statement

---

socio-, religio-, and ethno-centric thinking
Irrational belief that one's society, religion or ethnic group is superior.

discriminatory attitudes
Forms of intolerance based on ignorance and insensitivity.

94

I know why people think I'm arrogant. It's because they're stupid!
~Anonymous

Ethnic and religious stereotypes need to be dismantled in an era of multiculturalism and globalization.
Courtesy of Ed Kashi VII/Corbis Images.

made by our interlocutor and attack the interpretation which is most damaging to his or her position. Put more simply, if someone makes a claim that can be taken or understood in more than one way, we may wish focus on the interpretation, which is least acceptable and most damaging to their argument and the opposing position that it supports. To do this is to violate the **principle of charity**.

Whenever it's possible to interpret what someone has said in more than one way, it is best or "most charitable" to give the person the benefit of the doubt. This is a courtesy that should be extended our way as well. If we are still able to find fault even with most generous interpretation of our opponent's statement, then our own argument becomes stronger and our position more cogent. If our criticisms only apply to the most damaging interpretation and not to the alternative more generous one, then we might have to rethink our position.

We can regard the principle of charity as something like a **rule of rational engagement**. It is one rule worth adopting if we choose to be rational thinkers and reasonable in our dealings with others. Those who make it standard practice to go for the jugular and take people's complex or ambiguous statements in the most damaging ways lose credibility, at least in the eyes of those who value rational discussion. Accepting the principle of charity and arguing on the basis of it communicates respect for others and our desire to be fair and objective—good messages to convey especially when controversial issues are involved.

One tolerance that is intolerable is tolerance of intolerance.
~*Author*

principle of charity
Giving people the benefit of the doubt.

rule of rational engagement
Etiquette requirement in argument and debate.

95

Morals and Virtues for Character Development and Interpersonal Communications

Interpersonal communications and social interactions do not occur in a moral vacuum. Implicit norms are often operative without our thinking about them. For example, when you make a promise, the assumption is that you intend to keep it and the person to whom you made it quite properly has certain reasonable and justifiable expectations as a result. If you don't keep your promise, not only has a trust been violated, but a relationship might also be damaged as a result. Nobody likes to be lied to or to have his or her reasonable expectations unmet. If you make a promise to someone else, then the other person quite rightly deserves it to be kept, barring any unforeseen and uncontrollable circumstances, of course. One could say you have a "moral duty" to keep the promise. In general terms, morality places boundaries on what is and what is not acceptable behaviour.

In what follows, we'll examine a few moral notions that will be helpful to keep in mind if we wish to treat others in an ethically acceptable fashion and communicate with them following certain generally accepted moral norms. We'll also look at a few virtues worth developing. Before we do, let's start with the moral principle of respect for persons.

3.3   *Respect for Persons* Centuries ago, the great philosopher Immanuel Kant searched for the ultimate foundation of morality. Eventually, he grounded it on a rational principle called The Categorical Imperative (Kant, 1785). Kant expressed this imperative in various forms, but the best known perhaps is called: **Respect for Persons**. According to Kant, *we all have a duty to treat people as ends in themselves and never merely as means to our own ends.* Kant was particularly concerned with sexual exploitation where one person treats another not with human dignity but as an object of sexual gratification. He writes: "Sexual love makes of the loved person an object of appetite: as soon as that appetite has been stilled, the person is cast aside as one casts aside a lemon which has been sucked dry." For Kant, to be tossed away after being sexually used and abused is a gross violation of respect for persons.

respect for persons
Treating people as ends in themselves, never merely as means to our own ends.

It's important to be clear here about what it means precisely to use people. In a sense, we all "use" other people and in ways which nobody would object to. For instance, I may use my neighbor's daughter for baby-sitting purposes. I may pay her for looking after my children as I go out with my wife and friends to dinner. In this case, nobody's dignity is violated; nobody is cast aside as a worthless object; and no trust has been violated—assuming I pay up, of course! We all use other people in this way, whether it's getting somebody else to cut our grass or clear snow from our driveways in the winter. This kind of "using" is quite acceptable.

96

By contrast, Kant is drawing our attention to instances of where we use people and in the process disrespect their humanity or violate their rights. Slavery is a very good example of how the principle of respect for persons can be violated. In this instance, slave owners are exploiting other human beings for their own benefit. They force others to act against their will. The rights and wishes of those others are not recognized and respected; rather they are suppressed or go unacknowledged.

Essentially, violating the principle of respect for persons entails using others against their will to achieve our own ends. While this violation most often applies socially, Kant also states that we have a duty to respect ourselves. Even if we freely and knowingly choose to be used and then allow ourselves to be discarded like a half-eaten piece of fruit, he would argue that we don't have an appropriate sense of self-respect. We don't have an appreciation of our own inherent dignity as a human being. Breaking the principle of respect for persons can thus entail violating ourselves as well as others. Neither option is a good one.

What statement do you make to others if you don't respect yourself or treat yourself in a respectful fashion? What kind of treatment should others expect? Heck, you don't even respect yourself! Let's just say the optics are not good and the expectations are a bit worrisome. Creating worry in others and presenting yourself poorly is not what you want to do assuming you have personal and professional goals to achieve.

A general recommendation to be made, then, is that respecting yourself and other human beings is a good and moral thing to do. You're not likely to be criticized or ostracized from others because you respect them and treat them with dignity. Just the opposite is true. By treating yourself and others properly you're more likely to be respected yourself and considered a person of trust. To the extent such positive perceptions of you are generated in others, the better off you will be.

Please note that the venerable Kant would not have you adopt the principle of respect for persons just because of its positive consequences for you, however. He would argue that the principle is good and justifiable in itself and that it should be recommended for that reason alone. Whatever its justifiability, it will stand you in good stead with others. Try it and see. The point is that moral behaviour can be regarded as good in itself, not good just because of the results. We should be moral even when it doesn't pay! Some have said that the true judge of a person's moral character is what the person does when nobody is looking. Let me add, when nothing of personal benefit hinges on it.

3.3 **_The Ethical Reciprocity Principle_** What I'm calling the **ethical reciprocity principle** is better known in religious circles as The Golden Rule—at least within Christian denominations. It states simply that _you should do unto others, as you would have others do unto you._ The ethics of reciprocity

ethical reciprocity principle
Doing to others as you would have them do unto you.

can be found in virtually all the other major religions of the world. For instance, the Buddhist would say: *Hurt not others in ways that you yourself would find hurtful.* In Islam the equivalent is *None of you [truly] believes until he wishes for his brother what he wishes for himself* (Number 13 of "Imam Al-Nawawi's Forty Hadiths"). In Judaism it's stated as follows: *What is hateful to you, do not to your fellow man. This is the law: all the rest is commentary.* (Talmud, Shabbat 31a). With respect to Native American spirituality, Black Elk says: *All things are our relatives; what we do to everything, we do to ourselves. All is really One.*

Regardless of its particular wording or religious equivalent, the idea of ethical reciprocity is that *we should treat others as we ourselves wish to be treated.* Suppose, for example, you are about to lie to someone. You can check on the moral acceptability of this act by asking yourself whether you would like to be on the receiving end of the lie. If not, then what you're about to do is wrong and ill advised. The same could be said about making mean-spirited fun of someone else in public. Would you like to exchange roles and be mocked in front of your friends and onlookers? Again, if not, then you should not engage in such behaviour. Whatever we want to do to others that we wouldn't want done to ourselves violates the principle at issue here. You don't need to belong to a particular religion to get the point.

One can see the reciprocity principle as an essential part of secular morality, even if it has religious equivalents. Whatever its wording or whatever its origin, apparently a long history of moral thinking upholds its value. Its functionality is tried, tested, and true. For this reason, its application is recommended in our social interactions and in our moral and ethical dealings with others. What you should avoid is acting on *The Leaden Rule*, which states: *Treat others, as you would never wish to be treated yourself.* Unfortunately, this is something we all do from time to time, some of us more than others.

Integrity Hypocrisy is not something we like. When people say one thing and then do the opposite, we say they don't *walk the talk*, as it were. They're hypocritical and certainly no moral example of whatever they preach. Because of this, it's hard to admire them or even trust them. When politicians recommend fiscal restraint and belt-tightening and then go off to vote themselves raises and increase the national debt with deficit financing, we all bristle at their audacity. We ask: How do they get away with saying one thing and doing another? Failure to provide satisfactory answers to this question has left many entirely cynical of the political process.

The human relations lesson we learn from politics is that we should try to maintain our **integrity** in our dealings with others. Clearly, it's not in our interest to have people respond to us with cynicism and distrust. Saying one thing and doing another is certainly going to irritate and confuse others, not to mention breed suspicion. If we wish to present ourselves as persons with integrity, we need to ensure that our actions match our words. We need to

3.3

integrity
Walking the talk; doing what we preach.

Reprinted with permission of Paul McKenna and Scarboro Missions

honestly express our feelings in appropriate ways. We need to keep our promises and do what we said we were going to do. We also need to be consistent in what we say and do, not changing our positions from one moment to the next or one day to the next. Doing this lacks integrity. Changing one's mind over and over again gives the impression of being scatter-brained, not altogether stable.

When consistency over time between our words and actions is achieved, we show greater integrity to the world. Others then have more reason to trust and respect us. One might say: *Virtue pays!* Virtue is in your own self-interest and it's good for others. Everybody wins when virtue is at play. Short-term benefits might possibly accrue to you by being inconsistent and hypocritical, but in the long run the costs are very likely to outweigh the benefits. Winning a battle is not winning the war, as they say. Likewise, acting without integrity may get what you want right now in this instant, but it may not get you the long-term ultimate happiness and satisfaction that you want out of life in the end. Such action will almost certainly get you less trust and affection—not what you want.

Scientific Proof for Karma? York U Study Finds Small Acts of Kindness Have Big Impact on Emotional Well-Being

TORONTO, May 17, 2011—Practicing small acts of kindness will make you a happier person, and the boost in mood stays with you for months, according to research out of York University.

More than 700 people took part in a study which charted the effects of being nice to others, in small doses, over the course of a week. Researchers asked participants to act compassionately towards someone for 5–15 minutes a day, by actively helping or interacting with them in a supportive and considerate manner. Six months later, participants reported increased happiness and self-esteem.

"The concept of compassion and kindness resonates with so many religious traditions, yet it has received little empirical evidence until recently," says lead author Myriam Mongrain, associate professor of psychology in York's Faculty of Health. "What's amazing is that the time investment required for these changes to occur is so small. We're talking about mere minutes a day," she says.

Participants' levels of depression, happiness, and self-esteem were assessed at the study's onset, and at four subsequent points over the following six months; those in the compassionate condition reported sig-

Reprinted by permission of York University Media Relations, May 17, 2011.

nificantly greater increases in self-esteem and happiness at six months compared to those in the control group.

So why does doing good for others make us feel good about ourselves?

"The simplest answer is that doing noble, charitable acts make us feel better about ourselves. We reaffirm that we are 'good,' which is a highly-valued trait in our society. It is also possible that being kind to others may help us be kind to ourselves," Mongrain says. She notes that previous studies have demonstrated a causal relationship between compassionate behaviours and charitable self-evaluations.

"Compassion cuts both ways," she says. "If you make a conscious decision to not be so hard on others, it becomes easier to not be so hard on yourself. Furthermore, providing support to others often means that we will get support back. That is why caring for and helping others may be the best possible thing we can do for ourselves. On a less selfish level, there is something intrinsically satisfying about helping others and witnessing their gratitude," says Mongrain.

Not surprisingly, research has also shown that compassionate activities increase the level of meaning in one's life, which in turn elevates levels of happiness.

Researchers expected that those with needy personalities would experience greater reductions in depressive symptoms and greater increases in happiness and self-esteem as a result of being kind to others.

"We hypothesized this would occur as a result of the reassurance [needy personalities] might extract from positive exchanges with others," Mongrain says. "We did see some reduction in depressive symptoms for anxiously attached individuals, but further research is needed to see if there is any long-term benefit."

The study, "Practicing Compassion Increases Happiness and Self-Esteem," is forthcoming in the spring issue of the *Journal of Happiness Studies*. It is co-authored by York University researchers Jacqueline Chin and Leah Shapira. The research was funded by the Social Sciences and Humanities Research Council of Canada (SSHRC).

3.3 **Responsibility** In conversation, people are often quick to uphold and defend their rights. It's frequently said that: *You owe me! They owe me! The world owes me!* And so on. As people demand more and more as part of their basic rights, a greater sense of entitlement has arisen. Things that once were considered favours, benefits or privileges are now considered requirements, ones that if not provided, point to the fact that something is terribly wrong. Parents and

responsibility
Duties and obligations comprising the flip side of freedom.

teachers frequently complain about the culture of entitlement that has arisen from middle class life and the luxuries it has provided. Many of those luxuries have become necessities, at least in the minds of those who have been pampered and protected by doting helicopter parents throughout their childhood upbringing and even into their adult lives.

An unpleasant surprise usually occurs when young adults leave the nest at home for the first time. They discover that life does *not* owe them a living. Nobody is there to pick up their dirty underwear off the floor. Unrelated persons at school or at work are not about to give them everything they want on demand. Indeed, most of the people encountered in their lives outside the home don't really care much about any one of our particular pampered little darlings. What they've come to expect can no longer be taken for granted. Nobody is jumping through hoops backwards to give them what they want. *All of this is just so unfair! Why are people so mean? Why can't I have what I want, when I want it? Just let me do what I want, when I want to do it! Who are you to tell me what I have to do or what I should want to do? I want it bigger and better and faster and cheaper…and I want it now! And I want it for less money!* All of these outcries are symptomatic of the mindset of entitlement—one that doesn't work very well in what can be called: mature *adult-world*.

In this regard, I'm amused to think about what someone once said about France's gift of the Statue of Liberty to the United States of America. As we know, it was situated in New York on the east coast just off of Manhattan Island. The individual lamented the fact that France did not offer a second statue for the west coast: The Statue of Responsibility. Such a monument would have served as a constant reminder that liberties are the flip side of responsibilities. In other words, with liberties come responsibilities. Just as we have certain rights and freedoms, we are responsible to uphold and defend those rights for others. The road of moral relations is not a one-way street. Human circulation is bi-directional. We can't simply go where we want without watching out for others coming from the opposite direction. They have rights to the road of life as well. I trust you catch my drift here.

Being responsible is going to require some objectivity and cognitive de-centring talked about earlier. Responsible living is not just about me. It must take into account the rights and interests of others. It involves obeying the rules, meeting expectations, and fulfilling professional duties. It's about showing up on time, doing what you said you were going to do, keeping promises, treating others politely or with care, paying your bills, and the list goes on. Responsible living is all about common courtesy and being decent. A civil and ordered society has a number of implicit norms operating, norms which any responsible person is expected to abide by. Acts of civil disobedience may be in order when social norms are unjustified or discriminatory, for instance, but generally speaking it's good policy to stick with them.

Responsible behaviour promotes smooth interactions and more harmonious relations with others. **Responsibility** creates consistency and consistency produces things like confidence and security in others. Such things are much appreciated. Presenting yourself as irresponsible makes you look immature. You turn out to be a risky proposition for others. Lacking personal responsibility is not likely to help you land a job or enhance your chances in getting an apartment. You're more likely to get what you want through responsible action.

3.3 *Truthfulness* To a very large extent, integrity and responsibility hinge on **truthfulness**. It's not very responsible to lie to superiors when jobs have not been properly performed, for instance. It's also not very responsible to make up stories to get us off the moral hook when we don't show up as promised or when we fail to do what we said we would do. Becoming a person of integrity and responsibility entails being honest, and that means telling the truth, even when it's inconvenient.

truthfulness
Predisposition to be honest and not to lie.

Those who lie and make up stories to shirk responsibility are not generally looked upon favourably. Liars can't be trusted; they may even pose threats. Statements made by known liars are typically dismissed as false or discounted in value. This is unfortunate in instances where liars are actually telling the truth. Nobody knows for sure when a truth is told or when a lie is delivered, however. The reaction is understandable. Most everything claimed by a known liar is treated with suspicion. To be a 'suspect' in the eyes of others is not good for you. Little is gained in the long term from lying. A hefty price might have to be paid, *liar, liar, pants on fire!*

3.3 *Fairness* We can't demand that other people like us, love us or do favours for us, but we can complain if and when they treat us unfairly. **Fairness** is a minimal moral requirement in our dealings with others. All of us like to get our fair share of whatever it is, whether it's time, money or resources, for instance. If another person gets more of something than we do, when we're both deserving of the same, we often get upset charging that the unequal portion is unfair. If you've ever had an unfair boss, coach or teacher, say, you know just how upsetting unfair treatment can be. When our peers are treated as teachers' pets or favoured sons and daughters, we can feel slighted. Others receive special and undeserved treatment, treatment of which we may have been more worthy. They get notice and attention that perhaps should be more rightly directed at us.

fairness
Minimal moral requirement to give each their due.

Fairness is also about distributing assets equally, unless of course there's good justifiable reason to offer more to some than others. It's about getting your fair share. For example, if there are four people at the dinner table and there are four pieces of pie, each person would seemingly be entitled to his or her piece of dessert. Someone dieting might wish to give up their right to a piece of pie, but nobody could just take an extra piece and still be fair to the others. Someone who did would likely be described as greedy and selfish, oblivious to the rights of others. Everybody is entitled to his or her "just desserts"!—Please forgive the play on words.

Fairness is also about rewards and punishments. A lot of controversy has surrounded the bonuses paid to business executives after recent government bailouts in the United States. Under circumstances of recession and government bailout, many regarded the corporate compensation packages paid out in bonus money as undeserved. Some individuals even called for the firing of big corporate executives charged with creating the recession in 2008 in the first place. In the eyes of some it was totally *unjust* to reward those suspect of either breaking laws pertaining to financial investment or at least bending them to their personal advantage, and the country's disadvantage.

The lesson to be learned from Wall Street management with its bonus compensation packages is that other than the corporate elites who benefit, most other people resent unfair treatment and unjust practices. When it comes to wrongdoing in any company, organization or institution, the penalty (fine or suspension, etc.) should fit the crime, as it were. When it comes to success and positive performance, the rewards should be in proper proportion as well. Widespread dissatisfaction can be bred when it's not. Intuitively it doesn't make sense when those responsible for a financial crisis get huge rewards and those who suffer as a result get little to nothing in compensation. It just isn't fair.

Notwithstanding what we've witnessed with recent economic events, you can still do much to further your future by learning to be fair in your handling of other people. Fairness on your part can enhance your leadership potential, while at the same time increase your likeability quotient. We all wish to be treated fairly and we tend to trust and respect those who treat us this way; in fact, we might even come to admire them. Clearly, drawing respect, trust and admiration from others is good. This we do by being fair-minded and treating others in ways they deserve to be treated.

(3.3) ⋯⋯ *Moderation* In addition to operating according to certain ethical principles like fairness and respect for persons, it is also worthwhile to cultivate a number of character traits. We'll consider only a few here.

moderation
Finding the middle between extremes of deprivation and over-indulgence.

One trait worth cultivating is the virtue of **moderation**. Centuries ago, Aristotle called it *The Golden Mean*. Today, we would more likely label it *The Principle of Moderation*. Contrast this with going to extremes, overdoing it, or over indulging in things like food, drink, and sleep. Excessive consumption and extreme living, as it were, can no doubt be fun and pleasurable. Such a lifestyle might help to garner notice and make you popular *with some*. You might like to be thought of as an 'animal' or 'crazy-person' who is completely outrageous, overly self-indulgent and overstated in how you dress, for example. These days, pushing the envelope, as they say, and going over the top is one way to get noticed. I guess it comes down to whose notice do you wish to gain.

adult-world
The world of work, family, and mature responsible living.

Somehow with age and maturity, the excesses of youth become less attractive for many in what I've called: **adult-world**. During one's student days it may have been "fun" to get so drunk that one vomited on someone else's carpet before passing out, but that sort of fun somehow begins to wane as the years wear on. Once amused friends, now homeowners, are apparently more likely to get upset when others damage their property with adolescent lack of self-control. Try going to a company party or corporate function and drink to excess to see what happens. At best, you're likely to become a topic of gossip regarding your inappropriate behaviour. At worst, you may eventually end up looking for a new job after having made the wrong impressions on your superiors at work. Expectations in adult-world require that one show some restraint and self-control. This is a measure of a person's maturity and responsibility—things valued in professional and work related environments. So, overdo it at your own risk!

3.3 ..... *Courage* The notion of **courage** often comes to mind in the context of war and military action. It takes great courage to face the enemy and risk your own life. Going back to Aristotle for a moment, he says that courage is the golden mean between cowardice on the one extreme and foolhardiness on the other extreme. The courageous person is not a coward, but neither is he or she a fool, rushing in where others fear to tread. It's worth noting that courageous people do experience fear; they're just able to overcome it when necessary. Most soldiers, even those bestowed with medals, will admit to having being afraid in battle. Their heroism comes from overcoming their fears.

courage
Intestinal fortitude required to stand up for oneself or do what's necessary, but difficult, unpleasant or unwanted.

In everyday contexts, courage is not typically about risking your life in war torn regions of the world. It's more about finding the intestinal fortitude to stand up for ourselves or to do something we're reluctant to do. We may be fearful about speaking our minds or engaging in some sort of new activity that takes us out of our comfort zone. For instance, maybe we're a little timid about heights and so are reluctant to climb the stairs of a Mayan pyramid while on vacation. Doing so requires courage—overcoming a fear that normally limits us. If we muster up the courage to get past our fear, we may find it extremely satisfying in the end to realize that the only thing we had to fear was fear itself. The task may have turned out to be relatively easy. The mere prospect of going up was the frightening challenge and that fright was all in our heads.

Developing courage has the advantage of making more experiences available to us. With courage, we are less limited and open to more possibilities. We place ourselves in situations where self-overcoming yields incredible feelings of reward and accomplishment. Self-confidence grows alongside the development of courage. Things like greater self-confidence and courage may even impress others who are yet to overcome their own fears and anxieties. Though not your intent, you may even end up looking like a hero through your expressions of courage. You may develop the strength to say and do things that others are too afraid to say and do. For this you could be held up as a role model. So, like morality, virtue pays!

Courage is certainly useful in leadership roles. Sometimes leaders must take unpopular stands for the long-term good, for instance. Meeting resistance

If you don't have enemies, you don't have character.
~Paul Newman, American actor

If you accept everything, you stand for nothing.
~Anonymous

head on requires courage. The ability to deal productively with opposition is one mark of effective leadership. Efforts to develop it can start with independent critical thought and a refusal to submit to mindless conformity and irrational groupthink. Standing alone and in opposition to others is not always easy. It requires courage. For example, making demands on others for proof before going along with the crowd or with what the majority of others believe may expose you to group ridicule, something not so nice. Not everyone has the strength or courage to stand isolated and exposed. Do you?

3.3 .... *Prudence* Prudence is another virtue worth developing. It relates to rational discernment, or to put it another way, being able to discriminate between what's harmful and what's best for you or your rational self-interest. Prudent individuals don't speak or act rashly. Careful thought and consideration are given prior to making statements or committing to particular actions. The prudent person does not wish to say or do things that will be personally harmful or jeopardize his or her future. **Prudence** is what has us invest in retirement savings plans. It is the same prudence, which has us drive our cars below dangerous speeds. Prudence is what has us prepare for natural disasters like floods and hurricanes. In general, when we look after our personal welfare, we're being prudent.

prudence
Using rational discernment to avoid harm and maximize personal benefit.

Without prudence, we might otherwise behave in thoughtless and impetuous ways and thereby get ourselves into trouble. Acting reflexively on a momentary whim or desire might get us into long-term difficulty or have us behave in ways we later regret. For example, getting caught up in the excitement of an erotic moment might lead to physical pleasure, but if there's unprotected sex involved, it might also leave one suffering with HIV AIDS. For a brief moment of pleasure, one's life could be horribly changed forever. Allowing this to happen is not prudent. Having the discernment and willpower not to engage in activities that could endanger your future would indeed be indicative of this virtue.

Prudent individuals do not take foolish risks or put themselves in harm's way for no good reason or for the satisfaction of fleeting self-indulgent desires. Prudent people also manage to do things that they might not prefer, but do them anyway because they're good to do. Take regular exercise, for example; it may not always be fun, but good for one's health nonetheless. The prudent individual takes care of his or her body in order to enjoy life and maximize longevity.

Mind Your Manners

manners
Culturally defined conventions of polite behaviour.

One could argue that **manners** are nothing more than arbitrary cultural conventions. What is polite and acceptable in one culture is not in another. It's rumored at least that in some cultures, like the Bedouin, it is quite acceptable to burp after a meal to communicate satisfaction; in other cultures such behaviour might be considered the epitome of rudeness. Given that accepted norms related to manners only interfere with what we might more naturally prefer to do or that they simply serve to put limits and constraints on us, it might be tempting for some people to dismiss the need to abide by them regarding them as unnecessary and irrelevant in today's world.

No doubt proper manners vary from place to place and that proper etiquette has evolved from earlier times to the present. Does that mean we should forget about them altogether? Let me suggest you do so at your own peril. Rudeness puts you on the wrong road and the destination to which it takes you is not really where you want to go in the end!

(3.4) **_Etiquette and Electronics_** In this electronic age of cell phones, laptops, and portable media devices, it's sometimes difficult to get people's attention. It can be challenging to communicate with someone when they're plugged in and tuned out. College hallways are filled these days with students who often seem oblivious to what's going on around them. Even from a distance, one can frequently hear loud music pounding from headphones. It's perhaps not that all uncommon to see some students watching online television while at the same time doing Internet research for a project. With cell phone easily within reach, any person can watch television, enjoy music in one ear, listen via cell phone to a friend with the other, all while simultaneously reading text messages on a laptop.

All of this **electronic multi-tasking** can be immensely seductive. On the surface, it may appear that doing so many things at the same time reflects our sophistication or the technological progress we've made. The price to be paid, however, is becoming largely oblivious to what is going on in our immediate surroundings. Let's just say the scattered attention created by multiple electronic devices is not conducive to focused concentration. Multitasking technophiles are not having Zen moments in all of their instantaneous and fast-paced operations and activities. It's surprising that more people don't fall down stairs or bump into each other on the street when distracted with all of their electronic gadgets.

electronic multi-tasking
Using numerous electronic devices simultaneously.

Cell phones, in particular, can cause such distractions that their use while driving has been deemed dangerous and illegal in many provincial and state jurisdictions. Police understand that "multi-tasking" while driving—texting and calling friends, for example, is not a good idea. A single moment's inattention could cause an accident and possibly even injure someone or worse yet, take a life. So, while the prevailing accepted norm is that all these electronics are cool, they are not necessarily so cool in particular situations like driving a car. The broader lesson would seem to be that there are appropriate and inappropriate circumstances where electronics should and should not be used. The reason does not always relate to safety considerations, however.

107

Using electronics in certain places can be considered extremely rude. Having someone's mobile ringtone go off during a classroom lecture creates a disturbance, annoying to the class, not to mention the professor delivering the lecture. The same applies to a theatrical performance. Nobody likes to overhear someone else's irritating telephone conversation during dramatic moments on stage. Choosing to take a call, as is surprisingly done on occasion, reflects perhaps the height of impoliteness. The act is so incredibly selfish. The nonverbal message is that: *My call is more important than respecting your right to listen or enjoy the performance in an undisturbed fashion.* To the professor the message is: *My call is more important than anything you have to say.* Communicating to others that what they have to say is unimportant is not advised. Nobody likes to be discounted. Being distracted with personal gadgetry while conversing is one way to do just that—discount others that is.

With respect to school, if and when you are expecting an emergency call, it is best to inform the professor prior to class and to put your cell phone on vibrate mode. Having to leave class in order to take the emergency call with prior notice and permission doesn't leave the professor irritated by your interruption. Anticipating a possible interruption and informing those who might be inconvenienced is one way of showing that you are a considerate individual, not an insensitive slob who doesn't care much how one's actions affect others.

Another place not to use cell phones is in the bathroom, especially if it's a public bathroom. Clearly, the camera function many phones have is strictly forbidden for legal reasons as well as for etiquette considerations. Let's just say the sights and sounds one might experience in a bathroom are not meant to be shared with others. The call should certainly wait until one's business in the bathroom is done! Eliciting a disgusted gag reflex from your listener on the other end of the call is not what you want to do. Speaking while leaned up against a urinal doesn't send the right message.

Finally, with respect to being present, let it be said that just as its impolite to speak with someone while looking around that person or over that person's shoulders, so too is it rude not to be paying complete attention to the person to whom we're speaking. It's difficult to pay complete and focused attention to one person when talking to another on a cell phone or text messaging a third party while walking down the street with your conversational partner. It really doesn't matter whether he or she cares; neither does it matter that you wouldn't be bothered. Even if both of you accept rude behaviour, that fact doesn't change the fact the behaviour is rude. If you're so confident that "half-listening" to your friend while texting or calling is okay, then try it at your next job interview or while discussing a raise with your boss. I suspect you'd be concerned about the consequences. If so, the point is understood.

I cannot stress enough that the answer to life's questions is often in people's faces. Try putting your iPhones down once in a while, and look in people's faces. People's faces will tell you amazing things. Like if they are angry, or nauseous or asleep.
~Comedian Amy Poehler, Harvard Convocation Address, 2011

108

Tacky Use of Technology

Take a moment to think about times you were annoyed, offended or inconvenienced by others' rude use of technology. Where were you exactly? What was the situation? What were you doing or saying at the time? How did technology interfere with the communication process? Be specific.

What lessons can you learn from other peoples' rudeness? What should you try to avoid in the future? What should you make sure to do?

(3.4) ····· ***Punctuality*** It's always a good idea to try to be on time, whether it be for class, for an appointment or when getting together informally with friends. Showing up punctually at a prearranged time communicates the message that the meeting or get-together is important; that we care to attend or be present. Not only is it courteous, showing up when expected gives evidence that we're responsible. If we send the message that we're responsible, we instill confidence in others that we can be counted on to appear when we say we will.

punctuality
Being on time.

How many times have you been frustrated because you were left waiting for someone who didn't show up as promised or came so late that scheduled dinners or planned activities had to be delayed? Of course, unexpected traffic jams, subway breakdowns, and flat tires do occasionally happen. Such things can slow us down and make us late. When they do, we don't begrudge people their lateness because of them. It's when lateness is chronic that it becomes a problem. Others are forced to put things on hold, make alternative arrangements, or hope for the best. It's not nice to keep people waiting or to put other people in situations of inconvenience. In addition to being disrespectful, you're conveying the message that other people's time is not important, or at least not important to you.

Further, lateness communicates the message that my time is more important than yours. It might also communicate that one is disorganized and/or lacks proper time management skills. None of these messages are good ones to convey. Hence, taking the trouble to be punctual is advised. Punctuality communicates courtesy, responsibility and good time management—all desirable things.

(3.4) ····· ***Politeness and Right Speech*** Rare, if ever, is the situation where being polite will get you into trouble. Just the contrary is true. Saying "Please" and "Thank you," for instance, sends the message that you're well mannered and polished. So does holding the door for someone whose arms are filled with

politeness
Displaying good manners, being appropriate, showing respect or offering deference toward others.

packages. People generally like to be treated with dignity and **politeness** is one way to enhance it. Small tokens of kindness go a long way in telling others what kind of person you are.

Taking time to address people properly by their titles and by making the effort to pronounce hard to pronounce names correctly, once again, one shows respect for the worth and dignity of others. Individuals generally take pride in their names and clearly identify with them. Mispronouncing someone's name without a second's effort is one way to discount another person and show disrespect. I'm always impressed, when listening to CBC radio in Canada, when I hear how announcers are usually able to pronounce difficult multi-syllable names of all ethnic extractions so precisely, in a way that would do the composer or musician proud. The pronunciations give the impression that the announcer has the same linguistic and ethnic background from which the name originated; this is often not so.

What's also impressive to people is when you actually remember their names. Remembering someone's name, addressing him or her by it, and using the correct pronunciation of the name usually make the person feel good. Remembering and using a person's name is psychologically stroking. Think of when recent acquaintances or professors remembered yours. Didn't you feel somehow uplifted? A smile probably came across your face. Try then, to remember and use peoples' names when you meet them. They'll be impressed that you remembered. They will also feel better about themselves. This is an all win proposition.

Still on the subject of talking with others, there are just some topics that shouldn't be discussed in certain situations. Asking someone how much money they earn is impolite at the best of times. Someone else's income is none of your business. Or, asking whether or not a person is a virgin at a funeral is not acceptable. Again, such an intrusive question is none of your concern. Asking it at a funeral should be self-evidently inappropriate. Other more important things should be on people's minds during times of death and sorrowful loss. To be thinking and talking to others about sexual matters while they are mourning is boorishly insensitive. When speaking to others, be sure the topics are situation appropriate and not any sort of invasion of privacy. Try to be more sensitive to the surrounding circumstances and people involved.

gossip
Unkindly talking about others behind their backs.

Gossip is never recommended as a topic of conversation either. The person targeted by the gossip is not usually present to defend himself against what's being alleged. The people engaged in the gossip are often taking a kind of perverse pleasure in laughing at someone behind their back, delighting in someone else's misfortune. Gossiping may also involve reading into the intentions of others, rightly or wrongly, and then pronouncing judgment on those intentions, however accurately or inaccurately they have been surmised. This is dangerous business. The gossipers could be wildly wrong.

Whatever bad intentions were imputed to others could be completely and utterly false. People's lives and careers can be destroyed by misinformation spread by gossip. If you would not like your life ruined by lies told about you behind your back, then you shouldn't indulge in telling lies behind other people's backs. Taking pleasure in lies or in people's misfortunes tells others much about your character. What it says is not good.

To maintain **right speech** we should also avoid swearing or using otherwise coarse language. There are people who are offended by four letter words, for instance, and we should not want to be offending people in our day-to-day interactions with them. Close friends and family members who know you well might be more forgiving with respect to your foul language, but there's no guarantee that others will be or that others will see and appreciate your "pristine character" behind all of your offensive street-talk. Gutter language belongs in the gutter many would say. Of course, you are free to continue offending people with your profanities, but doing so is not likely to get you what you want. Swearing is certainly not going to send the message that you are a polite and polished person. Where such a person is sought, you will more likely be overlooked.

right speech
Avoiding gossip, as well as coarse and offensive language.

3.4 *Sensitivity to Diversity* On the subject of sensitivity it's always advised to avoid off-color ethnic jokes or humour with sexist, racist, or gender biased innuendo. You may end up telling an ethnic joke, for instance, not knowing that the person, you're telling it to, comes from the ethnic background you've just disparaged; he or she may not look Italian, German, Polish, or Arabic etc. When you tell such bad jokes, you risk offending people with your discriminatory humour. Even if the person is not directly offended by your joke, he or she may have friends or in-laws that do belong to the group you just slighted. Nobody likes to be mocked; neither do people like their friends and relatives to be subjected to racist, sexist and other discriminatory comments. It's certainly not advised to have fun at someone else's expense.

sensitivity to diversity
Treating differences with courtesy and respect, avoiding stereotyping.

The sensitivity issue just addressed pertains to the need to respect religious, cultural, linguistic, and gender identity diversity. People are not wrong or somehow inferior just because they're different in appearance, speak differently or just because they don't share all of your values, beliefs or sexual orientation. Being different does not necessary mean that others are somehow inferior, worthy of ridicule.

Further, just because one or two individuals from a particular group do something which is unethical or illegal doesn't mean we can stereotype and paint all people from that group with one and the same brush stroke. Doing so is dehumanizing and does psychological and emotional violence to innocent individuals. Doing so also reflects the fact that the person stereotyping lacks rationality and/or appropriate critical-analytical thinking skills. A sensitive, intelligent thoughtful person does not stereotype and unjustifiably discriminate against others. Surely, you don't wish to be thought of as a

111

stupid insensitive boor with no respect for others. Such self-presentation is not likely to further your life's options. It's best then to acknowledge and esteem others for who they are, no matter the diversity. You don't need to always agree with others, but you do need to respect the rights of people different from you.

appearance
The way you look and present yourself to others.

(3.4)

Appearance Much is communicated to others by your **appearance**. It's always advised to be clean and hygienic. Regular bathing or showering and tooth brushing and fixing one's hair are all pretty good things to do if you don't want to repulse others or disgust them with how you look or smell. Of course, you can't always judge the content of a person's character by how they look, but you also can't help but form first impressions either. Given this, it's probably a good idea to make sure that you are at least clean and presentable when making forays into the public domain.

Circumstances will no doubt determine what's appropriate in terms of dress. What one wears at a wedding banquet is probably not going to be the same as what one wears at a sports tournament or beach side resort. The situation will often dictate how formal or informal we should dress. It will also likely determine what is appropriately modest or immodest. How one should dress when going to a singles' bar is probably not how one should dress in church or at mosque, temple or synagogue. Discretion is thus advised. Dressing inappropriately for the occasion or circumstance may leave others with the impression that you have poor judgment—not an impression you wish to make.

(3.4)

Bragging and Name-Dropping It's often said that people with real power don't need to impose their authority. Similarly, it could be argued that people who are truly impressive don't need to brag and name drop in order to prove how extraordinary they actually are. There are some, who may feign interest in your other associations with important people, and some may even be truly impressed, but nonetheless, just as people are not necessarily guilty by association, they're not necessarily impressive by association either. Knowing and hanging around a celebrity does not make *you* one. Being around intelligent people doesn't make *you* smart.

It's recommended that when meeting people for the first time you don't start immediately trying to impress them by giving a list of your greatest accomplishments in life. Before establishing some sort of relationship, the other person may simply not care how "great" you really are! Furthermore, the need to impress may be perceived as a form of psychological defensiveness on your part. It may appear that you are trying to prove to yourself, as well as to others, how "special" you really are. You need to put the shoe on the other foot and imagine meeting someone for the first time and having the first hour of your conversation focus on all the achievements of your new acquaintance. It's likely that it wouldn't be too long before you were bored and disengaged. Constant and continual self-referring talk is not the most interesting in the world, certainly not to others.

On this note, be careful not to use other people's **bragging** as a springboard to jump into yours. Have you ever met individuals who use anything you say to brag about themselves? Not so much fun, is it? Well, if it's not fun for you, the opposite is not fun for them. So, don't brag if you don't wish to become a pain to others.

The dynamics of bragging are interesting. One brags, consciously or unconsciously, to establish one's worth or place in the pecking order of life. The person on the receiving end of the bragging often has not achieved the same things that the braggart is boasting about—otherwise they wouldn't be impressed. So, the braggart's indirect message can be: *I'm better than you. I've done something you haven't or can't.* Once communicated, the braggart now wants us to be impressed, right after putting us down in effect. It's like getting slapped in the face out of the blue and our slapper now expecting compliments with respect to how impressed we are with his or her ability to slap. That is the reason bragging is so offensive. The diminished are expected to pay homage to the diminisher! Ouch! Insofar as **name dropping** is meant to impress us with the fact that our diminisher has contacts that we the diminished don't, it too is a subtle put down with the expectation of admiration. Ouch again! If bragging is one of your personal traits, try humility for a while and see how people respond differently to you. Ironically, by not trying to be impressive, other people will be impressed.

bragging and name-dropping
Trying to impress people with your personal accomplishments or your associations with important or famous people.

Study Guide

Key Terms

character is destiny (84)
morals (85)
manners (85)
attitude adjustments (85)
character development (85)
cognitive egocentrism (86)
self-centred (87)
self-serving bias (87)
objectivity (88)
defensiveness (88)
projection (88)
perfectionist (89)
insincerity (90)
deceit (90)
histrionics (90)
groupthink (91)

conformity (91)
bandwagon effect (92)
mindless conformity (92)
healthy skepticism (92)
peer pressure (93)
aggressive arrogance (94)
socio-centric (94)
religio-centric (94)
ethno-centric (94)
discriminatory attitudes (94)
principle of charity (95)
rule of rational engagement (95)
respect for persons (96)
ethical reciprocity principle (97)
integrity (98)

responsibility (101)
truthfulness (103)
fairness (103)
moderation (104)
adult-world (104)
courage (105)
prudence (106)
manners (106)
etiquette (107)
electronic multi-tasking (107)
punctuality (109)
politeness (110)
gossip (110)
right speech (111)
sensitivity to diversity (111)
appearance (112)

Fill-in-the-Blank Questions

Instructions: Fill in each blank with the appropriate response from the list below.

Progress Check 3.1

punctuality
bragging
electronic multi-tasking
histrionics
conformity
healthy skepticism
aggressively arrogant
principle of charity
objectivity
defensive
perfectionist

sensitivity
appearance
gossip
Heraclitus
choices
character development
cognitively egocentric
self-serving bias
respect for persons
ethical reciprocity principle
integrity

insincerity   responsibility
deceit   prudence
moderation   fairness
courage

1. _____ claimed that character is destiny.

2. Individual character is reflected by our _____, as well as by our words and deeds.

3. _____ is important to mastering human relations.

4. People who are unable to see things from the perspectives of others are _____.

5. When individuals always claim personal credit for their successes and always blame others for their failures, they probably exhibit a _____.

6. Being able to see things from the vantage point of others and giving our own perspective no special value reflects _____.

7. Those who unconsciously project onto others things they don't like about themselves are being _____.

8. Finding fault and not giving credit where credit is due is a tendency of the _____.

9. People-pleasing can sometimes be a veiled form of _____ and _____.

10. Screaming and yelling at people we're displeased with is an example of emotional _____.

11. Jumping on the bandwagon and mindlessly going along with everyone else is indicative of _____.

12. _____ requires us to ask questions and get fuller information before deciding or pronouncing judgment.

13. Being a know-it-all and wanting to shove your opinions down other people's throats makes one _____.

14. Giving people the benefit of the doubt when they say something unclear or ambiguous is to apply the _____.

15. Refusing to use people in ways that violate they're dignity is consistent with the principle of _____.

16. Treating others as we ourselves would like to be treated reflects the _____.

17. "Walking the talk" or practicing what one preaches displays _____.

18. _____ requires us to recognize the rights and interests of others.

19. _____ is about giving people what they deserve.

20. _____ is a virtue that requires us to control our appetites.

21. Taking unpopular stands requires _____.

22. The virtue of _____ would have you further your rational self-interest.

23. _____ can cause one to be distracted and less present to others.

24. _____ is respectful and communicates to others that their time is important.

25. One way to violate right speech is to _____.

26. It's important to display _____ with respect to other people's religions and ethnic backgrounds.

27. Though you can't judge a person by his or her _____, first impressions are nonetheless important.

28. _____ is a way of inflating oneself and diminishing others.

True/False Questions

Instructions: Circle the appropriate letter next to each statement.

T F   1. Character is something with which you are born. You can't improve or develop it.

T F   2. Character is reflected by our intentions, words, and deeds.

T F   3. Children and others who cannot see the world from the perspective of others exhibit cognitive egocentrism.

T F   4. Defensiveness is a psychological posture one should assume when criticized.

T F   5. Valuing perfection necessarily makes you a perfectionist.

T F   6. One of the best things you can do to hone your human relations skills is to learn how to fake sincerity.

T F   7. It's best always to repress one's negative emotions

T F   8. It's always in your best interest to go along with everyone else and not create waves.

T F   9. Skepticism and cynicism are roughly equivalent to each other.

T F 10. Believing you are right and being willing to shove your views down other people's throats is typical of aggressive arrogance.

T F 11. The principle of charity requires one to do a certain amount of volunteer work each year.

T F 12. When you treat people with dignity and treat them as ends in themselves, you're showing respect for persons.

T F 13. The ethical reciprocity principle is more or less the same as The Golden Rule.

T F 14. Integrity is about consistency between what you say and what you do.

T F 15. Responsibility is in large part fulfilling your duties to others.

T F 16. Fairness is about giving people what they deserve.

T F 17. Finding a happy middle, not too much or too little, is the primary goal of prudence.

T F 18. Courage is a virtue limited to war and conflict.

T F 19. Prudence is a way of pursuing your rational self-interest.

T F 20. It's cool to use electronic devices no matter where, no matter with whom.

T F 21. Punctuality is important only for subordinates, not bosses.

T F 22. Gossip is a violation of right speech.

T F 23. Being careful not to offend someone by telling a racist or ethnic joke shows sensitivity.

T F 24. One's personal appearance and dress should always be left to the discretion of the individual.

T F 25. Bragging and name-dropping are good ways to impressive others.

Summary

1. What is character?
   - The moral and attitudinal dimension of personality
   - Something reflected in our thoughts, words, and deeds
   - A psychological posture or orientation toward the world
   - A kind of a default position evident in our reactions to events that impact on us

2. What are some attitudes that need to be changed or eliminated?
   - Egocentrism
   - Psychological defensiveness
   - Perfectionism
   - Insincerity and deceit
   - Histrionic predispositions
   - Group think and conformity
   - Aggressive arrogance
   - Haughtiness and superiority (displayed by bragging and name-dropping)

3. What are some useful attitudes and orientations that should be developed for purposes of mastering human relations?
   - Objectivity
   - Authenticity and commitment to truth
   - Rational self-control
   - Autonomy and Independence
   - Healthy skepticism
   - Sensitivity in regard to diversity
   - Charity

4. What are some moral principles important to human interactions?

- Respect for persons
- The reciprocity principle/The Golden Rule
- Integrity
- Truthfulness

5. What are some virtues that contribute to personal growth and good human relations?

- Fairness
- Moderation
- Courage
- Prudence
- Responsibility

6. What are some good manners worth developing so as not to offend others?

- Focusing and being present to others
- Punctuality
- Using right speech
- Respecting people's differences and responding to them with sensitivity
- Personal hygiene (e.g., showing up clean and presentable)
- Humility and deference to others (e.g., Letting others take center stage versus engaging in aggressive self-assertion or establishing superiority through bragging)

Related Readings

Aristotle, *Nicomachean Ethics, (trans. Terence Irwin)* Hackett Publishing Company: Indianapolis, 1985

Buron, Kari Dunn, *A 5 Is Against the Law!: Social Boundaries: Straight Up! An Honest Guide for Teens and Young Adults,* Autism Asperger Publishing Company; illustrated edition (January 2007).

Falikowski, Anthony, *Higher Reality Therapy: Nine Pathways to Inner Peace,* O-Books, Washington, 2010

Kant, Immanuel *Foundations of the Metaphysics of Morals,* (trans. By Lewis White Beck) The Library of Liberal Arts: The Bobbs-Merrill Company, Indianapolis, 1954

Piaget, Jean *The Construction of Reality in the Child,* Ballantine Books: New York, 1954

Post, Peter Essential Manners for Men: What To do, When To Do It, and Why, Publisher: William Morrow

Rawls, John *A Theory of Justice,* Harvard University Press, Cambridge, Mass., 1971

Riso, Don Personality Types: Using the Enneagram for Self-Discovery, Houghton Mifflin: Boston, 1987

Stohr, Karen *On Manners,* Publisher: Routledge (Oct. 25, 2011)

The lady doth protest
too much methinks.
~William Shakespeare

Psycho-Logical Defensiveness:
Unconscious and Irrational Factors in Interpersonal Communication

4

Chapter Overview

"Psycho-Logical" Defensiveness
Can Be Offensive to Others

- Self-Diagnostic 4.1
  How Defensive Am I?

Unconscious and Irrational
Defensiveness

Application Exercise 4.1
Dream Work

PSYCHO-logical Defence
Mechanisms

- Repression
- Rationalization
- Projection

- Reaction Formation
- Displacement
- Identification
- Regression
- Fantasy Formation
- Intellectualization/Isolation
- Denial
- Sublimation

Defence Mechanisms in
Summary

Application Exercise 4.2
Name the Defence Mechanism

Application Exercise 4.3
Dealing with Defensiveness

Thinking Straight Can Help You Relate

- Self-Diagnostic 4.2
  How Reasonable Am I?

Fallacies and Psycho-LOGICAL Defensiveness

- *Ad Hominem* Fallacy
- Straw Man Fallacy
- Circular Reasoning/Begging the Question
- Two-Wrongs Fallacy
- Slippery Slope Fallacy
- Fallacy of Appealing to Authority

- Red Herring Fallacy
- Fallacy of Guilt by Association

Application Exercise 4.4
Identify the Fallacy

Study Guide

- Key Terms
- Progress Check 4.1
- Summary
- Related Readings

Learning Outcomes

After successfully completing this chapter, you will be able to

(4.1) Identify the psychological defences you use to ward off anxiety

(4.2) Provide a working definition of defensiveness

(4.3) Explain the psychodynamics of defensiveness and illustrate how they serve as obstacles to effective human relations

(4.4) Engage in some preliminary dream analysis to help uncover repressed sources of anxiety giving rise to defensiveness

(4.5) Identify defensiveness in everyday behaviour

(4.6) Deal more effectively with defensiveness in yourself and others

(4.7) Explain the general nature and purpose of logical fallacies

(4.8) Outline and describe specific forms of fallacious reasoning

(4.9) Identify fallacies in everyday arguments and conversations

Focus Questions

1. What is defensiveness? What kinds are there?

2. What is the purpose of defensiveness?

3. Is human consciousness completely transparent to itself? What implications does this have in understanding defensiveness?

4. What are some PSYCHO-logical defence mechanisms? Which one(s) do you see most in your daily interactions with other people?

5. What is fallacious reasoning? What is its impact on interpersonal communication?

6. What are some examples of fallacious reasoning? Can you give any personal illustrations not found in the text?

"Psycho-Logical" Defensiveness Can Be Offensive to Others

noise
The psycho-logical obstacles that interfere with productive dialogue and harmonious relations with others.

psycho-logical defensiveness
The unconscious influences (the psycho part) and irrational thought processes (the logical part) that hinder our ability to get along with others and to communicate effectively with them.

unconscious influences
The "psycho" part of psychological defensiveness, which hinders one's ability to get along with others and to communicate effectively with them.

irrational thought processes
Bad thinking resulting from fallacious reasoning and other forms of ill-logic.

In Chapter 1 of this book, we began with an examination of the self and how it can influence person perception. In Chapter 2, we engaged in a process of self-analysis through an examination of personality type theory. We learned what we, as individuals, bring to our human interactions. Using the psychological insights of Myers, Briggs and Jung, we found ways to make our communications with others psych-smart. By applying type theory to our communications, we were able to develop greater sensitivity to psychological diversity.

Now, in what follows, we will examine a few of the "psycho-logical" obstacles that interfere with productive dialogue and harmonious relations with others. Theorists often refer to these obstacles as **"noise"** in the communication process. Note that I have purposely hyphenated the title of this chapter to read **"Psycho-Logical" Defensiveness**. I have done this to underscore the point that there are both **unconscious influences** (the psycho part) and **irrational thought processes** (the logical part) that hinder our ability to get along with others and to communicate effectively with them. By identifying and exposing these unconscious influences, and also by learning to make our irrational thought processes more rational, we can gain better control of our lives and reduce the amount of "nonsense" in our dealings with people. Let us begin, then, by exploring the nature and extent of our defensiveness by completing Self-Diagnostic 4.1.

Self Diagnostic 4.1 — How Defensive Am I?

Aim: The purpose of this self-diagnostic is simply to get you thinking about the degree to which you display defensiveness in your personal life. Results are not scientific, but merely suggestive. They are just a first step to help you determine how defensive you become in response to stress, conflict and anxiety-provoking situations.

Instructions: For each of the following statements, indicate how true each is for you. Be honest. Failure to be so is highly defensive!

1 = Never true
2 = Almost never true
3 = Sometimes true
4 = Usually true
5 = Almost always true

Score

_____ 1. When I get sexually aroused, I start thinking about something else.

_____ 2. Whenever I experience anger, I keep it inside, choosing not to express it.

_____ 3. I can offer explanations very easily and often for why I commit acts I recognize deep down as being wrong.

_____ 4. I put things off, reasoning that I can start tomorrow or make up then what I should have done today.

_____ 5. I misread people by attributing to them thoughts, feelings and intentions that are not their own, but really mine.

_____ 6. I feel threatened when I'm in the presence of people I don't like.

_____ 7. I am very polite and courteous to adversaries when I would rather attack.

_____ 8. When I feel afraid or insecure, I pretend I'm happy-go-lucky, joking around and laughing.

_____ 9. When I have a bad day at school or work, I unload my frustrations on younger or less powerful people in my circle of family, friends and acquaintances.

_____ 10. I've been known to attack defenceless people, either verbally or emotionally for no good reason.

_____ 11. I am a hero worshipper—imitating sports stars, musical artists or others of high repute.

_____ 12. If I didn't belong to a clique or in-group of some kind, I would feel left out, naked or exposed.

_____ 13. When I get upset, I either go drinking and partying or just start acting silly.

_____ 14. When mad, I pout and refuse to talk about what upsets me.

_____ 15. On days when things are not going well, I dream about better times in the future.

_____ 16. I often replay and win arguments in my mind well after they have finished.

_____ 17. I like to find theories and explanations for my unacceptable behaviours, thoughts and feelings.

_____ 18. I don't believe mistreatment directed at me should be taken too seriously. I maintain that sociological, psychological and economic factors cause people to do what they do.

_____ 19. I refuse to admit publicly that family and friends do things that are wrong and personally embarrassing.

_____ 20. I pretend not to hear things or see things I don't like.

_____ 21. I try to transform my undesirable impulses into actions that are socially acceptable.

_____ 22. I use creative or constructive outlets (e.g., painting, jogging) to vent my frustrations.

They defend their errors as if they were defending their inheritance.
~Edmund Burke

How to Score

All the above statements reflect defensive acts or tendencies. Add all the numbers that you placed in the Score column. Divide by 22. Round your score, if necessary. This method of calculation will give you your average score. An average score of 1 suggests that you are almost never defensive or possibly that you are unaware of your defensiveness. A score of 2 means that you are rarely defensive. A score of 3 indicates occasional defensiveness. A score of 4 reflects strong defensive tendencies, while a score of 5 could mean that you are defensive almost all the time.

Remember that your results are tentative and need to be verified. You may wish to discuss your results with someone you trust and know well. Note that statements are grouped in pairs, each relating to a particular defence mechanism that you'll learn about in this chapter. Which defences did you score highest on?

Questions	Defence Mechanism Reflected
1 and 2	Repression
3 and 4	Rationalization
5 and 6	Projection
7 and 8	Reaction Formation
9 and 10	Displacement
11 and 12	Identification
13 and 14	Regression
15 and 16	Fantasy Formation
17 and 18	Intellectualization/Isolation
19 and 20	Denial
21 and 22	Sublimation

defensiveness
The psyche's unconscious effort to protect the self from disquieting anxiety.

anxiety
The ego experience that serves to alert individuals to sources of imminent danger that must be counteracted or avoided.

124

diversionary and intimidation tactics
Irrational ploys used to persuade people and win arguments.

distortions of reality
Twisted perceptions based on insecurity and irrationality.

Unconscious and Irrational Defensiveness ·····4.2

Defensiveness is something we should all try to reduce in our psychological and interpersonal lives. For our immediate purposes, it can be defined simply as the psyche's unconscious effort to protect the self from disquieting **anxiety**, either through **diversionary and intimidation tactics** or by **distortions of reality**. As you'll soon see, defensiveness takes on many forms, but whatever the form, you can probably already appreciate how irritating it can be to be around people who unwittingly try to reduce anxiety by twisting things, by constantly attacking others, or by rationalizing their actions. Such people tend to be insecure and abrasive. For reasons we don't always understand, they seem to take things too personally. Being around defensive people can lead to conversations that are very one-sided and uninteresting, making interactions with them emotionally draining. As the title of this section suggests, being defensive can be offensive to others. It is important, therefore, that you learn more about defensiveness so that you can reduce it in yourself. You probably don't want your own defensiveness to get in the way of positive and fruitful relationships; nor do you want it to prevent you from achieving your goals. It can be enormously helpful to understand your own defensiveness, reduce it in yourself, and be able to work productively with it when found in others.

In advance of our discussion of the "psycho" part of psycho-logical defensiveness, it is only fitting to make brief reference to the work of Sigmund Freud. His pioneering work in **psychoanalysis**, developed and furthered by daughter Anna, has helped us to understand the unconscious dimensions of life and how we often twist reality in order to feel better about ourselves. According to Freud, not all of our psychological experience takes place at a **conscious** level. Some things are found at the **preconscious** level and others are deeply buried in the **unconscious**. What is conscious is what we are currently experiencing with respect to our feelings, thoughts and sensations. What is preconscious is that which we can call up at will. For instance, if now asked, you could no doubt give someone your birthdate or telephone number—things that were probably not occupying your conscious mind just a moment ago. However, what is unconscious is currently unavailable to self-awareness. The fact that there are things happening in the unconscious mind is important to remember. Frequently, in response to underlying fears and anxiety-provoking situations, we unwittingly resort to the use of psychic defences that help us to cope. These defences reduce unpleasant feelings or shield them from conscious awareness.

Unfortunately, an overreliance on unconscious defensiveness as a **coping mechanism** can lead to gross distortions of reality. A failure to appreciate the role played by unconscious defensiveness in our lives can also prevent us from functioning in healthy, autonomous ways. Buried fears and anxieties may dictate our actions and thoughts in ways we don't recognize. By learning more about defensiveness and by reducing it in ourselves, we can free ourselves from unconscious debilitating forces and we can learn to perceive situations and other people with less anxiety-based distortion.

Sigmund Freud was the founder of psychoanalysis.

psychoanalysis
Sigmund Freud's theory that psychic life can be represented by three levels of consciousness: the conscious, the preconscious and the unconscious.

preconscious
The level that lies just beneath the level of conscious awareness.

conscious
This level of mental activity is the one that includes all of the sensations and experiences we are aware of at any given moment.

unconscious
The level of consciousness which, according to Freud, is the most significant. He believed that many aspects of human behaviour are shaped and determined by drives, internal urges to satisfy biological needs, and instincts, innate tendencies of behaviour, found outside the realm of conscious awareness.

coping mechanism
The psychic defence that we use to reduce unpleasant feelings or to shield them from our conscious awareness.

The poets and philosophers before me discovered the unconscious. What I discovered was the scientific method by which the unconscious can be studied.
~Sigmund Freud

We wouldn't worry about what other people thought of us if we knew how seldom they did.
~Anonymous

125

Figure 4.1
A Glossary of Freudian Terms

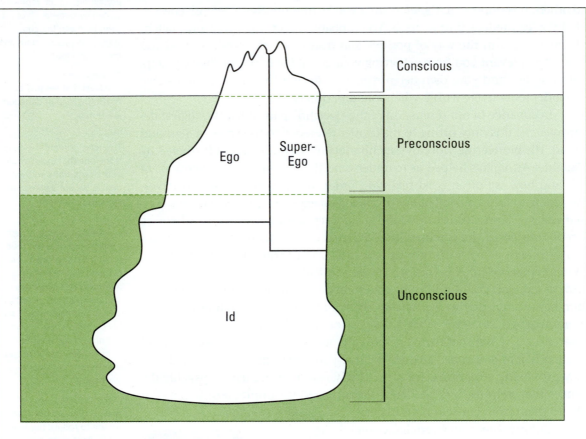

Levels of Consciousness

CONSCIOUS: Includes thoughts, feelings, sensations and experiences that we are aware of at any moment in time.

PRECONSCIOUS: Lies just below the level of conscious awareness. Contents of preconscious can be called into conscious awareness with a minimum of effort.

UNCONSCIOUS: Comprises drives and instincts outside the realm of conscious experience. Access to it can be gained indirectly by free association, dream analysis and other psycho-therapeutic techniques.

STRUCTURE OF PERSONALITY ID: Refers to the biological components of personality (e.g., sex drive). It operates on the pleasure principle and is irrational and impulsive. The Id makes up the largest part of the psyche; it is most influential in determining behaviour.

SUPEREGO: Houses our moral conscience and ego ideals. It is instrumental in making value judgments and helping us to distinguish between right and wrong. It operates on the perfection principle.

EGO: The rational part of personality. It operates on the reality principle. It serves to balance all parts of the personality to minimize anxiety.

Dream Work

4.4

Background: Sigmund Freud believed that mental activity is largely unconscious. He also argued that access to the unconscious (where defensiveness originates) must be indirect. Interpreting dreams is one indirect approach to the mind that can help you to understand better its unconscious workings. Dream analysis can enable you to locate sources of anxiety against which you unconsciously defend yourself. Of course, dream analysis is best done with the assistance of professionally trained experts. Our less-than-expert efforts here are for preliminary consideration only. Sweet dreams!

Instructions

1. Before going to sleep tonight, place a pad of paper and a writing instrument next to your bed. You could also use an electronic recording device, if available.
2. Tell yourself that you will remember your dreams for the night. Everybody dreams but we don't always remember what we've dreamt. (I've found that telling myself to remember is helpful.)
3. Immediately after waking up, record any dreams you had on paper or electronically. You may wish to fill in details about your dream later in the day.
4. Analyze your dreams by asking yourself the following questions:

   a. Are my dreams disconnected or is there a sequence to them?
   b. What parts of my dreams reflect the activities of the previous day? Is this significant?
   c. How do my dreams reflect my personal wants or attitudes toward others?
   d. What meaning could I give to my dreams?

5. Do this dream work for several weeks. Continue your analysis and interpretation. Look for any recurring themes and patterns. They may help you to uncover repressed material.
6. Record your personal insights in journal form.

Source: This activity is a variation of "Dream Journal" by Frager and Fadiman (1997).

PSYCHO-logical Defence Mechanisms

Since anxiety is inherently unpleasant, human beings have developed strategies to reduce its intensity. One strategy requires us to confront or run away from the threats that face us. We thereby eliminate difficulties, lower the chances of their future occurrence, or decrease the prospects of additional anxiety in the future.

psychological defence mechanisms
Collectively, the second strategy used for coping with anxiety (the first being to confront or run away from the threats that face us). They include repression, rationalization, projection, reaction formation, displacement, identification, regression, fantasy formation, intellectualization/isolation, denial and sublimation.

ego
A part of the psychic self. This psychological structure aims to gratify the wishes of the id within the restrictions of external reality and the moral requirements of the superego.

A second strategy for coping with anxiety is to employ **psychological defence mechanisms**. They include repression, rationalization, projection, reaction formation, displacement, identification, regression, fantasy formation, intellectualization/isolation, denial and sublimation.

As mentioned, defence mechanisms operate on an unconscious level. This explains why defensive people are largely unaware of their defensiveness. Also recall that defence mechanisms distort the reality of the anxiety-provoking situations that give rise to the mechanisms in the first place. When we use defence mechanisms, then, we unconsciously seek to protect ourselves against any real or perceived threat by falsifying the nature of the threat. Freud calls that part of the psyche that uses psychological defence mechanisms the **ego**.

It may be somewhat comforting to note that everybody uses defence mechanisms. If we didn't, we could all be overwhelmed by anxiety. The danger for us comes from an overreliance on the mechanisms. If we become too dependent on them, they could cause gross distortions in our perceptions of reality and we could begin to lose touch with what's really going on. People displaying excessive defensiveness often show symptoms of neurosis (Frager and Fadiman, 1997). It is important, therefore, to learn about the defence mechanisms discussed below and to become sensitive to your reliance upon them.

(4.3) ······ Repression

repression
A primary ego defence that makes all other psychological defensiveness possible. It is the central mechanism used by the ego to prevent anxiety-provoking thoughts from entering the conscious level of awareness.

Repression is the primary ego defence that makes all other psychological defensiveness possible. It is the central mechanism used by the ego to prevent anxiety-provoking thoughts from entering the conscious level of awareness. These thoughts may arise in reaction to in our biological instincts or painful events experienced in our past. Unacceptable sexual desires, for instance, may be repressed to the unconscious, as could childhood traumas. It is important to emphasize that "repressed" people are not aware of their own anxiety-provoking conflicts in the psyche, nor do they consciously remember the emotionally traumatic past events now buried in the unconscious recesses of the mind. As Freud (1915: 147) put it, "The essence of repression lies simply in turning something away and keeping it at a distance from the consciousness."

Despite its very real potential for harm, the use of repression helps us cope with everyday problems. Let's suppose, for example, that a friend said something spiteful to us. We might conveniently forget what was said to maintain the relationship. However, we might also "forget" to show up at the friend's pool party to which we were invited shortly after the remarks were made. In both such cases, repression would have a role to play.

Repression can also act as a temporary coping mechanism in response to conflict and pain stemming from our individual histories. Unpleasant things may have happened to us that are too horrible to bear consciously.

Distancing ourselves psychologically for a time may help us to survive, even if we remain emotionally wounded. Recognizing the lasting psychological scars of emotional trauma, a lot of the "inner child" work done these days by therapists and social workers aims to un-repress forgotten traumatic episodes in the lives of emotionally damaged individuals. Bringing painful memories to conscious awareness and learning to deal with them can have a healing, therapeutic effect.

Obstacles Repressed materials that are not brought to conscious awareness do not just disappear or slowly fade away with time. They remain active in the unconscious. Psychic energy is continually spent to prevent their emergence into conscious awareness. This strain drains much of the ego's resources and, therefore, less energy is available for more constructive, self-enhancing, creative behaviours (Hjelle and Ziegler, 1992). After all, "It's hard to expand your horizons when you're busy defending your borders."

As well as draining your creative energies, repression has the negative effect of precluding any possible resolutions to conflicts still buried in the unconscious. If you don't know what's disturbing you, it's difficult to make the appropriate adjustments in your life. Affected by anxiety, the true source of which is not understood, repressed people tend toward rigidity, lack of spontaneity and an inability to meet the challenges of life head-on. They may consequently seem awfully "stiff" or reserved to those communicating with them.

Even more seriously, highly repressed people may develop other unhealthy psychological and physical symptoms. According to psychoanalytic theory, phobias (e.g., fear of snakes) are derivative of repressed feelings, as are hysterical reactions. Psychosomatic illnesses (e.g., asthma and arthritis) may also be linked to repressed anxiety (Frager and Fadiman, 1997). Psychosexual disorders (impotence and frigidity) probably have a basis in repression as well.

In his treatment of patients, Freud discovered that repressed impulses find outlets in dreams, slips of the tongue and in other manifestations of what he described as the "psychopathology of everyday life" (Hjelle and Ziegler, 1992). You might wish to engage in some dream analysis yourself to uncover any personal repressions. What are your nighttime fantasies or daydreams all about? What could the themes indicate? Also, try to catch yourself in the act of "changing the subject," "pretending that you didn't understand" or making it appear that you "didn't hear what someone said." Whatever was changed, not understood or not heard may give you some insights into yourself and the workings of your mind. You may be able to uncover some fears and anxieties that you never consciously knew you had.

The dream is the royal road to the unconscious.
~Sigmund Freud

129

4.3 ···· Rationalization

rationalization
A defence mechanism in which the ego enlists the powers of reason to attempt to cope with disquieting anxiety.

Rationalization is another defence mechanism people heavily rely on in their efforts to cope with disquieting anxiety. To protect ourselves from mental pain, we often try to explain away our personal failures, shortcomings and misdeeds. In our own defence, the ego-self produces "reasonable" but dishonest explanations and justifications to support behaviours recognized at an unconscious level to be wrong or undesirable in some way. To recognize and admit our failures, wrongdoings or unacceptable cravings consciously could be too painful to bear. Instead, the ego disguises our true motives, distorts the reality of situations, and makes things look more morally acceptable than they are. This self-deception helps us to cope with immediate anxiety; however, it is not productive to the extent that it shields us from recognizing the real reasons behind our feelings, thoughts and actions.

Two "fruitful" examples of rationalization are "*sour grapes*" and "*sweet lemons.*" Using the sour grapes rationalization, we try to minimize the worth of something we actually truly want or once aspired to achieve, but failed. After discovering the impossibility of getting what we want, we proceed to undercut its value. Aesop's fable serves us well here. Remember the fox who wanted to eat the grapes? When the fox discovered they couldn't be reached, he decided that they were probably sour anyway. It's emotionally easier to cope with the fact that something undesirable is out of reach than something we really want. Failing to get what we want produces frustration and anxiety.

Using the sweet lemon rationalization, people magically see the positives in things that were not considered very attractive or desirable in the first place. For example, people may be forced to do unwanted tasks only to react later by praising the benefits of doing them. In truth, there may have been little to be gained, but believing there was a benefit allows people to better cope with unpleasantness.

Source: PEANUTS reprinted by permission of United Feature Syndicate, Inc.

Obstacles One negative result of rationalization is impaired judgment. If we see life as a collection of sweet lemons and sour grapes, we may end up with a basket of rotten fruit. Describing objects of our desire as less desirable or making undesirable objects sound more desirable may help us to feel better temporarily, but it certainly won't enable us to see clearly, impartially and objectively. When rationalizing, our judgments become indirect reflections of our wants and frustrations more than accurate evaluations of objects and events in the external world. Impaired judgment, like impaired driving, is dangerous and may get you into a lot of trouble. This idea takes us to the ethical problems associated with rationalization.

If, say, we rely on rationalizations whenever we violate social norms or personal standards of conduct, then we cease to function as moral people. Rationalizing helps us to justify unjustifiable acts in our own minds. It helps us to get off the hook of moral responsibility for personal wrongdoing. Heavy reliance on rationalization spares us from guilt and self-blame. From the vantage point of others, however, refusing to accept responsibility for our wrongdoing can be perceived as immature, if not immoral. No doubt, appearing childish and unethical is not in your personal self-interest. These qualities are not likely to endear you to others. It is important, therefore, that you minimize rationalization in your efforts to reduce anxiety in your life and improve your interpersonal effectiveness.

4.3 Projection

Projection is the unconscious act of attributing to others one's own feelings, thoughts and motivations. With projection, undesirable aspects of one's own personality are displaced from inside the person onto other people, things and events outside. By externalizing what is in fact internal, people can deal with anxiety-provoking thoughts without having to admit or be aware of the fact that these disturbing thoughts are their own (Frager and Fadiman, 1997). Projection offers temporary relief from anxiety as it allows people to blame someone or something else for their own personal shortcomings (Hjelle and Ziegler, 1992). Projection thus seems to come in handy whenever the ego or self-esteem is threatened. See Figure 4.2 for an example of projection.

The danger with projection is that it may become too intense and habitual. If this occurs, then gross distortions of reality can result. As a result, people could even become psychologically ill or disturbed. They might, for example, become paranoid and attribute aggressive thoughts to others that originate within themselves. On a less serious note, projections could cause people to evade responsibility or to perform at less than optimum levels. Students who don't study for tests and who don't wish consciously to admit their irresponsibility might unfairly criticize their professor for being unprepared in class. The next time you criticize anyone about anything, it could be insightful

projection
The unconscious act of attributing to others one's own feelings, thoughts and intentions.

Projection makes perception and you cannot see beyond it. Again and again have you attacked your brother because you saw in him a shadow figure in your private world and thus it is you must attack yourself first for what you attack is not in others. Its only reality is in your own mind, and by attacking others you are literally attacking what is not there.
~*A Course in Miracles*

131

Figure 4.2
Projection

for you to ask, "To what extent is my criticism an accurate reflection of reality?" or "What does my criticism of another tell me about myself?"

Obstacles The use of projection could have negative social consequences for people relying on it too frequently. If, for example, you unconsciously attribute to others your own hostile, aggressive urges and impulses, you may develop unwarranted suspicions. You won't be very trusting as an individual, making it difficult for you to establish close relationships (Barocas, Reichman and Schwebel, 1990).

Excessive projection could also cause you to fall prey to social prejudice and scapegoating. Ethnic and racial groups provide convenient targets for the attribution of your own negative personal characteristics to others (Adorno, Frenkel-Brunswick, Levinson and Sanford, 1950, cited in Hjelle and Ziegler, 1992). For instance, people who feel inferior may project their inferiority onto selected racial, ethnic or religious groups. Ambitious types may blame the "system" or some stereotyped elitist group for their difficulties in achieving success. Projection deflects attention away from ourselves and helps us to feel better about our personal shortcomings. Unfortunately, these better feelings come at the expense of others.

Projection can also have negative career consequences. If you display an inability to judge other people's motives, you may suffer from poor work adjustment. When trying to read others (i.e., their wants, goals and preferences) you may end up simply projecting and perceiving yourself externalized in someone else. Misjudgment of people is surely a liability in the professional world. Vaillant (1977) discovered in a longitudinal study of sophomores that those who used projection to a significant degree "had the worst career adjustments." Also, we learn from research that people with above-average relationships apparently do not significantly use projection. For interpersonal and professional success, then, a reduction of projection is indicated.

Reaction Formation

4.3 **Reaction formation** is used by the ego to control the expression of forbidden impulses. This mechanism works in two ways. First, unacceptable impulses are repressed in the unconscious. Second, opposites to the impulses are expressed on a conscious level (Hjelle and Ziegler, 1992). For example, people who are threatened by their own sexual urges may become crusaders against pornography and liberal laws on sexual conduct. Others who are highly anxious about their violent tendencies may become pacifists or animal rights advocates. In a letter to Jules Masserman, a famous psychologist who did work on alcoholism in cats, an antivivisectionist's moral crusade "covers up" the person's apparent violent tendencies. Notice in the following letter the lack of love and compassion for the drunkard and the personal attack on Masserman.

reaction formation
This is used by the ego to control the expression of forbidden impulses. Unacceptable impulses are repressed in the unconscious, and opposites to the impulses are expressed on a conscious level.

> I read [a magazine article...on your work on alcoholism]....I am surprised that anyone who is as well educated as you must be to hold the position that you do would stoop to such a depth as to torture helpless little cats in the pursuit of a cure for alcoholics....
>
> A drunkard does not want to be cured—a drunkard is just a weak minded idiot who belongs in the gutter and should be left there. Instead of torturing helpless little cats why not torture drunks or better still exert your would-be noble effort toward getting a bill passed to exterminate the drunks. They are not any good to anyone or themselves and are just a drain on the public, having to pull them off the street, jail them, then they have to be fed while there and it's against the law to feed them arsenic so there they are....If people are such weaklings the world is better off without them....
>
> My greatest wish is that you have brought home to you a torture that will be a thousand fold greater than what you have, and are doing to the little animals....If you are an example of what a noted psychiatrist should be I'm glad I am just an ordinary human being without letters after my name. I'd rather be myself with a clear conscience, knowing that I have not hurt any living creature, and can sleep without seeing frightened, terrified dying cats—because I know they must die after you have finished with

133

them. No punishment is too great for you and I hope I live to read about your mangled body and long suffering before you finally die—and I'll laugh long and loud. (Masserman, 1961: 35)

Of course, not all advocates of peace or animal rights display reaction formation defensiveness. Many have genuine, legitimate ethical disagreements with war and the destruction of animals. The clue in determining the difference between true feelings and defensiveness is found in the degree to which the feelings are emphasized (Hergenhahn, 1993). Reaction formations have a tendency to be more intense and extravagant in their expression. There may be something compulsive or exaggerated in the feelings communicated. The threatening urge (e.g., sexual or aggressive) to be repressed must be obscured again, again and again (Frager and Fadiman, 1997). Unconsciously, there is the fear that the unacceptable urge or impulse will break through if repeated attacks on it, or denials of it, do not continue.

Obstacles There are negative social consequences to using reaction formation. Relationships may be crippled by the defensive person's rigidity. Reaction formation contributes to building an "all or nothing" attitude toward life that makes the defensive person unyielding and inflexible. Little compromise may be possible with those whose strong feelings about something are merely a cover-up for unconscious fears and anxieties. Reasoning with unconsciously defensive people may sometimes seem next to impossible. Try, for example, to rationally debate the issue of pornography with an individual whose moral zeal is based on personal guilt and insecurity. Not much will be accomplished.

displacement
The unconscious defence mechanism that occurs whenever an instinctual impulse is redirected from a more threatening activity, person or object to a less threatening one.

(4.3)······ ## Displacement

Like other defence mechanisms, **displacement** is an unconscious process. It too has much to do with our primitive, instinctual impulses. Whenever we feel the urge to meet the demands of the **id** (a term used by Freud to designate the part of the personality directed at biological need satisfaction), we invest **psychic energy** in need-satisfying objects. When objects that would directly satisfy the impulses of the id are not available, or when they include some threat or unpleasantness, we may shift our impulses onto other objects. This substitution is called displacement (Engler, 1999). Sigmund Freud used the term **cathexis** to describe the investment of psychic energy in objects that satisfy needs (Hergenhahn, 1998). If need-satisfying objects are not available, an intense longing may manifest itself in the form of thoughts, images and fantasies. Such thoughts persist until needs are satisfied. When needs are finally satisfied, psychic energy dissipates to become available for other cathexes.

id
The biological components of personality, the part of the self that contains our basic sexual and aggressive instincts.

psychic energy
This is invested in need-satisfying objects whenever we feel the urge to meet the demands of the id.

cathexis
The investment of psychic energy in objects that satisfy needs.

If the structure of personality contained only impulses of the biological id and conscious ego functioning, society would probably degenerate into some form of animalistic existence (Hergenhahn, 1998). Instinctual needs from the id would arise and these needs would continue to create tension within individuals until satisfied. Unbridled sexual and aggressive impulses, for example, could be directed at target objects for rape and assault. Furthermore, with only an ego to serve the needs of the id, there would be no regard for the welfare of other people and no distinctions made between acceptable and nonacceptable objects of need satisfaction.

Fortunately, the human psyche has developed a moral superego that functions to inhibit primitive urges, instincts and desires. This inhibition requires energy to be spent on preventing unacceptable cathexes. Energy that is used to prevent unacceptable cathexes is called **anticathexis** (Hergenhahn, 1998). If an unacceptable cathexis were allowed to emerge, the superego would ensure that anxiety would result. To reduce anxiety, the ego and the **superego** (a term used by Freud to capture the notion of moral conscience) combine their efforts to create an anticathexis that is sufficiently strong to inhibit the primitive cathexes of the id. Note that the original needs of the id do not vanish. Rather, the original cathexis is displaced onto other safer objects and activities. This displacement is illustrated in Figure 4.3, where dancing becomes a non-anxiety-provoking substitute (displacement) for sex, which causes significant anxiety through guilt.

anticathexis
Energy that is used to prevent unacceptable cathexis.

superego
The part of the psyche that deals with morality. It houses our personal system of ethical values.

Figure 4.3
An Example of Displacement

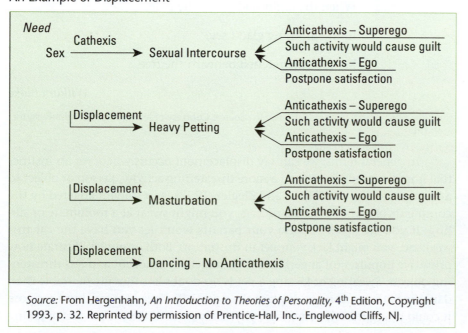

Source: From Hergenhahn, *An Introduction to Theories of Personality*, 4th Edition, Copyright 1993, p. 32. Reprinted by permission of Prentice-Hall, Inc., Englewood Cliffs, NJ.

reflection poem

A Poison Tree

I was angry with my friend;

I told my wrath, my wrath did end.

I was angry with my foe;

I told it not, my wrath did grow.

And I watered it in fears,

Night and morning with my tears.

And I sunned it with smiles,

And with soft deceitful wiles.

And it grew both day and night,

Till it bore an apple bright.

And my foe beheld it shine,

And he knew that it was mine.

And into my garden stole,

When the night had veil'd the pole;

In the morning glad I see;

My foe outstretched beneath the tree.

~William Blake

Source: Courtesy of Jeremy Tarcher Publishers, Inc.

In general terms, we can say displacement occurs whenever an instinctual impulse is redirected from a more threatening activity, person or object to a less threatening one (Hjelle and Ziegler, 1992). As a student angered by the comments of one of your instructors, you might swear at a roommate or sibling. If you are upset because your parents won't let you have the car this weekend, you might kick your pet in frustration. Both examples illustrate how primitive impulses (of anger) find their targets in innocent and less threatening objects. Swearing or kicking a pet is no doubt less morally desirable than dancing with someone to displace the unsatisfied need for sex, but I suppose it could be argued it is better than physically assaulting your parents or killing your cat. It's unfortunate that innocent objects often suffer from the displacements of others. By increasing awareness of this unconscious defence mechanism, perhaps we can reduce the injury and suffering of all.

A less common form of displacement involves "turning against the self" (Hjelle and Ziegler, 1992). In this case, hostile impulses toward other people are redirected at one's own person. The result can be things like depression and self-deprecation. If other innocent and less threatening objects are unavailable for displacement, the self can become its own target.

Obstacles Social and interpersonal manifestations of displacement can be rather unpleasant. First of all, innocent people are attacked, criticized, abused and hurt. They suffer merely by virtue of their relatively nonthreatening natures. Unjustified psychological assault can thus be destructive to interpersonal relationships. Second, people unconsciously relying on displacement tend to exhibit hypersensitivity to minor annoyances (Hjelle and Ziegler, 1992). For example, people criticized by overdemanding bosses may react violently to the slightest provocation from a spouse or friend. Target objects of hostility are simply substitutes for the boss who cannot be attacked. The boss has too much power and is therefore too threatening. If some "little comment" you innocently made once was met with undue anger or hostility, perhaps you witnessed displacement; alternatively you might have become the target of someone's defensiveness, the aim of which was to reduce that person's own level of anxiety. You benefit from knowing this by increasing your compassion for those experiencing psychological pain. You needn't take their aggressive outbursts personally. Through understanding, you might be able to help. At the same time, forgiveness becomes a real possibility. It's probably easier to forgive people you see as suffering than those you see simply as attackers launching unjustifiable assaults on you and others.

To understand all is to forgive all.
~*French proverb*

4.3 ## Identification

Identification is a psychological defence mechanism unconsciously used to decrease anxiety by increasing feelings of self-worth. It involves taking on the characteristics of someone admired or held in high esteem. (Hergenhahn, 1998). An obvious example of identification is the hero worship exhibited by school-age boys and girls (Barocas, Reichman and Schwebel, 1990). Typical heroes are rock stars and athletes. Young people are very motivated to learn everything they can about their heroes. They join fan clubs, purchase tapes and CDs, buy sports cards and memorize statistics and facts about those whom they idolize. Identification is clearly present when they adopt their favourite hero's hairstyle and dress or when they begin to imitate the hero's behavioural traits and speech patterns. Sometimes people identify with sports celebrities by "feeling part of the team" and basking in the sunshine of its glorious victories. Being on the side of the winner is one way to feel good about yourself and to

identification
A psychological defence mechanism that involves taking on the characteristics of someone admired or considered successful. By means of identification, people temporarily gain security and postpone the inevitable confrontation with the problem of forming an individual identity.

137

A child's identification with a parent helps to minimize anxiety and build self-esteem.

May God grant me power to struggle to become not another but a better man.
~*Samuel Taylor Coleridge*

convince yourself you're not a "loser." The fact that you don't actually play on the team or work for the organization may be unimportant details in the minds of those identifying themselves in such a way. The fact that team jerseys are worn is more significant for purposes of identification.

Identification doesn't disappear in adulthood. Older individuals may still identify with athletic teams, but more commonly with service clubs, professional organizations, successful individuals and political leaders. As with youngsters, adults unconsciously attempt to bolster feelings of self-worth through identification and thereby protect themselves from anxieties related to the self. Of course, identifications can fail in their hidden purpose by creating a certain vulnerability. If, for example, a political party suffers a humiliating defeat, any individual who is overidentified with that party may suffer a depression that reflects loss of self-esteem (Barocas, Reichman and Schwebel, 1990).

It is important to remember that the purpose of identification is to reduce anxiety. By assuming the characteristics of models who appear to us to be highly successful we can come to believe that we also possess their attributes (Engler, 1999). On this note, permit me to offer a personal example of my own defensiveness to help illustrate identification.

When I was 19, I made arrangements to take my girlfriend to a fancy restaurant for her birthday. Times were different then and, up until this occasion, I had never eaten in an expensive dining establishment. Pizza joints and "greasy spoons" were my usual places to frequent. In any case, I felt a little nervous about impressing my date. I wasn't quite sure how to act or what to say to the maitre d', my table waiter or to the host of people who kept filling our water and wine glasses. In addition, I was anxious about what to do with the multiple spoons, forks and knives surrounding my plate, which was complete with a decorative pewter cover. I can remember being very worried about exposing my ignorance about fine-dining etiquette. My ego was on the line and I felt it. In my anxiety, I kept looking around the restaurant to see what others were doing. I recall focusing on a distinguished gentleman nearby. He looked very confident. He appeared to have a good grasp of the situation and, unlike me, was actually enjoying his meal. Upon reflection, I now know that I unconsciously chose to imitate the behaviour of this man. In fact, after watching him take a closer look at a painting on the wall of the restaurant, I did likewise—after he left, of course! I guess I wanted to appear cultured and sophisticated like him. Now that considerable time has passed and my self-esteem remains more or less intact, I look back on my teenage defensiveness as a bittersweet memory. I see it as one young man's desperate attempt to feel good about himself by impressing his girlfriend. (By the way, the meal was terrible and the food was cold. I told the waiter that everything was fine and left a big tip to show my date I was a big spender!)

Apart from helping us to cope with anxiety, identification also has an important role to play in the formation of personality. When, as children, we identified with our parents and caretakers, we came to accept their values. This identification enabled us to limit or eliminate punishments that would otherwise come from expressing contrary and conflicting values. Therefore, this acceptance and internalization of parental values not only reduces the fear of retribution, but also helps to form the superego. Later on in life we develop our superego further by internalizing society's values and norms.

Obstacles Ironically, overuse of identification can contribute to problems of personal identity. If you're always trying to be like someone else, then you're not spending much time being yourself. This can lead to inauthenticity. You can't really know yourself or express who you are if you're always trying to imitate others. Emulating your heroes may give rise to playing roles and behaving in unnatural ways. It could also lead to certain pretences. Your attraction to others and emulation of them may erroneously lead you to conclude that you share their qualities. Being a hard-core fan of somebody does not make you that somebody, just as hanging around intelligent people doesn't make you smart.

Another potential problem related to identification is ostracism or separation from others. If you choose to be loyal to certain groups, you may have to reject others. They may have different values, norms and patterns of behaviour. Furthermore, strong identification with any group or person may make you a target for opponents of that person or group. If you wish to be a neo-Nazi skinhead, for example, don't be surprised if you're shunned by mainstream society. You may be stereotyped as much as you stereotype those outside your identified group.

I emphasize again that identification is a defence against anxiety. In this case, anxiety results from an unclear sense of self. While identification may temporarily relieve insecurity, it is not the final answer to the question of who you are. Identification is merely a diversion from mental pain. Finding your true self is therefore not some kind of frivolous philosophical pursuit, but an important life task. Failure to find yourself may relegate you to a life of anxious inauthenticity.

> This above all: to thine own self be true, And it must follow as the night the day, Thou canst not then be false to any man.
> ~*William Shakespeare*

4.3 ## Regression

Like other defence mechanisms, **regression** is used to defend against the conscious experience of anxiety. We use it to revert to an earlier, more childlike stage of development. This "going back" enables us to alleviate anxiety by retreating to a previous period in life that was experienced as being more secure and pleasant. At this earlier stage, there were fewer responsibilities and more parental/caretaker attention. Security came from being cared for and having one's gratification assured (Barocas, Reichman and Schwebel, 1990).

regression
A defence mechanism in which one reverts to an earlier, more childlike stage of development. This going back enables one to alleviate anxiety by retreating to a previous period in life that was experienced as being more secure and pleasant.

139

Calvin Hall (1954: 95–96) offers us a list of regression examples below.

> Even healthy, well-adjusted people make regressions from time to time in order to reduce anxiety, or, as they say, to blow off steam. They smoke, get drunk, eat too much, lose their tempers, bite their nails, pick their noses, break laws, talk baby talk, destroy property, masturbate, read mystery stories, go to the movies, engage in unusual sexual practices, chew gum and tobacco, dress up as children, drive fast and recklessly, believe in good and evil spirits, take naps, fight and kill one another, bet on the horses, daydream, rebel against or submit to authority, gamble, preen before the mirror, act out their impulses, pick on scapegoats, and do a thousand and one other childish things. Some of these regressions are so commonplace that they are taken to be signs of maturity. Actually they are all forms of regression used by adults.

Source: Copyright © 1954 by Harper & Row Publishers, Inc. Reprinted by permission of HarperCollins Publishers, Inc.

As with any defence mechanism, regression only temporarily relieves the experience of anxiety. It leaves the root cause unaddressed (Hjelle and Ziegler, 1992). Hence, anxiety-producing conflicts and situations are not truly resolved by regression, only obscured from conscious awareness. In cases of severely disturbed individuals, we may witness significant regression to early infantile states. People may begin to babble like babies or assume childlike appearances. Less serious examples of regression can be found in people who are fatigued or ill. When sick, people often experience an increased need to be pampered and cared for. Exhausted adults may become easily irritated and throw tantrums like overtired children. On this note, you might notice that even precocious children may revert to thumb sucking just before bedtime or when stressed. A classic example of childhood regression is bedwetting just

Source: "Cathy" by Cathy Guisewite. Reprinted by permission of Universal Press Syndicate.

before starting kindergarten. Unconsciously, the child may think, "If I wet my bed, I won't have to go to school because I'm too young and immature."

Obstacles Regression obviously interferes with human communication. Someone reduced to babbling or uncontrollably crying in a fetal position will not send coherent messages to those who would listen. Also, if highly anxious individuals display regressive symptoms by throwing tantrums, then it will be difficult to conduct level-headed conversations. Furthermore, if regressed people are preoccupied with the need to be cared for, they will appear very narcissistic or selfish to others. It is difficult to develop intimate relationships with those who only wish to take from others in order to satisfy their own security needs. Some people are simply put off by the immaturity of regressive behaviour. People displaying this behaviour may be avoided.

4.3 Fantasy Formation

Fantasy formation is a defence that involves "gratifying frustrated desires by thinking about imaginary achievements and satisfactions" (Weiten, Lloyd and Lashley, 1999). Through fantasy formation, we become what we're not, we have what we don't own, we accomplish what we've never done and we visit places to which we've never been. Fantasy formation provides yet another way of helping us to cope with anxiety. Let's suppose you just failed a test; dreaming about the day you graduate may help you to deal with the temporary setback. Or, think of somebody you particularly dislike; expressing your hostile feelings in fantasy is much better than physically or verbally assaulting the target of your aggression. Creative use of fantasy can sometimes be the key to dealing effectively with negative emotions and periodic frustrations.

> **fantasy formation**
> A device that involves gratifying frustrated desires by thinking about imaginary achievements and satisfactions.

Most obvious examples of fantasy are found with children. Often powerless to control others, they create imaginary playmates or animals who obey them (Barocas, Reichman and Schwebel, 1990). If threatened by guilt, they may conjure up monsters in their minds. Such fantasizing prepares children for reality and for the need to relieve pain.

Obstacles Extended use of fantasy formation can transport people psychologically away from real problems and real situations. Presented with the threat of anxiety, some people may use fantasy as a way of retreating from relationships of all kinds (Barocas, Reichman and Schwebel, 1990). In this case, problems and people are not directly faced. Avoidance and illusion are used to sweep the dirt of anxiety under the carpet of conscious awareness. Personal and interpersonal problems go unnoticed, leaving issues unresolved.

People relying heavily on fantasy formation as a defence mechanism may be difficult to communicate with. Their perceptions of reality may be highly unrealistic. Living in a future dream of success, they may overlook their current failures. Imagining how things could be, they may be blind to how things actually are. Pragmatic discussions, for example, ones that are based on facts and reality, may be difficult to hold with those living in a fantasy world.

4.3 ····· ## Intellectualization/Isolation

**intellectualization/
isolation**
A way of suppressing unpleasant emotions by engaging in detached analyses of threatening problems.

Intellectualization (or **isolation**) is a way of suppressing unpleasant emotions by engaging in detached analyses of threatening problems (Weiten, Lloyd and Lashley, 1999). This defence mechanism enables us unconsciously to "isolate" anxiety, separating parts of a situation from the rest of the psyche. Through this act of partitioning, little or no emotional reaction to the situation or event is consciously experienced (Frager and Fadiman, 1997). By isolating problems and conflicts from the rest of the personality, events can be recounted without feeling. The emotional detachment makes it seem like the situation or event involves a third party. By withdrawing more and more into the world of ideas, intellectualizing people need less and less to deal with the reality of their own feelings (Frager and Fadiman, 1997). Of course, there is nothing wrong in analyzing situations or intellectualizing about them. This problem occurs only when isolation is used unconsciously to protect the ego from acknowledging anxiety-provoking aspects of situations, events or interpersonal relationships. Thinking, in itself, is not necessarily a diversion from emotional experience.

The quotation below provides an illustration of intellectualization. In it, a person named Alan presents many great ideas about threatening matters (e.g., sex) but does not possess the feelings that normally accompany them. Let's see how.

> Alan offers a perfect example. At eighteen, one of his chief delights is to discuss philosophic ideas on love, politics, and death. But he thinks very little about his daily life. His lofty views on love in no way prevent him from being childish and callous with women.
>
> He wittily criticizes the middle-class marriage for its imperfections and hypocrisies. But he cannot move past the most obvious clichés in his own relationships. Perhaps most striking is the way Alan handles sex. He talks about it and reads books, including marriage manuals and intellectual histories translated from the French. When he is attracted to a woman, he tends to involve her in long discussions about the philosophic implications of sexual freedom and commitment. What Alan does is to intellectualize, or connect his feelings with abstract theories, with the result that he seldom experiences his feelings at all. (Barocas, Reichman and Schwebel, 1983: 118) While overdependence on intellectualization can become a general pattern of maladjustment, this defence is useful to the extent to which it enables the ego to become stronger and more mature. It can help to make later defensiveness unnecessary. Some have pointed out that intellectualization is developmentally appropriate in adolescence, but that it becomes less and less useful as the individual matures (Barocas, Reichman and Schwebel, 1990).

Obstacles Intellectualization can cause problems for effective interpersonal communication. For example, if people are not in touch with their real feelings, they will not be able to share them with others. Also, if individuals persist in analyzing and intellectualizing their lives, intimacy may suffer. Conversations may begin to sound more like theoretical debates. This need not be frustrating in itself; however, sensitive receivers of "intellectualized" defensive messages may become frustrated because they cannot make personal contact with the defensive people involved or appreciate what they are truly experiencing. Intellectualizing can create psychological distance.

4.3 Denial

The defence mechanism of **denial** blocks from the ego threatening events or facts found in external social reality (Atwater, 1999). Not accepting the fact that your ex-fiancée is having a sexual relationship with your best friend would be a case of denial. Here, threatening thoughts would surface in your conscious mind, but you would refuse to believe them. There would be a conscious effort to suppress what you'd experience as unpleasant.

Sigmund Freud did not claim to discover denial (Frager and Fadiman, 1997). Awareness of denial was enhanced by Darwin and Nietzsche's (a German philosopher) earlier observations about themselves. Darwin (cited in Frager and Fadiman, 1997: 25) wrote in his autobiography:

> I had during years followed a golden rule, namely, whenever I came across a published fact, a new observation or idea, which ran counter to my general results, I made a memorandum of it without fail and at once; for I had found by experience that such facts and ideas were far more apt to slip the memory than favorable ones.

Along the same vein, Nietzsche wrote the following:

> "I have done that," says my memory. "It is impossible that I should have done it," says my pride, and it remains inexorable [incapable of being moved]. Finally my memory yields. (Frager and Fadiman, 1997: 25)

As a defence mechanism, denial does offer certain adaptive advantages. In certain situations it can effectively reduce stress (Atwater, 1999). It can also enable people to live through difficult times and unbearable situations. For example, two psychiatrists at the Massachusetts General Hospital found that "major deniers" of heart trouble had better survival rates than those people who only partially or minimally denied.

Obstacles Overreliance on denial may indicate that mature problem-solving methods of dealing with life have not been learned and that some degree of maladjustment may be present (Barocas, Reichman and Schwebel, 1983). For instance, alcoholics who deny they drink too much are not doing themselves any favours. Physical symptoms can arise and social relationships can begin to suffer. People who eat too much and then deny it by blaming their weight

denial
The unconscious defence mechanism that blocks from the ego threatening events or facts found in external social reality.

143

on metabolism are probably not doing much in the long run to improve their self-esteem. In short, some painful realities have to be faced before they can be overcome. Not facing up to them probably doesn't help others and in most cases probably doesn't help you.

(4.3) ····· ## Sublimation

sublimation
A defensive strategy in which the ego diverts instinctual impulses into something advantageous to society. Sublimation involves a life-long defence against our broader realization that we cannot satisfy our urges and impulses in order to get what we want.

Sublimation is the only defensive strategy used by the ego to divert instinctual impulses into something advantageous to society (Hjelle and Ziegler, 1992; Hergenhahn, 1998). Freud (1930) argued that sublimation "is an especially conspicuous feature of cultural development; it is what makes it possible for higher psychical activities, scientific, artistic or ideological, to play such an important part in civilized life" (cited in Hergenhahn, 1993: 35). An example here would be the young person whose hostility toward a parent finds a productive outlet in legal struggles for the disadvantaged (Barocas, Reichman and Schwebel, 1990).

Another way of understanding sublimation is to see it as an "adaptive" use of the displacement defence mechanism, which was discussed earlier. By using displacement, aggressive or sexual impulses may be diverted from one object to another that is less threatening. Anger diverted from a parent or authority figure onto a younger, smaller or more innocent target may help to reduce the anxiety in the angry person, but such diversion does little for the new targeted object. By contrast, anger transformed into something socially useful (e.g., a crusade against violence) can be said to be sublimated.

Sublimation is not a defence mechanism that is called into action to protect a temporarily weak ego responding to crisis (Barocas, Reichman and Schwebel, 1990). Rather, it involves a life-long defence against our broader realization that we cannot satisfy our urges and impulses in order to get what we want. Through sublimation, we give up primitive satisfaction in favour of an investment in society. We find culturally sanctioned channels to express our basic needs.

Obstacles Noted already is the fact that sublimation is the most adaptive and advantageous of all defence mechanisms. If there is a downside to sublimation, perhaps it comes from the possibility that we could lose touch with the primitive, biological side of ourselves. We may lose sight of our instincts and urges, forgetting that we are physical, as well as social, beings. At worst, our zealous efforts to contribute culturally or socially could merely become a self-deception. What we are fighting for or doing may be only a substitution for what we unconsciously want.

Instinctual impulses can be sublimated into artistic and creative pursuits.

Defence Mechanisms in Summary

As we have learned, psychological defence mechanisms help us to reduce disquieting anxiety by distorting our perceptions of reality. They protect the psyche from internal imbalances and external tensions.

The defences avoid reality (repression), exclude reality (denial), redefine reality (rationalization), or reverse reality (reaction formation). They place inner feelings on the outer world (projection), partition reality (isolation), or withdraw from reality (regression). (Frager and Fadiman, 1984: 29)

Defence mechanisms not only help us to deal with unacceptable anxiety-provoking instinctual impulses, they also help us to master a variety of life conflicts. For instance, they can help us to contain ourselves emotionally when confronted with sudden life crises (e.g., a serious illness). They can help us to fashion changes in our self-image when required (e.g., after a demotion). Defences enable us to cope with unresolvable conflicts with significant others as well as to survive major conflicts of conscience stemming from our (mis)treatment of other people (Vaillant, 1977).

The danger of defensiveness arises when reality distortions become too great and too frequent. They diminish strength and rob energy from more creative and productive psychological functioning. As isolated responses to temporarily weakened egos, defence mechanisms have their uses. However, if they are unconsciously adopted as general strategies to deal with life, they are potentially unproductive and detrimental to personal well-being. They certainly can get in the way of effective interpersonal relations. See Table 4.1 for typical defences used in various kinds of anxiety-provoking situations.

Table 4.1

Defensive Response Patterns

Anxiety-Provoking Stimulus	Commonly Used Defences
Prohibited sexual urges or behaviour	Sublimation, repression, rationalization and projection
Feelings of inferiority	Fantasy, identification and regression
Guilt	Rationalization and projection
Failure	Intellectualization/isolation, projection and rationalization
Hostility	Sublimation, displacement, reaction formation, repression and fantasy
Disappointment	Intellectualization, fantasy and rationalization
Personal limitations	Denial, fantasy and regression

Source: Adapted from Coleman and Hammen (1974).

application
exercise

4.2

Name the Defence Mechanism

Aim: This exercise will help you identify defensiveness in everyday behaviour.

It should help you notice defensiveness in others and become more aware of it in yourself. This exercise can be done individually or in small groups. Allow time for discussion. Explanations should be offered for each selection.

4.5

a. Repression
b. Rationalization
c. Projection
d. Reaction formation
e. Displacement
f. Identification

g. Regression
h. Fantasy formation
i. Intellectualization/Isolation
j. Denial
k. Sublimation

Instructions: Place the correct letter next to each example of defensiveness. Letters correspond to the defence mechanisms listed above.

_____ 1. Michael always teases his sisters after his parents discipline him.

_____ 2. Mary's parents both died when she was young. When I asked her what it was like growing up with no parents, she said she couldn't remember. Years of her life seem to be a blank.

_____ 3. When the police officer told Mr. Boudreau that his son was found in possession of cocaine, he responded, "There must be some mistake! My boy does not do cocaine, never has, and never will. You simply don't have the right person."

_____ 4. Why do you keep saying I'm mad at you when I'm not?

_____ 5. I can't believe how friendly Kristine behaves toward Katherine face to face. She told me long ago how much she hates Katherine.

_____ 6. Barry: I can't believe you cheated on the exam. How could you do such a thing?
Andy: Everybody else was doing it.

_____ 7. Did you hear about Gloria? Can you believe that someone who had so many sexual partners herself is now a nun doing personal counselling with sex addicts?

_____ 8. Ever since Bill broke up with Angela, he's been drinking and playing poker with the boys every night.

_____ 9. Jim recently went to listen to a lecture given by the Maharesi Mahesh Yogi. He has now decided to grow his hair long and wear sandals and East Indian clothing.

_____10. Jennifer is experiencing great difficulties with her academic studies. She is failing every subject but one. She tells me that she manages to cope by picturing graduation in her mind and the great job she anticipates getting once her degree is in hand.

_____11. Whenever John is upset about anything, he always goes and finds a psychology textbook that explains his thoughts and emotions. Quoting chapter and page, he tries to illustrate the universal psycho-dynamics behind his unpleasant experiences.

Answer Key: 1. e, 2. a, 3. j, 4. c, 5. d, 6. b, 7. k, 8. g, 9. f, 10. h, 11. i

Dealing with Defensiveness

application
exercise
4.3

4.6 ····· **Aim:** The purpose of this activity is to help you deal more effectively with defensiveness in yourself and others.

Instructions: Get into small groups. Next to each defence mechanism listed, provide an example to illustrate its workings. The example can be real or hypothetical. Choose what feels comfortable. For each example, brainstorm ways you could deal with the defensiveness. First, see yourself as the one being defensive in the example. Second, see yourself as the one witnessing the defensiveness in another. What could you do to help yourself? What could you do to help another person?

Defence Mechanism	Example/ Illustration	Effective Handling (Yourself and Others)
1. Repression		
2. Rationalization		
3. Projection		
4. Reaction formation		
5. Displacement		
6. Identification		
7. Regression		
8. Fantasy formation		
9. Intellectualization/Isolation		
10. Denial		
11. Sublimation		

147

Faced with the choice be-tween changing one's mind and proving there is no need to do so, almost everyone gets busy on the proof.
~*John Kenneth Galbraith, Canadian-born Harvard economist*

miscommunication
Often results from faulty logic. A failure to convey an idea or argument success-fully so that the receiver un-derstands and accepts what is meant.

logical fallacies
Improper forms of reason-ing that people use to pro-tect their threatened selves when their viewpoints, in which they have a lot of ego invested, are being challenged.

Thinking Straight Can Help You Relate

In the preceding discussion, we looked at the "psycho" side of psycho-logical defence mechanisms. We saw how unconscious mental processes function to protect the conscious ego from anxiety. In the rest of this chapter, we'll be looking at the "logical" side of psycho-logical defensiveness. As you'll soon dis-cover, however, the logical side is not always so logical and the rational processes of thought used to protect and defend oneself or one's viewpoint can sometimes be irrational and lead to unjustifiable conclusions.

Much **miscommunication** arises from the faulty use of logic. Sometimes our conclusions do not follow from preceding premises, while, at other times, our assumptions are unfounded or unjustifiable. Often, we fail to communicate ef-fectively, solve problems or make good choices because the "facts" are in dispute.

Treatments of logic and rational thinking have traditionally been re-served for philosophy and critical reasoning courses. This is unfortunate, however, because thinking is part of life. It is an important element behind human action and social interaction. What we think, and how we think, fre-quently determine what we see, feel and do, and therefore, how well we get along with others. For our purposes here, I plan to have you look at a num-ber of **logical fallacies**. These are irrational thought processes that interfere with productive interpersonal communications. By learning to clean up our "logical acts," we can increase clarity and understanding, as well as improve our chances to share differing viewpoints in constructive ways. By knowing the differences between good and bad reasoning, we can defend ourselves against illogical attacks and irrational attempts to manipulate us. Good think-ing has a personal and social payoff.

Screaming and yelling seldom resolve differences of opinion.

Self Diagnostic

4.2 How Reasonable Am I?

4.7

Developing good reasoning skills can improve interpersonal communications. Good sense often makes for good relations. On the other hand, the use of bad logic in everyday interactions can contribute to irreconcilable differences, hurt feelings, personal attacks, dishonest and diversionary manoeuvres, as well as gross distortions of reality. In what follows, you will be presented with several examples of logical thinking that may or may not be rationally acceptable. Circle "A" next to examples that are acceptable and "U" next to those that are unacceptable. To find out if you can spot "sleazy logic" when you hear it, check your responses against the Answer Key that follows the examples.

A U 1. We shouldn't accept Professor Knowitall's argument that drinking coffee causes cancer. He's just a greedy and vain researcher trying to make a name for himself.

A U 2. Don't believe anything Mr. DeNile says. I know his relatives and they're all liars.

A U 3. If Wayne Gretzky, the greatest hockey player that ever lived, says that you must only play to win, then it must be so.

A U 4. You ought to be opposed to legalized gambling. Once you permit it, prostitution will necessarily follow. After that will come organized crime. In the end, legalized gambling will make our city's streets less safe than before.

A U 5. Listen, I dislike cheating as much as you do. But when everybody else cheats, you have to cheat in order to survive.

Answer Key

All the examples above present different forms of unacceptable reasoning. They each contain an informal logical fallacy.

1. U *ad hominem* fallacy
2. U fallacy of guilt by association
3. U fallacy of appealing to authority
4. U slippery slope fallacy
5. U two-wrongs fallacy

Note: To learn more about each fallacy, read the section in this chapter entitled Fallacies and Psycho-LOGICAL Defensiveness.

Fallacies and Psycho-LOGICAL Defensiveness

People often feel threatened when their viewpoints are challenged. If a lot of ego has been invested in a particular idea, or personal feelings are involved, improper forms of reasoning called logical fallacies may be used to rescue the threatened self. Fallacies are irrational. They involve thinking processes that lead to **unsound conclusions** and unacceptable positions. Fallacies are designed to persuade us emotionally and psychologically, not rationally (Johnson and Blair, 1993). People who use them try to divert attention from the real issues

unsound conclusions
Unacceptable conclusions based on fallacious reasoning.

149

intimidation
Attacking someone out of psychological defensiveness.

diversion
Illegitimately shifting attention from the main argument or issue to something else.

attack
One illogical strategy used in fallacious reasoning.

 4.8

ad hominem **fallacy**
An irrational way to argue in which you attack your opponent personally rather than criticizing your opponent's position.

Men stumble over the truth from time to time, but most pick themselves up and hurry off as if nothing happened.
~Winston Churchill

to something more favourable to themselves. Fallacies can also be used as forms of **intimidation**. Defensive people, worried about being wrong, may respond aggressively toward others. Putting someone else on the defensive requires one to be less defensive about oneself. Essentially, fallacies work through **diversion** and **attack**. As instruments of persuasion and rhetoric, they are unfortunately sometimes very effective. However, as ways of thinking, they are always wrong. Let's now look at some common fallacies you'll need to avoid or guard against in efforts to be more reasonable in your dealings with people.

Ad Hominem Fallacy

When you disagree with someone, the proper response is to criticize your opponent's position. If, instead of debating the issues involved, you attack your opponent personally, your actions are based on the ***ad hominem* fallacy**. For example, a wasteful person who resents the inconvenience brought about by recycling might refuse to support ideas and arguments presented by Pollution Probe on the grounds that all environmentalists are "'60s losers." Of course, the merits of an idea should not be judged by what generation the person advocating it comes from. Recycling is either good or bad in itself, regardless of when those advocating it were born. To better understand how *ad hominem* reasoning works, see Figure 4.4.

Despite the "ill logic" it contains, *ad hominem* reasoning is very common in everyday discussion and debate. This type of thinking process can be

Politicians may sometimes use faulty reasoning in their efforts to win elections.
Courtesy of Carolyn Kaster/Corbis Images.

Figure 4.4
Ad Hominem Fallacy

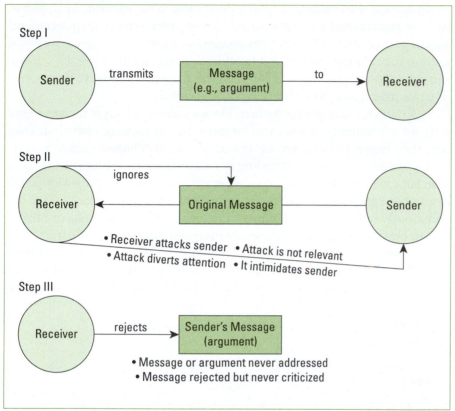

emotionally satisfying, insofar as it belittles or puts down people with whom we disagree. We find it unsettling to be forced to concede that an individual we dislike has made a valid point. Also, if we are highly committed to the viewpoint that's being attacked by another, we may erroneously perceive such an attack as a personal attack. In reflexive fashion, we may counterattack with an *ad hominem* verbal barrage of our own against the perceived threat. When we do, we allow irrationality, hostility and aggression to interfere with productive communication. Our own defensiveness becomes an offensive act targeted at others. Look for *ad hominem* attacks whenever people's personalities, characters, ethnic/racial backgrounds, underlying motives or special interests are criticized in response to messages perceived to be threatening. Also, don't allow yourself to be sidetracked when presenting your own viewpoints by defending yourself in response to others' *ad hominem* attacks on you. Stick to the issues.

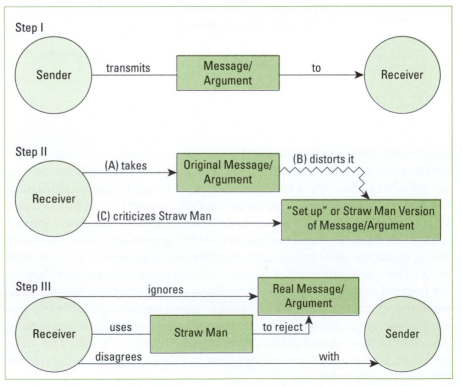

4.8 · Straw Man Fallacy

In discussion with others, we don't always like what we hear. In response, we may misrepresent what others have said in order to make their arguments appear unacceptable. We may then proceed to argue against the unsatisfying version to reject the original, but unaddressed, arguments. If we do, our reasoning is flawed. Our action is based on the **straw man fallacy**. The process of straw man reasoning is illustrated in Figure 4.5.

A caution might be in order here. Occasionally recipients of messages honestly do not understand what was intended by the message conveyed. They may then respond to what was never said. This kind of honest mistake may reflect a problem of listening, decoding or comprehension. It is unlike the straw man fallacy, in which one person is deliberately misrepresenting the viewpoints of another. I guess we get into foggy territory when misrepresentations occur unconsciously in psychological efforts to reduce anxiety. Conscious or unconscious, however, straw man fallacies are irrational distortions of the truth.

Suppose that a new provincial premier or state governor has just been elected to office. She supports tax increases for middle-income earners. In response someone says, "This doesn't surprise me! She's always been against

straw man fallacy
A form of "ill logic" in which one misrepresents what others have said in order to make their arguments clearly unacceptable. One may then proceed to argue against the unsatisfying version to reject the original, but unaddressed, arguments.

Figure 4.5
Straw Man Fallacy

Step I

Sender — transmits → Message/Argument — to → Receiver

Step II

Receiver — (A) takes → Original Message/Argument — (B) distorts it → "Set up" or Straw Man Version of Message/Argument

Receiver — (C) criticizes Straw Man →

Step III

Receiver — ignores → Real Message/Argument

Receiver — uses → Straw Man — to reject → Sender

Receiver — disagrees — with → Sender

working people belonging to unions and this is just another measure designed to undermine their interests. If we allow unions to crumble, democracy in this country will be threatened!" Notice that in the critic's reply, democracy, unions and working people are brought to our attention, not the rationale behind the tax increases. Presumably it is easier to argue in favour of democracy and union people than it is to argue against unwanted tax increases. By diverting attention to another topic and criticizing that, the original position supporting tax increases is rejected, though never properly addressed.

> We find comfort among those who agree with us, growth among those who don't.
> ~Frank Clarke

Since you can probably appreciate how annoying it is when others criticize what you never said, be sure to ask questions for clarification before criticizing others' arguments or viewpoints. Your criticisms are only valuable if they relate to what was actually intended by the claims or conclusions presented. Conversely, before allowing others to criticize your arguments and stated viewpoints, you could ask others to repeat in their own terms what they think you've said. If necessary, clarifications could be made. In the end, this extra step could reduce miscommunication and save time.

4.8 Circular Reasoning/Begging the Question

Have you ever been in arguments that seem to go nowhere but around in circles? If you have, perhaps someone in the argument was using **circular reasoning**, also known as the **fallacy of begging the question**. In circular reasoning people use as a premise of their argument the conclusion they are trying to establish. In other words, people assume as true in the beginning what they intend to prove logically at the end. When this is done, there is prejudgment (prejudice) on the issue being debated. The "logical" argument doesn't take you anywhere except back to what was assumed to be true at the outset. For this reason, begging the question is circular, taking us around and around. What we assume is what we set out to prove, and what we prove is what we originally assumed. Circular reasoning is perhaps most evident in religious discussions.

circular reasoning/ begging the question
Assuming to be true at the outset what one is attempting to prove or justify in the end.

B. Lever:
God Exists.

I. M. Agnostic:
How do you know God exists?

B. Lever:
Because it says so in the Bible.

I. M. Agnostic:
How do you know the Bible is telling you the truth?

B. Lever:
Because it's the inspired word of God.

In the previous example, B. Lever claims that God exists and uses the Bible to prove the point. The authority of the Bible is based on the premise or presupposition that God inspired it. Therefore, it's already assumed at the outset that God actually does exist (the point under debate). However, if B. Lever assumes to be true at the beginning what he is trying to prove at the end, nothing has been proven and we've just gone around in a circle. I don't mean to suggest that rational proofs cannot be given for God's existence, only that circular arguments don't work. Look at Figure 4.6 to better appreciate the process of circular reasoning.

(4.8) Two-Wrongs Fallacy

two-wrongs fallacy
A form of illogic in which a particular wrongdoing is defended by drawing attention to another instance of the same behaviour that apparently went unchallenged and was therefore accepted by implication.

Arguing based on the **two-wrongs fallacy** involves defending a particular wrongdoing by drawing attention to another instance of the same behaviour that apparently went unchallenged and was therefore accepted by implication. For instance, I remember that there were traditional initiation rituals for University of Toronto "frosh" (first-year students) that required minor acts of vandalism (e.g., painting a certain statue in Queen's Park). Once confronted about the justifiability of such acts, a student (guess who?) responded by saying that *frosh* had been doing it for years. Apparently, for him, the previous year's vandalism served as a justification for his own wrongdoing, namely, painting King Edward's horse red.

Figure 4.6
Circular Reasoning

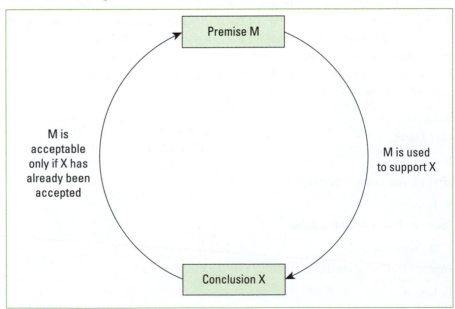

Highway speeders also provide us with an example of two-wrongs fallacious reasoning. When stopped for speeding, those charged often argue with the officer that they were just keeping up with traffic. In other words, they were doing nothing other than breaking the law just like everybody else. As you may have already learned from experience, most police officers will not accept this line of reasoning. The two-wrongs fallacy is illustrated in Figure 4.7.

4.8

Slippery Slope Fallacy

People who rely on the **slippery slope fallacy** display this form of illogic when they object to something because they incorrectly assume that it will necessarily lead to other undesirable consequences. For example, you may object to smoking marijuana. You could reason that such behaviour will surely lead to harder drug usage, addiction and eventually to a life of crime. Since crime is unwanted, you conclude that smoking marijuana is therefore wrong.

Notice that in this hypothetical example the major objection is to crime, the presumed eventual result of smoking marijuana. However, the conclusion drawn here is not inevitable. After experimenting once, you may choose to avoid marijuana in the future. Or you might decide to use it only occasionally in recreational ways. After smoking it, you could become a crusader

slippery slope fallacy
A form of illogic in which one objects to something because one incorrectly assumes that it will necessarily lead to other undesirable consequences.

Figure 4.7
Two-Wrongs Fallacy

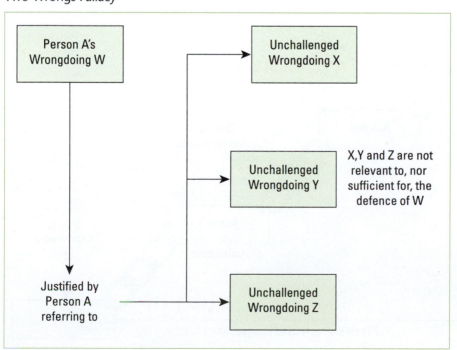

155

against mood-altering drugs. The point is that smoking marijuana is a separate and distinct act from harder drug use, addiction and crime. Each must be considered independently and evaluated on its own terms. While it may be that many criminals and addicts begin their lives of crime by smoking marijuana, not everybody who smokes marijuana becomes a criminal addict. Many law-abiding, non-addicted people have experimented with marijuana. Therefore, there is no necessary **causal connection** between marijuana and criminality. One does not necessarily have to lead to the other. If you can find a break in the causal chain that presumably links two unrelated acts, you uncover the presence of a slippery slope. See Figure 4.8.

causal connection

A cause and effect relationship.

4.8 Fallacy of Appealing to Authority

fallacy of appealing to authority

A rhetorical device in which one cites so-called expert advice or opinions to support one's argument.

When people get into arguments, they frequently rely on the **fallacy of appealing to authority** to justify their positions. Some appeals to authority are proper, while others are not. Proper appeals can be made to support factual claims within larger arguments. If in the previous example about marijuana, someone had wanted to condemn its use on medical grounds, scientific and empirical research data could have been presented to support claims

Figure 4.8
Slippery Slope Fallacy

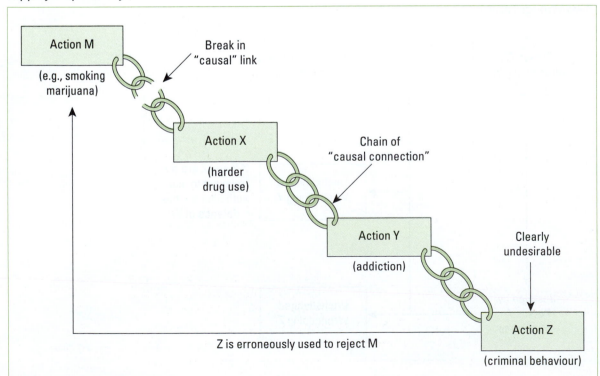

about marijuana's adverse physical effects. As long as the data presented were based on the recognized contributions of medical researchers in the field and accepted after peer review and evaluation, such data could have been justifiably used to support factual claims imbedded in the broader argument. Of course, recognized researchers do not always agree amongst themselves; that's the reason scientific method cannot yield "absolute" proof. Even when citing scientific data, then, it is important to exercise some caution. To appreciate why, just ask what current scientific studies say about the effects of drinking coffee, for example. Some studies suggest caffeine is harmful, while others disagree. In such cases, it is prudent to go with the weight of the evidence. Ask, "What do most studies suggest?" or "Is there overwhelming evidence one way or another?" When the data are highly suggestive one way or another, at least references to them go beyond personal opinion to a recognized body of knowledge. Authoritative appeals can best be made in the hard sciences. Statements made in these disciplines can be verified in principle and hypotheses can be tested. There are clear public standards to test the validity of claims made, even if those claims are only highly probable at best.

> Man is a credulous animal and tends to believe what he is told. Historically, philosophers...have taken great pains to point out that authority is at least as important a source of error as it is of knowledge. *~Joseph Brennan*

When questions of value are at issue, it is much more difficult, and usually unjustifiable, to make authoritative appeals. Normative assumptions and principles (for example, people should always behave in their own self-interest) cannot be proven true or false by empirical observation or scientific experiment. Whether or not people actually behave in their own self-interest cannot tell us whether or not they should. Where matters of value are concerned, authoritative appeals cannot be made in rationally acceptable ways. This idea also applies where interpretation and personal preferences play a role or where the boundaries of subject matter are in dispute. Where experts have no empirical means or scientific procedures to settle disputes, authoritative appeals should be avoided. Such disputes must be settled by reason and argument. The next time you get into an argument, you should ask yourself what kind of claim is being made. Is the claim factual in nature? If so, where can you obtain legitimate support? If the claim is normative or value-related, how should you proceed to justify your position or criticize that of another? Can you use a general value premise to justify a specific moral conclusion?

One improper appeal to authority involves the notion of democratic popularity. In this case, a conclusion is supported by an appeal to numbers. If a majority of people supports something, then that something is necessarily good, right or praiseworthy. Of course, numbers guarantee nothing. Historically speaking, majorities have been proven wrong. The fact that a majority of people in the southern United States once favoured slavery does not justify it. Reference to the will of the majority proves nothing. The moral status of slavery must be considered independently from its supporters. If 51 percent of the people in Lunenburg, Nova Scotia are in favour of cheating Revenue Canada on their income taxes, this fact alone does not make it right. The next time you think about trying to convince your parents, friends or spouse that you should be allowed to do something "just because everybody else says it's okay," reflect on the fallacy of appealing to authority. Could you give other reasons to support what you want to do?

Appeals to traditional wisdom are also fallacious. In this case, actions are justified by saying, "This is the way it's always been done." Other actions are rejected by saying, "We've never done things this way before." However, actions that are justified by reference to past conventions (i.e., socially accepted ways of doing things) are not necessarily justified at all. For instance, suppose someone said, "We should never have allowed a woman, especially Kim Campbell, to become prime minister of Canada because we never had a woman occupy that office before." Obviously, a history of gender bias and discrimination cannot properly serve as a justification for continuing this practice. While tradition often gives us many valuable insights, it can also present its own moral problems. In itself, traditional wisdom is not unconditionally valid. Be careful, though, not to throw the "traditional baby" out with the "dirty bathwater." Tradition does have its legitimate place in human experience.

A final criticism of authoritative appeals is directed at the fact that authorities often disagree among themselves when matters of value are at issue. If authorities cannot reach a consensus, we cannot rely on authoritative judgments to settle disputes. Maybe you could look for an authority over authorities, but even this would be a problem. Your ultimate authority (e.g., God) may not be accepted by others (e.g., atheists). In a tolerant, democratic, multicultural society, it is usually improper to use your chosen authority figure as a reference point for judgment when dealing with others. Commitments to your own beliefs should not violate the rights of others. The rules and regulations of your religious, political or military authorities, for example, may contain little rational moral force when applied to those who have different commitments. To put the danger of authoritative appeals into perspective, suppose someone's supreme authority were Luc Jouret, leader of the Solar Temple cult in Quebec. You will recall that his cult took part in a mass murder-suicide in 1994, with incidents in both Canada and Switzerland. Nobody knows all the details of what happened, but let's speculate for an instant that Jouret ordered his followers to kill themselves. Would this action, in itself, justify their actions? Rational thinking requires that we say no. In fact, many philosophers have often argued that suicide is inherently irrational and therefore unjustified. Trying to justify murder-suicide by reference to Jouret's authority would involve the use of fallacious reasoning. Refer to Figure 4.9 for a visual depiction of the fallacy of appealing to authority.

> A great many people think they are thinking when they are merely rearranging their prejudices.
> ~*William James*

(4.8) Red Herring Fallacy

red herring fallacy
see definition on opposite page.

The **red herring fallacy** is another favourite form of illogic used by rationally dishonest or unconsciously irrational individuals. The name of this fallacy comes from the sport of fox hunting. In this sport, hunters on horseback

Figure 4.9

Fallacy of Appealing to Authority

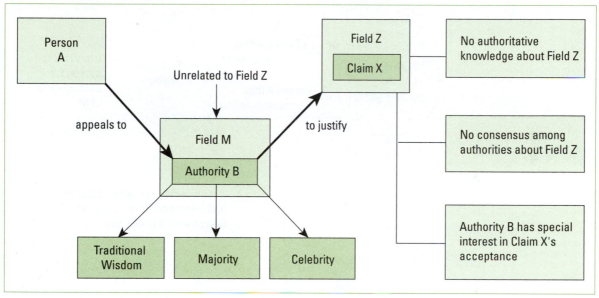

follow a pack of hounds tracking a fox's scent. In order to save the fox in the end, dried and salted red herring is drawn across the fox's tracks ahead of the pack. The herring is then pulled in a direction away from that which the fox took. The dogs are diverted by the stronger and fresher scent of the herring. The fox is saved and left to run another day.

In the red herring fallacy a controversial claim or position is defended by taking the offensive. This defence involves setting up a new issue that has only a tenuous connection with the original one. Since the original position is weak, the defender proceeds to argue for the new issue or position, which is more supportable. In other words, attention is deflected from the original position to a new one, which is probably less open to question and debate. Below is an example of red herring reasoning. Notice what the patriotic bartender does when he perceives his country is under attack. He diverts attention from the Canadian's allegations of crime, violence, discrimination and influence peddling to space technology, universities and military might. The latter can more easily support his claim that "America is the greatest." The Canadian's critical comments make such a claim highly questionable.

Detroit Bartender: The United States is the best country in the world.

Canadian Tourist: You must be kidding. The U.S. is falling apart at the seams. Murders are committed by the thousands every year. Women and minorities are discriminated against and lobby groups have too much power in Washington. On top of this, fear of being victimized by criminals in the

red herring fallacy
A logical fallacy in which a controversial claim or position is defended by taking the offensive. This defence involves setting up a new issue that has only a weak or tenuous connection with the original one. Attention is thereby deflected from the original position to a new one, which is probably less open to question and debate.

159

Figure 4.10
Red Herring Fallacy

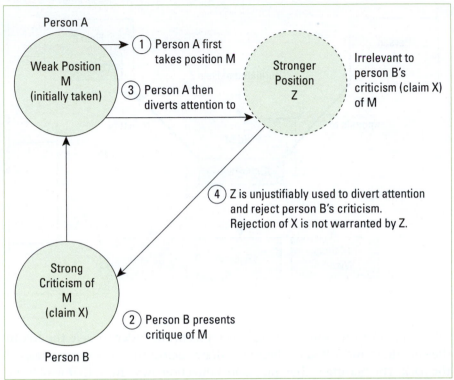

streets frightens people from walking outdoors in the evening. Face it, your nation is in decline.

Detroit Bartender: What are you talking about? We have the most military might in the world. We have the best universities and the most advanced space technology. America is the greatest.

The red herring fallacy is illustrated in Figure 4.10.

4.8 Fallacy of Guilt by Association

This form of illogic is generally used in adversarial situations in an attempt to discredit an opponent or that opponent's arguments, claims and positions; it draws attention to an alleged association that the opponent has with some group or individual that has already been discredited. The attempt to discredit is not direct as in typical *ad hominem* arguments; rather, the guilt of the discredited individual or group is transferred to the opponent.

Let us suppose that someone refused to vote "socialist" in the next election. His reason is that the "socialists almost sent England and France into bankruptcy." The unspoken claim is that if elected here, they will bankrupt this country too. Apparently, for this voter, socialist mismanagement across the ocean is enough to convict socialists here of incompetence. They are found guilty prior to doing anything wrong. It is possible, of course, that a socialist government could mismanage our country—some argue that Liberals and Conservatives have been doing so for years! But in any case, actions and policies of foreign socialist governments alone cannot serve as an adequate basis of judgment on domestic socialism. Our socialism may be different in significant ways. Our socialists may have learned from the mistakes of their European counterparts. Perhaps contemporary North American socialism has evolved into something more akin to capitalism? There could be almost no political communication between the two socialist groups named. Who knows? Simply put, you can't pin incompetence on Canadian or American socialists because of what foreign socialists have done. To do so is to argue based on the **fallacy of guilt by association**. Nonetheless, by using this diversionary tactic, fear can be created in the minds of unreflective voters and it may work as a means of persuasion. Creating fear is not very rational, but against people lacking the skills of logical self-defence, it often works. The fallacy of guilt by association is illustrated in Figure 4.11. See also Table 4.2 for some helpful hints on what to do (and avoid) during an argument.

fallacy of guilt by association
This form of illogic is generally used in adversarial situations in an attempt to discredit an opponent or that opponent's arguments, claims, and positions; it draws attention to an alleged association that the opponent has with some group or individual that has already been discredited.

Figure 4.11

Fallacy of Guilt by Association

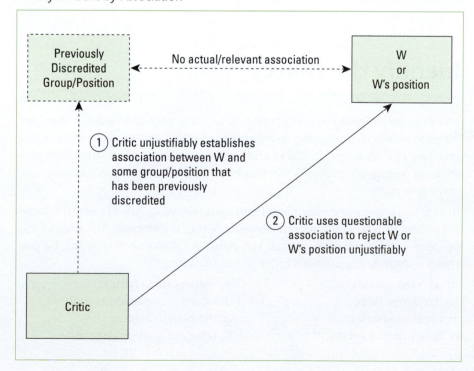

Table 4.2

Some Dos and Don'ts for Argument's Sake

Don't	Do
Attack or intimidate	Remain rational and emotionally detached
Divert attention from the real issues	Stay objective
Base arguments on emotional or psychological appeals	Listen to opposing viewpoints with openness
Build false or questionable claims into your argument	Analyze conflicting positions fairly and impartially
Take disagreements personally	Examine the logical thinking behind particular conclusions
Appeal to authorities unjustifiably	Look for fallacious reasoning
Attribute to others what they didn't say	Stick to the issues
Make illegitimate associations	Base your positions on sound arguments
Contradict yourself	
Change the subject when challenged	
Be inconsistent	
Use faulty causal reasoning	
Justify one wrongdoing with another	
Be diverted or intimidated by fallacious reasoning	

application exercise 4.4

Identify the Fallacy

4.9

This exercise will give you an opportunity to apply your knowledge and understanding of fallacious reasoning. Being able to identify fallacious reasoning will protect you against illogical attacks and irrational attempts to manipulate your thinking. Recognizing fallacies will also help you to minimize them in your own communication.

Instructions: Below are examples of fallacious reasoning. Identify which fallacies are present by placing the appropriate letter next to the example. This exercise can be done individually or in groups. For classroom discussion purposes, be prepared to provide explanations for each identification.

a. *ad hominem* fallacy

b. straw man fallacy

c. circular reasoning

d. fallacy of two wrongs

e. slippery slope fallacy

f. fallacy of appealing to authority

g. red herring fallacy

h. fallacy of guilt by association

_____1. You shouldn't accept the premier's or senator's arguments in favour of gay marriage. After all, he's a godless communist.

_____2. I can't believe you're in favour of having premarital sex. It's obviously wrong. The Pope says so.

_____3. Two students were having a disagreement about cars. Curtis said, "I can prove to you that a Honda Civic is faster than a Toyota Matrix. John owns a Civic and he told me that he has beaten every Matrix he has ever raced on the highway." Michael asked, "How do you know John is telling the truth?" Curtis replied, "Someone who drives the fastest car wouldn't have to lie."

_____4. We can't allow marijuana to be legalized. If we did, sooner or later everyone would become addicted to harder drugs and after that the crime rate would surely rise.

_____5. It's perfectly all right to go through stop signs on quiet streets; everybody else in town does it.

_____6. The consultant recommended that the company switch to voice mail as a way of receiving and sending internal messages. He claims that this change will make our operation more efficient. I can't believe this guy. He thinks every problem in the world has an electronic solution. Computers and telephones can't improve the economy or morale at work. I think we should reject his recommendation.

_____7. You don't seriously believe what André Cousineau says about promoting national unity. Remember, he's from Quebec and related to the leader of the Parti Québécois. That party wants Quebec to separate from the rest of Canada. We should reject anything he suggests.

_____8. What do you mean I'm not making sense? Did you hear your own nonsense yesterday when you said that you had an encounter with an alien? I think your credibility needs to be re-examined.

Answer Key: 1. a, 2. f, 3. c, 4. e, 5. d, 6. b, 7. h, 8. g

Study Guide

Key Terms

noise (122)

psycho-logical defensiveness (122)

unconscious influences (122)

irrational thought processes (122)

defensiveness (124)

anxiety (124)

diversionary and intimidation tactics (124)

distortions of reality (124)

psychoanalysis (125)

conscious (125)

preconscious (125)

unconscious (125)

coping mechanism (125)

psychological defence mechanisms (128)

ego (128)

repression (128)

rationalization (129)

projection (131)

reaction formation (133)

displacement (134)

id (134)

psychic energy (134)

cathexis (134)

anticathexis (135)

superego (135)

identification (137)

regression (139)

fantasy formation (141)

intellectualization/ isolation (142)

denial (143)

sublimation (144)

miscommunication (148)

logical fallacies (148)

unsound conclusions (149)

intimidation (150)

diversion (150)

attack (150)

ad hominem fallacy (150)

straw man fallacy (152)

circular reasoning/ begging the question (153)

two-wrongs fallacy (154)

slippery slope fallacy (155)

causal connection (156)

fallacy of appealing to authority (156)

red herring fallacy (158)

fallacy of guilt by association (161)

Fill-in-the-Blank Questions

Progress Check 4.1

Instructions: Fill in each blank with the appropriate response from the list below.

repression

fantasy formation

circular reasoning

reaction formation

straw man

identification

red herring

displacement

projection

two-wrongs

regression

rationalization

denial

ad hominem

intellectualization/isolation

1. People who behave in ways exactly opposite to their true feelings display _____.

2. Keeping disturbing or anxiety-provoking thoughts buried in the unconscious is called _____.

3. Reverting to immature patterns of behaviour in response to problems and difficulties is called _____.

4. Diverting strong negative emotions from a threatening target to a less threatening substitute is called _____.

5. Attributing your own thoughts, feelings and motives to another is labelled _____.

6. Imagining a pleasurable future as a way of escaping harsh current realities indicates _____.

7. Refusing to accept the facts as they present themselves is evidence of _____.

8. The act of objectifying emotions and dealing with them in detached, theoretical ways is called _____.

9. Individuals who enhance their self-esteem by forming real or imaginary alliances with groups and organizations exhibit _____.

10. The act of creating false but plausible excuses in order to justify unacceptable behaviour is called _____.

11. To assume as true at the beginning of an argument what you are setting out to conclude is to argue based on the fallacy of _____.

12. Taking someone's argument, changing it into something less acceptable, and then criticizing this less acceptable version as a way of rejecting the original is relying on the _____ fallacy.

13. Attacking an individual personally, rather than responding to that person's argument, is evidence of the _____ fallacy.

14. Trying to justify your wrong actions by referring to similar unpunished wrong acts performed by others is to fall prey to the _____ fallacy.

15. If you change the subject to something more defensible when someone criticizes your original viewpoint, then you are using the _____ fallacy.

True/False Questions

Instructions: Circle the appropriate letter next to each statement.

T F   1. Anxiety is caused by defence mechanisms.

T F   2. Sigmund Freud discovered the unconscious.

T F   3. Psychological defence mechanisms are used unconsciously.

T F   4. Repression enables us to bury anxiety-provoking conflicts and memories in the unconscious.

T F 5. Isolation is another term for rationalization.

T F 6. Hero worship is an example of identification.

T F 7. Breaking down in tears in response to news of a death in the family is an example of reaction formation.

T F 8. Displacement occurs when individuals forget why they are anxious.

T F 9. Fallacious reasoning is sometimes designed to intimidate.

T F 10. Winning arguments by making emotional appeals should be encouraged in rational debate.

T F 11. Attacking the person whose argument you find threatening is an example of using the slippery slope fallacy.

T F 12. Some arguments are better, or more rational, than others.

T F 13. To say that watching violence on TV necessarily leads to insensitivity, increased aggression and eventually to murder in the streets is to rely on the slippery slope fallacy.

T F 14. In the straw man fallacy, the sender of a message/argument tries to change it in response to criticism without others noticing.

T F 15. Appeals to authority in rational argument are permitted when matters of value and ethical principle are in dispute.

Summary

1. What is defensiveness?
   - psyche's unconscious effort to protect the self from anxiety either through diversionary and intimidation tactics or by distortions of reality
   - a coping mechanism used by the ego

2. Why is defensiveness undesirable?
   - it creates "noise" in the communication process
   - it adds to "nonsense" in our dealings with people
   - it's irritating and offensive to others
   - it blocks awareness of what really troubles us
   - it leaves us blind and insensitive to others' needs

3. How many levels of consciousness are there? At what level does defensiveness occur?
   - Sigmund Freud has identified three levels: conscious, preconscious and unconscious
   - defensiveness occurs at the unconscious level

4. What defence mechanisms were covered in this chapter?
   - repression
   - rationalization
   - projection
   - reaction formation

- displacement
- sublimation
- identification
- regression
- fantasy formation
- intellectualization/isolation
- denial

5. How does each of the defence mechanisms function? What obstacles does each present to personal growth and interpersonal communication?

Repression

Function: to keep anxiety-provoking thoughts buried in the unconscious

Obstacles:
- repression prevents psychological conflict resolution
- the ego's resources are diverted from more self-enhancing and creative behaviours
- relationships suffer due to rigidity, lack of spontaneity and inability to deal with challenges
- phobias, hysterical reactions and psychosomatic illnesses may develop

Rationalization

Function: to cope with anxiety by offering plausible but false explanations and justifications for unacceptable behaviours

Obstacles:
- judgment becomes impaired
- objectivity is reduced
- increased potential for ethical problems (excuses for wrongdoing)
- may contribute to immaturity (flight from responsibility)

Projection

Function: to attribute to others negative feelings, thoughts and intentions that actually originate in oneself

Obstacles:
- unwarranted suspicions of others may develop
- trust will diminish
- social prejudice and scapegoating will emerge
- ethnic and racial stereotyping occurs
- unable to judge other people's motives
- career adjustment suffers

Reaction Formation

Function: to reduce anxiety by behaving in a way that is opposite to how one really feels

167

Obstacles:
- rigidity and an "all or nothing" attitude develops
- does not allow compromise with others offering different viewpoints
- loses touch with true feelings

Displacement

Function: to divert emotional energy (e.g., anger) from an original threatening object to a less threatening substitute object

Obstacles:
- innocent people are victimized, attacked, criticized, abused and hurt
- person becomes hypersensitive to minor annoyances

Identification

Function: to increase feelings of self-worth and decrease anxiety by taking on the characteristics of someone or some group that is admired or considered successful

Obstacles:
- increasing problems of personal identity
- fosters unnaturalness, pretenses
- promotes separation from unidentified others
- promotes stereotypical behaviour

Regression

Function: to reduce anxiety by reverting to immature patterns of behaviour

Obstacles:
- interferes with communication (e.g., babbling like a baby is incomprehensible to others)
- indulges in unproductive rages and tantrums
- narcissism develops
- interferes with intimacy
- avoided by others

Fantasy Formation

Function: to alleviate anxiety caused by frustrated desires through imaginary achievements and satisfactions

Obstacles:
- it is unproductive because people and problems are not faced directly
- it encourages unreality; current failures and shortcomings are overlooked
- living in the fantasy of the future or the past may prevent productive living in the present

Intellectualization/Isolation

Function: to diffuse anxiety (unpleasant emotions) by engaging in detached analyses of threatening problems

Obstacles:
- lose touch with real feelings
- intimacy suffers, personal contact becomes difficult

Denial

Function: to protect the self from anxiety by refusing to perceive unpleasant reality

Obstacles:
- lack of mature response to problem solving
- contributes to poor adjustment (e.g., an alcoholic denying alcoholism)
- development of physical symptoms (e.g., obesity from denial that one eats too much)

Sublimation

Function: to divert instinctual impulses into something socially acceptable or advantageous to society

Obstacles:
- lose touch with the primitive, biological side of personality
- self-deception (diversion from what we really want)

6. What is a logical fallacy?

- a rhetorical device
- an irrational form of reasoning designed to persuade emotionally and psychologically, not rationally
- an argument used to divert attention
- an intimidation tactic

7. What are some examples of logical fallacies and how do they work?

- *ad hominem*: an attack of the person, rather than the person's ideas
- straw man: rejecting an argument by criticizing a distorted version of it
- circular reasoning: assuming to be true or acceptable in the beginning what one is attempting to prove or justify in the end
- two wrongs: justifying one wrongdoing by pointing to other cases of similar wrongdoing that went unchallenged or unpunished
- slippery slope: rejecting one thing because of an alleged necessary chain of connections with other undesirable things which, in fact, does not exist
- appealing to authority: inappropriately using someone's power, position or authority as a basis of justification, when such things have no relevance

Also, using tradition or the will of the majority as justification

- red herring: shifting attention from one's weak argument or position to a more acceptable one in order to defend the original argument or position
- guilt by association: attempt to reject a position or argument by inappropriately drawing an alleged association to someone or something which is undesirable, when in fact, such an association does not exist or is not relevant to the argument or position proposed

Related Readings

Adler, Ronald and Neil Towne (1996). *Looking Out, Looking In*, 8th edition. Fort Worth, TX: Holt, Rinehart and Winston.

Falikowski, Anthony (1998). *Moral Philosophy for Modern Life*. Scarborough, ON: Prentice Hall Allyn and Bacon Canada.

Freud, Anna (1971) [1936]. *The Writings of Anna Freud*, Volume II. "The Ego and the Mechanisms of Defense," revised edition. New York: International Universities Press, Inc.

Hergenhahn, B.R. (1998). *An Introduction to Theories of Personality*, 4th edition. Upper Saddle River, NJ: Prentice Hall.

Johnson, R.H. and J.A. Blair (1994). *Logical Self-Defense*, 3rd edition. Toronto: McGraw-Hill Ryerson Ltd.

> Strong lives are
> motivated by dynamic
> purposes.
> ~Kenneth Hildebrand

5

Motivation and Emotion in Human Relations

Chapter Overview

Motivational Mysteries

The Nature of Motivation

- Everybody's Motivated
- Reasons for Behaving
- Conscious and Unconscious Motivations
- Internal Versus External Locus of Control

Theories of Motivation: What Makes Me Tick?
- A Psychoanalytic Explanation
- Self-Diagnostic 5.1 Internal Control Index

- Maslow's Humanistic Theory of Motivation
- Life after Self-Actualization: Metamotivation and the Metaphysical Blues

Application Exercise 5.1
Picture, Picture in the Book

- Choice Theory of Motivation
- Pictures in Our Minds
- Human as Behavioural Control Systems: Taking Action

Application Exercise 5.2
The TBWA—Total Behaviour and Wants Analysis

Emotions and Emotional Intelligence

- Personal Competencies
- Social Competencies

Study Guide

- Key Terms
- Progress Check 5.1
- Summary
- Related Readings

Learning Outcomes

After successfully completing this chapter, you will be able to

(5.1) Explain the general nature of motivation

(5.2) Determine your locus of control

(5.3) Outline a psychoanalytic explanation of motivation

(5.4) Describe Abraham Maslow's humanistic theory of motivation

(5.5) Profile self-actualized individuals

(5.6) Identify your personal motivations using a thematic apperception test

(5.7) Give a choice-theory account of motivation

(5.8) Gain greater control of your personal behaviour

(5.9) Testify to the importance of emotional intelligence (EQ)

(5.10) List and explain personal competencies associated with EQ

(5.11) List and explain social competencies associated with EQ

Focus Questions

1. Do unmotivated people exist? Explain.

2. Is it true that people always know what motivates them? Why?

3. Is all behaviour caused? Can people make you glad, mad or sad? Are you forced by determining factors to do what you do? Discuss.

4. Is biology relevant or irrelevant to human motivation? Explain.

5. What explanation could be given for why people are seemingly always dissatisfied?

6. What does it mean to be self-actualized? Do you know any self-actualized individuals? What are they like?

7. How can human behaviour be governed like a thermostat?

8. Is intellect or emotion more important to vocational success and human relations effectiveness? Why?

9. What are some fundamental emotional competencies?

Motivational Mysteries

When Jamal was a young boy, everybody considered him to be an intelligent, above-average student. He worked hard and tried his best at everything he did. Jamal was a likable guy, the kind of person who brought out the best in others. At his grade eight graduation, virtually everyone picked Jamal as the one who would excel in high school and be most likely to succeed later in life. Once Jamal entered high school, however, things suddenly began to change. His grades became inconsistent, his attendance became unpredictable and his boundless curiosity and enthusiasm for learning all but disappeared. He started to avoid people and engaged in self-destructive behaviours. He got into some minor trouble with the law and started taking drugs. He developed an apathetic attitude toward his personal responsibilities and life in general. Jamal somehow managed to graduate from high school and miraculously was admitted to the local college. Nobody expects very much from him now. If he squeaks through, everybody will be happy. Jamal doesn't have a clue what he'll do after school.

Althea is Jamal's younger sister. She has always been an average student, never excelling in anything she does. A bit self-conscious and overweight, she used to present herself as a shy person with not much to say about anything. The fact that Jamal was intelligent and well-liked in grade school served only to reinforce Althea's own feelings of inferiority. When Althea entered high school, things changed for her as well, only this time for the better. Althea's grades took a leap upwards and she worked hard to earn straight As. Althea shed some weight and began putting a lot of emphasis on improving her physical appearance. She decided to exercise regularly, buy fashionable clothing and use makeup to help her look more attractive. Althea, too, graduated from high school. She entered the local transfer college and plans to earn a liberal arts degree before eventually going on to law school. Althea is energized and "hungry" to acquire the material benefits of professional success.

Stories such as these two are far from uncommon. Maybe you identified a little bit yourself with one of these fictional characters. Maybe there's a Jamal or Althea in your family or in your circle of friends. The point is that the Jamals and Altheas of the world leave us all wondering, "Why do people do the things they do?" Why, for example, are some individuals motivated to achieve and others not? Why do some aspire to achieve great things, while others couldn't care less. In this chapter, we'll look at different theoretical explanations that have been given for motivation and how they relate to human behaviour. This discussion should help you to understand why you (and others) do the things you do. With this understanding you will be able to take more effective control of your life. You will also learn how to become a positive motivational force in other people's lives. The information provided here, along with the application exercises and self-diagnostic, should help you to build a self-managed lifestyle, one that may not provide you with absolutely everything you want, but they will help you get much of what you really need.

5.1 # The Nature of Motivation

Highly successful motivational speakers sometimes make it sound as if **motivation**, the impetus to act, is a relatively easy concept to understand. These purveyors of personal success claim that "proven" behavioural techniques can be easily applied to anyone's life to maximize personal goal achievement. While their own success is witness to the fact that energy and enthusiasm are inspiring and motivational for many, I am not sure that life is so simple that their prescriptions for personal happiness should be so casually dispensed to a hungry public craving purpose and direction. Before going out to buy the next new and improved motivational book or CD on the market, you may wish to become an "informed consumer" of sorts. Acquaint yourself with some of the serious issues and psychologically important theories related to motivation discussed here.

motivation
The impetus to act.

Don't tell me what to do
or I won't do it!
~Adel Escent

Life can be pulled by goals
just as surely as it can be
pushed by drives.
~Viktor Frankl

Everybody's Motivated

In casual conversation we sometimes hear it said that "so-and-so is motivated," along with a lament for the fact that "so-and-so's brother or sister" is not. We also hear about motivated and unmotivated students or ambitious and unambitious employees. All this talk makes it sound like motivation is some kind of desirable character trait that not everyone possesses, and anyone who lacks it is psychologically flawed. It also raises the idea that people can be categorized by one of two personality types: motivated or unmotivated. This categorization would be highly simplistic, as an individual might be motivated today, but not tomorrow. Maybe that person is motivated at work, but not at school. Perhaps some tasks are approached with a desire to do well, while others are approached lackadaisically. In fact, maybe the same task is approached by the same individual on two different days in qualitatively different ways—on one day with interest and enthusiasm and on the next with apathy and careless ease. In short, motivational levels can vary within and between individuals. They can vary as well among situations, tasks and the times at which things are done. In view of this variance, it could be argued that we're all motivated, we're just not motivated to do the same things in the same ways, at the same times and with the same people. It's probably true to say that when we describe others as unmotivated, what we are really saying is that those others are not doing what we want them to do in the way we want them to do it, at the time we want it done.

Reasons for Behaving

Motivation obviously has a lot to do with behaviour. When searching for the motivation for a behaviour, we try to discover the reason behind it. However, finding the reason for behaviour is no easy task. I suppose you could simply ask people why they do the things they do. You might on occasion even get an honest reply! However, suppose the person responding to you is hiding his or her real intentions. Answers to your question will not be very helpful. Maybe the individual lacks sufficient self-insight and does not really understand the reasons behind the behaviour she exhibits. Do you always know why you do things you do? Lack of self-awareness, then, as well as dishonesty, can make it difficult to determine people's motivations. Furthermore, we might, as observers, unwittingly project onto others our own motivations as we respond defensively toward them (see Chapter 4). In this case, the motivations we witness and attribute to them would actually be our own staring us in the face.

Conscious and Unconscious Motivations

conscious and unconscious motivations
Motivations can be either conscious or unconscious. Conscious motivations lead us to do things wilfully and with self-awareness. With consciously motivated actions, we know what we're doing and can provide rationales and explanations for them. Unconscious motivations, by contrast, give rise to actions performed without self-awareness or self-understanding. Lacking insight into ourselves, we may exhibit behaviour that we later regret.

Motivations can be either conscious or unconscious. **Conscious motivations** lead us to do things intentionally and with self-awareness. With consciously motivated actions, we know what we're doing and we can provide rationales and explanations for them. **Unconscious motivations**, by contrast, give rise to actions performed without self-awareness and self-understanding. Lacking insight into ourselves, we may exhibit behaviour that we later regret. We may say to ourselves, "I don't know why I did that" or "How could I have said that?" Our own motivations can sometimes be mysteries to us as much as they are to others. Repressed fears, buried anxieties or latent hostilities, for example, may manifest themselves in personal behaviour without warning and thereby catch us by surprise. Psychiatrists such as Sigmund Freud and Carl Jung would argue that much of our behaviour is indeed unconsciously motivated. On an optimistic note, they both believed that clinical procedures could be used to bring a greater segment of human behaviour under the rational, conscious control of the ego. If we do not gain access to the unconscious, much of what appears to be freely chosen behaviour will in fact be determined by forces over which we have little control.

Internal Versus External Locus of Control

Speaking of control, the question arises as to whether motivation is an "inside" or "outside" job. When you do something wrong, for example, did "the devil make you do it?" When you aggressively attack someone either verbally or physically, is it because that person "made" you angry? Is that person, not you, responsible for what happened? Is some behaviour simply beyond your control, caused by outside influences? Believing this is the case, defence lawyers often plead for reduced sentences on behalf of their guilty clients. They frequently argue that external circumstances influenced their clients to commit some wrongdoing. They were in many respects innocent victims of circumstance. The "boys in the 'hood" made them do it. Society made them do it. The system made them do it. An alcoholic parent made them do it. Everything made them do it except they themselves. To hold this position would be to assume that they experienced an **external locus of control** for behaviour. By contrast, if people accept responsibility for their actions, they assume an **internal locus of control**.

People who display a high internal locus of control see themselves as self-governed. They do not feel coerced; nor do they believe that they are "victims of the system." What they do is a matter of personal choice. They really want to do what they're doing, feeling in charge of their destinies. The rewards derived from internally motivated activities often come from the activities themselves. We can observe that internally motivated people frequently do things for an action's intrinsic value. For example, when you behave virtuously, not to impress or to gain praise, but simply for the sake of duty, you implicitly recognize the inherent worth of your virtuous acts. Virtue, for you, becomes its own reward. Others may act virtuously by giving to charity, but they may do so because fellow workers at the office have shamed them into it or because they want the tax deduction. The same action can be motivated by very different reasons. Reasons for behaviour can be external and coercive, or internal and voluntary.

It's not my aim here to convince you that some motivations are good or that others are bad. Nor is it my intent to defend or discredit any one position on the nature of human motivation. In what follows, we'll examine several established motivational theories that seek to explain why we do the things we do. After completing our theoretical survey, a behavioural strategy for more effective, self-directed living will be introduced for your consideration and use.

external locus of control
The position that external circumstances or outside forces cause people to be the way they are or do the things they do.

internal locus of control
The position where people accept responsibility for their own actions.

5.3 Theories of Motivation: What Makes Me Tick?

A Psychoanalytic Explanation

If you have been going through this book in sequence, you have already encountered Freud's **psychoanalytic theory** in Chapter 4. There you learned about the different psychic structures and the various mechanisms of defence. Here, we'll look at what fuels the functioning of human personality. By examining what makes people tick, you'll better understand what makes you tick.

psychoanalytic theory
Freud's theory of personality explaining the different psychic structures and the various mechanisms of defence.

Self Diagnostic

5.1 Internal Control Index

(5.2)

Please read each statement. Where there is a blank, indicate what your usual attitude, feeling or behaviour would be.

A = Rarely (less than 10 percent of the time)
B = Occasionally (about 30 percent of the time)
C = Sometimes (about half the time)
D = Frequently (about 70 percent of the time)
E = Usually (more than 90 percent of the time)

1. When faced with a problem I _____ try to forget it.

2. I _____ need frequent encouragement from others to keep working at a difficult task.

3. I _____ like jobs where I can make decisions and be responsible for my own work.

4. I _____ change my opinion when someone I admire disagrees with me.

5. If I want something I _____ work hard to get it.

6. I _____ prefer to learn the facts about something from someone else rather than to have to dig them up myself.

7. I will _____ accept jobs that require me to supervise others.

8. I _____ have a hard time saying "no" when someone tries to sell me something I don't want.

9. I _____ like to have a say in any decisions made by any group I'm in.

10. I _____ consider the different sides of an issue before making any decisions.

11. What other people think _____ has a great influence on my behaviour.

12. Whenever something good happens to me I _____ feel it is because I've earned it.

13. I _____ enjoy being in a position of leadership.

14. I _____ need someone else to praise my work before I am satisfied with what I've done.

15. I am _____ sure enough of my opinions to try and influence others.

16. When something is going to affect me I _____ learn as much about it as I can.

17. I _____ decide to do things on the spur of the moment.

18. For me, knowing I've done something well is _____ more important than being praised by someone else.

19. I _____ let other peoples' demands keep me from doing things I want to do.

20. I _____ stick to my opinions when someone disagrees with me.

21. I _____ do what I feel like doing, not what other people think I ought to do.

22. I _____ get discouraged when doing something that takes a long time to achieve results.

23. When part of a group, I _____ prefer to let other people make all the decisions.

24. When I have a problem I _____ follow the advice of friends or relatives.

25. I _____ enjoy trying to do difficult tasks more than I enjoy trying to do easy tasks.

26. I _____ prefer situations where I can depend on someone else's ability rather than just my own.

27. Having someone important tell me I did a good job is _____ more important to me than feeling I've done a good job.

28. When I'm involved in something I _____ try to find out all I can about what is going on, even when someone else is in charge.

Internal Control Index (ICI)

Author: Patricia Dutteiler

Purpose: To measure locus of control

Description: The ICI is a 28-item instrument designed to measure where a person looks for, or expects to obtain, reinforcement. An individual with an external locus of control believes that reinforcement is based on luck or chance, while an individual with an internal locus of control believes that reinforcement is based on his own behaviour. Locus of control is viewed as a personality trait that influences human behaviour across a wide range of situations related to learning and achievement. There are two factors contained in the ICI, one called self-confidence, and a second called autonomous behaviour (behaviour independent of social pressure).

Norms: The ICI was developed and tested with several samples of junior college, university undergraduate, and continuing education students. The total N involved 1365 respondents of both sexes. Means are available that are broken down by age, group, sex, race, and educational and socioeconomic level, and range from 99.3 and 120.8.

Scoring: Each item is scored on a 5-point scale from A ("rarely") to E ("usually"). Half the items are worded so that high internally oriented respondents are expected to answer half at the "usually" end of the scale and the other half at the "rarely" end. The "rarely" response is scored as 5 points on items 1, 2, 4, 6, 8, 11, 14, 17, 19, 22, 23, 24, 26 and 27; for the remainder of the items, the response "usually" is scored as 5 points. This produces a possible range of scores from 28 to 140, with higher scores reflecting higher internal locus of control.

Reliability: The ICI has very good internal consistency with alphas of .84 and .85. No test-retest correlations were reported.

Validity: The ICI has fair concurrent validity with a low but significant correlation with Mirels' Factor I of the Rotter I-E Scale.

Primary reference: Duttweiler, P.C. (1984). "The Internal Control Index: A newly developed measure of locus of control," *Educational and Psychological Measurement* 44, 209–221. Instrument reproduced with permission of Patricia Duttweiler and *Educational and Psychological Measurement.*

Availability: Journal article.

179

Source: From *Educational and Psychology Measurement* by Corcoran and Fisher. Copyright 1987.

What I lack is not happiness, but peace of mind.
~Mortimer Adler, philosopher

energy model
A Freudian notion used to explain how the psyche or mind functions.

homeostasis
A state of equilibrium.

nirvana principle
The theory that the psychic structure of personality functions to reduce excitation and tension. The mental apparatus tries to maintain a relatively stable state of stimulation-free existence. Instincts are aroused so that we'll act in ways to re-establish homeostasis.

pleasure principle
A force in psychic life separate from, but complementary to, the nirvana principle according to Freud. He realized that pleasure is not only achieved when people rid themselves of disturbing tensions and an excess of stimulation (the nirvana principle), but also that some states of pleasure require an increase in excitation, rather than a reduction of stimulation. People who actively seek out tensions for the purpose of physical excitement live by this principle.

eros
Generic label including both the life and sexual instincts.

libido
In general terms, the libido is that which seeks physical and pleasurable feelings associated with the life instincts, both erotic and non-erotic.

Instincts—The Forces That Drive the Personality When Freud developed his concept of personality, he was influenced by prevailing views within the biological and physical sciences. He adopted a then-accepted **energy model** to explain the workings of the human mind. According to Freud, human beings can be conceptualized as complex energy systems that require energy to do psychological work such as thinking, perceiving, remembering and dreaming (Carver and Scheier, 1988). The energy that is used to perform psychologically is generated and released through natural biological processes. Energy is continually used and released.

In this model of motivation, instincts are responsible for generating the psychic energy necessary to keep the human body functioning. Given this, behaviour has a biological basis. Instinctual drives are activated by bodily needs that motivate people to seek gratification. Biological need states cause psychological desires or wishes to emerge. If the body is suffering from a liquid deficiency, for instance, a bodily need gives rise to thirst, an urge to rectify an imbalanced condition. Once our thirst is satisfied, the need temporarily goes away and we are no longer motivated to drink or seek out fluids.

Nirvana and Pleasure Principles Implicit in what has just been explained is the notion of **homeostasis**. If Freud is correct, human behaviour aims to achieve a state of equilibrium. The psychic structure of personality functions according to the **nirvana principle**, meaning that it seeks to reduce excitation and tension. The mental apparatus tries to maintain a relatively stable state of stimulation-free existence (Monte, 1987). This principle was first called the constancy principle, a term borrowed from psychophysicist Gustav Fechner. Freud initially saw the nirvana principle of behaviour as inextricably linked to pleasure. For him, when people rid themselves of disturbing tensions and an excess of stimulation, they experience pleasure. Freud (1924) later distinguished between the nirvana principle and what he called the **pleasure principle**. He recognized, in the second principle, that some states of pleasure require an increase in excitation, rather than a reduction in stimulation. People who actively seek out tensions for the purpose of physical excitement live by this principle. On this note, Freud went on to regard the nirvana principle and the pleasure principle as separate but complementary forces in psychic life (Monte, 1987: 102).

Kinds of Instincts: Eros and Thanatos To help us better understand instinctual life, Freud distinguished between two basic types of instinct: *eros* and *thanatos*. Falling under **eros** are the life instincts and sexual instincts. They aim toward survival, self-preservation, procreation and pleasure. Collectively they belong to what people commonly refer to as the **libido**. Notice that the libido is not purely sexual. Hunger and pain avoidance can be considered life instincts, though they are not associated with erotic urges. In general terms, then, the libido is that which seeks physical and pleasurable feelings associated with the life instincts, both erotic and non-erotic (Monte,

1987). Instincts that do not fall under eros are placed under the heading of *thanatos*, which includes our death instincts. As Freud once said, "The aim of all life is death" (cited in Monte, 1987: 102). At first glance, such a proposal may seem a little ridiculous, but let's consider it seriously for a moment.

If we go back to the nirvana principle, we find that instincts are aroused so that we'll act in ways to reestablish homeostasis—a "state of peaceful freedom from need" (Monte, 1987: 102). For instance, when tension mounts from hunger, we eat and the tension is removed. Under the pressure of instinct we constantly seek to achieve an earlier state of "organismic quietude" before the external world or internal needs made their disquieting demands upon us. Complete quietude—absolute freedom from need and tension and total independence from the world—comes only with death. Intuitively we understand this concept. We sometimes see expressions of peaceful bliss on the faces of deceased individuals. They look so still, so calm. We feel strangely uplifted and reassured, believing that they are now resting in peace, knowing perhaps that they did not live in peace. In a sense, death represents a final state of repose in which all struggles, tensions, torments and deprivations disappear.

A derivative of the death instinct is **aggression**. Tension can be reduced by a verbal, physical or symbolic attack. The objects of attack are usually others, though the self can be attacked as well. Aggressive urges that were once targeted at others could be redirected toward the self, resulting in acts of self-mutilation or even suicide. Expressions of humanity's aggressivity are present everywhere. People take dangerous drugs and laugh about their effects. Malicious people love to gossip and uncover "good dirt" that they can use against others. Individuals at work sabotage the efforts of colleagues. On the street, people physically assault their enemies. Contact sports are another obvious manifestation of the instinct of aggression. When I point to sports, I do not wish to pick on athletes. The next time you see a boxing match on television, watch the "bloodthirsty" spectators (some of whom would probably feel cheated if the fight ended in the first round with no blood or knock-out punch). Or the next time you're at a hockey game and a fight breaks out, watch the fans yell, scream and pound on the glass in the vicinity of the action. Many fans of the game do not object to violence; they want it. That's what they pay for and that's what they like to see. Just ask the NHL expert Don Cherry! I guess in some ways he is unwittingly championing the cause of Freudian psychoanalysis. Don Cherry a Freudian?

The notion that aggressive instincts are motivating may seem to contradict the nirvana or homeostasis principles of psychoanalysis. Common sense would seem to suggest that when people display aggression, they become more aroused and physically excited. Research shows just the opposite, however. Aggressive acts serve as a **catharsis** or emotional release. In one study, subjects were harassed by an experimenter while they were working on a task. What resulted was a significant increase in heart rate and systolic blood pressure (indicators of tension). Afterwards, subjects were placed in four

thanatos
According to Freud, one of the two basic types of instinct (the other being eros). Those instincts that do not fall under eros are placed under the heading of thanatos, which includes our death instincts.

aggression
According to Freud, a derivative of the death instinct. Aggressive acts show a catharsis or emotional release.

catharsis
An emotional release.

181

Figure 5.1

The Tension-Reducing Effects of Aggressive Acts

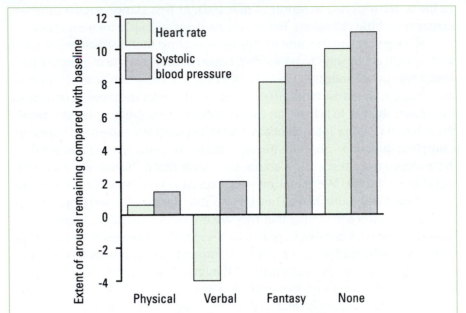

Source: From Carver and Scheier, *Perspectives on Personality.*Copyright 1988 by Allyn and Bacon. Reprinted by permission.

groups. One group was ostensibly allowed to attack its tormentor physically by administering an electric shock; a second group was allowed verbal attack through experimenter rating; a third group was allowed to act aggressively in fantasy; a fourth group was given no chance to act aggressively in any fashion. The results displayed in Figure 5.1 indicate that there is an emotional catharsis when people have an opportunity to retaliate.

Control Your Instincts Before Your Instincts Control You Recognizing that aggressive acts are emotionally cathartic should not suggest that we all become violent psychopathic killers, lashing out against people and objects in the world. Also, taking into account our instinctual sexual urges does not mean that we should sexually abuse others.

While life and death instincts constitute our ultimate source of motivational energy, they must be sublimated (see Chapter 4) into socially acceptable forms of expression. Police work, national defence, athletics and other competitive activities are good examples of ways to use aggression constructively. Artistic creation through photography, painting, movie making, writing or poetry would be good ways of sublimating sexuality, especially when expression of sexual urges would be inappropriate and morally prohibited. Instincts emanating from the id can also be better handled by raising levels of self-consciousness. The less that is denied or repressed in the unconscious, the greater rational control we have over our actions. Last, by reducing our defensiveness, we can learn to live with our biological nature and deal with it more effectively. Denying the reality of human biology is risky business; losing control of it is even worse. Think here of the roles that aggression and sexuality have played for famous people, such as former U.S. president Bill Clinton and O.J. Simpson, and what they have done to their careers and livelihoods. Maybe Freud was correct when he suggested that refusing to acknowledge the motivational force of biological instincts is just another expression of psychological defensiveness. Why is so much energy spent denying the importance of sexuality in human life?

Abraham Maslow
An important figure in the historical development of motivational theory. He viewed human nature as essentially good, and identified a hierarchy of human needs that motivate us to grow and develop.

5.4 Maslow's Humanistic Theory of Motivation

Abraham Maslow is another important figure in the historical development of motivational theory. In his classic books *The Farther Reaches of Human Nature*, *Motivation and Personality* and *Toward a Psychology of Being*, he presents a picture of human motivation that differs greatly from Freud's view.

Freud envisioned life as a constant struggle or conflict between the instinctive biological needs of the id and the moral demands imposed by the superego and society at large. He used clinical studies of neurotic and dysfunctional patients as the basis for his generalizations about human behaviour and motivation. By contrast, Maslow did not see psychological beings as people constantly at war with themselves and others. He viewed human nature as essentially good, not evil and destructive. While Freud painted a dark picture of humanity focusing on its frailties, shortcomings and pathologies, Maslow emphasized human strength and virtue. He concentrated on the bright side of human reality. To study neurotics (as Freud did), in order to find out what normal people are like would be, for Maslow, like studying high school dropouts to develop a psychological profile of successful college or university graduates. To correct what he

Abraham Maslow believed that all human beings are motivated to actualize themselves and to realize their potentialities.

183

saw as inappropriate psychoanalytic conclusions drawn from a "sick" population, Maslow began to study healthy and well-adjusted individuals (e.g., extraordinary people he knew, as well as outstanding historical figures). He believed that the study of psychologically healthy people could provide a more adequate science of psychology and a better understanding of human motivation.

The Hierarchy of Human Needs I've heard it said that people are never satisfied. Usually when this assertion is made, the person making it is expressing displeasure, bewilderment or some kind of disapproval. It's as if wanting something more or wanting something different is inherently wrong. Maybe you've been criticized yourself for being restless and itchy, always searching for something you don't have. If so, you might take some comfort in Maslow's characterization of human beings as "wanting animals" who rarely reach a state of complete satisfaction (Hjelle and Ziegler, 1981). If you're never satisfied, maybe you're not a spoiled brat or a selfish malcontent, but simply a typical human being. For Maslow, psychological states of equilibrium or nirvana are short-lived. As soon as one need is satisfied, another demands satisfaction. To be human is to continually desire something.

hierarchy of human needs
A structure of ascending needs developed by Abraham Maslow.

According to Maslow, our natural desires can be arranged in a **hierarchy of human needs**, a structure of ascending requirements. We have universal physiological needs, safety and security needs, social needs for love and belonging, esteem needs, cognitive needs, aesthetic needs and self-actualization needs. (Whether Maslow's hierarchical concept of motivation should be depicted with five or seven levels is open to discussion. In *Motivation and Personality*, he pays closest attention to physiological needs, safety and security needs, belonging and love needs, esteem needs and self-actualization needs. Cognitive and aesthetic needs are recognized as important, but are dealt with almost as an afterthought. Whether they belong to the higher levels of "basic needs" dealing with self-actualization or to the level of "meta-needs" beyond self-actualization is unclear to me. The cognitive needs for knowledge and understanding bear some resemblance to metaneeds for truth and meaning. Aesthetic needs seem to overlap with metaneeds for beauty and simplicity. For our purposes, I will put them at the higher level of the basic needs hierarchy). See these needs represented in Figure 5.2. We'll discuss each in a moment.

184

actualize
To actualize ourselves is to become all we are capable of becoming.

These innate needs motivate us to grow and develop. They serve to help us **actualize** ourselves, to help us become all that we are capable of becoming. Maslow does not see people as born inherently flawed or defective. They need not be redeemed, nor is there any instinctual devil that needs to be exorcised. For Maslow, the potential for healthy psychological growth and development is present at birth. Whether or not people fulfill themselves or actualize their potential will depend on the individuals themselves and on existing societal forces that will either serve to promote or inhibit self-actualization (Schultz, 1977). Different environments can stifle growth or encourage it.

As stated, the needs that have been listed as human motivators are hierarchical in nature. There is a **prepotency** to them, meaning that lower-level needs must be satisfied before higher-level needs become salient or important in people's lives. At any given time, then, one level of needs dominates any individual's life. Which level it is depends on what other needs have already been satisfied. The further one's needs are satisfied up the hierarchy, the more self-realized the individual is. Let us now look at Maslow's hierarchy more closely.

Level One: Physiological Needs

People at this level are most concerned with meeting their survival and **physiological needs**. They are preoccupied with obtaining such things as food and water. People struggling to survive may walk long distances for nourishment or for a life-saving sip of water. Physiological needs also include our need for air to breathe, and for sleep and sex. Without air we would obviously die. With continuous sleep deprivation, our mental and physical health would deteriorate. Without sex, the species would become extinct. (This statement has been true up until now; however, with new reproductive technologies such as in vitro fertilization, artificial insemination and newly developing cloning techniques, sex may become a redundant human need).

Level Two: Safety and Security Needs

In some cultures where people are starving and the struggle to survive is an ongoing daily battle, higher-order needs are not usually on their minds. If you're dying of thirst, realizing long-term ambitions does not occupy your attention. By contrast, in other cultures or societies where the basic needs of survival have been looked after, the physiological needs begin to play a less important role in daily life. **Safety and security needs** become prominent and exert themselves to ensure that there is stability, order, structure and certainty in one's environment. Children, for example, prefer routine and predictability. Uncertainty and unpredictability are difficult for

prepotency
The needs that have been listed as human motivators are hierarchical, and lower-level needs must be satisfied before higher-level needs become important.

physiological needs
The first level in Maslow's theory of motivation, these are the survival needs, which include food, water, air, sleep and sex.

Figure 5.2

Maslow's Hierarchy of Human Needs

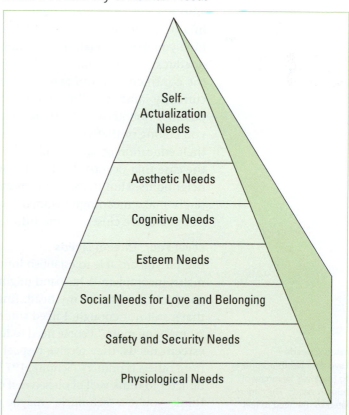

Source: From Hergenhahn, *An Introduction to Theories of Personality,* 4th Edition, Copyright 1993, p. 32. Reprinted by permission of Prentice-Hall, Inc., Englewood Cliffs, NJ.

safety and security needs
Level two needs according to Maslow's hierarchy of human needs. These needs become prominent after physiological needs have been met and exert themselves to ensure that there is stability, order, structure and certainty in one's environment.

social needs for belonging and love
Level three needs according to Maslow's hierarchy of human needs. Individuals who are motivated at this level crave intimacy and caring relationships with other people.

everyone to cope with, but especially so for them. Take children out of their established routines and they show signs of distress.

When we finally get our safety and security needs met, we free ourselves from much fear and anxiety. Before meeting these needs, it is hard to see the magnificent horizons of our future; we are too busy defending and protecting our physical and psychological borders.

Level Three: Social Needs for Love and Belonging

People whose survival is ensured and security is guaranteed can still find themselves dissatisfied. When the first two levels of needs are met, level three **social needs for belonging and love** begin to emerge. Individuals who are motivated at this level crave intimacy and caring relationships with others. People at this level need to feel a sense of belonging and togetherness with others. To avoid feeling lonely or socially ostracized, people will join clubs, groups and organizations.

In contemporary Canadian society, many of us experience difficulty meeting our level three needs. You may be a college or university student who has left all of your friends and family at home. Perhaps now you live in a basement apartment or residence where you know almost nobody. In time you may graduate as a business student, nurse, technician, social worker or educator, for example, and be forced to travel across the country, or even the continent, to find gainful employment. In this case, again, those who currently satisfy your love and belonging needs may be left behind, and quite possibly nobody will be there in your new location to make you feel that you belong or that you count. Even people who are not on the move due to their education or career find their level three needs frustrated. It's frequently the case that occupants of high-rise apartment buildings barely know their neighbours. Hundreds, if not thousands, of strangers can live close by and rarely make meaningful human contact. Being surrounded by people does not guarantee closeness and intimacy—a basic human need.

Level Four: Esteem Needs

Even if you are able to establish intimacy and a network of friends, life still remains incomplete. A husband might say to his wife, "I have a loving family, a good job, a roof over my head, financial security and food in my belly, but that's still not enough. I need something more!" At level four, esteem is the "something more." People need to feel good about themselves; in meeting their **esteem needs**, they receive respect from others. In Maslow's theory, esteem from others is primary (Schultz, 1977). This is understandable, for it can be very difficult to think well of ourselves if others don't. For example, if everybody else thinks you're a "schmuck," maybe you're not worthy of esteem. Some of the ways we try to gain the acceptance of others is by developing good reputations, achieving status or fame, gaining prestige or becoming a social success. We may also try to impress others by the car we drive, the clothes we wear, the neighbourhood we live in or by the knowledge and skills we display (Schultz, 1977).

esteem needs
Level four needs according to Maslow's hierarchy of human needs. They are related to the need to feel good about oneself.

Internal self-esteem is a universal need to feel worthy and adequate within ourselves. When this need is met, we feel confident and psychologically secure. We know ourselves well, living by no grand self-delusions or inflated conceptions of self. We're able to assess our abilities and weaknesses in objective terms. When the need for self-esteem is frustrated, we experience a lack. We may feel inferior, discouraged or helpless. People with low self-esteem typically have poor self-concepts. (Refer back to Chapter One for more detailed discussions of self-concept and self-esteem.)

Level Five: Cognitive Needs

Once people have their esteem needs met, then higher-level **cognitive needs** arise. These needs reflect our "impulse to satisfy curiosity, to know, to explain and to understand" (Maslow, 1987: 23). People who have level-five needs frustrated may exhibit symptoms of boredom, loss of zest and steady deterioration of the intellectual life and its tastes. According to Maslow, the need to know is present in infancy and adulthood. As he puts it, "Children do not have to be taught to be curious. But they may be taught, as by institutionalization, not to be curious" (Maslow, 1987: 25).

Maslow also places understanding under the heading of cognitive needs. He points out that the need to know impels us, on the one hand, to minute details, while on the other hand, it moves us more and more toward developing a world philosophy, or theological perspective. This need can be labelled a search for meaning—"a desire to understand, to systematize, to organize, to analyze, to look for relations and meanings, to construct a system of values" (Maslow, 1987: 25). Within the level of cognitive needs itself, a mini-hierarchy exists. The desire to know is prepotent over the desire to understand. Some discussions of Maslow's motivational theory leave out the cognitive needs as well as the aesthetic needs (see Ryckman, 2000). This is unfortunate for, as Maslow himself says, "The desire to know and to understand...are as much personality needs as the basic needs we have already discussed" (Maslow, 1987: 25).

Level Six: Aesthetic Needs

Maslow addresses the issue of **aesthetic needs** somewhat tentatively. He believes that clinical observation indicates that, at least in some individuals, there is a truly basic aesthetic need. He maintains that people can get "sick" from ugliness and that cures can be found in beautiful surroundings. If you have any doubt about this idea you might try to imagine yourself being raised in a poverty-stricken ghetto, surrounded by dirt and squalor, graffiti-covered abandoned warehouses and severely deteriorating apartment complexes. How would you feel? What would your outlook be like? The answers to these questions are likely not very positive. Falling under the aesthetic category are needs for symmetry and closure, as well as needs for completion, system and structure (Maslow, 1987).

cognitive needs
Level five needs according to Maslow's hierarchy of human needs. These needs reflect our impulse to satisfy curiosity, to know, to explain and to understand.

aesthetic needs
Level six on Maslow's hierarchy of human needs. These are the needs for symmetry and closure, as well as needs for completion, system and structure.

187

Level Seven: Self-Actualization Needs

Let's suppose that an individual—call her Kristine—has gained a lot of knowledge and has surrounded herself with beauty. Let's also say that she has developed positive self-esteem. She's respected and liked by others. Furthermore, Kristine belongs to many groups, has a solid network of friends, shares a loving intimate relationship with another person and is secure in her job, and certainly does not lack for the bare necessities of life. Yet Kristine is still dissatisfied. She wants something more. Since Kristine's needs at levels one through six are met, we would have to conclude that level seven **self-actualization needs** are probably becoming dominant in her life. At level seven, Kristine feels a need to actualize all of her potentialities; in other words, to become all of what she can be. Not to realize all her inborn potential would leave Kristine feeling frustrated. On this note, Maslow has written that "a new discontent and restlessness will soon develop unless the individual (Kristine) is doing what he or she, individually, is fitted for. Musicians must make music, artists must paint, poets must write if they are to be ultimately at peace with themselves. What humans can be, they must be. They must be true to their own nature. This need we may call self-actualization" (Maslow, 1987: 22).

As a college teacher I've met many Kristines. They are often returning students who are established and financially secure. They have families and friends. They are confident and able. They return to college to "grow" as people. They tell me that life before college was in some ways stifling them and interfering with their natural development as human beings. By coming to college they hope to realize themselves and their dreams.

self-actualization needs
Level seven needs according to Maslow's hierarchy of human needs. Individuals who are motivated at this level feel a need to actualize all of their potentialities; in other words, to be all they can be.

(5.5)   **A Psychological Portrait of Self-Actualized Individuals**

Self-actualized people

1. Perceive clearly and efficiently. They have an unusual ability to detect dishonesty and to see concealed or confused realities.
2. Accept themselves, others and nature without guilt or complaint.
3. Behave spontaneously, with simplicity and naturalness.
4. Focus strongly on problems external to themselves, not on their own egos. They are frequently on a "mission" or have some life task to complete.
5. Enjoy privacy and solitude more than does the average person.
6. Are autonomous and resist enculturation. They are not dependent upon the physical and social environment.
7. Display a fresh appreciation for life. They experience life with awe, pleasure and wonder.
8. Have mystical and peak experiences.
9. Possess a deep feeling for humanity. They truly wish to help the human race.
10. Are honestly respectful and humble before others.
11. Have deep relationships with a limited number of people.
12. Are ethically strong, possessing definite moral standards.

13. Distinguish clearly between means and ends, focusing mostly on ends.

14. Display an unusual sense of humour, one that is philosophical and not hostile in nature.

Source: Summary is based on material from Maslow (1987: 128–142 and 1968: 26).

5.6 Life after Self-Actualization: Metamotivation and the Metaphysical Blues

Maslow's work with self-actualized individuals eventually led him to theorize that extremely healthy people were motivated by different things compared with average, normal and unhealthy people. He called his motivational theory for self-actualizing people **metamotivation**. He also calls it **being motivation**, or B-motivation, for short. To enable you to understand what's meant by this concept, it's helpful to draw attention to a distinction that Maslow makes between growth or B-motivation and deficit or **deficiency motivation** (D-motivation).

D-motivation serves the purpose of rectifying deficiencies in the person. Deficits in the body (lack of food, for example) produce pain and discomfort, as do psychological deficits. In response to biological and psychological deficiencies, hungry people are motivated to eat and insecure people are motivated to achieve, please or impress. Generally speaking, people with average to below-average mental health are motivated by D-motives. Their behaviour aims primarily to gratify lower-level requirements.

By contrast, self-actualizers are motivated by higher-level needs. The term "needs" is used with caution here. Perhaps a better term would be "values." Self-actualizers do not live their lives preoccupied with reducing tensions or rectifying deficits. Rather, they aim to enrich and enlarge their experience of life (Schultz, 1977). Life for them is a kind of celebration; there's joy and ecstasy in simply being alive. As Schultz (1977: 66) puts it, "Self-actualizers are beyond striving, desiring, or wishing for something they need to correct a deficit; all their deficits have been corrected. They are no longer becoming, in the sense of satisfying the lower needs. Now they are in a state of being, of spontaneously, naturally, joyously expressing their full humanness. In that sense then, they are unmotivated." I may have witnessed an unmotivated self-actualized student in the hallway at school recently. She was wearing a T-shirt that read, "If I don't own it; I don't want it." I can only guess that all of her lower-level material needs were met. If her life reflected what her T-shirt said, apparently she lacked for nothing, or at least she wished for nothing that she didn't already have.

When people go after objects for purposes of need gratification, the objects become means to further ends. Were there no deficit, the objects wouldn't be sought. By contrast, metamotivation addresses itself to things that have being value (B-value). Such things have intrinsic worth as they are ends in themselves.

metamotivation
A motivational theory for self-actualizing people that deals with higher-order matters of being and value beyond basic needs.

being motivation
Maslow's motivational theory for self-actualizing people. (He also calls it metamotivation.) Maslow describes self-actualizers as people who do not live their lives preoccupied with reducing tensions or rectifying debts. Rather, they aim to enrich and enlarge their experience of life. Being motivation or metamotivation should be seen as involving states of being rather than intermediate steps to ultimate goals.

deficiency motivation
Motivation to rectify deficiencies in the person. Deficiencies in the body (lack of food, for example) produce pain and discomfort, as do psychological deficits. Generally speaking, people with average to below-average mental health are motivated by D-motives.

189

Metamotivation should be seen as involving states of being rather than intermediate steps to ultimate goals.

In some respects, B-values do act like needs, only on a higher plane. They can be referred to as metaneeds. Blocking of metaneeds does not produce neurosis or psychopathology, but rather a kind of **existential frustration** or **metapathology**. Schultz (1977) describes metapathology as "a rather formless malaise; we feel alone, helpless, meaningless, depressed, and despairing, but we cannot point to something and say, 'There! That person, or that object, is the cause of my feeling this way.'" Personally, I call this kind of existential angst the "metaphysical blues." To help you recognize the various metapathologies resulting from frustrated metaneeds, see Table 5.1.

existential frustration
According to Maslow, the resulting disquiet when metaneeds are blocked.

metapathology
A kind of existential frustration involving meaninglessness, loneliness and despair.

Table 5.1

Metaneeds or B-Values and Specific Metapathologies

Metaneeds or B-Values	Specific Metapathologies
1. Truth	Disbelief; mistrust; cynicism; skepticism; suspicion.
2. Goodness	Utter selfishness. Hatred; repulsion; disgust. Reliance only upon self and for self. Nihilism. Cynicism.
3. Beauty	Vulgarity. Specific unhappiness, restlessness, loss of taste, tension, fatigue. Philistinism. Bleakness.
4. Unity; Wholeness	Disintegration; "the world is falling apart." Arbitrariness.
4a. Dichotomy-Transcendence	Black-white thinking, either/or thinking. Seeing everything as a duel or a war, or a conflict. Low synergy. Simplistic view of life.
5. Aliveness; Process	Deadness. Robotizing. Feeling oneself to be totally determined. Loss of emotion. Boredom; loss of zest in life. Experiential emptiness.
6. Uniqueness	Loss of feeling of self and of individuality. Feeling oneself to be interchangeable, anonymous, not really needed.
7. Perfection	Discouragement; hopelessness; nothing to work for.
7a. Necessity	Chaos; unpredictability. Loss of safety. Vigilance.
8. Completion; Finality	Feelings of incompleteness with perseveration. Hopelessness. Cessation of striving and coping. No use trying.

Table 5.1

continued

Metaneeds or B-Values	Specific Metapathologies
9. Justice	Insecurity; anger; cynicism; mistrust; lawlessness; jungle worldview; total selfishness.
9a. Order	Insecurity. Wariness. Loss of safety, of predictability. Necessity for vigilance, alertness, tension, being on guard.
10. Simplicity	Overcomplexity; confusion; bewilderment, conflict, loss of orientation.
11. Richness; Totality	Depression; uneasiness; loss of interest in world. Comprehensiveness.
12. Effortlessness	Fatigue, strain, striving, clumsiness, awkwardness, gracelessness, stiffness.
13. Playfulness	Grimness; depression; paranoid humourlessness; loss of zest in life. Cheerlessness. Loss of ability to enjoy.
14. Self-sufficiency	Dependence upon the perceiver. It becomes his responsibility.
15. Meaningfulness	Meaninglessness. Despair. Senselessness of life.

Source: "Metamotivation (Table 1)" from *The Farther Reaches of Human Nature* by Abraham H. Maslow. Copyright 1971 by Bertha G. Maslow. Used by permission of Viking Penguin, a division of Penguin Putnam Inc.

application
exercise
5.1

5.7

Picture, Picture in the Book

Instructions: Below you see an illustration. Take a few seconds to look at it and then answer the questions that follow. Don't just describe what you see. Use your creative imagination to produce a detailed story.

Source: Adapted with permission of the Tests and Scoring Division, McBer and Company, 137 Nenbury St., Boston MA 02116.

1. What do you think is happening in this illustration?

2. What events could possibly have preceded this situation? Did something happen in the past? If so, what?

3. What do you believe the man in the picture is thinking? Does he want something? Does he need something? How does he feel?

4. Is something about to occur? What, exactly?

Volunteers may offer to read their stories to other members of the class.

Debriefing: The exercise you just completed is similar to a Thematic Apperception Test (TAT) originally developed by R. Murray. This test requires individuals to describe ambiguous pictures. If members of your class shared their stories with you, you can readily appreciate how ambiguous the photo is and, as a result, how many different interpretations can be given for it. In fact, there are no "correct" descriptions or interpretations. The idea is that people will project their own needs onto the content of the stories that they have created. The TAT is thus like a motivational inkblot test. By using it, you can begin to learn something about your own motivations. Maybe there is something in your story that reveals your underlying needs?

According to David McClelland (1962), people's needs are learned from the culture or society in which they're raised. Three of them emphasized by McClelland are the need for achievement, the need for affiliation and the need for power. The need for achievement captures the drive everyone has to excel, to rise above, to succeed or to achieve in view of some pre-selected standards of accomplishment or perfection. The need for affiliation is all about the desire to create and maintain interpersonal relationships that are friendly, caring and close. Finally, the need for power encompasses any individual's desire to make others behave in ways they would not have behaved without personal influence or control.

If you have high achievement motivation, your story may sound something like this one produced by a business executive.

> The man is an engineer working at his desk on a Saturday morning. The picture is of his family. He has a problem and is concentrating on it. It is merely an everyday occurrence—a problem which requires thought. How can he get the bridge to take the stress of possible high winds? He wants to arrive at a good solution to the problem by himself. He will discuss the problem with a few other engineers on Monday and make a decision which will be a correct one—he has the earmarks of competence.

If you have a high need for affiliation, your story may run along the lines of the one below.

> The engineer is at work on Saturday when it is quiet and he has taken time to do a little daydreaming. He is the father of the children in the picture. He has a happy home life and is remembering some tender moments with his wife and kids. He is also looking forward to getting home to see everyone. He plans, on the following day, Sunday, to use the afternoon to take his family for a short trip.

Finally, if you're highly motivated by power, your projected interpretation may read something like this scenario.

> We have an engineer or architect here. He is trying to establish the best way to present his plan at the design committee meeting coming up soon. He has to persuade committee members that his plan is the best. He believes that the force of his ideas will defeat any skeptics. He doesn't anticipate any difficulty putting to rest criticisms that might come up. He thinks that if he wins the day with his plan, then nobody will stand in his way as he moves up the corporate ladder.

Source: Adapted from "Business Drive and National Achievement" by David McClelland, *Harvard Business Review*, July/August 1962, pp. 99–112.

5.8 ## Choice Theory of Motivation

choice theory
A theory of human motivation developed by William Glasser.

The last model of motivation we'll consider in this chapter is William Glasser's **choice theory**. Glasser is a world famous psychiatrist and founding president of the Institute for Reality Therapy, now known as the William Glasser Institute. His motivational model of human behaviour provides us not only with therapeutic applications, but with educational, correctional and organizational ones as well. So whether you're training for a career in business, social work, allied health, education, or law and security, for example, you should find this treatment of choice theory helpful. (Note: in 1998, Dr. Glasser renamed his motivational model. It was formerly called control theory.)

Our Basic Needs William Glasser (1989) says, "Built into our genetic instructions, into the very core of our being, is a group of basic needs that we must satisfy continually." This group of **basic needs** includes

basic needs
Fundamental motivations that are genetically encoded.

1. The need to survive and reproduce.
2. The need to belong, love, share and cooperate.
3. The need for power.
4. The need for freedom.
5. The need for fun.

need to survive and reproduce
This need finds its biological roots in the most ancient part of our brain. Much of its activity occurs without us being aware of it. It sends messages to the newer part of the brain (the cerebral cortex) to get needs met by seeking the appropriate environment.

The Need to Survive and Reproduce

The **need to survive and reproduce** finds its biological roots in the most ancient part of our brain, which is located at the top of the spinal cord. Brain structures there keep our bodily machinery functioning and healthy. Vital operations such as breathing, digesting, perspiring and regulating blood pressure are controlled by this "old brain." Much of its activity occurs automatically, without us being aware of it. For instance, our immune systems go to work whenever foreign bacteria invade our bodies, and our heart rate goes up when we exercise to supply our greater requirements for oxygen.

With human biological evolution, a cerebral cortex or "new brain" has developed to help the old one meet needs. Suppose, for instance, that you haven't eaten for a long time. Your old brain will detect this lack of nutrient as a threat to your survival. Since the old brain is not the seat of consciousness, nor the initiator of any intentional behaviour, it sends what Glasser calls a "help me" signal to the new brain. In this case, the signal is recognized as hunger. Once recognized, our conscious new brain directs us to search for food. We are motivated to seek out in the environment that which will satisfy our basic survival need of hunger. The process works the same with thirst, air, sex and physical comfort.

William Glasser is the founder of reality therapy and president of the William Glasser Institute.

The Need to Belong

While it's easily recognized that the need to survive is basic and genetically programmed, Glasser argues that it's not prepotent in Abraham

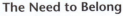

Maslow's sense. Survival needs can be and sometimes are overridden by other social needs, such as the **need to belong**. Glasser points out that most people who attempt suicide describe devastating loneliness as the reason. He concludes that "the need for friends, family, and love—best described as the need to belong—occupies as large a place in [your] my mind as the need to survive" (Glasser, 1989). Just as people are motivated or "genetically instructed" to eat and drink, so too are they directed to belong, love, share and cooperate.

need to belong

Just as people are genetically instructed to eat and drink, so too are they directed to belong, love, share and co-operate.

The Need for Power

For Glasser, everyday experience vividly demonstrates that people have a **need for power**. Wealthy individuals can sometimes spend a lot of money trying to get into positions of political influence. Managers may try to exert their power by getting subordinates to do what they otherwise wouldn't do. We constantly compare ourselves with others to see who's stronger, better, more attractive, richer or who lives in the more exclusive neighbourhood. As Glasser points out, while nonhuman animals struggle for power in terms of territorial behaviour, it is only humans who compete for power simply for the sake of power itself. History is a testimony to this; so too are contemporary "empire builders," whether they're found in government, business, politics, the battlefield or on the street.

need for power

One of the group of basic needs as identified by Glasser. For Glasser, everyday experience demonstrates clearly that people have a need for power. Human beings are the only species to desire power for the sake of power itself.

The Need for Freedom

As with power, the **need for freedom** is apparent everywhere. People will often say that they don't want to be tied down and don't want to be told what to do. Wars and revolutions are sometimes fought in the name of freedom and political liberty. People from ethnic and racial minorities frequently talk about the "struggle" that is really a name for their quest for freedom from oppressors. No matter where you go, it seems, somebody is searching for freedom. Life is virtually an endless struggle of removing obstacles, taking detours or coping with adversity so that we can eventually do what we want to do, when we want to do it.

need for freedom

One of the group of basic needs as identified by Glasser. People constantly seek to remove obstacles, take detours or cope with adversity so that we can eventually do what we want to do, when we want to do it.

The Need for Fun

By including the **need for fun** under the heading of basic needs, Glasser seems to take us away from some of the more traditional motivational theories. (Do you think the death instinct was fun for Freud?) Glasser notes that most of us do not feel as driven by this need as by the need for power, freedom or belonging, but he nonetheless believes that it is as much a basic need as any other (Glasser, 1989). He states, "I believe that fun is a basic genetic instruction for all higher animals because it is the way they learn." If you doubt this statement's truth, talk to any primary school teacher. I'll bet you that person often uses games and fun as a way of promoting learning. To support his claims, Glasser points to research done with female apes and monkeys. If they are isolated and deprived of normal social play in early development, they fail to learn even the simplest of social interactions, such as mothering their

need for fun

One of the group of basic needs as identified by Glasser. While he notes that most of us do not feel as driven by this need as by the need for power, he states that it too is a basic, genetic instruction for all higher animals because it is the way they learn.

Satisfying the need for fun can keep you feeling young.

offspring. Since humans are primates, research with monkeys and apes is highly suggestive. Glasser claims that forgetting how to play and have fun in life is a sign of mental deterioration, especially in older people (Glasser, 1989: 14).

Pictures in Our Minds

We have seen how, for Glasser, all of our basic needs are produced by genetics and biology. They are universal throughout the human species. What is not universal is how people satisfy their basic needs. At birth, infants do not know how to meet their needs. They feel uncomfortable, and instinctively cry and show other symptoms of distress. In time a child may begin to associate a particular face with food, physical comfort or security. A mental **picture** may be taken of the caretaker as an agent of need satisfaction. Once the child is mobile, he may seek out the caretaker whenever physical security or physical nourishment needs must be satisfied. If this occurs, we have evidence that a need-satisfying picture of the caretaker has been stored in what Glasser metaphorically refers to as the "picture album" in the child's head.

Everyone possesses a mental picture album. In that album we store images of what we want and things that have satisfied one or more basic needs in the past. These pictures are not exclusively visual. Our sensory apparatus makes for quite an extraordinary device that can record not only visual pictures, but also auditory, gustatory, olfactory and tactile pictures. Pictures are

picture
Visual, auditory, gustatory, olfactory and tactile images recorded by our sensory apparatus. Glasser believes that they serve as specific motivations for all we attempt to do with our lives.

196

important for Glasser because they serve as the specific motivations for all we attempt to do with our lives (Glasser, 1989). Throughout our lifetime, we probably develop hundreds, if not thousands, of pictures that satisfy an individual need.

The picture album of wants we put together begins to make up a selective part of our memories—the **ideal world** or **quality world** that we want right now. Glasser says that the power of pictures as a motivator for action is complete. Every day we make endless efforts to satisfy our wants. We may sometimes do what, in the estimation of others, are crazy and wild things in order to get what we want. We may even behave in ways that endanger our lives. The point is that pictures in our minds don't necessarily have to be rational or sane. They don't have to make sense. Someone may satisfy his need for power by trying to become recognized as the greatest mass murderer of this century; another may seek power by winning a college basketball championship. Different pictures and different wants take us in different directions to our commonly sought, ultimate destination of basic need satisfaction.

The pictures in our minds do not necessarily remain there forever. As we live our lives, we continually add and occasionally subtract pictures that are no longer satisfying. Sometimes this removal is necessary, especially in therapeutic situations. People sometimes develop unrealistic pictures of what they want and what would be satisfying. Getting what's currently wanted may be very difficult, if not impossible. If a spouse has died, for example, relying on that person to continue satisfying one's needs would make little sense. Memories are satisfying, but you can't build a satisfying life on memories. Another picture of a loving, caring person may have to be found and placed in the internal world if future belonging needs are going to be met. As people commonly say after a period of bereavement, "It's time to get on with my life." To live in the past (preoccupied with the picture of how life was) is counterproductive to living in the present.

Humans as Behavioural Control Systems: Taking Action

If what we're getting from life is roughly equivalent to what we want, we experience relatively little frustration, limited displeasure and we are more or less in effective control of our lives. However, to the extent that our perceptions of reality are radically different from what we want, as defined by pictures in our internal quality world, we experience pain and frustration. The greater the frustration, the greater the impetus or motivation to act. Our **behavioural system** is activated so that we can get what we want.

According to Glasser, when people are understood as behavioural control systems, we can better appreciate why they do the things they do. He imagines the human structure as very similar to a thermostat. When a

. . . life without a picture to satisfy the need to belong is really life without hope.
~William Glasser

ideal/quality world
According to Glasser, the quality world represented by the picture album of wants we put together to make up a selective part of our memories.

197

behavioural system
Our total behaviour comprising thinking, feeling, acting and our physiological reactions.

thermostat is set at 22 degrees and the air temperature is the same, the furnace sits idle. However, once the thermostat senses that the air temperature has dropped, instructions are sent to the furnace to turn on. Likewise, when people aren't getting what they want, they fly into action. Furthermore, just as thermostats turn off once the proper temperature is reached, so too do people stop behaving once they get what they want. For example, if you like sweet lemonade but the glass you just bought tastes sour, you can add a teaspoon of sugar. You taste the lemonade again. If it is sweeter but still too sour for your taste, you can add another teaspoon. You keep doing this until the lemonade is just the way you want it. At this point, you stop adding sugar. The behavioural system shuts down when your wants are satisfied.

As adults, we have during our lifetime placed many actions into our behavioural systems. Think of your behavioural system as the repertoire of actions you've accumulated over the years, actions that have proven to be need satisfying. We can call upon any action in our behavioural system at any time to satisfy our wants. Adding sugar is but one example of an action to rely on whenever you want to decrease sourness. (Someone else could add an artificial sweetener.) Unfortunately, we don't always have actions ready in our behavioural systems to deal with all our frustrated wants and emotional pains. If you're just breaking up with your first boyfriend or girlfriend, you've never encountered this situation before. You may not know how to behave. You need to care and be cared for, so what do you do? When previous behaviours don't work to satisfy our wants (e.g., calling to apologize, but having the apology rejected), newly organized behaviours have to be created to deal with the frustration and pain. The reorganized behaviours can seem silly or stupid to others; however, for the person engaged in them, they represent a best attempt at the time to get basic needs met.

Behaviour Is Total When it comes to behaviour, people often make what Glasser would consider illegitimate distinctions. For instance, people often separate how they think from how they feel, or how they feel from how they act, or how they act from how they function physically. For Glasser, thinking, feeling, doing and functioning physiologically are all interdependent parts of what he calls **total behaviour**. In any given situation, a particular aspect of behaviour (e.g., feelings) is dominant, but it's not divorced from all of the other components of total behaviour. For instance, if you are sad, what is the reason for your sadness? What are you thinking that is making you sad? Even if you are unable to articulate in precise terms the thinking behind the sadness, it doesn't mean that there's no thinking at all. Be sure, too, that the body is responding physiologically to sadness. It's a fact that sad and depressed people tend to get sick more often than happy people because their immune systems are affected by emotional states. Are you tired right now as you read? What if I informed you that you had just won $3.7 million? Chances are pretty good, I'll bet, that you'd suddenly wake up and feel energized. Thinking about your winnings would brighten you up fairly quickly. We see

total behaviour
According to Glasser, people often consider illegitimate distinctions when they attempt to separate how they think from how they feel, or how they feel from how they act. For Glasser, thinking, feeling, doing and functioning physiologically are all interdependent parts of what he calls total behaviour.

then how thinking and feeling can affect the body.

Conversely, body functioning can affect your thinking. How? Bodily fatigue and hunger affect your thinking and emotions. If you're like many, you probably get irritable, impatient or pessimistic when tired or hungry. Doesn't the world look a lot better after a nutritious meal and a good night's sleep?

To put total behaviour in choice theory context, Glasser posits that internal pictures of our wants steer our behaviours in certain directions. He uses the metaphor of a car to explain this idea. He says that basic needs are like the engine of an automobile because they provide the energy or motivational force for the vehicle. The wants act as the steering wheel that determines the direction the automobile will take. Thinking, feeling, acting and physiological responses serve as the wheels of transportation to get us to our destination and get us what we want. See Figure 5.3 for an illustration of the choice-theory auto.

Figure 5.3

Choice-Theory Auto

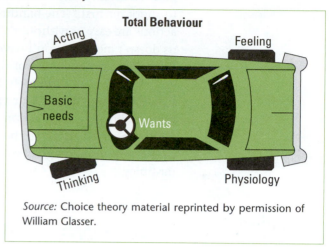

Source: Choice theory material reprinted by permission of William Glasser.

Behaviour as a Feedback Loop Once we behave in some fashion to get what we want, we then examine, either consciously or unconsciously, the consequences of our actions. We perceive the effects of our actions and then evaluate them. Some of our perceptions will turn out to be positive, some will be negative, while others will be neutral. How perceptions are evaluated depends on what's in our quality world. If we're getting what we want, the evaluation is positive. If our actions do not get us what we want, the evaluation is negative. If our actions have little or no impact on our wants, the evaluation is neutral. The point to underscore here is that internal values and wants determine whether our perceptions are appraised as good or bad. We keep behaving until we get what we want.

Glasser believes that human motivation has an internal locus of control. Pictures represent wants and wants are what propel us into action. Nothing in the real world makes us sad, glad or happy or forces us to do certain things. We are not like Pavlovian dogs automatically responding to stimuli. An insult (stimulus) may or may not affect us; it all depends on the value we place on it. If we value the opinion of the one who insulted us, we may be hurt (response). If we don't, the insult leaves us unaffected (another possible response). Similarly, a red light is not a stimulus event that automatically causes us to stop in response. In any emergency, we may choose to ignore the light to get to our destination more quickly, if this is what we want. People respond to wants, not to external stimuli. To illustrate this, let us take an extreme example: Even bandits can't force you to do anything. Glasser once related the story of someone who refused to surrender a wallet when held up at gunpoint. Defiantly, the victim said, "No, you can't have my wallet; you'll have to shoot me first." The bandit fled. Don't think, from this example, that all actions are easy or without risk. But just because someone is trying to coerce us doesn't mean we don't have choices. Our choices may be limited and difficult. The consequences of these choices may be mixed or unpleasant. In any event, we are ultimately in control. We choose what we want and we value what we choose. Our values filter our perceptions, and our internal pictures impel us into action. While what happens to us is sometimes beyond our control, how we choose to respond is our responsibility. Acceptance of this responsibility gives us freedom and power to determine our personal destinies.

application
exercise
5.2

The TBWA—Total Behaviour and Wants Analysis

5.10

This tool can be used to promote individual effectiveness through basic need satisfaction. It is a self-exploratory exercise based on William Glasser's choice theory of behaviour and human motivation. The TBWA will help you identify a current want and become aware of the actions you're taking to get what you want. It will also enable you to evaluate the effectiveness of your current actions and plan for future success in terms of getting what you desire. Follow the directions as described.

Step 1: Identify a Want
Consider an important want you currently have. It could be a thing, an ideal or a positive situation. If this step is difficult, think of what you dislike or don't want. If you got rid of what you don't want, what would you have? What you would have is in fact what you want. Once you've clearly established a want in your mind, write it below.

I want _____

Step 2: Describe Your (Total) Behaviour in Relation to Your Stated Want
In relation to my stated want above, what am I likely to be

Thinking: _____

_____

Feeling: _____

_____

Doing: _____

_____

Experiencing Physically: _____

_____

Step 3: Evaluate Your Total Behaviour

Given what I'm thinking, am I more or less likely to get what I want? Explain.

_____

_____

Given what I'm feeling, am I more or less likely to get what I want? Explain.

_____

_____

Given what I'm doing, am I more or less likely to get what I want? Explain.

_____

_____

Given what I'm experiencing physically, am I more or less likely to get what I want? Explain.

_____

_____

Now provide a summary evaluation of your total behaviour.

When I'm feeling physically and emotionally as I am, thinking what I'm thinking and doing what I'm doing, what's the result? How does my total behaviour affect what I want? Are my feelings, thoughts and actions helping or hindering me from getting what I want? Explain.

_____

_____

Step 4: Plan for Want Satisfaction

If my total behaviour is enabling me to get what I want, I am in more effective control of my life. If, by contrast, my total behaviour leads me to serious frustration, dissatisfaction, anger, depression or withdrawal, I am in less effective control of my life. In this case, I need to make some new behavioural plans and commit myself to following them. Even if my wants are somewhat satisfied, better planning can offer me even more need satisfaction and more effective control.

In broad terms, what new plan will I now make to get what I want?

_____

_____

What specifically will I do (today, tomorrow or in the next few days) to get what I want?

_____

_____

How could I sabotage my own plans? What excuses could I possibly make for not following them?

Will I accept my own excuses? Yes _____ No _____ Probably _____
Given my answer above, am I more or less likely to get what I want?

_____

_____

Am I fully committed, then, to getting what I want?

_____

_____

If I accept my excuses, if I am not fully committed to getting my wants satisfied, or if my total behaviour hinders me from meeting my basic needs, who is truly responsible for the resulting frustration? Who must change? Who must take alternative courses of action?

_____

_____

Debriefing: The TBWA process can be simplified using the acronym WDEP, which stands for

W — Wants: What do I want?
D — Doing: What am I doing?
E — Evaluation: Is what I'm doing helping or hindering me?
P — Planning: How must I plan for success?

The TBWA assumes that

- All human behaviours are internally motivated. We are not victims of the environment, socioeconomic circumstances or early childhood histories.

- A human is designed as a control system that operates in the world to satisfy wants or pictures of what is wanted at a given time.

- Human beings are responsible for their thoughts, feelings and actions. Behaviour is holistic and can be self-controlled. Actions, thoughts, feelings and physiological reactions are all part of the same total behaviour.

- At any given time, we are either in more or in less effective control of our lives.

- While wants vary from person to person and from time to time, basic needs remain the same.

- Personal and professional success in life requires that we gain more effective control.

(5.9) Emotions and Emotional Intelligence

It is with the heart that ones sees rightly. What is essential is invisible to the eye.
~Antoine de Saint-Exupéry

In the previous section we learned from William Glasser that emotions are very much related to motivation. They are also intimately related to what we think, how we act, and how we feel physically. Daniel Goleman is another contemporary researcher who has emphasized the importance of emotion in matters of personal adjustment and interpersonal effectiveness. Let us now explore what insights he has to offer us in our continuing efforts to master human relations.

As mentioned in the Introduction of this book, it comes as an unpleasant surprise to many college graduates that specialized knowledge and practical skills training alone are not enough to ensure vocational success. Studies have suggested that even one's IQ or intelligence quotient cannot reliably predict who will or will not succeed in life. Having a high IQ may contribute to academic achievement, but clearly living a successful life cannot be limited to this one outcome involving performance at school. Daniel Goleman writes: "When IQ test scores are correlated with how well people perform in their careers, the highest estimate of how much difference IQ accounts for is about 25 percent. A careful analysis, though, suggests a more accurate figure may be no higher than 10 percent, and perhaps as low as 4 percent...[A] study of Harvard graduates in the fields of law, medicine, teaching, and business found that scores on entrance exams—a surrogate for IQ—had zero or negative correlations with their eventual career success" (Goleman, 2000: 19).While this finding may leave some intelligent book-smart individuals feeling uneasy, it can also have the effect of providing hope for everyone, regardless of intellectual or scholastic ability. The problem is that focus on academic intelligence—the type emphasized in schools—offers little preparation for the vicissitudes of life (Goleman, 1997: 36). Daniel Goleman suggests that "emotional intelligence" matters immensely, more than IQ, when it comes to our personal destiny. He writes:

> Much evidence testifies that people who are emotionally adept—who know and manage their own feelings well, and who read and deal effectively with others people's feelings—are at an advantage in any domain of life, whether romance and intimate relationships or picking up the unspoken rules that govern success in organizational politics. People with well-developed emotional skills are also more likely to be content and effective in their lives, mastering the habits of mind that foster their productivity; people who cannot marshal some control over their emotional life fight inner battles that sabotage their ability for focused work and clear thought (Goleman, 1997: 36).

Highly influenced by Howard Gardner's (1985) book, *Frames of Mind: The Theory of Multiple Intelligences,* and the work of Yale psychologist Peter Salovey, Daniel Goleman has put together an **emotional competence framework**

emotional competence framework
A table consisting of personal and social emotional competencies.

204

Figure 5.4

The Emotional Competence Framework

Personal Competence	**Social Competence**
These competencies determine how we manage ourselves.	*These competencies determine how we handle relationships.*
Self-Awareness	**Empathy**
Knowing one's internal states, preferences, resources, and intuitions	*Awareness of others' feelings, needs, and concerns*
Emotional awareness: Recognizing one's emotions and their effects	**Understanding others:** Sensing others' feelings and perspectives, and taking an active interest in their concerns
Accurate self-assessment: Knowing one's strengths and limits	**Developing others:** Sensing others' development needs and bolstering their abilities
Self-confidence: A strong sense of one's self-worth and capabilities	**Service orientation:** Anticipating, recognizing, and meeting customers' needs
Self Regulation	**Leveraging diversity:** Cultivating opportunities through different kinds of people
Managing one's internal states, impulses and resources	**Political awareness:** Reading a group's emotional currents and power relationships
Self-control: Keeping disruptive emotions and impulses in check	**Social Skills**
Trustworthiness: Maintaining standards of honesty and integrity	*Adeptness at inducing desirable responses in others*
Conscientiousness: Taking responsibility for personal performance	**Influence:** Wielding effective tactics for persuasion
Adaptability: Flexibility in handling change	**Communication:** Listening openly and sending convincing messages
Innovation: Being comfortable with novel ideas, approaches, and new information	**Conflict management:** Negotiating and resolving disagreements
Motivation	**Leadership:** Inspiring and guiding individuals and groups
Emotional tendencies that guide or facilitate reaching goals	**Change catalyst:** Initiating or managing change
Achievement drive: Striving to improve or meet a standard of excellence	**Building bonds:** Nurturing instrumental relationships
Commitment: Aligning with the goals of the group or organization	**Collaboration and cooperation:** Working with others toward shared goals
Initiative: Readiness to act on opportunities	**Team capabilities:** Creating group synergy in pursuing collective goals
Optimism: Persistence in pursuing goals despite obstacles and setbacks	

Source: Daniel Goleman, Working with Emotional Intelligence, *New York: Bantam Books, 2000.*

which can be used to foster development in **emotional intelligence**, or **EQ** as it's being called (see Figure 5.4).The framework presents emotional intelligence as comprising a number of personal and social competencies which Howard Gardner dubbed "intrapersonal" and "interpersonal" intelligence respectively. The former involves the individual's ability to examine and know his own feelings, while the latter entails looking outward, toward the behaviour, feelings and motivations of others (Gardner, 1985: 240–241). In what follows, I will borrow heavily from **Daniel Goleman** as we explore the subcomponents constituting each type of intelligence.

emotional intelligence
The ability to know and manage one's own feelings, while reading and dealing effectively with others.

Daniel Goleman
Researcher and author of *Emotional Intelligence.*

5.10   Personal Competencies

Self-Awareness **Personal competencies**, as laid out by Goleman, determine how we manage ourselves. They include (1) **self-awareness**, (2) **self-regulation** and (3) **motivation**. With respect to the first, one could argue that self awareness—the recognition of how our emotions impact on what we are doing—is the fundamental emotional competence (Goleman, 2000: 55).Without this competence, we may allow our emotions to run wild, doing and saying things that we later regret. How many times have you witnessed people screaming in anger while simultaneously denying that they are angry at all? In such cases, there is clearly a lack of self-awareness regarding felt emotions. If people are unaware of their own feelings, they may be oblivious to their effects, both on themselves and others. Individuals could be eating themselves up inside with anger and repulsing others without even knowing it. They could be sabotaging themselves emotionally without the

personal competencies
Emotional competencies which determine how we manage ourselves.

self-awareness Conscious recognition of one's internal states, preferences, resources and intuitions.

self-regulation The process of managing one's internal states, impulses and resources.

205

slightest clue that something is wrong. "People who are unable to know their feelings are at a tremendous disadvantage. In a sense, they are emotional il-literates, oblivious to a realm of reality that is crucial for success in life as a whole, let alone work" (Goleman, 2000: 56).

Lack of emotional self-awareness may also cause us to suffer physically. Failure to become aware of our emotional discomfort may manifest in chronic headaches, anxiety attacks, lower back pain or other psychosomatic symp-tomatology. For healthier living, it is important, therefore, to become more aware of our feelings. They can serve as an inner barometer, helping us to gauge how things are going for us personally at any given time. If we don't know how we feel or, let's say, we suffer from **alexithymia**—a confused awareness of our emotional states—then our inner world becomes constricted in a fashion. Emotional states, whether benign or unpleasant, become blurred; nuances of emotion become elusive, and so we become unable to use our gut sense to guide our thinking and action (Goleman, ibid.: 57).

Feelings are related to values. By becoming more aware of our feelings, we may be better able to clarify to ourselves what matters most to us. If, for example, there is a discrepancy between what you are doing and what you actually value, what could arise is an "...uneasiness in the form of guilt or shame, deep doubts or nagging second thoughts, queasiness or remorse, and the like" (Goleman, ibid.: 58). By knowing your innermost self and following that inner sense of what is worthwhile, it's possible to minimize emotional disturbance. Being aware of how you feel and knowing what you value is especially important in working life. As Goleman (2000: 59) states, "The less aware of what makes us passionate, the more lost we will be. And this drifting can even affect our health; people who feel their work is repetitive and boring have a higher risk of heart disease than those who feel that their best skills are expressed in their work."

Those possessing a high degree of self-awareness display a second ca-pacity: **accurate self-assessment**. People exhibiting this competence are aware of their strengths and weaknesses; they are self-reflective and able to learn from experience. They are also receptive to honest feedback, to new perspectives on things and to continuous learning and self-development. In addition, those who are able to accurately self-assess typically show a sense of humour and perspective about themselves, not taking themselves too seri-ously. They know what inner resources and abilities they possess and are aware of limiting factors within themselves.

Psychological defensiveness is one thing that interferes with accurate self-assessment. We certainly don't mind taking credit for our successes; how-ever, more often than not we blame our failures on others or uncontrollable circumstances. Of course, it may sometimes be that our successes were really due to luck and our failures were in some part of our own making. In such cases, we all share a tendency toward denial, a defensive but emotionally comforting strategy protecting us from the distress that acknowledging the hard truth would bring.

alexithymia
A psychiatric term for peo-ple with a confused aware-ness of their own feelings.

Stars know themselves well.
~Robert Kelley

accurate self-assessment
Correct identification of one's strengths and limitations.

206

There are numerous factors militating against accurate self-assessment.[1] Robert E. Kaplan has identified some of the more common ones exhibited by otherwise successful executives. One is **blind ambition.** People suffering from this feel the need to compete at all costs. They have a tendency toward boastfulness and arrogance, exaggerating their own contributions. Others are often perceived in oversimplified terms—either as friends or foes.

blind ambition
An exaggerated desire to compete or achieve, even at the expense of others.

Highly successful people can also undermine themselves by lacking awareness of the fact that they set **unrealistic goals** for themselves and others, failing to appreciate what it takes to get the job done. Individuals who are relentlessly striving to achieve may become vulnerable to burnout, compulsively working at the expense of everything else in life. Those who are on the brink of burnout themselves may also drive others too hard; they may become insensitive to the emotional harm done to those others.

unrealistic goals
Target objectives that cannot be achieved.

Still another emotional blind spot is a failure to recognize one's **hunger for power.** In pushing our own personal agendas, we may exploit others to get our own way. This power-mongering could also manifest in a kind of insatiable need for recognition. If addicted to glory—with its attendant reputation and status—we may foolishly take credit for other people's successes and unjustifiably blame others for our personal setbacks. If we are preoccupied with appearances and the need to look good, we may distort reality and fall prey to the material trappings of success.

hunger for power
A desire for control or dominance often reflecting an insatiable need for recognition.

A final emotional blind spot identified by Kaplan deals with the **striving for perfection.** People who feel insecure about making mistakes may become enraged by criticism, whether it is warranted or not. They may refuse to admit failure, rarely confessing to having personal limitations. Think about your own experience with people who, in their own minds at least, are never wrong or overly confident about their abilities. Are such people individuals with whom you would prefer to associate? Are they more or less likely to enhance their life prospects? Would they stand to gain by becoming more self-aware regarding the impressions they make on others? The answers to these questions would all seem to suggest that developing emotional awareness is something very much in our own self-interest. To the extent this is true, what we learn from this insight is that we should value the opinions of others and want to hear how others perceive us. We can then use this information to engage in a process of continual self-improvement.

striving for perfection
An attempt to achieve flawlessness; sometimes accompanied by outrage at personal criticism.

Having examined several blind spots vis-a-vis accurate self-assessment, let us now consider another aspect of self awareness: **self-confidence.** People displaying this personal competence possess a strong sense of their self-worth. They believe in their skills and capacities, even if their skill levels do not always match their confidence levels. Individuals who exhibit self-confidence do not hesitate to express unpopular views; they don't mind going out on a

self-confidence
A strong sense of one's self-worth and capabilities.

---

[1]The ones mentioned here relate to a study done by Robert Kaplan and referred to by Daniel Goleman. See pp. 65-67, *Working with Emotional Intelligence.*

limb for what they believe is right. Self-confident individuals are able to make decisions, notwithstanding all of the uncertainties and pressures that might present themselves. As you engage in the process of self-reflection, in your efforts to master human relations, you should ask yourself how often you experience feelings of helplessness. Do you often feel powerless or are you ever paralyzed in your activities by self-doubt? If so, then you probably lack self-confidence.

While lacking self-confidence is not a good thing, neither is having excessive self-confidence. It's not good to be so overly self-confident that you come across as arrogant and brash. A proper level of self-confidence manifests itself in a strong self-presentation. Those exhibiting appropriate self-confidence project what might be termed "presence." This presence gives self-confident people charisma and the ability to inspire confidence in those whom they encounter. Self-confident people regard themselves as efficacious, able to take on new challenges. There is a readiness to master new skills and to take on new enterprises. Self-confident people have a tendency to compare themselves favourably with others and are undaunted by competition. What you also find is that self-confident people are decisive without appearing arrogant or defensive. This isn't to suggest that self-confident individuals are confident about everything. As Goleman (2000: 70–71) points out, our sense of self-efficacy is domain specific: "How well we think we can do on the job does not necessarily match how well we believe we might do in a parallel activity elsewhere in life."

Self-Regulation

Self-Control: A second major category of personal competence, with its own list of subcompetencies of emotional intelligence, is self-regulation—the ability to manage one's internal states, impulses and resources (Goleman, ibid.: 26). Certainly **self-control** is an important aspect of this regulation. It enables us to keep disruptive emotions and impulses in check. People who display this competence are able to manage their impulsive feelings and distressing emotions effectively. They are able to stay calm and composed even when confronted with personally challenging situations. Self-control involves the ability to think clearly and stay focused under pressure.

self-control
The ability to keep disruptive emotions and impulses in check.

Emotional self-control does not entail repression or denial of our true feelings. One could argue that feelings are feelings, they are not right or wrong in themselves. It's what we do with our feelings that makes them productive or damaging. Anger, for instance, may not necessarily be bad in all instances. It can serve as a powerful motivator, especially when it flows from the urge to right an injustice or to bring equity to an unfair situation. Anger at the sight of crime is what helps to maintain a law-abiding society. Even anxiety, if not too great, can be useful; it can sometimes heighten productivity and increase our creative insights and intuitions. Some people perform at their best "under pressure."

Emotional self-control should also not be equated with over-control. Over-control would simply stifle our feelings and extinguish our spontaneity. Surely joy, excitement, surprise and the like are emotional experiences which we would not wish to deny, suppress or extinguish. Research suggests, in fact, that over-control of the emotions can have negative physical, psychological and interpersonal consequences. For instance, when emotional suppression is chronic, it can impair thinking, undermine intellectual performance and disrupt smooth social interactions (James Gross and Robert Levenson, 1997: 106). Proper emotional self-control would have the opposite effects.

Trustworthiness and Conscientiousness The personal competency of self-regulation also contains what might be seen as moral or ethical components: **trustworthiness** and **conscientiousness.** Self-regulating people with this competency are able to maintain a high level of integrity, taking responsibility for their personal performance. Those individuals whom we would describe as trustworthy act ethically and are generally above moral reproach. Trustworthy persons manage to build trust on account of their reliability and authenticity. What you see is what you get. There are no phony fronts and no mind-games to be played. Furthermore, you can count on such people. They are reliable and dependable. When trustworthy people make mistakes, they admit them. They are also prepared to confront others guilty of unethical behaviour.

In addition to being trustworthy, people displaying a high degree of self-regulation are conscientious, able to meet their commitments and keep their promises. Such persons do not slough off responsibility, but rather hold themselves to account, even when objectives are not met. Conscientious people also tend to be organized and careful in their work.

If you wish to present yourself as credible, it is very much in your interest to maintain your personal integrity. Let people know what you value and how you feel. Stand up for your principles and don't dishonestly mask your intentions. If you become known as someone who often conceals important information or someone who fails to fulfill personal commitments, you will undermine the trust that others put in you—certainly not in your own self-interest. In the long run, morality pays!

Adaptability and Innovation Two more subcompetencies falling under the general heading of self-regulation include **adaptability** and **innovation.** In general, they involve remaining open to novel ideas and approaches and being flexible in response to change (Goleman, 2000: 95).

Innovative persons are certainly not creatures of habit. They actively seek out and develop fresh new ideas—if necessary, from a wide variety of sources. Rather than always doing things in the traditional, old-fashioned way, they often entertain original procedures or solutions to problems that might arise. A trademark of innovators involves their creative ability to achieve results. Innovative individuals possess a knack for simplifying complex problems, often by finding original connections or patterns that go unnoticed

trustworthiness
The personal competence of maintaining standards of honesty and integrity.

conscientiousness
Taking responsibility for personal performance.

adaptability
Flexibility in handling change.

innovation
Reflected by being comfortable with novel ideas, approaches and new information.

209

by others. Those lacking this emotional competence of innovation tend not to see the forest for the trees, missing out on the larger picture of any problem or situation. The failure to take a broader perspective can slow progress, as can the fear of risk, which may cause anyone to shy away from novelty. Unfortunately, those who are uncomfortable about taking risks often become the chronic critics and negativistic naysayers. Psychological defensiveness and an overly cautious stance toward life may cause these critics and naysayers to scoff at, and undermine, innovative ideas, however good they may be.

When we work in flow, the motivation is built in—work is a delight in itself.
~Daniel Goleman

Closely related to innovation is adaptability. If the old solutions no longer work and traditional ways of doing things are simply ineffective, then flexibility may be required. The rapid changes occurring in a modern society like ours necessitates that we stay flexible, smoothly handling multiple demands, shifting priorities and the like. You know you lack adaptability if you are haunted by fear or anxiety stemming from psychological discomfort with change.

Motivation A third general category of personal competence within the Emotional Competence Framework is motivation. Subcompetencies falling under motivation include achievement drive, commitment, initiative and optimism. It shouldn't be too surprising that emotional intelligence involves motivational factors given that the words "motive" and "emotion" both share the same Latin root, *motere*, meaning "to move." As Goleman (ibid.: 107) says: "Emotions are, literally, what move us to pursue our goals; they fuel our motivations, and our motives in turn drive our perceptions and shape our actions."

To better understand what "moves" you, it is useful to make a distinction between internal and external motivations. Things like grades, scholarships, incentives, reviews, promotions, stock options and bonuses, for instance, are examples of external motivators. They do motivate us, sometimes by helping us to "keep score" or monitor our progress. There certainly is satisfaction to be gained from the knowledge that we're progressing, improving or getting better, so attaining higher grades or earning sales bonuses become visible, external proof that we've achieved. Notwithstanding this, however, motivational experts have found that doing a job just for the pay, say, can ultimately leave individuals bored and frustrated. When financial survival is an issue, money may be enough as a motivator. Once low-level needs regarding (financial) security are met, however, money is often not enough to motivate someone. In this case, internal motivators become the most powerful. When one does a task not simply for its instrumental value (e.g., earning a paycheque, achieving required grades for admission) but for the pleasure entailed in it, upbeat moods can be fostered within happier and more interested individuals. On this account, it's preferable to do what you have a passion for, even if greater external rewards are found elsewhere. Evidence for this comes from a study of 700 men and women in their sixties who, when asked near the end of their careers what produced the most satisfaction at work, cited the creative challenge and stimulation of the work itself. Following this came pride in getting things done, developing friendships and mentoring or helping people on the job. Way down the list come status and financial reward.

Achievement Drive How motivated we are is often closely associated with our desire to achieve. This could translate into one's striving to improve or meeting a standard of excellence appropriate to a particular task or activity. Those with high achievement drive are results-oriented, displaying a high need to meet their stated objectives. They set challenging goals for themselves and are willing to take calculated risks. Another feature of achievement-driven persons is the energy they are willing to expend pursuing information and resources to do better or to work more efficiently. By contrast, those lacking this competence tend to be lackadaisical and unrealistic. They tend to look for the easy way out or else they set unrealistically ambitious goals for themselves.

Commitment It's almost become common sense to suggest that how successful and meaningful your life will be in the future depends on one's level of commitment, especially at work. Committed people are those who align their personal goals with the goals of a group or organization. If you're "on-board" with the business, company, institution or organization that employs you, you're more likely to make sacrifices or go the extra mile. Committed persons are able to find a sense of purpose in a larger mission. They actively seek out opportunities to fulfill the group's mission or the mission of the larger body to which they belong. Commitment is not something that can be dictated. It is emotional in nature. In work situations, some individuals regard themselves as "stakeholders," not just employees.

To build commitment, it is important to develop self-awareness. As Goleman (ibid.: 120) says: "Employees who know their own guiding values or purpose will have a clear, even vivid sense about whether there is a 'fit' with an organization. When they feel a match, their commitment is spontaneous and strong."

Initiative and Optimism Two more subcompetencies falling under the heading of motivation are **initiative** and **optimism**. If you are someone displaying initiative, then you're prepared to seize opportunities that present themselves. Often, you pursue goals and achieve them by going to the next level, as it were; you go beyond what's minimally required. While others do what's expected of them, you do that special extra.

Individuals with initiative tend to be more proactive, not reactive. While many of us only act when we have to or when external circumstances make unavoidable demands on us, those with initiative act before they are forced, often taking anticipatory action to avoid problems *before* they arise. Because of their anticipatory far-sightedness, they are able to take advantage of opportunities before they are visible to others.

The problem with being reactive and lacking initiative is that it puts one in a situation of always operating in crisis mode—falling behind and

initiative
Preparedness to go beyond what's minimally required without request.

optimism
A positive attitude related to resilience and hope.

211

constantly being forced to manage unforeseen emergencies. If people are always operating in a reactive crisis mode, it's possible that a sense of hopelessness could emerge. They may see themselves as helpless and victims of circumstance.

With all of the fear and uncertainty in the world, optimism is certainly an important emotional competence to develop. If you're always pessimistic or irrationally perceive gloom-and-doom scenarios in the future whatever the imagined case, you will wear heavily on yourself and others. Realism and pessimism are not always identical. On top of that, expectations of a better day or a better performance may play into a self-fulfilling prophecy created and realized by yourself. In any case, optimists tend to function with hopes of success, rather than fears of failure. Setbacks are perceived in terms of manageable circumstances, not evidence of fatal personal flaws.

Optimism is clearly related to hope. In view of whatever setback we experience, optimism and hope are what enable us to persist and bounce back. Optimistic people are distinguished by how they interpret their disappointments and failures. Such things are not the end of the world; rather lessons to be learned for the next time.

Mortals can keep no secret. If their lips are silent, they gossip with their fingertips; betrayal forces its way through every pore. ~Sigmund Freud

(5.11) ⋯⋯ ## Social Competencies

social competencies
The ability to read and handle the feelings of others.

empathy
An awareness and understanding of others' feelings, needs and concerns.

social skills
Abilities to effectively handle emotions in other people.

Empathy We've already learned that emotional intelligence involves not only personal but **social competencies** as well. In this section, we'll examine the importance of the latter in terms of building **empathy** and **social skills**. Let's begin with empathy.

Empathy is a notion that broadly refers to an awareness of others' feelings, needs and concerns. Empathic people are able to detect emotional clues that often go unnoticed by others. The ability to sense what others feel without their saying so is vital and captures the essence of empathy. These unspoken feelings may be expressed by someone's tone of voice, by his or her facial expressions or through other non-verbal indicators (see Chapter 9). Goleman describes empathy as a kind of social radar. As he puts it: "...empathy requires being able to read another's emotion; at a higher level, it entails sensing and responding to a person's unspoken concerns or feelings. At the highest levels, empathy is understanding the issues or concerns that lie behind another's feelings." (Goleman, 2000: 135).

The social competence of empathy involves a number of subcompetencies. Those who display empathy are able to understand others, develop others, leverage diversity and demonstrate political awareness.

Understanding Others If you exhibit an understanding of others, you can not only sense their feelings, but are able to adopt their perspectives and take active interest in their concerns. People possessing this competence are good listeners who can pick up on subtle emotional cues. Sensitivity is what enables them to see the world through another's eyes. A combination of this sensitivity and good listening skills permits empathic people to help others based on an understanding of others people's specific needs and feelings.

If one lacks the ability to understand others through active listening, one can appear uncaring or indifferent. Such a perceived attitude may then result in others becoming less communicative. If you truly wish to understand others, you will have to go beyond what is said by asking questions, restating in your own words what you hear them communicate and by asking others whether your restatement of their thoughts is accurate. This is what active listening is all about. Just sitting or standing still, passively—or, worse, impassively—absorbing someone's comments is not likely to further understanding of others.

Developing Others The social subcompetency of developing others is vitally important in situations of leadership. Whether you function as a parent, boss or organizational administrator, serving others' developmental needs and bolstering their abilities is crucial to success. Those who develop others take time to acknowledge and reward people's strengths and accomplishments. Criticism, both positive and negative, is given as useful feedback, not as harsh attack or disingenuous attempts to ingratiate oneself. The skill of developing others also involves mentoring, giving timely coaching and fostering a person's skills. Satisfaction comes from knowing that we have created the conditions and provided the helpful support for someone else to excel. Knowing that we had a small part to play in someone else's success can be a gratifying experience. The social payoffs can be enormous as well. Those mentored are likely to become more loyal and experience more satisfaction themselves. In work-related situations, this translates into lower turnover rates and greater degrees of trust. Empathic individuals concerned with developing others are genuine; their interest in those they guide and for whom they have empathy is real, without hidden agendas or other self-promoting intentions.

Service Orientation The social competence of empathy also involves an **other-centredness**—what in the business world is called a **service orientation**. Having this competency is what allows one to anticipate, recognize and meet the needs of others. In a retail situation, for example, a service-oriented sales associate would attempt to understand what customers need and then match those needs to services or products that are offered. Service-oriented salespeople try to build relationships, winning loyalty through increased customer satisfaction. Making a quick sale by manipulating people to buy things they don't really want or need for the sake of a sales commission is antithetical to the service-oriented spirit.

Those with a service orientation take the feelings of others to heart. They are able to de-centre from their own point of view, noting, for instance, signs of discomfort in response to suggestions. They are able to do this while expressing a friendly emotional tone. What service-oriented people do not do

other-centredness
A perceptual focus on another individual or group with the willingness to put that individual or group first.

service orientation
A psychological predisposition to anticipate, recognize and meet the needs of others.

213

is create an "us-versus-them" mentality where others are viewed as adversaries to be used and manipulated. The needs of the other become important concerns to be respectfully acknowledged, rather than summarily dismissed.

leveraging diversity
Using personal and group differences to everyone's advantage.

Leveraging Diversity Another aspect of empathy involves **leveraging diversity**. In today's pluralistic, multicultural world—one that seems to be shrinking in size with the continuing impact of globalization—learning to properly handle diversity may no longer be an option, but a requirement. History informs us only too well as to the damage done to individuals when others fail to appreciate their differences. Stereotypes can certainly have a disabling effect. Claude Steele (1997) has demonstrated this empirically. In one of his studies, he had college men and women who were skilled in mathematics solve problems taken from a graduate school qualifying exam. One half of the group was told the test usually revealed gender differences. The other half was told nothing. The findings indicated that women's scores turned out to be significantly lower than the men's, but only in the first half of the group—the half informed about gender differences. Those women in the second half of the group who weren't thinking in terms of gender issues performed as successfully as the men (Steele, 1997).When the same type of "threatening message" was given to black test-takers, the same performance-lowering effect occurred. Steel concluded that stereotypes about women and blacks (and presumably other groups) can give rise to debilitating anxiety, one that impairs personal performance. On this note, Goleman (2000) writes: "...people are particularly vulnerable to doubting their own abilities, questioning their talents and skills—thus undermining their own sense of capability. Their anxiety acts as a spotlight, both for themselves and (at least in their minds) those who are watching to see how well or how poorly they will do (Goleman, 2000: 157). If people are stereotyped and subjected to "rumours of inferiority" over extended periods, they may become intimidated, suffering emotionally and being adversely affected in many areas of life.

Of course, those who are visibly different or stereotypically defined must learn to overcome any negativity arising from other people's intolerance and bigotry—not an easy task and certainly not one that can be adequately dealt with here. On the other side of things, however, there are many things we can all do to leverage diversity to everyone's advantage. In developing this competence, we need to respect people regardless of their varied backgrounds. We need to better understand diverse world views and become sensitive to group differences. Rather than regard diversity as a threatening presence, we should try to seize the opportunities which diversity presents and make efforts to create environments where many different kinds of people can prosper. Whenever possible, we should challenge bias and intolerance, tying to become more open-minded and accepting. An important goal in leveraging diversity is achieving "success through others who are different from yourself" (Goleman, 2000: 158). There is strength, creativity and innovation in difference, things that in today's competitive world may yield a significant advantage. Simply put, one should be inclined to welcome diversity, not fear it, attack it, or withdraw from it. Effectively dealing with diversity is to your personal advantage.

Political Awareness Another social competency which is very much to your advantage to develop is **political awareness**. It is certainly useful when trying to achieve success, whether in institutional or corporate settings. Having political awareness involves being able to empathize on an organizational level, as well as on an interpersonal one. People who display this skill are able to accurately read key power relationships. They are in-tune to the political realities and dynamics vital to behind-the-scenes networking and coalition building. Those with political awareness display the ability to appraise situations objectively, free from personal distortions, biases and unfounded assumptions. This objectivity enables the politically astute to appreciate and balance the many and diverse perspectives of peers, bosses, subordinates, clients and competitors. Also, those who are politically aware recognize the implicit ground rules for what is acceptable and what is not within, say, the occupational setting. To empathize at an organizational level means that one is generally attuned to the climate and culture of the organization. Politically aware individuals are sensitive to the competing conditions and power struggles that exist. They perceive the political divides defining various alliances and rivalries. With this information, politically savvy people can better understand the underlying issues and what really matters to key decision-makers.

political awareness
Empathy at an organizational level.

In his discussion of political awareness, Goleman (2000: 162) provides a cautionary note. "Political animals" who play the game of organizational politics usually do so for purposes of self-interest and advancement. As a result, they may ignore information not pertinent to their personal agendas. They may also tune out the feelings of others around them except when they become relevant to their own ambitions. The result is that these political animals are often regarded as self-centred, uncaring and insensitive to others—things not conducive to furthering one's ambitions.

Goleman also points out, however, that simply ignoring or disdaining organizational politics can be a liability too. Without an appreciation of the politics of the situation, efforts to mobilize others or achieve one's goals will likely be misdirected or inept. As Goleman puts it: "...what's needed is a keen sense of the informal structure and the unspoken power center in the organization."

Everyone brings joy to others. Some when they arrive; others when they leave.
~Anonymous

215

Social Skills Social skills constitute the final broad subcategory within Daniel Goleman's emotional competence framework. They involve handling emotions effectively in *other* people. Those with social skill are adept at inducing desirable responses from others. They are masterful at transmitting emotional signals, making them powerful communicators, leaders who are able to sway their audiences. Goleman accepts as a primal fact that we all influence each other's moods, for better or worse. Using empirical evidence he argues that moods and emotions are "catching" and can be passed from one person to another like a virus. For example, in one study, three strangers volunteered for a study on mood. They were asked to sit quietly for two minutes. It was found that the most emotionally expressive person transmitted his or her mood to the other two over the course of the two minutes (Howard Friedman and Ronald Riggio, 1981). To the extent that emotions and moods are contagious, we are all interconnected, continually priming each others' emotional states, most notably with smiling. As Goleman points out, smiles are most contagious emotional signal of all. Smiling has a virtually irresistible power to make other people smile in return. Smiling, in itself, somehow primes the pump of positive feelings in others.

influence
A social skill enabling one to persuade others.

Influence One social skill of significant importance is the notion of **influence**. It involves using effective techniques of persuasion. Often, these techniques are not purely rational. A good sound argument may not always be enough to win people over. It's frequently necessary to appreciate what other kinds of appeals must be made to persuade others. A person needs to notice when rational arguments are falling on deaf ears and when emotional appeals can add impact. The one doing the persuading may have to bring passion to a project or proposal. That person may need to generate enthusiasm for outperforming a competitor. A social activist, for instance, might have to induce some moral outrage over some social injustice being perpetrated in society. By an expression of our own confidence, resolve and determination, we may try to elicit respect from our peers or an authority so that we may wield power more effectively. Purely rational techniques of persuasion may not always move the apathetic and fearful or those hostile and suspicious of our motivations. If we are to influence others, we must create the emotional climate which makes compliance and change possible. Failure to appreciate the feeling dimensions of decision making is to exhibit a kind of emotional illiteracy.

Those who are emotionally literate, by contrast, and adept at influencing people are able to sense or even anticipate audience reactions to their conveyed messages. Superior communicators know when a good argument is not enough and what must be done to effectively carry everyone toward an intended goal. This may involve impression management, a little drama, building coalitions or mustering behind-the-scenes or grass-root support. The idea here is that if you involve people in at least some of the steps of the process you're undertaking, they will become committed missionaries for you.

In his book, *Working with Emotional Intelligence*, Goleman discusses a number of obstacles which prevent one from being persuasive. These obstacles should be avoided, of course. You can undermine your own power of influence by failing to build coalitions; by developing an overreliance on familiar strategies, when occasions call for the use of new ones; by being bullheaded about promoting a point of view, no matter what the feedback; by failing to inspire interest; or simply by having a negative impact on others.

Communication People with a high emotional intelligence quotient are superior communicators. They are able to get the best out of people by eliciting their energy and creativity from them. Nobody likes to be shut out of conversations; people would rather be openly received and listened to. One study suggests that a full third of people's evaluations regarding whether or not someone is an effective communicator hinges on listening skills (Haas and Arnold, 1995). Does the individual ask astute questions? Is the person open-minded and understanding? Is he or she willing to seek suggestions without the presence of interfering preoccupations and interruptions?

Good communicators are able to regulate their moods. Regardless of one's mood—however elevated or depressed it might be—it's a good idea to remain cool and collected. Doing so leaves one in a better state of preparedness, ready to respond to any situation regardless of the circumstances. "Keeping our cool" also enables us to stay flexible in our own emotional responses. If we retain our composure, while others are losing theirs, we may give off a reassuring sense of self-control. People who are wildly tossed by their emotional states are often much less available and less able to respond to the demands of the moment.

Having good communication skills is not limited to extraverted, outgoing people. In fact, sometimes such people can be their own worst enemies. There are situations wherein communication effectiveness is negatively correlated with being highly extraverted. As Goleman points out, in posh executive retreat settings, outgoing and talkative staff are sometimes experienced as annoyingly intrusive. When and where people are looking for privacy, staff needs to be available, friendly and helpful, but otherwise inconspicuous (Stewart and Carson, 1995).Thus, on occasion, it's advantageous to underplay one's presence. Good communicators know when *not* to talk and when it's time to listen.

Conflict Management The topic of conflict management is something to which an entire chapter is devoted later in this book. Since, however, it represents one of Goleman's social skill competencies of emotional intelligence, we will briefly deal with it here before moving on.

According to Goleman, conflict management is all about negotiating and resolving disagreements. People possessing this competence are able to deal with difficult people and tense situations with diplomacy and tact. Whereas some individuals like a good fight, those skilled in this competency seek to de-escalate matters, while at the same time bringing disagreements into the open. Rather than repress conflicts or add fuel to the fires of animosity, good conflict managers try to orchestrate win-win solutions through open discussion and debate.

As a way of developing the skill of effective conflict management, Goleman offers the following suggestions: To cool down heated emotions

217

Leadership is giving energy.
~Birgitta Wistrand, CEO

in a conflictual situation we should first tune into our own feelings and express them clearly, but with sensitivity. This act will have a calming effect. There's something emotionally cathartic about saying what's on our minds or telling others what's troubling us. At the same time as we express our concerns, we should also display a willingness to work things out with the other parties involved. Again, we don't wish to escalate differences with more aggression. Thirdly, it's important that viewpoints be stated in neutral language, one which avoids an argumentative tone. In the end, the objective is to find fair solutions or equitable ways of resolving the dispute at issue, ones that each of the conflicting parties embrace. Such results constitute what's called "win–win solutions" (see Chapter 10).

Leadership As with conflict management, leadership is also an important topic which receives greater in-depth attention in a later chapter. But because, again, it is one of Goleman's social skills belonging to his emotional competence framework, we will briefly discuss it here as a prelude of what's to come.

Individuals with leadership skills are able to inspire and guide. People possessing this competence lead by example. They are able to generate enthusiasm and clearly articulate shared visions and mission statements for whatever company, organization, group or institution with which they are affiliated. One doesn't have to be a president or chief executive officer to lead. Anyone can display leadership qualities—what is needed is that the person be willing to step forward when called upon.

In today's complex changing world, the art of leadership often relates to *how* a person implements change, not the change itself. Skillful leaders are sensitive to undercurrents of emotion and are able to recognize how their decisions affect people psychologically and at an emotional level. Leaders who can sense collective, but unspoken, feelings, and articulate for the group or people involved, establish their credibility and demonstrate that they understand the concerns of those they lead. Once leaders are able to show they understand, it's easier for them to spark people's imaginations and inspire them to move in a desired direction. As Goleman suggests, it takes more than simple power to motivate and lead.

Effective leadership in the emotional domain is *not* about faking sensitivity and concern. If one wishes to inspire and move others, the feelings must be genuine. To be a charismatic messenger, the leader must behave on the basis of authentic belief (Wasielewski, 1985). Really believing in the emotional message is what distinguishes the charismatic leader from the self-serving manipulative one.

In covering leadership, Goleman points to a number of common feelings. One deals with assertiveness. Some leaders are less effective than they could be because they fail to be emphatically assertive when necessary. Sometimes action is required and the leader may be the one to initiate it. Lack of assertiveness may be viewed by some as lack of confidence or ability.

Sometimes leaders are guilty of passivity. They may be more concerned with being liked than with getting the job done right. Unfortunately, giving priority to being liked means that one is prepared to tolerate poor performance, rather than confronting it productively.

Change Catalyst People who have a high emotional quotient or high EQ are able to initiate and manage change. They display the courage to challenge the status quo when it's recognized that there's a need for change. Rather than become paralyzed by fear or enslaved by routine, effective change catalysts remove obstacles and become champions of change, enlisting others in its collective pursuit.

Change catalysts have to be passionate about the change they embrace. For them, change takes on the quality of a mission. They accept the task of modelling the change expected of others. This requires that effective change leaders develop deep commitments and high levels of motivation. To make change happen, leaders must be optimistic, while remaining realistic and having an instinct for organizational politics.

Goleman talks about the change catalyst in the context of *transformational leadership*. He says that transformational leaders are able to rouse people through the sheer power of their enthusiasm. Rather than order or direct people, they choose instead to inspire. We find that transformational leaders are both intellectually and emotionally stimulating in articulating their visions of how things could or should be. Certainly, they are committed to nurturing relationships with those they lead, often appealing to people's sense of meaning and value. Goleman (2000: 196) writes: "Work becomes a kind of moral statement, a demonstration of commitment to a larger mission that affirms people's sense of sharing a valued identity."

Building Bonds Another aspect of emotional intelligence involves the ability to nurture instrumental relationships, that is, to bring people together in order to achieve specific targeted ends. In essence, this is a talent for social coordination. People with high EQ in this area are able to create psychological closeness, nurturing feelings of trust. Bonded individuals are "sympatico," as it were, and even when they go off in separate life directions, they still remain in touch. Remaining in touch helps to build networks of personal contacts that produce a kind of personal capital or reservoir of good will and trust which we may wish to dip into at some later date.

For people who are shy or introverted by psychological type, cultivating relationships will be especially challenging. Reclusive individuals and withdrawn introverts must learn to initiate contact and extend invitations to others, not simply sit back and wait for them in a state of relative passivity. Conversations must go beyond work-related matters. Time spent together may sometimes have to occur socially if those socially less adept truly wish to enlarge their web of relationships.

People sometimes fail to build bonds because they are overly protective of their work time and personal agendas. They may consequently turn down most requests to help or work cooperatively. This can build resentment in others and therefore stunt relationships. What "bond-builders" are able to do is balance their own work responsibilities with carefully chosen favours to others. They are thereby able to build goodwill accounts with other individuals who become important resources later (Kelly, 1998). This goodwill should not be achieved in any strained or artificial way. It hinges on empathy and emerges naturally during the course of casual interactions and conversations about family, sports, children, and all the other everyday things of life.

Collaboration and Cooperation Very closely related to building bonds are notions of collaboration and cooperation. These things involve working with others toward shared goals, not just one's own personal objectives. "Cooperative collaborators" are adept at balancing goal-achievement with attention to relationships. They easily collaborate, sharing plans, information, and resources. Contrast this with others who are a little stingy about sharing such things or even their ideas. It's difficult to work together with people who are psychologically distant and retentive. It is therefore important to practice promoting a friendly cooperative climate wherever you are. Try to identify and nurture opportunities for collaboration.

Groups of individuals who share, cooperate and collaborate on projects are likely to be more emotionally resilient. As Goleman points out, groups that enjoy life and have fun together—who enjoy each other's company and who can joke together and share good times—amass the emotional capital not just to excel in good times, but survive the difficult times as well. Groups that have not developed emotional ties are more likely to fall prey to paralysis or become dysfunctional and disintegrate under pressure. Emotional bonds are certainly crucial to morale and effectiveness in many social situations.

Team Capabilities The last social competency comprising emotional intelligence involves the ability to create **group synergy** in pursuing collective goals. Individuals possessing this competence are able to build team identity and commitment. They share credit with the group to which they are affiliated; they do not simply grab it for themselves. Team players are able to draw others into active and enthusiastic participation within the group. They model qualities such as respect for others, helpfulness and cooperation.

Daniel Goleman suggests that the "team achievement" outlook constitutes a shared competitive drive, strong social bonds, and confidence in one another's abilities (Goleman, 2000: 218). Anyone with team skills is competitive, but evenhanded in matching people to the best role given their talents. Team players have a strong affiliative need, simply liking people for their own sake. This need, in turn, makes them better able to manage conflicts and help others to offer mutual support. This has a harmonizing effect for everyone involved. Power, when exerted, is not used in an intimidating way or purely out of self-interest, but rather in the interests of the group.

None of us is as smart as all of us.
~Proverb

group synergy
The activity, energy and superior performance which results when individuals cooperate in pursuit of common goals.

220

In speaking about "Star Teams," Goleman (2000: 219) says: "As with individuals, so with groups." He suggests that what sets star teams apart from mediocre or dysfunctional ones has much to do with their emotional competence. Someone with good team capabilities needs to be able to build the following emotional competencies into the group. Star teams display:

- empathy or interpersonal understanding
- cooperation in a unified effort
- open communication, setting explicit norms and expectations
- a drive to improve
- self-awareness, recognizing their strengths and weaknesses as a team
- initiative and proactive tendencies
- self-confidence as a group
- flexibility in how they go about their collective tasks
- organizational awareness
- a desire to reach out and build bonds to other teams within any organization, company or institution

It's easy to see when teams are in trouble. Healthy debate is transformed into open warfare. Disagreements are expressed as thinly veiled personal attacks. Discussing points of disagreement becomes an exercise in political gamesmanship or intellectual grandstanding. When groups go off-track, they lose sight of their mission and their common bonds and they become poisoned by distrust and acrimony. Someone with team capabilities is able to limit all of this, creating a positive group synergy, the accomplishments of which are greater than any one individual.

Study Guide

Key Terms

motivation (175)
conscious and unconscious motivation (176)
external locus of control (177)
internal locus of control (177)
psychoanalytic theory (177)
energy model (180)
homeostasis (180)
nirvana principle (180)
pleasure principle (180)
eros (180)
libido (180)
thanatos (181)
aggression (181)
catharsis (181)
Abraham Maslow (183)
hierarchy of human needs (184)
actualize (184)
prepotency (185)
physiological needs (185)
safety and security needs (185)
social needs for belonging and love (186)
esteem needs (186)

cognitive needs (187)
aesthetic needs (187)
self-actualization needs (188)
metamotivation (189)
being motivation (189)
deficiency motivation (189)
existential frustration (190)
metapathology (190)
choice theory (194)
basic needs (194)
need to survive and reproduce (194)
need to belong (195)
need for power (195)
need for freedom (195)
need for fun (195)
picture (196)
ideal world (197)
quality world (197)
behavioural system (197)
total behaviour (198)
emotional competence framework (204)
emotional intelligence (205)
Daniel Goleman (205)
personal competencies (205)

self-awareness (205)
self-regulation (205)
motivation (205)
alexithymia (206)
accurate self-assessment (206)
blind ambition (207)
unrealistic goals (207)
hunger for power (207)
striving for perfection (207)
self-confidence (207)
self-control (208)
trustworthiness (209)
conscientiousness (209)
adaptability (209)
innovation (209)
initiative (211)
optimism (211)
social competencies (212)
empathy (212)
social skills (212)
other-centredness (213)
service orientation (213)
leveraging diversity (214)
political awareness (215)
influence (216)
group synergy (220)

Fill-in-the-Blank Questions

Progress Check **5.1**

Instructions: Fill in each blank with the appropriate response from the list below.

emotional intelligence
motivations
healthy
hierarchy of human needs
personal competencies
thematic apperception test
total behaviour
locus of control
aesthetic needs
instinct
pictures
empathy

moral components
nirvana principle
prepotency
vicarious consequences
basic needs
thermostat
metamotivations
alexithymia
desirous
thanatos
accurate self-assessment
other-centredness

1. Human behaviour can have conscious and unconscious _____.

2. Debate as to whether behaviour is motivated internally or externally centres on the notion of _____.

3. The _____ is a Freudian concept used to explain how people are motivated to reduce disturbing tensions and excess stimulations in their lives.

4. A(n) _____ has its source in some bodily need or deficit.

5. _____ is another name for the death instinct.

6. Abraham Maslow's humanistic account of motivation is based on the study of _____ individuals.

7. To be human is to be continually _____ of something.

8. According to Maslow, human behaviour is motivated by a(n) _____.

9. In Maslow's scheme, needs possess a _____. Lower ones must be satisfied before higher ones.

10. The requirement people have for such things as beauty, symmetry and elegance points to our _____.

11. Self-actualized persons are not without needs. They are driven by _____ or B-values.

12. _____ matters more than IQ when it comes to vocational success.

13. "Self-awareness" is something that falls under David Goleman's category of _____.

14. _____ is the condition which causes a confused awareness of our emotional states.

15. Blind ambition, unrealistic goals, hunger for power and striving for perfection are factors which militate against _____.

16. Trustworthiness and conscientiousness are _____ of emotional intelligence.

17. The ability to sense what others feel without their saying so captures the essence of _____.

18. If you anticipate, recognize and meet the needs of others, you display _____.

19. The _____ can be used to determine people's needs for achievement, power and affiliation.

20. According to William Glasser, all human behaviour is internally motivated by _____.

21. In choice-theory terms, people develop motivating _____ of what they want, which in turn satisfy what they basically need.

22. Glasser is opposed to stimulus-response accounts of behaviour. His choice theory holds that human behaviour is regulated more like a _____.

23. A choice-theory account of motivation does not completely separate thinking and feeling or doing and physiological reactions. They are all seen as related parts of _____.

True/False Questions

Instructions: Circle the appropriate letter next to each statement.

T F   1. There are two kinds of people, motivated and unmotivated.

T F   2. When it comes to motivation, we always know why we do the things we do.

T F   3. People with a high internal locus of control see themselves as self-governed.

T F   4. The Freudian nirvana principle states that the human organism functions to reduce tension and excitations.

T F   5. Aggressive acts can serve as a catharsis.

T F   6. Abraham Maslow is a behaviourist.

T F   7. According to Maslow, lower-level needs are prepotent with respect to self-actualization needs.

T F   8. Maslow's theory explains why it is wrong never to be satisfied with what one has.

T F   9. B-values act in the same way as needs, only on a lower plane.

T F 10. For William Glasser, the need to survive is prepotent as compared with the need to belong.

T F 11. Choice theory was developed to help people take control over others.

T F 12. The instinct of *eros* deals exclusively with sexuality.

T F 13. Like Freud, Abraham Maslow based his studies on neurotic patients.

T F 14. Self-actualized people tend to have deep relationships with lots of people.

T F 15. David Goleman developed the idea of multiple intelligences.

T F 16. Self-awareness, self-regulation and motivation are examples of personal competencies within the emotional competence framework.

T F 17. "Presence" gives self-confident people charisma and the ability to inspire confidence in others.

T F 18. One who is able to use psychological, cultural and linguistic differences to his or her advantage knows how to leverage diversity.

T F 19. Moods and emotions are "catchy" and can be passed from one person to another like a virus.

T F 20. Influence has nothing to do with persuasion.

Summary

1. What can be said generally about the nature of motivation?
   - everybody is motivated
   - it can be conscious or unconscious
   - the locus of motivational control may be internal or external

2. What does Sigmund Freud say about human motivation?
   - personality is driven by instinctual energy
   - instincts belong either to *eros* (life) or *thanatos* (death)
   - behaviour is based on nirvana and pleasure principles
   - instincts must be sublimated for acceptable social expression
   - aggression and sexuality are two powerful motivations in everyone's life

3. How does Abraham Maslow conceptualize motivation?
   - people are driven by needs
   - needs are found on a hierarchy
   - lower-level needs must be satisfied before higher-level needs become potent motivating forces
   - humans can be classified as "wanting animals"
   - once lower-level D-needs are satisfied (e.g., survival and esteem), higher-level B-motivations kick into operation (e.g., the need for truth, beauty and goodness)
   - failure to live by B-motivations can lead to metapathologies

4. How does William Glasser conceptualize motivation?
   - everyone is motivated
   - motivation ultimately stems from basic need satisfaction
   - needs give rise to wants represented by motivating mental pictures
   - when wants are frustrated, people are motivated to act

- behaviour is not a mechanical response to stimuli; it works in the same way as a control system or thermostat
- behaviour is energized when wants go unsatisfied
- we are ultimately in control of our behaviour, the motivating pictures we place in our mental picture albums, and we are responsible for how we choose to respond to people, situations and events in our lives
- people are either in more or in less effective control of their lives

5. What competencies are associated with emotional intelligence?
There are two broad categories: Personal and Social
Personal competencies include: self-awareness, self-regulation, and motivation
- Self-awareness: emotional awareness, accurate self-assessment, self-confidence
- Self-regulation: self-control, trustworthiness, conscientiousness, adaptability, innovation
- Motivation: achievement drive, commitment, initiative, optimism
- Social competencies include: empathy and social skills
- Empathy: understanding others, developing others, service orientation, leveraging diversity, political awareness
- Social Skills: influence, communication, conflict management, leadership, change, building bonds, collaboration, cooperation and team capabilities.

Related Readings

Freud, Sigmund (1973). *New Introductory Lectures on Psychoanalysis*. London: Penguin Books.

Glasser, William (1981). *Stations of the Mind: New Directions for Reality Therapy.* New York: Harper & Row.

Maslow, Abraham (1968). *Toward a Psychology of Being.* Van Nostrand Reinhold Co.

Rathus, Spencer and Jeffrey Nevid (1992). *Adjustment and Growth: The Challenge of Life*, 5th edition. Fort Worth, TX: Holt, Rinehart and Winston.

Are you... Stressed out and sleepless in Saskatchewan? Nervous in Nova Scotia, New York, Newfoundland, or Nunavut? Terrified in Tennessee? Quivering in Quebec? Yowling in the Yukon? Anxious in Alabama? Burned out in British Columbia? Manic in Missouri? Peeved in Prince Edward Island? Or, obsessed in Ontario? Don't worry, be happy!...Stress is in the mind of the beholder.

~I.M. Nervus

Stress and Lifestyle Management:
Good News for Jitterbugs and Adrenalin Junkies

Chapter Overview

Stressed Out About School?

The Nature of Stress

Understanding Stress in Terms of Stressors

- Life-Event Stressors
- Occupational Stressors
- Psychological Stressors
- Daily Hassles

Stress as a Response: General Adaptation Syndrome (GAS)

- The Alarm Reaction
- The Resistance Phase
- The Exhaustion Stage
- Self-Diagnostic 6.1 Stress...Let Me Sum It Up!

Distress Versus Eustress

Stress as an Interaction

Ways to Cope with Stress: Effective and Ineffective Strategies

- Coping Strategies with Limited Effectiveness
- Effective Coping Strategies
- Self-Diagnostic 6.2 How Is My Current Thinking Contributing to My Personal Stress?

Application Exercise 6.1
Practice in Cognitive Coping

Application Exercise 6.2
Achieving Calm Through Focused Attention

Study Guide

- Key Terms
- Progress Check 6.1
- Summary
- Related Readings

Learning Outcomes

After successfully completing this chapter, you will be able to

(6.1) Explain the nature of stress from three theoretical perspectives

(6.2) Gauge your stress level using Holmes and Rahe's Social Readjustment Rating Scale

(6.3) Determine if, and to what extent, stress is affecting your academic performance

(6.4) Distinguish between stress and eustress

(6.5) List and describe effective and ineffective strategies to cope with stress

(6.6) See to what extent your thinking style is contributing to your personal stress levels

(6.7) Practise cognitive strategies for coping with stress

(6.8) Use meditation for purposes of stress reduction

Focus Questions

1. Do students have a relatively stress-free life compared with other adults? Explain.
2. What is meant by saying that stress is a response?
3. How can stress be understood as an interaction?
4. Is stress simply caused by stressors? Please explain.
5. How is personality related to stress?
6. What is the physiology of stress as described by researchers such as Hans Selye?
7. Is all stress bad? Why or why not?
8. What are some ineffective ways to cope with stress?
9. What are some effective coping strategies?
10. How does Albert Ellis help us to manage stress?
11. How is thinking style related to stress?
12. What is cognitive reframing?
13. How is autogenic training similar to and different from meditation?
14. What can be learned about stress management from William Glasser?

Stressed Out About School?

Imagine this scenario: You just woke up in response to your neighbour's barking dog. Looking at your clock, you realize your alarm did not go off. As you leap out of bed, you remember that you have a test to write in precisely one hour. School is a 65-minute drive away. Skipping breakfast and your daily shower, you feverishly start to dress, only to discover stains on both sleeves of your sweater. Hurrying to gather your books together, you jump into your car. In disbelief, you discover the battery is dead. You ask your mom if you can use her car. She says okay, but then you find that you're riding on empty. You stop at a service station and use your last five dollars to buy gas— so much for lunch! Once you get back on the road, you see that cars are lined up bumper to bumper and you learn that all possible detours are under construction. Eventually, you make it to class only to get blown away by your instructor, who lectures you on the virtues of punctuality. So, in view of all this, may I ask how are we feeling today?

Contrary to what some people may think, student life is not always simple and easy, as the example above illustrates. Students really don't have it easy and, like everyone else, they experience stress stemming from the demands of everyday life. In what follows, we'll look at the nature of stress, its contributing factors, its consequences and what you can do to handle it. Being able to deal with stress in constructive ways will help you to live a more productive and satisfying life. Also, learning to understand and manage your stress will help you to function better socially and interpersonally. Like defensiveness, stress is a "noise" factor in interpersonal communications. If you're stressed, you're probably not listening very attentively to others as you're probably preoccupied with your own worries, concerns and anxieties. You may simply miss a lot or you might misinterpret the intention of what was said given your agitated state of mind and body. If you want to listen effectively and properly understand what people mean to say, it's to your advantage to remain calm and receptive. This state can be achieved by methods of stress management, something we'll get to shortly.

As long as man is capable of anxiety, he is capable of passing through it to a genuine human destiny.
~Northrop Frye

(6.1) ···· ## The Nature of Stress

stress
Definitions may come from three different perspectives, the stressor, the response or the interaction between the stimulus event and the individual experiencing it.

Stress is an experience that many of us know intimately, yet it is difficult to explain. A review of the literature on stress indicates that definitions of it tend to come from three different perspectives. Some researchers explain stress from the viewpoint of the *stressor* itself. This viewpoint operates on the assumption that there are stimulus events in the world that cause stressful responses in people. By contrast, a second perspective focuses on stress in terms of *responses*. From this perspective, the stress is not in the stressor, but in the reactions of the individual experiencing it, whether they be emotional, psychological or behavioural. Finally, a third perspective conceptualizes stress in terms of an *interaction* between the stimulus event and the individual experiencing it. Between the stressor and the stressful reaction comes the perception and cognitive appraisal of the person. Whether or not a stressor is perceived and experienced as stressful depends on what the person thinks about it. Later we'll look at the importance of cognitive appraisals as we learn how thinking styles can affect how well we cope with stress. Until then, let's get back to the business of defining stress itself.

Understanding Stress in Terms of Stressors

The first perspective on stress research to be discussed emphasizes the role of stressors. **Stressors** can be classified in different ways. For our purposes here, let's categorize them under four headings: life-event stressors, occupational stressors, psychological stressors and daily hassles.

Life-Event Stressors

6.2

Holmes and Rahe's research (1967) suggests that **life-event stressors**, or various life changes and events, can create stress within individuals. Their findings indicate that as the number of significant life changes increases (what they call LCUs or life change units), the risk of illness grows. They have found that people can suffer ill effects from stressors for as long as one year after their initial appearance. To help us assess the stress potential of various events in our lives, Holmes and Rahe have constructed what they call the social readjustment rating scale (see Table 6.1).

You might wish to check off those items that pertain to you and add up your score using the values attached to each. If your score is somewhere between 150 to 199, you are probably experiencing a mild life crisis right now. A score between 200 and 299 reflects the likelihood of a moderate crisis, and any score over 300 points, a major crisis. (These norms take into account differences in age, sex and race.)

Occupational Stressors

If you're a typical college or university student, chances are pretty good that you have a part-time job. If you do, there's probably no great need to point out that work can be stressful and that you face **occupational stressors**.

stressors
Those situations or events that may potentially cause stress, which may be categorized as follows: life-event stressors, occupational stressors, psychological stressors and daily hassles.

life-event stressors
The various life changes and events that can create stress within individuals. According to Holmes and Rahe as the number of significant life changes increases, the risk of illness grows.

To be totally without stress is to be dead.
~Hans Selye

231

occupational stressors
Work-related stressors including the physical environment, interpersonal relationships and technology.

Table 6.1

Social Readjustment Rating Scale

Rank Value	Life Event	Mean
1	Death of spouse	100
2	Divorce	73
3	Marital separation	65
4	Jail term	63
5	Death of close family member	63
6	Personal injury or illness	53
7	Marriage	50
8	Fired at work	47
9	Marital reconciliation	45
10	Retirement	45
11	Change in health of family member	44
12	Pregnancy	40
13	Sex difficulties	39
14	Gain of new family member	39
15	Business readjustment	39
16	Change in financial state	38
17	Death of close friend	37
18	Change to different line of work	36
19	Change in number of arguments with spouse	35
20	Mortgage over $10 000	31
21	Foreclosure of mortgage or loan	30
22	Change in responsibilities at work	29
23	Son or daughter leaving home	29
24	Trouble with in-laws	29
25	Outstanding personal achievement	28
26	Wife begins or stops work	26
27	Begin or end school	26
28	Change in living conditions	25
29	Revision of personal habits	24
30	Trouble with boss	23
31	Change in work hours or conditions	20
32	Change in residence	20
33	Change in schools	20
34	Change in recreation	19
35	Change in church activities	19
36	Change in social activities	18
37	Mortgage or loan less than $10 000	17
38	Change in sleeping habits	16
39	Change in number of family get-togethers	15
40	Change in eating habits	15
41	Vacation	13
42	Christmas	12
43	Minor violations of the law	11

Source: Reprinted with permission from *Journal of Psychosomatic Research*, Vol. 11, pp. 213–218, Holmes and Rahe, "The Social Readjustment Scale," 1967, Elsevier Science Ltd., Pergamon Imprint, Oxford, England.

Consider the physical environment in which you work. Fluorescent lighting, excessive noise, uncomfortable temperatures and stale air are all factors that can act as stressors. Perhaps your boss is unreasonable. Maybe he overworks you, issues conflicting demands, doesn't specify clearly what should be done or somehow places you in a compromising position of role conflict. At work you might also experience difficulties with your fellow employees, or with those working under your authority. Bad interpersonal relations can be stressors indeed. Finally, at the beginning of the twenty-first century, rapid technological advances have also become stressors. We may be given little opportunity to do things for any period of time in any kind of stable, established ways. New technologies and continually updated software programs may almost always keep us vigilant and on our toes, ready for the next required adjustment. In this kind of environment, people fear "falling behind."

Psychological Stressors

Type A and Type B Personalities A number of years ago cardiologists Meyer Friedman and Ray Rosenman (1974) suggested that people who display certain behavioural patterns and who suffer from certain **psychological stressors** are more likely to suffer (stress-induced) heart attacks. They distinguished between **Type A personalities** and **Type B personalities**, claiming that those people with the former type were more likely than the latter to suffer from heart disease. To whatever extent you display tendencies to behave in ways listed below, to that same extent you are a Type A personality (see Friedman and Rosenman, 1974: 100–102).

> You are a Type A personality if you

1. Explosively accentuate key words in ordinary speech.
2. Always walk, talk and eat rapidly.
3. Are impatient about the rate at which most things get done.
4. Frequently try to do two or more things at once.
5. Are preoccupied with your own thoughts and often try to swing conversations to topics that interest you.
6. Feel guilty when relaxing.
7. Fail to notice interesting and beautiful objects in your surroundings.
8. Are constantly seeking to get things, rather than to enjoy them as they are.
9. Try to do more and more in less and less time.
10. Feel challenged by other Type A personalities.
11. Exhibit characteristic gestures or nervous tics such as clenching your fists or banging your hand on a table.
12. Take pride in being able to do things better because you are faster.
13. Translate everything everyone does in terms of "numbers" (e.g., time, amount, distance).

Source: Reprinted by permission of Alfred A. Knopf.

psychological stressors
Potential sources of stress such as pressure, frustration and conflict.

Type A personalities
Cardiologists Friedman and Rosenman group people who display a particular complex of personality traits, including excessive competitive drive, aggressiveness, impatience and a hurrying sense of time urgency into a category they call Type A personalities. They are also more likely than people with Type B personalities to suffer from heart disease.

Type B personalities
Individuals who are able to play for fun, who can relax without feeling guilty and who rarely suffer from a sense of time urgency with the impatience that comes with it. This personality is a mirror image of the Type A personality according to Friedman and Rosenman.

Friedman and Rosenman (1974: 14) say that a Type A personality exhibits

. . . a particular complex of personality traits, including excessive com-petitive drive, aggressiveness, impatience, and a harrying sense of time urgency. Individuals displaying this pattern seem to be engaged in a chronic, ceaseless, and often fruitless struggle with themselves, with oth-ers, with circumstances, with time, and sometimes with life itself. They also frequently exhibit a free-floating but well-rationalized form of hostility, and almost always a deep-seated insecurity.

Source: Reprinted by permission of Alfred A. Knopf.

By contrast to the Type A personality, the Type B personality rarely suf-fers from a sense of time urgency with the impatience that accompanies it. Type B individuals carry with them no free-floating hostility. They have no need to display themselves or to discuss their achievements publicly. At play-time, Type B people actually play for fun, not necessarily to win and exhibit superiority. They are also able to relax without feeling guilty. In short, we see in the Type B personality a mirror opposite of the Type A. Type Bs are free of the habits and traits that harass the severely stressed Type A person (Friedman and Rosenman, 1974).

Some relatively recent studies have failed to show a link between Type A behaviour and heart disease. Critics of these studies claim that people in-volved in them were not accurately classified as Type A or Type B in the be-ginning, therefore negating any conclusions (Coon, 1997). Some evidence suggests that it's the anger and hostility components of Type As that correlate with heart attacks, not the other aspects of this personality profile (see Chesney and Rosenman, 1985; Friedman and Booth-Kewley, 1987; and Wright, 1988). In view of the fact that hundreds of other studies have supported the hy-pothesis about Type A being linked to heart disease, let's say that the jury is still out on this one. Nonetheless, if you are a Type A personality, you may wish to consider changing some of your behavioural patterns. As Dennis Coon (1997) points out, one large-scale study of heart attack victims found that the rate of repeat heart attacks could be significantly reduced by modifying Type A behaviours. Perhaps by changing Type A behaviours at the outset, the first "big one" could be avoided as well!

Pressure Regardless of whether you exhibit a Type A or a Type B personality, you've probably felt **pressure** at some point in your life. Maybe your parents have pressured you to do well at school or to make concrete plans for your future. Perhaps you've been under pressure to juggle many different respon-sibilities at the same time. People may think of you as "superman" or "super-woman" as they form great expectations and heap loads of them upon you. It could be that you are "supposed to" produce, regardless of the difficulties and competing demands. In situations such as these, pressure is all about expec-tations and demands and how they make us behave in certain ways.

pressure
The expectations and de-mands of us, and how they make us behave in certain ways.

There are two subtypes of pressure (Weiten and Lloyd, 2000): the *pressure to perform* and the *pressure to conform*. In the first instance you may be expected to successfully complete tasks and execute responsibilities in a quick and efficient manner. For instance, you may have to meet quotas, deadlines or achieve minimal standards of quality. As a student, you may be under pressure to earn at least a B average in your studies to be considered as a candidate for a post-graduate program. Police officers are sometimes pressured to meet their quotas of traffic tickets. Academics can be pressured to submit grant applications before specified deadlines.

Pressure can also relate to conformity. People are often pressured to conform to others' expectations. Fears, anxieties and insecurities about how we should dress, act, speak or think often arise when we are unclear about what others expect of us. We may wish to please, obey authorities or just fit in, but remain uncertain as how to do so exactly. Even if we are clear about others' expectations, we may still have fears about not being able to live up to them. If the expectation for a male executive is to wear a jacket and tie to work, he may still worry about whether or not they coordinate properly or whether they fit the required corporate image.

Regardless of whether people are under pressure to perform or conform, preliminary research suggests a strong relationship between pressure and psychological symptomatology (Weiten, 1988; Weiten and Dixon, 1984). In fact, pressure may be more strongly tied to stress-related disturbances than change as measured by Holmes and Rahe's social readjustment rating scale.

Frustration **Frustration** can often be a stimulus event that leads to stress. Generally speaking, "frustration occurs in any situation in which the pursuit of some goal is thwarted" (Weiten and Lloyd, 2000). Whenever you are denied what you want, your goal is not attained and you become frustrated. If you are actually able to get what you want, but are forced to wait longer than you would like before getting it, frustration results again.

frustration
A stimulus event that leads to stress. Frustration results when your goal is not attained.

Two common kinds of frustration involve *failure* and *loss* (Weiten and Lloyd, 1994). If you want to pass a test, but fail, you can experience stress over the failure and over the fact that your chances of graduating may be jeopardized. On the other hand, your girlfriend or boyfriend may break up with you and leave you at a loss, stressed out about what to do next.

Conflict In Chapter 10, we will look at the nature of **conflict** in a bit more detail. There we learn that it can result when we must choose between two positives, the lesser of two evils, or when we must make any other choice that has both positive and negative elements attached. Conflicts can be internal or interpersonal. I may want something but my moral conscience may tell me that it's wrong. The guilt or self-blame I lay on myself as a result could be a source of stress. By contrast, the conflict I experience may not be within my psyche, but between us. You and I may want the same thing at the same time (e.g., a job) when only one of us can have it. Whenever we experience "me against you" or "us against them" situations, stress is also likely to result.

conflict
A potential psychological stressor that may occur when we must choose between two positives, the lesser of two evils, or when we must make a choice that has both positive and negative elements attached. Conflicts may be internal or interpersonal.

235

We may fear that we may not get our share of scarce resources, or that others will overpower us. Anxious about the eventual outcomes, we experience stress.

Daily Hassles

daily hassles
The commonly occurring, everyday frustrations in life that collectively can be as upsetting as major life traumas.

Studies in stress research seem to suggest that **daily hassles** and frustrations in life can be collectively as upsetting as major life traumas (Delongis et al., 1982; Lazarus, 1981). From a broader objective point of view, having to wait in bumper-to-bumper traffic is really a rather trivial inconvenience. However, don't tell that to angry daily commuters when someone cuts into traffic in front of them. Especially for impatient (Type A) people, having to wait is stressful. The wait could be in traffic, in the line at the grocery store or on the phone. When communicating with a Type A person over the phone, put that individual "on hold" at your own risk. Being forced to wait is one of life's daily hassles that drives some people crazy.

It's all right to have butterflies in your stomach. Just get them to fly in formation.
~Dr. Rob Gilbert

Stress as a Response: General Adaptation Syndrome (GAS)

general adaptation syndrome (GAS)
The theory developed by Canadian Hans Selye as a way of explaining the body's reaction to stress. According to Selye, stress is the nonspecific response of the body to any demand made upon it. The GAS has three basic stages: the alarm reaction, the resistance phase and the exhaustion state.

Of all the definitions of stress, the one provided by Canadian stress researcher Hans Selye (1974, 1976) has been one of the most influential. A professor at McGill University and director of the Institute of Experimental Medicine and Surgery at the University of Montreal, he developed his theory of the **general adaptation syndrome (GAS)** as a way of explaining the body's reaction to stress. According to Selye (1974: 27), "Stress is the nonspecific response of the body to any demand made upon it." To say that stress involves a nonspecific response means that regardless of the stressor, the bodily reaction remains the same. Bodily responses to earthquakes, firings, poisonous snakes, bungee-jumping and term tests are all physiologically identical. Stress induced by fear or apprehension, regardless of its source, produces the same effects. You can't look at a stress-induced bodily reaction and say, "Oh, this one comes from an earthquake" or "That one results from test anxiety." The body's response to stress is stereotypically the same. The general adaptation syndrome has three basic stages: the alarm reaction, the resistance phase and the exhaustion stage.

alarm reaction
The stage, according to the GAS theory, at which the autonomic nervous system prepares the body for the fight-or-flight response. Physiologically, blood pressure increases, muscles tense, heart rate increases, blood coagulability increases, adrenalin is secreted, respiration rate increases, digestion is inhibited, corticosteroids are secreted, blood flow increases to skeletal musculature and perspiration increases.

The Alarm Reaction

You will understand the stage of **alarm reaction** better (and the GAS more broadly) if you place it in a biological, evolutionary context. To begin with, the body is genetically programmed to maintain a homeostatic balance. We

Hans Selye

Dr. Hans Selye (1907–1982) was a pioneering visionary in the field of medicine and stress research. His work has helped us to understand how the body reacts negatively to stress. His research has also opened up the way for many new types of treatment programs for stress-related diseases. During his lifetime, Selye was a professor at McGill University and director of the Institute of Experimental Medicine and Surgery at the University of Montreal. He held doctoral degrees in philosophy and science, as well as in medicine. Selye received 16 honourary degrees in addition to many awards, medals and honourary citizenships. He was also made a Companion of the Order of Canada, the country's highest honour.

all carry within ourselves something like a "biological thermometer" that regulates such things as our body temperature, heart rate and respiration. When all is well, things operate more or less smoothly. However, when a stressor (e.g., a frightening stimulus) is presented, the homeostatic balance of the body is upset as it prepares to deal with the presented threat.

To understand how, let's go back to prehistoric times to meet Conan the cave dweller. Let's suppose that our friend Conan was suddenly confronted by a sabre-toothed tiger. Faced with this predicament, Conan could choose to stay and fight the predator or take flight to save himself. To help him meet the demands presented by this frightening stressor, Conan's autonomic nervous system would kick in and prepare him for a *"fight-or-flight response."* Conan's digestion would slow so that more blood could be directed to his muscles and brain. His respiration rate would increase to supply increased oxygen to the muscles. His heartbeat would accelerate and his blood pressure would soar, forcing blood to the parts of the body that needed it. Perspiration would increase to cool the body; muscles would tense in preparation for action; chemicals would be released into the blood to make it clot more rapidly in case of injury, while sugars and fats would be poured into the bloodstream to provide fuel for quick energy needs. In short, Conan's body would prepare to meet the demands of the life-threatening situation. Such bodily preparations would serve to enhance the chances of Conan's continued survival. If Conan stayed and slayed the beast, the threat would be over and his body would return to its normal homeostatic balance. If Conan chose to flee the situation, the same thing would happen. (See Table 6.2 for a list of physiological reactions that follow a stressor.)

In contrast to our friend Conan, however, we at the start of the twenty-first century are not likely to be confronted by prehistoric predators, but

Table 6.2

The Physiology of the Alarm Reaction

blood pressure increases	respiration rate increases
muscles tense	digestion is inhibited
heart rate increases	corticosteroids are secreted
blood coagulability increases	blood flow increases to skeletal musculature
adrenalin is secreted	perspiration increases

rather by personal ghosts, environmental demons and organizational bogeymen (metaphorically speaking, of course). There may be some kind of beast (e.g., an imposing uncle) or dragon (a pushy aunt) that we have to contend with. Maybe we are afraid of some personal ghosts in our psychological closets, or perhaps we feel unsure about ourselves, afraid to take risks where others are involved. It could be that our boss at work is an ogre who is constantly on our case, so much so that we're worried that we might get fired. We could also be anxious about the state of the economy. With all the past corporate downsizing and global restructuring, we may feel trapped and victimized about our future prospects. Add to this our apprehension about falling behind at school, keeping up with technological advances and getting our finances in order, and Conan's tiger begins to look a little bit like a pussy cat, don't you think?

I don't wish to suggest that our early ancestors lived an easy life compared to us, but at least Conan's fears were temporary and short-lived. Once the tiger was killed or an escape was accomplished, life returned to normal. For us, some stressful situations (e.g., traffic jams) do come and go relatively quickly; others, though, can last for days, weeks, months or even years. We may find ourselves in stressful and threatening situations (e.g., a bad economy) from which we cannot easily escape or about which we cannot do much. The result is that our bodies, like Conan's, make ready for a "fight-or-flight" response—but for a very long time. What should normally be a brief, temporary state of physiological arousal to deal with an external threat becomes for us a longer-term scenario. Our bodies are often constantly on red alert to attack the threat or flee from it if necessary.

Threats to Conan were tangible and real because when the tiger disappeared, so did the threats. This means that Conan's body was given the chance to rest and return to normal. For us, as highly evolved relatives of Conan, things become somewhat more complicated. The evolution of our cerebral cortex allows us to anticipate and predict dangers and threats, which certainly has biological advantages. It allows us to prepare for dangers before they present themselves. We can plan our escapes and ready ourselves for challenges and confrontations. On the downside, however, the evolved human brain also leads us to perceive threats and dangers that are nonexistent in reality, but present only in our minds. In other words, it's possible to be afraid of nothing except what we imagine to be true or think likely to occur. The saying, "You have nothing to fear but fear itself" seems especially relevant here. At this juncture, you might wish to ask yourself how much time you have wasted thus far in your life worrying about things that have never happened. I trust you get my point! We can literally worry ourselves sick over nothing. The ultimate source of our stress may sometimes not be out there, but in our minds. If the alarm reaction continues for any significant length of time, physical symptoms may result. For example, people could develop sleep disorders, hypertension, headaches, low-grade fevers, aching joints or loss of appetite. (More will be said about symptoms shortly.)

The Resistance Phase

When a stressor persists, the body adapts by moving into the **resistance phase** of the GAS. In this phase, the bodily signs characteristic of the alarm reaction virtually disappear (Selye, 1974). Resistance actually rises to above normal. Neural and glandular systems become hyperactive. We remain in a constant state of overstimulation and are continually mobilized for defence. Thus, in the resistance phase we have learned to cope with the stressors in our lives, and do so by functioning at higher-than-normal levels of physiological arousal.

resistance phase
One stage of the general adaptation syndrome, as developed by Hans Selye. In this stage, bodily signs characteristic of the alarm reaction stage virtually disappear.

The Exhaustion Stage

Although it would be great if human beings possessed unlimited energy, in reality they do not. Following long-term exposure to stressors to which the body has adjusted, the body eventually exhausts its energy supply. This happens because the glands of the body are not given an opportunity to rest and restore their normal levels of activity. The result is that they become overtaxed and no longer function well. In the **exhaustion stage**, physical signs and symptoms of stress originally evident in the alarm reaction reappear (Selye, 1974). The difference is that many of these symptoms are now irreversible. Damage to the body can be permanent. The ultimate consequence is death. If high blood pressure—one symptom of prolonged stress—is called the "silent killer" by doctors, perhaps stress—as one factor that gives rise to it (no pun intended)—should be named the "deadly co-conspirator." Stress and high blood pressure are partners in crime and all of us are potential victims. (see Figure 6.1 for an illustration of the GAS.)

exhaustion stage
The stage, according to the GAS theory, at which physical signs and symptoms of stress originally evident in the alarm reaction reappear. The difference is that now many of these symptoms are irreversible. Damage to the body can be permanent. The ultimate consequence is death.

239

Self
Diagnostic
6.1

Stress . . . Let Me Sum It Up!

(6.3) **Aim:** This self-diagnostic will help you reflect on the amount of stress you have experienced recently in your personal life and as a post-secondary student. Findings suggest that the amount of stress reported by college students is directly related to their general health. Furthermore, stress seems to be related to academic performance (see Napoli, Kilbride and Tebbs, 1992). Students who experience many life changes and stressful events tend to get lower grades than do those who experience fewer changes and fewer stressors. This self-diagnostic will help you to compare your stress level with that of other students.

Instructions: Below are 47 events that can affect your stress level. Check those that apply to you. For each event that is checked, multiply its numerical value by the number of times it occurred to you within the last year. If, for example, you changed your living conditions (number 21) twice, then multiply 42 x 2 to get 84. After making your selections and doing the multiplication, add all your subtotals together to get a grand total. Scores below 347 place you in the low stress category. Scores above 1435 put you in the high stress category as compared with other post-secondary students. If you have been ill lately or if your grades have fallen, perhaps stress has something to do with it.

Event		Numerical Value
✓1	Entered college	50
2	Married	77
3	Trouble with your boss	38
✓4	Held a job while attending school	43
5	Experienced the death of a spouse	87
✓6	Major change in sleeping habits	34
✓7	Experienced the death of a close family member	77
✓8	Major change in eating habits	30
9	Change in or choice of major field of study	41
10	Revision of personal habits	45
11	Experienced the death of a close friend	68
12	Found guilty of minor violations of the law	22
✓13	Had an outstanding personal achievement	40
14	Experienced pregnancy or fathered a pregnancy	68
✓15	Major change in health or behaviour of a family member	56
16	Had sexual difficulties	58
17	Had trouble with in-laws	42

18	Major change in number of family get-togethers	26
19	Major change in financial state	53
20	Gained a new family member	50
21	Change in residence or living conditions	42
22	Major conflict or change in values	50
23	Major change in church activities	36
24	Marital reconciliation with your mate	58
25	Fired from work	62
26	Were divorced	76
27	Changed to a different line of work	50
28	Major change in number of arguments with spouse	50
29	Major change in responsibilities at work	47
30	Had your spouse begin or cease work outside the home	41
31	Major change in working hours or conditions	42
32	Marital separation from mate	74
33	Major change in type and/or amount of recreation	37
34	Major change in use of drugs	52
35	Took on mortgage or loan of less than $10 000	52
36	Major personal injury or illness	65
37	Major change in use of alcohol	46
38	Major change in social activities	43
39	Major change in amount of participation in school activities	38
40	Major change in amount of independence and responsibility	49
41	Took a trip or a vacation	33
42	Were engaged to be married	54
43	Changed to a new school	50
44	Changed dating habits	41
45	Trouble with school administration	44
46	Broke or had broken a marital engagement or a steady relationship	60
47	Major change in self-concept or self-awareness	5

Source: Reprinted with permission from *Journal of Psychosomatic Research*, Vol. 19, p. 97, Vince Napoli, James Kilbridie and Donald Tebbs, "The Influence of Recent . . . ," 1975, Elsevier Science Ltd. Pergamon Imprint, Oxford, England.

241

Figure 6.1
Hans Selye's Model of the General Adaptation Syndrome

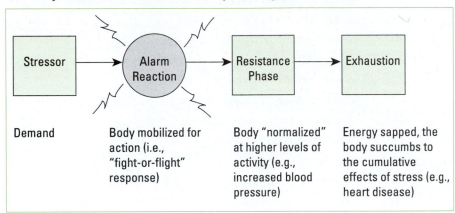

| Demand | Body mobilized for action (i.e., "fight-or-flight" response) | Body "normalized" at higher levels of activity (e.g., increased blood pressure) | Energy sapped, the body succumbs to the cumulative effects of stress (e.g., heart disease) |

6.4 Distress Versus Eustress

Stress is like the tension on a violin string. You need enough tension so that you can make music, but not so much that it snaps.
~Anonymous

The fact that Selye (1976) defines stress as a "nonspecific response of the body to any demand" means that stress is something that cannot be avoided. Life constantly makes demands on us. As a result, our biological homeostasis is continually being upset whether we are aware of it or not. As Selye said, to be totally without stress is to be dead. You shouldn't stress yourself, therefore, trying to lead an entirely stress-free life. To want to do this is to dream the impossible dream.

If stress is unavoidable, you may be inclined to think that we're all headed toward the exhaustion stage of Selye's general adaptation syndrome. This is not necessarily so. To begin with, stress is not all bad, as you might think. There are **high sensation seekers** who actively pursue experiences that many people would find very stressful (Weiten, Lloyd and Lashley, 1991). These "adrenalin junkies" prefer, and may even need, higher levels of stimulation to maintain their well-being. They may skydive, bungee-jump or drive race cars in order to relax. If they experience too little stimulation, they may fall prey to **hypo-stress**, a stress brought on by boredom (Lafferty, 1984). Of course, **low sensation seekers** prefer a peaceful, slower-paced life. Selye labels adrenalin junkies "race horses." He calls low-sensation seekers "turtles." In short, a lifestyle that would be exhausting to one person may be healthy to another. This difference raises the next point.

Stress may in fact play a role in healthy human functioning. Let's use the analogy of a muscle. If you don't use it, the muscle will atrophy and lose its strength. Likewise, an unused mind will not fully develop. As for stress, some tension or resistance is necessary for healthy functioning. A certain amount of stress keeps us operating at peak performance levels (Lafferty, 1984). Being pushed or challenged can help us to "get up" for the game or to get "pumped

high sensation seekers
People who actively pursue experiences that others would find stressful.

hypo-stress
Stress brought on by boredom. Potentially experienced by high sensation seekers who need higher levels of stimulation to maintain their well-being.

low sensation seekers
Individuals who prefer a peaceful, slower-paced lifestyle.

242

Adrenalin junkies find excitement relaxing and stress-reducing.

up" for the presentation. Of course, how much stress any one person requires to do her personal best is an individual matter.

Recognizing that the same stressor (e.g., skydiving) may have different effects on individuals, Selye (1976) distinguishes between distress and eustress. Stressors that lead to **distress** elicit uncomfortable feelings and harmful physical consequences. Distress is bad. It is something that we dislike and seek to avoid. By contrast, stressors that lead to **eustress** produce positive feelings and no apparent ill-effects (the prefix "eu" means good in Greek). When we're experiencing eustress, we typically develop a motivating surge of energy that can improve the efficiency and quality of whatever we're doing (Lafferty, 1984). It is important to note again that one person's distress can be another's eustress. This brings us to the third perspective on stress, one where stress is located not exclusively in the stressor, nor entirely in the bodily reactions of the stressed individual, but in the interaction between the stressor and the person involved.

Stress as an Interaction

According to interactionist accounts of stress, how much stress is experienced and whether a specific stimulus event will give rise to eustress or distress hinges on any particular individual's appraisal of it. Thus, responses to the same potential stressor will vary from person to person depending on how the stressor is interpreted and evaluated. According to Lazarus and Folkman

distress
As distinguished from eustress (by Selye), stressors that lead to this state produce uncomfortable feelings and harmful physical consequences. Distress is bad. It is something that we dislike and seek to avoid.

eustress
As distinguished from distress (by Selye), stressors that lead to this state produce positive feelings and no apparent ill-effects. When we're experiencing eustress, we typically develop a motivating surge of energy that can improve the efficiency and quality of whatever we're doing.

243

(1985), upon initial exposure to a potential stressor or stimulus event, we first appraise it by determining its relevance to us. Is the event or stimulus relevant or irrelevant to us given our position and circumstances in life? Second, if the stimulus event is found to be relevant, we must determine whether or not it is threatening. On the basis of this determination, we decide whether or not the event is stressful. After this initial appraisal, we are likely to make a secondary appraisal. We assess our coping resources and options for dealing with the stressor presented. The fewer the resources and the greater the threat, the more intense the stress becomes. You can see here that **cognitive appraisal** plays an important role in an interactionist account of stress. In what follows, we'll examine a number of key variables that affect our cognitive appraisals of potentially stressful stimulus events: interests, values, personal wants, beliefs, familiarity, controllability, predictability and imminence.

cognitive appraisal
The notion of mental evaluation in the interactionist account of stress.

Interests Diverse **interests** lead people to appraise the same situation in different ways. Let's say, for instance, that you and I hear the same bad news about a fall in stock market prices. I may panic and become distressed about the situation, whereas you might be left essentially unaffected. Since you have no money invested, you have nothing to lose in the price fall. However, as I perceive (appraise) the situation, I stand to lose a lot of money. Consequently, I become worried, angry and upset at my stockbroker for not anticipating the crash. From this illustration, we can clearly see how interests can come between (potential) stressors and (alternative) responses. When I perceive my interests are jeopardized by poor stock market performance, I respond in a way that you probably would not. (I'm assuming of course that you're a poverty-stricken student, even if you do drive a better car than I do!)

interests
Those things that one values or considers to be personally beneficial.

Values **Values** can also act as intervening variables between stressor and response. If I value your opinion and you say something nice about me, I'm likely to respond favourably to what you say. However, suppose you say something very negative and critical about my teaching performance or the content of this textbook; then, I am quite likely to experience some distress. If I didn't value your opinion, your critical comments would be irrelevant to me, leaving me unaffected. However, since I value your evaluations, negative ones cause me psychological and emotional discomfort. Note that it's not what is said that pains me, but the value placed on what is said. Of course, the value judgment resides in my mind. You might also wish to note that this entire situation could be reversed. What your instructor says about your academic work may or may not stress you, depending in large part on the importance you place on the instructor's evaluations. If you do not value the instructor's opinions or if you do not care about your grades, you will not be distressed by any negative appraisal.

values
Can act as intervening variables between stressor and response when experiencing stress.

244

personal wants
According to an interactionist account of stress, whether or not a stimulus event contributes to distress, eustress or no stress often depends on personal wants.

Personal Wants Whether or not a stimulus event contributes to distress, eustress, or no stress at all often depends on our **personal wants**. If you are a friendly but shy person, content with doing routine tasks at work, for example, being required to assume a prominent leadership role with new responsibilities could be quite distressful. By comparison, if you see yourself as an aggressive mover and shaker who desires a high level of material and professional success, being asked to assume the same leadership role would be quite eustressful. You may appraise the new responsibilities not as a threat, but as an opportunity to rise to the occasion, a chance to demonstrate your talents, skills and abilities. When it comes to stress, the equation is this: the same situation plus different wants equals different reactions.

Beliefs Your **beliefs** can also affect the kind and amount of stress you experience. If you believe in a punishing and vengeful God, for example, you will feel differently about an action that could be considered immoral (e.g., premarital sex) than would an atheist who does not believe that God exists. Whether or not an action, as a stimulus event, eventually results in guilt and fear (emotional symptoms of distress) or joy and elation (eustress) depends again not on the event itself, but on how the belief intervenes between the stimulus and the response. Shortly we'll look a little more closely at a number of irrational beliefs that contribute to people's distress. Getting rid of irrational beliefs is one way to reduce the amount of unwanted stress in our lives.

Familiarity Research has shown that **familiarity** with potentially stressful events reduces the amount of threat people are likely to feel (Weiten, Lloyd and Lashley, 1991). When we are familiar with challenges and events as they present themselves, we can often make difficult obstacles easier to overcome. If you've been there and done it before, going there and doing it again may not be so threatening. Going to a new college with new people, accompanied by new expectations and unfamiliar circumstances, is probably a lot more stressful for most compared with going back to visit your old high school. Walking down recognizable hallways and experiencing familiar sights and sounds is typically less threatening than going into unknown territory. I remember the first time I travelled to Europe. Being a stranger there was occasionally a bit scary for me. Returning as I did years later for a second visit, the same places were not as intimidating. I felt more relaxed and stress-free.

Controllability How much control you have over your affairs can also affect the amount and type of stress you experience. Generally speaking, the more **controllability** you have, the less stress you tend to feel. Ask people who say their lives are out of control how stressed they are. Chances are pretty good they'll admit to high levels of stress and anxiety. By contrast, if you feel that you're in effective control of your life, you are probably experiencing greater levels of happiness and personal well-being. An exception to this is found with people who have control (responsibility), but who worry about external evaluations by others. If you know that you are responsible and in control, you cannot blame others for your failures and inadequacies. Having someone else to blame instead of ourselves can be less stressful, even if it is dishonest.

beliefs
According to an interactionist account of stress, your beliefs can affect the kind and amount of stress you experience. Whether or not an action, as a stimulus event, eventually results in guilt and fear or joy and elation depends on how the belief intervenes between the stimulus and the response.

familiarity
Research has shown that being familiar with challenges and events as they present themselves can often make difficult obstacles easier to overcome.

controllability
The amount of control you have over your affairs can affect the amount and type of stress you experience. Generally speaking, the more controllability you have, the less stress you tend to feel.

predictability
One variable that affects our cognitive appraisals of potentially stressful stimulus events.

Predictability Whether or not a potential stressor is experienced as (dis)stressful also can depend on **predictability**. Usually people like to be warned when something unpleasant is about to occur. When a devastating situation can be anticipated, it is generally easier to cope with. If a company is making plans to downsize, and informs employees that many workers will be let go, layoffs are less likely to be taken personally. Laid-off individuals may be spared feelings of inadequacy and poor self-esteem. In fact, positive steps could be taken to prepare for what is likely to come. A job search could begin and prospects could be explored. By the time the layoff is actually announced, those who could predict it might be well on their way to establishing new careers and new directions in their lives. Compare this scenario with individuals who one day are called into the office unexpectedly and fired. Of course, some people would rather not know things in advance. I guess this just serves to support the interactionist thesis. Predictability's role in stress cannot be properly understood apart from the individual's attitude toward it.

imminence
According to an interactionist account of stress, when you have prior knowledge or advance warning that a threatening event is going to occur, the closer the threat comes, the more stress results.

Imminence **Imminence** is the last key factor we'll discuss here that is important to the interactionist account of stress. Let's say that you do have prior knowledge or advance warning that a threatening event is going to occur. The closer the threat comes, the more stress results. It is a surprise to many when they discover that experiencing a stressful event is in fact far less stressful than anticipating it. Worrying about going to the dentist, for example, may prove to be worse than the actual discomfort involved in replacing a worn filling. We may be pleasantly surprised that the experience wasn't as bad as we anticipated. See Figure 6.2 on depicting stress as an interaction.

6.5 — Ways to Cope with Stress: Effective and Ineffective Strategies

Researchers such as Hans Selye are correct when they say that stress is a necessary and unavoidable part of life, and, therefore, we are well-advised to begin developing coping strategies. If we can't live without stress, we might as well learn to live with it. We certainly don't want to be overwhelmed by distress or to suffer its long-term ill effects. In what follows, we'll look at some effective and ineffective coping strategies people use to deal with stress. This section will give you an opportunity to reconsider your coping efforts in order to determine if you ought to be doing something else or continue doing something more. Maybe you'll discover that what you're doing is in fact not getting you what you want.

Coping Strategies with Limited Effectiveness

In their desperation to reduce and eliminate stress, people often engage in behaviours that work temporarily but make things worse later on. Temporary re-

Figure 6.2

An Interactionist Model of Stress

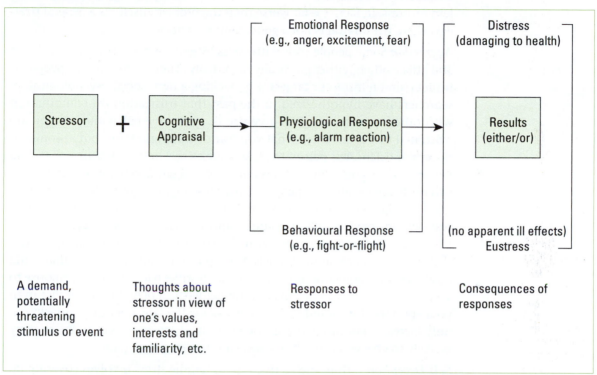

lief is no substitute for long-term solutions. What works for the moment can have negative consequences for the future. Let's see how.

Withdrawal Nobody should be a masochist. If a stressor is unnecessarily causing you mental pain or physical illness, it might be wise simply to remove yourself from the stressful situation. Maybe you're involved in a relationship or marriage within which there are irreconcilable differences. If loving feelings are quickly fading, or if they have vanished entirely, it might be wise to get out. To accept unnecessary pain and suffering is to cause yourself avoidable stress. Maybe you're in a job or studying a subject at school that doesn't fit your temperament and personality. Leaving may be the best thing for you. To say that quitting, leaving and getting out are occasionally advised is not to suggest, however, that these forms of withdrawal and escape are, generally speaking, the best means of coping with stress. You can't always deal with stressful situations by "checking out." People who do are often described as immature and irresponsible. A mature and responsible approach to life requires that we deal with stress in direct and intelligent ways. The reason some people give up on life is that they believe there is nothing they can do to change the situation causing their stress. Researcher Martin Seligman (1975) calls this response to stress "learned helplessness." As people no longer try to effect positive change in their lives, they are more likely to become anxious and depressed. Extreme withdrawal can lead to psychosis, which is obviously no solution to the problem of stress. In fact, it is far worse than the problem itself. As a general strategy, then, withdrawal is not a good coping strategy.

Aggression Some people cope with stress by getting mad. They may lash out and attack others, either physically or verbally. They intend to hurt people or inflict pain on innocent targets (e.g., kicking a pet). Social psychological researchers have hypothesized in the past that frustration (in combination with other factors) can often give rise to aggressive behaviours. If you are frustrated by being denied what you want, you might strike out at some innocent or defenceless person to make yourself feel better. Of course, if feeling better requires you to hurt others and behave aggressively toward them, you can easily appreciate how people in your life might begin to disappear. From their vantage point, stress does not justify your hurting them. Cursing, verbally abusing or physically assaulting someone may help you to feel better momentarily, but you must live with the stress of the subsequent guilt and shame, not to mention the ostracism and possible criminal charges that could ensue. Furthermore, others could choose to strike back at you in response to your own aggression. They may no longer wish to play the role of victim in your episodes of stress-induced violence. Being the target of others' attacks can only increase your own stress in the long run. Aggression as a coping strategy is likely to give you only short-term gain for long-term pain.

Self-Deception A third ineffective way to handle stress involves covering up any anxiety through self-deception. We can ignore stress, put it to the side, push it down, and escape from it by being dishonest with ourselves. This fact is most vividly illustrated by examples of Freudian psychological defence mechanisms (see Chapter 4). If we see our own behaviour as somehow deficient or unacceptable, we can rationalize it rather than consciously accept the stress that it produces. If we feel anxious and worried after being chewed out by our instructors at school, we can go home and unload our stress and pent-up hostility on our family (displacement). We can always refuse to accept the feelings associated with stress and behave exactly opposite to the way we feel (reaction formation). We can also choose to escape stressful situations in our imaginations by fantasizing our way out of them. When things get unpleasant for us, we can always intellectualize our predicament and provide logical-sounding explanations instead of coming to terms with the pain or hurt resulting from stress. On top of all this, we may choose to manage our stress by denying that unpleasant emotions exist. By refusing to acknowledge the emotions, at some level we may think that stress and related anxiety will just disappear.

As psychoanalysis suggests, anxiety covered up by psychological self-deception does not just disappear. Defensiveness consumes energy. Over time, our resources dwindle until unpleasant feelings and urges manifest themselves in thoughts, feelings and actions. After years of repression and denial, the ego may not be able to control stressful feelings. Irrational urges may take control of our lives in the form of neurotic obsessions, compulsions and, at worst, in psychotic symptomatology. To deny, repress, displace and otherwise lie to ourselves about the stressful anxiety in our lives is to set ourselves up for later psychological difficulties. Extensive use of psychological defensiveness is no solution to the stress problem; it's only a cover-up.

Effective Coping Strategies

Cognitive Approaches to Stress Management Instead of withdrawing from life, aggressing against others or playing a game of self-deception, there are other, more constructive ways to cope with the stress in our lives. In view of what interactionists have to say about stress, we'll first take a look at cognitive approaches to stress management. Our goal will be to learn how to make psychological appraisals of life's potential stressors in more reasonable and productive ways. To the extent that we are able to accomplish this goal, we will be able to promote more rational and responsible living. In addition, we'll also explore how stress can be better handled through behavioural modification strategies and lifestyle management. By altering not only what we think, but also what we do, we can effect positive change with respect to how we deal with the problem of stress. Effective stress management is important, for it can significantly affect the quality of our lives.

Albert Ellis's A-B-C Model of Emotional Response

Albert Ellis, now deceased, was an internationally recognized psychologist and the developer of rational-emotive therapy (now called rational-emotive behaviour therapy, REBT). According to him, people feel the way they do largely because of how they think. He said that "what we label our emotional reactions are mainly caused by our conscious and unconscious evaluations, interpretations and philosophies" (Ellis, 1973: 56). When we feel anxious, worried or stressed, it is frequently due to the irrational assumptions we make and the foolish beliefs to which we cling. If we could identify our irrational assumptions and beliefs and then abandon them, we would begin to live a more rational lifestyle, one with significantly less stress and less negative emotion. By clinging to irrationality, we become architects of our own stress. We create more stress for ourselves than necessary. To help us understand how this is so, Ellis designed an **A-B-C model of psychological functioning** that he incorporated into his system of rational-emotive therapy. By using this model, Ellis believed, we can positively change our emotional reactions to stress. We do this by altering our appraisals of potentially stressful events.

The "A" in Ellis's model stands for the activating event. Given what we know already about stress, we might label it the "potential stressor." According to Ellis, an activating event is anything with the capacity to disturb or upset an individual. It could be a failing grade on a test, a missed bus or a

...for there is nothing either good or bad, but thinking makes it so.
~*William Shakespeare*

249

A-B-C model of psychological functioning
Developed by Albert Ellis and used as part of his system of rational-emotive psychotherapy. An activating event (A) will lead to a particular consequence (C) depending on the belief (B) of the individual.

Albert Ellis believed that stress and unpleasant emotion result from irrational thinking.

irrational beliefs
Unreasonable beliefs leading to unnecessary emotional upset.

If you are pained by any external thing, it is not the thing that disturbs you, but your judgment about it. And, it is in your power to wipe out this judgment now.
~Marcus Aurelius

confrontation with a gang member. Common sense might seem to dictate that such stressors would automatically cause some sort of stressful response. This would be consistent with an S-R (stimulus-response) understanding of human behaviour. Contrary to this common-sense perspective, however, Ellis claimed that between the activating event (the stimulus) and the response or emotional consequence (labelled "C") comes a cognitive appraisal. This appraisal is based on a "belief" about the stressor. The belief component of Ellis's model is, not surprisingly, labelled "B."

Now, depending on what exactly is believed (B) about the activating event (A), the consequences (C) will vary. In other words, the same activating event can lead to different emotional consequences depending on how it is interpreted and appraised. See Figures 6.3 and 6.4 for an illustration of common-sense S-R thinking and how it differs from Ellis's A-B-C model.

In Ellis's (1991) book, *Reason and Emotion in Psychotherapy*, a number of **irrational beliefs** are listed—these are ones that contribute to unnecessary emotional upset. For each irrational belief, Ellis provided us with a more rational alternative, one that will probably lead to less stress and ill-feeling. For Ellis, the belief that "It's catastrophic when things don't turn out the way I'd like them to" was irrational and likely to lead to emotional pain and disappointment. The alternative belief: "Frustrating situations are challenges that can be useful for personal change" was more productive. Such a belief is more likely to be emotionally calming and stress reducing. It is also irrational to believe that you must be loved and approved of by everyone. The better alternative is to accept the notion that you can't please all of the people, all of the time. By believing that you should develop self-respect by being good, say, or by doing what should be done, and by accepting the idea that feelings

Figure 6.3
Common Sense S-R Thinking About Stress

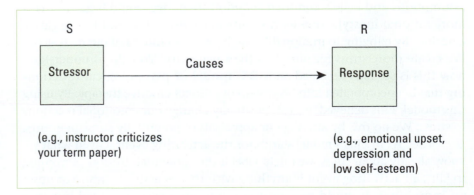

Figure 6.4

A-B-C Model of Emotional Responses to Stress

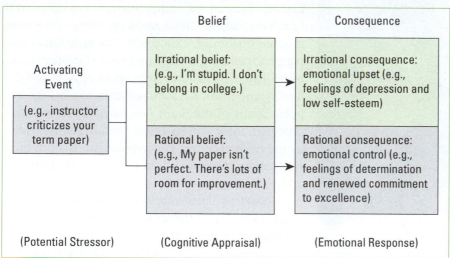

of self-worth should not entirely hinge on the fickle opinions of others, you liberate yourself from a lot of psychological misery.

Human Synergistics

In the early 1980s, a program of stress management called SCOPE was developed by Lorraine Colletti and Ronald Phillips. SCOPE stands for System for Creating Organizational and Personal Effectiveness. A key component of this stress program is the stress processing report (SPR). In consultation with Hans Selye, J.C. Lafferty and his staff developed the SPR to help people identify their particular **thinking styles** so that they could assess the extent to which their own thinking was contributing to the stress in their lives. Lafferty hypothesized that if a potential stressor could give rise either to distress or eustress, as Selye discovered, a critical factor determining the outcome was "thinking." One's thoughts about any given stressor could cause it to be emotionally energizing or upsetting. This hypothesis was supported by empirical research done with a group of managers and executives (Lafferty, 1984). Apparently, not all such people who experience stress succumb to the physical symptoms usually associated with it. According to Lafferty's findings, there are healthy and unhealthy ways to think about the stressors in anyone's life. Certain thinking patterns are more likely to cause distress than others. By changing your thinking patterns, then, you can more effectively manage the stress in your life.

The Role of Thinking in Distress When an event is perceived, the mind internalizes it and then sends signals to the body. The body, in turn, attempts to interpret the signals. When people think negatively about stimulus events and potential stressors, they often engage in a form of "self-talk," which is

thinking styles
According to Lafferty, the manner in which one regards or thinks about a particular stressor determines whether the outcome is distress or eustress. By changing your thinking styles, Lafferty argued, you can more effectively manage the stress in your life.

Men are disturbed not by things, but by the view which they take of them.
~Epictetus, Stoic philosopher

Dr. Lorraine Colletti-Lafferty and the late Dr. J. Clayton Lafferty, psychological practitioners whose work on stress was influenced by the insights of Hans Selye.

self-defeating. They may say things like, "I must be perfect in everything I do," "I must always finish first and beat all the competition," "I'm no good if I can't do that," or "If we break up, there's no reason to keep on living." Such self-talk contains catastrophic thinking, unreasonable assumptions and unrealistic conclusions. Regardless of how self-defeating and irrational such self-talk may be, the hypothalamus of the brain nonetheless receives and processes information about stressors as provided by the cerebral cortex. The hypothalamus sends messages about these supposed threats to the pituitary and adrenal glands, which combine to create the physiological alarm reaction of the body (Selye's idea). Even if the threat is not real, the body responds as if it were. The body responds to "thinking" about the stressor, not to the stressor itself. Optimistically speaking, this means that if we begin to engage in more positive self-talk and if we change our self-defeating thinking patterns, we can reduce our levels of distress, regardless of the stressors in our lives. While we may not be able to change the world, we can always change our thinking about it. Controlling our thoughts can significantly help us to control our stress levels. Researchers at Human Synergistics appear to confirm the insight offered earlier that "stress lies in the mind of the beholder" or, as some would say, "It's all in your head." The notion that stress is an "inside job" can be graphically illustrated. See Figure 6.5.

Think About Thinking: The Purpose of the Stress Processing Report (SPR) To help us better understand how thinking can affect stress and stress-related symptomatology, Lafferty et al. (1988) developed the SPR. The basic mission of the SPR is to measure, with reliability and validity, the key ingredients in human thought processes. Human Synergistics has aimed this di-

Figure 6.5
Human Synergistics Stress Equation

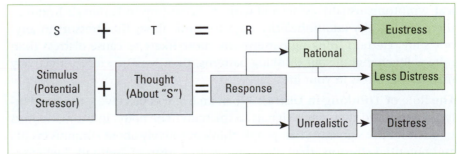

agnostic instrument and its associated support program (SCOPE) at helping participants to change their thinking and behaviour so that they are less prone to the negative effects of change and stress.

Lafferty et al. (1988) have grouped 19 different thinking patterns into four major clusters: self, others, process and goals. Of major importance to our mental health is how we think about ourselves. Self-perceptions and our personal belief system affect how we deal with the stressors in our lives. In terms of others, our social perceptions can affect our relationships and how we feel about them. The process or way we go about our lives, and how we accomplish what we have chosen to do, all influence our stress levels, as will our goal directedness. If we have goals, know what we want and have a plan to get there, stress levels will lower (Lafferty et al., 1988). Table 6.3 shows the domains of thought that belong to each cluster.

Cognitive Reframing

When you're feeling stressed, you might want to try **cognitive reframing**. This requires you to take another look at the situation. Any "bad" set of circumstances can be reframed to reveal potential benefits. Losing your job may seem like a terrible tragedy from one point of view. From another, it becomes an opportunity to explore other new and exciting career possibilities. Recently, I taught a student who was unsuccessful in a sports injury management program. In my conversations with her, I sensed the disappointment and anxiety she felt as a result of her "failure." In time she discovered, however, that she was very good at psychology and philosophy; in fact, she excelled in her

cognitive reframing
Taking another look at a potentially stressful situation to reveal potential benefits. The emotional upset of stress may be reduced by looking at life from a broader perspective or at least from a different one.

Table 6.3

Domains of Thought for Four Major Clusters

Self Cluster	Others Cluster
self-image	inclusion
past view	interpersonal (thoughts)
control	intimacy
approval	trust
growth	
effectiveness	
Process Cluster	**Goals Cluster**
receptiveness	satisfaction
synergy	directedness
cooperation	expectations
time orientation	future view
time utilization	

...to gain insight into the depths of our reality...requires a very calm and quiet mind. It is impossible to see into the depths of a pool of water when it is turbulent.
~S.N. Goenka

meditation
An effective strategy to cope with stress in which, by concentrating attention, we develop the ability to overcome the mind's usual habit of jumping from one thought to another. When the incessant activity of the mind is stilled, the meditator experiences that aspect of being that is prior to and distinct from his or her thoughts and from attention itself.

deep relaxation
The state, which may be achieved through meditation, that has been described as transcendental awareness, cosmic consciousness or "satori."

254

newly adopted general arts and science program. Today she plans to attend law school and become a lawyer after earning her degree. Had this student recognized at the time that her failure opened a door to an exciting future, she probably wouldn't have been so anxious and disappointed. Reframing our little setbacks within the general scheme of life, or travelling into the future in our minds to look back on the problems we face today, can help us to cope. The emotional upset of stress can be reduced by looking at life from a different and/or broader perspective.

Physical and Behavioural Approaches to Stress Management
Practise Meditation

Sometimes it's difficult, if not impossible, to think your way out of stress. In fact, thinking may be part of your problem. Maybe you are obsessive in your thoughts. Perhaps your mind always races and it's difficult for you to relax or fall asleep. Engaging in more thinking will probably not help you very much; it may even make things worse.

An entirely different, "nonthinking" approach to stress management is **meditation**. The kind of meditation I'm referring to here does not deal with any kind of intellectual contemplation or rational reflection about the universe. When we meditate to reduce stress, we're not analyzing concepts or seeking truth. We're not examining beliefs or studying cognitive thought processes. (I'm getting stressed just thinking about it!) Rather, we practise meditation for stress reduction to gain "mastery over attention" (Pelletier, 1992: 193). Meditation focuses on concentration. People who meditate learn to fix their attention firmly upon a given task for progressively longer and longer periods of time. By concentrating attention, we develop the ability to overcome the mind's usual habit of jumping from one thought to another. When the incessant activity of the mind is stilled, the meditator experiences that aspect of being that is prior to and distinct from her thoughts and from attention itself (Pelletier, 1992: 193). At the most profound levels, this state of **deep relaxation** has been described as transcendental awareness, cosmic consciousness or "satori." Some believe that the deep inner peace achieved by meditation can open the doorway to higher levels of self-knowledge not possible through rational thought or cognitive thought processes. Whether you believe this or not is unimportant for our purposes here. The fact is that scientific research supports the notion that meditation can help reduce arousal levels associated with stress. I'll say more about this in a moment; for now, let's look at a couple of ways we can learn to fix our attention for purposes of stress reduction.

Types of Meditation While meditation practice is a relatively recent phenomenon in North America and the Western world, many Eastern religions have practised it for centuries. They have found different ways to focus attention. In one form of Zen meditation, people focus on common external objects such as landscapes, mountaintops or ocean horizons. By contrast, Tibetan

Self Diagnostic
6.2

How Is My Current Thinking Contributing to My Personal Stress?

One way for you to determine whether your current thinking is insulating you from stress or contributing to it would be to complete the entire Stress Processing Report (available from Human Synergistics in Plymouth, MI). While this is not possible given space limitations imposed by the text, Dr. Colletti-Lafferty has extracted from the SPR two domains of thinking and kindly produced, especially for us here, a mini self-diagnostic. It is based on the SPR and can help us to begin assessing the extent to which our thinking in two selected domains contributes to personal stress.

The two domains are "directedness" and "expectations" in the goals cluster. Directedness refers to the sense of where we're going and the sense of certainty we have about getting there. Expectations refer to the anticipation and assurance of achieving reasonably challenging objectives. These two domains, like the others, proceed on a continuum from the negative to the positive. Thinking in the negative direction will produce stress, while thinking in the positive will limit, and may even insulate us from, stress.

Instructions: Draw a circle around the number that best describes the extent to which you agree with each statement.

0   Don't agree at all

1   Slightly agree

2   Somewhat agree

3   Agree

4   Strongly agree

0	1	2	3	4	I know what I want to do with my life.
0	1	2	3	4	Setting goals is difficult for me because things are always changing.
0	1	2	3	4	I feel little sense of direction or purpose in my life.
0	1	2	3	4	I think about how things could be and work toward that image.
0	1	2	3	4	I take concrete steps to move toward the future I have planned.
0	1	2	3	4	I have few personal goals that are important to me.
0	1	2	3	4	Where I am going with my life seems vague and uncertain.
0	1	2	3	4	I feel I'm not very good at the things I do.
0	1	2	3	4	I worry about failing before I even start.
0	1	2	3	4	At home or at work I'm successful at the tasks I take on.
0	1	2	3	4	I am confident even when I take on difficult tasks.
0	1	2	3	4	The possibility of failing prevents me from trying new things.
0	1	2	3	4	I have trouble doing things as well as I would like.
0	1	2	3	4	I can succeed at almost anything I try.
0	1	2	3	4	When I make an effort to do something, I can perform at the level I expect.

Total Score: _____

255

A score between 20 and 32 indicates that you have a clear-cut sense of where you are going and a sense of continuity about getting there. In other words, you display goal-directed behaviour. A score of 0 to 20 indicates less direction in life with more vagueness and undetermined goals. The lower the score, the more probable the chance of experiencing greater stress around this issue.

Prescription for Change: To develop a sense of direction, you must first change your self-defeating thought patterns and set some goals for yourself. Begin with a modest personal goal. List the steps necessary to reach it. Visualize the results and take action to achieve them. Enjoy the satisfaction of achievement and you'll be motivated to tackle more goals. If you think about yourself in a more positive fashion and become more self-accepting, you will probably experience less distress and fewer unpleasant emotions compared to people who reject themselves and others. Remember, how you think about life is a choice, and the choice is yours.

Source: Reprinted with permission of Human Synergistics.

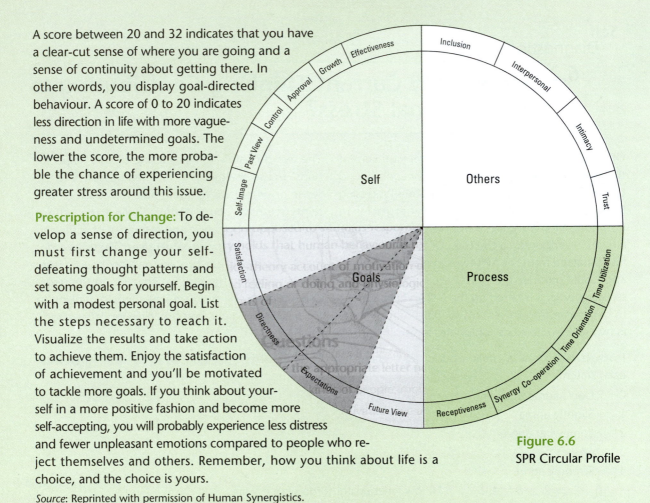

Figure 6.6
SPR Circular Profile

Just in case you're discouraged about your current thinking patterns, here's the story of a man who

Failed in business in 1831	Was defeated again for Congress in 1846
Was defeated for the Legislature in 1832	Was defeated a third time for Congress in 1848
Failed again in business in 1834	Was defeated for the Senate in 1855
Lost his sweetheart in 1835	Was defeated for vice-president in 1856
Had a nervous breakdown in 1836	Was defeated for the Senate in 1858
Was defeated in an election in 1838	Was elected President of the United States in 1860
Was defeated for Congress in 1843	

The man was Abraham Lincoln. And you think you've got problems! What do you imagine Honest Abe was thinking?

Practice in Cognitive Coping

6.7 **Part I:** Read the brief description of the situation presented below and then answer (in private) the questions that follow.

Situation: You walk into an upstairs bedroom at a house party to find your boyfriend or girlfriend hugging someone else.

Questions

1. How will you respond?

2. What will you say?

3. How will you feel?

4. What will your physical state be?

5. What thoughts would or did you have just before responding?

6. What assumptions did you make upon seeing the two of them together?

Part II: Form small groups. Explore and identify the different assumptions people made about the situation.

Questions

1. What different assumptions could be made about this situation?

2. Are all the possible assumptions about the situation negative? Explain.

3. What other assumptions could one make about the situation that your group has not identified?

4. What new thoughts follow from these assumptions?

5. Would these new and different thoughts give rise to different emotions? If so, how?

6. What thoughts about this situation could reduce stress?

7. Select those thoughts about this situation that would reduce emotional upset. Pick thoughts that are reasonable, mature and responsible.

Buddhists practise their power of concentration by using a **mandala**, a geometric figure that has spiritual or philosophical importance (see Figure 6.7). Buddhists may also use a **mantra** or a silently repeated sound such as "ohm" (Greenberg, 1999). Adapting this last strategy into secular, nonreligious practice, many North Americans simply close their eyes and silently repeat words such as "in, out" while breathing. The chosen words or sounds are not really important. Their purpose is to focus awareness.

mandala
A geometric figure that has spiritual or philosophical importance, used in meditation to focus awareness.

mantra
A silently repeated sound, such as "ohm," used in meditation to focus awareness.

Figure 6.7
A Mandala

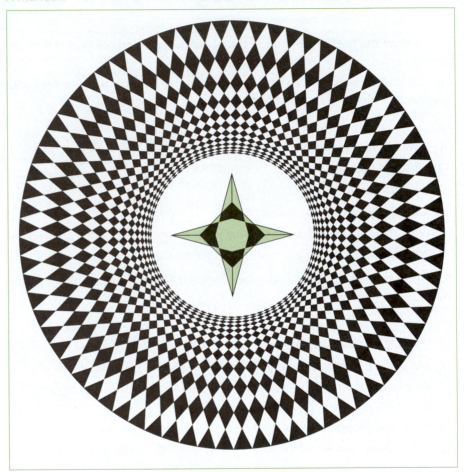

If you choose to focus on a mantra or mandala when meditating, internal and external stimuli may sometimes divert your attention. When this happens, no resistance should be offered. Simply allow distractions to flow through you. Become aware of them and then let them go. In time and with practice, distracting thoughts should become less frequent. Deep concentration will also serve to filter out external noise.

Now that you have some idea of what a meditation is, we will conduct one in Application Exercise 6.2. In this meditation, we'll learn to focus our attention by becoming aware of our breathing and different parts of the body. We won't be using external objects or mantras, but the calming effects should still be the same.

Achieving Calm Through Focused Attention

6.8

Aim: This meditation exercise has two purposes. It will help you to practise **focused attention** and it will enable you to experience first-hand the calming effects of meditation.

Instructions: Have the instructor or a student volunteer slowly read the text below. If available, play relaxing background music, such as Pachelbel's "Canon in D" or something from the *Solitudes* series of tapes produced by Canadian Dan Gibson.

Please take a moment to find a comfortable position in your chair...pause...you might like to sit with a straightened back. Unfold your arms and uncross your legs. Now, what I'd like you to do is take a deep breath...hold it...exhale...hold...inhale...hold for a moment...exhale...hold...inhale...hold...exhale. I invite you now to close your eyes. As you take note of the darkness, begin to focus on your breathing...Feel the air as it passes through your nostrils...Is there a difference in temperature between the air inhaled and the air exhaled? Focus on this for a moment...

Now direct your attention to your face and head...Are there any areas that are tense? Are your eyes pulsating? Are your lips twitching? Is there a stiffness at the back of your skull where your head attaches to your neck? Focus on these tension areas...Now, every time you exhale, I want you to imagine you're blowing out those tensions...

Focus now on your neck...How does it feel? Do you need to swallow? Is there a lump in your throat? Imagine any tensions you have draining downward. Feel how heavy your neck is...Let's visualize now how all these squeezed-down tensions are moving down your arms and out your fingertips...Feel your arms relax.

Now focus on your stomach. Do you hear any noises...feel any sensations? Can you picture your diaphragm moving up and down as you breathe? Concentrate now on your seat. Are your buttocks comfortable? Do you need to move or readjust yourself? Do so, if necessary...How do your legs feel? Is there pressure on your knees?...

How about your calves?...Focus on your toes. See if you can feel each one in isolation from the others...Every time you breath and exhale see the little remaining tension trickle down, out your toes... Enjoy for a moment the calm that has come through focused concentration...Feel the tranquillity and inner peace...Rest assured that you can achieve this state of calm any time you wish. All you need to do is to sit still and focus...When you are ready, open your eyes refreshed and energized, present to the moment, yourself and others. Notice how things appear different to a calm mind.

focused attention An effective strategy for coping with stress in which we make ourselves aware of our breathing and different parts of the body.

259

Exercise and Physical Activity

You will recall from our discussion of Hans Selye's general adaptation syndrome that when stressful demands are placed upon us, the body responds with the alarm reaction in preparation for fight or flight. Our levels of physiological arousal increase to adapt to the stressors which present themselves. Recall how heart rate and perspiration increase along with blood pressure. A number of physiological changes prepare us to deal with whatever threat is at hand.

In response to threats and related stress, some of us strike out at others, attacking physically or verbally. As we've learned, aggressing against others is not a very effective physical way of coping. A better alternative for letting off steam before we explode (in anger) is to engage in **physical exercise**. We can use our physiological arousal productively in sports and in other exercise activities. By means of such things we can beneficially use our bodies in some active way without hurting others (Greenberg, 1999).

If you're a serious runner or know of someone who is, you've probably heard of the "jogger's high." Those who jog often experience a feeling of well-being while exercising. Personally speaking, as a jogger for more than 30 years, I experience the "high" immediately upon starting the cool-down phase of my jog (i.e., when I walk home the last half kilometre or so). I recognize this feeling, I know what it is and I purposely jog to experience it and feel euphoric. To suggest that a feeling of euphoria can accompany strenuous physical exercise is not an exaggeration. While jogging, the brain releases endorphins into the bodily system. Endorphins are a little like morphine. They serve to dull pain and to produce feelings of well-being (Greenberg, 1990). If you wish to get naturally high, then you should exercise. Feeling euphoric is certainly better than feeling stressed and anxious. Of course, due care should be taken as well. Illness or fragile health may place restrictions on what types of exercise are best for you. Consult your physician before embarking on any kind of rigorous exercise program.

Clinical Biofeedback Techniques

Another way of reducing physiological levels of arousal associated with stress is through **clinical biofeedback procedures**. Biofeedback is based on the premise that many autonomic or involuntary nervous-system functions can be brought under conscious control. By using mechanical devices to monitor such things as brain wave patterns, heart rate, muscle tension and body temperature, people can learn to make physiological changes in their bodily systems (Pelletier, 1992). In other words, by becoming aware of internal bodily processes that we don't usually notice, we can bring them under voluntary control (Davis, Eschelman and McKay, 1988). Biofeedback helps us discover which parts of our nervous system are more or less relaxed. It can help us to gain awareness of what total relaxation feels like and can assist us in achieving that state. By means of biofeedback procedures, we can learn to lower

physical exercise
An alternative method of letting off steam, using physiological arousal productively in sports and other exercise activities.

clinical biofeedback procedures
The use of electronic and mechanical devices to monitor and gain control of autonomic nervous system functions.

such things as muscle tension and blood pressure whenever we need to respond to a stressful situation. The assumption is that changes in our physiological state will be accompanied by positive changes in our mental and emotional states, whether conscious or unconscious.

EMG (**electromyogram**) training is one biofeedback technique. The EMG is a machine that monitors skeletal muscle tension. Connected to the EMG are sensing electrodes that are placed on the forehead, jaw and trapezius muscles of the person using the machine. Muscles at these locations typically tighten and become tense when responding to stressful situations. By learning to reduce tension at these sites, greater relaxation can be induced. Another biofeedback technique involves EEG training or using the **electroencephalogram**. The EEG can help you to create brain wave patterns associated with states of calm. It has been used to treat insomnia and epilepsy. A third biofeedback technique makes use of the GSR or **galvanic skin response**. In this case, a skin graph or dermograph monitors minute changes in the concentration of salt and water in the body's sweat gland ducts (Davis, Eschelman and McKay, 1988). An imperceptible electrical current is passed through the skin. When sweat glands become more active, the GSR machine registers the skin's increased ability to conduct electricity. Remember that according to Selye's notion of the alarm reaction, we perspire more when nervous, in order to cool the body. Increased perspiration will show up in changes to the GSR. The lower the measurable voltage of electrical skin conductibility, the less sweat gland activity. By controlling our GSR, we can thereby control physiological reactions associated with stress. If you are interested in learning more about biofeedback techniques, I suggest you look at *The Relaxation and Stress Reduction Workbook* by Davis, Eschelman and McKay, *Mind as Healer, Mind as Slayer* by Pelletier, and *Comprehensive Stress Management* by Greenberg.

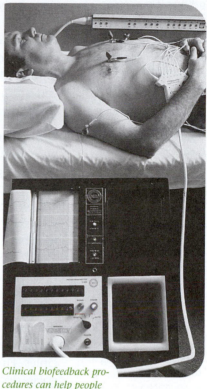

Clinical biofeedback procedures can help people learn to make physiological changes in their bodily systems.

electromyogram
A technique used in clinical biofeedback. The EMG is a machine that monitors skeletal muscle tension. Connected to the EMG are sensors or electrodes that are placed on the forehead, jaw and trapezius muscles of the person using the machine. By learning to reduce tension at these sites, greater relaxation can be achieved.

electroencephalogram
A technique used in clinical biofeedback. The EEG can help you to create brain wave patterns associated with states of calm.

Autogenic Training
Autogenic training (AT) is another effective means for dealing with the problem of stress. It was developed by the German psychiatrist Johannes H. Schultz in 1932 to help people adapt to an overstressed environment (Pelletier, 1992). Through autogenic training, people can learn to regulate their autonomic nervous systems and normalize physical, mental and emotional processes that become imbalanced due to stress (Davis, Eschelman and McKay, 1988). The goal of AT, then, is much like that of meditation. If practised correctly, AT achieves "a state of mind and body which have many of the same

galvanic skin response
A technique used in clinical biofeedback. In this case, a skin graph or dermograph monitors minute changes in the concentration of salt and water in the body's sweat gland ducts. An imperceptible electrical current is passed through the skin. When sweat glands become more active, the GSR machine registers the skin's increased ability to conduct electricity.

autogenic training
People learn to regulate their autonomic nervous systems and normalize physical, mental and emotional processes that become imbalanced due to stress.

WDEP method
A strategy for handling stress based on reality therapy principles.

characteristics as the low arousal state achieved through meditation" (Pelletier, 1992: 231). Whereas meditation uses the mind to relax the body, AT uses physical sensations to first relax the body before using visual imagery to expand the relaxed state of the mind. In both meditation and AT, the results are similar. They both reduce blood pressure, respiration rates, muscle tension and serum cholesterol levels. Brain wave activity (i.e., alpha waves) associated with states of relaxation increase in both instances as well.

Reality Therapy's WDEP Method of Lifestyle Management and Stress Control
In learning how to handle stress, we've looked at some effective and ineffective coping strategies. Before we conclude this discussion, I would like to suggest that negative emotions related to stress can be reduced by taking greater and more effective control of our lives. People who perceive themselves as powerless or out of control tend to be more stressed than do those who have a self-directed and self-managed lifestyle. In order to take more effective control of your life, I strongly suggest you reflect on the work of William Glasser, as discussed in Chapter 5. Recall that Glasser developed reality therapy. By using a choice-theory systems approach to explaining human behaviour and motivation, he shows us how to get what we want from life in more rational, responsible and effective ways. To manage the stress in our lives better, we could use the **WDEP method** based on reality therapy principles. First, we must identify our wants. We must become clear about our goals, desires and aspirations. Second, we must examine our actions or total behaviour, as Glasser would say. What are we doing to get what we want from life? Third, we must evaluate our actions. Is what we are currently doing helping us or hindering us from getting what we want? Finally, if what we're doing is not working, and thereby creating stress for us, we must plan for success. We must come up with alternative courses of action and we must act on the best alternatives. By using reality therapy's WDEP strategy, we can use what is, in effect, a problem-solving strategy to deal with the stress in our lives. Using choice-theory psychology, we can learn to control stress before it controls us!

Study Guide

Key Terms

stress (230)
stressors (231)
life-event stressors (231)
occupational stressors (231)
psychological stressors (233)
Type A personalities (233)
Type B personalities (233)
pressure (234)
frustration (235)
conflict (235)
daily hassles (236)
general adaptation syndrome (GAS) (236)
alarm reaction (236)
resistance phase (239)
exhaustion stage (239)

high sensation seekers (242)
hypo-stress (242)
low sensation seekers (242)
distress (243)
eustress (243)
cognitive appraisal (244)
interests (244)
values (244)
personal wants (244)
beliefs (245)
familiarity (245)
controllability (245)
predictability (246)
imminence (246)
A-B-C model of psychological functioning (249)

irrational beliefs (250)
thinking styles (251)
cognitive reframing (253)
meditation (254)
deep relaxation (254)
mandala (257)
mantra (257)
focused attention (259)
physical exercise (260)
clinical biofeedback procedures (260)
electromyogram (261)
electroencephalogram (261)
galvanic skin response (262)
autogenic training (262)
WDEP method (262)

Fill-in-the-Blank Questions

Progress Check **6.1**

Instructions: Fill in each blank with the appropriate response from the list below.

type A personality
general adaptation syndrome
eustress
ineffective coping strategies
irrational beliefs
thinking styles
clinical biofeedback
endorphins
meditation
occupational stressors

interactionist
defence mechanisms
mandala
fight-or-flight
stressors
reframe
alarm reaction
conform
cognitive appraisal
control

263

1. According to one account, stress is caused by _____.

2. In the context of work, bad lighting, stale air and uncomfortable temperatures are all examples of _____.

3. Stressed individuals who are impatient, competitive and aggressive probably have a _____.

4. Stressed people are sometimes under pressure to perform and _____.

5. Hans Selye has explained the stress response in terms of the _____.

6. In the context of Selye's work, increased blood pressure, increased heart rate and increased adrenalin secretions, when combined, help to create the _____ (or fight-or-flight response).

7. Not all stress is bad. Good stress is called _____.

8. According to the _____ account of stress, values, beliefs, wants and interests all intervene between stressors and reactions to particular stimulus events.

9. Self-deception, withdrawal and aggression are all examples of _____.

10. Self-deception is accomplished by the use of _____.

11. According to Albert Ellis, much of our stress is self-induced because of catastrophic thinking and _____.

12. The "B" element in Ellis's A-B-C model of emotional responses to stress involves a form of _____.

13. According to Clayton Lafferty at Human Synergistics, there are healthy and unhealthy _____ that can either insulate people from stress or contribute to it.

14. When you look at the same stressful situation from a different angle or from a different perspective, you are trying to _____ the situation.

15. One nonthinking approach to stress management is called _____.

16. A _____ is a geometric figure used to induce states of relaxation.

17. Physical exercise can give us a sense of well-being, in part due to the release of _____ into the bodily system.

18. According to advocates of _____, autonomic nervous system functions can be brought under conscious control.

19. Standard exercises of autogenic training can be used to reverse the physiological _____ response.

20. According to William Glasser, people can reduce the stress in their lives by taking more effective _____.

True/False Questions

Instructions: Circle the appropriate letter next to each statement.

T F   1. Student life is stress-free.

T F   2. According to Selye, the human organism needs some stress to remain alive.

T F   3. Marriage, divorce, retirement and change are all examples of life-event stressors.

T F   4. Type B personality types are at a higher risk than Type A personality types of having heart attacks.

T F   5. Daily hassles are a normal part of living. They give rise to no stress.

T F   6. During the resistance phase of the GAS, bodily symptoms present in the alarm reaction disappear.

T F   7. Eustress can be energizing.

T F   8. The same things cause stress for all people.

T F   9. According to the interactionist account of stress, cognitive appraisal comes between potential stressor and emotional response.

T F 10. Usually the more familiar we are with a stressful situation, the less stress we experience.

T F 11. Being able to predict a stressful event always creates greater stress.

T F 12. The closer the threat, the greater the stress.

T F 13. Withdrawing from a stressful situation is usually the best thing to do.

T F 14. In response to stress, some people get mad and behave aggressively toward others.

T F 15. We can discard a lot of stress in our lives by ridding ourselves of irrational beliefs.

T F 16. According to the interactionist account, stress is caused by a single stimulus.

T F 17. There are healthy and unhealthy ways to think about time.

T F 18. Stressful situations can be "cognitively reframed" to create less stress.

T F 19. Meditation works exactly like autogenic training.

T F 20. Stress can be reduced by taking more effective control of our lives.

Summary

1. How can stress be defined?
   - as a stressor
   - as a response
   - as an interaction

2. What are the major categories of stressors?
   - life-event stressors
   - occupational stressors
   - psychological stressors
   - daily hassles

3. Which personality type is most likely to suffer from heart disease? What is this personality type like?
   - Type A
   - accentuates key words, talks and walks rapidly, is impatient, preoccupied, hostile, aggressive, has nervous ticks, translates performance into numbers and is competitive

4. Apart from personality type, what are some other psychological factors contributing to stress?
   - pressure
   - frustration
   - conflict

5. What makes up the general adaptation syndrome?
   - alarm reaction (fight-or-flight response)
   - resistance phase
   - exhaustion stage

6. What occurs in the alarm reaction?
   - blood pressure increases
   - muscle tension increases
   - heart rate increases
   - blood coagulability increases
   - adrenalin secretions increase
   - digestion slows
   - corticosteroids are secreted
   - perspiration increases
   - blood flow to skeletal musculature increases

7. How are distress and eustress different?
   - distress is bad and takes a physical toll
   - eustress is good, energizing and doesn't harm the body

8. How does cognitive appraisal affect stress?
   - cognitive variables (e.g., values and beliefs) determine whether a stimulus will be experienced as stressful

9. What are some intervening variables affecting cognitive appraisals?
   - interests
   - familiarity
   - values
   - controllability
   - personal wants

- predictability
- beliefs
- imminence

10. What are some ineffective ways to cope with stress?
- withdrawal
- aggression
- self-deception

11. What are some effective coping strategies?
- monitor and discard irrational beliefs (Ellis)
- develop a stress-insulating thinking style (Human Synergistics)
- cognitively reframe stress-causing situations
- practise meditation
- engage in exercise and physical activity
- use clinical biofeedback techniques
- use autogenic training
- take control of your life using WDEP strategy

Related Readings

Ader, R. (1993). "Conditioned Responses." In Healing and the Mind, edited by B. Moyers. New York: Doubleday.

Berenbaum, H., and J. Connelly (1993). "The Effect of Stress on Hedonic Capacity." *Journal of Abnormal Psychology*: 102, 474–481.

Charlesworth, Edward A. and Ronald G. Nathan (1984). *Stress Management*. New York: Athenaeum.

Culligan, M. and K. Sedlacek (1976). *How to Kill Stress Before It Kills You*. New York: Grosset & Dunlap Publishers.

> Eventually everyone begins to recognize, however dimly, that there must be a better way.
> ~*A Course in Miracles*

7

Cultivating Character, Meaning and Purpose in Life

Chapter Overview

The Self and Self-Transcendence

The Enneagram: A Path to Personal Liberation

- Relationship to Traditional and Contemporary Psychology
- How Did You Get Your Type?
- Self-Diagnostic 7.1 What's My Enneagram Type?
- The Wings
- Levels of Development
- Paths of Integration and Disintegration
- The Problem with Your Personality

Application Exercise 7.1 Self-Expressions

Life...and May I Ask, What's the Meaning of This?

- Dr. Frankl and the Soul
- The Three Dimensions of Life
- Existential Neurosis
- Meaninglessness in Modern Society
- Roots of Meaninglessness
- How to Find and Create Meaning in Your Life
- Meaning Is Found in Work, Love and Suffering

The Heroic Journey: Living Based on Archetypal Psychology

- What Is Archetypal Psychology? What Can It Do for Me?
- The Kingdom Is Sick
- The Hero's Journey as a Model for Living
- The Call to the Quest
- Psychological Archetypes: Inner Guides for the Journey

- Self-Diagnostic 7.2
  What Kind of Hero Are You, Anyway?

Application Exercise 7.2
My Life Story Is a Heroic Myth

Study Guide

- Key Terms
- Progress Check 7.1
- Summary
- Related Readings

Learning Outcomes

After successfully completing this chapter, you will be able to

7.1 Outline enneagram theory and describe its relationship to traditional and contemporary psychology

7.2 Form a hypothesis of your enneagram personality type

7.3 Find personal direction in view of your enneagram type

7.4 Identify healthy and unhealthy expressions of your enneagram personality type

7.5 Use the insights of Viktor Frankl's logotherapy to deal more effectively with the spiritual concerns of life

7.6 Locate the sources of meaninglessness in contemporary life

7.7 Work toward greater meaning in your life

7.8 Promote self-development using archetypal psychology's concept of "the heroic journey"

7.9 Determine which psychological archetypes are dominant in your life at this time, thereby establishing the stage you are at in life's journey

Focus Questions

1. How is personality conceptualized in enneagram terms?
2. What role does meaning play in life? Where is it found?
3. In what ways is the hero myth useful for living?
4. How is self-knowledge liberating?
5. What are the dark and shadowy sides of human personality?

The Self and Self-Transcendence

personal liberation
Freeing ourselves from the limiting aspects of our personalities—what spiritual writers often refer to as the ego or false self.

ego
The false self from which we must become liberated in order to realize our full human potential.

false self The ego, inevitably developed through our interactions with our families, friends, cultures and societal institutions. In our efforts to adapt to our social worlds, we all move away from our true selves.

false consciousness
The state at which you arrive by falling prey to self-deception or lying to yourself. When suffering from this state you may be doing and saying all the right things, but for a lot of dishonest reasons you won't admit to. In addition, you may overly identify with one or two aspects of your personality and thereby neglect other important dimensions of your humanity. If so, this would leave you unwhole and unfulfilled.

bad faith
False consciousness characterized by self-deception.

In this final chapter of Part One, we turn now to matters of character, meaning and purpose in life. This will involve pursuing three very lofty goals. The first is **personal liberation**. This liberation has nothing to do with political struggle or socioeconomic injustice. Rather, the liberation we'll be addressing involves freeing ourselves from the limiting aspects of our personalities—what spiritual writers often refer to as the **ego** or **false self**. This self inevitably develops through interactions with our families, friends, cultures and societal institutions. In our efforts to adapt to our social worlds we all move away from our true selves. We learn to play mind games. We put on social masks. We detach ourselves from our innermost feelings. We unwittingly fall prey to those things that will hurt us most. We become obsessive in our thoughts and compulsive in our actions as we defend ourselves against the world. We do all this to protect our precious ego selves. It is from the limiting and harmful aspects of our personalities, therefore, that we wish to become liberated.

Perhaps on the surface, at least, you're currently quite happy. Maybe you like being extraverted or introverted in attitude, Promethean in temperament, or visionary in leadership style (see Chapter 11). Moreover, you may take pride in your psychological preferences and personality traits. In your everyday experience of life you may not feel particularly limited or constrained. You may feel that you're very much in control of your own destiny. Yet studies in existential, transpersonal, archetypal and spiritual psychology would suggest you are constrained, even if unknowingly. According to these psychologies, there is often more going on in the self (personality) than meets the eye. For example, without knowing it you may be falling prey to a lot of self-deception (e.g., maybe you're trying to convince yourself you're happy when you're not). Lying to yourself can lead to **false consciousness** or what existentialists call **bad faith**. When suffering from this state you begin to believe your own lies about yourself. For instance, you may not be upset for the reasons you think. You may not truly be motivated by what you believe. You may be doing and saying all the right things, but for a lot of dishonest reasons you won't admit to. In addition, you may overly identify with one or two aspects of your personality and thereby neglect other important dimensions of your character. If so, this would leave you unwhole and unfulfilled. Or, in protection of the self, you may behave in ways that are injurious to your health or detrimental to your long-term well-being. In short, all this bad faith, defensiveness and underdevelopment produces a false self with which we identify. We call this the "ego self" or "I."

As you can well appreciate, failure to see our own psychological enslavement may be the worst kind of bondage. Not knowing that you're bound is far worse than being bound and knowing it. It's like not knowing that you don't know. To continue the analogy, if you know what you don't know, at least you can take steps to obtain information and thereby rectify the situation. So too with personal freedom. Once you know how you've been imprisoned by your personality, you can then take positive steps to free yourself and realize your full potential. Creating an awareness of the limits imposed by our personalities will therefore be one of our goals. Now is the time for all of us to face the enemy ourselves, for indeed, we often are our own worst enemy.

To help us face the enemy we'll turn to the spiritual psychology of the enneagram. The **enneagram** (pronounced ANY-a-gram) is an ancient and powerful symbol of human character that can facilitate the process of **self-transformation**. This symbol can help us to identify the traps set for us by our egos. It can show us how to avoid these traps, offering hope and direction for future liberation from our limiting personalities. The enneagram can also bring to our awareness the spiritual dimensions of life, an awareness that has fortunately grown in recent years and prompts this discussion. If you've ever wondered about your identity, human nature or the purpose of life itself, you have indeed faced spiritual questions.

Our second goal in this chapter is to find greater meaning in our lives. To this end, we'll focus on the work of existential psychiatrist Viktor Frankl. He claims that the greatest meaning in life is found in **self-transcendence**. By getting beyond our egos and by overcoming ourselves, we can commit to things, forget our self-preoccupations and ultimately experience happiness in life. Frankl diagnoses society as suffering from a "metaphysical malaise of meaninglessness" and provides a prescription to remedy this widespread existential ailment. If you personally feel apathetic and bored with life, or if you're depressed and fatalistic, Frankl's insights will prove helpful to you.

Our third goal in this chapter is to find dignity, purpose and hope in our lives. To do so, we will look at the **archetypal/transpersonal psychology** of Carol Pearson. She uses the metaphor of the "hero's journey" to map our developmental stages and transitional periods of life interpreting human development in terms of a spiral process. We all begin life by establishing ego boundaries, then develop what she calls soul, before we reach the final destination of the real or **authentic self**—that which allows us to experience wholeness and integrity as individuals. It's a bit misleading to say "final destination," for achievement of the authentic self then allows us to go back and redefine our ego boundaries and enrich our souls in new ways not possible before the development of self. In time, continuing soul and ego developments make possible new experiences and expressions of the authentic self. The journey to wholeness is for Pearson a spiralling process that ends only in death. "It ain't over 'til it's over!" so to speak. People are not like pastries baked in an oven; there never comes a moment in time when we're baked to perfection. The human journey is itself the destination. To think you've ever finally "made it" in life or that for once and for all you've "got your act totally together" is probably a self-deception. Your life is like an incomplete masterpiece, beautiful for what it is, but incomplete nonetheless.

The longest journey begins with the first step.
~Chinese proverb

enneagram
A geometric symbol with spiritual significance used in transformational psychology.

self-transformation
The process of personal change facilitated by the enneagram.

self-transcendence
According to Frankl, the manner in which we find the greatest meaning in our lives. By getting beyond our egos and by overcoming ourselves, we can commit to things, forget our self-preoccupations and ultimately experience happiness in life.

archetypal/transpersonal psychology
A developmental transpersonal psychology that outlines the key stages of human development, each having its own lesson, task or gift. Its heroic journey concept is a universal metaphor (as evidenced in myth, art and literature) that can be used as a model for living in our complex modern world. It is best seen as an educational tool that helps people to discover themselves and their mission in life.

authentic self
The real self—the final destination according to archetypal psychology—that which allows us to experience wholeness and integrity as people.

You have no enemy except yourself and you are the enemy indeed to him because you do not know him as yourself.
~A Course in Miracles

 The Enneagram: A Path to Personal Liberation

Enneagram Theory
A type of psychology that uses a geometric symbol to represent nine basic personality types and their interrelationships.

Enneagram Theory provides a system of transformational/spiritual psychology that uses a geometric symbol to represent nine basic personality types and their interrelationships. The term is derived from the Greek words *ennea*, meaning nine, and *gram*, meaning graph or drawing. The symbol begins with a circle. Around the circle are placed nine equidistant points, each having a number. The numbers refer to different personality types, so somebody could be a one, an eight, or a five, for example. Note that no number is better or worse than any other; the numbers are value-neutral. On the enneagram, the number nine is top and centre. Number one is found to the right of it, while the rest of the numbers follow clockwise in sequence. Within the circle itself, you will find an equilateral triangle and another six-pointed shape. See the enneagram symbol below in Figure 7.1.

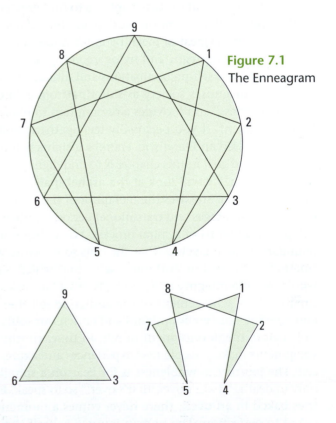

Figure 7.1
The Enneagram

Who's really behind the ego-mask?

Source: Figures 7.1, 7.2, 7.3, 7.4. Don Richard Riso, best-selling author of *Personality Types, Understanding the Enneagram, The Riso-Hudson Enneagram Type Indicator* and *Enneagram Transformations*.

Relationship to Traditional and Contemporary Psychology

The enneagram has ancient origins. Some believe it dates back to the Islamic Sufi Brotherhoods in the fourteenth and fifteenth centuries, while others believe the enneagram originates even earlier with Greek thinkers like Plato, Plotinus and Pythagoras, the last of whom thought that all things in the universe could be explained in numerical terms—a thesis which modern day physics and mathematics seems to support. Whatever its origins, the enneagram's psychological insights were introduced to the west by the George Ivanovich Gurdjieff in 1916. Building upon what they've learned about the enneagram from spiritual teachers like Gurdjieff and others who came into contact with it, current enneagram developers, such as Don Richard Riso and Russ Hudson (2000), have incorporated the works of Karen Horney, Sigmund Freud, Oscar Ichazo, Claudio Naranjo and Carl Jung into their theories in efforts to explain the psychodynamics of the various enneagram personality types. In this vein, Riso has pointed out that his descriptions of the enneagram types correlate not only with Jungian types (described in Chapter 2) but also with personality disorders as described in the Diagnostic and Statistical Manual of Mental Disorders, essentially the bible of the psychiatric profession. For example, the eight (in its unhealthy expressions) corresponds to the antisocial personality disorder, while a dysfunctional one displays symptoms characteristic of the compulsive personality disorder. Renee Baron and Elizabeth Wagele (1994) have also tried to correlate Jungian personality types with enneagram types. See Figure 7.2 for an illustration. Your enneagram type may thus help to verify your Myers-Briggs Jungian type and vice versa. For purposes of type verification, complete Self-Diagnostic 7.1, What's My Enneagram Type?

One's own self is well hidden from one's own self: of all mines of treasure, one's own is the last to be unearthed.
~Friedrich Nietzsche

...forget not that no concept of yourself will stand against the truth of what you are.
~A Course in Miracles

Clad in this "self," the creation of irresponsible and ignorant persons, meaningless honours and catalogued acts—strapped into the straight jacket of the immediate. To step out of all this, and stand naked on the precipice invulnerable, free: in the Light, with the Light, of the Light. Whole, real in the Whole. Out of myself as a stumbling block, into myself as fulfilment.
~Dag Hammarskjold

How Did You Get Your Type?

To understand how you developed your type, it's helpful first to arrange the nine personality types into three triads. Riso and Hudson (1996) call them the instinctive triad, the feeling triad and the thinking triad. See Figure 7.3 on page 278.

In each of the triads, one type overexpresses the characteristic faculty of the triad, another underexpresses it and the third is most out of touch with it. See Figure 7.4 on page 278.

We all have instinctive abilities, as well as the ability to think and to feel. However, during our childhoods, we began to emphasize one faculty over the other two. The triad in which your personality type is found represents the overall way you consciously and unconsciously adapted to your family and the world (Riso, 1996). It's not that the other two triads disappear but, as Riso puts it, "all three faculties operate in an ever-changing balance to produce our personality" (1987: 26). The faculty that emerges and becomes dominant

Figure 7.2

Enneagram Types in Relation to Jungian, Myers-Briggs Personality Types

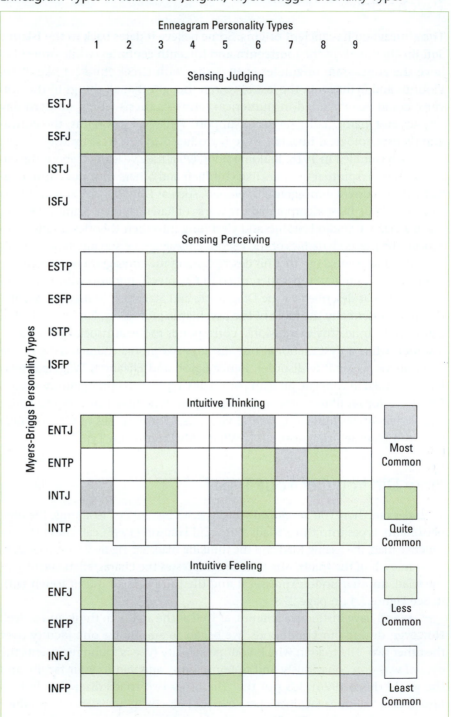

Self Diagnostic

7.1 What's My Enneagram Type?

Aim: This self-diagnostic will enable you to form an initial hypothesis of your enneagram personality type. The results will be useful in finding whole new liberating directions for personal self-transcendence. They should enable you to remove self-created obstacles to your higher development as a spiritual being.

Instructions: Listed below are 45 statements. Next to each one, indicate how well it reflects what you're like as a person. The person we're addressing here is not your "social self," "family self," or "school self," but the "self inside" that you know to be the most authentic expression of who you are.

1 = Not like me at all
2 = Not very much like me
3 = A little bit like me
4 = Frequently like me
5 = Almost always like me

3 1. It's important for me to be morally correct. I want to do the right things for the right reasons.

4 2. How others see me is important.

4 3. I focus more on goals than on relationships.

2 4. I want to understand myself. I want others to understand me as well.

4 5. I am very observant, seeing things most people overlook.

1 6. I am a traditionalist, strongly identifying with groups, institutions and friends.

1 7. I am unpredictable, spontaneous and fun-loving.

3 8 I am direct, able to motivate and take charge when necessary.

2 9. Keeping the peace is very important to me.

5 10. I try to achieve perfection in my work. Others should do the same.

5 11. I wouldn't want to live with people who don't care about or appreciate me.

5 12. It's important that I make something of myself.

4 13. Beauty and taste are important to me. My physical surroundings strongly influence my moods.

3 14. I have a deep desire to gain knowledge and to understand the world around me.

5 15. I am severely hurt when betrayed by others.

5 16. In my opinion, people need to lighten up.

3 17. I enjoy opposition and confrontation.

2 18 I avoid disagreement and confrontation whenever I can.

1 19. I tend to be formal and idealistic.

4 20. It's important that I make people feel comfortable and welcome.

3 21. I try to make good first impressions on people.

___1___ 22. I'm easily bothered or hurt by intrusions.

___1___ 23. I hold on tightly to what I have acquired.

___4___ 24. I need people to give me clear-cut guidelines so I know where I stand.

___4___ 25. I like and enjoy people and they usually like and enjoy me.

___5___ 26. I hate being used or manipulated by others.

___5___ 27. I'm usually perceived as friendly and easygoing, though on occasion I can be extremely stubborn.

___3___ 28. I get upset when people break the rules.

___2___ 29. People sometimes see me as an interference, when I'm only trying to help.

___4___ 30. I can adapt to whatever group of people I'm with.

___4___ 31. I am often envious of what others have.

___5___ 32. Being alone is not a problem for me. I love my privacy.

___1___ 33. I'm more sensitive to danger and threat than most other people.

___1___ 34. I really hate being bored, having no plans and having nothing to do.

___3___ 35. I need to be in control and to exhibit my strengths.

___3___ 36. I prefer to be optimistic rather than pessimistic.

___2___ 37. I do what I say I'll do almost all of the time.

___4___ 38. I easily show my feelings.

___4___ 39. I'm competitive.

___2___ 40. I often appear melancholy, sad or emotionally intense.

___1___ 41. I have a tendency to intellectualize my problems.

___1___ 42. I'm a practical, "meat and potatoes" kind of person.

___5___ 43. I enjoy physical activity.

___4___ 44. I emphasize practical results over abstract ideals.

___2___ 45. I often need help or encouragement to get started on things. Once I get started, I'm usually OK. Getting started is the problem.

Scoring: The numbers of the preceding statements have been arranged into columns. Next to each statement number, place the numerical value you gave to it reflecting your level of agreement.

1: The Perfect Idealist	2: The Nurturing Helper	3: The Motivating Star
1. 3	2. 4	3. 4
10. 5	11. 5	12. 5
19. 1	20. 4	21. 3
28. 3	29. 2	30. 4
37. 2	38. 4	39. 4
Totals 14	19	20

4: The Sensitive Artist	5: The Observant Thinker	6: The Wary Loyalist
4. _2_	5. _4_	6. _1_
13. _4_	14. _3_	15. _5_
22. _1_	23. _1_	24. _4_
31. _4_	32. _5_	33. _1_
40. _2_	41. _1_	42. _1_
Totals _13_	_14_	_12_

7: The Enthusiastic Generalist	8: The Assertive Leader	9: The Easygoing Peacemaker
7. _1_	8. _3_	9. _2_
16. _5_	17. _3_	18. _2_
25. _4_	26. _5_	27. _5_
34. _1_	35. _3_	36. _3_
43. _5_	44. _4_	45. _2_
Totals _16_	_18_	_14_

My highest total is ___20___ under the ___motivating star___ column.

To discover what your enneagram type is like, read the descriptions below.

1. **Perfect Idealist** Rational, hardworking, ethical, serious, emotionally rigid or unexpressive; can be wise and discerning; often impatient, angry and humourless

2. **The Nurturing Helper** Caring and nurturing; friendly, self-sacrificing and altruistic; can also be possessive, proud and manipulative, creating dependency relationships

3. **The Motivating Star** Adaptable and chameleon-like; motivated by success; ambitious and image conscious; can be overly competitive, emotionally shallow, driven, opportunistic and arrogant

4. **The Sensitive Artist** Typically shy and introverted; quiet and gentle, inspired and creative; sees self as special, introspective; can be moody, melancholic, inhibited and self-pitying

5. **The Observant Thinker** Intellectual, insightful and curious; independent and innovative; great capacity for knowledge and system building; can be emotionally distant, isolated, eccentric and awkward with people

6. **The Wary Loyalist** Dependable and trustworthy; committed, reliable, security oriented, dependent on others, endearing; can also be defensive and suspicious, creating "in" and "out" groups; may hide fear by acting tough

7. **The Enthusiastic Generalist** Usually energetic and enthusiastic with a real *joie de vivre;* playful and spontaneous, likable and optimistic; can be infantile, excessive and self-centred or insensitive to others

8. **The Assertive Leader** Aggressive, powerful, forthright and decisive; strong, assertive and resourceful; can become belligerent and confrontational; overly controlling

9. **The Easygoing Peacemaker** Stable, accommodating and trusting; blends into surroundings; at one with the world; avoids conflict, minimizes upset; can also be stubborn, inattentive, impenetrable and neglectful

277

Figure 7.3
The Psychological Triads

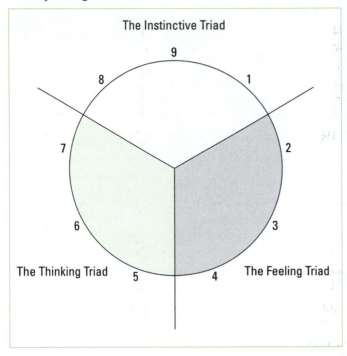

Figure 7.4
What Each Type Does

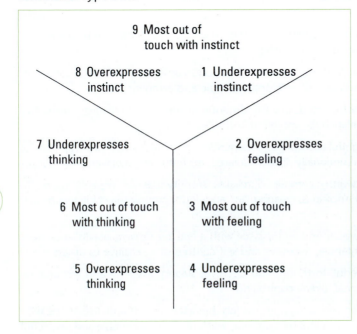

in our lives is a product of biology and early childhood experience. Concerning the latter influence, enneagram developers such as Riso (1996) give special importance to **childhood orientations** toward the parents when it comes to the development of type. You may, for example, have bonded and felt closely connected to the nurturing figure (usually the mother) or the protective figure (usually, though not necessarily, the father) in your life. Perhaps you positively connected with both. By contrast, maybe you felt disconnected from either one or both, or perhaps you felt ambivalent toward either one or both. Whatever the case, these initial childhood orientations to the nurturing and protective figures in your life helped to form your adult personality. Important to understand is the fact that the identifications that are, or are not, formed in childhood have little to do with the quality of parental caretaking. You could strongly identify with an abusive parent or disconnect with a loving one in whom you simply do not see yourself.

The Wings

According to enneagram theory, nobody is a "pure" personality type. Riso (2000) maintains that anyone's personality is a unique blend of his basic type and one or two of the types adjacent to it on the circumference of the enneagram. For example, the five can be coloured by its four or six wing, or both in differing degrees.

When the wings of personality are taken into account, we can understand how two people with the same basic personality type can exhibit subtle differences or different shades of the same character. For instance, a five with a strong four wing "looks" different from a five with a strong six wing. The traits of the four and five conflict with one another. Fives tend to withdraw and distance themselves from experience, whereas fours internalize everything to intensify their feelings (Riso and Hudson, 1996). Combining elements of the two produces one of the richest subtypes. Possibilities for outstanding artistic achievement (number four trait) are combined with intellectual achievement (number five trait). Riso and Hudson (1996) identify Glenn Gould, the late great Canadian classical pianist, as a five with a four wing. By contrast, a five with a six wing constitutes a personality type that is one of the most difficult to communicate with or to maintain a relationship with. The person's fiveness creates problems of trust, while the six wing reinforces anxiety, thereby making risk-taking in relationships difficult (Riso and Hudson, 1996). An example of a five with a strong six wing is Sigmund Freud, a psychological theorist whom we've already studied.

Levels of Development

Every enneagram personality type has within it levels of development. You can express your personality in healthy, average and unhealthy ways (Riso and Hudson, 2000). For instance, a healthy eight acts differently from an unhealthy eight or an average eight. At the highest level of development, the eight is heroic and magnanimous. At the lower levels, an eight can become confrontational, domineering and intimidating. At worst, the eight can become a sociopath (Keyes, 1992) or an antisocial personality (Riso and Hudson, 1994).

What is so powerful about the enneagram is that it offers an explanation of the psychodynamics of the descent into dysfunction. On the upside, it also offers directions for climbing out of the abyss, overcoming the unhealthy debilitating expressions of our personalities and ultimately achieving personal liberation from ourselves.

Paths of Integration and Disintegration

According to enneagram theory, people change but their personalities remain the same for life. A seven cannot suddenly become a four, for instance. However, your personality is not fixed. As we just learned, people can move from unhealthy to healthy expressions of their personalities. As well, very healthy people can move beyond their basic personalities in the direction of integration, or choose the **path of integration**. Under stress or great anxiety, people can also choose the **path of disintegration** by moving in the direction of disintegration. In other words, people can grow or deteriorate and, in the process, they can begin to display behaviours characteristic of other personality types. Given this, in order to fully understand the workings of your

childhood orientations
The psychological relations established between children and nurturing and protective caregivers, usually the parents.

path of integration
According to enneagram psychology, the direction healthy people take to move beyond their basic personalities. The paths of integration are 1-7-5-8-2-4-1 and 9-3-6-9.

path of disintegration
According to enneagram psychology, the direction people under stress or great anxiety may take that leads toward deterioration. The paths of disintegration are 1-4-2-8-5-7-1 and 9-6-3-9.

Figure 7.5

Paths of Integration and Disintegration

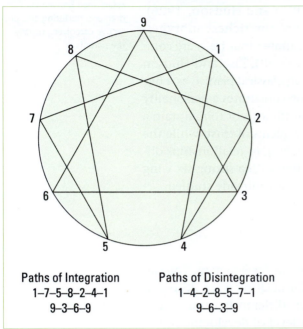

Paths of Integration
1–7–5–8–2–4–1
9–3–6–9

Paths of Disintegration
1–4–2–8–5–7–1
9–6–3–9

...there is nothing on which people are so fixated as their self-image. We are literally prepared to go through hell just so we don't have to give it up. Ernest Becker rightly calls it "character armour." It determines most of what we do or don't do, say or don't say, what we occupy ourselves with and what we don't. We're all affected by it. The question is: Do I have the freedom to be anything else than this role and this image?
~Richard Rohr

personality, you need to know your basic type, your wing(s), your personal direction of integration (i.e., how you grow and develop by going beyond your basic type), and your direction of disintegration. See Figure 7.5 for an illustration of the paths of integration and disintegration.

From Figure 7.5 we see that as individuals become healthier or unhealthier, they can move in different directions from their basic types. Riso and Hudson (1987: 38–39) provide an example of how type six can integrate or disintegrate by either moving ahead to nine or deteriorating to three.

A brief example will illustrate what these movements mean. At personality type six, one line is drawn to nine, and another to three. This means that if a six were to become healthy and begin to actualize his potentials, he would move to nine, the direction of integration specified by the enneagram, activating what personality nine symbolizes for the six. When the enneagram predicts that a healthy six will move to nine, we find that this is precisely the kind of psychological development we see in individuals who are sixes. Many of the six's problems have to do with insecurity and anxiety, and when the six moves to nine he or she becomes relaxed, accepting, and peaceful. This six at nine is more self-possessed and less anxious than ever before.

Conversely, the line to three indicates the six's direction of disintegration. If a six were to become not merely neurotic, but even more unhealthy, he or she would do so by "going to three." The six's anxiety has made him extremely suspicious of others, and his feelings of inferiority and insecurity are rampant.

A move to three marks a neurotic six's need to bolster his self-esteem by an extreme narcissistic overcompensation. The six at three will maliciously strike out at people to prove how tough he can be, and to triumph over anyone he thinks has threatened him. In short, the six at three becomes dangerously aggressive and psychopathic.

Source: Riso (1987, 1990). Quotations from *Personality Types, Understanding the Enneagram, The Riso-Hudson Enneagram Type Indicators* and *Enneagram Transformations.*

The Problem with Your Personality

Sadly, many of us fall under the spell of our personalities. We use them to defend ourselves from fully realizing how fearful we are. We adopt ingenious strategies for inflating the ego as a defence against insecurity and loneliness (Riso, 1987). In the process, we create self-fulfilling prophecies bringing about the very things we fear most and losing what we most desire. Riso (1987: 346) says:

> Looking at each of the personality types as a whole teaches us what we can expect if we inflate our ego at the expense of other values. By coercing others to love them, twos end by being hated. By aggrandizing them-selves, threes end by being rejected. By exclusively following their feel-ings, fours end by wasting their lives. By imposing their ideas on reality, fives end by being out of touch with reality. By being too dependent on others, sixes end by being abandoned. By living for pleasure, sevens end by being frustrated and unsatisfied. By dominating others to get what they want, eights end by destroying everything. By accommodating them-selves to others too much, nines end as undeveloped, fragmented shells. By attempting to be perfect with humanity, ones end by perverting their humanity. The way out of these inexorable conclusions is to become con-vinced that only by transcending the ego can we hope to find happiness. As wisdom has always recognized, it is only by dying to ourselves that we find life.

In studying the enneagram we find a path for personal growth. The en-neagram exposes each personality type's self-deceptions, dead-end pursuits and destructive self-defeating tendencies. Identifying your enneagram type should therefore not be experienced as fun. The enneagram is not a game. The en-neagram can reveal much about you that is not very pleasant. Talking about the feelings that should result when one honestly comes to terms with his or her enneagram number type, Richard Rohr (1992: 13) says that

> [w]hoever is not humiliated has not yet found his or her "number." The more humiliating it is, the more one is looking the matter right in the eye. Anyone who says, "It's wonderful that I'm a Three" is either not a Three or hasn't really understood what I'm saying about type Three...The Enneagram uncovers the games we find ourselves tangled in. It will initially be experienced as embarrassing and perhaps shameful. For a time there will even be a loss of energy and motivation until we relearn how to operate from truth.

If you refer back to the descriptions of the enneagram types provided in Self-Diagnostic 7.1, you will see that each type has much to be disturbed and embarrassed about. For example, at lower levels of development, ones can be impersonal, rigid and impatient; twos can be manipulative and controlling; threes may be calculating, arrogant and opportunistic; fours are sometimes self-pitying and impractical; fives can be awkward and eccentric; sixes often scape-goat and rebel; sevens can be infantile and insensitive; eights are sometimes hard-hearted and openly belligerent; while nines can be stubborn, inattentive and neglectful.

281

Not wishing to leave you here completely humiliated and embarrassed (though if I were a dysfunctional eight, this option might be tempting!), let me suggest to you that by leaving behind a false self, filled with its deceptions, illusions, obsessions, misguided wants and compulsions, a kind of spiritual rebirth becomes possible. Repeating the ancient wisdom to which Riso draws our attention, "It is only by dying to ourselves that we find life" (Riso and Hudson, 1996). Nothing less than existential rebirth is required. To lay bare the psychological games we have played for so long and to see how our natural gifts have unconsciously been used as weapons of psychological self-defence against our basic fears is in itself liberating. Life can become more serene, for when we confront the lies of our life, when we expose our absurdity and when we finally see how ridiculous we can sometimes be, then we are in a position to call upon others to do the same (Rohr, 1992). Finally, we grow to love our true selves (not artificially created self-images) and to love others for who they really are. Ultimately, by shedding the character armour of our personalities, we free ourselves to the experience of love and joy in our lives.

We should be prepared for some difficulty on the road to our spiritual rebirth. The enneagram would have us travel into unknown territory. We may have to express feelings, do things or relate in ways that are foreign to our current self-concepts. We may have to overcome past habits, confront old attitudes and identifications, and learn to leave the old ways behind (Riso and Hudson, 1996). Only by transcending our ego selves, however, can we find lasting happiness, peace and redemption (Rohr, 1992).

7.3

Enneagram Travel Tips for Life

For Ones

1. Relax! The world will survive without you. Not everything will end in disaster if you're not there to be involved.

2. Stop telling yourself and others what should be done. It's not healthy. Instead of saying, "I should...," try saying, "I want to...." Rather than insisting, "That's wrong," say instead, "I don't like it when...." Make your judgmental statements more like statements of personal preference.

3. Inject some humour into your life. Don't always be so serious.

4. Get in touch with your feelings. They may not be perfect or rational, but they're nevertheless yours. Ignoring them doesn't mean that they will not exert unconscious influence. Come to terms with your anger in particular.

5. Take a class in stress reduction or engage in some sports and leisure activities. Stop working or doing whatever it is you do so compulsively.

For Twos

1. Do some pleasurable and self-satisfying things without others. Do something for yourself for a change.

2. Stop expecting a return for your generosity or kindness toward others. Don't guilt people into appreciating you; they likely won't appreciate either you or what you've done for them. At best, they'll feel guilty. At worst, they'll resent the guilt you've instilled.

3. If you become the target of unfair treatment, speak up immediately and rationally express your concerns.

4. Don't be possessive with your friends and loved ones. Share them with others.

5. Don't kid yourself about the benefits you derive personally by being nice or helpful to someone else. There's a payoff in being a self-sacrificial martyr. What's the payoff for you?

For Threes

1. Remember that no self-image can ever replace the truth of who you really are. Tell that to your image consultant!

2. Try not to manipulate people on your climb to the top. At the top of the ladder there's only one way to go, namely down. On your descent you might run into some of the people you passed on your way up to personal glory.

3. Give back to the community some of what the community has given to you. Do not feel entitled to get what you want at the expense of others (Riso and Hudson, 2000).

4. Quit trying to be impressive. People may see you as a braggart—little could be more detrimental to your personal pursuit of success.

5. Don't let your competitive instincts cause bad feelings and contempt for others. Respect your opponents.

For Fours

1. Focus on the present. Avoid self-pity. If your needs were not met in the past, treat yourself with love and compassion now.

2. Get active and don't wait until you're in the mood. The right feelings may never come. Dedicate yourself to some type of meaningful work. Live by this dictum: "When the going gets depressed, the depressed get going."

3. Try not to take people's comments and behaviours so personally. "You would worry less about what others thought of you if you knew how seldom they did." Your propensity toward defensiveness is irritating to others; it doesn't help you either.

4. Give yourself time to be creative. Ideally, find work that uses your creative talents.

5. Don't overwhelm people with your emotions. For an emotional outlet, write letters to yourself that you don't mail (Baron and Wagele, 1994).

For Fives

1. Remember Gurdjieff's insight: "Books are like maps, but there is also the necessity of travelling." Do more and think less.

2. Get in touch with your body. Take up sports, physical activities and creative pursuits.

3. If you want to understand, concentrate on observing without judgment. Analyze less what you see.

4. Reject your natural tendency to withdraw. Support and nurture others. Try to approach and co-operate.

5. Remember that someone having less knowledge than you doesn't make that person less worthy. Don't use your knowledge as a way of building yourself up as you put others down. You probably like doing this, but this habit hasn't made you any friends lately or helped you to win any popularity contests.

For Sixes

1. Don't mask your insecurity with a tough façade. Accept and come to terms with your anxiety. Use it to energize yourself into productive action.

2. Surround yourself with people who are accepting, trustworthy and encouraging (Baron and Wagele, 1994).

3. Try to develop more trust in your life. Risk rejection as you try to develop close and meaningful relationships.

4. Don't allow yourself to get into patterns of negative thinking.

5. Don't "suck up" to authorities or worship them. Smart authorities will recognize your behaviour for what it is. Be your own self-respecting person. Remember, authorities can be wrong; they certainly conflict with one another.

For Sevens

1. Don't string yourself out doing too many things at the same time.

2. Don't let your "joie de vivre" or your pleasurable pursuits get in the way of duties and responsibilities.

3. Start to control your impulses. A Nike commercial once suggested that you "Just do it," but if you just do it without thinking, you may end up regretting what you've just done.

4. Try not to make happiness your ultimate life goal. It is a by-product of giving yourself to something worthwhile (Riso, 2000).

5. Be grateful and appreciative for what you have. Try to heed this Chinese proverb: "Before you wish for any one thing, first examine how happy are those who already have it." Here's another sobering Chinese zinger for you: "Want anything long enough and you don't."

For Eights

1. Remember that not everything in life is a contest. Allow others to take control sometimes. See what it's like to be a follower. Imagine what it would be like to be your follower.

2. Don't use your power to hurt or intimidate people. People will not accept your control if they hate you.

3. Keep in mind that you have a tendency to become restless and impatient with others' incompetence or inability. Showing this side of yourself may scare people away or interfere with their performance.

4. Don't confuse honesty with rude bluntness. Try expressing criticism softly and tactfully. As for appreciation, express it loudly and frequently.

5. Monitor your tendency to pick fights with others. Ask yourself what you're trying to prove when you say or do provocative things.

For Nines

1. Take action when things aren't right. Don't just sit there wishing and hoping for better times.

2. Show initiative rather than always waiting for others to make the first move. Have others join you in your actions for a change.

3. Accept your negative feelings and impulses. If you don't express them, they will surface unexpectedly and interfere with the peace and harmony you want in your relationships.

4. Set goals and deadlines for yourself. Stick to them.

5. Don't allow yourself to be distracted from problems. Deal with them head-on. Remember, conflict is an opportunity for positive change.

285

Enneagram Types Before the Party cartoon

Enneagram Types After the Party cartoon

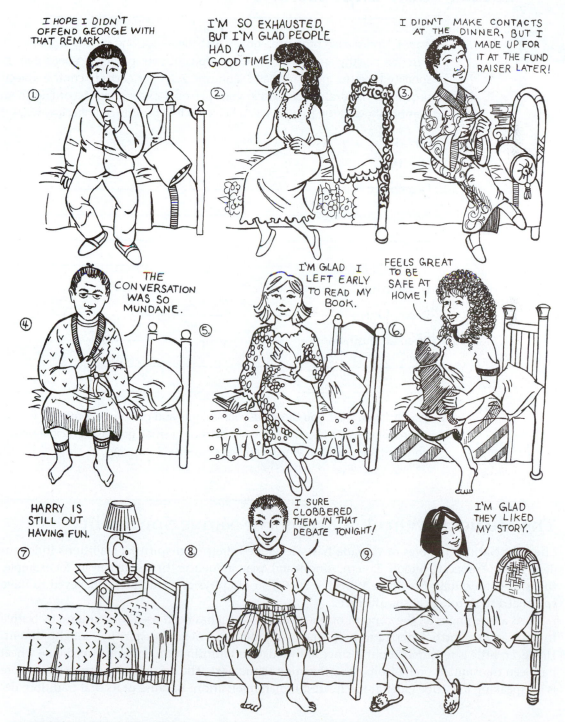

Source: From *Enneagram Types* and *Before/After the Dinner Party* from *The Enneagram Made Easy* by Renee Baron and Elizabeth Wagele. Copyright 1994 by Renee Baron and Elizabeth Wagele. Reprinted by permission of HarperCollins Publishers, Inc.

application exercise 7.1

7.4

Self-Expressions

Part I: Under each of the categories that follow list one or two adjectives that describe healthy and unhealthy expressions of your particular enneagram personality type (for help, see Self-Diagnostic 7.1). For each descriptive adjective provide an illustration of it using your personal experience. According to your number, how in the past have you behaved in a healthy or unhealthy way?

My type: _____

Healthy

Descriptors: ——————————————————————

Personal Illustrations: ————————————————

——————————————————————————

——————————————————————————

Unhealthy

Descriptors: ——————————————————————

Personal Illustrations: ————————————————

——————————————————————————

——————————————————————————

Part II: If you wish, you can share your insights and personal information with others in the class. This may be done in pairs or in small groups. Participation is optional. Share only that which you feel comfortable sharing.

The Medicine Wheel: A Symbol of Native Spirituality

The First Nations peoples of Canada have developed their own spiritual traditions independently from European, Middle Eastern, African and Asian influences. In Saskatchewan, for example, the Moose Mountain Medicine Wheel, a 2000-year-old physical structure, is believed to have spiritual and astrological significance.

As a teaching tool, the concept of the medicine wheel has been used for centuries by Native Indians across North America to help them gain self-awareness and spiritual enlightenment. However, little is recorded about it since knowledge and information about the medicine wheel has been transmitted orally from one generation to the next. The best way for you to learn more is by speaking to a tribe elder at the nearest Indian reservation. Because of its oral tradition, details and descriptions of the medicine wheel differ between regions and tribes. In her discussions of the medicine wheel, Mary E. Loomis (1991) shares with us Native teachings as revealed to her by Harley Swiftdeer, a Cherokee medicine man.

Loomis tells us that the medicine wheel is first of all a circle. On the circle are placed the so-called Powers of the Four Directions: North, South, East and West. Native spiritualists believe everything that exists can be organized according to these powers. For example, if you look at the medicine wheel included here, you will note that each direction has a colour associated with it (i.e., white, black, yellow and red). These colours represent the four races of humanity. The rainbow centre represents people of mixed race.

Each direction on the wheel provides specific life lessons for us to learn. The sun and fire of the East Power illuminate possibilities and spark the imagination. The Power of the West, using earth and blackness, teaches us the value of introspection and connection with the earth. The South Power, with plants that nourish us, teaches us to be trusting and innocent, while the Power of the North, using animal symbols, teaches us about perfection, wisdom and logic. At the centre of the wheel is found sexual energy. This catalytic energy is a creative force that combines masculine and feminine potentials in harmonious balance. By using the medicine wheel, we can learn to balance and harmonize the emotional, physical, mental, spiritual and sexual components of the human personality. The medicine wheel can facilitate the development of psychological wholeness and health. (For more information on the medicine wheel, read *Dancing the Wheel of Psychological Types* by Loomis.)

Figure 7.6

The Medicine Wheel: Powers of the Four Directions

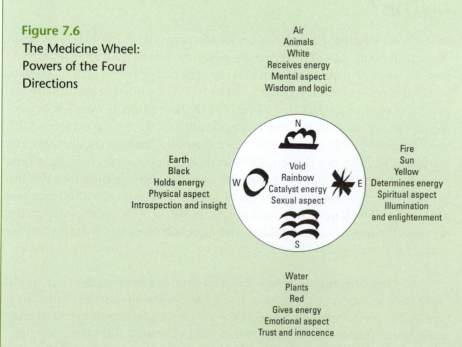

Source: From Mary E. Loomis, *Dancing the Wheel of Psychological Types*, copyright 1991 by Mary E. Loomis, p. 5. Reprinted by permission of the publisher, Chiron Publications.

Books are like maps but there is also the necessity of travelling.
~Gurdjieff

Sometimes you have to go miles out of your way to go a short distance correctly.
~Edward Albee

In closing this discussion of the enneagram, let me leave you with some direction for each numbered type to follow on the continuous journey to personal freedom.

The two needs to overcome its tendency toward self-deception by moving toward the self-understanding of the healthy four. The three needs to overcome its malicious envy of others by moving toward the loyalty and commitment of the healthy six. The four needs to overcome its self-destructive subjectivity by moving toward the objectivity and self-discipline of the healthy one. The five needs to overcome its nihilism by moving toward the courage of the healthy eight. The six needs to overcome its suspicion of others by moving toward the receptivity of the healthy nine. The seven needs to overcome its impulsiveness by moving toward the involvement of the healthy five. The eight needs to overcome its egocentricity by moving toward the concern for others of the healthy two. The nine needs to overcome its complacency by moving toward the ambition of the healthy three. And the one needs to overcome its inflexibility by moving toward the productivity of the healthy seven (Riso, 1987: 348).

Life...and May I Ask, What's the Meaning of This?

Among all my patients in the second half of life, that is, over thirty-five, there has not been one whose problem in the last resort was not that of finding a religious outlook on life.
~C.G. Jung

In the book entitled, *The Unheard Cry for Meaning*, Viktor Frankl tells us about 60 students at an American university who were interviewed after attempting suicide. Some 85 percent of them said the reason they tried to kill themselves was that for them "life seemed meaningless." This finding was particularly surprising in view of the fact that 93 percent of these students were actively engaged socially, performing well academically and were on good terms with their families. Frankl believes that these stunning findings should serve as a wake-up call from our dreams. The North American dream for a long time has been material in nature. A majority of people believe that if we just improve the socioeconomic situation of people, everything will be fine and everyone will be happy. As Frankl puts it, however, "The truth is that as the struggle for survival has subsided, the question has emerged: survival for what? Ever more people have the means to live, but no meaning to live for" (Frankl, 1997).

In view of Frankl's experiences and findings with students, it would seem that neither money, success, nor a good social life can guarantee happiness. Even when people struggle for an entire lifetime to get what they want, the question still remains: "What do they want it for?" Unfortunately, many people do not seriously ask the "what for" question until middle age or later. When they do, they usually recognize at some level of consciousness that "having it all still isn't enough." They are surprised by the prospect that they have been travelling in the fast lane of life but that all along their destination has been a dead end. Life then takes on the quality of a "**spiritual emergency**." The mind and body may be functioning more or less adequately, but from neglectful malnourishment, the spirit finds itself in critical condition. Pills, profits and pleasures that often work to sustain physical and mental life prove to be ineffective when healing the spiritually diseased patient.

In hopes of saving you from a midlife crisis, or at least from a little bit of grief between now and then, let's turn our attention to the work of Viktor Frankl, world-famous psychiatrist and developer of **logotherapy**—a psychotherapeutic method of counselling that focuses on the spiritual problem of meaning.

spiritual emergency
The occurrence that takes place when the spirit finds itself in critical condition even though the mind and body are functioning more or less adequately. Many people seem to encounter this phenomenon in mid-life.

logotherapy
A psychotherapeutic method of counselling that focuses on the spiritual problem of meaning.

7.5 Dr. Frankl and the Soul

So far in this text, there has been a lot of talk about basic needs. Recall, for example, how Freud argued that human beings are motivated by drives and instincts. Much of life, he maintained, is determined by the pleasure principle emanating from the id. Recall also how Abraham Maslow conceptualized his hierarchy of human needs. He talked about the basic needs of survival, safety and security, esteem and self-realization. William Glasser brought to the motivational table of life his own set of basic needs including fun and freedom, as well as power, survival, care, love and belonging. What Viktor Frankl claims is that deep within every person is an innate need to find meaning in life. He calls this the **will-to-meaning** (Frankl, 1986). A major problem in contemporary life, perhaps in your own, is that meaning escapes us. The search for meaning therefore becomes one of our most important life tasks.

will-to-meaning
According to Frankl, the innate need to find meaning in life.

The Three Dimensions of Life

Viktor Frankl (1986) brings to our attention the fact that life has three dimensions: the somatic or physical, the mental and the spiritual. He believes that modern psychology and psychiatry have overemphasized the importance of the mind and body to the virtual exclusion of spirituality. This is unfortunate, according to Frankl (1986), since spirituality is what makes us distinctively human. Rats and weasels do not ask about the meaning of life, but humans do.

In today's fast-paced, results-oriented world, people who ask why things happen or ask questions of meaning are often regarded as disturbed, neurotic or maladjusted in some way. The point, it seems, is to get on with living and to quit worrying about life's significance.

For many there is no purpose in asking about the value of life. In response, Frankl would say that "to be concerned about the meaning of life is not necessarily a sign of disease or of neurosis. It may be; but then again, spiritual agony may have little connection with a disease of the psyche. The proper diagnosis can be made only by someone who can see the spiritual side of man" (Frankl, 1986).

Existential Neurosis

In the context of classical psychoanalysis, blocking the expression of biologically based drives gives rise to frustration that in turn can lead to clinical neurosis. Similarly, Frankl holds that when the will-to-meaning is blocked, **existential frustration** results. If such frustration is strong and persistent enough, a type of existential neurosis may arise. He says, "When existential frustration results in neurotic symptomatology, we are dealing with a new type of neurosis which we call '**noögenic neurosis**'" (Frankl, 1973: xii).

(7.6) ⋯⋯ ## Meaninglessness in Modern Society

Young people growing up in the last decade of the twentieth century were said to be a part of a lost generation, or X-generation, as it's been dubbed. Many of them suffered from what Frankl would label a **collective neurosis**. This neurosis is characterized by four symptoms. The first is *planlessness*. Some people just live day–to-day showing little or no energy or enthusiasm for life. For them, there are no five-year plans or long-term goals. Many people simply live for today and today alone. A second symptom of collective neurosis involves developing a *fatalistic attitude*, essentially a feeling of helplessness. Fatalistic people feel powerless. They believe that their lives are controlled by forces beyond their control. These forces may be internal conditions or external circumstances. Having no plans and no control, people often display *collective thinking* as a third symptom of mass neurosis. Fearing their own individuality, and trying to escape personal responsibility, they immerse themselves in the crowd. They become like others simply doing what others do. Finally, a life with a frustrated need for meaning may manifest itself as *fanaticism*. In contrast to those who surrender their personalities to the crowd, the fanatic ignores others who are different. The fanatic may even hate and attack those who do not follow "the chosen path." Here, differences become the basis of hatred, a sick response to perceived meaninglessness. Thus, if Frankl is correct, it may be that neo-Nazi racists, for example, are really just frightened people responding antisocially to the fear of emptiness in their lives. They may be trying to fill a painful vacuum with aggressions and racial hatred. Behind the tough exterior may be fearful and lost individuals.

Roots of Meaninglessness

Frankl believes that **meaninglessness** in life has several root causes. The first, interestingly enough, has to do with evolutionary biology. In contrast to animals, humans are not so determined by genetics and hormones. Whereas animals unavoidably and necessarily respond to instinctual urges, humans have evolved in ways that allow them to rise above biology. We can choose not to eat when hungry, not to drink when thirsty, not to attack aggressively when provoked and not to engage in mating rituals when sexually aroused—try stopping an animal from making these choices! In short, instincts no longer tell us what we must do.

Second, Frankl points out that in society today, traditional values and institutions are declining in importance in people's lives. A good example is organized religion. It no longer has the influence it once had, providing guidance and direction. In fact, it is often a target for cynical attack. Furthermore, the traditional nuclear family has been under siege in recent years. Once defined by bloodline, it now seems that any convenient arrangement of loving and caring people living together, regardless of gender combination, constitutes a family. Add to this dramatic changes in sexuality and ever-changing societal attitudes, and we can readily understand how some people have become confused by life. They no longer know what is right or wrong, good or bad. Simply, they no longer know what they should do.

So placed in a position where they no longer do what they must do by force of biology, and no longer knowing what they should do given the changing values and crumbling institutions of society, people no longer know what they want to do. They are lost and cast adrift on the turbulent sea of life. They see no way home and can find no shelter from the storm. In response to this frightening and dangerous situation, they fall ill to collective neurosis, made up of **conformity** and **fanaticism** (mindless obedience). They no longer accept personal responsibility for themselves or their lives. They become followers and foolish imitators in their desperate attempt to escape the anxiety of decision making in an uncertain world.

7.7 ···· ## How to Find and Create Meaning in Your Life

A number of years ago on a CBC show entitled *Man Alive*, host Roy Bonisteel asked Viktor Frankl where meaning could be found. In response, Frankl said it can be found anywhere by anyone. Meaning can be found on the mountaintops and in the valleys of life. It can be found in the dingiest hut or in the fanciest mansion. Meaning is possible whether you're rich or poor, beautiful or ugly, male or female, hearty or sick, young or old, intelligent or unintelligent. Meaning is not the exclusive preserve of philosophers, geniuses, or rich and accomplished people. In fact, Frankl points out that, according to letters he's received, some of the deepest meaning is found by convicted prisoners in jail, those sentenced to be executed and living on death row. Given that meaning can be found even in prison, he laments the fact that so many young people today lack meaning in their lives, so much so that even when surrounded by the abundance of life in the twenty-first century, they still

meaninglessness
The state in which we do not find any meaning in life. According to Frankl, the experience of meaninglessness has fundamental root causes including evolutionary biology, declining traditional values and the weakening of the traditional nuclear family. Placed in a position where they no longer do what they must do by force of biology, and no longer knowing what they should do given the changing values and crumbling institutions of society, people no longer know what they want to do.

conformity
An aspect of the collective neurosis experienced by people faced with meaninglessness. They no longer accept personal responsibility for themselves or their lives. They become followers and foolish imitators in their desperate attempt to escape the anxiety of decision making in an uncertain world.

fanaticism
Mindless obedience. According to Frankl, a life with a frustrated need for meaning may manifest itself as fanaticism. In contrast to those who surrender their personality to the crowd, the fanatic ignores others who are different. The fanatic may even hate and attack those who do not follow the chosen path.

find cause to kill themselves. Given this tragic situation, it's vitally important that we find meaning in our lives, but how can we begin the search?

Self-Transcendence As a logotherapist and existential psychiatrist, Frankl recognizes that meaning cannot be imposed on individuals. Nobody can prescribe life's meaning for someone else. There is not one single meaning that applies to everybody. Since all people are different, meaning is unique to each and every individual. Each person is challenged by life in different ways by the particular set of circumstances in which he finds himself. No two people find themselves in exactly the same situation as we've all been dealt a different hand in life. Only the requirement to respond is universal.

According to Frankl, some people respond to life by seeking meaning in the pursuit of happiness. By feeding their appetites and satisfying their desires, or by indulging in the pleasures of the body, some hope to find meaning. These people think of life in terms of "I want," "Me first" and "Gimme gimme," believing that, "Whoever dies with the most toys wins" and "You only live once, so you might as well go for the gusto and get everything you can."

In contrast to the pleasure-seeking self-indulgence of the crowd just mentioned, others try to find meaning in self-absorption. It could be argued that a whole segment of the book-publishing industry is devoted to narcissistic people who wish to analyze themselves, interpret themselves, intellectualize themselves—in short, to absorb themselves in themselves. For Frankl, this kind of self-absorption, along with the pursuits of the self-indulgent crowd, cannot ultimately lead to meaning and lasting life satisfaction. He likens self-absorbed people to the boomerang. He points out, contrary to popular belief, that the job of the boomerang is not to return to the hunter who throws it. If the boomerang returns, it means that the hunter failed to hit the prey he was aiming at. So too with individuals. When people focus on themselves too intently rather than on a target mission or life task external to themselves, they fail in their endeavour. Frankl prescribes **self-transcendence** as a requirement for meaningful and satisfying life. Frankl believes it's necessary to forget oneself, to quit caring so much about one's personal wants and needs if meaning is to be found.

Obsessively focusing on the self will, in the end, be self-defeating. It's not that your basic needs and wants should be totally neglected, only that preoccupation with them will not help you find meaning.

Future Orientation When the locus of meaning is placed outside the individual, life begins to take on a **future orientation**. One begins to perceive a gap between the way things are and the way things ought to be, or between the way one is and how one should be. This perceived gap between "is" and "ought" produces in the person a kind of healthy tension. People begin to feel motivated to act. They find reasons to get up in the morning, get active and start changing things. They want to make things better for the future. Looking

---

When the people lack a proper sense of awe, then some awful visitation will descend upon them.
~Lao Tzu

. . . man should not ask what he may expect from life, but should rather understand that life expects something from him.
~Viktor Frankl

self-transcendence
According to Frankl, the manner in which we find the greatest meaning in our lives. By getting beyond our egos and by overcoming ourselves, we can commit to things, forget our self-preoccupations and ultimately experience happiness in life.

future orientation
A view toward bridging the gap between what is and what could or should be at some point in the future.

for improvements, they constantly find new purposes to fulfill. Compare this to people who dwell in the past, either living in a pleasant fantasy that no longer exists, or bitterly resenting a personal history that cannot be undone. Neither option yields very much meaning, if any at all. Lamenting an unsatisfying present or complaining about current frustrated wants doesn't yield very much meaning either.

Meaning Is Found in Work, Love and Suffering

For Frankl, meaning in life is ultimately found in work, love and, if necessary, in suffering. Let's look at work first. **Work** provides all of us with an opportunity to find meaning in our lives. Through work we can express our personal creativity and realize values that are important to us. If you're an artist, your work enables you to fulfill your potentialities. If you're devoted to saving the planet, working for Greenpeace, say, will help you champion a cause you consider important. Note that not all work is inherently creative or important in itself. Fortunately, it's not the work that yields meaning; rather, it's the way in which the work is performed. Show me somebody at work, at any job, who doesn't care or who just goes through the motions, and I'll show you a bored and dissatisfied person. On the other hand, show me a student, a janitor, an executive or parent who takes pride in her efforts and personal

work According to Frankl, one of the means through which we can find meaning in life. Through work we can express our personal creativity and realize values that are important to us. It's not the work itself that yields meaning; rather, it's the way in which the work is performed. Work affords us all the opportunity for self-transcendence. Finding a cause or mission to which we want to commit ourselves is one of our ultimate life tasks.

Meaning is not found in work itself, but in the way it is done.

best, an individual who goes the extra mile without being asked, and I'll show you a person who's motivated and enthusiastic about life.

Work affords all of us the opportunity for self-transcendence. By investing ourselves in our work, we can get beyond our petty self-preoccupations. We can enrich our personal lives and the lives of others by giving ourselves to something greater than ourselves. Life can indeed take on the quality of a mission. We can commit and dedicate ourselves to worthwhile values and ideals. We can thereby give dignity to life and find purpose in our actions. Serving a cause greater than ourselves can provide a reason for living. Finding a cause or mission to which we want to commit ourselves is one of our ultimate life tasks. This doesn't necessarily entail jumping on some kind of social bandwagon or becoming a pavement-pounding crusader. Your mission may be played out quietly and in private. It's all up to you. The expression of meaning is a personal choice.

Love is a second source of meaning. It too provides an opportunity for self-transcendence. In true love we forget ourselves. We experience someone else in his or her uniqueness. Rather than preoccupy ourselves with what we want or need, we focus on the other person. We give, share and care. We try to do for the other and take pleasure in doing so. In this context, Frankl (1997) talks about the problem of sexual dysfunctions in intimate sexual relations. When people pursue sexual pleasure as an end in itself, when they try to impress their partner or when they seek self-satisfaction above all else, they often become sexually dysfunctional.

According to Frankl, it is precisely by not caring about yourself or your "performance" that you find the most satisfying sexual intimacy with another. For Frankl, happiness is a by-product of self-transcendence. When happiness (say through sex) is pursued directly, as a target objective, failure and misery are sure to result. The **pursuit of happiness** is regarded as a contradiction in terms. Happiness can't be pursued, he says; instead it must ensue from giving oneself to another in love, or, as I mentioned before, by offering oneself in service to a cause or mission greater than oneself. To worry about how happy you are today or how much pleasure you're currently enjoying is to make a wrong turn in life.

Love is but one example of an **experiential value**. Other such values in which we find meaning include goodness, beauty and truth. Glorious sunsets, cultural achievements, scientific discoveries, literary works, natural wonders, heroic acts, saintly examples of humanity and profound insights into human nature are all things that make life wondrous and worth living. They leave us awestruck, filled with joy, inspired about the future and eager to partake in the mystery of life. It is by losing ourselves in culture, nature, art and research that we find meaning.

Finally, meaning can be found in certain **attitudinal values**, especially those relating to how we respond to unavoidable suffering. Viktor Frankl says (1986) that "facing your fate without flinching is the highest achievement

love A source of meaning as identified by Frankl. It provides an opportunity for self-transcendence. In true love we forget ourselves. We try to do for the other and take pleasure in doing so.

Two things fill the mind with ever new and increasing admiration and awe . . . the starry heavens above and the moral law within.
- Immanuel Kant

pursuit of happiness
According to Frankl, a contradiction in terms. Happiness can't be pursued, he says; instead it must ensue from giving oneself to another in love or devoting oneself to a cause or immersing oneself in work.

experiential value
According to Frankl, values in which we find meaning, examples of which include love, goodness, beauty and truth.

attitudinal values
Reflected in how we respond to unavoidable suffering, these values may provide a means through which we find meaning in our lives.

that has been granted to man." When **suffering** can be avoided, he thinks it should be. If you're sick and medication can make you well, you should take the medication. Unnecessary suffering does not yield any meaning. To accept avoidable suffering is masochistic. However, if you are faced with unavoidable suffering (e.g., incurable cancer or unemployment), meaning can be found in how you face your distress. The challenge presented by life here is to transform the tragedy into a personal triumph. To face suffering and difficulty with cheerful courage, in your particular style, is to make for greatness. It serves as a heroic example to others. Your response to suffering and life's difficulties can be inspiring. Frankl uses his own Nazi concentration camp experience of suffering to illustrate how such terrible circumstances can bring out either the best or worst in people. Those who saw purpose in their suffering—to educate the world after the war—were more likely to survive. Those who saw no future and no purpose in their suffering were less likely to survive. Your **mission** in life, then, is to see the purpose in every tragedy, the gift in every problem and to respond in ways that ennoble yourself and others. You're on the existential stage of life and the whole world is waiting for your response.

suffering
According to Frankl, meaning can be found in how we face pain and misfortune.

mission
In the context of transpersonal/spiritual psychology, your ultimate purpose or life task.

7.8 The Heroic Journey: Living Based on Archetypal Psychology

In this final section of the chapter we'll examine the **archetypal psychology** of Carol Pearson. She is the author of the well-known books *The Hero Within: Six Archetypes We Live By* and *Awakening the Heroes Within: Twelve Archetypes to Help Us Find Ourselves and Transform Our World*.

archetypal psychology
A developmental transpersonal psychology that outlines the key stages of human development, each having its own lesson, task or gift. Its heroic journey concept is a universal metaphor (as evidenced in myth, art and literature) that can be used as a model for living in our complex modern world.

What Is Archetypal Psychology? What Can It Do for Me?

Carol Pearson's archetypal theory is a developmental transpersonal psychology. It "take[s] a technique of literary criticism, combine[s] it with the central premises of Jungian psychology, and appl[ies] it to people" (Pearson, 1993). In addition to Jung, other influences on Pearson's psychological thinking include Joseph Campbell (author of *The Hero with a Thousand Faces*) and David Olfield, whose creative mythology methods enabled Pearson to work with archetypes and mythical material in experiential ways. Archetypal psychology outlines key stages of human development, each having its own lesson, task or gift. Pearson believes that the archetypal psychology's **heroic journey** concept is a universal metaphor (as evidenced in myth, art and literature) that can be used as a model for living in our complex modern world. It can help us realize current developmental challenges in our lives. It can open

heroic journey
A universal metaphor that can be used as a model for living.

Macbeth:
Canst thou not minister to a mind diseased,

Pluck from the memory a rooted sorrow,

Raze out the written troubles of the brain.

And with some sweet oblivious antidote

Cleanse the stuffed bosom of that perilous stuff

Which weights upon the heart?

Doctor:
Therein the patient Must minister to himself.

Macbeth:
Throw physic to the dogs; I'll none of it.

~William Shakespeare, Macbeth, Act 5, Scene 3

metaphysical blues
An equivalent expression for free-floating existential anxiety.

Everyone who takes a journey is already a hero. ~Carol Pearson

A disciple once complained, "You tell us stories, but you never reveal the meaning to us." Said the master, "How would you like it if someone offered you fruit and masticated it before giving it to you?" ~Anthony DeMello

alienation
A feeling of separation, distance, or isolation.

existential vacuum
A description Frankl might apply to the state in which those members of the kingdom (according to archetypal psychology) who are worst off—disconnected from their souls and disconnected from the world as well. The lives of such people are empty and unrewarding.

up new ways to personal growth. It can prepare us for more effective citizenship and for leadership roles in a democratic society. Archetypal psychology can also create a greater tolerance for diversity. It shows us that people differ not only racially, culturally and linguistically, but psychologically as well. At the higher reaches of human nature, archetypal psychology can be useful as a guide to spiritual development. It can transform us and help us transform the world. Archetypal psychology is best seen as an educational tool that helps people to discover themselves and their mission in life.

The Kingdom Is Sick

Archetypal psychology begins with the observation that there's sickness in the kingdom, so to speak. Frankl might describe this sickness as collective neurosis; other humanistic psychologists might refer to it as existential anxiety. I call it the **metaphysical blues**. According to Pearson's observations, some people in the kingdom (society) have grown ill because they are without "soul." Like Goethe's Faust, they have sold their souls to the devil for personal gain. While they have made it in the world by achieving fame and fortune, they nonetheless feel empty inside. They do all the right things and go through all the right motions, but in the end it's movement without meaning (Pearson, 1991). They just don't know what all their moving and shaking is for. To say that these people have sold out to the devil is not to suggest that they're necessarily destined for hell, as conceptualized by Christians, Jews and Muslims. Rather, it means that life remains unfulfilled for them. They remain unwhole, experiencing some kind of lack, one that is disturbing to the very core of their being. This is hell enough. This is hell on earth.

Another disease in the human kingdom is **alienation**. People with this existential ailment feel connected to their souls, but cut off from the world (Pearson, 1991). They feel love, and experience life intensely, but they can't find meaningful work and satisfying relationships. They just can't "connect." They experience the external world as an imposition, placing constraints on their freedom. They consequently feel separate and apart.

Finally, you have those in the kingdom who are the worst off. These people are disconnected from their souls and disconnected from the world as well. The lives of such people are empty and unrewarding. Frankl would probably say they suffer from an **existential vacuum**. They don't know how to be true to themselves or how to make their way in the world (Pearson, 1991). They don't know who they are, how to relate, what they should do or what the meaning of life is.

The Hero's Journey as a Model for Living

If you currently suffer from one of the plagues devastating the kingdom, take heart. Self-knowledge, meaning and purpose are all possible and within your grasp. We can all find our way in life learning from heroes. Pearson explains:

Stories about heroes are deep and eternal. They link our own longing and pain and passion with those who have come before in such a way that we learn something about the essence of what it means to be human, and they also teach us how we are connected to the great cycles of the natural and spiritual worlds. The myths that can give our lives significance are deeply primal and archetypal and can strike terror into our hearts, but they can also free us from unauthentic lives and make us real. If we avoid what T.S. Eliot called this "primitive terror" at the heart of life, we miss our connection to life's intensity and mystery. Finding our own connection with such eternal patterns provides a sense of meaning and significance in even the most painful or alienated moments, and in this way restores nobility to life. (1991: 2)

Source: Pearson quotations from "Twelve Archetypes" and "Archetypes and Their Stories" from *Awakening the Heroes Within* by Carol S. Pearson. Copyright 1991 by Carol S. Pearson. Reprinted with permission of Harper Collins Publishers, Inc.

We can find our place in the world, then, through stories about mythical heroes. By means of them we can feel rooted in history and eternity. Our personal life stories are not unlike those of heroes who came before us. Our lives may not be as celebrated as the lives of mythic heroes, but they are in many ways essentially the same. Their quests are our quests. Their struggles are our struggles. The obstacles they overcome (e.g., dragons) are metaphors for the problems that we face. By seeing how our lives and the lives of others are heroic, we can begin to forge links between ourselves and all people of the world, regardless of time and place (Pearson, 1991). We can at last find our connection to humanity. We can begin to live in responsible community with one another. Through identification with heroes we can restore dignity and nobility to life. And when we do this, we heal ourselves and transform the world at the same time.

In classical mythology, how happy or how well a kingdom was often depended on the health of the king or queen. If the monarch was sick, injured or wounded, the kingdom degenerated into a wasteland. For the kingdom to be saved, it was typically necessary for a hero to undertake a quest. Some kind of challenge had to be met or some type of sacred object had to be found. Of course, many difficulties usually confronted the hero along the way. In the end, the hero had to return to the kingdom to heal the king or queen or take that monarch's place as ruler (Pearson, 1991).

Pearson sees parallels between the mythic hero's journey and life today. Stories of heroes reflect psychosocial realities. Our world is the ailing kingdom; our mission is the hero's quest. She continues:

Our world reflects many of the classic symptoms of the wasteland kingdom: famine, environmental damage to the natural world, economic uncertainty, rampant injustice, personal despair anfd alienation, and the threat of war and annihilation. Our "Kingdoms" reflect the state of our collective souls, not just those of our leaders. This is a time in human history when

Try to apply seriously what I have told you, not that you might escape suffering—nobody can escape it—but that you may avoid the worst—blind suffering.
~C.G. Jung

It's not where you are. It's where you're headed that matters.
~Joseph R. Smallwood, former Premier of Newfoundland

The destination is not the goal, for all the learning is in the journey.
~Taoist saying

299

heroism is greatly needed. Like heroes of old, we aid in restoring life, health, and fecundity to the kingdom as a side benefit of taking our own journeys, finding our own destinies, and giving our unique gifts. It is as if the world were a giant puzzle and each of us who takes a journey returns with one piece. Collectively, as we contribute our part, the kingdom is transformed.

The transformation of the kingdom depends upon all of us. Understanding this helps us move beyond a competitive stance into a concern with empowering ourselves and others. If some people "lose" and do not make their potential contribution, we all lose. If we lack the courage to take our journeys, we create a void where our piece of the puzzle could have been, to the collective, as well as our personal, detriment. (Pearson, 1991: 2–3)

The point should be stressed here that one's "heroic journey never ends. As soon as we return from one journey and enter a new phase of our lives, we are immediately propelled into a new sort of journey, the pattern is not linear or circular but spiral" (Pearson, 1991: 3). New journeys start at new levels, present new obstacles, new treasures and new transformative abilities.

The Call to the Quest

call to the quest
According to archetypal psychology, the challenge we must all take on by embarking on our own heroic journeys. We must take on the challenges, confront the dragons, find our treasures and finally return home from our quest to offer our gifts.

delusions of insignificance
Thinking that you're a nobody or a "psychological serf" and that this means you don't have to do anything in the kingdom of the world except feel lost and empty.

It is important for all of us to accept the **call to the quest** and to embark on our heroic journeys. We must take on the challenge, confront the dragons, find our treasures and finally return home from our quest to offer our gifts. We thereby transform the kingdom. To accept any **delusions of insignificance** is to engage in self-deception and ultimately to retreat from personal responsibility. To do so would be to give up our freedom. I guess if you think you're a "nobody" or just a "psychological serf" you don't have to do anything in the kingdom of the world except feel lost and empty. If contemporary society's values have turned you into a self-disrespecting person or if you think of yourself as little more than a commodity to be sold in the job market to the highest bidder, more's the pity. Pearson contends that we must come to respect the human mind and soul as much more than tools of material acquisition. Those of us who have been duped into believing we are unimportant unfortunately "seek to fill our emptiness with food, or drink, or drugs, or obsessive and frantic activity. The much lamented pace of modern life is not inevitable—it is a cover for its emptiness. If we keep in motion, we create the illusion of meaning" (Pearson, 1991: 4).

Some people will at first experience the call to the quest as an urge to improve themselves or their personalities. Society encourages us to measure up to standards of beauty and success. Life can become for many a kind of self-improvement project. By improving self-images, playing our roles better or by living up to perfectionistic standards imposed by others, some of us try to become what we're not. For Pearson, the point of life is not to become someone other than who you are, but to find your true self and discover what you were put on the face of the earth for. We are who we are. It's impossible for us to become someone else. We do not have to measure up to anything. We only have to be true to ourselves. We are not wrong. We are not misplaced. God did not make a mistake. We are all heroes. We are all here to embark on our life journeys. As I said before, we must face our dragons, find our personal treasures and heal the ailing kingdom. By our mere presence in the kingdom we are charged with the responsibility of transforming the world. (And you were bored, thinking you had nothing to do today!)

Psychological Archetypes: Inner Guides for the Journey

From her literary studies of the mythic hero's journey, Pearson has identified 12 **psychological archetypes** that influence our personal life travels. They include the Innocent, Orphan, Warrior, Caregiver, Seeker, Destroyer, Lover, Creator, Ruler, Magician, Sage and Fool. Each archetype "has a lesson to teach us, and each presides over a stage of the journey" (Pearson, 1991: 5). Archetypes are visible everywhere. They are outward manifestations of inner psychic realities. They are reflected in the recurring images of art, literature, myth and religion. We see them represented in all cultures and in all periods of history.

In Chapter 1, you learned how cognitive structures (i.e., mental concepts and ideas) can shape and organize incoming sensory stimuli in different ways. The mind provides the form or mould into which the contents of

It furthers one to have somewhere to go.
~The I Ching

This thought, that the only thing you are called to become is the individual that only you can be, places profound worth on each of us.
~Margaret Frings Keyes

You are more than you have become.
~The Lion King

psychological archetypes
The twelve archetypes that influence our personal travels, according to Pearson. They are outward manifestations of inner psychic realities. They are reflected in the recurring images of art, literature, myth and religion. We see them represented in all cultures and in all periods of history. They include the Innocent, Orphan, Warrior, Caregiver, Seeker, Destroyer, Lover, Creator, Ruler, Magician, Sage and Fool.

Gandalph from The Lord of the Rings

experience are poured. Well, archetypes work something like this. They are mental forms or patterns that condition what we perceive and how we experience the world. As different archetypes gain prominence in our psychological lives, we tend to focus on different things, establish different priorities, think in different ways and experience different emotions. As each archetype becomes operative in our psyche, it "brings with it a task, a lesson and ultimately a gift" (Pearson, 1991: 7). Collectively, the archetypes teach us how to live and realize the full human potential within ourselves.

According to Pearson, which archetypes become operative in anyone's psychic life at any given moment is determined by where the person is in terms of her heroic journey. At the **preparation stage**, the Orphan, Innocent, Caregiver and Warrior take prominence. At the **journey stage**, we find the Seeker, Destroyer, Lover and Creator. Finally, at the **return stage** of our personal journeys, the Ruler, Magician, Sage and Fool are most influential.

At this point, it might be fun and revealing for you to do Self-Diagnostic 7.2, a shortened adaptation of Pearson's Heroic Myth Index, as found in the appendix of *Awakening the Heroes Within*. This exercise will start you thinking about where you are in your life's journey and what things occupy your attention, given the dominant archetypes in your life. If you wish, you can verify your initial hypothesis by completing the Heroic Myth Index prepared by Pearson and her associates.

preparation stage
The first stage of Pearson's heroic journey. In this stage the Orphan, Innocent, Caregiver and Warrior take prominence.

journey stage
Developmental stage captured by soul archetypes. A sense of yearning and movement toward authenticity become salient.

return stage
According to Pearson, that stage along the heroic journey when the Ruler, Magician, Sage and Fool are most influential.

Self Diagnostic 7.2

What Kind of Hero Are You, Anyway?

7.9 **Instructions:** Next to each statement below indicate your level of agreement or disagreement. Do these statements describe you or not? Do they reflect your feelings, thoughts and attitudes?

1 = Strongly disagree
2 = Disagree somewhat
3 = Not quite sure
4 = Agree somewhat
5 = Strongly agree

Note: Be honest when completing this instrument, but try to avoid number 3 whenever possible. Choosing this number too frequently will not provide a very accurate archetypal profile.

1. _____ Thriving on chaos is something that makes sense to me.
2. _____ I often experience states of inner tranquillity.
3. _____ I'm good at leading people.
4. _____ I have faith in my intuitions or gut-level feelings about things.

5. _____ I hate playing roles; I prefer to be real and genuine with people.

6. _____ There are many things going on in my life right now; I feel disoriented.

7. _____ It's difficult for me to say "no" to people.

8. _____ Without self-discipline, there is little chance of personal success.

9. _____ Love makes the world go round.

10. _____ It's time for me to make a change and back away from certain significant others in my life.

11. _____ Life has not dealt me a fair hand.

12. _____ I tend to see the bright side of things.

13. _____ When situations get boring or lifeless, I try to get things going and generate activity.

14. _____ I try not to judge people, but accept them with all their imperfections.

15. _____ I like it when people look up to me for direction.

16. _____ Helping myself enables me to help others.

17. _____ I can sometimes accomplish a lot in ways that seemingly require little work or effort on my part.

18. _____ It's time for me to let go of attachments, things and activities that no longer fit me or my personality.

19. _____ I'm a giving person. I like to share before asking anything in return.

20. _____ I defend my beliefs and values, even when personal risks are involved.

21. _____ I'm aware of my sexiness and sensuality.

22. _____ I like to go my own way and find my own answers.

23. _____ I worry that people will leave me high and dry when they no longer need me.

24. _____ I think people are essentially good; if they hurt others they do so out of ignorance more than anything else.

25. _____ I'm a fun person, though sometimes perceived as irresponsible.

26. _____ I tend to see things from a distance, in objective terms.

27. _____ I know how to find the right person for the right job.

28. _____ I'm the kind of person who makes things happen and precipitates change.

29. _____ I have so many good ideas, I find it difficult to act on all of them.

30. _____ I sometimes think of myself as a loser, since I fail to live up to my self-expectations.

31. _____ I typically put others before myself.

32. _____ I'm not reluctant to stand up to objectionable people.

33. _____ I live to love, because love is life.

34. _____ I often feel restless, like I need to go somewhere or do something else.

35. _____ Most of the time I feel like I'm on my own with little help coming from anywhere.

36. _____ I think most people are trustworthy.

Scoring: Statements have been grouped together according to the archetypes they reflect. Next to each statement number, place your answer. Add the columns. Provide combined totals where instructed.

Self Archetypes (Return Stage)

Fool	1 _____	Ruler	3 _____
	13 _____		15 _____
	25 _____		27 _____
	_____ Total		_____ Total

Sage	2 _____	Magician	4 _____
	14 _____		16 _____
	26 _____		28 _____
	_____ Total		_____ Total

Combined Totals for Self Archetypes _____

Soul Archetypes (Journey Stage)

Creator	5 _____	Destroyer	6 _____
	17 _____		18 _____
	29 _____		30 _____
	_____ Total		_____ Total

Lover	9 _____	Seeker	10 _____
	21 _____		22 _____
	33 _____		34 _____
	_____ Total		_____ Total

Combined Totals for Soul Archetypes _____

Ego Archetypes (Preparation Stage)

Innocent	12 _____	Warrior	8 _____
	24 _____		20 _____
	36 _____		32 _____
	_____ Total		_____ Total

Orphan	11 _____		*Caregiver*	7 _____
	23 _____			19 _____
	35 _____			31 _____
	_____ Total			_____ Total

Combined Total for Ego Archetypes _____

Scoring Summary

Highest score: _____   Dominant archetype: _____

Lowest score: _____   Least influential archetype: _____

Highest combined score: _____   (Ego, Self or Soul) _____

Lowest combined score: _____   (Ego, Self or Soul) _____

Currently, I am at the (preparation, journey, return) _____ stage of my heroic life quest. (To determine your answer, look at the combined totals for ego, self and soul archetypes.)

Interpretation

See Table 7.1 for the goals, fears, problems, life responses and gifts associated with each of the archetypes, including the one that is dominant for you. By looking at the same things associated with your lowest score, you can learn what is either not important to you right now or possibly repressed. Also, read the descriptions of the stages below to understand better where you are in your life, psychologically speaking. Pay closest attention to the stage that captures your highest combined score.

Ego Stage: If you are at the ego stage of development, your life right now is focused on establishing boundaries between yourself and the world. You're learning to adapt and to get your needs met. You are building the "container" for your future life.

Soul Stage: At this developmental stage you are trying to connect with the eternal. Life may be seen as a mystery to you. You are probably experiencing a sense of yearning. The will-to-meaning is likely consciously present at this time. You may be shedding a false identity and moving toward authenticity.

Self Stage: At this stage, you are moving into a whole new mode of being. Life is no longer a struggle. You appreciate its abundance. Your true inner self is coming out naturally and openly now. It's time to express yourself in the world and to give your gifts to the world.

305

Table 7.1

The 12 Archetypes

Archetype	Goal	Fear	Dragon/Problem	Response to Task	Gift/Virtue
Innocent	Remain in safety	Abandonment	Deny it or seek rescue	Fidelity, discernment	Trust, optimism
Orphan	Regain safety	Exploitation	Is victimized by it	Process and feel pain fully	Interdependence, realism
Warrior	Win	Weakness	Slay/confront it	Fight only for what really matters	Courage, discipline
Caregiver	Help others	Selfishness	Take care of it or those it harms	Give without maiming self or others	Compassion, generosity
Seeker	Search for better life	Conformity	Flee from it	Be true to deeper self	Autonomy, ambition
Lover	Bliss	Loss of love	Love it	Follow your bliss	Passion, commitment
Destroyer	Metamorphosis	Annihilation	Allow dragon to slay it	Let go	Humility
Creator	Identity	Inauthenticity	Claim it as part of the self	Self-creation, self-acceptance	Individuality, vocation
Ruler	Order	Chaos	Find its constructive uses	Take full responsibility for your life	Responsibility, control
Magician	Transformation	Evil sorcery	Transform it	Align self with cosmos	Personal power
Sage	Truth	Deception	Transcend it	Attain enlightenment	Wisdom, nonattachment
Fool	Enjoyment	"Nonaliveness"	Play tricks on it	Trust in the process	Joy, freedom

Source: Tables 7.1, 7.2. Carol Pearson (1991). *Awakening the Heroes Within: Twelve Archetypes to Help Us Find Ourselves and Transform Our World.* New York: Harper San Francisco.

My Life Story Is a Heroic Myth

Part I

Instructions: Begin by drawing a timeline on a sheet of paper. One end of the line represents birth. The other end represents death. Place an "X" on your timeline at the appropriate spot, given your age. Now think of all the significant events and important people in your life. Mark these events and people on the timeline.

Part II

Once you've completed your timeline, write a one or two page autobiography using the information you've recorded. When you're done, translate your life story into mythic language. I've provided an example below of what you're expected to do.

Life Story

I was born into an average family. My mother was a school teacher and my father worked as a conductor on the railroad. As the youngest child, nobody paid much attention to me. My mom was working all day and my dad was away for days at a time....

Mythic Language Translation

Once upon a time, there was a very special child, born with a promise and a light within him that was so bright that it blinded all others and they did not dare to look at him. Even his mother, who knew of the way things worked, and his father, who officiated on caravans to distant realms, could not see him (Houston, 1987: 112).

Your life story:

_____

_____

Your life story translated into the mythic language:

_____

_____

Part III

Compare your life myth with those of the various archetypes (see Table 7.2). If your life contains many painful episodes, smashed illusions and the unveiling of a lot of phoniness, your formative myth may be a variation of the Destroyer's plot. If your life has been about proving yourself, getting your way or fighting against the world, maybe you have been living a variation of the Warrior's plot.

Table 7.2

Archetypes and Their Stories

Innocent	Paradise lost but faith retained; paradise regained.
Orphan	Paradise lost, resulting despair and alienation; gives up hope of paradise; and works with others to create better conditions in world as it is.
Warrior	Goes on journey; confronts and slays dragon; rescues victim.
Caregiver	Sacrifices and does what others ask; feels maimed or is manipulative of others; gains the capacity to choose to live as feels right and life-enriching.
Seeker	Feels alienated in community by perceived pressure to conform; goes off on journey alone; finds treasure of autonomy and vocation; finds real family and home.
Lover	Yearns to love; finds love; separated from love, and (in tragedy) dies or (in comedy) is reunited with loved one.
Destroyer	Experiences great loss and pain; loses illusions and inauthentic patterns; faces death and learns to make death an ally.
Creator	Discovers true self; explores ways of creating a life that facilitates the expression of that self.
Ruler	Is wounded and kingdom is a wasteland; takes responsibility for kingdom and own woundedness; kingdom is restored to fertility, harmony and peace.
Magician	Overcomes debilitating illness; through healing and transforming self learns to heal and transform others; experiences destructive effects of hubris or insecurity; learns to align will with that of universe.
Sage	Seeks truth through losing self; recognizes own subjectivity; affirms that subjectivity; experiences transcendent truth.
Fool	Lives for pleasure but without rootedness in self, community or cosmos; learns to commit and bond with people, nature, universe; is able to trust the process and live in harmony with universe; finds joy.

Part IV

Now that you have begun to identify the myth by which your life operates, answer the following questions to gain personal insight.

1. In my myth, what am I scripted to be? (e.g., Victim, Villain or Warrior)

2. Is my role in the script limiting in any way? If so, how?

3. What is the gift, lesson or treasure in this script?

4. What results personally if I choose to live by no other script?

5. What new challenges must I accept now to transform myself into an even greater hero? What other heroes are calling out to me for life responses?

According to Pearson, the heroic journey is not just some interesting and playful notion; it is a sacred task that should not be taken lightly, though it does not always have to be taken seriously. Just ask your resident psychic Fool! Advantages of identifying the heroic story of your life include the following:

1. You will be less likely to undercut or undervalue yourself.
2. You will be less likely to get confused by trivial and nonessential concerns.
3. You will be less likely to be manipulated by others.
4. You won't be talked into becoming less than you could be (Pearson, 1991).

If you are like many people, you have been travelling life until now without a map. Lacking a sense of history or destiny, you may not have felt grounded. Maybe you have not really understood where you have been, where you are now and where you're going in the future. By looking at life as a heroic journey, you can relate to the past and to the future. You can see where you are right now along the way, what dragons must be fought and what potential treasures can be discovered. Good luck on your journey, young Braveheart!

Study Guide

Key Terms

personal liberation (270)
ego (270)
false self (270)
false consciousness (270)
bad faith (270)
enneagram (271)
self-transformation (271)
self-transcendence (271)
archetypal/transpersonal
    psychology (271)
authentic self (271)
enneagram theory (272)
childhood orientations
    (279)
path of integration (279)
path of disintegration (279)
spiritual emergency (291)

logotherapy (291)
will-to-meaning (291)
existential frustration
    (292)
noögenic neurosis (292)
collective neurosis (292)
meaninglessness (293)
conformity (293)
fanaticism (293)
self-transcendence (294)
future orientation (294)
work (295)
love (296)
pursuit of happiness (296)
experiential value (296)
attitudinal values (296)
suffering (297)

mission (297)
archetypal psychology
    (297)
heroic journey (297)
metaphysical blues (298)
alienation (298)
existential vacuum (298)
call to the quest (300)
delusions of insignifi-
    cance (300)
psychological archetypes
    (301)
preparation stage (302)
journey stage (302)
return stage (302)

Fill-in-the-Blank Questions

Progress Check 7.1

Instructions: Fill in each blank with the appropriate response from the list below.

triads
levels
self-image
archetypal
wing
gift
kingdom
spiritual

disintegration
mass neurosis
suffering
delusions of insignificance
inner guides
enneagram
meaning

1. The _____ is a Greek symbol used to describe nine different personality types.

2. Don Riso uses the concept of the _____ to talk about secondary personality characteristics.

3. The nine enneagram personality types can be categorized in terms of thinking, instinctive and feeling _____.

4. According to Riso, within each personality type there are healthy, average and unhealthy _____.

5. When an enneagram type two "goes" to eight, that type takes a path of _____.

6. According to Richard Rohr, the problem with people is that they get fixated on their _____.

7. According to Viktor Frankl, the most human of all needs is the need for _____.

8. For Frankl, the _____ dimension of life has been sorely neglected in contemporary society.

9. Meaninglessness is evidenced by the _____ of society.

10. Frankl believes meaning can be found in love, work and potentially through _____.

11. _____ psychology uses the hero's journey as a metaphor of life.

12. The reason people do not experience themselves as heroes, according to Carol Pearson, is because they suffer from _____.

13. Psychological archetypes can act as _____ on our personal journeys.

14. Each psychological archetype has a _____ to offer us.

15. Your task in life is to transform the _____.

True/False Questions

Instructions: Circle the appropriate letter next to each statement.

T F   1. Some enneagram types are better than others.

T F   2. Don Richard Riso is the sole inventor of the enneagram.

T F   3. Unhealthy enneagram types bear some resemblance to dysfunctional types as described by the Diagnostic and Statistical Manual of Mental Disorders.

T F   4. People's basic personalities change as they get older.

T F   5. Enneagram type sixes are most out of touch with thinking.

T F   6. People can express their personalities in healthy or unhealthy ways.

T F   7. It's fun and exciting to discover your true enneagram personality type.

T F   8. Viktor Frankl's system of counselling, called logotherapy, deals seriously with problems of meaning.

T F   9. People who search for meaning suffer from clinical neurosis.

T F 10. People suffering from an existential vacuum have no purpose in life. They are without direction.

T F 11. Suffering can yield no meaning, according to Frankl.

T F 12. Archetypal psychology is a transpersonal theory of human development.

T F 13. According to archetypal psychology, we are all called to be heroes in life.

T F 14. Heroic myths can ground us psychologically in history and in destiny.

T F 15. Certain psychological archetypes are to be repressed and avoided at all cost.

Summary

1. Why is it necessary for people to get beyond their personalities or ego selves?
   - for personal liberation
   - our personalities are limiting in some ways
   - to get in touch with our true selves
   - the ego personality leads to game playing, self-deception, compulsivity and obsessions
   - to realize their full potentials
   - self-preoccupation is self-defeating

2. How is the enneagram related to contemporary psychology?
   - recent developments are based on the insights of Karen Horney, Sigmund Freud and Carl Jung
   - the enneagram correlates to the *Diagnostic and Statistical Manual of Mental Disorders*

3. How do people get their enneagram type?
   - as a product of biology and early childhood experience
   - types of connection found with nurturing and protective figures have an influence on which triad one will find oneself in

4. What is a wing?
   - the aspect of your personality reflecting secondary traits and characteristics, which may have a large or small role

5. What are the levels of personality development?
   - healthy
   - average
   - unhealthy

6. What are the paths of personality integration?
   - 1 - 7 - 5 - 8 - 2 - 4 - 1
   - 9 - 3 - 6 - 9

7. What are the paths of personality disintegration?
   - 1 - 4 - 2 - 8 - 5 - 7 - 1
   - 9 - 6 - 3 - 9

8. What unfortunate consequence results if we inflate our ego and fall under the spell of our personality?
   - we bring about the very things we fear most and we lose what we most desire

9. What is the most basic of all human needs and drives, according to Frankl?
   - the will-to-meaning

10. People whose need for meaning is frustrated suffer from
    - mass neurosis, fatalism, helplessness and conformity
    - an existential vacuum/existential frustration
    - planlessness
    - directionlessness
    - noögenic neurosis

11. What are the three dimensions of life for Frankl?
    - the somatic or physical
    - the mental
    - the spiritual

12. What are the roots of meaninglessness?
    - evolutionary biology
    - waning values and declining traditional institutions
    - lack of clarity about personal wants

13. How does one find meaning?
    - through self-transcendence (e.g., getting beyond petty self-preoccupations, narcissism and self-indulgence)
    - adopt future orientation
    - see distinction between "is" and "ought"

14. Where is meaning to be found?
    - in love, work and suffering, if need be

15. What is archetypal psychology? What does it do?
    - a new, cutting-edge developmental, transpersonal psychology
    - it takes literary criticism, combines it with Jungian psychology, and applies it to people
    - it uses the "hero's journey" as a metaphor for life and applies this metaphor in the construction of a developmental model of human life

16. Why must we all take our heroic journeys?
    - to heal ourselves
    - to find our personal treasures
    - to heal the kingdom
    - to reach wholeness

- to find our roots and our destinies
- to find dignity and nobility in living
- to get over our delusions of insignificance

17. What is a psychological archetype?
    - a pattern, form or cognitive structure that organizes our perceptions
    - an inner reality reflected in external recurring images (e.g., wise men, fools and warriors)

18. How do the psychological archetypes function?
    - they condition our perceptions
    - they offer gifts
    - they suggest directions
    - they make us focus on other aspects of life and experience

Related Readings

Frankl, Viktor (1967). *Psychotherapy and Existentialism: Selected Papers on Logotherapy.* New York: Simon and Schuster.

Hurley, Kathleen and Theodore Dobson (1991). *What's My Type?* New York: Harper San Francisco.

Keen, Sam and Ann Valley Fox (1989). *Your Mythic Journey: Finding Meaning in Your Life through Writing and Story Telling.* Los Angeles: Jeremy Tarcher.

Naranjo, Claudio (1991). *Ennea-Type Structures: Self-Analysis for the Seeker.* Nevada City, CA: Gateways/IDHHB Inc.

Palmer, Helen (1995). *The Enneagram in Love and Work: Understanding Your Intimate and Business Relationships.* New York: Harper-SanFrancisco.

Pearson, Carol (1991). *Awakening the Heroes Within: Twelve Archetypes to Help Us Find Ourselves and Transform Our World.* New York: Harper San Francisco.

Pearson, Carol (1998). *The Hero Within: Six Archetypes We Live By. 3/e.* New York: HarperCollins.

They are playing a game. They are playing at not playing a game. If I show them I see they are playing a game, I shall break the rules and they will punish me. I must play the game of not seeing that I play the game.
~R.D. Laing

Games People Play:
Better Relationships Through Transactional Analysis

8

Chapter Overview

Transactional Analysis
- Ego States
- Self-Diagnostic 8.1 What's My Dominant Ego State?

Application Exercise 8.1 Exploring Your Ego States

Types of Transactions
- Complementary Transactions
- Crossed Transactions
- Ulterior Transactions

Strokes

Life Positions
- I'm Not OK—You're OK
- I'm Not OK—You're Not OK
- I'm OK—You're Not OK
- I'm OK—You're OK

Games
- If It Weren't for You
- Blemish: A Put-Down Party Game
- "Why Don't You"—"Yes, But"
- Rapo
- See What You Made Me Do
- High and Proud

Roles Played in Psychological Games

How to Break Up Psychological Games

Application Exercise 8.2 Ego States and the Effective Memorandum

Application Exercise 8.3 Events and Ego-State Reactions

Study Guide
• Key Terms
• Progress Check 8.1

• Summary
• Related Readings

Learning Outcomes

After successfully completing this chapter, you will be able to

(8.1) Provide a definition of, and an historical background for, transactional analysis

(8.2) Identify your dominant ego state as revealed by your personal egogram

(8.3) Outline the basic features of the child, adult and parent ego states

(8.4) Associate typical behaviours with each ego state

(8.5) Analyze and describe types of communication transactions

(8.6) Explain the nature and types of strokes, as well as their importance to healthy psychological development

(8.7) Describe four basic life positions by which people orient to others in the world

(8.8) Give examples of psychological games and explain why they are counterproductive

(8.9) Discuss the roles played in psychological games

(8.10) Break up psychological game playing

(8.11) Write more effective memoranda that are ego-state sensitive

(8.12) Identify ego-state reactions in others

Focus Questions

1. What is an ego state? What kinds of ego states are there? Can you describe each?

2. How do ego states function? How do they influence interpersonal communication?

3. What are some common verbal expressions, voice patterns and body language cues associated with each of the ego states?

4. What is a transaction? What kinds of transactions are there? Can you explain them?

5. Which kinds of transactions lead to good communication? Which do not? Why?

6. What are strokes? What kinds are there? Why do we need them?

7. What are life positions? Can you name and explain each? How do life positions develop?

8. What are games? Can you name some? How and why are they played?

317

(8.1) ····· # Transactional Analysis

transactional analysis
A broad theory of personality and interpersonal relations that emphasizes patterns of communication.

Transactional analysis is a "broad theory of personality and interpersonal relations that emphasizes patterns of communication" (Weiten, Lloyd and Lashley, 1991: 265). Originally conceived by Canadian-born and educated psychiatrist Eric Berne (1910–1970) during the 1950s, it underwent numerous changes and refinements over the years. While initially developed for research purposes and therapeutic applications, T.A. gained widespread acceptance in the general population. Well-known books based on transactional analysis include *Games People Play* (Berne, 1964), *I'm OK—You're OK* (Harris, 1973) and *Born to Win* (James and Jongeward, 1971). In recent years, transactional analysis has lost some of its popularity. Nevertheless, it is still used by many human service practitioners who continue to see its practical value. Let's now discover how transactional analysis can help us in our continuing efforts to master human relations.

Ego States

Have you ever resented being talked down to? When frustrated or upset, have you ever responded childishly by pouting or throwing an adult version of a temper tantrum? Perhaps you like to use the word "should" a lot, using the pointed index finger for authoritarian emphasis. Maybe your general pattern of communication is to speak matter-of-factly about whatever is being discussed. The important point to note here is that what we say and how we respond to what others say originate in what Eric Berne (1961) refers to as **ego states.** By learning more about ego states, we can better understand where communication messages are coming from, psychologically speaking. We can modify our own message delivery, if necessary, and make intelligent decisions about how to respond to others. Recognizing that social communication does not occur in a psychological vacuum will also help us very shortly to better understand the nature of crossed and ulterior communications, as well as the unfortunate games people play when interacting with one another. Before learning more about ego states, you are now invited to do Self-Diagnostic 8.1.

ego states
According to Transactional Analysis, the personality of a fully grown person is something like a psychological trinity, comprising three unique aspects, or ego states; namely, Parent, Adult and Child.

(8.3) ·····   According to transactional analysis, the personality of a fully grown person is something like a psychological trinity. It comprises three unique aspects, or ego states as Berne (1964) calls them. They include the Child ego state, the Adult ego state and the Parent ego state. As you will learn shortly, the Child and Parent both have sub-states that are reflected in your personal egogram. With respect to the basic three ego states, each one develops in a consistent, predictable sequence (Gilliland, James and Bowman, 1989). Ego states function like three distinct beings within each one of us (Levin, *Becoming the Way We Are*, 1988). For example, the Parent within us judges, the Adult figures out solutions, while the Child expresses feelings and needs. Let's now look

Eric Berne

Showcase profile

Eric Berne (born Eric Lennard Bernstein) was born on May 10, 1910, at his family home in Montreal, Quebec. The descendant of Polish immigrants, he earned his bachelor's degree, his medical degree and his Master of Surgery degree by the age of 25 from McGill University. In 1936, Berne started a psychiatric residency at the Psychiatric Clinic of Yale University School of Medicine. In 1941, he accepted the position of Clinical Assistant in Psychiatry at Mt. Zion Hospital in New York City. Also in that year, he began his training in psychoanalysis under the famous Erik Erikson at the New York Psychoanalytic Institute. From 1943 to 1946, Berne served in the U.S. Army Medical Corps, where there was a great need for psychiatrists during World War II. After serving with the army, Berne moved to California, where the early developments of transactional analysis began. In 1964, Berne established the International Transactional Analysis Association, a body that still exists today with chapters in Canada and throughout the world. Years after the introduction of transactional analysis, many practitioners from the fields of psychiatry, business, education and social work continue to apply its principles in their personal and professional lives.

Source: Encyclopedia Americana, 1994 edition. Copyright 1994 by Grolier Incorporated. Reprinted by permission.

Self Diagnostic

8.1

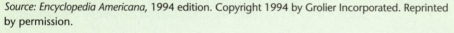

What's My Dominant Ego State?

8.2

This instrument will increase your self-awareness and self-understanding. Results suggest which ego state is likely dominant in your life at this time. The scores will help you to identify areas for self-improvement. They will also help you to establish behavioural strategies for enhancing interpersonal relations. Your dominant ego state will be the one from which much of your communication originates and the one from which you often respond to others when interacting socially. The notion of ego state can be understood as the operating psychological structure that organizes your perceptions, processes information and reacts to the world. In truth, we function in a variety of ego states; however, we sometimes tend to rely on one more than the others. This reliance has important social consequences, as you will soon see.

Instructions: Described on page 320 are five situations with different possible reactions to each. Next to each reaction, indicate how likely it would be for you to respond in that fashion or in one similar to it. When finished, complete the scoring.

1 = I definitely would not react in this way or in any similar way

2 = I might react in this way or in a similar way

3 = I would be likely to react in this way or in a similar way

4 = I would almost surely react in this way or in a similar fashion

319

1. Your Human Relations instructor doesn't show up for the appointment you scheduled to discuss your term paper. What would you say to yourself?

_____ a. It's okay that she forgot about the meeting. The instructor has been under a lot of stress lately and probably needed a break.

_____ b. Not showing up is totally irresponsible! Lazy teachers these days can't even keep simple appointments.

_____ c. I wonder if the instructor misplaced her appointment book? Perhaps car trouble caused the missed appointment? I'll check it out.

_____ d. Great, the instructor didn't show up. Now I've got an extra hour to do whatever I want.

_____ e. Okay, fine! See if I show up for our next scheduled appointment!

2. Your brand new computer breaks down. What do you think?

_____ a. I hate garbage clones. Wait until I give that salesperson who sold it to me a blast.

_____ b. Wow! Can you believe it? My computer is already *kaput*. It always amazes me how these things work anyway.

_____ c. I guess I'll call the service department this afternoon for repairs.

_____ d. I think the manufacturer of these clones should be notified that they don't work as advertised. They probably use cheap components to maximize profits. It's wrong to sacrifice quality for profit.

_____ e. Well, I guess technology isn't perfect. Mistakes are sometimes made. I'll see if I can help the computer store identify the problems.

3. Rumour has it that the grade results on the first term test are very low. What would you do?

_____ a. Attend the next class to find out what happened.

_____ b. Plan to justify your belief that the test was unfair.

_____ c. Go to class because you're curious how others will react once the tests are handed back.

_____ d. Tell the instructor how to construct better tests in the future.

_____ e. Go to class in order to raise hell about the results.

4. You are not accepted into the college program of study for which you applied. How would you respond?

_____ a. I would either get very angry and upset or perhaps I would get depressed and cry.

_____ b. I would ask the admissions committee the rationale behind my non-acceptance and then take steps to increase my chances next time.

_____ c. I would forget about the refusal very quickly and get excited about other possibilities.

_____ d. I would criticize the selection process.

_____ e. I would console other friends and acquaintances who were not accepted either.

5. You and a few others have just been laid off from your part-time jobs. What would you probably say to yourself?

_____ a. This job stinks, anyway!

_____ b. I guess I have some new financial problems to deal with.

_____ c. Money and work—easy come, easy go! Isn't life so unpredictable? Time for a pastry!

_____ d. They should at least have given us some warning.

_____ e. Maybe I should have the others who've been laid off over to my
place for a farewell party. This might make everyone feel better.

Scoring: Each situation above has five possible reactions (a to e). Next to each possible reaction you placed a number indicating the chances you would respond in that way or in a similar fashion. Record your values below.

Add the columns to obtain your ego-state scores. After referring to the model egogram below, plot your scores on My Personal Egogram (Figure 8.1) to create a similar bar graph.

1.	a. _____	b. _____	c. _____	d. _____	e. _____
2.	e. _____	d. _____	c. _____	b. _____	a. _____
3.	d. _____	b. _____	a. _____	c. _____	e. _____
4.	e. _____	d. _____	b. _____	c. _____	a. _____
5.	e. _____	d. _____	b. _____	c. _____	a. _____
Total	_____	_____	_____	_____	_____
	Nurturing Parent (NP)	Critical Parent (CP)	Adult Ego State (A)	Natural Child (NC)	Adapted Child (AC)

Figure 8.1

My Personal Egogram

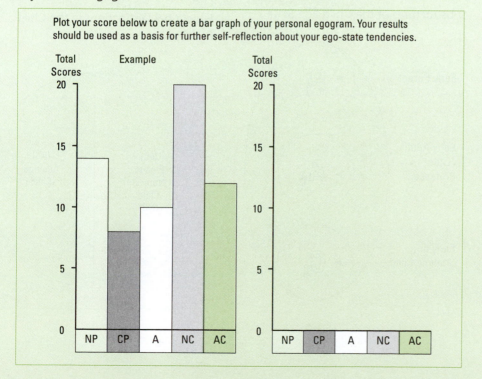

Plot your score below to create a bar graph of your personal egogram. Your results should be used as a basis for further self-reflection about your ego-state tendencies.

Figure 8.2

The Three Ego States Forming Personality

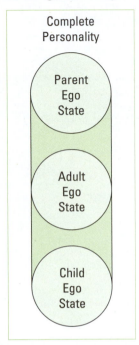

at each of the three ego states in a bit more detail. It is important to understand their nature before we go on to examine their influence on interpersonal communication. See Figure 8.2.

The Child Ego State The **Child ego state** is the first structural element formed within our personalities. This state has its own inner sequence of development. At first, we see its rudimentary beginnings in observable behaviours such as crying, sucking and gurgling. These behaviours reflect the earliest substructure of the fully formed Child. It is called the Early or Somatic Child (see C_1 in Figure 8.3).

Whenever you find people behaving like crybabies, they are likely behaving that way as a function of their Early Child ego state (Gilliland, James and Bowman, 1989). In time, infants begin to explore themselves and their environments. They start to form that aspect of the Child ego state labelled the Early Adult or "Little Professor" (A_1 in Figure 8.3). The Little Professor processes information on a preverbal level and makes decisions based on it. Young children display an intelligence of action that they cannot express in words. It's fascinating to watch children solve problems with their hands. The Little Professor possesses both creative and intuitive potential. However, it is possible that this Little Professor may sometimes record faulty information and choose to act on incorrect data.

Child ego state
The first structural element formed within our personalities. This state has its own inner sequence of development, the first being the Early or Somatic Child, the second being the Early Adult or Little Professor, and the third being the Early Parent. How this state functions in interactions with others and the world is explained by making a further distinction between the Free Child (or Natural Child) and the Adapted Child.

Figure 8.3

Substructures of the Child Ego State

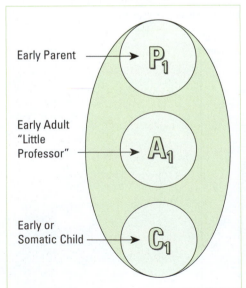

Early Parent → P_1

Early Adult "Little Professor" → A_1

Early or Somatic Child → C_1

Figure 8.4

Functional Distinctions in the Child Ego State

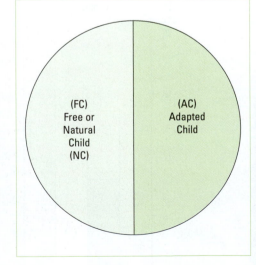

(FC) Free or Natural Child (NC)

(AC) Adapted Child

The third substructure of the Child ego state is the Early Parent (P_1 in Figure 8.3). This aspect of the Child is formed by children's early perceptions of parental behaviours and feelings before the development of language. The Early Parent contains both nurturing and negative messages that the child interprets and internalizes (Goulding and Goulding, 1979).

In the formation of the Child ego state, we find a permanent record of events during early development. It's as if the Child ego state has **taped events** of what the child's parents or caretakers said and did. Using scientific evidence obtained from Wilder Penfield's neurological studies on epilepsy at McGill University in Montreal, transactional analysts claim that early childhood memories are stored in their natural forms as ego states (see the Showcase Profile on Wilder Penfield).

When grown individuals are put into situations similar to those encountered in childhood, taped events of feelings that were recorded in the brain are replayed in the present. Someone's current dislike of being told what to do, for example, may reflect earlier negative feelings toward parental authority. In the Child ego state we find the "recordings of the child's early experiences, responses, and the 'positions' taken about self and others" (James and Jongeward, 1971: 18).

taped events
A permanent record of events during early development that is found in the formation of the child ego state.

Like the children in the picture above, the natural child in all of us enjoys fun and excitement.

Showcase profile

Wilder Graves Penfield

Wilder Graves Penfield (1891–1976) was the American-Canadian neurosurgeon who devised a surgical method of treating epilepsy. Born in Spokane, Wash., on January 26, 1891, he graduated from Princeton University in 1913. As a Rhodes Scholar at Oxford, he was greatly influenced by Sir William Osler and was introduced to the study of the brain by Sir Charles Sherrington, who pioneered in neurological studies of decerebrate animals. He received his medical degree from Johns Hopkins in 1918 and spent a year's internship under Harvey Cushing at Peter Bent Brigham Hospital in Boston before returning to Oxford to study neurophysiology.

For seven years Penfield practised neurosurgery in New York City before being named in 1928 as professor of neurology and neurosurgery at McGill University, where he taught until 1954. In 1934 he established, with the aid of the Rockefeller Foundation, the Montreal Neurological Institute, which stressed a multidisciplinary approach to the nervous system. He served as its director until 1960. Penfield died on April 5, 1976, in Montreal.

Penfield was one of the first neurosurgeons to apply neurophysiological techniques to the study of the human brain. Through his innovative work on the development of surgical techniques for the removal of scar tissue from the brains of epileptics, he employed electrical stimulation of the exposed cerebral cortex of patients undergoing surgery. He used this procedure both to minimize surgical damage and to map out the anatomy of the brain and locate such functional areas as the motor, sensory, and speech centres.

His career-long interest in identifying the neural substrates of consciousness led him to propose a "centrencephalic" system to explain consciousness. This system stressed the role of the upper brain stem, as opposed to the cortical areas, in the integration of higher functions; although the system was controversial at the time of its proposal, current opinion generally supports this explanation.

Source: Encyclopedia Americana, 1994 edition. Copyright 1994 by Grolier Incorporated. Reprinted by permission.

How your Child ego state functions in interaction with others and the world can be better explained by making a functional distinction between the Free Child (FC) or Natural Child (NC) and the Adapted Child (AC). See Figure 8.4. Also refer back to your personal egogram.

When we function with our **Free** or **Natural Child** in control, we tend to display curiosity, or a need for intimacy, fun, joyfulness, fantasy and impulsivity (Lussier, 1990). A liability of staying in our Free Child too much or for

Free Child/Natural Child
The part of the personality that is spontaneous, open and fun.

too long is that others may begin to perceive us as irresponsible or out of control. In contrast to the Free Child, the **Adapted Child** may be whiny, defiant or placating. The Adapted Child may appear pouty, sad or display an innocence marked by an impassive and motionless posture. Thus, when we behave in our Adapted Child state we are either extremely compliant or rebellious. We may look ashamed or exhibit a demanding attitude. If you have ever seen anyone who appears guilty, depressed and robot-like, or if you witness someone having a tantrum, you are observing the Adapted Child at work.

Adult Ego State The operation of our **Adult ego state** makes us behave in rational and thoughtful ways. We gather and store information. We engage in factual inquiry and we do so in an objective, emotionally detached fashion. The Adult in us reasons things out and evaluates probabilities (Lussier, 1990). The Adult also acts as referee between the demands of the Parent ego state and the wants of the Child ego state. As Gilliland, James and Bowman (1989: 115) put it, the Adult ego state "provides the 'how to' for the personality by asking 'why' questions and considering consequences." Harris (1969) says that by means of the Adult we can begin to tell the differences between life as it was taught and demonstrated to us (Parent), life as we felt it, wished it or fantasized about it (Child), and life as we figure it out for ourselves (Adult).

It might be helpful to see the Adult as a data-processing computer. It makes decisions after computing information from all three ego state sources. The updating function of the Adult examines the data in our Parent to see whether they are sound and applicable today. Then the data are accepted, rejected or modified accordingly. Lessons we were taught as youngsters may be counterproductive, unhealthy or downright wrong today. The Adult ego also appraises the Child to see whether or not the feelings located there are appropriate to current circumstances (Harris, 1969).

The Parent Ego State The **Parent ego state** contains all the rules we've learned concerning how things should and shouldn't be. This ego state houses our morality and standards of acceptable behaviour, defining for us what is important. It gives us instructions about what we should know and do in order to survive and function successfully in our culture. Whenever we talk about values that are important to us or whenever we discuss matters of principle, the Parent ego state is at work.

Like the Child ego state, the Parent can be broken up into two functional elements. These two elements are called the **Nurturing Parent** (NP) and the **Critical** or **Controlling Parent** (CP). When people operate in their Nurturing Parent ego state, they behave in a caring, concerned and protective manner. By contrast, the Critical Parent may have us present ourselves as oppressive, prejudiced, powerful, intimidating or controlling (Gilliland, James and Bowman 1989). The Critical Parent in us distrusts our own thinking. It calls upon external authority to enforce its demands.

Adapted Child
One of the functional distinctions in the Child ego state. The adapted child may appear pouty, sad or display an innocence marked by an impassive and motionless posture.

Adult ego state When operating, this ego state makes us behave in rational and thoughtful ways. The Adult also acts as referee between the demands of the Parent ego state and the wants of the Child ego state.

Parent ego state
The personality structure from which derive our morals and nurturing tendencies.

Nurturing Parent
One of the functional elements of the Parent state. When people operate in this ego state, they behave in a caring, concerned and protective manner.

Critical Parent/Controlling Parent
One of the two functional elements of the Parent ego state. When people operate in this state, they may present themselves as oppressive, prejudiced, powerful, intimidating or controlling.

Figure 8.5

Structural and Functional Depictions of Ego States

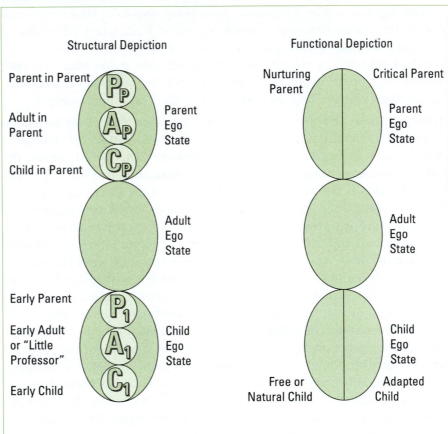

With respect to its structure, the Parent ego state can be subdivided into three parts. As the Parent develops we incorporate into this ego state messages from caretakers and parental figures that reflect Child, Adult and Parent type responses. When operating in our Parent ego state we may copy our parents' and caretakers' functioning in *their* Parent state (P_p), *their* Adult state (A_p) or *their* Child state (C_p). For instance, imagine someone scolding another as his mother used to do in her Critical Parent state or scolding as the mother did in her frustrated Child state (Gilliland, James and Bowman, 1989). The scolding in both cases comes from the Parent ego state. Differences in the way the scolding occurs depend on what was recorded and internalized from the parent. See Figure 8.5 for both a structural and functional depiction of the three ego states. Also look at Table 8.1 for a summary of typical behaviours associated with each ego state, including the Parent.

8.4

Table 8.1

Typical Behaviours Associated with Each Ego State

Ego States	Common Verbal Expressions	Characteristic Voice Patterns	Body Language Clues
Critical Parent	That's nice, bad	Judgmental	Points or wags finger
	That's cute, good	Admonishing	Frowns, squints
	You should	Critical	Feet apart, hands on hips
	You ought	Condescending	Slaps, spanks
	You never	Loud	Serious looking
	Be quiet, good	Disgusted, sneering	Arms crossed, closed posture
	Don't you	Scheming	Foot tapping
	Ridiculous	Comparing	Looks up in disgust
	You must	Demanding	Pounds table
Nurturing Parent	Uses words that are:		
	Reassuring	Soft	Arms open
	Comforting	Concerned	Palm outward
	Consoling	Soothing	Holds hands
	Loving	Encouraging	Hugs, holds, kisses
	Supporting	Sympathetic	Cradles
	Nonjudgmental		Smiles, touches, strokes, nods approvingly
Adult	Asks questions:		
	How	Modulated	Relaxed
	What	Appropriate	Stroking the chin
	Where	Corresponds to feelings	Finger pointing to head area
	Who	Controlled, calm	Looks up (as if in search of answers)
	Why	Straight	
	It seems to me	Confident	Brow wrinkles when thinking

327

Table 8.1

continued

Let's see what we find			Supporting head with hands
The solution is			Attentive
I wonder			
Natural Child	I wish	Loud or quiet, depending on mood	Showing off
	I want	Laughs	Rolls, tumbles
	I hope	Cries	Walks freely, easily
	I can't	Rages	Posture open, ready to swing into action
	I won't	Giggles	Flops easily and comfortably on chair or floor
	Wow		Skips
	Gee		
	Whoopee		
Adapted Child	Compliant words:		
	Yes, OK, You're right	Annoying	Showing off
	I'll do it, I'm wrong	Repetitive	Pouting
	Defiant, rebellious words	Sweet	Fights aggressively
		Placating	or
	No, Make me	Angry	Withdraws timidly
	I won't, You're wrong, I don't care	Defiant	Chip on shoulder
		Loud or soft	or
	Other expressions:	Total silence	Passive conformity
	Help me, It's your fault, You'll be sorry		Teary eyed Looks innocent

Source: Don Hamachek. *Encounters with the Self,* 3rd edition, copyright © 1987 by Holt, Rinehart and Winston. Reproduced by permission of the publisher.

Exploring Your Ego States

This activity is designed to help you get in touch with the three basic ego states that make up your psychological self. They've been there for a long time, so it's time you got to know them. By experiencing and recognizing them in yourself, you'll begin to see them in others.

Instructions: Bring to mind an important decision you need to make. Use this decision to fill in the blanks below. What exactly is your required decision?

1. We can hear the voice of our Child ego state when it talks about feelings, wants and needs. For example, it might say, "I feel happy, sad, mad, glad, frightened or delighted," "I want more money, a vacation, a fancy car and a promotion at work" or "I need to eat better, sleep more, get more exercise and have more fun."

Now fill in the blanks below (with respect to the decision to be taken).

My Child feels

_____

_____

My Child wants

_____

_____

My Child needs

_____

_____

2. The voice of the Adult ego state sounds like a computer. It calculates, measures, predicts, reasons and reports our thinking. For example, it might say that $7+5=12$, the meteor shower will occur August 11 and the roads are wet and slippery.

Now fill in the blank below (with respect to the decision to be taken).

My Adult thinks

_____

_____

329

3. The voice of the Parent ego state addresses values and moral considerations. For example, it might say, "I should do my homework, arrive to work on time, look after my personal hygiene, go to church and never commit murder."

Now fill in the blank below (with respect to the decision to be taken).

My Parent says I should

_____

_____

4. Now that you have heard your Child, Adult and Parent speak on the important decision to be made, listen carefully again to uncover any conflicts among the three parts of your self. What, if any, conflict is contained?

What does your Child need or feel?

_____

What does your Adult think?

_____

What does your Parent demand or prohibit?

_____

What will you do?

_____

Source: This exercise is a variation of one found in Levin (1988: 5–6).

(8.5) ···· # Types of Transactions

Now that we are familiar with all three ego states, we can move on and examine communication patterns that involve them. Berne writes that when people verbally communicate with each other, **transactions** take place.

transactions
Units of social intercourse, as identified by Berne.

> The unit of social intercourse is called a transaction. If two or more people encounter each other...sooner or later one of them will speak, or give some other indication of acknowledging the presence of others. This is called the transactional stimulus. Another person will then say or do something which is in some way related to the stimulus, and that is called the transactional response. (Berne, cited in Harris, 1969: 33)

It is important to note that transactional stimuli and transactional responses arise from ego states. Our job and the task of transactional analysts is to appraise "which ego state implemented the transactional stimulus and which executed the transactional response" (Berne, 1964: 29). There are several types of transactions, depending on how ego states interact and what was really intended by the messages transmitted. Here we'll look at complementary transactions, crossed transactions and ulterior transactions.

Complementary Transactions

There are two types of **complementary transactions**. In the first type, the receiver of a message responds to it from the same ego state the sender used in transmitting the message. For example, the sender sends a Parent message and the receiver responds in the Parent mode. Complementary transactions of this sort can also take place at the level of Adult and Child. See Figure 8.6 below.

A second type of complementary transaction is based on unequal relationships. For instance, the transaction could be from Parent to Child or vice versa. It might also be from Child to Adult or Adult to Child. In all unequal complementary transactions, the lines of communication are still parallel. Whether transactions are equal or unequal, the first rule of T.A. is that when source stimulus and receiver response occur in a parallel fashion, transactions are complementary and can go on indefinitely (Harris, 1969). For an illustration of unequal complementary transactions, see Figure 8.7.

In his book *I'm OK—You're OK*, Harris provides an example of a complementary transaction occurring between two women complaining to each other about how their bus is going to arrive late at its destination. This

complementary transactions The communication pattern in which the source stimulus and receiver response occur in a parallel fashion. These transactions can go on indefinitely and may take place either in equal or unequal relationships.

Figure 8.6

Type 1 Complementary Transactions

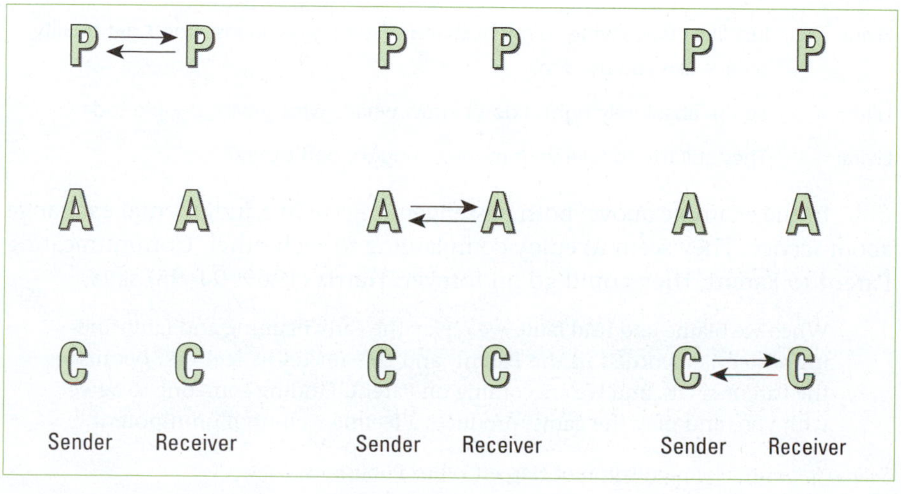

Figure 8.7

Type 2 Unequal Complementary Transactions

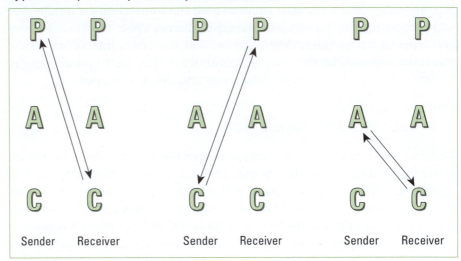

transaction occurs in a parallel fashion at the Parent ego state level. A paraphrase of Harris's example is found below.

Elvira: While glancing at her watch, mumbling to herself and catching the eye of the female passenger next to her, she sighs wearily.

Lilith: Sighs back in response; adjusts herself and looks at her watch.

Elvira: We're going to be late again.

Lilith: It always happens.

Elvira: Have you ever seen this bus arrive on time?

Lilith: Never have.

Elvira: Just like I was saying to my husband yesterday—you just don't get quality service like you used to.

Lilith: You're absolutely right. I don't know what's wrong with people today.

Elvira: They still like to take your money, though, don't they?

In the example above, both passengers engage in a judgmental exchange about service. They seem to enjoy complaining to each other. Communicating Parent to Parent, they could go on forever. Harris (1969: 94–95) says:

> When we blame and find fault, we replay the early blaming and fault-finding which is recorded in the Parent, and this makes us feel OK, because the Parent is OK, and we are coming on Parent. Finding someone to agree with you, and play the game, produces a feeling well-nigh omnipotent.

Source: Reprinted by permission of HarperCollins Publishers.

Crossed Transactions

In **crossed transactions**, the lines of communication are not parallel. Rather, they cross or intersect each other at some point. Instead of promoting further communication, crossed transactions disrupt it. Thus, a second rule of T.A. "...is that communication is broken off when a crossed transaction occurs" (Berne, 1964: 30). Crossed transactions come in two types. A Type 1 crossed transaction is illustrated in Figure 8.8.

In a Type 1 crossed transaction the message stimulus is Adult-to-Adult. In the example below, an appropriate response to the question regarding the whereabouts of the book would have been something like "No, I don't" or "The last time I saw it, it was on your desk in class." Instead, what we have is a receiver who flares up and responds in a Child-to-Parent fashion. As Figure 8.8 shows, the two vectors of communication cross. Communication is thereby broken off. If communication is to resume, either the sender must become Parental to complement the receiver's Child or the receiver's Adult ego state must be activated as a complement to the sender's Adult.

In a Type 2 crossed transaction, an Adult-to-Adult stimulus message is answered with a Parent-to-Child response. Let's modify the example about the textbook to illustrate the point. See Figure 8.9.

In both Type 1 and Type 2 crossed transactions, communication about the book stops. Either a digression must be made about who got blamed for what or talk must resume about who's acting like a child. The location of the book becomes a dead issue. See Figure 8.10 for additional illustrations of crossed transactions.

crossed transactions The communication pattern in which the lines of communication are not parallel, but instead intersect or cross each other at some point. Instead of promoting further communication, crossed transactions disrupt it.

Figure 8.8

Type 1 Crossed Transaction

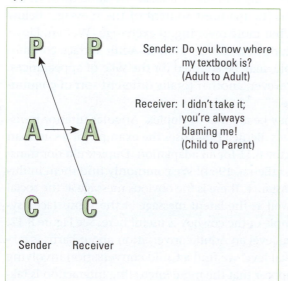

Sender: Do you know where my textbook is? (Adult to Adult)

Receiver: I didn't take it; you're always blaming me! (Child to Parent)

Figure 8.9

Type 2 Crossed Transaction

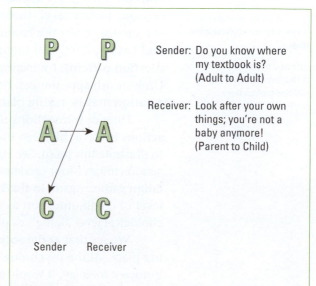

Sender: Do you know where my textbook is? (Adult to Adult)

Receiver: Look after your own things; you're not a baby anymore! (Parent to Child)

333

Figure 8.10

More Crossed Transactions

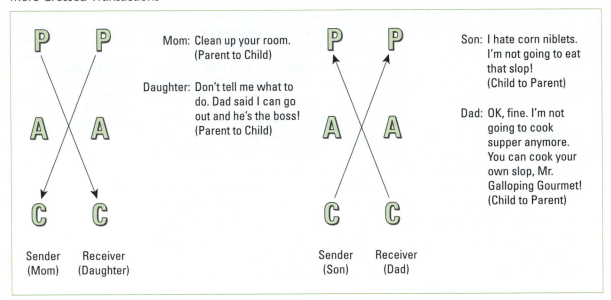

Mom: Clean up your room.
(Parent to Child)

Daughter: Don't tell me what to do. Dad said I can go out and he's the boss!
(Parent to Child)

Son: I hate corn niblets. I'm not going to eat that slop!
(Child to Parent)

Dad: OK, fine. I'm not going to cook supper anymore. You can cook your own slop, Mr. Galloping Gourmet!
(Child to Parent)

Sender (Mom)   Receiver (Daughter)

Sender (Son)   Receiver (Dad)

Ulterior Transactions

ulterior transactions
Complementary transactions that include hidden messages intended to serve ulterior motives.

hidden messages
Ulterior communications intended to serve ulterior motives.

ulterior motives
A hidden desire served by ulterior transactions.

Ulterior transactions are complementary transactions that include **hidden messages** intended to serve **ulterior motives** (Weiten, Lloyd and Lashley, 1991). Ulterior transactions use more than two ego states simultaneously (Berne, 1964). When observing ulterior transactions we discover surface level and subsurface level messages being communicated at the same time. At the obvious surface level, there is the manifest content of the message. Below the surface occurs the latent but more meaningful exchange (Weiten, Lloyd and Lashley, 1991). In ulterior transactions, Adult-to-Adult surface communication patterns, for example, may be adopted for the sake of appearances. Underneath appearances, however, another totally different sort of communication may be taking place.

Ulterior transactions may be angular or duplex. Angular ulterior transactions involve three ego states. Berne (1964) uses the example of a salesman to illustrate this point. See Figure 8.11 for an adaptation. Duplex ulterior transactions involve four ego states (Berne, 1964). We commonly find them in flirtation games. Again, in this instance, there is the obvious message at the social level of communication as well as the latent message at the subsurface psychological level. Berne's example of the cowboy is useful here. See Figure 8.12.

We see that at the social level an Adult conversation about barns is taking place. At the psychological level we find a Child conversation involving innocent foreplay. It would appear that the more interesting interaction is taking place at the hidden or subsurface level.

334

Figure 8.11

Angular Ulterior Transactions

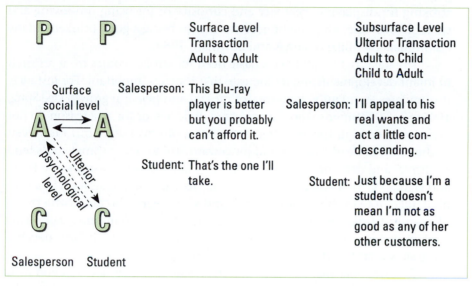

		Surface Level Transaction Adult to Adult		Subsurface Level Ulterior Transaction Adult to Child Child to Adult

Salesperson: This Blu-ray player is better but you probably can't afford it.

Student: That's the one I'll take.

Salesperson: I'll appeal to his real wants and act a little condescending.

Student: Just because I'm a student doesn't mean I'm not as good as any of her other customers.

Figure 8.12

Duplex Ulterior Transactions

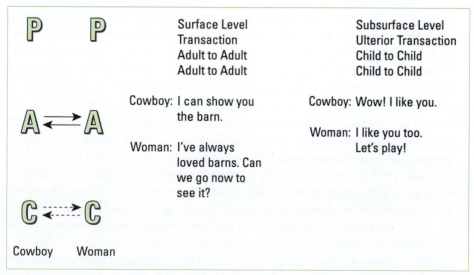

Surface Level Transaction
Adult to Adult
Adult to Adult

Subsurface Level Ulterior Transaction
Child to Child
Child to Child

Cowboy: I can show you the barn.

Woman: I've always loved barns. Can we go now to see it?

Cowboy: Wow! I like you.

Woman: I like you too. Let's play!

8.6 ······ # Strokes

Whatever the nature of people's communication transactions (complementary, crossed, ulterior), the basic motivation behind the social interaction is the need for **strokes** (Dusay and Dusay, 1979: 377). All three ego states require

strokes
The actual or symbolic touch that is the basic motivation behind social interaction.

stroking for optimal development. The Parent might need strokes for being a good listener, caretaker, advice giver or character model. The Child may crave stroking for displaying creativity and curiosity or for being fun-loving and spontaneous. The Adult might need strokes for being a good thinker and decision-maker (Gilliland, James and Bowman, 1989).

The idea that we all have a basic need for strokes comes from research in infant development. Studies indicate that touch is important. For instance, it stimulates an infant's chemistry for mental and physical growth (see Spitz, 1945: 53–74). "Infants who are neglected, ignored, or for any reason do not experience enough touch, suffer mental and physical deterioration even to the point of death" (James and Jongeward, 1978). Their spinal cords tend to shrivel and deteriorate. This condition is known as **marasmus** (see Freed and Freed, 1973). If you ever have a chance to visit a neonatal ward in a hospital, take note of the nurses, parents and volunteers who are instructed to physically "stroke" premature infants for about 15 to 20 minutes daily. This stroking helps them to thrive. Without stroking, premature infants develop more slowly and, with extreme neglect, may not survive.

Transactional analysts claim that the need for strokes does not end with infancy. As ego states develop, the Parent, Adult and Child in us all require stroking for healthy growth and development. A gentle and caring touch continues to be a positive stroke for us throughout our lifespan. As we emerge from infancy, however, we begin to experience strokes often on a more subtle and symbolic level (Gilliland, James and Bowman, 1989). Whenever we enter the awareness of another person and express the message verbally or nonverbally that "I know you're there and I recognize you," we provide a life-sustaining stroke (Gilliland, James and Bowman, 1989). While this stroke could be a nonverbal touch, it could also be a wish or letter. It could come in the form of a thank-you, an effort to remember a name, or it might be delivered as a specific verbal reinforcer (Harris and Harris, 1985). Listening in an attentive fashion is perhaps one of the finest strokes you can give to another person (James and Jongeward, 1971). We all like to be listened to and taken seriously. It's annoying to speak with people who aren't paying attention, who are preoccupied or who look right through us. Such things **discount** the importance of what we're saying. They can also discount us personally.

Strokes come in different forms and are delivered under varying sets of circumstances. Some strokes come as freebies, some are earned and still others are requested (Freed and Freed, 1973). The freebies are the best. You get these strokes from people for just being you. **Freebie strokes** don't require you to impress anybody or to do anything. A second kind of stroke is an earned one. **Earned strokes** are obtained by getting good grades, for instance, or by winning or doing things for people. Strokes can also be gained by simply asking for them. Children frequently ask their parents, "Do you love me?" When parents respond, "Of course we love you. You're very special to us," a stroke is delivered. When you ask professors what they think of your work,

marasmus
The condition in which infants who are neglected, ignored, or for any reason do not experience enough touch, suffer mental and physical deterioration even to the point of death.

If you touch me soft and gentle

If you look at me and smile at me

If you listen to me talk sometimes before you talk I will grow, really grow.

~Bradly (age 9)

(Source: James and Jongeward, 1978)

discount
To devalue someone by refusing to provide strokes. In a conversational situation, a parent may discount the importance of what a child is saying by failing to pay attention or by looking right through the child.

freebie strokes
Unearned and unsolicited positive reinforcement.

earned strokes
Actively seeking stroking by getting good grades, winning or doing things for people.

From infancy onward we all have a basic need for strokes; that is, a need to be held, cuddled, touched and cared for.

your aim is **requested strokes**. There is nothing wrong with this approach; strokes leave us feeling happy and contented. In T.A. jargon, these feelings are referred to as **warm fuzzies**.

In contrast to warm fuzzies, which are pleasant, some strokes can be unpleasant. These are referred to as **cold pricklies** (Steiner, 1977). Such strokes, though negative, at least make us feel alive. If we can't get the warm fuzzies we need, we'll do what it takes to get cold pricklies. As Freed and Freed said, "Any stroke is better than no stroke" (1973: 12). This point can be illustrated by the individual who'd rather be hated than not be noticed at all. The overlooked child may act up to get parental attention, even if punishment follows.

Life Positions

8.7

The nature and frequency of the strokes we receive from early infancy onward establish for us our **life positions** in relation to the world. Our personal life position results from the decisions made in response to how parents and caretakers reacted to our initial expressions of feelings and needs. We either got warm fuzzies (positive strokes), cold pricklies (negative strokes) or nothing at all (abandonment or lack of response). Our stroking history, then, contributes significantly to the formation of four possible life positions.

requested strokes
Strokes gained by asking for them.

warm fuzzies
The happy and contented feeling we get from earned, requested or freebie strokes.

cold pricklies
Unpleasant strokes. Such strokes, though negative, at least make the individual feel alive.

life positions
One of four possible stances we assume in relation to the world based on our responses to our parents' and caretakers' reactions to our expressed feelings and needs.

I'm Not OK—You're OK

During early development, children are at the mercy of others. They are small, weak and incapable. By comparison, adults are big and strong, possessing what seems to the child like infinite abilities. Since they deliver the strokes children need, adults are OK. If children's needs are not met, they may decide that the lack in their lives is their fault. In this case, this conclusion is drawn: I'm not OK.

In adulthood, the I'm Not OK—You're OK life position may be lived out by withdrawal (Harris, 1969). People in this position may find it too painful to be around OK people, especially since they don't perceive themselves to be OK. They may also live in a world of fantasy, saying to themselves that life will be good "if I..." or "when I...." They may provoke people so that others turn on them. Resulting negative stroking reinforces the I'm Not OK life position. (Remember, negative strokes are better than no strokes at all.)

Individuals adopting the I'm Not OK—You're OK stance in life frequently seek out friends and associates with a big Parent (Harris, 1969). Not-OK people are typically eager and willing to comply with the demands of others. As Harris (1969) puts it, "Some of our best people are where they are because of these efforts to gain approval." Unfortunately, the approval-seeking Not-OK person is committed to a lifetime of endless mountain climbing. After reaching the summit of one mountain, another mountain presents itself. The Not-OK position can never provide lasting satisfaction because "No matter what I do, I'm still Not-OK" (Harris, 1969).

I'm Not OK—You're Not OK

Infants who receive relatively little stroking sometimes find that as they get a bit older and mobile, the stroking all but disappears. "If this state of abandonment and difficulty continues without relief through the second year of life, the child concludes I'm Not OK—You're Not OK (Harris, 1969). After reaching this conclusion, the Adult stops developing. It ceases to grow since its primary function of getting strokes is frustrated. There is no source of stroking to be found.

People in the I'm Not OK—You're Not OK position tend to give up on life. They may lose hope. They may barely survive or display symptoms of extreme withdrawal, ending up in mental institutions. They may also show regressive behaviour patterns that point to a longing to get back to very early infancy where at least some minimal stroking occurred.

I'm OK—You're Not OK

If children are mistreated, they may decide unconsciously that others are Not OK. The conclusion that they (i.e., the children) are OK themselves probably comes from **self-stroking** (Harris, 1969). Commenting on how battered children, for example, stroke themselves, Harris (1969:72) writes:

> I believe this self-stroking does in fact occur during the time that a little person is healing from major, painful injuries such as are inflicted on a youngster who has come to be known as "the battered child"....I believe that it is while this little individual is healing, in a sense "lying there licking his wounds," that he experiences a sense of comfort alone and by himself, if for no other reason than his improvement is in such contrast to the gross pain he has just experienced. It is as if he senses, "I'll be all right if you leave me alone. I'm OK by myself."

> *Source:* Copyright © 1967, 1968, 1969 by Thomas A. Harris, M.D. Copyright renewed 1995 by Amy Bjork Harris. Reprinted by permission of HarperCollins Publishers, Inc.

People adopting the I'm OK—You're Not OK life position could be described as **survivors**. Unfortunately, such survivors may wish to "strike back" at the cruel world later in life. They have witnessed toughness and know very well how to be tough themselves. Deep-seated hatred may become a life-sustaining force, even though it is masked by politeness or social etiquette. Underscoring the energizing power of hatred, Caryl Chessman said, "There is nothing that sustains you like hate; it is better to be anything than afraid" (cited in Harris, 1969: 73). The hatred that sustains this position is often found in incorrigible criminals. Described as people lacking a moral sense of right and wrong, they are convinced that they are always OK, regardless of what they do. Where fault is to be found, it is always found in others.

A serious problem that arises when people adopt this life position is that they set themselves up for **stroke deprivation**. If it is true that a stroke is only as good as the stroker, and if there are no OK people, it follows that there are no OK strokes (Harris, 1969). If people in the I'm OK—You're Not OK position gather together an entourage of praising and stroking "yes men," even then the strokes delivered are not accepted at face value. In fact, the more the "yes men" stroke, the more they may be despised. The attitudinal stance toward others is nicely captured by the saying "Come close so I can let you have it" (Harris, 1969: 73).

I'm OK—You're OK

This life position offers us considerable hope. While the first three positions form unconsciously as a product of our stroking histories, the fourth is a product of conscious decision. It is "based on thought, faith, and the wager of action" (Harris, 1969: 74). Harris describes the adoption of the I'm OK—You're OK position as a conversion experience. It includes not yet experienced possibilities as well as the abstractions of philosophy and religion. In this life position, OK-ness is not bound by personal experience. We can transcend our histories and circumstances to make life OK for us and OK for

self-stroking
A phenomenon that may occur among children who are mistreated. It is believed to happen when they are healing from major, painful injuries such as are inflicted on a youngster known as a battered child. The healing child may experience a sense of comfort alone and by himself, if for no other reason that his improvement is in such marked contrast to the gross pain he has just experienced. This self-stroking may lead children to arrive at the I'm OK—You're Not OK life position.

survivors
Persons who have established an "I'm OK—You're Not OK" life position, likely because they were mistreated as children and have unconsciously decided that others are not okay. The conclusion that they're okay themselves probably comes from self-stroking.

stroke deprivation
Absence of touch, which in an infant may result in marasmus. In adults, stroke deprivation is more verbal and symbolic.

everyone else. This does not mean that we can simply discard our pasts by choosing this position. Harris (1969: 76) points out that:

> [T]he not OK recordings in the Child are not erased by a decision in the present. The task at hand is how to start a collection of recordings which play OK outcomes to transactions, successes in terms of correct probability estimating, successes in terms of integrated actions which make sense, which are programmed by the Adult, and not by the Parent or Child, successes based on an ethic which can be supported rationally. If we now wish to work toward adopting the "I'm OK—You're OK" position, we should be forewarned that instant OK feelings cannot be guaranteed. We must acknowledge the presence of "old tapes" playing in our memories. What we can try to do is turn unpleasant tapes off when they threaten to undermine the faith we have placed in our new ways of thinking. In time, the gradual growth and development of the Adult will result in a new happiness and a more satisfying way of life.
>
> *Source:* Copyright © 1967, 1968, 1969 by Thomas A. Harris, M.D. Copyright renewed 1995 by Amy Bjork Harris. Reprinted by permission of HarperCollins Publishers, Inc.

(8.8) Games

In order to get necessary life-sustaining strokes to feel OK, people sometimes get involved in "game playing." The game playing referred to here is not fun. The intent is serious and the playing field is found on the level of the unconscious. We're playing for keeps, only we don't know we're in the game.

Games involve recognizable patterns of human communication. Eric Berne describes game playing below (1976: 69).

games
An ongoing series of complementary ulterior transactions progressing to a well-defined, predictable outcome. People may turn to game playing as a way of getting the strokes they need.

> A game is an ongoing series of complementary ulterior transactions progressing to a well-defined predictable outcome. Descriptively it is a recurring set of transactions, often repetitious, superficially plausible, with a concealed motivation; or, more colloquially, a series of moves with a snare, or "gimmick." Games are clearly differentiated from procedures, rituals, and pastimes by two chief characteristics: (1) their ulterior quality and (2) the payoff.
>
> Procedures may be successful, rituals effective, and pastimes profitable, but all of them are by definition candid; they may involve contest, but not conflict, and the ending may be sensational, but it is not dramatic. Every game, on the other hand, is basically dishonest and the outcome has a dramatic, as distinct from merely exciting, quality.

For Berne, people become involved in game playing because there is precious little opportunity for intimacy in daily life. Intimacy may simply not be available for some people, or perhaps it is psychologically impossible for particular individuals. The result is that people can spend a great deal of their social life seriously playing games. In fact, game playing may become necessary for maintaining mental health. Psychic stability may be so precarious and life positions so tenuously maintained that to deprive some people of their games may be to plunge them into irreversible despair (Berne, 1964).

Transactional analysis has identified a variety of games. Berne (1964) classifies games under the following headings: life games, marital games, party games, sexual games, underworld games, consulting room games and good games. Ken Ernst (1972) has paid special attention to games that students and teachers play. He calls them troublemaker games, put-down games, tempter games, I-know-best games, helping games and close-to-student games. If you wish to master a detailed knowledge of games, I suggest you read Ernst and Berne in the original. For our purposes here, we'll look at a few of the more popular, commonly played games that interfere with honest and productive communication.

If It Weren't for You (IFWY)

If It Weren't for You is classified by Berne as a marital game, one frequently played by marriage partners. It can also be played between children and parents or between boyfriends and girlfriends. In all cases, there is typically a long-term established relationship.

When playing this game, one person charges another with restricting his or her behaviour. Let's suppose, for example, that a wife mentions the fact that a high school friend is about to graduate from medical school. In response, the husband says, "That's wonderful." This response sets the stage for the wife to assert with anger and frustration, "If it weren't for you, I too could be a doctor today." (While her husband is barely surviving as a guitar player in a failing band, the wife has been working as a waitress to pay the rent and buy groceries). With her response, the wife brings up an old source of bitterness and conflict between them.

When people play games, there are psychological payoffs. Remember, too, there is dishonesty. In this example, the wife is actually afraid of going back to school. She unconsciously fears the challenge is too great. The result is that she engages in self-deception to suppress hidden insecurities and maintain her self-esteem. Dishonestly blaming her husband for her own missed opportunities can also provide the game-playing wife with a bargaining advantage in future communication transactions.

As Berne (1964) points out, many men and women select domineering partners who restrict their behaviour so that they can play a lifetime of *If It Weren't for You/Him/Her*. In fact, the person allegedly doing the restricting is doing the game player a kind of service. The domineering person who forbids or somehow prevents the other from doing something actually feared helps the game player suppress awareness of that fear. However, if the domineering partner ceases to restrict behaviour and allows the game player to do whatever she wants, then the game is over and the underlying fears and phobias are

341

uncovered. The game player can no longer attack the dominant partner. The sources of fear must then be confronted face to face. Since it is easier to blame others than to face your own fears, *IFWY* is a favourite game people play.

Blemish: A Put-Down Party Game

Like other games, *Blemish* is played in an unconscious and dishonest fashion. Unfortunately, it causes a lot of petty discord in everyday life (Berne, 1964). This game is played from the vantage point of the depressive Child ("I am no good" or "I'm not OK") that is protectively transformed into the Parental position ("They are no good" or "They are Not OK"). The task for the game player here is to prove the thesis of the second position.

Blemish game players are often perfectionists. They may be looking for the "perfect knight in shining armour" or the "flawless and radiant princess" of their dreams. Before perfectionistic *Blemish* players get too close to anyone, they look for flaws in that person, either physical or psychological (Ernst, 1972). Since *Blemish* players are not OK in their own minds, they do not feel comfortable unless they are around others who are at least as Not OK as they are. When it comes to intimacy, "Closer relations are first encouraged, but when the person comes closer the Parent panic-button is pushed and the 'Blemish' is used as ammunition" (Ernst, 1972: 61). In other words, the fault is found and distance is maintained.

Creative players of this game can use almost anything about a person as a blemish. They can criticize and distance people because of their social status, education, colour, ethnicity, acne or hairstyle.

I guess transactional theory supports folk wisdom here: "People who criticize others usually don't like themselves." This is certainly true with *Blemish* players. The advantage of *Blemish* is that it wards off depression about being Not OK. It also has the psychological payoff of avoiding intimacy that could expose the game player's own blemishes. According to Berne (1976), this game is usually based on sexual insecurity and its aim is reassurance.

"Why Don't You"—"Yes, But" (YDYB)

"Why Don't You"—"Yes, But" is also a party game that can be played on all kinds of occasions. Of all games, this one is best understood by transactional analysts (Berne, 1964). It was the first game to be identified for analysis. Personally speaking, before I ever learned anything about T.A., I knew a YDYB player who was a very good friend of mine. I'm amused to remember how he would always say "yeah, but" whenever suggestions were made about solving his problems. In response to almost any recommendation, he would shout out "Yeah, but...yeah, but" until he could get the person's attention. The following is an example of someone playing this game.

Farquar:	My sister always insists on having Christmas dinner at her place, but she always messes up the meal and usually most of the food ends up tasting terrible.
Skivington:	Why doesn't she take a cooking class?
Farquar:	Yes, but she doesn't have time.
Skivington:	Why don't you buy her a cookbook?
Farquar:	Yes, but she probably wouldn't read it.
Skivington:	Why don't you suggest a catering service provide this year's Christmas dinner?
Farquar:	Yes, but that would cost too much.
Skivington:	Why don't you lighten up on your sister's main course; bring your own dessert, and fill up on that?
Farquar:	Yes, but that would hurt her feelings.

Typically, an exchange between a "yes, but" player and another ends in silence (Berne, 1964). The silence may be broken, in this case, by a comment like, "Well, I guess some people just can't cook!" Berne (1964: 116–117) says the following about this game:

> YDYB can be played by any number. The agent presents a problem. The others start to present solutions, each beginning with "Why don't you...?" To each of these White [the game player] objects with a "Yes, but...." A good player can stand off the others indefinitely until they all give up, where-upon White [the game player] wins. In many situations she [or he] might have to handle a dozen or more solutions to engineer the crestfallen silence which signifies her [or his] victory....

Since *YDYB* players reject, with rare exceptions, all solutions to their problems, the game must have some kind of ulterior purpose. The game is not really played as an Adult search for solutions, but rather as a means of gaining reassurance and gratification for the Child. This is the payoff. The manifest transaction may sound Adult-to-Adult in nature, but in truth, game players present themselves as a Child too incapable or inadequate to meet the demands of problem situations. Others are transformed into wise Parents anxious to dispense wisdom for the benefit of the game player. Figure 8.13 depicts both social and psychological levels of *YDYB* transactions. Note that a "Why don't you..." comment acts as a Parent-to-Child stimulus that elicits the Child-to-Parent response, "Yes, but..." (both at the ulterior level).

In playing *YDYB*, both participants are usually unconscious of the ulterior transactions. The initiator of the game gains pleasure in rejecting all suggestions. The larger payoff doesn't come, however, until after all others have racked their brains and failed to find acceptable solutions. The resulting silence confirms for the game player that others are inadequate; they are unable to solve his problem. When this is "proven," the *YDYB* player "wins."

Figure 8.13
Social and Psychological Levels of *YDYB* Transactions

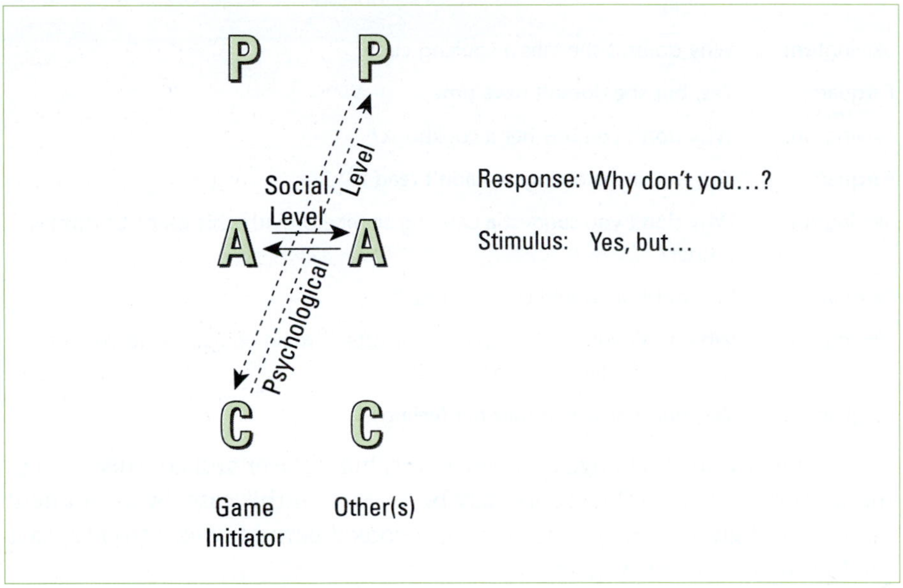

Response: Why don't you...?

Stimulus: Yes, but...

Rapo

Berne (1964) classifies *Rapo* as a sexual game. According to him, it is a form of flirtation carried out between men and women. (In principle, this kind of flirtation game could also be played by homosexuals.) Other possible names for this game are *Kiss Off,* or *Indignation*. A fairly harmless form of this game is often played at social gatherings. It is made up of mild flirtation. Players signal their availability and take pleasure from the pursuit of others. As soon as those others commit themselves, the game is over. Polite *Rapo* players may say to their pursuers something like, "I appreciate your compliment and thank you very much," while moving on to the next conquest (Berne, 1964: 26).

In another, more serious variation of *Rapo*, the initiating game player gets only secondary satisfaction from the advances of others. The primary satisfaction comes from delivering the rejection. A woman might say to a man, for example, "Buzz off, buster!" A man may, after some flirtation, say, "Take a hike, honey!" The *Rapo* player gets the other person into a much more serious commitment and then enjoys observing the discomfort created by the rejection.

See What You Made Me Do (SWYMD)

Another form of dishonest game playing in interpersonal relations is *See What You Made Me Do*. In its classical form, it is very much a marital game, though it can also be played between parents and children or between workers and bosses. When used in work contexts, *SWYMD* is classified as a life game (Berne, 1964).

As with *Rapo*, there are degrees of seriousness exhibited by *SWYMD* game players. First-degree players begin by wanting something, such as privacy. Someone else frustrates this want by interrupting. At the same time, the initiating game player makes a mistake in his work and conveniently blames the interrupting player for the mistake, even though the interruption actually has little or nothing to do with the error. By blaming the other person, the initiator discourages future interruptions and gets what's wanted, namely, privacy.

Second-degree *SWYMD* players use this game as more than an occasional protective mechanism. *SWYMD* becomes a way of life. Their strategy is to defer decisions and responsibilities to others. If things work out well, there is a payoff. The initiator enjoys the results of good decisions and related actions. If things don't turn out well, there's still a payoff because someone else can be blamed for what went wrong. Eric Berne (1964) does not regard this game as an end in itself. For the second-degree player, it merely offers passing satisfaction on the way to "I told you so" or "See what you've done now."

The game of *SWYMD* is often found in real-life work situations. For example, bosses may ask their subordinates for suggestions on improving productivity or performance. On the surface, they may appear to be good managers who operate democratically. Beneath the surface appearance, however, these game-playing bosses use employee suggestions to terrorize those beneath them. Mistakes are used against those who tried to be helpful. People may be criticized or harshly dealt with. In this case, bosses use the guise of democratic management to relieve themselves of personal responsibility. When things go wrong, it's not their fault, but the fault of others. That's the payoff.

Third-degree *SWYMD* is very serious. It may be played by paranoid individuals against people rash enough to give them advice. The paranoid may use the advice given to them in order to combine a second game with the first. The second game is called *You Got Me into This* (UGMIT). The *SWYMD-UGMIT* combination is a wickedly effective game as far as psychological dishonesty is concerned. In this combined game, blame and condemnation of others is combined with fear and paranoia. The serious third-degree player probably needs professional help.

345

High and Proud

Before concluding this section on games, I thought it might be interesting to look at one that you might observe in your college or university classrooms. In his classic work, *Games Students Play*, Ken Ernst (1972) draws our attention to High and Proud, a nifty little game used by students to gain the moral high ground above recognized authorities. In this game, students provoke situations of conflict in which the evidence for wrongdoing on the part of the enemy (i.e., the authoritarian professor or educational administrator) is beyond question. Confrontations are so designed and manipulated that any reasonable observer of the dispute would be aroused by the enemy authority's over-reaction. Gaining support of a "reasonable public" enables the High and Proud player to win.

High and Proud is illustrated in the following example of fraternity president Stu Dent, and professor of administrivia Dr. Dic Tator. First of all, Stu Dent arrives at his first class with skinhead and satanic tattoos proudly displayed. He's wearing torn jeans and a ripped T-shirt. Stu refuses to follow the dress code at his exclusive private college. He will not wear a jacket and tie as required by school regulations. Within minutes of arriving, he invites a number of his classmates to smoke marijuana after class. His language is foul and he seems to enjoy breaking all the rules laid down by administration. By the combination of all these actions, Stu is well equipped to bait school authorities.

Dr. Dic Tator, on the other hand, is obligated to enforce the rules of his educational institution. He is required by his Parent ego state or the Parent rules of the school to respond punitively to Stu, who is flagrantly violating authority. Of course, objective evaluation clearly indicates that being a skinhead does not interfere with learning. Also, scientific evidence suggests that smoking marijuana isn't any more harmful than smoking cigarettes. Four-letter words are only offensive to those who choose to be offended by them. With all this information ready to access and present as a defence, Stu Dent causes Dic Tator to overreact. Stu becomes the martyr and Tator becomes the villain. The stronger the overreaction by Tator and school authorities, the better for Stu. "This type of reaction demonstrates that there is something wrong with the Parent-type person" (Ernst, 1972: 82). Ernst classifies High and Proud as belonging to the "tempter variety" of games.

Roles Played in Psychological Games

Now that you are aware of some of the psychological games people play, you need to understand that people adopt particular **roles** when they get involved. For example, do you know someone who always seems to get picked on by others? Perhaps you know people who spend a lot of time themselves picking on others or putting them down. You may also know a person who typically intervenes when other people are having problems. If you have met or seen individuals such as those just described, you've quite likely witnessed game players in action. When getting into a game, people can adopt the role of **persecutor**, **victim** or **rescuer**. Of course, some people are truly persecuted (e.g., due to race); others are truly victimized (e.g., by sexual abuse); still others really function heroically as rescuers (e.g., from physical danger). These

---

roles
One of the three stances (persecutor, victim or rescuer) that people adopt in game playing.

persecutor
One of the illegitimate roles played in psychological games in which the individual sets unnecessarily strict limits on behaviour, enforces rules with sadistic brutality and makes others suffer because they are weaker.

(8.9)

victim
One of the illegitimate roles adopted in psychological game playing. For example, people who do not qualify for a job but falsely claim they are denied it because of race, sex or religion are acting as victims.

rescuer
A person who, in the guise of being helpful, keeps others dependent upon him, doesn't help them, and in fact may resent helping.

Some students get strokes playing High and Proud when they're feeling not OK.

people are not playing games. What is also true, however, is that people sometimes assume illegitimate roles they can act out as part of their psychological game playing. Illegitimate or phony roles are outlined below by James and Jongeward (1975: 114).

Persecutors: People who set unnecessarily strict limits on behaviour; who enforce rules with sadistic brutality; who make others suffer because they are weaker.

Victims: People who do not qualify for a job but falsely claim they are denied it because of race, sex or religion. People who feel continually put upon.

Rescuers: People who, in the guise of being helpful, keep others dependent upon them, don't really help them and in fact may resent helping. Phony roles are always part of a game.

8.10 How to Break Up Psychological Games

In *The People Book*, James and Jongeward (1975: 139) offer us some helpful suggestions for breaking up games. They are listed and briefly explained.

Use the Adult ego state to break up games Use your Adult to understand the nature and purpose of games. Consider your own favourite game role. Examine how the game roles of others complement yours. Try to discover how the

347

games you get involved in produce bad feelings in the end. Use your Adult to figure out other options besides game playing. Try out new patterns of behaviour.

Stop playing the complementary hand. Cross transactions instead You can stop playing someone else's game by refusing to play the complementary hand. If someone else is playing "Yes, but," that person wants you to give advice that will be rejected for purposes of the game. Either don't give the advice or put the problem back on the shoulders of the would-be game player. You could answer, for example, "I really don't know what I'd do" or "What do you think is best?" These responses will cause a crossed transaction and end unproductive communication.

Don't play the victim, persecutor or rescuer To end game playing, stop seeing yourself as a victim, acting helpless and dependent when, in fact, you are able to support yourself. Second, don't play the illegitimate role of persecutor, criticizing those who don't need or deserve it. Furthermore, don't reinforce your role as rescuer, giving help to those who don't need it. Don't help someone if you'll resent giving assistance.

Stop exaggerating Game players exaggerate the strengths and weaknesses of others as well as themselves. You can help stop game playing by quitting the exaggeration. For example, if you are constantly putting yourself down (e.g., "How stupid of me!") and blaming yourself inappropriately, you're probably playing an illegitimate role in some psychological game. Stop it. This exaggeration doesn't help yourself or others.

Don't misuse time If you choose to give up your psychological game playing, you'll find you have much more time to do other productive things. You might develop a new skill, exercise your talents, form new friendships or spend more time in leisure activities.

Stop collecting negative strokes If you are a game player, you must learn to get more positive strokes. If someone else you know is playing games, you can refuse to deliver the negative strokes they want and find ways of giving positive strokes. The danger is that all strokes might disappear when game playing ceases. Remember negative strokes are better than no strokes at all, but a life shouldn't be based on negative strokes and their acquisition.

To get positive strokes, be more generous in giving them Positive stroke givers attract positive strokes from other people. Mutual positive stroking can help to create and sustain long-lasting relationships. "To have friends, a person must learn how to be a friend."

Ego States and the Effective Memorandum

8.11 Whatever you eventually do for a living, you will probably be required at some time to communicate with others in writing. One such format is the memorandum. It is commonly used in all kinds of organizational and institutional settings.

Memoranda are not always well received. Sometimes people object to the tone of a particular memo as much as they do to its content. The tone of a memorandum likely has something to do with the "voice" of the ego state used to create it. It is important, therefore, that you recognize the ego states imbedded in your written communications. It is also important that you activate the desired ego states in your readers in order to make your memos more effective.

Instructions: Read the memorandum below. Then identify

1. The ego state from which the memo was written.

2. The ego state likely activated in the reader.

3. The probable effectiveness of the memo.

"Do Your Part" Memo

To: All Parents and Teachers at Sunnybrook Cooperative Daycare

From: The President of Sunnybrook

This memo is to remind you to get excited about our Christmas fund-raising auction. I expect all parents and co-op teachers to encourage their neighbours, friends and relatives to come out to the auction and support our fund-raising efforts.

As long as you keep bringing in money, you needn't worry about Sunnybrook closing. Good daycare is hard to come by, so it's in your interest to work hard.

As a member of this cooperative, it's your duty to keep us financially afloat. Make sure to do your part!

Signed: The President

After personal reading and analysis of the memo, form small groups to discuss your answers. When group discussion on the memo is completed, have everyone work together to rewrite the memo in a way that makes it more effective. Be prepared to discuss your group's improvements using "ego state" language.

Events and Ego-State Reactions

Part A

(8.12)

Any one situation or stimulus event can elicit three possible ego-state reactions. Under each situation listed below are different responses. Your job is to identify each as either Parent, Adult or Child in nature. You will have to imagine the tone of voice used and the gestures that accompany each response.

1. A 19-year-old son loses an important application.

_____ a. "What's wrong with you? Why can't you keep track of things for which you are responsible?"

_____ b. "You could telephone the college's lost and found to see if anybody turned it in."

_____ c. "I don't know where your stupid application is! I didn't take it. Why do you always blame me?"

2. A ride to school doesn't show up on the day of a big test.

_____ a. "I'm not going to give you gas money for this week's rides."

_____ b. "Why didn't you show up?"

_____ c. "I can't count on you for anything! You've elevated irresponsibility to an art form."

3. Someone you thought was your friend ignores you in the hallway.

_____ a. "Were you busy thinking about the assignment tomorrow?"

_____ b. "What's the matter? Aren't I good enough for you?"

_____ c. "I really think you should be more courteous to your friends if you wish to keep them."

Part B

Your task here is to create three situations of your own. For each situation, provide a Parent, Adult and Child response. Your responses to each situation could be read out in class. For a bit of fun and learning, have others identify them.

Situation One

_____

_____

Response A:
Response B:
Response C:

Situation Two

_____

_____

Response A:
Response B:
Response C:

Situation Three

_____

_____

Response A:
Response B:
Response C:

Answer Key: 1. P,A,C. 2. C,A,P. 3. A,C,P.

Study Guide

Key Terms

transactional analysis (318)
ego states (318)
Child ego state (322)
taped events (323)
Free Child/Natural Child (324)
Adapted Child (325)
Adult ego state (325)
Parent ego state (325)
Nurturing Parent (325)
Critical Parent/ Controlling Parent (325)

transactions (330)
complementary transactions (331)
crossed transactions (333)
ulterior transactions (334)
hidden messages (334)
ulterior motives (334)
strokes (335)
marasmus (336)
discount (336)
freebie strokes (336)
earned strokes (336)
requested strokes (337)
warm fuzzies (337)

cold pricklies (337)
life positions (337)
self-stroking (339)
survivors (339)
stroke deprivation (339)
games (340)
roles (346)
persecutor (346)
victim (346)
rescuer (346)

Progress Check 8.1

Fill-in-the-Blank Questions

Instructions: Fill in each blank with the appropriate answer from the list below.

child
parent
transactions
life position
game playing
adult
persecutor
intimacy
self-stroking
complementary

ulterior
strokes
marasmus
transactional analysis
rational
victim
crossed transactions
unequal relationships
ego states
crossed

1. _____ is a broad theory of personality and interpersonal relations that emphasizes patterns of communication.

2. According to transactional analysis, personality comprises three _____.

3. The "Little Professor" belongs to the _____ ego state.

4. The Adult ego state is _____.

5. The _____ ego state is like a data-processing computer.

6. The caregiver who gives support and concern to another is functioning in the role of Nurturing _____.

7. According to Eric Berne, the Canadian-born psychiatrist, communication can be analysed in terms of _____.

8. When lines of communication are not parallel, we can describe them as _____ transactions.

9. Transactions that include hidden messages can be described as _____ transactions.

10. Parallel communications are _____.

11. The basic motivation behind any social interaction is the need for _____.

12. The belief that I'm OK—You're Not OK is a _____.

13. Infants who fail to prosper and sometimes die due to lack of strokes suffer from _____.

14. People with an I'm OK—You're Not OK life orientation often engage in _____.

15. In order to get life-sustaining strokes, people sometimes get involved in _____.

16. People who illegitimately claim to be discriminated against play the role of _____.

17. Demanding that other people adhere to your unrealistic and demanding rules places you in the role of _____.

18. _____ can help you to put an end to psychological game playing.

19. People get involved in game playing because they often lack _____ in their lives.

20. It is possible to have complementary transactions in _____.

True/False Questions

Instructions: Circle the appropriate letter next to each statement.

T F   1. Interpersonal communication occurs in a psychological vacuum.

T F   2. According to T.A., we should try to mature and go beyond our Child ego state.

T F   3. Functionally speaking, the Child ego state can be separated into two elements: the Natural Child and the Adapted Child.

T F   4. The Adult ego state serves as referee between the demands of the Parent ego state and the wants of the Child ego state.

T F   5. When operating in our Parent ego state, we are always punitive and judgmental.

T F   6. Complementary transactions are impossible in unequal relationships.

T F   7. When two people complain to each other about others, they are communicating Parent to Parent.

T F   8. Ulterior transactions include hidden messages.

T F   9. Ulterior transactions are always negative or hurtful.

T F 10. Negative strokes are better than no strokes at all.

T F 11. Marasmus is a form of hypnosis used in persuasion.

T F 12. You can give a positive stroke to another by listening carefully to what that person says.

T F 13. The strokes we do or don't get in childhood help to establish our life positions.

T F 14. People adopting the I'm OK—You're Not OK position can be described as survivors.

T F 15. A psychological game is an ongoing series of complementary ulterior transactions progressing to a well-defined predictable outcome.

T F 16. Once game playing starts, there's no way to end it.

T F 17. *If It Weren't for You* is a game that helps people divert attention from their own fears and insecurities by blaming others.

T F 18. *Blemish* is a game played by people from the vantage point of the I'm Not OK life position.

T F 19. *"Why Don't You"—"Yes, But"* players sincerely want your advice to help them solve problems.

T F 20. First-degree *Rapo* is a form of mild flirtation.

T F 21. *See What You Made Me Do* is a game sometimes played to get privacy.

T F 22. *High and Proud* is a game used to make others look unreasonable by baiting them and taking the moral high ground.

T F 23. In the context of game playing, we can be truly helpful to victims by adopting the role of rescuer.

T F 24. Psychological games help to promote healthy relationships.

T F 25. People are always aware of the games they play.

Summary

1. What is transactional analysis?
   - it is a broad theory of personality and interpersonal relations that emphasizes patterns of communication

2. What are the three ego states?
   - Parent (Critical and Nurturing)
   - Adult
   - Child (Adapted and Natural)

3. How do each of the ego states function?
   - the Adult calculates, referees, decides and figures out solutions
   - the Parent judges, gives instructions, cares and nurtures, and criticizes
   - the Child responds spontaneously and displays curiosity, joyfulness and rebelliousness

4. What kinds of communication transactions are there?
   - *complementary*: sender and receiver communicate from the same ego state, or messages are parallel though originating from different ego states
   - *crossed*: messages intersect and cause a break in communication
   - *ulterior*: hidden messages serve ulterior motives; they are latent messages, but provide a more meaningful exchange

5. Why are strokes important?
   - they are required for healthy growth and development
   - infants who do not experience strokes can develop a condition known as marasmus
   - some examples are a touch, wink, letter, thank-you, an effort to remember someone's name, and listening attentively

6. What kinds of strokes are there?
   - *freebies*: you get these strokes for just being you
   - *earned*: you obtain these for doing something
   - *requested*: these strokes are asked for
   - *warm fuzzies*: these strokes leave us feeling good
   - *cold pricklies*: although they are negative strokes, they make us feel alive

7. What life positions can we take in relating to the world?
   - I'm Not OK—You're OK
   - I'm Not OK—You're Not OK
   - I'm OK—You're Not OK
   - I'm OK—You're OK

8. What are games? What are some examples?
   - they are unconscious, serious and deceptive ways of getting life-sustaining strokes
   - games have an ulterior quality and a payoff
   - examples are *If It Weren't for You, Blemish, Why Don't You—Yes, But, Rapo, See What You Made Me Do*, and *High and Proud*

9. What roles are played in psychological games?
   - *victim*: the person wrongly feels put down or put upon
   - *persecutor*: the person sets unrealistic standards and rules to justify punitive behaviour
   - *rescuer*: the person keeps others dependent by helping them

10. How can you break up psychological games?
    - use your Adult ego state
    - cross your transactions and stop playing complementary roles
    - don't play victim, persecutor or rescuer
    - stop exaggerating
    - don't misuse time
    - stop collecting negative strokes; instead, be more generous giving positive strokes

Related Readings

Bennett, Dudley (1980). *Successful Team Building Through T.A.* New York: Amacom.

Harris, A.B. and T.A. Harris (1985). *Staying OK.* New York: Harper & Row Publishers.

Keepers, Terry and Dorothy Babcock (1986). *Raising Kids OK.* Menlo Park, CA: Menalto Press.

Wagner, Abe (1981). *The Transactional Manager: How to Solve Problems with Transactional Analysis.* New York: Prentice Hall Press.

… women speak and hear a language of connection and intimacy, while men speak and hear a language of status and independence.
~*Deborah Tannen*

Gender, Culture and Nonverbal Cues in Communication

9

Chapter Overview

Gender Communications: He Said, She Said

• Interpreting Your Responses

Application Exercise 9.1
Dad or Joe: Who Should Go?

• Morality in a Different Voice: Carol Gilligan
• Gender Differences in Language Usage: You Just Don't Speak My Language

Culture and Communication: Inside Looking Out, Outside Looking In

• What Is Culture?
• Intercultural Communication
• How to Improve Intercultural Communication

Nonverbal Communication: You Don't Say!

• The Nature of Nonverbal Communication

Application Exercise 9.2
Don't Talk to Me!

• The Relationship Between Verbal and Nonverbal Communication
• Classifying Nonverbal Communication

Application Exercise 9.3
Clothes Talk

Self-Diagnostic 9.1
How Tactile Are You?

Study Guide
• Key Terms
• Progress Check 9.1

• Summary
• Related Readings

Learning Outcomes

After successfully completing this chapter, you will be able to

(9.1) Appreciate how gender impacts on interpersonal communications

(9.2) Account for male-female differences in moral thinking by reference to early identity formation

(9.3) Give examples of gender differences in language usage

(9.4) Discuss the importance of culture to interpersonal dynamics

(9.5) Provide four different forms of intercultural communication

(9.6) Give illustrations of miscommunication stemming from intercultural transactions

(9.7) Improve intercultural communication

(9.8) Define nonverbal behaviour

(9.9) Better understand the functional relationship between verbal and nonverbal communication

(9.10) Classify types of nonverbal behaviour

(9.11) "Read" people better on the basis of their clothing and physical appearance

(9.12) Illustrate how space and time send nonverbal messages

(9.13) Explain how we communicate by touch

Focus Questions

1. How do women speak in "a different voice" from men?

2. What accounts for male and female differences when communicating about interpersonal (moral) conflict?

3. How do men and women speak a different language, according to Deborah Tannen?

4. Why must culture be taken into account in the context of interpersonal communication?

5. What are some examples of intercultural miscommunication?

6. How can your intercultural communication be improved?

7. What are the different types of nonverbal communication?

8. Can you illustrate how statements can be made nonverbally? How so?

9. Given your usual physical appearance, posture and paralanguage, as well as your use of space and time, what nonverbal messages do you send to others? What specifically could you do to change these messages?

reflection poem

Coming and Going

i have noticed

that men

somewhere around forty

tend to come in from the field

with a sigh

and removing their coat in the hall

call into the kitchen

You were right

Grace

it ain't out there

just like you've always said

and she

with the children gone at last

breathless

puts her hat on her head

the hell it ain't!

coming and going

they pass

in the doorway

~Ric Masten

Source: From *Ric Masten Speaking*, Papier-Mache Press.
Copyright Sunflower Inc., 37931 Palo Colorado Rd.,
Carmel, CA 93923.

In this chapter, we'll be addressing matters of gender, culture and nonverbal communication. At first glance, these topics may appear to be dissimilar. However, many illustrative examples can be provided to reveal how they're actually quite closely connected. Gender relations, for instance, are often dictated by cultural norms. Who gets served first at dinner is a function of age and gender in Japan. Where men and women sit in an Israeli synagogue hinges on custom and religious tradition. Like gender relations, nonverbal signals can also depend on cultural factors. For example, when I was growing up in Brantford, Ontario, the "thumbs up" signal meant "Go to hell." (I remember delighting in its naughty use as a kid!) Years later, when I travelled to Europe, I was surprised to discover that it meant "Good luck." I guess Canadians import hand signals the way they do European fashions insofar as the thumbs-up signal apparently now means "Good luck" in Paris, Ontario, just as it does in Paris, France. We'll continue to discuss nonverbal cues a little later on in the chapter, but for now, let's examine more closely the effects of gender on interpersonal communication.

9.1 Gender Communications: He Said, She Said

How people communicate and get along with one another can be affected by **gender**, that is, one's sex or sexual identity. Studies suggest that men and women use language differently, that their behaviour is often influenced by gender-role expectations, and that they tend to interpret the moral dimensions of life in different terms (Gilligan, 1983; Tannen, 1990). These differences are important to note, for if we want to reduce gender-based misunderstandings we should take into account the contrasting perceptual tendencies, communication styles and reasoning patterns of men and women. Let's begin, then, by examining how men and women tend to perceive interpersonal conflicts differently, especially when matters of morality are concerned. To facilitate your understanding, do Application Exercise 9.1 before reading on.

gender
One's sex or sexual identity. Studies suggest that men and women use language differently, that their behaviour is often influenced by gender-role expectations, and that they tend to interpret the moral dimensions of life in different terms.

Interpreting Your Responses

The dilemma in Application Exercise 9.1 comes from the work of the late Lawrence Kohlberg (1976). Kohlberg was a Harvard psychologist who studied moral reasoning development for more than two decades. He used the "Joe dilemma" and others like it to gain information about the evolution of thinking when it comes to people's reasoning about moral matters. On the basis of his research, he concluded that **moral reasoning** progresses sequentially through six stages, falling under three basic levels of development.

moral reasoning
Reasoning that deals with ethical issues (e.g., conflicting rights).

361

**application
exercise
9.1**

Dad or Joe: Who Should Go?

Instructions: Read the moral dilemma below. After you have answered the questions privately, discuss your answers with others. You might wish to divide the class into smaller all-male and all-female groups. This division would help you to see if any gender-based differences arise. If the class is broken up into smaller gender-based groups, have each subgroup report to the class as a whole in order to compare answers.

1. Joe is a 14-year-old boy who wanted to go to camp very much. His father promised him he could go if he saved up the money himself. Joe worked hard at his paper route and saved up the $40 it cost to go to camp, with a little money left over. However, just before camp was going to start, his father changed his mind. Some of his friends decided to go on a special fishing trip, and Joe's father was short the money it would cost. So he told Joe to give him the money he had saved from the paper route. Joe didn't want to give up going to camp, so he thought of refusing to give his father the money.

    Should Joe refuse to give his father the money or should he give it to him? Why?

2. Further discussion about this dilemma can be generated by adding the following information:

    Joe lied and said he only made $10 and went to camp, with the $40 he made. Joe had an older brother named Bob. Before Joe went to camp he told Bob about the money and about lying to their father. Should Bob tell their father?

At level one (pre-conventional morality), people respond to cultural labels of good/bad and right/wrong. They interpret these labels with respect to the physical or hedonistic consequences of action or in terms of the physical powers of those who make and enforce the rules. Wrong is defined by what gets punished; right is defined by what gets praised, rewarded or is allowed. At level two (conventional morality), people try to live up to the expectations of their family, group or nation. They act out of loyalty and for the maintenance of the existing social order. Good behaviour is that which pleases or helps others. Good is also defined by that which conforms to existing laws and rules of conduct. At level three (post-conventional morality), people define their own moral values and principles apart from any particular authority, group or cultural norm. Moral judgments are rational and objective. At level three, moral judgment is not biased by personal interest (level one) or group loyalty (level two). Instead, judgments possess a universal prescriptive quality. They apply to all people regardless of space-time considerations. Appreciating this information now, you may wish to review your personal responses to Application Exercise 9.1 in terms of Kohlberg's scheme. Where does your reasoning fall?

Morality in a Different Voice: Carol Gilligan

If you did not score as highly as you might have liked on Kohlberg's scheme, you can take some comfort (especially if you're female) in the fact that Carol Gilligan, another noted Harvard researcher, has been critical of Kohlberg's work. She points out that females tend to score at lower levels of development than males in terms of Kohlberg's stage theory. Rather than accept these findings, Gilligan criticizes the moral assumptions underlying the theory itself. She draws attention to the fact that women have a tendency to speak to moral issues "in a different voice" from men, as she puts it. Perhaps you found this yourself when comparing male and female responses to the "Joe" dilemma in class. According to Gilligan, the different **moral voice** of women is what actually causes the lower scores. Since women make different psychological assumptions about morality, they display different reasoning patterns than do men. Unfortunately, male researchers such as Kohlberg have not been sensitive to these differences in the past. The result is that male norms have been used to judge moral reasoning adequacy.

With the new insights offered to us by feminists such as Gilligan, ignored differences between the sexes are presently being taken seriously in social scientific research. Theories and research methodologies, once considered sexually neutral in their scientific objectivity, are now being found to reflect consistent observational and evaluative biases. This appears to be true with Kohlberg.

Kohlberg's initial experimental studies were based on an all-male sample of subjects. This fact, once unnoticed or considered unimportant by the scientific community, is now astonishing in its gender bias. Making broad generalizations about people's moral reasoning development based on a small sample of males is clearly unacceptable. Furthermore, the dilemmas like "Joe" were also constructed by Kohlberg himself. He did not permit subjects to define the moral domain or to interpret moral conflict in their own terms. The dilemmas were all hypothetical, impersonal and abstract. These facts are important, for, as Gilligan points out, women tend to view moral situations more personally and concretely. Gilligan's critique of Kohlberg thus underscores the contaminating effects of the male bias and the abstract, unreal nature of the hypothetical situations.

The "different voice of morality" that Gilligan addresses is characterized more by theme than by gender (Gilligan, 1983). As she says, "Its association with women is an empirical observation ... But this association is not

moral voice
The different voice of morality identified by Carol Gilligan to highlight a distinction between two approaches to morality. One, which is typically but not necessarily female, views moral situations more personally and concretely. The other, which is typically but not necessarily male, views moral situations more impersonally and abstractly. This insight has led to the discovery in social scientific research that theories and methodologies, once considered sexually neutral in their scientific objectivity, actually reflected consistent observational and evaluative biases.

363

absolute...[T]he contrasts between male and female voices are presented here to highlight a distinction between two modes of thought and to focus on a problem of interpretation rather than to represent a generalization about either sex." In other words, male and female differences in moral reasoning can be observed though there's nothing necessary or innate about them. Nothing prevents women from displaying "typically male" reasoning patterns or men from displaying "typically female" reasoning patterns. Gilligan refers to Nancy Chodorow's (1974) work on identity formation to help account for apparent masculine and feminine differences in moral thinking.

9.2

identity formation
According to Chodorow, gender differences in identity formation affect interpersonal relations and moral thinking. For females the early attachment and identification with the same-sex mother provides them with a stronger basis for experiencing other people's needs or feelings as their own. In defining themselves as masculine, males separate themselves from their mothers. The net result is that male development entails more emphasis on the process of separation, individuation and a more defensive firming of experienced ego boundaries.

According to Chodorow, **identity formation** in males and females is quite different. For females, identity formation occurs in a context of ongoing relationships. As she puts it, "[M]others tend to experience their daughters as more like, and continuous with, themselves (Chodorow, cited in Gilligan, 1982: 7). As daughters form their female identities, they perceive and experience themselves as being much like their mothers. The process of identity formation thus involves a significant element of attachment.

When it comes to boys, "mothers experience their sons as a male opposite" (Chodorow, cited in Gilligan, 1982: 8). Boys, in defining themselves as masculine, separate themselves from their mothers. They curtail "their primary love and sense of empathic tie." The net result is that male development entails more emphasis on the process of separation, individuation and a "more defensive firming of experienced ego boundaries" (Chodorow, 1974). If Chodorow is correct about male and female differences regarding the period of early identity formation, we can better understand how girls emerge from it with a greater capacity for empathy built into their primary definition of self. The early attachment and identification of girls with their same-sex mother provides them with a stronger basis for experiencing other people's needs or feelings as their own. Early identification with a same-sex parent means that girls tend to experience themselves "as less differentiated than boys, as more continuous with and related to the external object-world, and as differently oriented to their inner object-world as well" (Chodorow, cited in Gilligan, 1982: 9).

Male and female differences regarding early identity formation affect interpersonal relations as well as moral thinking. "Since masculinity is defined through separation while femininity is defined through attachment, male gender identity is threatened by intimacy while female gender identity is threatened by separation. Thus, males tend to have difficulty with relationships, while females tend to have problems with individuation (Gilligan, 1982: 8). Male and female differences, with respect to identity formation, take us back to the inherent problems of Kohlberg's research on moral reasoning. Gilligan claims that by designing hypothetical dilemmas to emphasize justice considerations (legalistic rights, fairness and competing interests), Kohlberg has set up situations requiring detachment, rational objectivity, impartiality and the cold impersonal application of rules and principles. The legalistic, "rights" element in each of the dilemmas caters to the masculine psychology of separation. The better or more adequate moral solution to any dilemma is determined by justifications based on abstract principles of justice and fairness. Any reasoning that is subjective, personal, contextual, emotional or relationally based is deemed less adequate or less developed (because it's reflective of conventional, level-two thinking). Male life is thus taken as the norm. Abstract principles are preferred to real people and their personal interests.

In contrast to Kohlberg, who thought of morality as a development from hedonism to a rule-regulated morality, Gilligan sees feminine morality as a progression from selfishness to the recognition of social responsibility (Lefrancois, 1999). Using research on women's reasoning for having or not having an abortion, she has identified three stages in female moral development. In the initial stage, women are moved primarily by selfish concerns, e.g., "This is what I want, what I need, and what I should do, or what would be best for me." In the second stage, women increase their recognition of responsibility to others. The third and final stage of female moral reasoning displays a woman's wish to do the greatest good for both herself and others. Below, Lefrancois, from the University of Alberta, sums up the male and female differences as they emerge from the work of Gilligan and Kohlberg.

> It seems that, in general, girls are more responsive to social relationships and to the social consequences of their behaviour, more concerned with empathy and compassion, perhaps more in touch with real life, and less concerned with the hypothetical...Boys are perhaps more concerned with law and order than with the personally meaningful dimensions of morality. (Lefrancois 1999)

We learn from Gilligan and Kohlberg that people can construct social morality differently. A Kohlbergian level-two, stage-three response (based on a need to maintain relationships) is not necessarily less mature, less adequate or less developed than a response that appeals to abstract principles—at least not when viewed from a feminine perspective. As in so many areas of life, inter-gender communication may call for some compromise and mutual understanding. Perhaps we should all learn to appreciate the feminine **morality of care** and **relationship** as well as the masculine **morality of impersonal justice**. If we took these differences into consideration, perhaps men would appear less cold and uncaring, and women would appear less inconsistent and immature. Maybe we need to care more about reason, and reason with more care.

morality of care
The feminine moral voice, which speaks to morality from a subjective, personal, contextual, emotional or relational basis.

relationship
The intimate, social aspect of human social morality.

morality of impersonal justice
The masculine moral voice, which speaks to morality from a detached, rationally objective, impartial and coldly impersonal application of rules and principles.

Anima and Animus

anima
According to Carl Jung, the feminine qualities, attributes and intentions that men and women each possess as a part of their psyches.

animus
According to Carl Jung, the masculine qualities, attributes and intentions that men and women each possess as a part of their psyches.

According to Carl Jung, the founder of analytical psychology, both men and women display psychic characteristics usually attributed to the opposite sex. Thus, psychologically speaking, men are not entirely masculine or exclusively male, since they posses feminine qualities, attributes and intuitions. These things make up the **anima**. Because of culture and tradition, however, men are encouraged to repress traits of the anima that could be described as weak, soft or feminine. Women, on the other hand, are not entirely feminine or exclusively female. They possess an **animus** as part of their psyche. We find in the animus all that is thought to be traditionally male. While the anima produces moods in men, the animus produces opinions in women.

There are dangers associated with both the anima and animus. First, it's possible that the psyche may fall under the exclusive influence of either one of these psychological archetypes. A man dominated by the anima may lose his masculinity; if dominated by the animus, he may lose his tenderness and intuitive powers. A woman dominated by the animus may lose her femininity; if dominated by the anima, she may lose her objective rational capacities. A general point to be made here is that balance is required. The anima and the animus are different, but complementary, aspects of the unified self. If the anima or animus is repressed, both men and women will fail to achieve psychological wholeness. They will remain incomplete or somehow imbalanced. A healthy and whole person is psychologically androgynous, someone who displays a balance of male and female characteristics. Refer to the graphic of the self for an illustration.

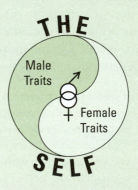

Gender Differences in Language Usage: You Just Don't Speak My Language

The unlike is joined together, and from differences results the most beautiful harmony...
~*Heraclitus*

The preceding discussion was used to raise awareness of the fact that men and women tend to think differently about morality and interpersonal relations. In contrast to men, women speak in "a different voice," as Carol Gilligan puts it. In this part of the chapter, we'll continue to look at gender differences with respect to how men and women use language in everyday contexts. Knowing about language differences is important. First, it can help you to understand others better. Second, by being sensitive to your own language characteristics, you can better appreciate the impressions you make on others. Third, if you increase your understanding of others through a study of language differences, and others come to appreciate and understand you more, mutual empathy becomes a real possibility (Weaver, 1996).

9.3   In her best-selling book entitled *You Just Don't Understand: Women and Men in Conversation*, writer and researcher Deborah Tannen discusses a number of male and female differences in language usage. Her first observation is remarkably consistent with Gilligan's work. Tannen (1990: 42) says, "[W]omen speak and hear a language of connection and intimacy, while men speak and hear a language of status and independence..." Parallels can easily be drawn between a feminine morality of care and the language of connection, and between a masculine morality of rights and the language of independence (separation). A second observation made by Tannen is that male-female communication can be plagued by what she calls **asymmetries** (1990: 49–73). Because male and female speech lacks similarity of form, men and women often talk to each other at cross-purposes. For an example of an asymmetrical communication, read the dialogue below:

asymmetries
Gender-based dissimilarities with respect to the form of language communication.

He: *I'm really tired. I didn't sleep well last night.*

She: *I didn't sleep well either. I never do.*

He: *Why are you trying to belittle me?*

She: *I'm not! I'm just trying to show I understand.*

Source: Tannen, 1990: 51

In the example above, the female had a particular intention behind her response. She was trying to establish a connection with the male, making an effort to show him that she understood his problem through her own experience. The male, on the other hand, took no comfort in the woman's response. He thought she was "trying to take something away from him by changing the uniqueness of his experience" (Tannen 1990: 51). In this case, the man filtered the woman's attempt to establish connections through his concern with preserving personal autonomy and independence. Of course, problems of asymmetry can be reversed. Women can become annoyed or frustrated because men do not respond to their troubles by offering corresponding troubles—something they would appreciate.

public speaking
Speaking in and before groups of people, the kind of speaking which, according to Tannen, is more comfortable for men than for women.

private speaking
The language of conversation, this is the option that more women feel comfortable with, according to Tannen.

A third gender difference in language, Tannen (1990: 77) observes, involves speaking in private or in public. She says, "More men feel comfortable doing '**public speaking**,' while more women feel comfortable doing '**private speaking**.'" Another way of capturing these differences is by using the terms **report talk** and **rapport talk**. According to Tannen, rapport talk (done in private) is a language of conversation. It helps to establish connections and negotiate one's way within relationships. It emphasizes matching experiences. She explains, "From childhood, girls criticize peers who try to

report talk
According to Tannen, this usually takes place publicly, and men are more comfortable using this. It is used to exhibit knowledge and skill, preserve independence and maintain status in the hierarchical social order.

rapport talk
According to Tannen, the language of conversation, or private speaking, which more women feel comfortable with. It helps to establish connections and negotiate relationships.

367

stand out or appear better than others." Rapport talk tends to occur at home in private because that's where the closest connections are. By contrast, report talk usually takes place publicly. A man who barely speaks at home may appear confident and quite vocal to others as he uses report talk to exhibit knowledge and skill, preserve independence and maintain status in the hierarchical social order. "From childhood, men learn to use talking as a way to get and keep attention." Thus, they become more comfortable in later life speaking in larger groups.

gossip talk
A form of conversation that can form the core of friendship and which can serve as a useful function in establishing intimacy.

Gender differences can also be found in **gossip talk**. Both sexes gossip; only their subjects tend to differ. Men may gossip about business matters or sports, while women have a tendency to talk about feelings and what is currently happening in their lives. Such gossip talk forms the core of friendship (Tannen 1990: 96–122). Here we see that gossip needn't necessarily be destructive for it can serve a useful function in establishing intimacy.

Male and female language usage differences are evident in the context of lecturing and listening as well. "[M]en are more comfortable than women in giving information and opinions and speaking in an authoritative way to a group, whereas women are more comfortable than men in supporting others" (Tannen, cited in Weaver, 1996). Related to the business of who's talking and who's listening, Tannen points to research on gender and language that apparently reveals that men don't listen very well, as they tend to interrupt women more than women interrupt men (Tannen, 1990: 189). Interruptions should not be taken lightly, especially in close relationships. They can transmit metamessages to those whom we interrupt—messages like "I don't care enough to pay attention," "I don't want to listen" or "I'm not interested in what you're saying." Nobody likes to hear these metamessages because we all like to be heard and valued as persons (Tannen, 1990: 189). When speaking to someone you care about, you might choose to be a little more careful about your interruptions.

Masculine and feminine values, together and in balance, yield complementary benefits that enrich life. When either overwhelms the other, neither is life-giving. In our society—deprived of soul and therefore of a conscious understanding of the feminine—we've been looking at the feminine through the wrong lens, the lens of masculine understanding. However, just as masculine values were never intended to be evaluated through a feminine perspective, feminine values can't be understood from a masculine viewpoint.
~Kathleen Hurley and Theodore Dobson

Source: What's My Type, by Kathleen V. Hurley and Theodore E. Dobson. Copyright 1991 by Enneagram Resources, Inc. Reprinted by permission of HarperCollins Publishers, Inc.

Finally, when speaking in public situations, women are expected to be less boastful than men. Whereas males often use self-aggrandizing information to achieve status, females typically do not "wear their achievements on their sleeves," so to speak (Weaver, 1996). Unfortunately, they do tend to be underestimated as a result. When addressing gender language differences, Richard Weaver (1996) cautions us about our generalizations, and I think his caution is well recommended. After all, people are individuals and do not always fit the generalizations. What people do or say may vary from time to time, place to place and group to group. Furthermore, gender studies on language are at this point still inconclusive—gender tendencies seem to be present in some studies but not in others. Finally, group composition (the number of males and females) can also influence speech patterns. For example, language differences may be less evident in groups where gender mix is about equal. Be sure, then, not to make any gross generalizations or to predict people's behaviour solely on the basis of gender.

Culture and Communication: Inside Looking Out, Outside Looking In

9.4

If Canada or the United States were a purely homogeneous society, that is, if everyone dressed the same, spoke the same language, professed the same faith, originated from the same ethnic and racial background and shared the same sexual preferences and inclinations, communication would likely be an uncomplicated matter. However, as former prime minister Joe Clark once stated, the nation of Canada is a "community of communities." We are, in fact, both **pluralistic** societies and **multicultural** ones. If we are to live in a democratic fashion and communicate effectively with one another as friends, neighbours and citizens, we must learn to deal with cultural diversity. We must make honest efforts to listen to each other, accepting differences, working with them and using them to enhance the quality of our collective lives.

Not only has pluralism forced us to focus on the importance of culture in communications, but so too has economics. In a global economy, consisting of multinational corporations, foreign markets and international trade agreements, many people are forced to do their business in other countries and with many other cultures. They must travel and remain constantly mobile. They must be able to understand, adapt to and accommodate people and circumstances in which they find themselves. **Economic interdependence** now requires us to communicate more effectively across different cultures. Furthermore, advances in technology and telecommunications have brought the world to our doorstep. We can witness events as they happen, live from around the world, by simply turning on the TV. Computers and the Internet allow us to communicate across borders and gain access to information in amounts and at rates that would have dumbfounded earlier generations. We can attend teleconferences and communicate in real time with people thousands of miles away. If we are not to misunderstand them, we must learn to appreciate the cultural contexts out of which communications arise.

Politics also point to the importance of culture on communication. In a nation such as Canada, regional differences often cause tension and conflict. For example, there are Maritimers and Quebeckers, First Nations peoples and Westerners, groups whose needs and demands are often very different. In federal governmental affairs, it seems sometimes that every region wants to have a "voice," but is not willing to really listen to others. In light of this, one could argue that the survival of Canada depends on better communication among its diverse populations in various regions of the country.

It may be doubtful, at first, whether a person is an enemy or friend. Meat, if not properly digested, becomes poison; But poison, if used rightly, may turn medicinal.
~Saskya Pandita

pluralistic
Referring to a society comprised of many languages, faiths, ethnic and racial backgrounds, sexual orientations and inclinations.

multicultural
A society that is culturally diverse.

economic interdependence
Our global economy, consisting of multinational corporations, foreign markets and international trade agreements, requires us to communicate more effectively across different cultures.

politics
Governmental affairs can point to the importance of culture in communication.

369

What Is Culture?

culture
A group of people living in a more or less defined and recognizable lifestyle. This group is collectively bonded by their shared values, ideals, beliefs, behaviours and accepted ways of doing things.

enculturation
The transmission of culture from one generation to the next.

acculturation
The process by which an individual's culture is modified through direct contact or exposure with another culture.

Since we're focusing here on the importance of culture to communication, it makes sense to define what we mean by culture. **Culture** refers to a group of people living a more or less defined and recognizable lifestyle. This group is collectively bonded by their shared values, ideals, and beliefs, and by their accepted ways of communicating and doing things. All of the above are transmitted from one generation to the next (DeVito, 1997). Culture is not genetically determined; nor is it inborn or innate. Through our experiences with parents, teachers, peers, religious authorities and social institutions, we absorb the culture we have been raised in and become part of it ourselves, contributing to the **enculturation** of the next generation.

Related to enculturation is the notion of **acculturation**. In this process, an individual's "culture is modified through direct contact or exposure to another culture" (DeVito, 1997: 255). Immigrants to this country, for example, may acculturate by assimilating to our Canadian lifestyle and adopting many of our values as their own. Also, a member of one ethnic subcultural community may acculturate to another by incorporating some or any of its ways. I recently heard of a wedding, for example, between a Polish-Canadian woman and a Jamaican-Canadian man. At the wedding reception, cabbage rolls were served while reggae music was played in the background. The combination probably represents, symbolically at least, some kind of cultural bridging or mutual acculturation between two subcultural groups. Members of both communities adopted preferences of the other and made them part of their own experience.

A language professor once suggested to me that you could tell when someone had successfully acculturated into any given society, saying that people are not acculturated until they understand the newly adopted culture's sense of humour. Personally speaking, I tend to agree. I remember how alienated I once felt in Quebec years ago as a student when I couldn't appreciate the jokes that were told at social gatherings, though I understood the vocabulary that was used. Cultural context (i.e., history and politics) added humour to otherwise neutral language, making a joke that could not be grasped by at least one anglophone from Ontario.

9.5

intercultural communication
Communication between or among international, interracial, inter-ethnic, religious, occupational or gender groupings.

There are four different forms of **intercultural communication** (DeVito, 1998). The first form is international and could refer to communication between Germany and Japan or between Ukraine and Italy, for example. The second form is interracial and could refer to the communication between blacks and Chinese people or between Native people and whites. The third type is inter-ethnic and could refer to communication between French-Canadians and Finnish-Canadians. The fourth type is religious and could be the sort of communication that takes place between Buddhists and Jews, Catholics and Protestants, or Hindus and Muslims. Occupational groups also form subcultures in a society. It's always interesting to hear doctors and lawyers communicate, for instance, especially in court! The technical "computerese" spoken by programmers is always an intriguing contrast to the "psycho-babble" spoken by behavioural scientists. Communication can also take place between a dominant culture and a particular subculture, such as the heterosexual and gay communities. Finally, it's possible to distinguish communication on the basis of gender groupings, such as between men and women, as we did in the preceding section. What needs to be stressed here is that communication can and often does go beyond simple transactions between two individuals. Not only does psychological type filter communication, but so too does the culture and cultural subgroup to which one belongs. See Figure 9.1 for a depiction of the communication process incorporating a cultural overlay.

9.6 Intercultural Communication

Miscommunication can sometimes arise when people from different cultures or subcultural groups interact. Language may not be understood, intentions may be misread or customs may be unconsciously violated.

Figure 9.1
The Communication Process with Cultural Overlay

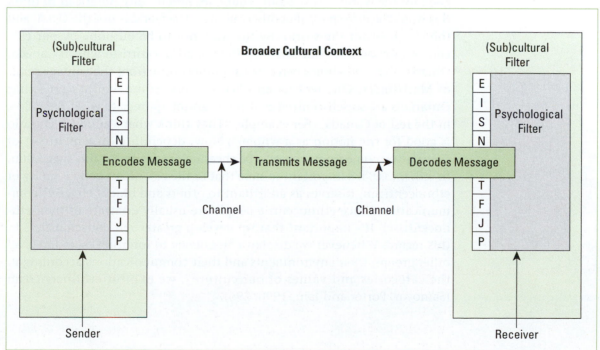

For example, an American tourist in Japan might stop to take pictures of a Buddhist wedding in progress. For the American, weddings are a time of joyful celebration. Taking pictures comes naturally and spontaneously on such happy occasions. However, for Buddhists, weddings have a different purpose and picture taking is offensive to them. To do what seems innocent to the American is wrong to the Japanese Buddhist. From this illustration, we can appreciate how cultural diversity can sometimes be a source of unfortunate misunderstanding. (Samovar, Porter and Jain, 1990: 395).

ethnocentrism

The social equivalent to psychological egocentrism in which people, racial minorities, occupational groups, subcultures and religious denominations, for instance, see the world strictly from their own perspective.

Communication can also suffer from **ethnocentrism**. Think of this as the social equivalent to psychological egocentrism. Egocentric people can only see the world from their own self-referring perspective. Like children, they can't see the broader picture. Their perceptions are slanted by subjectivity and personal bias. They are unable to detach themselves from their own wants, preferences, values and beliefs to see things as others see them. If we expand psychological egocentrism to include the collective psyche of a culture, nation or particular subgroup within it, we create a kind of ethnic egocentrism or ethnocentrism for short. Peoples, races, minorities, occupational groups, subcultures and religious denominations, for instance, may suffer from ethnocentrism. Around the globe you often hear people criticizing U.S. citizens, objecting to a viewpoint that they rightly or wrongly attribute to them, namely, "What's good for America is good for the world." This claim is dubious, and for any American to think this would be disrespectful of other cultures. The world is not the U.S.A. and the U.S.A. is not the world. By the way, not to be outdone by our U.S. cousins, we too have our own examples of ethnocentrism within Canada. Ontarians are sometimes perceived as ethnocentric from the vantage point of Maritimers, Quebeckers and Westerners. Some would argue that Ontarians are so self-centred that they cannot appreciate what life is like in the rest of Canada. (For example, "They think what's good for Ontario is good for the nation as a whole.") Now, depending on which part of Canada you come from, you may be cheering or sneering at this suggestion. In either case, it's important to note that to the extent anybody is guilty of ethnocentrism, it serves as an irritant to others and blocks effective communication. Since ethnocentric people are usually unaware of their ethnocentrism, it's important that we develop greater self-consciousness in this regard. Whenever we display a "tendency to interpret or to judge all other groups, their environments and their communications according to the categories and values of our culture", we exhibit ethnocentrism (Samovar, Porter and Jain, 1990: 296).

Perception of difference is yet another potential obstacle to effective intercultural communication (Samovar, Porter and Jain, 1990: 396; also see DeVito, 1992: 258–260). When dealing with unfamiliar cultures, we sometimes tend to perceive differences as greater than they really are (Samovar, Porter and Jain, 1990: 297). We then allow these unrealistic differences to inhibit communication. We lack the trust to communicate and get along. Unfortunately, creating a **false perception of difference** is sometimes politically or militarily useful, even if ethically questionable. If soldiers are indoctrinated to believe that the enemy is inhuman, that "it" does not value life or that "it" is inferior to one's own group, attack becomes easier. A violent encounter is facilitated when the other group is depersonalized, dehumanized and made to look different—something like a monster.

While it is true that some differences are fabricated for questionable instrumental purposes, occasionally we do ignore real differences between ourselves and others. We may wrongly assume similarities exist and that differences don't. DeVito says, "When you assume similarities and ignore differences, you implicitly communicate to others that yours are the right ways and that their ways are not important to you" (DeVito, 1997). Let me give you an example. As a professor, I have always been concerned by American speakers who cite U.S. statistics when addressing Canadian audiences. They often make generalizations about Canada by asking Canadians to divide U.S. statistics by 10 since in terms of population, we are about one-tenth the size of the U.S. In fact, Canadian college and university students have read so many foreign textbooks that cite U.S. research statistics that they do this division almost automatically. I have received many papers that cite U.S. data from my students. The American misperception that Canadians are very similar has apparently led some Canadians, namely my students, to believe it themselves.

However, if we compare murder statistics from both countries, for example, we find enormous cultural differences. In 2003, Statistics Canada reported that 548 murders were committed across the country. In the United States, 16,503 persons were murdered in the same year, or approximately thirty times more, though the population is roughly only ten times larger than ours. The net result is that murder rates are about 3 times higher in the United States as compared with Canada, adjusting for population differences. Hence, with respect to murders at least, we are not just like Americans—only one-tenth the size.

A word of caution is in order here. Describing the United States as a more violent culture than ours does not mean that every American is violent. When it comes to perceiving those in other cultures, we should be careful not to **stereotype**—to make generalizations about people and ignore individual differences. Not all Americans carry guns, nor do they all kill

perception of difference
A potential obstacle to effective intercultural communication. When dealing with other cultures we sometimes tend to perceive differences as greater than they really are.

false perception of difference
An international obstacle to effective communication in which a difference, say between cultures, is reported as being greater than it is. While it may work militarily or politically, it is ethically questionable.

stereotype
A perceptual error in which we lump different individuals together by wrongly attributing to them common characteristics.

innocent people in the streets. Within any culture there is a great deal of diversity. On this note, it would be dangerous to say that all Canadians favour a constitutional monarchy, especially if you said this to a political militant in Quebec. Furthermore, to suggest that all Canadians are bilingual simply because Canada is a bilingual society is wrong.

On the subject of language, you should note that we cannot discount intercultural differences in the meanings attributed to words. It could be argued that meanings do not exist in words themselves, but in the people using them. For instance, the word "religion" may mean different things to different individuals. To pop-singer Edie Brickell it is a "smile on a dog"; to Karl Marx it's "the opiate of the masses"; and for believing Catholics it's an "institution" created by God. Words are often laden with values and underlying connotations. As I mentioned earlier, nonverbal language also involves intercultural differences that can cause miscommunication. In this country a "V" sign made with the index and middle fingers stands for victory, or for the number two. To some South Americans, it is an obscene gesture (DeVito, 1997). To use inappropriate nonverbal language in a particular cultural context could get you into serious trouble.

Failure to appreciate and take into account all the differences observed above adds to another general problem with intercultural communication, namely, lack of empathy (Samovar, Porter and Jain, 1990: 397). **Empathy** involves an element of role taking. People who empathize with others are able to understand others' feelings and place themselves in others' shoes. Whenever you say things like "I know how you feel" or "I've been there; I know what you mean," you express empathy. Of course, empathizing is difficult for an ethnocentric person, who cannot shift from his own cultural perspective and really appreciate what things look like from another cultural vantage point. If we stereotype others, empathizing is also difficult, if not impossible. If we fail to see people as they truly are and ascribe to them inappropriate cultural stereotypes, given individual diversity within cultures, we will fail to understand them, their thoughts and their feelings. In interacting with others, we may project onto them many of our own fears, insecurities and misguided notions.

empathy
The ability to understand another's feelings or to place oneself in another's shoes.

9.7 How to Improve Intercultural Communication

Given the virtual inevitability and necessity of intercultural dialogue and interaction, a mastery of human relations demands that we take positive steps to break down barriers to effective communication. Listed below are some helpful recommendations (Samovar, Porter and Jain, 1990: 399–404).

1. Know Thyself In many ways self-knowledge is a prerequisite for effective communication, both intercultural and interpersonal. If we are unaware of our ignorance or prejudicial tendencies, for example, we will not notice when our social perceptions are based on incomplete information or unjustifiable stereotypes. If we are blind to our negative attitudes toward homosexuals, for instance, we may not be aware of how our **precommunication attitudes** colour transactions between us and them (assuming the "us" is heterosexual). An accepting precommunication attitude among homosexuals may help to establish positive tones in communication that could be difficult to achieve between heterosexuals and homosexuals, if the former were unconsciously fearful of the latter. A climate of fear and distrust usually acts as an impediment to effective social interaction. It is well advised, then, that you learn as much as you can about yourself so that latent fears, buried hostilities and unconscious insecurities and tensions can be reduced.

Knowing yourself also involves being aware of the image you present to others. For example, how are Canadians perceived abroad? How are Sikhs perceived in Manitoba? How are New Yorkers regarded in Los Angeles? How are French Canadians looked upon in Alberta or British Columbia? Or how are lawyers perceived by engineers? If we wish to improve our intercultural or intergroup communication and understand the reactions of others toward us, we must have some idea of how other people see us (Samovar, Porter and Jain, 1990: 400).

If we know that others are likely to be hostile toward us or to project certain images upon us, we can take steps to diffuse any anger and dispel any undesirable stereotypes and preconceived notions. For instance, we could try to empathize with the other groups to understand the basis of their anger or negativity, putting ourselves in their shoes to see ourselves as they do. Using humour is another possibility. Personally speaking, I find self-deprecating humour to be an effective means of relieving tension. If we can laugh about our differences and intercultural misperceptions, we can begin to create a warmer atmosphere for more productive communication. I think many black, Jewish and physically-challenged comedians have understood this principle for a long time. By listening to blind comedians joke about their blindness, for instance, we learn to appreciate their experience of life and, as a result, develop a better understanding of people who are blind. An increased understanding of others can often facilitate better communication.

2. Use a Common Language It's obviously difficult to communicate with people if you don't speak their language, as North Americans travelling in Europe can attest. People can try to make themselves understood with the help of dictionaries and hand gestures, but interactions could clearly run much more smoothly if people spoke the same language. When travelling abroad, then, a crash course in the language of the country you plan to visit or work in could be quite beneficial.

Within any country, linguistic barriers can also exist. Take any major metropolitan centre, for example. City neighbourhoods are sometimes identified by their ethnic and linguistic characteristics. In Toronto, people often

precommunication attitudes
The attitudes (conscious or unconscious) we bring to interpersonal or intercultural social interaction. Negative attitudes, such as ignorance or prejudicial tendencies act as an impediment to effective communication.

375

You will also see bilingual signs in Toronto's Greektown.

refer to Chinatown and Little Italy. In those areas, a good portion of the population speaks either Chinese or Italian. Street signs are bilingual (English and Chinese, or English and Italian) while governmental agencies and stores offer services in the foreign languages represented there. In fact, some immigrants to Canada settle in ethnic communities and lead productive lives without ever learning either one of Canada's two national languages.

My maternal Lithuanian-Canadian grandmother, for example (who recently passed away at the age of 101), barely spoke a word of English and no French. She lived in Canada for more than 40 years. For her, telephone conversations were complicated by her lack of English. On the other hand, she got along fine within her Lithuanian community.

Language difficulties derive not only from different national origins, but also from people belonging to different professional and technical fields. Specialists in any given field often use jargon. **Jargon** is really a kind of sub-language that can create barriers if it is used to impress or confuse others (DeVito, 1992: 261). Good illustrations of sub-language can be found in insurance policies and legal documents. Academics and physicians also tend to use their own technical languages to say the simplest things. An orthopaedic surgeon may refer to the crest of your hip bone as the "anterior-superior iliac spine"; a general practitioner may use "medicalese" when telling you that you suffer from a "bilateral periorbital haematoma." If you don't ask for clarification on this one, you may not know you have a black eye. Using "computerese" jargon,

jargon
Specialized, technical language belonging to a particular field or discipline.

376

let me suggest that we should try to make our communications with others more "user friendly," especially when interacting with people outside our areas of technical expertise. Opt for the simplest and clearest way to say things. We should shift from our own point of view and try to understand what our jargon sounds like to others. We shouldn't assume that others always understand our specialized terminology. People are sometimes too embarrassed to admit their ignorance.

As an academic who sometimes uses jargon (this book is full of it—literally, I hope not figuratively), I wish to draw your attention to the fact that technical sub-languages do have their legitimate place. Terms and concepts are sometimes invented to describe and label (in exact terms) experiences, phenomena and events in the world. People who use technical language may be trying to develop a certain precision in their speech, to establish clarity and label new discoveries for those within their disciplines. Jargon that is confusing to you as a layperson may be perfectly understandable to an expert. The use of jargon, in itself, is not good or bad. It depends on the people involved and the situational context. If you're currently having difficulty understanding classroom lectures, your instructor may not be trying to show off by using big words. Maybe jargon is needed to capture a certain idea accurately. Perhaps the instructor is unaware of the impact her speech is having on the class. The instructor may be trying to communicate in a classroom situation in the same way that she communicates with colleagues at professional conferences. Therein may lie the problem. On the other hand, you may wish to expand your vocabulary and adopt your instructor's technical jargon as your own.

3. Take Time Before Pronouncing Judgment Finally, when dealing with people from different cultures and cultural sub-groups, it's probably a good idea to delay or suspend judgment. We shouldn't jump to conclusions about others and presume to know what they are like. I once had a theatre arts student take my philosophy class as a required general education course. Having barely introduced myself in the first class, the student abruptly interrupted me and said he wanted nothing to do with me or my course. He informed me that his older sister had once dated a philosopher and that the "guy was a pompous jerk." Barely able to pronounce my name, never having spoken to me before and not allowing me a chance to introduce him to the study of philosophy, he dismissed me in one verbal assault. I guess in his mind all philosophers are pompous jerks. Now this may or may not be true, but I never got the opportunity to prove his point! The suggestion I'd like to make is that before we evaluate any culture or subgroup (e.g., philosophers), we should take the time to familiarize ourselves with those who belong to it. We should try to get to know their values and ideals. Otherwise, we are likely to arrive at false conclusions. (My own experience indicates that only 37.3 percent of philosophers are pompous jerks, not 100 percent as the student concluded!) In any

377

case, preconceived notions, precommunication attitudes and prejudgments about this group obviously had a negative influence on this student's perceptions of me in my class. The student jumped to what I like to believe is an incorrect conclusion.

Point of View

Art of Communication Is as Varied as the World's Culture

by Arthur Black

According to Marshall McLuhan, "Language is a form of organized stutter." McLuhan was right. Every syllable of spoken word we know, from Hamlet's soliloquy on the battlements to Jean Chrétien's sound bites on Prime Time News—nothing but organized stutter.

How did that come to be? Nobody knows precisely when Grok the Caveman grew tired of waving his hairy arms around and decided to use grunts, growls, and snorts to express himself, but anthropologists know that the human throat was capable of speech anywhere from 20,000 to 35,000 years ago, so it's a safe bet that we nattered at each other for several thousand years before somebody got a bright idea and said, "I say chaps, how be we call all these noises we're making 'English'?"

And not just English. There are some 9,000 languages and dialects spoken around the world. The most popular is Mandarin Chinese. English is second, then Hindi, Russian, and Spanish.

Ottawa Valley Speak is not in the top 100.

Not all languages are spoken either. The deaf and the mute have sign language. Boy Scouts and aircraft carrier signalmen use semaphore. Various Indian tribes used to communicate by smoke signal. There is Morse Code, Braille, NHL referee hand signals.

And there is the drum.

Most of us in North America don't consider the drum to be a prime source of communication among human beings. For us, the drum is a loud, rather tiresome quasi-musical instrument employed to drown out other musicians. It owes its current popularity to Mister Ringo Starr, a large-nosed Liverpudlian, who regularly assaulted a drum kit on behalf of the Beatles.

But we in North America don't know diddley-squat about drums.

They do in West Africa. The Akan people—who are found throughout the West African countries—have been using drums to talk with each other for centuries.

Very effectively, too. A good West African drummer can pound out a message that will carry for nearly 40 miles. That message will, in turn, be picked up by other drummers in all directions who will each transmit it to their "listening audience."

In hours a message can sweep across thousands of miles without the benefit of telephone poles, highways, or communications satellite.

And how does a drum message "read"? Not cut and dried like Morse Code. More like a soliloquy from Hamlet. West African drumspeak is highly poetic and beautiful. A plane crash translates as "a canoe that flies like a bird has fallen out of the sky."

And when the much-revered President of the Ivory Coast died last year, the tribal drums throbbed out a dirge that translated as—"The great elephant has lost its teeth. The leopard has lost its spots. The baobab (tree) has crashed down."

A little more majestic than "KENNEDY SHOT!" wouldn't you say?

Reminds me of my most memorable encounter with a non-spoken language. Actually, it was a second-hand encounter. I heard the story from two wandering Canucks I met on a Spanish freighter waddling along the west coast of Africa. The two Canadians had been living on the island of Gomera—a tiny, volcanic atoll among the Canary Islands. They told a story of climbing one of the many rugged mountains on the island.

What they couldn't understand was how every villager they met seemed to be expecting them. Odd, considering they were climbing a goat path and there were no roads or telephones on their route. When they reached a village on the top of the mountain, they were astounded to find that the townsfolk had killed and cooked a goat in their honor. Yes, the head man told them, they'd been expecting "two foreigners." "Bienvenido."

But how? How could they know?

The two Canucks were masters of suspense. They waited until I paid for a round of drinks in the ship's saloon before they explained.

It was whistling. The people on the island of Gomera speak a language of whistles called silbo. The piercing whistles carry so well across valleys (or up mountains) that a "speaker" can be heard up to five miles away.

I wonder what Marshall McLuhan would say about that.

Source: Reprinted by permission of Arthur Black.

Nonverbal Communication: You Don't Say!

Have you ever had the uncomfortable experience of receiving mixed messages? Perhaps an individual told you one thing yesterday, but another completely different thing today. Contradictory messages of this sort often result in emotional upset and confusion. The ambiguity or inconsistency causes a psychological fog, so to speak, making interpersonal navigation unsure and potentially dangerous. Sometimes the mixed messages we receive are more subtle and complex. One message may be verbal, the other nonverbal. There may be a gap between what people say and how they say it, or between what they say and what their body language communicates. For example, if you've ever witnessed people grit their teeth, clench their fists or stare without blinking, and then say, "I'm not mad," you can appreciate what I mean. People's nonverbal messages often belie what they say. It is possible, of course, to have consistency between verbal and nonverbal behaviour. What is expressed nonverbally can match what's actually said. For example, an angry person may act angrily and speak in angry terms (e.g., $*#@!).

In what follows, we'll explore the nature of nonverbal communication and its various expressions. What you'll learn in this section should help you to become a keener observer of people. Your increased powers of observation should help you to read people better, to be more sensitive to them and to hear what is not said, but communicated indirectly through nonverbal cues. Being sensitive to your own nonverbal communication will also help you to manage your behaviour more effectively. You'll become better able to govern the impressions you make on others. This ability could help you to get through certain "doors of life." In a very informal study done by TV celebrity hostess Oprah Winfrey, efforts were made to find out what it takes to get into some of the finest nightclubs and hotspots in America. She discovered that attitude (the way you carry yourself) was a determining factor. It wasn't always what people said that got them through the door, but how people handled themselves. Demeanour and deportment often meant direct entry. (A cash bribe didn't hurt either!)

9.8 The Nature of Nonverbal Communication

As stated, messages between people can be sent at verbal and nonverbal levels. Verbal communication deals with words, which can be spoken or written. They can be sent in face-to-face conversation, over the telephone, by fax or through the mail. Thus, while some verbal communication can be vocal (i.e., oral), it can also be nonvocal, say, electronic (Stewart and D'Angelo, 1997).

nonverbal communication
Communication without words. Nonverbal messages are sent through a number of channels. For example, information may be sent by means of gestures, physical movements, facial expressions, eye movements, uses of space and time, personal appearance and touch. They may be sent intentionally or unintentionally.

Nonverbal communication can be defined as "communication without words" (Adler and Rodman, 2000). Like verbal communication, it can also have vocal dimensions. Accompanying what anyone says is the tone of voice, volume, pitch, rate and articulation, which is referred to as paralanguage, something we'll look at in a moment. Nonverbal communication is multi-channelled (Adler and Rodman, 2000). Nonverbal messages are sent through a number of sub-channels. For example, information may be sent by means of gestures, physical movements, facial expressions, eye movements, uses of space and time, personal appearance and touch. In contrast to paralanguage, these expressions of nonverbal communication are nonvocal. Nonverbal messages can also be sent intentionally or unintentionally as people are not always aware of the nonverbal messages they send. In any case, nonverbal communication cannot simply be turned off. Nonverbal messages occur spontaneously, with or without the person realizing it (Weiten, Lloyd and Lashley, 1999). Complete Application Exercise 9.2 now to prove this point.

Don't Talk to Me!

This exercise can be done very easily in small or large groups. Select the person sitting next to you as your partner. If numbers are uneven, the instructor may participate as well. On cue, spend one minute looking at your partner without saying a word. Do not communicate verbally. Then record on a piece of paper all of the impressions, feelings and thoughts that were transmitted to you by your partner. In other words, what was communicated nonverbally? Share your observations first with your partner. Then listen for your partner's reactions. Did you and your partner read each other accurately? Willing participants can share what they learned with the rest of the class.

Application Exercise 9.2 illustrates how nonverbal communication is multichannelled and how it provides a constant source of information about yourself and others. If you didn't really want to do this exercise or thought you didn't participate fully, chances are pretty good that your nonverbal cues told your partner this. What did your face say? What did you tell your partner by your posture and eye movements? In the debriefing portion of this exercise you may have learned that nonverbal communication is ambiguous, especially if you misread your partner. Inferences made about other people based on their nonverbal cues are sometimes wrong. People may remain silent because they're shy, angry, insecure, reluctant, introverted, or, as in this case, because they're instructed to be that way. Silence, like other nonverbal communication, can be hard to read. Be careful, then, not to jump to conclusions, for it's precarious to make assumptions about people based solely on nonverbal factors. What is said, who says it, and the context in which it's said, should be considered as well.

Nonverbal communication has a social function (Adler and Rodman, 2000). By means of dress, posture and facial expression, for instance, we can present ourselves as friendly and outgoing. We may try to manage our identities and our projected images. In addition, we may use nonverbal communication to define the kind of relationship we wish to establish. If we want to remain distant and uninvolved, we can avoid all physical contact. By contrast, if we want to welcome someone, a warm handshake, hug or smile will do the trick. Finally, we may use nonverbal communication to express our feelings and attitudes; sometimes we do this unconsciously. Without knowing it, we can express our disinterest or enthusiasm by what our body "says." Through eye contact we may show interest in another person; by eye-contact avoidance, we may communicate apathy, discomfort, upset or preoccupation.

Culture also affects nonverbal communication, an idea that was hinted at earlier. As we learned, certain hand gestures can mean different things in different cultures. As well, various cultures may have characteristically different forms of nonverbal communication. In one study, researchers observed Fiorello LaGuardia, the mayor of New York City from 1933 to 1945, who spoke fluent English, Italian and Yiddish. They watched films of his campaign speeches with the sound turned off. Without actually hearing LaGuardia's addresses, the observers were able to identify the language he was speaking by his nonverbal behaviour (Birdwhistell, 1970, cited in Adler and Rodman, 2000). Do you know any immigrants or first-generation Canadians? Do they import into English some of their nonverbal behaviours from other linguistic and cultural contexts? Is their nonverbal communication with you different from how it is with those from their culture of origin? What, if anything, have you observed? What impact have these differences had on your interpersonal communications?

On the issue of culture and nonverbal communication, I would like to stress one last point. While differences do exist, some nonverbal behaviours are seemingly universal; apparently meaning the same thing everywhere. For example, in every culture, laughter and a smiling face are universal signs of positive emotion. A sour expression conveys displeasure, no matter where you go (Adler and Rodman, 2000). Charles Darwin hypothesized that nonverbal expressions such as these functioned as survival mechanisms, allowing early humans to communicate feelings or states of emotion before the development of language.

The Relationship Between Verbal and Nonverbal Communication

......(9.9)

Implicit in what has been covered so far is the idea that verbal and nonverbal communication are related. At a bare minimum they can be consistent or inconsistent with each other. Here I'd like to discuss, in a bit more detail, the function of nonverbal communication as it pertains to its verbal counterpart. Nonverbal communication can do a number of things. It can accent, complement, contradict, regulate, repeat or substitute for the spoken word (DeVito, 1998). Let's see how.

To **accent** a verbal message, we could bang a fist on a table to underscore our objection. We could also throw a nerf ball at the television while complaining about the officiating of the game being televised. Another thing we do nonverbally is **complement** what we say. For instance, we could laugh while telling a joke or shake our head when expressing disbelief. As you already know, verbal messages can **contradict** what we do nonverbally. We might display a devilish grin when saying "Trust me!" As a student you might insist to your instructor that you are interested in the course, yet always look out the window during class. Nonverbal communication can also **regulate**. Leaning

accent
To underscore a verbal statement by nonverbal behaviour cues.

complement
Adding nonverbal cues to our communication that assist in delivering our meaning. For instance, we may laugh as we tell a joke, or shake our head when expressing disbelief.

contradict
Nonverbal cues that convey a meaning opposite to the verbal communication. For instance, delivering the words "Trust me" with a devilish grin.

regulate
The manner in which we may nonverbally express our desire to direct a communication by indicating that we are ready to listen.

forward in your chair and raising your hand may indicate that you are anxious to answer a question. Your body language may be saying, "I wish to speak now." Leaning back in your seat and orienting to the speaker may communicate, "It's your turn; I'm ready to listen." Nonverbal communication can **repeat** what you say. If you were a server in a restaurant, you might ask, "Was that one cheeseburger or two?" first raising your index finger and then your middle finger (or your thumb and index finger, if you prefer!) Finally, nonverbal communication can interact with verbal communication through substitution. Instead of saying "yes" or "no," for instance, we could indicate our choice by nodding our head or shaking it. We needn't actually say anything. Our answer can be transmitted nonverbally. So you see, verbal and nonverbal communication can be interconnected.

repeat
Through nonverbal communication, you can say the same thing you just said through verbal communication.

9.10 Classifying Nonverbal Communication

We can better understand nonverbal communication by classifying it in terms of the following eight categories: paralanguage, environment, artifactual communication, physical appearance, posture and body movement (kinesics), space communication (proxemics), time communication (chronemics) and touch communication (haptics).

Paralanguage How we say something can be as important as what we say. Volume, rate, pitch, articulation and emphasis are all important. They add communication value to our verbal messages. The sentences below illustrate the point that the same statement can communicate different ideas, depending on where the emphasis falls. As you read the variations of the same statement, emphasize the italicized words.

1. *Cynthia* took the human relations course for personal growth.
2. Cynthia took the *human relations* course for personal growth.
3. Cynthia took the human relations course for *personal* growth.
4. Cynthia *took* the human relations course for personal growth.
5. Cynthia took *the* human relations course for personal growth.

How is each statement different? What different things are communicated by emphasizing different parts of the same sentence?

Paralanguage, or the manner in which you say something, involves not only emphasis, but also volume. Soft and loud talk may communicate very different things. Asking someone, in a whisper, to shut the door communicates something very different compared with screaming the same request at the top of your lungs. In the latter case, the speaker conveys upset or anger, and in the former case only a simple request.

The speed (or rate) at which you speak also falls under paralanguage. It is important because of the impressions it creates. Studies have indicated that people who speak more quickly are stereotyped as more competent than slower

paralanguage
The manner in which something is said; the volume, rate, pitch, articulation and emphasis.

383

speakers (see Mulac and Rudd, 1977, cited in Adler and Rodman, 1994: 456). Of course, if you speak too quickly, others will be less able to understand you and follow what you're saying. This reminds me of the time I was teaching at Sir Wilfred Grenfell College in Corner Brook, Newfoundland. As most Canadians already know, Newfoundlanders have a unique accent. Being a mainlander, I sometimes found conversations difficult to follow as rapid speech, combined with a regional dialect, made things virtually incomprehensible. Appreciating the kind of difficulty mainlanders experience, a fish-processing company that advertised its products on TV once had a Newfoundland fisherman promote its food products while subtitles ran across the bottom of the screen to help those outside Newfoundland understand what he was saying.

It wasn't only the rate of speech that caused difficulty for me in Newfoundland, but also the accent and articulation. Within Canada, indeed within many nations, regional and ethnic dialects are found that convey nonverbal messages, and not always favourable ones. The "Georgia Cracker" accent or "Southern drawl" is often regarded as less favourable or less desirable in the United States as compared with a Midwest accent. In fact, many Canadian newscasters are deliberately hired by U.S. stations in part because of their neutral-sounding accents. The late Peter Jennings, Morley Safer, Hillary Bowker, J.D.(John) Roberts and Mary Garafalo (the latter two both formerly with CityTV in Toronto) now work for U.S. networks.

articulation
One of the categories of paralanguage that involves our pronunciation. When we articulate, we may leave off parts of words (deletion), we may replace a part of a word (substitution), we may add parts to words (addition) or we may slur our words.

substitution
An aspect of articulation in which we replace parts of words with other sounds. For instance, the ending of a "th" word might become a "t" sound.

Articulation involves our pronunciation. When we articulate, we may leave off parts of words (deletion), we may replace a part of a word (substitute), we may add parts to words (addition) or we may slur our words (Adler and Rodman, 1994). A common deletion involves words that end in "ing." Hoping, thinking and praying become hopin', thinkin' and prayin'. In my own case, I often use deletion as a way of making my speech more friendly and informal. In more formal, professional settings, I usually make an effort to articulate clearly all my "ing" endings for fear of appearing uneducated or a little "rough around the edges."

Substitution is another aspect of articulation that occurs when parts of words are replaced by incorrect sounds. The "th" ending of a word may become a "t." Found at the beginning of a word, "th" may become a "d" sound. A classic book out east, *Death on the Ice*, is pronounced by some Newfoundlanders as "*Det own dee Ice.*"

Addition is another aspect of articulation that involves adding extra parts to words that don't belong; for example, you would say "normalicy" instead of normalcy or "sufferage" instead of suffrage (the right to vote in political elections). In northern Ontario, people sometimes say "youse" instead of "you." Addition also makes use of "tag questions." Canadians are notorious for saying "eh" at the end of their sentences. Sometimes we add words like "right" or "you know" (for example, "I saw this guy, right" or "He was a big dude, you know") to the end of sentences. The danger with additions is that they can become irritating to listeners, eh? (The American translation is "huh.")

Slurring is yet another aspect of articulation. When we slur, words run together or overlap. The word "of" is often transformed by slurring. "This kind of thing" becomes "This kinda thing." "Sort of" becomes "sorta." "Want to" changes to "wanna." Slurring can become problematic if it makes you look unintelligent or interferes with comprehension.

Pitch is the last dimension of paralanguage we'll look at here. Pitch points to the highness or lowness of your voice and tends to be related to rate and volume. When people speed up their speech or increase their volume, pitch tends to rise. Since pitch is also associated with muscle tension in the throat (specifically in the vocal folds), nervous speakers may sometimes squeak while talking. It's important to take pitch into account when communicating. A continuously high, squeaking pitch may irritate others, while a low drone may put them to sleep. It's best to modulate your pitch, as well as your rate and volume, according to the demands of the situation and the messages to be relayed. Be aware of what you're saying, how you're saying it, to whom you're speaking and what impression you are giving off by virtue of your nonverbal speech characteristics.

pitch
A dimension of paralanguage that points to the highness or lowness of your voice and can be related to rate and volume.

Environment People don't communicate in a vacuum. Their communications obviously take place in a particular physical location or **environment**. Sometimes the location can have a significant impact on the quality and nature of the interaction itself. If you've ever said in conversation, "Here is not the place to be discussing this," you've recognized at an intuitive level what constitutes a proper or improper environment for certain kinds of interpersonal communications. You probably appreciate how environment can affect our moods, actions and choice of words. For example, some things that you say on the street, you would never say in church. Also, you may find that you are more relaxed, more friendly, in a better mood or more polite in certain locations as compared with others. You may communicate differently on a beach in Nassau in contrast with your office at work or in the college library. In fact, company executives who recognize this often hold professional retreats off-location to boost morale and to create an environment conducive to better human relations.

environment
The physical location within which communication takes place.

Things falling under physical environment include "furniture, architectural style, interior decorating, lighting conditions, colours, temperature, additional noises or music, and the like, in which the interaction occurs" (Knapp and Hall, 1996). Obviously, inanimate objects cannot talk, yet don't we often say things like, "This furniture makes a statement," or "The decor in this room tells me a lot about you; you're obviously an artsy/practical/tasteful person." We can also make statements about ourselves nonverbally by how we arrange our environments—by the materials, fabrics and shapes we include in it or by the surfaces of objects found there. Suppose, for example, that you were invited to someone's apartment for coffee. What impression would be made on you if you drank from fine, imported china cups worth $200 each? What would you think if you were given a used paper cup instead? What would the

385

What does this work environment communicate to you?

artifactual communication
The decoration of space involving the physical environment, including, but not limited to, colour, clothing and bodily adornment.

386

two different cups say to you? On the subject of materials, don't many people attribute higher status to genuine leather compared with vinyl or rubber imitation? Don't we seem to place certain value judgments on materials in this culture and describe people who know how to select and choose properly among them as discriminating consumers, or people with taste? Don't we tend to be impressed by those who can distinguish between quality and cheap substitutes? Real wood communicates something different from inexpensive veneer. Of course, what it communicates is open to interpretation. Remember, nonverbal communication is fraught with ambiguity.

Artifactual Communication The decoration of space involving the physical environment is sometimes discussed under **artifactual communication** (DeVito, 1993). I've included it under the category of the communication environment. Under artifactual communication we'll focus on colour, clothing and bodily adornment.

Colour
Colours can have different meanings conveying different messages often depending on culture. For instance, green can mean environmentally friendly or envious. Yellow transmits the idea of divinity at the Vatican in Rome, while the same colour describes a coward in North America. Furthermore, the same colours can mean different things within any one culture. On the subject of yellow, I recall one evening calling out, "Go, Yellow!" in support of my fellow Bruins hockey players during one of my men's league hockey games (our sweaters were predominately yellow). Another player on the bench asked if I could use the word "gold" instead of "yellow." He didn't like the negative connotations of yellow. As a matter of fact, I recall team morale being somewhat down because the league did not issue us the modern-era black NHL Bruins' uniforms, but the vintage yellow version instead. (Black is regarded by many as tough and intimidating.)

The importance of colour should not be discounted, especially when it comes to clothes. Whether or not we accept a person may depend on the colours he wears. I recall when Frank Miller became leader of the Conservative Party in Ontario. He had a habit of wearing red-and-blue plaid sports jackets that became targets of humour and political satire. Miller was disparagingly described by some as looking like a farmer or a used car salesman. Of course, there is nothing wrong with farmers or salespeople, but in government many people want leaders to look like leaders and this means wearing certain colours and not others. Miller quietly changed much of his wardrobe, probably on the advice of image consultants. The importance of colour to occupation has been noted by Bernice Kanner, a colour expert. In the context of the U.S. legal profession she writes, "If you have to pick the wardrobe for your defence lawyer heading into court and choose anything but blue, you deserve to lose the case" (DeVito, 1998). Apparently black is so powerful a colour that it can work against the lawyer's interests with the jury. Brown isn't authoritative enough, while green could give rise to negative reactions (DeVito, 1998: 111). It might be interesting for you to consider what colours you most often wear and what colours you'd never be caught dead in. What colours, if any, send unappealing messages to you? Look around the room the next time you're in class; what colours are most often worn by others? What do these colours tell you?

Beware of all enterprises that require new clothes.
~Henry David Thoreau

Clothing

Clothing can also send messages to others revealing how modest or immodest you are, how liberal or conservative you are, to which cultural or subcultural groups you belong, or what your income bracket is likely to be. People make inferences about you all the time. They do this in part by the way you dress. In one study, college students perceived an instructor who was informally dressed as enthusiastic, friendly, fair and flexible. When the same instructor dressed formally, college students perceived the person to be knowledgeable, prepared and organized (Devito, 1998: 111). Correctly or incorrectly, we say that "clothes make the person." While I think you'd agree this phrase is a bit of an overstatement, it's hard to deny that our perceptions of people are influenced by clothes. I once heard an upper-middle-class woman express skepticism about a social worker who was assigned to help her. She said something along these lines: "How can someone wearing sandals and blue jeans possibly be of any use to me?" Obviously, this woman's interactions with the social worker were undermined by her perceptions. From her perspective, the social worker lacked credibility due to the way he was dressed. In another place and with other people, he may have appeared "cool," but the woman was not interested in "cool" and consequently was not interested in talking to him.

Bodily Adornment

In addition to clothing, jewelry also constitutes part of bodily adornment. Wearing an inexpensive Timex watch may communicate to others that you are frugal and practical, while wearing a Rolex or Gucci timepiece may say that you are wealthy and established. In fact, some people like to look wealthy and established even if they're not, which is the reason why a black market exists for "label" merchandise. It's possible to buy a fake Gucci

Farewell: Wearing his trademark tartan jacket, Frank Miller filled his briefcase while vacating a Queen's Park office on his last day as Progressive Conservative leader, Nov. 21, 1985, soon after an election ended the party's 42-year reign.

387

watch (one made by another manufacturer but displaying the Gucci label) for a fraction of what the genuine one costs. (I know this because I have been approached to buy one!) People buy the label and wear the watch to communicate nonverbally that they're successful. Many of us hear and accept that message. Other artifacts of personal adornment that send out messages include such things as hairpieces, false eyelashes, lipstick and attaché cases (Knapp and Hall, 1996). The attaché case may say, "I'm in business," while an obvious wig might communicate, "I don't like my real hair and I'm insecure about it."

physical appearance This is closely tied to clothing, colour and adornment. There are some things about appearance that we can change or mask, but other things we can't. Body type, attractiveness, height, weight and skin colour can communicate messages about ourselves.

Physical Appearance Closely tied to clothing, colour and adornment is **physical appearance**. Some things about our appearance we can change or mask through clothes, for example, but other things we can't. We communicate messages about ourselves simply by our body type, attractiveness, height, weight and skin colour. Hair can be dyed another shade but its texture and thickness cannot really be changed all that much. Even hair transplants can create an unnatural look. In many ways our genetic heritage fixes our physical appearance. We may be destined to be tall or short, thick or thin, pretty, handsome or modest in our attractiveness to others (as culturally defined). Some research suggests that certain people may be genetically predisposed to be heavier, rather than lighter. Some people apparently have more fat cells than others. Let's look now at how physical appearance affects nonverbal communication.

Physical appearance has a lot to do with body type. People's body types can fall under one of three basic categories: endomorph (fat), ectomorph (thin) and mesomorph (athletic). See Figure 9.2 on page 391 for a visual depiction of each type.

In studies, people who were shown silhouette drawings of each of the body types were asked to rate them on a variety of scales. See Table 9.1, Knapp and Hall's (1996) findings on what each of the body types communicated to people and how each was perceived.

Certainly another important dimension of physical appearance is **attractiveness**. Physically attractive people are often perceived as possessing many desirable traits. Attractiveness seems to say, "Look, I'm more interesting, poised, sociable, independent, exciting and sexually warm than unattractive people" (Brigham, 1980: 365). People also tend to believe that attractive individuals are more intelligent and more pleasant. Studies indicate, for instance, that essays allegedly written by attractive women receive higher grades and better evaluations than those written by unattractive women (Landy and Sigall, 1974, cited in Weiten, Lloyd and Lashley, 1999). Apparently, good looks communicate competence.

attractiveness

A pleasing physical appearance tends to be a nonverbal cue indicating such other desirable traits as intelligence, independence, sociability and sexual warmth.

Height is another feature of physical appearance that influences what's communicated in interpersonal relations. Some women feel embarrassed about dating shorter men, while men often feel the same way about dating taller women. Everyday experience illustrates, then, that height can affect

Clothes Talk

Following are descriptions of people dressed and adorned in different ways. If you saw these people, what would you think to yourself? What would their appearance say to you? Share your answers with classmates.

9.11

1. A young woman is dressed in a very short, tight, blue-jean skirt. She is wearing black nylons and black high-heeled shoes. Her black top is lacy and see-through, revealing a black bra underneath. She is wearing heavy makeup: bright red lipstick, dark eye shadow, false eyelashes and a painted mole on one cheek. What is this young woman saying to you nonverbally?

_____

_____

2. A young man is wearing black Doc Martens, black socks, black jeans, a black T-shirt and black leather jacket. One ear is pierced with some kind of silver earring symbolizing death. His hair is completely shaven except for a goatee and he has adorned his arms with numerous satanic tattoos. What is this young man saying to you nonverbally?

_____

_____

3. A male student enters the class. He is wearing Birkenstock sandals, faded blue jeans and a tie-dyed shirt. His long hair is pulled back in a ponytail and he carries with him an army bag filled with philosophy books. The only facial hair is a little tuft just under his lower lip. What is this male student expressing to you nonverbally?

_____

_____

4. A female student sits near you in the cafeteria. She places a Louis Viutton bag next to her. Her hair is dyed blond and she has blue-tinted contact lenses. She's wearing a gold necklace, a Piaget watch and a one-carat diamond ring. This student is also wearing a dark blue suit with dark nylons and pumps. Her blouse is white and its frilly collar flops out onto her jacket. She pulls out a gold lighter and French cigarettes while apparently looking for something in her soft leather wallet. What is this female student saying to you?

_____

_____

389

Table **9.1**

What Each of the Body Types Communicates

Endomorph	Mesomorph	Ectomorph
fatter	stronger	thinner
older	more masculine	younger
shorter	better looking	more ambitious
more old-fashioned	more adventurous	taller
less strong physically	younger	more suspicious
less good-looking	taller	more tense
more talkative	more mature	more nervous
more warmhearted	more self-reliant	less masculine
sympathetic		more stubborn
more good-natured		inclined to be difficult
agreeable		more pessimistic
more dependent on others		quieter
more trusting of others		

Let me have men about me that are fat; Sleek-headed men and such as sleep o'nights; Yon Cassius has a lean and hungry look; He thinks too much; such men are dangerous.
~*William Shakespeare, Julius Caesar, Act 1, Scene 2*

partner selection and interpersonal attraction. (Don't be surprised, however, if you find short men preferring tall women or tall women preferring short men.) For some people, height is associated with leadership. Trait theorists have tried to link particular physical characteristics like height to the ability to lead. While correlations remain suspect, you may wish to compare the average height of CEOs and successful business executives with low-level employees and middle managers. Is it true that successful professionals tend to be taller? What does height say about a person? Why does the taller candidate in U.S. presidential elections usually win? Why do some women fantasize about men who are tall, dark and handsome, not short, dark and handsome, or short, fair and plain? Height, like other nonverbal factors in communication, is ambiguous and culturally bound. What does it mean to you?

Skin colour is yet another physical characteristic that communicates nonverbally. Simply being "lily white" in some neighbourhoods may say to others that you're spoiled, privileged or "white trash." To a racist individual, or to one guilty of stereotyping, someone's skin colour may say, "You can't trust me," or "I'm dangerous." Skin colour may not be vocal, but, paradoxically, it can sometimes speak very loudly, for better or for worse.

"Weight" also speaks to people. One's weight may nonverbally communicate the message, "I like and take care of myself" or "I have no self-respect and abuse my body." Caution is advised, however. I remember my mother not being impressed by some of the thin girls I dated in high school. My Eastern European mama would describe them as "skinny chickens." Their

390

Figure 9.2
Body Types

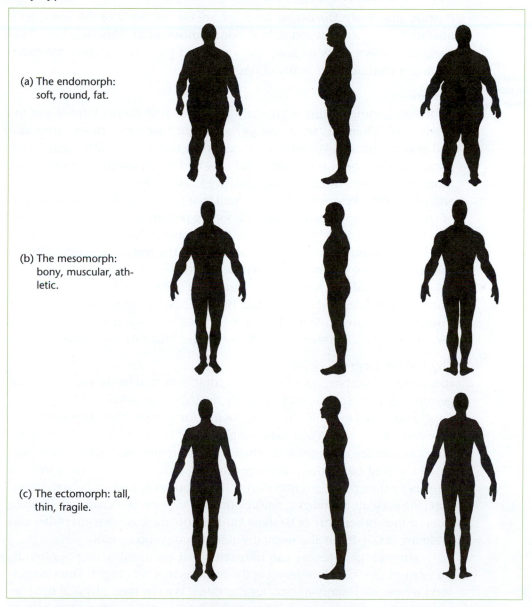

(a) The endomorph: soft, round, fat.

(b) The mesomorph: bony, muscular, ath-letic.

(c) The ectomorph: tall, thin, fragile.

Source: Figures 9.2, 9.4, 9.5 from *Nonverbal Communication in Human Interaction*, Fourth Edition, by Mark L. Knapp and Judith A. Hall. Copyright 1996 by Holt, Rinehart and Winston, Inc. Reproduced by permission of the publisher.

light weight told her that they were obviously underfed and lacked the stamina necessary to bear children and do hard work. I believe my dates thought their thin bodies were communicating something else. We see here how nonverbal communication is ambiguous. A single factor such as thinness can communicate different messages to different individuals.

Posture and Body Movement Since we are on the topic of the body, let's now move into a discussion of how **bodily movement (kinesics)** has a language all its own. How we hold our bodies and the ways in which we move them can communicate many different things.

Posture

A forward-leaning posture is generally associated with higher interest and involvement. When we "sit up and pay attention," we move closer physically and psychologically. We tell the other person that "we're with them." This posture has also been associated with liking and, interestingly, to lower status in situations where those interacting do not know each other very well (Knapp and Hall, 1996). Research indicates as well that posture is a key communicator of emotional states. A person with a drooping posture communicates sadness. One with a rigid, tense posture communicates anger (Knapp and Hall, 1996). During a conversation, one person may "mirror" the posture of another. When this happens, one communicates rapport or attempts to build it.

How would you feel if one evening you were on a date, say, and after leaning forward toward your partner, he or she did likewise? How would you interpret this move? What other "right moves" could you make to communicate your friendly intentions? (We won't get into this any further here!)

Physical Gestures

In addition to posture, body language is communicated by the use of physical gestures. Before Gene Siskel's untimely death, when Siskel and his partner, Roger Ebert, used to signify "two thumbs up" for a movie, they were expressing approval for the film. When someone gives the "Trudeau salute" (showing the raised middle finger), anger and defiance are communicated. (This gesture was made a part of our national heritage during a train trip taken across western Canada by then prime minister Pierre Elliot Trudeau.) Preening behaviour like applying makeup, rearranging one's clothes or combing one's hair may indicate interest in another party or be some kind of unconscious come-on (Adler and Rodman, 2000). It can also mean disinterest and preoccupation.

Through gestures, we can illustrate what we mean. Using our hands, for example, we can show how big the fish was that we caught. Through gestures we can also communicate our emotions. We can meet physical needs as well by, say, scratching our head when it's itchy. Finally, gestures can help us to regulate communication. By raising our arm and displaying the palm, we can tell others to stop—the movement that traffic cops make at intersections. By means of a sweeping arm movement, they tell us to go through.

Face and Eye Movements

Face and eye movements have as much communication value as posture and other physical gestures, if not more. The eyes, for example, send many kinds

---

bodily movement (kinesics)
Posture and physical gestures that can nonverbally communicate such things as our emotions or emotional states.

of messages. You can elicit feedback or convey to others that the channel of communication is open. You can provide signals about the nature of a relationship or psychologically reduce the distance between yourself and another. A combination of rolling your eyes and giving a knowing glance to another across a room can say, "I'm with you. Can you believe what's happening?" or "I'm on your side." Even when eye contact is avoided, messages continue to be sent. Eye avoidance can express disinterest. It can also express nervousness or guilt. Sometimes we avoid eye contact to enable others to maintain their privacy. When we're in close quarters, such as in an elevator, we often avoid eye contact to maintain our own privacy as well.

Like many aspects of nonverbal communication, gender and culture affect how we use our eyes to communicate. In North American culture, direct eye contact usually communicates honesty and forthrightness. In Japanese culture, it indicates lack of respect. In times of grief, women tend to make more eye contact than men and usually maintain it for longer periods. This appears to be so whether they are speaking or listening to others (DeVito, 1998).

An interesting hypothesis about eye movements has been raised by neurolinguistic programmers (NLPs) Joseph O'Connor and John Seymour (1993). They claim that people move their eyes in different directions depending on what they are thinking and how they are processing information. To illustrate their point, they ask people to think of the first thing they see as they walk through the front door of their homes. They say that in thinking about the answer, right-handed people usually look up and left. When asked how it would feel to have velvet next to their skin, people typically look down and to the right. According to O'Connor and Seymour (1993), visual cues let us know how people access information. See Figure 9.3 for a visual representation of NLPs' claims about eye movements and information access.

The face is also an important vehicle of nonverbal communication. By means of facial expressions, we communicate universal emotions such as surprise, disgust, happiness, sadness, fear and anger. However, facial expressions can be difficult to read sometimes, if for no other reason than that they can change so quickly. People also try to mask their true feelings by putting on a "false face" or a "good front." When facial expressions become somewhat exaggerated, it usually indicates that efforts are being made to deceive. If you want to read faces better, examine them carefully when those observed are not likely to be thinking about the way they look at a particular moment in time. Look for quick flashes of emotional expression that differ from the ones the person observed is seeking to convey. You might also pay close attention to contradictions found on the face itself. The message sent by the eyes may not be consistent with the one sent by the mouth and eyebrows (Adler and Rodman, 2000).

9.12 ⸱⸱⸱⸱⸱ *Space Talk: Close Encounters and Space Invaders* Next we'll discuss **space communication (proxemics)**. We can communicate much by our use of space. Each one of us lives in a kind of invisible space bubble that either expands or

space communication (proxemics)
We each live in a kind of invisible space bubble that either expands or contracts, depending on particular conditions and circumstances. Such factors determine the size of the bubble we choose, or the distance we maintain from others.

393

Figure 9.3
The Eyes Say It All

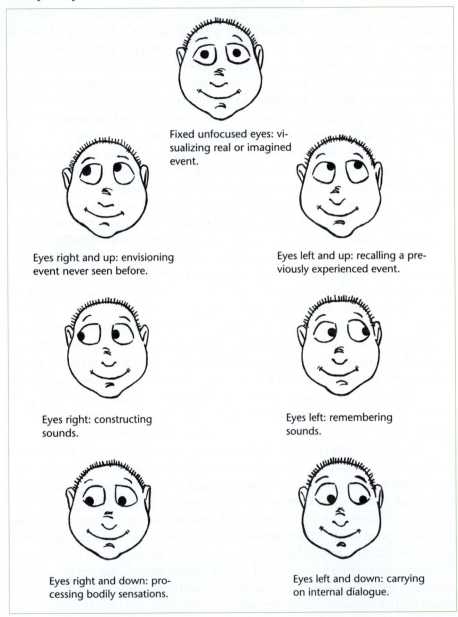

Fixed unfocused eyes: visualizing real or imagined event.

Eyes right and up: envisioning event never seen before.

Eyes left and up: recalling a previously experienced event.

Eyes right: constructing sounds.

Eyes left: remembering sounds.

Eyes right and down: processing bodily sensations.

Eyes left and down: carrying on internal dialogue.

contracts, depending upon particular conditions and circumstances. Knapp and Hall (1996) have identified a number of primary factors that affect space and space communication. I've provided an example for each factor.

1. **Sex** In natural settings, females predominantly choose to interact with other people (of either sex) more closely than males do.

2. **Age** Young children interact more closely than adults. Interaction distance appears to expand incrementally from about the age of six to early adolescence. By that time, adult norms seem to be operative.

3. **Culture and Ethnic Background** Diverse cultures' norms produce different distances for communication. Cultures may be loosely described as "contact" or "noncontact" in nature. People in contact cultures (southern Europeans, Latin Americans) tend to face one another when communicating, interact in closer proximity, touch more often and make more eye contact. People in noncontact cultures, by contrast, make less eye contact and touch less often.

4. **Topic or Subject Matter** Topic can influence conversational distance. Student subjects, for example, were given negative, positive and neutral comments upon entering a room. Studies showed that "[s]tudents given the negative comment sat furthest from the experimenter while those who were praised sat closest." After being insulted, people generally assume a greater distance than usual from the person with whom they're communicating.

5. **Setting for Interaction** In formal or unfamiliar settings, people maintain a greater distance from unknown others and a closer distance to known others.

6. **Physical Characteristics** Obese people are accorded greater interaction distances. People interacting with stigmatized individuals choose greater initial speaking distances than with non-stigmatized "normal" people. This distance diminishes as the length of interaction increases.

7. **Attitudinal and Emotional Orientation** People choose to maintain greater distance when communicating with people perceived as unfriendly. Variations in our emotional conditions can also influence how close or how distant we wish to be with others. States of depression, fatigue, excitement or joy all have their spatial expressions. It's interesting to note that individuals who choose to maintain closer distances are frequently perceived as warmer, more empathetic and more understanding.

8. **Characteristics of the Interpersonal Relationship** Strangers begin conversations farther away from each other than do acquaintances. Findings suggest that "closer relationships are likely to be associated with closer interaction distance" (Hall, 1969).

9. **Personality Characteristics** In conversation, introverts display a tendency to stand farther away than extraverts. They seem to prefer greater interpersonal distances.

Spatial Distances

Having just learned a little bit about "space talk," we can now see better how the distances we maintain from others in interaction with them depend on a variety of factors and circumstances. The specific distances we maintain have been given names by anthropologist Edward T. Hall (1969). They are **intimate distance**, **personal distance**, **social distance** and **public distance**.

intimate distance

The first category of spatial distance we maintain from one another. At this distance (range: skin contact to 1/2 m) the close phase includes the space for such things as lovemaking, wrestling, comforting, and protecting. At the far phase, touch can be achieved by hand extension. This is not usually a distance considered proper for stranger-to-stranger interaction.

personal distance

The second category of spatial distance as identified by Edward T. Hall. At this distance (range: 1/2 to 1 1/3 m) perceptual acuity is still very strong. At the far phase of this distance, we can keep someone at arm's length, if we wish. It is also at this distance that we discuss subjects of personal interest and involvement.

social distance

The third category of spatial distance we maintain from one another as identified by Edward T. Hall. At this distance (range: 1 1/3 to 2 1/3 m) visual acuity begins to diminish. It is here that we typically conduct business and interact at social gatherings.

public distance

The fourth category of spatial distance. This is the distance (range: 4 to 8 1/3 m) your college or university instructor probably uses in the classroom. From this distance nonverbal communication must be exaggerated or amplified to be perceived, and people are able to take evasive or defensive action if threatened.

Below are brief descriptions of each. Each distance has what Hall refers to as a "close phase" and a "far phase." The former moves toward greater closeness, the latter toward lesser closeness.

Intimate Distance (skin contact to 1/2 m) The close phase of intimate distance includes the space we use for such things as lovemaking, wrestling, comforting and protecting. At the far phase, touch can be achieved by hand extension. This is not usually a distance considered proper for stranger-to-stranger interaction.

Personal Distance (1/2 to 1 1/3 m) One can still hold or grasp the other person at this distance. Perceptual acuity is still very strong. At the far phase of this distance, we can keep someone at arm's length, if we wish. It is also at this distance that we discuss subjects of personal interest and involvement.

Social Distance (1 1/3 to 2 1/3 m) At this distance, visual acuity begins to diminish. It is here that we typically conduct business and interact at social gatherings. When maintaining social distance it is important to maintain eye contact and to speak up in order to be heard. A feature of social distance is that it liberates us from nonstop interactions with those surrounding us, and does so without making us seem rude.

Public Distance (4 to 8 1/3 m or more) This is the distance your college or university instructor probably uses in the classroom. If one moves away more than 8 1/3 m, interpersonal communication becomes difficult. Public distance allows people to take evasive or defensive action if threatened. From this distance, nonverbal communication must be exaggerated or amplified (e.g., facial expressions, gestures and posture) if it is to be perceived. We tend to reserve this distance for public figures and for formal occasions.

Territoriality

Not only do people seek to maintain spatial distance from one another, but they also try to grab space itself. The possessive reaction to occupy space and objects within it is referred to as **territoriality**. By means of territoriality we communicate ownership and status (DeVito, 1997). We do this in a variety of ways. Whether territoriality is an innate predisposition or something learned is a continuing topic of debate in the world of psychology between ethologists and behaviourists respectively.

If you own a pet, you've probably already witnessed territoriality in action. Dogs will defend their turf against the mail deliverer or the person who brings your daily newspaper. They will bark, snarl and sometimes bite. While humans don't usually do such things (though I know some who do!), they have their own way of protecting their territories and threatening potential intruders. For example, my son Michael once wanted me to buy a doormat for the entrance to our house. It had a gun printed on it with the words, "We don't call 911." We can also protect and defend our territories by posting "No Trespassing" or "Beware of Dog" signs. My personal favourite sign indicating territorial possession was found on a Harley Davidson motorcycle owned by a gang member. It read, "Life after death? Touch this bike and find out." (The language was actually a bit more colourful, but some editorial licence was necessary to protect the innocent!)

There are three different types of territories: primary, secondary and public (DeVito, 1997). Primary territories are ones you would call your own. They belong exclusively to you. Things included in your primary territory could be your Playstation system, iPod or desk. Secondary territories don't actually belong to you; nonetheless, you have used or occupied them so much that they become associated with you. The first seat in the first row of the class is not technically yours. You don't own it, you don't have legal rights to it. Yet people may recognize it as "yours" because you always sit there. I once went to an English pub in a small town south of London. Without knowing it, I took the seat of a regular customer. Upon arriving at "his" seat, he communicated nonverbally—his expressions of annoyance and irritation communicated his disapproval—that I was sitting in the wrong place. Public territories are open to all. The West Edmonton Mall does not belong exclusively to you or me, nor does the movie theatre down the street or the lawn at the provincial or state legislature. We all have access.

People indicate possession of territory by use of markers. You might leave your books on a chair, for example, or spread them across a desk in the library to indicate occupancy as well as a desire to be alone. We can mark possessions in many other ways as well. Maybe you label your gym bag and sporting equipment with your name, or place a fence between your property and your neighbour's yard. Still another way to mark your territory is by personalizing the space you occupy, such as your college residence. You may recall a scene from the movie *Wolf*, where Jack Nicholson, in wolf-like fashion, marked his territory in the men's bathroom by urinating on the walls and floor. This form of territorial marking is OK for wolves, but is considered ill-advised for normal humans!

Status and Space

The size of the territory we mark off is quite often a reflection of status. Success is frequently symbolized by the physical dimensions of the office, desk or property we own. In any organization, higher status individuals are not likely to possess the smaller desk, workspace or residence. Furthermore, with respect to status, territorial invasions are "socially and professionally permissible" only when higher status individuals encroach on the space of lower status individuals. The opposite is not true. While the boss may take and use the secretary's pen without asking, the secretary is well advised not to do likewise. Tolerated invasions of space are status-dependent. Notice I use the description "tolerated." It's probably rude, at any time, to borrow without asking or to encroach without permission. The fact that people do it to demonstrate status or dominance does not make it right, justifiable or polite.

territoriality
The possessive reaction to occupy space and objects within it, by means of which we communicate ownership and status.

397

Applying the Golden Rule is probably a good idea here: "Do unto others as you would have others do unto you."

Time Talk In North American society, time is a highly valued commodity. In fact, we often say, "Time is money." Given the importance attributed to it, we often use **time communication (chronemics)** to express nonverbal messages, both intentional and unintentional. Our personal use of time is frequently influenced by the psychological orientation we take toward it. Some of us see time in exact terms. Nine o'clock means nine o'clock. Others see time as diffused or approximate. Nine o'clock could mean anything between 8:45 and 9:15. When two people adopt different time orientations, frustration can arise. If one person has a diffused orientation toward time and promises to meet you at around 9:00, that person may in her mind be only 15 minutes late when she arrives at 9:30. Let's say you are highly punctual and make it a point to arrive 10 to 15 minutes early for all your appointments. In this case, you could end up waiting 45 minutes for someone who believes they are almost on time. If the latecomer doesn't understand your upset, it's probably because time is not perceived the same way. Thus, when arranging meetings and appointments, it's probably a good idea to clarify what you mean by a specified time. Personally speaking, I have a relative who is chronically late for everything. The strategy adopted by many members in the family is to say, "If you're not here by whatever o'clock, we'll get started without you," or "We'll meet you there" or "We'll see you when you arrive."

Time and Culture Sometimes culture can affect our use of time and the messages sent by it. A number of years ago I taught a First Nations Canadian at Brock University in St. Catharines. According to his experience, many traditionally minded Six Nations people on the reserve, near Brantford, relate to time differently than most of us do. He explained to me how a number of his Native friends could not understand why their employers were so upset whenever they arrived late for work. If they were being paid for eight hours of work, they were quite willing to work hard for eight hours. The "white man's" preoccupation with starting on time at 7:00 a.m. or 9 a.m. every day was puzzling for my student's friends. Why people always had to eat lunch at 12 p.m. or relax for 15 minutes at 3:15 p.m. every day was a bit of a mystery. The natural flow of life seemed to be disrupted by the need to do things according to a schedule. Of course, for many whites in mainstream culture, punctuality, efficiency and productivity are largely defined in terms of time. People working by different time lines are therefore sometimes described as irresponsible, inefficient and unproductive. Perhaps some crosscultural miscommunication could be alleviated by a more creative use of time, or one that respects the values of all. We see this happening in fact with "flex-time" work schedules and flexible vacation periods. Time off is also being granted more and more to people of different faiths and cultures so that they can celebrate their traditions. Not allowing time off can communicate things like disrespect or contempt

time communication (chronemics)
The way in which we use time (which is influenced by our psychological orientation toward it) may indicate nonverbally things about us, such as our culture and perceived status.

for differences. If this is what an employer is communicating nonverbally, we shouldn't be surprised if a loyal and motivated workforce fails to emerge.

Status and Time

Time can be used to communicate status. Executives and highly placed people often make it a point to arrive fashionably late. An early arrival could indicate eagerness and anticipation. Some think it's undignified to be a "keener." If you're concerned about communicating your own personal importance to others, you may think others should eagerly anticipate your arrival. To wait for others is to place yourself in a diminished position.

We often witness time being used as a status symbol in professional relationships. For example, instructors can arrive late to class and expect no protest. If students arrive late, however, speeches, threats and grade deductions may follow. Also, so-called "important" people may see you by appointment only, while it is permissible for you to drop by without notice on equal-status peers and colleagues. Furthermore, although it's allowable for prospective bosses to keep you waiting outside their offices, it would not be well-advised for you to show up late for an interview and keep them waiting. This type of delay would send the wrong message.

Finally, status seems to exempt "important" people from having to endure the waiting that most of us face in life. An acquaintance recently told me of a woman who called her husband's restaurant for a reservation. The wait for a table was going to be at least 90 minutes. When the woman identified herself as Dolly Parton, a table was made available immediately. Time talks. In this case, it says you're too special and important to be kept waiting. This may not be fair in any moral or ethical sense, but seems to be the way it is in the real world.

9.13 *Touch Communication* The importance of **touch communication (haptics)** to healthy human development was briefly alluded to in Chapter 8. Recall the observation that infants desperate for strokes (human touch) often fail to thrive when physical contact is not forthcoming from caretakers. Institutionalized infants during the late nineteenth and early twentieth centuries who were deprived of physical strokes often suffered from marasmus (a Greek word meaning "wasting away"). Some even died. In Ashley Montague's *Touching: The Human Significance of the Skin*, findings reveal that at Bellevue Hospital in New York, "mortality rates for infants under one year fell from 30 to 35 percent to less than 10 percent" following the institution of "mothering" on the pediatric wards. Touching, caressing and holding seemed to keep these babies alive. Incredible as it may seem, touch appears to be necessary for survival.

Touch is also important to human communication. By means of touch, such as shaking someone's hand, we can show appreciation. We can console our friends or give support by lending a shoulder to lean on. A gentle caress could indicate our interest or sexual attraction. A physical nudge or soft push could be a form of playful aggression. A slap on the back may be someone's way of giving

Touch can communicate emotion and help to solidify relationships.

... paradise is attained by touch.
~Helen Keller

encouragement. By means of touch we can also communicate things like inclusion, affection, compliance, attention, greeting and departure (Weaver, 1996). Studies and observations of touch point to some positive effects. For instance, librarians who touched patrons when returning library cards were evaluated more favourably. Waitresses who touched diners received bigger tips; psychologists who touched students discovered greater compliance, while therapists who touched their clients accelerated the process of healing. This last finding underscores again the "therapeutic" benefits of touch. On this note, when tactile people ("touchers") were compared with "nontouchers," it was found that the latter "report more anxiety and tension in their lives, less satisfaction with their bodies, more suspicion of others, and are more socially withdrawn and more likely to be rigid or authoritarian in their beliefs" (Knapp and Hall, 1996).

Of course, not all touch is beneficial, as survivors of child molestation and sexual abuse will attest. They may be suspicious of touch for very good reasons. Thus, it is a good idea to ask permission before touching someone whom you suspect might respond negatively to your physical contact.

As you might have guessed, touch, as a form of nonverbal communication, is also affected by culture and gender. In one study, Sidney Jourard counted the frequency of contact between couples in cafés in various cities throughout the world. He reported the following: in San Juan, Puerto Rico, couples physically made contact 180 times every hour; in Paris, France, the frequency was reduced to 110; in Gainesville, Florida, people touched two times; in London, England, they didn't touch at all. (Knapp and Hall, 1996.) In another study, Japanese and U.S. students were observed for their touching patterns (Barnlund, 1975, cited in Knapp and Hall, 1996). Americans apparently touch about twice as much as the Japanese. They are also more accessible to touch. See Figure 9.4.

When it comes to touching, we also find gender differences. For example, females tend to engage in more same-sex touching than do males. They also tend to respond more favourably to touching than do men (at least in North America). Men and women are similar insofar as both respond favourably to touch when the one who originates it has higher status (Weiten, Lloyd and Lashley, 1991).

Figure 9.4

Physical Contact Patterns in Japan and the United States

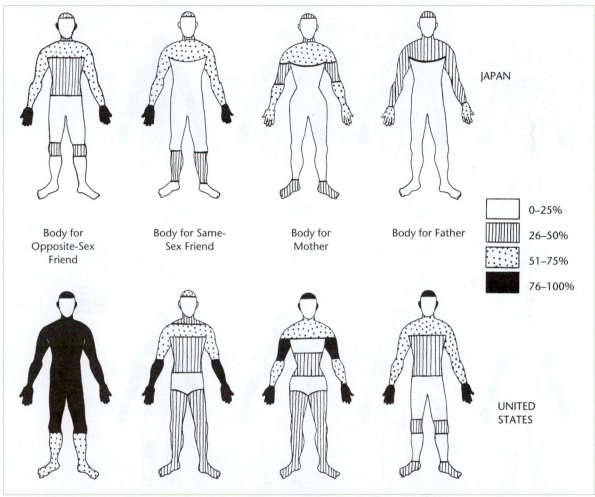

Interested in knowing what body parts people think are most often touched, Jourard administered a questionnaire to students, who revealed which (of 24) body parts they had seen or touched on others or that others had seen or touched on them within a one-year period. The "others" were designated as father, mother, same-sex friend and opposite-sex friend. Findings indicated that females are significantly more accessible to touch by all people compared to males. Most touching occurred between friends. Many fathers were recalled as touching little more than the hands of subjects. Jourard's findings are visually displayed in Figure 9.5.

401

Figure 9.5
Areas of the Body Involved in Bodily Contact

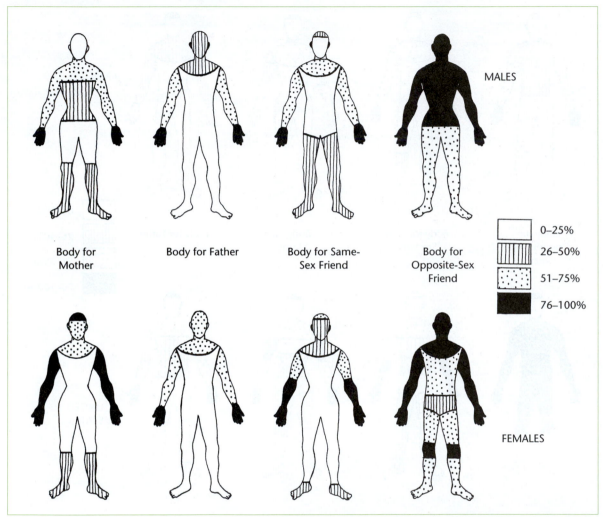

Body for Mother

Body for Father

Body for Same-Sex Friend

Body for Opposite-Sex Friend

MALES

FEMALES

0–25%

26–50%

51–75%

76–100%

Self
Diagnostic
9.1

How Tactile Are You?

Instructions: This instrument comprises 18 statements concerning how you feel about touching other people and being touched yourself. Please indicate the degree to which each statement applies to you by considering whether you

1 = strongly agree
2 = agree
3 = are undecided
4 = disagree
5 = strongly disagree

_____ 1. A hug from a same-sex friend is a true sign of friendship.

_____ 2. Opposite-sex friends enjoy it when I touch them.

_____ 3. I often put my arm around friends of the same sex.

_____ 4. When I see two friends of the same sex hugging, it revolts me.

_____ 5. I like it when members of the opposite sex touch me.

_____ 6. People shouldn't be so uptight about touching people of the same sex.

_____ 7. I think it is vulgar when members of the opposite sex touch me.

_____ 8. When a member of the opposite sex touches me, I find it unpleasant.

_____ 9. I wish I were free to show emotions by touching members of the same sex.

_____ 10. I'd enjoy giving a massage to an opposite-sex friend.

_____ 11. I enjoy kissing a person of the same sex.

_____ 12. I like to touch friends that are the same sex as I am.

_____ 13. Touching a friend of the same sex does not make me uncomfortable.

_____ 14. I find it enjoyable when my date and I embrace.

_____ 15. I enjoy getting a back rub from a member of the opposite sex.

_____ 16. I dislike kissing relatives of the same sex.

_____ 17. Intimate touching with members of the opposite sex is pleasurable.

_____ 18. I find it difficult to be touched by a member of my own sex.

Scoring

To score your self-diagnostic, follow these procedures:

1. Reverse your scores for items 4, 7, 8, 16 and 18. Use these reversed scores in all future calculations.

2. To obtain your same-sex touch avoidance score (the extent to which you avoid touching members of your sex), total the scores for items 1, 3, 4, 6, 9, 11, 12, 13, 16 and 18.

3. To obtain your opposite-sex touch avoidance score (the extent to which you avoid touching members of the opposite sex), total the scores for items 2, 5, 7, 8, 10, 14, 15 and 17.

4. To obtain your total avoidance score, add the subtotals from steps 2 and 3.

The higher the score, the higher the touch avoidance—that is, the greater your tendency to avoid touch. In studies by Andersen and Leibowitz (1978), who constructed this test, average opposite-sex touch avoidance scores for males were 12.90 and for females was 14.85. Average same-sex touch avoidance scores were 26.43 for males and 21.70 for females.

Touch Tips

Since touch, like other forms of nonverbal communication, is ambiguous and because so much hinges on the people and circumstances involved, it's virtually impossible to set down concrete guidelines for appropriate touching. At best, a number of general considerations can be put forward. These should help you decide when or when not to touch. Any given instance of touching could be appropriate or inappropriate depending on

a. the nature of the relationship between the person touching and the one being touched

b. the circumstances in which the touching occurs

c. the response of the one touched

d. the amount of pressure used

e. the length of the touch

f. the part of the body that is touched

g. what part of the body does the touching

Source: From "The Development and Nature of Construct Touch Avoidance" by Peter Anderson and Ken Leibowitz as in *Environmental Psychology and Nonverbal Behaviour* 3: 89–196, 1978. Reprinted by permission of Human Sciences Press, Inc. and the authors.

Study Guide

Key Terms

gender (361)
moral reasoning (361)
moral voice (363)
identity formation (364)
morality of care (365)
relationship (365)
morality of impersonal
   justice (365)
anima (366)
animus (366)
asymmetries (367)
public speaking (367)
private speaking (367)
report talk (367)
rapport talk (367)
gossip talk (368)
pluralistic (369)
multicultural (369)
economic interdepen-
   dence (369)
politics (369)
culture (370)

enculturation (370)
acculturation (370)
intercultural communi-
   cation (370)
ethnocentrism (372)
perception of difference
   (373)
false perception of dif-
   ference (373)
stereotype (373)
empathy (374)
precommunication atti-
   tudes (375)
jargon (376)
nonverbal communica-
   tion (380)
accent (382)
complement (382)
contradict (382)
regulate (382)
repeat (383)
paralanguage (383)

articulation (384)
substitution (384)
pitch (385)
environment (385)
artifactual communica-
   tion (386)
physical appearance
   (388)
attractiveness (388)
bodily movement
   (kinesics) (392)
space communication
   (proxemics) (393)
intimate distance (396)
personal distance (396)
social distance (396)
public distance (396)
territoriality (397)
time communication
   (chronemics) (398)
touch communication
   (haptics) (399)

Fill-in-the-Blank Questions

Instructions: Fill in each blank with the appropriate response from the list below.

Deborah Tannen
men
care and relationship
ethnocentrism
jargon
paralanguage
Lawrence Kohlberg
body type
acculturation
Carol Gilligan
public distance

women
articulation
artifactual
kinesics
neurolinguistic programmers
ambiguous
justice and fairness
nonverbal communication
empathy
cultural context
Charles Darwin

Progress
Check
9.1

405

1. According to _____, moral development occurs sequentially in terms of three basic levels of development.

2. _____ claims that cognitive-developmental reasoning has an inherent gender bias.

3. According to _____, women speak a language of connection and intimacy, while men speak and hear a language of status and independence.

4. _____ have a tendency to interrupt _____ more often in conversation.

5. In matters of interpersonal conflict, men speak more the language of _____, while women are more interested in matters of _____.

6. Through the process of _____, a person from one culture is modified through direct or indirect exposure to another.

7. The process of interpersonal communication takes place in a broader _____.

8. When people are only able to see things from their own cultural perspective, not objectively, they exhibit _____.

9. _____ involves an element of role taking, placing ourselves in the shoes of the other.

10. _____ is a type of sub-language that can cause problems with interpersonal communication.

11. _____ can be vocal or nonvocal.

12. Tone of voice, pitch and rate are included under the umbrella of _____.

13. Nonverbal cues are not always easily read because they are often _____.

14. According to _____, nonverbal expressions served as early survival mechanisms, prior to the development of language.

15. When we leave off parts of words, add parts that shouldn't be there or slur words, we are guilty of bad _____.

16. What we "say" by colour, clothing and bodily adornment is an aspect of _____ communication.

17. Endomorphy, mesomorphy and ectomorphy are all examples of _____.

18. The study of body movement is called _____.

19. According to _____, eyes move according to how people think and process information.

20. The space kept between you and your instructor during class is called _____.

True/False Questions

Instructions: Circle the appropriate letter next to each statement.

T F 1. The need to seize and occupy space is called territoriality.

T F 2. Space is often used as a symbol of status.

T F 3. Because of concerns over child abuse and sexual violence, it's always a good idea to refrain from touching other people.

T F 4. According to Sidney Jourard's crosscultural observations, French couples touch each other in cafés more often than do couples of any other nationality.

T F 5. The "V" sign made with the right hand is a universal sign for victory.

T F 6. Male-female differences in moral reasoning are innate (i.e., genetically determined), according to Carol Gilligan.

T F 7. According to Carl Jung, both men and women possess innate tendencies stereotypically attributed to the opposite sex.

T F 8. According to Deborah Tannen, asymmetries in male-female communication often lead to miscommunication.

T F 9. Ethnocentric people have superior powers of observation.

T F 10. Knowing yourself better can improve social communication.

T F 11. The expression "user friendly" is an example of jargon.

T F 12. Sometimes we receive mixed messages because what people communicate verbally is inconsistent with their nonverbal messages.

T F 13. Nonverbal communication is never vocal.

T F 14. Nonverbal communication can be used to accent, complement, regulate, contradict, repeat or substitute for the spoken word.

T F 15. Use of time can indicate status.

T F 16. Attractive people are usually looked upon with greater suspicion than are unattractive people.

T F 17. Being thin always sends a positive message.

T F 18. Preening behaviour could be interpreted as a conscious or unconscious come-on.

T F 19. It's possible to refrain from nonverbal communication.

T F 20. People who arrive chronically late are irresponsible.

407

Summary

1. Why is a consideration of gender important to human relations development?
   - men and women use language differently
   - they behave according to different gender-role expectations
   - they tend to perceive and interpret interpersonal conflict differently

2. How do people differ in their moral reasoning?

   Moral reasoning can occur at three basic levels of development:
   - The Pre-conventional Level: reasoning in terms of reward and punishment or in terms of payback and instrumentality
   - The Conventional Level: reasoning in terms of being nice and obeying the rules
   - The Post-Conventional Level: reasoning in which duties and responsibilities are negotiable; universal justice considerations become paramount

3. How do Carol Gilligan's views of morality differ from those of Lawrence Kohlberg? Morality is

Gilligan	Kohlberg
subjective	objective
personal	impersonal
concrete	abstract/hypothetical
relational/contextual	rational/universal
care-based	justice-based
focused on social responsibility	focused on individual rights

4. How do men and women tend to use language differently, according to Deborah Tannen?
   - women speak a language of "connection and intimacy"; men talk in terms of "status and independence"
   - male and female communication is often asymmetrical; women like people to express matching experiences as a way of showing empathy, men tend to see this as a form of discounting experience
   - men tend to be more comfortable doing public speaking (report talk) while women usually prefer private speaking (rapport talk)
   - topics of gossip differ for males and females
   - men like to give information and opinions; women are more comfortable in supporting
   - men interrupt more than women
   - men are more self-aggrandizing; women are less boastful

5. What form does intercultural communication take?
   - international (e.g., between Germany and Japan)
   - interracial (e.g., between blacks and Asian people)
   - interethnic (e.g., between French-Canadians and Finnish-Canadians)
   - interreligious (e.g., between Catholics and Protestants)
   - interoccupational (e,g., between doctors and lawyers)
   - intergender (i.e., between males and females)

6. What are some problems related to intercultural communication?
   - language
   - misread intentions
   - violations of values and customs
   - misunderstandings
   - ethnocentrism
   - perceiving differences as greater than they are
   - ignoring important differences
   - different meanings attributed to the same word
   - differing nonverbal cues
   - stereotyping and lack of empathy

7. How can intercultural communication be improved?
   - know yourself better (your prejudices, precommunication attitudes and projected image)
   - use a common language (minimize jargon and agree to meanings of terms)
   - suspend judgment (take your time before making evaluations)

8. What is the nature of nonverbal communication?
   - it is language without words
   - it may or may not be vocal (tone, pitch)
   - it is multichannelled
   - it is ambiguous
   - it has a social function (e.g., it can express fear or define a relationship)

9. What is the relationship between verbal and nonverbal communication?
   - nonverbal communication can accent, complement, regulate, contradict, repeat and substitute for the spoken word

10. What are the possible classifications for nonverbal communication?
   - paralanguage
   - environment
   - artifactual communication

- physical appearance
- posture and body movements
- space communication (proxemics)
- time communication (chronemics)
- touch communication (haptics)

11. What are the different spatial distances?
   - intimate distance (skin contact to 1/2 m)
   - personal distance (1/2 to 1 1/3 m)
   - social distance (1 1/3 to 2 1/3 m)
   - public distance (4 to 8 1/3 m or more.)

12. What is territoriality? What kinds are there?
   - territoriality is the possessive reaction to occupy space and objects within it
   - a way of communicating status and ownership
   - the three types are primary, secondary and public

Related Readings

Ardrey, Robert (1997). *The Territorial Imperative*. New York: Kodansha America, Inc.

Chodorow, Nancy (1974). "Family Structure and Feminine Personality." In *Women, Culture and Society*, edited by M. Z. Rosaldo and L. Lamphere. Stanford: Stanford University Press.

Duska, Ronald, and Mariellen Whelan (1975). *Moral Development: A Guide to Piaget and Kohlberg*. New York: Paulist Press.

Kohlberg, Lawrence (1976). "Moral Stages and Moralization: The Cognitive-Developmental Approach." In *Moral Development and Behaviour*, edited by T. Lickona. New York: Holt, Rinehart and Winston.

Montagu, Ashley (1971). *Touching: The Human Significance of the Skin*. San Francisco: Harper & Row.

People who think they
know it all are espe-
cially annoying to
those of us who do.
~Anonymous

How to Resolve Conflicts

Chapter Overview

The Experience of Conflict

The Nature of Conflict

Types of Conflict

- Psychological
- Social
- Approach-Avoidance
- Functional Versus Dysfunctional
  Conflict

Benefits of Conflict

Psychological Orientations to
Conflict

- Constructive Orientation
- Passive-Defensive Orientation

- Aggressive-Defensive
  Orientation

Application Exercise 10.1
My Personal Experience of
Conflict

Conflict Management Styles

- Self-Diagnostic 10.1
  What's My Conflict
  Management Style?

- The Conflict Management
  Menagerie

Application Exercise 10.2
Pick the Most Appropriate Conflict Resolution
Style

Win-Win Conflict Resolutions

Application Exercise 10.3
Type Tips for Conflict Resolution

Study Guide

- Key Terms
- Progress Check 10.1
- Summary
- Related Readings

Learning Outcomes

After successfully completing this chapter, you will be able to

- (10.1) Provide a definition of conflict
- (10.2) Outline the various types of conflict
- (10.3) State the benefits of conflict
- (10.4) Explain and give three examples of psychological orientations to conflict
- (10.5) Provide descriptive outlines of five conflict management styles
- (10.6) Identify your dominant and backup conflict management styles
- (10.7) Go through the steps to arrive at win-win conflict resolutions
- (10.8) Use psychological-type insights for purposes of conflict resolution

Focus Questions

1. What is the nature of conflict?
2. What types of conflict can be identified?
3. Are there any advantages to conflict? Explain and illustrate.
4. How do people orient themselves to conflict? Is there one orientation better than the others? Why?
5. Is there more than one style of managing conflict? If so, what are those styles? Can you briefly describe them?
6. What are the various components of win-win conflict resolutions?

413

The Experience of Conflict

conflict
Opposition, contention or strife; a fighting or struggle for mastery.

Benjamin Franklin once said that there are two unavoidable things in life: death and taxes. I'd like to add a third item to Ben's list, namely **conflict.** Talk to any person on the street about what's good or bad, useless or worthwhile, and you'll almost certainly find differences of opinion. At social gatherings, where politics or religion is the issue, disputes can rarely be avoided. Amazingly, even family discussions about next year's vacation destination can sometimes flare up into screaming matches. One person may insist on going to the Rockies, while another may prefer to go to the east coast. Our everyday experience would seem to suggest, then, that conflict is something that cannot be escaped in our interactions with others. Conflict is a common occurrence.

The gem cannot be polished without friction—nor a man without trials.
~Chinese Proverb

In Chapter 4, we looked at a number of psycho-logical defence mechanisms people often employ when conflicts and strong disagreements lead to anxiety and other unpleasant emotions. We learned how people do things such as twist reality, divert attention or intimidate others when involved in disputes or confrontations of egos. In this chapter, what we'll do is look more carefully at the nature of conflict itself. We'll see how theorists have conceptualized conflict, how people adopt different psychological orientations toward it, and how there are different methods and styles of conflict resolution. By understanding such things, we'll be better able to manage conflict and to deal with it in our personal and professional lives, as well as in our informal interactions with friends and family.

(10.1) The Nature of Conflict

Whoever is dissatisfied with himself is continually ready for revenge.
~Friedrich Nietzsche

Though commonplace, conflict is not something that permits precise and easy definition. *The New Webster's Encyclopedic Dictionary of the English Language* defines it as "a fighting or struggle for mastery."

It is also defined as "combat, a striving to oppose or overcome; active opposition; contention; strife." As a verb, to conflict means "to meet in opposition or hostility; to contend; to strive or struggle; to be in opposition; to be contrary; to be incompatible or at variance." From this definition, we get the general idea that conflict somehow involves opposing forces and differing objectives. Let us now explore in a bit more detail what this variance, opposition and struggle is all about.

The Six Men of Indostan

It was six men of Indostan

To learning much inclined,

Who went to see the elephant

Though all of them were blind

That each by observation

Might satisfy his mind.

The first approached the elephant

And, happening to fall

Against the broad and sturdy side,

At once began to bawl:

"Why, bless me! But the elephant

Is very much like a wall!"

The second, feeling of the tusk

Cried: "Ho! What have we here

So very round and smooth and sharp?

To me, 'tis very clear,

This wonder of an elephant

Is very like a spear!"

The third approached the animal,

And, happening to take

The squirming trunk within his hands

Thus boldly up he spake:

"I see," quoth he, "the elephant

Is very like a snake!"

The fourth reached out his eager hand

And felt about the knee:

"What most this wondrous beast is like

Is very plain," quoth he:

415

"Tis clear enough the elephant

Is very like a tree!"

The fifth who chanced to touch
the ear

Said: "E'en the blindest man

Can tell what this resembles
most—

Deny the fact who can:

This marvel of an elephant

Is very like a fan!"

The sixth no sooner had begun

About the beast to grope

Than, seizing on the swinging tail

That fell within his scope,

"I see," quoth he, "the elephant

Is very like a rope!"

And so these men of Indostan

Disputed loud and long,

Each in his own opinion

Exceeding stiff and strong,

Though each was partly in the
right,

And all were in the wrong.

~John G. Saxe

Figure 10.1
The Six Men of
Indostan

Source: John G. Saxe from *The Hokusai Sketchbooks* by James A. Michener.
Charles E. Tuttle, Publisher. Copyright James A. Michener.

10.2 Types of Conflict

Psychological

Perhaps the best place to start our explorations is with the individual. Some conflict that occurs in life happens internally. We call this **psychological conflict**. This type of conflict could be going on inside you right now with nobody else around even noticing. For example, you may be having erotic fantasies about someone in the class, but be experiencing guilt because such fantasies violate your religious values and beliefs. In this case, your biological sexual instincts may be at odds with your moral standards. This kind of psycho-sexual conflict is captured nicely in the New Testament of the Christian Bible. In St. Paul's letter to the Galatians (5:16 in the Good News Bible), it is written, "For what our human nature wants is opposed to what the spirit wants, and what the spirit wants is opposed to what our human nature wants. These two are enemies, and this means you cannot do what you want to do." To express the same Christian insight in Freudian psychoanalytic terms, the "id is in conflict with the superego" (see Chapter 4). For Freud, life itself is a continuing saga of conflict. The conscious rational ego must balance the opposing parts of the psyche and reconcile primitive biological urges with the demands presented by civilized society. According to Freud, our personalities are always in conflict to some degree.

Social

Some conflictual experience in life occurs between or among people, not strictly within them. You and your siblings may, for example, be strong rivals, always fighting over things like who gets the next new cell phone or who gets the bigger bedroom in the new house. This "me against you" type of conflict involving two different individuals can be described as **interpersonal conflict.**

Sometimes the conflicts we face are not of the "me against you" variety, but rather involve "us against them." This type of social or interpersonal conflict entails **intergroup conflict**. Land developers may be at odds with residents' groups, or business associations may be at war with community planners about proposed changes to the downtown core of a city.

Still another variation of social conflict is "me or you versus them." In this case, there's an individual opposing a group of some sort. Let's say that you're doing a group project. Everyone but you is willing to do the least possible work to complete only the minimal requirements of an assignment. For them, grades don't matter. On the other hand, grades do matter to you and you want to do the best possible job by exceeding the instructor's expectations. In this situation, different wants create the oppositional forces.

Sometimes, all group members agree on their wants and goals, but they still cannot agree on how best to achieve them. Let's say that, as a member of

psychological conflict
Internal conflict. According to Freud, life itself is a continuing saga of conflict. The conscious rational ego must balance the opposing parts of the psyche and reconcile primitive biological urges with the demands presented by civilized society.

Conflict is the gadfly of thought. It stirs us to observation and memory. It instigates to invention. It shocks us out of sheeplike passivity, and sets us at noting and contriving.
~*John Dewey*

interpersonal conflict
Fighting, or a struggle for mastery, between people.

intergroup conflict
Struggle or opposition between two or more groups.

No conflict is so severe as his who labours to subdue himself.
~*Thomas à Kempis*

I am never upset for the reason I think.
~*A Course in Miracles*

My idea of an agreeable person is a person who agrees with me.
~*Benjamin Disraeli*

417

the student union, you and some members of your governing council wish to effect change at your school immediately; others belonging to the union desire the same change, but wish to proceed more slowly. Your faction is militant and extreme, while the other faction within the group is more moderate. In other words, you all want the same thing, but differ on strategies to get it. This type of opposition can be described as **intragroup conflict**. See it as the social equivalent of **intrapsychic conflict**, where the disequilibrium is all inside.

Approach-Avoidance

Whether conflict is social or psychological in nature, some people have found it useful to think of it in terms of desirable and undesirable characteristics, or approach-avoidance features. In this light, conflict can be described as approach-approach, avoidance-avoidance or approach-avoidance. See Figure 10.2 for an illustration.

    Let's consider **approach-approach conflict** first. Suppose you want to go out on a date with a special somebody, for example, but you also want to go skiing with other friends at the same time. We'll assume that taking your date skiing is not possible. In this case, two desirable things are wanted, but only one option can be chosen.

    When we face two equally unattractive alternatives, we face **avoidance-avoidance conflict**. You may not wish to study for an exam; nor do you wish to mow the lawn. Nonetheless, you are asked by your parents to do one or the other (some choice, eh!), or you won't be allowed to use the family car.

intragroup conflict
Fighting or struggle for mastery within the same group (the social equivalent of intrapsychic conflict, where the disequilibrium is all inside).

intrapsychic conflict
Conflict that takes place within the individual. See also psychological conflict.

approach-approach conflict
A type of conflict in which two desirable things are wanted, but only one option can be chosen.

avoidance-avoidance conflict
A type of conflict in which one is faced with two equally unattractive alternatives.

Figure 10.2
Types of Conflict

Approach — Approach
"I want this" but "I also want that"

Avoidance — Avoidance
"I don't want this" and "I don't want that"

Approach — Avoidance
"I want this" but "I don't want what this entails"

A third kind is **approach-avoidance conflict**, which you may experience, for example, if you wish to change college or university programs. The problem is that you're insecure about setting off on a whole new course (no pun intended). Obviously, there are attractive and unattractive aspects to either choice. If you stay in your current program, you will continue to be dissatisfied, though confident. If you move on, you'll be energized and enthusiastic, though insecure. In some respects, "you're damned if you do and damned if you don't."

If you're at all worried about how others may react to your conflict-related decisions, you may wish to take comfort in the poem by Kent Keith that I've re-titled "Conflict Resolutions for Life."

approach-avoidance conflict
A type of conflict in which there are attractive and unattractive aspects to both choices involved.

reflection poem

Conflict Resolutions for Life

People are unreasonable, illogical and self-centred.

Love them anyway.

If you do good, people may accuse you of selfish motives.

Do good anyway.

If you are successful, you may win false friends and true enemies.

Succeed anyway.

The good you do today may be forgotten tomorrow.

Do good anyway.

Honesty and transparency make you vulnerable.

Be honest and transparent anyway.

What you spend years building may be destroyed overnight.

Build anyway.

People who really want help may attack you if you help them.

Help them anyway.

Give the world the best you have and you may get hurt.

Give the world your best anyway.

The world is full of conflict.

Choose peace of mind anyway.

~Kent Keith

419

Functional Versus Dysfunctional Conflict

dysfunctional conflict
The type of fighting or struggle for mastery that hinders group performance and upsets personal psychological functioning.

Because conflict is often associated with disruptions and unpleasant feelings, many people try to avoid it as much as possible. Common experience tells us that conflict can frequently be counterproductive. This kind of **dysfunctional conflict** hinders group performance and upsets personal psychological functioning. If you're "torn apart" by conflict, you may not be able to concentrate on your studies or do your job at work. If there is great animosity between individuals in an organizational department, differences between them may become irreconcilable. Productive teamwork and co-operative efforts may become next to impossible to achieve.

functional conflict
Conflict that is productive and leads to improvement or innovation.

interactionist perspective
View that conflict can contribute to innovation, creativity, energy and growth.

By contrast, writers and researchers have noted that there also exists **functional conflict** (Robbins, 1998). Some companies, such as IBM, see such conflict from an **interactionist perspective**. At IBM, conflict is encouraged, "...on the grounds that a harmonious, peaceful, tranquil, and cooperative group is prone to becoming static, apathetic, and nonresponsive to the needs for innovation" (ibid.: 446). From this view, a small and optimum level of conflict can help to keep groups viable, self-critical and creative. To determine whether a (social) conflict is functional or dysfunctional, it is helpful to look at group performance. If the conflict serves to achieve group objectives in the end, then it is functional. If it gets in the way and undermines group performance, then it is dysfunctional.

(10.3) ····· # Benefits of Conflict

By making a distinction between functional and dysfunctional conflict, the idea is captured that not all conflict is necessarily bad. Optimistically speaking, conflict needn't be destructive at all in some cases. When handled properly, it can be an occasion for growth and development. Conflict, like argument, should be seen as an opportunity, not an obstacle. On this note, David Johnson (1999) has listed the benefits of conflict, when skilfully managed. They are paraphrased as follows.

420

What sort of thing would life really be with your qualities ready for a tussle with it, if it only brought fair weather and gave those higher faculties of yours no scope?
~William James

1. Conflicts enable us to become aware of problems within relationships.
2. Conflicts serve as a catalyst for positive change. Maybe we need to experiment and do things a little differently (for our good and the good of others).
3. Conflicts are energizing and can motivate us to deal with immediate problems.
4. Conflicts add spice to life. They stimulate interest and curiosity.

5. Conflicts can be cathartic. A good argument may relieve minor tensions associated with interacting with other people. (Isn't it enjoyable to make up after a good "fight"?)

6. Conflicts can cause decisions to be made more carefully and thoughtfully.

7. Conflicts promote self-knowledge. For example, they heighten awareness concerning what angers us, what frightens us and what is important to us.

8. Conflicts are potentially energizing and fun, if not taken too seriously. Competitive games and sports can be enjoyable when conflict is involved.

9. Conflicts can improve relationships in the long term. People learn that relationships can hold up under stress. Conflicts can clear the air of unexpressed resentments.

10.4 Psychological Orientations to Conflict

Whether or not people see value in conflict will largely depend on their psychological orientations toward it. Clayton Lafferty and Ronald Phillips (1990) at Human Synergistics in Plymouth, Michigan, have identified 12 individual styles of approaching conflict, which they group into three basic orientations. Before we examine each one in turn, however, let us first spell out what is meant by the notion of **orientation** itself.

For our purposes here, it will be helpful to conceptualize a **conflict orientation** as something psychological. When faced with conflict, we all display certain **predispositions**. Some of us are inclined to approach people with whom we disagree, while others are more inclined to withdraw or attack those who choose to dispute with us. The notion of psychological orientation also involves one's **beliefs** and **perceptions**. There are those who see opportunity and challenge in conflict, whereas others believe that it is something essentially destructive and undesirable. Furthermore, when faced with conflict, some of us wish to resolve differences and get on with things. By contrast, others apparently have a real need to win or come out on top. In other words, people have different **motivations** in their dealings with conflict. **Intentions** vary as do corresponding **behaviours**. A psychological orientation to conflict can be defined, then, by our perceptions, motivations and predispositions, as well as by our beliefs and intentions. See Figure 10.3 for an illustration of psychological orientations to conflict.

Nobody's psychological orientation to conflict is carved in stone. It is possible to change from one orientation to another. For example, if you've fallen into some bad habits where conflict is concerned—say, stomping away in anger—you can learn new behavioural patterns and effect necessary attitude adjustments to more productively handle conflict in the future.

orientation
The psychological stance toward conflict that each individual possesses, based on his or her beliefs, perceptions, motivations, intentions and behaviours. The three conflict orientations are: constructive, passive-defensive, and aggressive-defensive.

conflict orientation
Conflict orientation is psychological and involves one's perceptions, motivations and predispositions, as well as beliefs and intentions.

predispositions
A natural inclination, this is one of the factors used in defining conflict orientation.

beliefs
One of the elements that contributes to one's psychological orientation to conflict.

perceptions
The means by which we become aware of our physical and social surroundings.

motivations
The impetus to act.

intentions
Part of one's psychological orientation toward conflict.

behaviours
Our predisposition to act in a certain way is evidence, in part, of our psychological orientation to conflict.

421

Figure 10.3
Psychological Orientations to Conflict

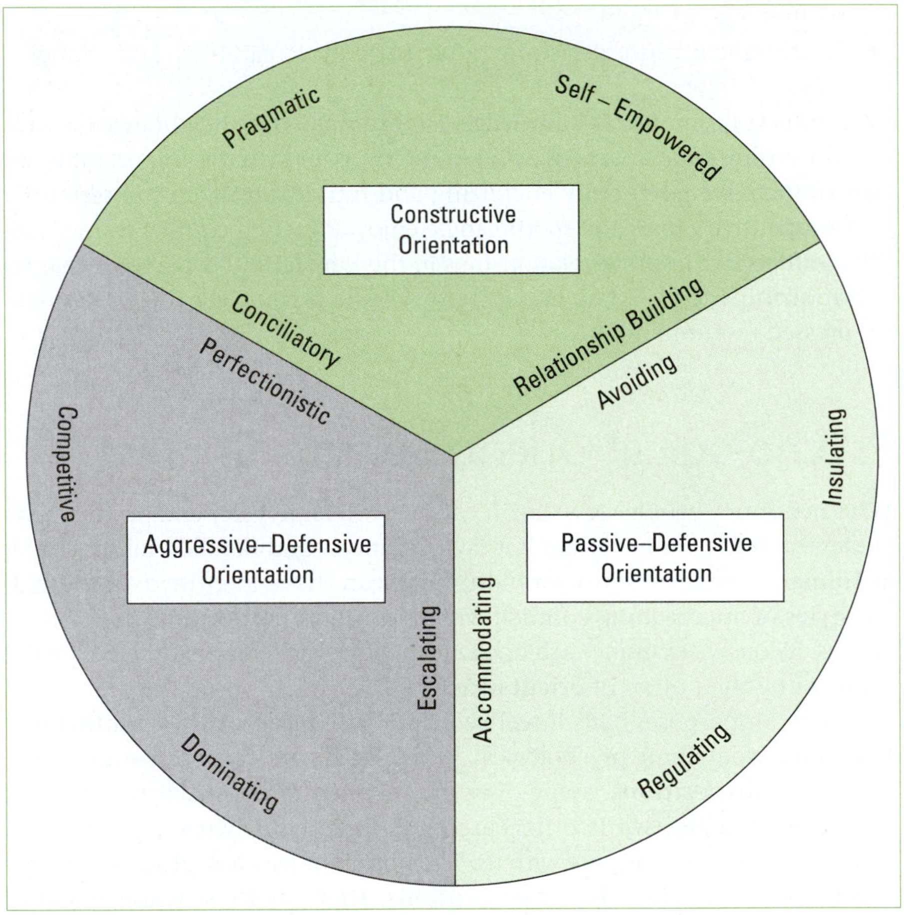

Constructive Orientation

constructive orientation to conflict
The vantage point which regards conflict as something normal and commonplace.

realistic
Using analytical abilities to clarify and discuss issues.

pragmatic approach
The approach taken by people who adopt the constructive orientation to conflict.

Since we've already had a chance to consider the potential benefits of conflict and because we're on the topic of handling conflict productively, perhaps it's best to start with the **constructive orientation to conflict** resolution. From this vantage point, conflict is regarded as something normal and commonplace. It is viewed as useful for achieving longer-term interests. People with a constructive orientation are **realistic**, using their analytical abilities to clarify and discuss issues. Adopting the **pragmatic approach** means that feelings are expressed in honest and direct ways. The pragmatism also means that those adopting this orientation dissociate their self-worth from any results arising from the dispute. Not getting one's own way is not a blow to self-esteem or a slight against one's ego.

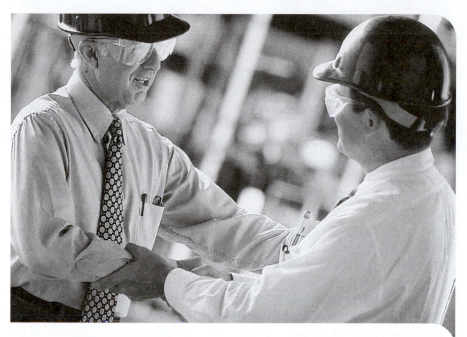

Individuals with a constructive orientation work together to resolve differences.

Another important characteristic about people choosing a constructive orientation is that they are **self-empowered**. This means they are "**internally centred**," so to speak. They recognize that their power comes from inside themselves and not from associations with others, wealth or expertise. Self-empowered individuals respect their opponents in conflictual situations, refusing to become hostile and defensive toward them. They tend to address differences with patient sensitivity.

Constructively oriented people are **conciliatory**. They assume that people are basically well-intentioned and that they prefer to work through differences in a **fair** and **reasonable** fashion. Instead of being offended by caustic behaviour, these individuals look for the underlying needs and desires motivating it. An insult, for instance, would not be taken at face value, but appreciated in terms of what's going on inside the person who issued it. By standing back from the unpleasantness often associated with conflict, constructive people maintain an **objective perspective**. They make efforts to diffuse passions and facilitate negotiations by refusing to be diverted by irrelevant side issues. Finally, constructively oriented people place great value on loyalty to the relationship. For them, few issues are important enough to break the bonds of a friendship.

---

self-empowered
A characteristic of individuals who adopt a constructive orientation to conflict. They are internally centred, recognizing that their power comes from inside themselves and not from associations with others, wealth or expertise.

internally centred
A characteristic of people choosing a constructive orientation. They recognize that their power comes from inside themselves and not from associations with others, wealth or expertise.

conciliatory
Individuals with a constructive orientation to conflict assume that people are basically well-intentioned and that they prefer to work through differences in a fair and reasonable fashion.

fair
The manner in which individuals with a constructive orientation to conflict tend to work through differences.

reasonable
The fashion in which constructively oriented people work through differences. They use their analytical abilities to clarify and discuss issues.

objective perspective
People with a constructive orientation are able to distance themselves from the unpleasantness often associated with conflict and refuse to be diverted by irrelevant side issues.

423

Passive-Defensive Orientation

passive-defensive orientation
People with this orientation view conflict as threatening. They hold the belief that conflict is unnecessary and destructive.

accommodating
A conflict resolution strategy stressing the importance of relationships and minimizing the value of personal goals.

insulate
A tendency of individuals with a passive-aggressive orientation to conflict to hide from controversies and disputes.

avoiders
People who withdraw from conflict or deny it.

regulate
A strategy adopted by passive-defensive individuals to avoid conflict by staying in the background, trying to shame antagonists into more co-operative behaviour.

aggressive-defensive orientation
An orientation that tends to intensify or escalate conflict. Individuals with this orientation believe that competence—particularly intellectual prowess—is key to their acceptance by others.

escalate
To intensify conflict by means of aggressive-defensive behaviour.

aggrandize
A desire common to aggressive-defensive individuals—the primary strategy is to build themselves up at their opponent's expense, camouflaging their own inadequacies by highlighting those of others.

A less-than-constructive psychological approach to conflict is the **passive-defensive orientation**. Rather than seeing conflict as normal and possibility-generating, people with this orientation view conflict as threatening. They avoid getting involved and make efforts to "calm troubled waters." The belief is held that conflict is unnecessary and destructive.

People with a passive-defensive orientation are **accommodating**. With an aim to maintain a climate of perpetual harmony, they have a tendency to passively acquiesce and do what others expect. They are upset by conflict and believe that little good comes from it. For accommodating individuals, self-worth is measured by others' acceptance and approval.

Passive-defensive individuals try to **insulate** themselves from controversies and disputes. Conflict is regarded as a power struggle in which they are powerless to defend their own interests. Insulating persons often feel frightened and helpless and, as a result, try to remain unnoticed and inconsequential. Passive-defensive people are always "hiding out." This fact points to the notion that passive-defensives are **avoiders**, frequently withdrawing from conflict or denying that it exists. Since conflict is seen as unnecessary and destructive, they flee from it whenever possible. Others are allowed to handle disputes. Passive-defenders **regulate** things by staying in the background, trying to shame antagonists into more co-operative behaviour. Seldom, then, will you find passive-defensive individuals balking at authority. Instead, you're more likely to find them behaving as loyal, law-abiding employees or citizens, seeking out dependent relationships with those more powerful than they are.

To increase the probability of constructive conflict outcomes, passive-defensive individuals need to do the following:

- Recognize that conflicts can be useful
- State their interests clearly and forcefully
- Stand up for themselves and for what's important
- Recognize that power can be given away
- Stop believing that others will necessarily protect their interests
- Accept that conflict does indeed exist, if others say it does

Aggressive-Defensive Orientation

In stark contrast to the passive-defensive orientation that minimizes conflict, the **aggressive-defensive orientation** will intensify or **escalate** it. Aggressive-defensive individuals believe that competence—particularly intellectual prowess—is the key to their acceptance by others. We see in escalators a desire to **aggrandize** themselves at their opponent's expense. The primary strategy here is to camouflage their own inadequacies by highlighting those of others. You can tell when you're around escalating, aggressive-defensive types, for they tend to create a highly adversarial climate of attack and counterattack.

Another variation of this orientation is found in the **dominator**. Dominators seek the high ground of **power** and **authority**. They attempt to dictate the terms of their relationships. High-level dominators take every opportunity to attack the power of opponents either directly or by indirect means. Dominating aggressive types live by the ethic "Might makes right," using **force** to manipulate others.

From the vantage point of the aggressive-defensive orientation, conflict is about **competition**. Conflict becomes a context in which people either gain or lose status. When involved in any conflictual situation, the primary motivation is to gain recognition and the admiration of others. Winning is important for it is associated with self-worth. According to the competitive aggressive-defensive type, there is no such thing as a win/win solution.

Finally, some individuals express their aggressive-defensive orientation through **perfectionism**. They set unrealistic standards and demand the impossible from others. No outcome is ever accepted as good enough, while the belief is held that an ideal solution to conflict is indeed possible. By explicitly or implicitly communicating that others have failed or fallen short, a position of (dishonest) superiority can be maintained. Because perfectionistic individuals make unrealistic demands on themselves too, they never feel good enough and, hence, suffer from low self-esteem. In their minds, it is better to have others feel inadequate than to feel inadequate oneself.

dominator
A variation of the aggressive-defensive orientation to conflict. The dominator seeks the high ground of power and authority.

power
An inappropriate basis from which aggressive-defensive individuals seek to dictate relationships.

authority
An inappropriate basis for rational justification when values or normative issues are concerned.

force
An aggressive mode of manipulating others.

competition
The way in which individuals who possess the aggressive-defensive orientation view conflict. To these individuals, conflict becomes a contest in which people either gain or lose status.

perfectionism
The way in which some individuals express their aggressive-defensive orientation. They set unrealistic standards and demand the impossible from others. By explicitly or implicitly communicating that others have failed or fallen short, a position of (dishonest) superiority can be maintained.

Athletes sometimes resolve their conflicts with the use of physical force.

10.5

application exercise

10.1

My Personal Experience of Conflict

Your task in this exercise is to bring to mind a memorable conflict that you've experienced sometime in your life. This is a conflict you're willing to comment on and share with others in the class. (You needn't get too personal or too detailed!) Answer the following questions:

1. What was the conflict about?

2. How did you feel? What were your thoughts? What did you do? How did you act?

3. What type of conflict were you involved in? Was it functional or dysfunctional, psychological or interpersonal, approach-avoidance or something else?

4. Were there any benefits arising from the conflict? If so, explain. Was the conflict destructive? Why?

5. What sort of psychological orientation did you assume in the conflictual situation? If others were involved, what attitudinal stance did they adopt? How did these orientations facilitate or hinder conflict resolution?

Things aggressive-defensive people can do to achieve more constructive resolutions to conflict include the following:

- Don't confuse force with power. "…[T]he more force used to assert your interests, the less power you have to sustain them."
- Separate your personal worth from the outcome of a conflict.
- Apply standards of fair conduct.
- Explore differences rather than force win/lose settlements.
- Be willing to accept less than perfect solutions.
- Respect the interests of others.
- Learn to accept feelings as facts.

426

10.6

Conflict Management Styles

In view of the fact that people display different psychological orientations to conflict and differing behavioural tendencies—to approach, attack or withdraw from others who are involved—it is perhaps not surprising that different conflict management styles have been identified. (see Lafferty and Phillips, 1990;

David Johnson, 1999; Stephen Robbins, 1998; and M.A. Rahim, 1983.) To identify your own personal conflict management style, do Self-Diagnostic 10.1.

Self-Diagnostic 10.1 can help you to begin identifying your dominant and backup **conflict management style**. Here, we'll look at each of your preferred styles as well as others to promote further self-understanding. We'll examine the basic features of each style, the ego states energized by each style, the types of situations created by the different conflict resolution approaches, the advantages and disadvantages of each style, and suggestions about when each style could best be used. (If you wish, refer back to Chapter 8 to refresh your memory with regard to psychological ego states.)

Writers and researchers in the field of human relations have identified at least five different conflict management styles (Lussier, 1995; Johnson, 1999):

1. Forcing (or competing)
2. Avoiding (or withdrawing)
3. Accommodating (or smoothing)
4. Compromising
5. Collaborating (or problem confronting)

Each of these styles takes into account the two major concerns people have when they get into conflict: **goals** and **relationships**. When you experience interpersonal conflict, you typically have a goal that is at odds with another person's goal. Your goal may or may not be highly important to you. As well, when you are in conflict, you're usually required to take into account relationship considerations. Either the relationship in the conflict situation is, or is not, important to you. Looking at the importance of goals in light of the importance of relationships allows us to identify the five conflict management styles listed. Johnson (1999) has associated, in a playful and creative way, different animals with each one. (No offence to the animals intended!) See Figure 10.4.

According to Johnson, the particular conflict strategy you should use in any given situation depends on how important goals and relationships are to you. For him, each conflict management style has its proper place. It's probably not well-advised to behave in the same fashion in every conflict you encounter. Johnson says, "To be truly skilled in conflict management, you need to be competent in all five strategies and be able to vary your behaviour according to the person and the situation. You do not want to be an over-specialized dinosaur who can deal with conflict in only one way" (Johnson, 1990: 248). An important point to note here is that you have choice. Conflict resolution styles are not inborn or innate, but learned. If you have learned only one and rely too heavily on it, it's probably best that you familiarize yourself with the others and practise them when appropriate. Although Self-Diagnostic 10.1 will help you to identify your two most preferred styles, nothing prevents you from using others.

---

conflict management style
The strategy one chooses to use in any given situation, depending on how important goals and relationships are to that individual. The styles are: accommodating teddy bear, collaborating owl, compromising fox, competing shark and avoiding turtle.

goals
One of the two major concerns people have when they get into a conflict (the other being relationships).

relationships
Concerns that must be taken into account when you are in conflict.

427

Self Diagnostic 10.1

What's My Conflict Management Style?

(10.6)

Instructions: Listed below are 15 statements. Each statement provides a possible strategy for dealing with conflict. Give each statement a numerical value (i.e., 1 = Always, 2 = Very often, 3 = Sometimes, 4 = Not very often, 5 = Rarely, if ever) depending on how often you rely on it. Don't answer as you think you should; answer as you actually behave.

_5_ a. I argue my case with peers, colleagues and co-workers to demonstrate the merits of the position I take.

_2_ b. I try to reach compromises through negotiation.

_1_ c. I attempt to meet the expectations of others.

_2_ d. I seek to investigate issues with others in order to find solutions that are mutually acceptable.

_3_ e. I am firm in resolve when it comes to defending my side of an issue.

_3_ f. I try to avoid being singled out, keeping conflict with others to myself.

_2_ g. I uphold my solutions to problems.

_1_ h. I compromise in order to reach solutions.

_1_ i. I trade important information with others so that problems can be solved together.

_3_ j. I avoid discussing my differences with others.

_2_ k. I try to accommodate the wishes of my peers and colleagues.

_3_ l. I seek to bring everyone's concerns out into the open in order to resolve disputes in the best possible way.

_3_ m. I put forward middle positions in efforts to break deadlocks.

_2_ n. I accept the recommendations of colleagues, peers and co-workers.

_2_ o. I avoid hard feelings by keeping my disagreements with others to myself.

Scoring: The 15 statements you just read are listed below under five categories. Each category contains the letters of three statements. Record the number you placed next to each lettered statement. Calculate the total under each category.

							TOTALS
Forcing Shark	a.	_5_	e.	_3_	g.	_2_	_10_
Collaborating Owl	d.	_2_	i.	_1_	l.	_3_	_6_
Avoiding Turtle	f.	_3_	j.	_3_	o.	_2_	_8_
Accommodating Teddy Bear	c.	_1_	k.	_2_	n.	_2_	_5_ .
Compromising Fox	b.	_2_	h.	_1_	m.	_3_	_6_

Results: My dominant style is _accomdatili_ (lowest score) and my backup style is _compricic_ (Second lowest score).

Interpretation of Results: Read the section of the text entitled "The Conflict-Management Menagerie," on pages 429–432.

Source: Based on the work of David Johnson (1984), Stephen Robbins (1993) and M.A. Rahim (1983).

Figure 10.4

A Menagerie of Conflict Management Styles

Source: David Johnson. *Reaching Out.* Copyright 1999 by Allyn and Bacon. Reprinted by permission.

The Conflict Management Menagerie

The Competing Shark Sharks are highly goal-oriented people who use a **forcing** (or **competing**) conflict management style where conflicts are concerned. Relationships take on a much lower priority for them. Sharks do not hesitate to use aggressive behaviour to resolve conflicts. They try to achieve their goals at all costs. Unconcerned with the feelings and needs of others, they are unco-operative, autocratic or authoritarian. They can also be very threatening and intimidating. They seek to force resolutions onto problems. Sharks have a need to win and for them this means that others must lose; in other words, Sharks create win-lose situations in their dealings with conflict. They

forcing/competing
A conflict management style characterized by aggressive behaviour.

429

I don't have a warm personal enemy left. They've all died off. I miss them terribly because they helped define me.
~*Claire Booth Luce*

do so by employing the Critical Parent and Adapted Child ego states. This is where the aggression comes from, as well as the need to satisfy their own wants at the expense of others, if required (Lussier, 1995).

One advantage of this conflict style is that better decisions can be made (assuming the Shark is right) as compared with less effective, compromised decisions. A deterrent to using this style is that it may breed resentment and hostility toward the person (leader) using it. The forcing style is appropriate to use when

- the conflict involves personal differences that are difficult to change.
- fostering intimate or supportive relationships is not critical.
- others are likely to take advantage of noncompetitive behaviour.
- conflict resolution is urgent, in emergency situations, or when decisive action is vital.
- unpopular decisions need to be implemented.

avoiding/withdrawing
A conflict management style that is unassertive and unco-operative.

The Avoiding Turtle Turtles adopt an **avoiding** (or **withdrawing**) conflict management style, choosing to ignore conflicts rather than resolve them. Metaphorically speaking, they withdraw into their shells. Turtles' need to avoid or delay confrontation usually leaves them unco-operative and unassertive. Since they stay away from contentious issues, they give up their personal goals and relationships; they do this while displaying the passive behaviour of the Adapted Child or Nurturing Parent ego state. By leaving conflicts alone, they create lose-lose situations.

One advantage of Turtle avoidance is that it may help to maintain relationships that would be hurt by efforts at conflict resolution (Lussier, 1995). On the downside, conflicts remain unresolved. Furthermore, Turtles overusing this style may find that people are walking all over them. Leaders who don't face the fact that subordinates are breaking the rules must live with the consequences of their inaction. Turtle avoidance can appropriately be used when

- the personal stakes are not high or the issue is trivial.
- confrontation will hurt a working relationship.
- there's little chance of satisfying your wants.
- disruption outweighs the benefits of conflict resolution.
- gathering information is more important than an immediate decision.
- others can more effectively resolve the conflict.
- time constraints demand a delay.

accommodating/smoothing
A conflict resolution strategy stressing the importance of relationships and minimizing the value of personal goals.

The Accommodating Teddy Bear Teddy Bears use an **accommodating** (or **smoothing**) conflict management style, placing a great deal of importance on human relationships. However, their own goals are of little importance. The Teddy Bear tries to resolve conflicts by giving in to others. Anyone using this style of conflict resolution operates passively in the Adapted Child or the Nurturing Parent ego state. The general approach is unassertive and co-operative. The result of this approach is a win-lose situation. The Teddy Bear loses, but the other party involved in the conflict wins.

As with the other conflict management styles already discussed, there are advantages and disadvantages associated with this one. On the upside, accommodating helps to maintain relationships. On the downside, giving in to another in conflict may not be productive. The Teddy Bear may need a better solution. Overreliance on accommodation may lead others to take advantage of Teddy Bears, which is certainly not in their personal best interest.

Lussier (1995) and Thomas (1977) offer us suggestions as to when accommodating is the best conflict style to use:

- When maintaining a relationship far outweighs the importance of all other considerations.
- When suggestions and changes are not important to the accommodator.
- When trying to minimize losses in situations where you are outmatched and losing.
- When time is limited.
- When harmony and stability are valued.

The Compromising Fox Foxes use a **compromising** conflict management style because they are concerned with both goals and relationships. They try to resolve interpersonal conflicts through concessions. They are willing to forfeit some of their goals while persuading the other person in conflict to give up part of his. Conflicts are resolved by both sides getting something. Foxes will accept sacrifice in order to achieve agreement.

compromising
The conflict management style adopted by foxes, who are very concerned with both goals and relationships. They try to resolve interpersonal conflicts through concessions.

This process of compromise elicits both assertive and co-operative Adult ego-state behaviours. Win-lose or lose-lose situations may be created by the compromises found. When both parties give up what they want and get what they don't want, a lose-lose compromise results. In this case, nobody is really satisfied with the resolution. When each party gets some of what's wanted and loses some, you could say a win-lose situation results.

Compromise, as a conflict resolution strategy, is beneficial because relationships are maintained and conflicts are removed relatively quickly. The problem is that compromise sometimes creates less than ideal outcomes. Game playing may also result. Understanding that things will have to be given up, people may make exaggerated and unrealistic demands, hoping to get what they really want. Use compromise when

- important and complex issues leave no clear and simple solutions.
- all conflicting people are equal in power and have strong interests in different solutions.
- there are time constraints.

collaborating/problem confronting The conflict management style adopted by Owls, who view conflicts as problems to be solved.

Wise people seek solutions; The ignorant only cast blame.
~Lao Tzu

The Collaborating Owl Owls adopt a **collaborating** (or **problem confronting**) conflict management system valuing both their goals and relationships. Owls view conflicts as problems to be solved. Collaborators try to resolve disputes by finding solutions agreeable to all parties. They use their Adult ego state to find win-win situations. They believe that a conflict is not settled until people get what they want and all tensions and negative feelings have been extinguished. The disadvantage is that solving every conflict consumes a great deal of time and effort. Collaboration is useful when

- maintaining relationships is important.
- time is not a concern.
- peer conflict is involved.
- trying to gain commitment through consensus building.
- learning and trying to merge differing perspectives.

For a summary statement of conflict management styles, associated ego states, resulting situations, and occasions when indicated, see Table 10.1.

Table 10.1

Conflict Management Styles

Conflict Management Style	Associated Ego States	Resulting Situations	When Indicated	Pros and Cons
Competing Shark	Critical Parent Adapted Child	Win-Lose	High Goal / Low Relationship Concerns	Pro: Better Decisions Con: Resentment and Hostility
Avoiding Turtle	Adapted Child Nurturing Parent	Lose-Lose	Low Goal / Low Relationship Concerns	Pro: Relationship Maintenance Con: Unresolved Conflict
Accommodating Teddy Bear	Nurturing Parent Adapted Child	Win-Lose	Low Goal / High Relationship Concerns	Pro: Preserves Relationship Con: Exploitation of Accommodator
Compromising Fox	Adult Ego State	Win-Lose Lose-Lose	Moderate Goal / Moderate Relationship Concerns	Pro: Conflict Resolution, Relationships Maintained Con: Less-than-ideal Outcomes, Game Playing
Collaborating Owl	Adult Ego State	Win-Win	High Goal / High Relationship Concerns	Pro: Best Resolutions Con: Time and Effort Required

Pick the Most Appropriate Conflict Resolution Style

10.7   Your task in this exercise is to analyze the following case study in light of what you've learned on the subject of conflict and conflict management. What sort of conflict or conflicts are we dealing with? Explain, given the facts, which conflict management style is the best one to use. What led you to your conclusion?

> Mr. Wonderful is the teacher of your general education elective in philosophy offered by the computer studies department. Try as he might, his class is not going very well by mid-term. Mr. Wonderful has noticed that several students in the class always sit close to each other and disrupt proceedings by their rude behaviour and sarcastic questions intended not to clarify matters, but to embarrass the instructor and others. On top of this, students in the elective class don't get along well together. They come from various streams of study within the computer studies department. Some students are fresh out of high school, while others are direct entry, meaning that they already possess either a diploma or degree at the time of course enrollment. Still others are "mature students" who qualified for admission to computer studies by virtue of their age and experience. Often, you can hear arguments among the students who group themselves according to stream. In fact, physical fights have even broken out in the hallways. Mr. Wonderful wishes the conflict would end, that a civilized environment for learning could be reestablished and that everybody would get back to their schoolwork.

In your own words, describe the conflict situation. What should Mr. Wonderful do? What conflict management style would be reflected by these suggested actions? Why do you favour this style in this case?

Win-Win Conflict Resolutions

The ideal resolution to conflict is **win-win**. In this case, everybody benefits and nobody loses. Of course, unequal power relationships, time constraints and other concerns sometimes make win-win resolutions to conflicts difficult to manage. However, when conflicting parties are peers or colleagues with essentially equal power, and when they have a desire to achieve mutually beneficial outcomes, the collaborating or problem confronting style of conflict management is to be preferred; this style makes win-win outcomes most probable.

    David Johnson (1999) has done an excellent job of explaining the steps involved in using the win-win confronting/collaborating style of conflict resolution. The step-by-step discussion that follows draws heavily from his work.

win-win conflict resolution
The ideal resolution to a conflict in which everybody benefits and nobody loses.

433

> **Seven Steps to Constructive Conflict Resolution Using the Collaborative Style**
>
> 1. Confront the opposing party.
> 2. Define the conflict together.
> 3. Communicate personal positions and feelings.
> 4. Express co-operative intentions.
> 5. Understand the conflict from the other party's viewpoint.
> 6. Be motivated to resolve the conflict and to negotiate in good faith.
> 7. Reach an agreement.

He that wrestles with us strengthens our nerves, and sharpens our skill. Our antagonist is our helper.
~Edmund Burke

Step 1: Confront the Opposing Party If you're going to resolve any conflict constructively using the collaborative strategy, the first thing you have to do is to let the other person(s) know that a conflict exists. If the other party doesn't know that you're bothered or upset about something, then from that person's perspective, there is no conflict and nothing is wrong. When you properly confront another person, what you must do is express your view of the conflictual situation and relate your feelings about it, while inviting the other party to do the same.

Of course, whether you choose to confront depends on the quality of relationship, the importance you place on it, and how the person is likely to respond to the confrontation. As a general rule, the stronger or more solid the relationship, the more forceful the confrontation may be. As Johnson (1999) points out, however, if the other party in the conflict displays high anxiety and a low motivation for change, or if the confrontation will not be used as an invitation for self-examination, then confrontation should be avoided. "Whether you decide to open your mouth or button your lips depends on the other person and the situation" (Johnson, 1990: 239).

Step 2: Define the Conflict Together After you have confronted the other person, your second task is to define the conflict in a mutually agreeable fashion. Both of you must agree on what the problem, in fact, is. This must be done fairly and objectively and in a way that doesn't make anyone feel defensive.

When you try to arrive at a common definition of the problem, make efforts to avoid insults, veiled statements and negative value judgments. Personal attacks and prejudgments on the issues are not likely to take you very far down the road of constructive conflict resolution. Furthermore, when defining the conflict, try to be as clear and specific as possible. Leaving things vague or implicit may lead to misunderstandings and crossed communications. As part of defining the conflict situation, accurately describe your feelings

434

and, for purposes of verification, reflect back to the other person her feelings as you experience and understand them. Try as well to control your passions as you describe your own actions and the actions of the other person that contribute to the conflict as you see it.

Step 3: Communicate Personal Positions and Feelings During the process of conflict resolution, positions taken on issues may change, as may feelings on them. It is important, therefore, to keep the lines of communication open. If you're going to disagree with another person's position, you must know what that position is.

The same is true if you wish to suggest changes to that position or if you wish to criticize it. If you don't understand how the other person's thoughts, feelings, wants or goals differ from your own, then the chances of reconciling your differences are jeopardized. Similarly, if the other person doesn't properly appreciate where you stand, or how your stand has changed, finding satisfactory solutions to the conflict will be much more difficult.

While exploring your positions in a conflict situation, seek to uncover precisely what your differences are. Also look for commonalities and points of agreement. Identify which behaviours, on both sides of the conflict, parties find objectionable. Explore possible solutions to the expressed conflict that would prove satisfying to all parties concerned. Think about the things both you and the other person need to do to resolve the conflict.

Step 4: Express Your Co-operative Intentions If you're going to adopt a constructive orientation to conflict resolution in dealings with people whom you value, then you don't want differences to terminate or somehow undermine your relationships with them. It's a good idea, therefore, to make it clear to others that you don't wish to threaten friendships and ongoing associations. Make it known that you want to work together to reach a settlement that is agreeable to all. Show optimism and confidence that the conflict can eventually be resolved with the net effect of strengthening the bonds you have already established.

Step 5: Understand the Conflict from the Other Party's Viewpoint Problems with conflict resolution sometimes arise because people remain "**cognitively egocentric**"; that is, they tend to see problems and conflicts only from their own psychological standpoint. They have difficulties "de-centring" from their own point of view to see things more objectively, from different angles and from other perspectives. I suspect that the more emotionally invested a person is in his own position, the more difficult it is for that individual to appreciate things from alternative vantage points. Certainly, if you wish to constructively resolve conflicts, you cannot ignore, fail to recognize or discount the perspectives of others. Such actions would violate the spirit of mutually respectful win-win negotiations.

Step 6: Be Motivated to Negotiate in Good Faith It is important in win-win negotiations not to use dishonesty, deception or misrepresentation. Trying to

If we could read the secret history of our "enemies" we should find in each man and woman's life sorrow enough to disarm all hostility.
~Henry Wadsworth Longfellow

cognitively egocentric
The tendency to see problems and conflicts only from one's own psychological standpoint.

435

People who use appropriate conflict management techniques can enhance their interpersonal effectiveness.

bad faith
A psychological climate contributing to dishonest negotiations.

honourable intentions
A necessary ingredient used in negotiating in good faith. In order to negotiate in this way, the individuals must not use dishonesty, deception or misrepresentation.

436

fool people into believing they have gotten what they wanted, when you know this isn't true, is bargaining in **bad faith.** Healthy and long-lasting relationships cannot be based on lies, half-truths and broken promises. It is important, therefore, to be motivated by **honourable intentions.** Also, ask yourself if you really want to perpetuate the conflict. What would you gain by ending the conflict? What would the other person gain? What would you and the other person lose if you prolonged the dispute? Are the losses worth it? Are you both motivated, then, to come out as winners? Understand that people's motivations to terminate conflicts can change. If you can increase the gains for resolving conflict or show how the costs of continuing the conflict are likely to increase, you might be able to motivate conflicting parties to make quicker changes that would lead to a settlement of the conflict.

Step 7: Reach an Agreement Once you have defined and confronted the problem, communicated personal positions and associated feelings, expressed co-operative intentions, understood the problem from alternative vantage points, negotiated in good faith, and shown your resolve to reach a solution, then it is time to finalize an agreement. A win-win agreement requires that everyone be satisfied and that they be committed to abide by the agreement. A successful resolution specifies clearly the shared position adopted. It also specifies how people will act differently in the future and how co-operation will be restored if someone backslides and acts inappropriately. It is also advantageous if conflicting parties can agree to meet later on in order to discuss how co-operation can be strengthened.

Symptoms of Inner Peace

Be on the lookout for symptoms of inner peace. The hearts of a great many have already been exposed to inner peace and it is possible that people everywhere could come down with it in epidemic proportions. This could pose a serious threat to what has, up to now, been a fairly stable condition of conflict in the world.

Some Signs and Symptoms of Inner Peace

- A tendency to think and act spontaneously rather than on fears based upon past experiences
- An unmistakable ability to enjoy each moment
- A loss of interest in judging other people
- A loss of interest in judging self
- A loss of interest in interpreting the actions of others
- A loss of interest in conflict
- A loss of ability to worry (a serious symptom)
- Frequent, overwhelming episodes of appreciation
- Contented feelings of connectedness with others and nature
- Frequent attacks of smiling
- An increasing tendency to let things happen rather than make them happen
- An increased susceptibility to the love extended by others as well as the uncontrollable urge to extend love to others

Caution

If you have some or all of the above symptoms, please be advised that your condition of inner peace may be so far advanced as to not be curable. If you are exposed to anyone exhibiting any of these symptoms, remain exposed only at your own risk.

Type Tips for Conflict Resolutions

10.8 By this point in your efforts to master human relations you have become quite familiar with matters of psychological type and the notion of differing cognitive and behavioural preferences. This familiarity can help you to better appreciate the psychology of conflict as well as accommodate differing preferences in an effort to resolve interpersonal disputes. In *Type Talk at Work*, Otto Kroeger and Janet

Thuesen say that "any conflict-resolution model that does not consider personality differences is doomed to fail" (Kroeger and Thuesen, 1993: 128). This claim may be somewhat overstated; nonetheless, personality is clearly one important variable to be taken into account when trying to resolve any interpersonal conflict. In fact, sometimes personality differences are the causes of conflicts. What the thinker may interpret as simply making a case, for instance, the feeler may understand as provoking an argument.

To prevent any defensiveness here, I'd like to emphatically state that no one type has a monopoly on starting conflicts, nor does any one type excel at dealing with them. Conflict can unfortunately bring the worst out in all of us. For example, TJs (thinking—judging types) tend to become overly rigid, while extraverts can become excessively loud and needlessly aggressive (Kroeger and Thuesen, 1993). In their work, Kroeger and Thuesen have identified five steps to conflict resolution. This strategy is type sensitive. The five steps are listed below. Following the steps, I've paraphrased their recommendations for all types involved in conflict resolution.

Five Steps to Conflict Resolution

1. Define the issues involved.
2. Try to put the issues into a typological framework, ideally pinpointing them to a letter preference.
3. Examine the probable cause of the conflict, in typological terms if possible.
4. Ask each party involved to identify with the other's point of view.
5. Seek compromises or contracts that can move the conflict toward resolution.

A type-sensitive strategy for resolving conflicts requires that

- **extraverts** stop to look and listen. Care must be taken to appreciate the other person's point of view.
- **introverts** express themselves. They must be heard by extraverts, who sometimes won't let them get a word in edgewise.
- **sensors** get beyond the facts. Facts are sometimes misleading or perceived differently by different people. Look to extenuating circumstances. Other issues besides the facts may need to be taken into account.
- **intuitives** address the issues; they do not cloud the issues with vague generalities. They must try to deal with the specifics that contribute to the conflict at hand.
- **thinkers** allow for the possibility of expressing emotion. They must understand that expressing emotion and dealing with it is integral to successful conflict resolution.

- **feelers** be direct and confrontative. They must say what's on their minds. They shouldn't apologize for their feelings. Rather, they should just state them. Frankness will be appreciated.

- **judgers** recognize that they're not always right. They must stop seeing life and situations in purely black-and-white terms. They must accept the fact that judgers can be wrong.

- **perceivers** must learn to take a stand. They cannot forever remain flexible and undecided. Sooner or later decisions must be made and actions must be taken.

Personal "Shoulds" for Conflict Resolution

In the spaces provided below, list the four letters of your psychological type. Next to each letter, indicate what you should do or consider when faced with conflict, given the type-sensitive suggestions listed earlier. (Refer to Chapter 2, if necessary, to find your psychological type.)

My psychological type is	When in conflict with others, I should
____ (E or I)	(What should I do about my E or I attitude?) _____ _____
____ (S or N)	(What should I notice about my S or N perceptions?) _____ _____
____ (T or F)	(What should I realize about my T or F decision-making tendencies?) _____ _____
____ (J or P)	(How should I deal with my J or P orientation to the external world?) _____ _____

439

Study Guide

Key Terms

conflict (414)
psychological conflict (417)
interpersonal conflict (417)
intergroup conflict (417)
intragroup conflict (418)
intrapsychic conflict (418)
approach-approach conflict (418)
avoidance-avoidance conflict (418)
approach-avoidance conflict (419)
dysfunctional conflict (420)
functional conflict (420)
interactionist perspective (420)
orientation (421)
conflict orientation (421)
predispositions (421)
beliefs (421)
perceptions (421)
motivations (421)

intentions (421)
behaviours (421)
constructive orientation to conflict (422)
realistic (422)
pragmatic approach (422)
self-empowered (423)
internally centred (423)
conciliatory (423)
fair (423)
reasonable (423)
objective perspective (423)
passive-defensive orientation (424)
accommodating (424)
insulate (424)
avoiders (424)
regulate (424)
aggressive-defensive orientation to conflict (424)
escalate (424)
aggrandize (424)
dominator (425)

power (425)
authority (425)
force (425)
competition (425)
perfectionism (425)
conflict management style (427)
goals (427)
relationships (427)
forcing/competing (429)
avoiding/withdrawing (430)
accommodating/ smoothing (430)
compromising (431)
collaborating/problem confronting (432)
win-win conflict resolution (433)
cognitively egocentric (435)
bad faith (436)
honourable intentions (436)

Progress Check 10.1

Fill-in-the-Blank Questions

Instructions: Fill in each blank with the appropriate response from the list below.

psychological
dysfunctional
passive-defensive
conflict management styles
wrong

self-knowledge
constructive
collaborating
win-win
aggressive-defensive

conflict orientation   intragroup
competing shark   conflict
approach-approach

1. If we oppose people, strive to overcome them or struggle for mastery over them, then we are engaged in _____.

2. The poem "The Six Men of Indostan" illustrates that people who disagree among themselves can be partly right, but all be _____ in the end.

3. Conflicts that occur inside oneself or in one's mind are _____.

4. Conflicts that arise among members of one single group can be labelled _____.

5. Having to decide between two desirable items—only one of which can be had—is the very definition of _____ conflict.

6. Conflict that interferes with a group's performance and productivity is _____.

7. Conflict can promote _____ by heightening awareness of what upsets or frightens us.

8. A _____ is defined by a person's beliefs, perceptions, motivations and behaviours toward others in situations of disagreement and dispute.

9. Somebody who is realistic, pragmatic, self-empowered, fair and conciliatory displays a(n) _____ orientation to conflict.

10. Somebody who is accommodating and avoidant when it comes to conflict displays a(n) _____ orientation.

11. Some people intensify and escalate conflict. They often use force. These people adopt a(n) _____ orientation.

12. David Johnson has identified five _____.

13. Lafferty and Phillips's notion of the aggressive-defensive orientation is most closely related to Johnson's style of the _____.

14. The _____ conflict management style is most like the constructive orientation.

15. The ideal resolution to conflict is _____.

True/False Questions

441

Instructions: Circle the appropriate letter next to each statement.

T F   1. The best way to deal with conflict is simply to ignore it.

T F   2. To say that someone is "cognitively egocentric" is to suggest that the person is selfish.

T F   3. Some Myers-Briggs personality types are more likely than others to start conflicts, while other types are usually better at resolving them.

T F 4. With proper human relations training, conflict can be avoided most of the time.

T F 5. Conflict somehow involves opposing forces and differing objectives.

T F 6. Conflict always takes place between two or more individuals or groups.

T F 7. From an interactionist perspective, an optimum level of conflict can help to keep groups viable and creative.

T F 8. Conflicts can cause decisions to be made more carefully and thoughtfully.

T F 9. The behavioural tendency to personally attack people who disagree with you reflects the aggressive-defensive orientation to conflict.

T F 10. Refusing to engage in conflict and withdrawing from it reflects the constructive orientation to conflict.

T F 11. From the aggressive-defensive orientation, people try to aggrandize themselves at the expense of others.

T F 12. The compromising (fox) conflict management style is the one most likely to lead to win-win solutions.

T F 13. David Johnson believes that no one strategy is best for resolving all disputes.

T F 14. The accommodating (teddy bear) style of conflict management places a great deal of importance on human relationships.

T F 15. The collaborating (owl) style of conflict management is best to use when time is limited.

Summary

1. What is the nature of conflict?
   - defined as combat, a striving to oppose or overcome
   - to meet in opposition or hostility
   - to be incompatible or at variance

2. What are some types of conflict?
   - psychological, intrapsychic
   - social: interpersonal, intergroup, intragroup
   - approach-approach, approach-avoidance, avoidance-avoidance
   - functional versus dysfunctional

3. What are the benefits of conflict?
   - problem awareness
   - change catalyst
   - energizing and motivating
   - stimulating and interest generating

- cathartic
- improves quality of decisions
- promotes self-knowledge
- enhances fun
- potentially improves relationships in the long run

4. What constitutes a psychological orientation to conflict?
   - predispositions, beliefs, perceptions, motivations, intentions and behaviours

5. How do people psychologically orient to conflict?
   - constructive orientation: realistic, pragmatic, self-empowered, conciliatory, fair, reasonable, objective
   - passive-defensive orientation: accommodating, insulating, avoidant, regulating
   - aggressive-defensive orientation: escalates conflict, self-aggrandizing, dominating, competitive, perfectionistic

6. What are five conflict management styles identified by David Johnson?
   - forcing/competing: goal oriented, unco-operative, win-lose
   - avoiding/withdrawing: ignore conflicts, sacrifice goals and relationships, lose-lose
   - accommodating/smoothing: values relationships over goals, unassertive, unco-operative, win-lose
   - compromising: values goals and relationships, uses concessions, assertive and co-operative, win-lose or lose-lose
   - collaborating: problem confronting, works toward consensus, win-win

7. How are win-win conflict resolutions achieved?
   - use the collaborating style: confront the opposing party; define the conflict together; communicate personal positions and feelings; express co-operative intentions; understand the conflict from the other party's viewpoint; be motivated to resolve the conflict and to negotiate in good faith; reach an agreement

Related Readings

Adler, Ronald B. and George Rodman (2000). *Understanding Human Communication*, 7th edition. Toronto: Harcourt Brace College Publishers.

Adler, Ronald B. and Neil Towne (1998). *Looking Out, Looking In*, 9th edition. Toronto: Harcourt Brace College Publishers.

Gordon, Thomas (1989). *P.E.T. Parent Effectiveness Training*. New York: New American Library.

Napoli, Vince, James M. Kilbride and Donald E. Tebbs (1992). *Adjustment and Growth in a Changing World*, 4th edition. St. Paul: West Publishing.

Weeks, Dudley (1992). *The Eight Essential Steps to Conflict Resolution*. New York: G.P. Putnam's Sons.

"Come to the edge," he said. They said, "We are afraid." "Come to the edge," he said. They came. He pushed them And they flew.

~Guillaume Apollinaire

Leadership Skills Development

Chapter Overview

Life and Leadership
- Defining Leadership
- Leadership Versus Management

Application Exercise 11.1
Take Me To Your Leader

Approaches to Leadership

- Trait Leadership Theory
- Behavioural Leadership: Theory X and Theory Y

Application Exercise 11.2
Boss-Behaviour Analysis

- Three-Factor Theory
- The University of Michigan Studies
- Situational Leadership

Application Exercise 11.3
Following the Leader at Camp Athabasca

- Leadership by Temperament Style: Keirsey and Bates

- Self-Diagnostic 11.1 Assessing Your Leadership Temperament

Study Guide

- Key Terms
- Progress Check 11.1
- Summary
- Related Readings

Learning Outcomes

After successfully completing this chapter, you will be able to

(11.1) Define leadership

(11.2) Distinguish between leadership and management

(11.3) List the functions of management

(11.4) Outline and describe six approaches to leadership

(11.5) Decide on the best form of situational leadership to use in a case study example

(11.6) Assess your leadership temperament

(11.7) Modify leadership appreciation strategies to fit psychological temperament types

Focus Questions

1. Why is the study of leadership important to the mastery of human relations?

2. How can leadership be defined? How is it related to management?

3. Is there more than one way to lead people? How so?

4. What are some of the behavioural assumptions leaders make about their followers? Which assumptions would *you* make about people?

5. Which leadership theory do you like best? Would your preference be most effective? Explain why.

445

Life and Leadership

Experience suggests that no matter who you are or what you do for a living, chances are pretty good that you will be required to assume a leadership role at some time in your life. You may become a leader among your friends, a class leader at school, a neighbourhood organizer, the head of a family, or someone expected to provide direction at work or in some civic organization operating within your local community. Given the likelihood that leadership demands will be placed upon you in the future, if not right now, you are well advised to develop an understanding of the nature and process of leadership. It is important that you prepare yourself for carrying out leadership roles in order to maximize your effectiveness. This preparation may indeed turn out to be instrumental to your personal and professional success.

From the moment of their birth, some are marked for subjugation and others for command.
~Aristotle

11.1 Defining Leadership

Leadership is one of those vague concepts that everyone seems to understand intuitively, but which few can define precisely. Over the years, many models and approaches to leadership have been developed. In this chapter, we'll be looking at a few of them, but before we begin, it will be helpful to provide a simple working definition of leadership.

leadership
The ability to influence the actions of others. People displaying leadership can cause others to work toward common goals in social, institutional and organizational settings. Leaders can get others to do things that they wouldn't otherwise do.

Leadership involves the ability to influence the actions of others (Benton and Halloran, 1991). People displaying leadership can cause others to work toward common goals in social, institutional and organizational settings. Leaders can get others to do things that they otherwise wouldn't do. Examples of great Canadian leaders include Pierre Elliot Trudeau (former prime minister), and Nellie McClung (political activist who helped win women the vote in Alberta in 1916). Great American leaders include former president Abraham Lincoln and wealthy investor and philanthropist, Warren Buffet.

11.2 Leadership Versus Management

Common sense might seem to dictate that leadership has something to do with management functions. You may be inclined to think that departmental heads, institutional directors, presidents of corporations and assembly-line bosses are typical examples of people who act as leaders in our society. It would appear that higher authority and greater levels of responsibility make someone a leader. Yet some writers and researchers on the subject of leadership would take issue with such a notion. They would not accept the idea that managers are destined to become leaders simply by virtue of their institutional or organizational roles (Barr and Barr, 1989). While it may be true that some managers function as effective leaders, other managers may manage but fail to lead. You may also have individuals in your group, neighbour-

Leadership is the ability to decide what is to be done, and then to get others to want to do it.
~Dwight D. Eisenhower

446

hood or class who hold no special title, no authority or no formal responsibility—in short, people who are not charged with the task of managing anyone or anything—but who are still recognized as leaders. Furthermore, you may know people who have both management and leadership abilities, but no opportunity to use them. Thus, given the possibilities, we have

1. individuals who manage, but do not lead.
2. individuals who lead, but do not manage.
3. individuals who both lead and manage.
4. individuals who have both leadership and management abilities, but no people who follow them.

In Figure 11.1 you can see the four categories of individuals depicted graphically. In case you're still a little unclear about the differences between management and leadership, here is a quote from Lee and Norma Barr (1989: 9): "**Management** affects work; leadership affects people. Management maintains orderly work systems; leadership maintains an enlivening, unfolding, dynamic development of people. They work well together, but they are not the same."

Now, before examining the leadership of people more closely, let us briefly look at some managerial functions for purposes of contrast and comparison. One function of management is **planning**. This could be short or long term. The manager involved with short-term planning decides what needs to

11.3

management
The maintenance of orderly work systems, through such functions as planning, organizing, implementing, communicating, controlling and evaluating.

planning
One of a manager's key functions, which may involve (in the short-term) deciding what needs to be done, where it will be done, who will assume responsibility for doing it, the time frame within which the work will be done, how required tasks will be performed, and which resources will be needed to complete them. In the long term, planning requires managers to ask questions about the general direction to be taken by the organization, future needs, resource development and financial matters.

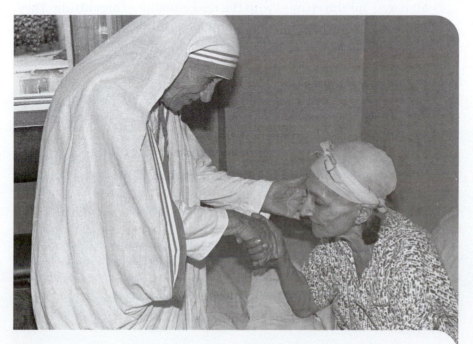

I know God will not give me anything I can't handle. I just wish He didn't trust me so much.
~Mother Teresa

447

A leader herself, the late Mother Teresa followed instructions from an even "higher authority."

Figure 11.1

Leadership, Management and People

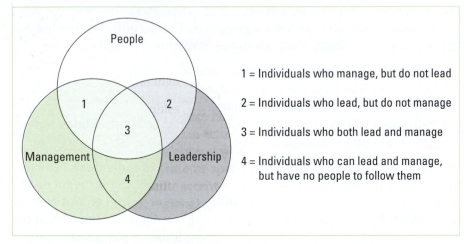

1 = Individuals who manage, but do not lead

2 = Individuals who lead, but do not manage

3 = Individuals who both lead and manage

4 = Individuals who can lead and manage, but have no people to follow them

> Leadership is the process of influencing people to give their energies, use their potential, release their determination, and go beyond their comfort zones to accomplish goals. Leadership is a dynamic process. It affects, risks, drives, inspires, threatens, supports, and leads. Leadership draws trust, acknowledgment, risk, and loyalty from the led.
> *~Lee and Norma Barr*

be done, where it will be done, who will assume responsibility for doing it, the time frame within which the work will be done, how required tasks will be performed, and which resources will be needed to complete them. Long-term planning requires managers to ask questions about the general direction to be taken by the organization, future needs, resource development and financial matters (Barr and Barr, 1989).

organizing A process of providing structure within which to implement plans.

Managers are also charged with the responsibility of **organizing**. They must provide structures within which to implement their plans. They may have to list priorities, establish procedures and set performance guidelines.

application exercise

11.1

Take Me to Your Leader

Pretend that you are taking me to meet the leader you admire most. How would you describe this leader? What is it about him or her that makes this person your favourite? What does the person do? What does that person say? What emotions does the person elicit? How does your favourite leader get people to do things they otherwise wouldn't do?

Would you be willing to make any generalizations about great leaders based on your individual favourite? If so, what general statements would you be willing to make? Jot down your answers on a piece of paper and share them with others in the class. Are there any personal leadership qualities commonly identified in the favourites selected by your classmates? If so, what are they? Why are these qualities important?

THE BEST AND WORST LEADERS

A leader is best

When people barely know he exists,

Not so good when people obey and acclaim him,

Worse when they despise him.

But of a good leader, who talks little,

When his work is done, his aim fulfilled,

They will say:

We did it ourselves.

~Lao-Tzu

GETTING THE JOB DONE

The Story of Everybody, Somebody, Anybody and Nobody

There was an important job to be done.

EVERYBODY was asked to do it.

EVERYBODY was sure that SOMEBODY would do it.

ANYBODY could have done it, but NOBODY did it.

SOMEBODY got angry about that because it was EVERYBODY's job.

EVERYBODY thought that ANYBODY could do it, but NOBODY realized that EVERYBODY wouldn't do it.

It ended up that EVERYBODY blamed SOMEBODY when NOBODY did what ANYBODY could have done.

~Anonymous

If a person wants to lead somebody, he must first lead himself.
~Anonymous

implementation
One of a manager's key functions, in that he or she must delegate tasks, is to assign necessary responsibilities and convey practical instruction to get plans moving in the right direction. Implementation requires managers to function as consultants and guides.

communicate
It is by means of communication that managers assign work, correct performance, negotiate differences, present ideas and confront non-productive behaviour.

control
A manager must ensure that goals and plans are achieved and that quality is maintained.

evaluate
A manager must determine whether goals are being met and whether performance is adequate, and take corrective action when they are not.

managerial functions
The responsibilities of a manager (i.e., planning, organizing, implementing, communicating, controlling and evaluating) that are inherent in the work, rather than being inherent in the person.

managerial skills
Those human relations skills necessary to effective management.

Once matters are planned and organized, managers perform their next duty through **implementation**. They may have to delegate tasks, assign necessary responsibilities and convey practical instructions to get plans moving in the right direction. Implementation requires managers to function as consultants and guides (Barr and Barr, 1989).

Of course managers must continually **communicate** while performing their functions. Information must be transmitted and ideas must be exchanged. By means of communication, managers "assign work, correct performance, negotiate differences, present ideas and confront non-productive behaviour." (Barr and Barr, 1989: 8).

Managers also **control** and **evaluate**. They must ensure that goals and plans are achieved and that quality is maintained. When goals are not being met or when substandard performance is at issue, then managers must take corrective action.

On the subject of management proper, Lee and Norma Barr (1989: 8) make a second interesting distinction between **managerial functions** and **managerial skills**. They say: "Managerial functions [like those discussed] are

449

inherent in the work; managerial skills are within the person." For them, excellence in managerial functioning is not enough in today's world. While getting things done efficiently is important and desirable, it is no longer enough if one is to gain the competitive edge or to achieve the highest quality in performance or product. Renewed emphasis must be placed on people skills and human resource development. All the plans, organizational structures, standards and performance appraisals in the world will not work if the human side of leadership is ignored. The efficient manager must therefore master human relations skills to be an effective leader.

11.4 Approaches to Leadership

As someone preparing to assume a leadership role in society, you may be somewhat uncertain about the best way to do it. While learning by trial and error can provide you with much valuable experience, you should rest assured that there's no need to repeat others' mistakes or to "reinvent the wheel." For decades now, extensive research on leadership has been conducted and valuable insights have been fashioned into various models of leadership. It is helpful and time saving to review some of the classical models here. By examining different conceptions of leadership, you'll be able to extract what's personally useful as you begin to develop your own approach.

Trait Leadership Theory

Historically, many efforts have been made to identify personal characteristics that make someone an effective leader. The practical benefits of such efforts are clear. If you can find the common traits of successful leaders, then you can select individuals who would do a good job functioning in leadership roles.

trait leadership theory
The theory that leaders are born, not made, and that they possess certain distinctive physical and psychological characteristics that contribute largely to their leadership effectiveness.

According to **trait leadership theory**, leaders are born, not made. They possess certain distinctive physical and psychological characteristics that contribute largely to their leadership effectiveness. Traits such as persuasiveness, self-reliance, appearance and dominance have been analyzed and considered important to leadership.

Unfortunately, after decades of effort and hundreds of trait studies, findings about the importance of traits to leadership remain inconclusive (Lussier, 1990). Nobody has been able to arrive at a universal list of traits that all effective leaders possess. While "height" was once singled out as an identifiable trait of leaders, it has been noted that Napoleon was short. Add the more recent leadership of Michael (Pinball) Clemons, the coach of the Grey-Cup-winning Toronto Argonauts in 2004—a diminutive man—and you can see that height does not prevent short people from becoming successful leaders. Furthermore, when lists of leadership traits were compiled, it was found that many people who possessed all of them were not necessarily suc-

Source: Reprinted with special permission of King Features Syndicate.

cessful in leadership roles (Lussier, 1990). The importance of traits also became suspect when people were found to be successful in one leadership position, but not in another. This suggested that something other than traits was influencing leadership effectiveness.

In 1971, Edwin Ghiselli published his results from a now classic study of more than 300 managers from 90 different businesses. He concluded that there are traits that tend to be important to effective leadership, though not all are prerequisites for success. Traits deemed by Ghiselli to be significant are listed below in order of importance.

1. **Supervisory ability** Effective leaders complete tasks through others. They are able to perform management functions well.
2. **Need for occupational achievement** Good leaders typically seek responsibility. They are motivated to work hard and succeed.
3. **Intelligence** Effective leadership usually results from good judgment and from sound reasoning and thinking abilities.
4. **Decisiveness** Successful leaders display good problem-solving skills and competence in decision making.
5. **Self-assurance** Effective leadership is associated with self-assurance (i.e., feeling confident that one is able to cope with problems and display self-confidence to others).
6. **Initiative** Good leaders tend to be self-starters. They work with a minimum of supervision.

Behavioural Leadership: Theory X and Theory Y

In a classic work entitled *The Human Side of Enterprise*, Douglas McGregor (1960) offers us a theory of **behavioural leadership.** He suggests that all managerial decisions and actions are ultimately based on fundamental assumptions about human nature and human behaviour. In other words,

supervisory ability
Effective leaders complete tasks through others. They are able to perform management functions well.

need for occupational achievement
Good leaders typically seek responsibility. They are motivated to work hard and succeed.

intelligence
Leadership trait characterized by good judgment as well as sound thinking and reasoning abilities.

decisiveness
Good problem-solving skills and competence in decision making.

self-assurance
The confidence that one is able to cope with problems and display self-confidence to others.

initiative
Good leaders tend to be self-starters. They work with a minimum of supervision.

behavioural leadership
A management theory based on psychological assumptions about human behaviour.

451

theory X
The traditional autocratic approach to leadership that assumes people have an inherent or natural dislike of work and will avoid it if they can.

theory Y
The participative approach to leadership that assumes mental and physical work are as natural as play, given favourable conditions, and that people will exercise personal initiative and self-control when there is commitment to organizational or institutional goals.

traditional autocratic approach
The theory X approach to leadership, according to McGregor, in which the leader assumes "mediocrity of the masses."

paternalistic attitude
Authoritarian control displayed by individuals who take the theory X (Traditional Autocratic Approach) to managerial leadership.

In Aristotelian terms, the good leader must have ethos, pathos and logos. The ethos is his moral character, the source of his ability to persuade. The pathos is his ability to touch feelings, to move people emotionally. The logos is his ability to give solid reasons for an action, to move people intellectually.
~Anonymous

managerial leaders operate according to certain psychological principles, beliefs about people, and understandings of what makes human beings tick. Such principles, beliefs and understandings are grouped under the headings **theory X** and **theory Y**. Let's now look briefly at each.

Theory X: The Traditional Autocratic Approach

- According to the **traditional autocratic approach**, people have an inherent or natural dislike of work and will avoid it if they can.

- Because of people's aversion to work, they must be coerced, controlled, directed and threatened; otherwise, they will not put forth sufficient effort to achieve organizational goals.

- People typically prefer to be directed, to avoid responsibility, to show little ambition, and to seek security above all else.

In general terms, a theory X approach to managerial leadership is built upon the assumption of the "mediocrity of the masses" (McGregor, 1960: 34). While managers and leaders may pay lip service to the ideal that all human beings have equal worth and are deserving of respect, those adhering to theory X assumptions actually adopt a **paternalistic attitude** toward subordinates. For them, democratic treatment of individuals often results in permissiveness and inefficiency. Authoritarian control, sometimes disguised as benevolent paternalism and direction, is preferable. People need to be told what to do and how to do it. Add threat to the business of control and the job will get done. According to McGregor, theory X is by no means a defunct managerial philosophy. Though it may sound harsh to those holding contemporary social values, theory X management continues to be practised today.

Theory X could be described as traditional autocratic management. The traditional leader uses rewards, promises, incentives, threats and other coercive devices to achieve organizational and institutional goals. McGregor points out that the "carrot and stick" understanding of human motivation, which underlies theory X, works fairly well when people are struggling to satisfy lower-level needs for safety and survival. However, it "...does not work at all once man has reached an adequate subsistence level and is motivated primarily by higher needs." (McGregor, 1960: 41). When people have their basic needs met, leaders are well-advised to adopt a different set of behavioural assumptions—those falling under theory Y.

Theory Y: A Participative Approach
Affluence, as well as an established sense of safety and security in the minds of followers, requires that managerial leaders shift their motivational emphasis to the social and psychological ego needs of those with whom they work. These needs relate to self-esteem, self-respect, autonomy, achievement, knowledge, status, recognition, association, appreciation and self-fulfillment (McGregor, 1960: 38). If managers fail to satisfy these higher-order needs, people will feel deprived and their

deprivation will be reflected in diminished personal performance. Organizational goals may not be met; quality may suffer. Under conditions of higher-need deprivation, rewards and punishments, related to survival and physiological needs, are not likely to be effective. The alternative assumptions of theory Y, which would probably be more effective, are listed below:

- Mental and physical work are as natural as play, given favourable conditions.
- People will exercise personal initiative and self-control when there is commitment to organizational or institutional goals.
- Under suitable conditions, people can learn not only to accept, but actually to seek out, responsibility.
- The capacity for creative problem solving within organizations is widely—not narrowly—distributed throughout the population.
- Under current conditions of modern life, the potentialities of people are only partially realized. They have much more to offer given the chance.

From our brief overview of theory X and theory Y, we can appreciate how the behavioural and motivational assumptions that leaders make about people affect the ways in which they behave. Theory X and theory Y assumptions give rise to differing attitudes and predispositions toward people. It's not necessary, however, that theory X managers come across as "dictators." They may be very friendly in their paternalism. Also, don't assume theory Y management will always produce the best results. People often fail to live up to their potential (Timm and Peterson, 1999). In any case, it's probably rare to find somebody who operates strictly by theory X or theory Y assumptions. Most people probably fall somewhere on a continuum between the two (Callahan and Fleenor, 1988).

Boss-Behaviour Analysis

application
exercise
11.2

Probably by now in your life you've had at least one part-time job. Maybe you've worked in the retail industry as a salesperson, in the restaurant business as a server, cook or dishwasher, or maybe you've had a temporary seasonal job such as one selling tickets at the Calgary Stampede or the Canadian National Exhibition in Toronto. Regardless of your particular job, if you've worked for someone else, then you've had a boss—or "leader," if you will. Think about that boss now. Did that person operate on theory X or theory Y assumptions about people? Explain and illustrate. Was your boss's leadership style effective? Why or why not?

Three-Factor Theory

Recognizing that most leaders probably operate on principles falling somewhere between theory X and theory Y, Robert Tannenbaum and Warren Schmidt (1973) developed a **three-factor theory** of leadership that identifies five points between the two extremes of boss-centred leadership (theory X) and subordinate-centred leadership (theory Y). See Figure 11.2.

According to Tannenbaum and Schmidt, a wide range of factors determines whether autocratic leadership, participative leadership or something in between is most effective. These factors are listed next.

- **Manager factors** Personal values, levels of security/insecurity, individual leadership tendencies, confidence in subordinates.
- **Subordinate factors** Need for independence, willingness to take on responsibility and make decisions, tolerance for ambiguity, interest in problem solving, comprehension of and commitment to departmental, institutional/organizational goals, relevant knowledge and experience, as well as expectations.
- **Situation factors** Time constraints, group effectiveness, organizational type, and nature of the problem.

As a potential leader, these factors can be useful for you to consider. You can use them to analyze and assess situations to determine which styles of leadership will work best. If something must be done in a hurry, for ex-

Figure 11.2

A Continuum of Leadership Tactics

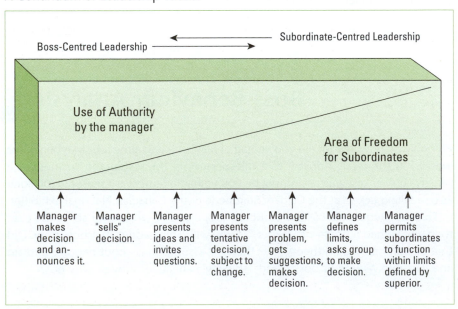

ample, then a directive or autocratic style could be the most appropriate as there may be little or no time for consultation. Time constraints on decision making can be an important factor to consider in determining preferred leadership styles.

The University of Michigan Studies

Job-Centred Versus Employee-Centred Styles of Leadership In the 1940s, the University of Michigan conducted a large-scale research program dealing with problems of administration. This study is now considered a classic. Under the direction of Rensis Likert (1961), researchers wanted to discover the principles and methods of managerial leadership that resulted in optimum performance. The research compared styles of leadership with specific performance variables in the best and worst departmental units of several organizations. Things such as productivity, job satisfaction, employee turnover, absenteeism, cost and waste were examined.

The Michigan Studies concluded that there are two basic leadership styles used by managers: (1) The **job-centred style** (not to be confused with Tannenbaum and Schmidt's boss-centred) and (2) the **employee-centred style**. Managers using the former were found to be very directive. They closely supervised their workers and sometimes resorted to negative uses of power (e.g., punishment). Job-centred leaders typically emphasized schedules and critically evaluated performance. These leaders were definitely **task-oriented**.

By contrast, employee-centred managers were more person-centred. They didn't mind delegating responsibility and placing confidence in others. Employee-centred managers showed a concern for the welfare of employees, including their individual needs, advancement and personal growth. While job-centred leaders tended to make assumptions about people falling in line with theory X, employee-centred managers were much more likely to accept theory Y assumptions.

The Michigan Studies suggest that employee-centred leadership is preferable to job-centred leadership. Work units headed by employee-centred leaders tend to be more productive than those headed by job-centred leaders. No guarantees are possible, however. One-third of the employee-centred units were low in performance, while one out of eight job-centred units was high in performance. The conclusion we derive from this research is that variables apart from leadership are probably involved in performance.

The Michigan Studies Leadership research done by Rensis Likert, focusing on job-centred versus employee-centred management.

job-centred style Form of task-oriented leadership often resorting to negative uses of power.

employee-centred style Person-centred leadership approach as defined by Rensis Likert.

task-oriented The orientation displayed by managers who prefer the job-centred style of management. These leaders typically emphasize schedules and critically evaluate performance.

Situational Leadership

If no one leadership style can guarantee success or optimal performance, then perhaps the effectiveness of any particular style depends on the situation.

455

situational leadership
The theory that effective leadership requires a leader to select the right style in a particular situation that depends on the followers' maturity.

maturity
A technical term used in situational leadership. The degree of a person's task-relevant maturity is determined by assessing each of the following factors: his or her achievement motivation, responsibility, ability, and education and experience.

achievement motivation
One component of Hersey and Blanchard's notion of task-relevant maturity.

responsibility
One of the factors used to assess maturity (i.e., Do the people involved show a willingness to assume responsibility?).

ability
In the context of situational leadership, the skill or knowledge an individual brings to a particular task.

education and experience
One of the factors used to assess maturity (i.e., Does the individual or group have the education or experience necessary to complete this task?).

relationship building
When appropriately mixed with task directing, it can increase the probability of effective leadership.

task directing
Appropriately mixed with relationship building, it can increase the probability of effective leadership.

This is exactly the position taken by the theory of **situational leadership**, developed by Paul Hersey and Kenneth H. Blanchard (1982). For them, effective leadership requires a leader to select the right style that depends on the followers' "**maturity**." Maturity is a technical term that will be explained in a moment. The point is that in the leadership equation, followers cannot be ignored. It is they who either accept or reject the leader. "Regardless of what the leader does, effectiveness depends on the actions of his or her followers. This is an important dimension that has been overlooked or underemphasized in most leadership theories" (Robbins, 1993).

According to Hersey and Blanchard (1982), we can choose appropriate leadership styles in particular situations by first establishing the maturity levels of the individuals and groups who will perform specific tasks and functions. Note that the term "maturity" refers to task-relevant maturity. Situational leaders ask: "How mature is the person or group relative to the function, goal or objective assigned?" Maturity takes the following into account:

- **Achievement Motivation** Ask: Does the individual or group set high, but attainable, goals?
- **Responsibility** Ask: Do the people involved show a willingness to assume responsibility? To what extent are individuals and groups committed to take on specific tasks? (A question of psychological maturity.)
- **Ability** Ask: What level of relevant knowledge or skill and ability does this individual or group bring to this particular task? (A question of job maturity.)
- **Education and Experience** Ask: Does the individual or group have the education or experience necessary to complete the task?

Maturity is a useful concept. It can help leaders determine the appropriate mixture of **relationship building** and **task directing** when it comes to increasing the probability of effectiveness (Timm and Peterson, 1982). As maturity varies from task to task, and from this individual and group to that individual or group, so too will preferred leadership styles and associated communication patterns. An important objective of leadership in this context is to move people toward ever-increasing levels of maturity—both psychological and job-related.

There are four levels of maturity (M1, M2, M3, M4). Read what follows to learn more about what each displays.

M1 At this low level, individuals or groups are both unable and unwilling to assume responsibility for performing a function. They are neither confident, nor competent.

M2 At this low to moderate level, people are unable but nonetheless willing to do necessary job tasks. They are motivated, but lack necessary skills.

M3 At moderate to high levels of ability and willingness, individuals are able but unwilling to do what the leader requests.

M4 At high levels of maturity, people are both able and willing to do what is asked of them. They are intrinsically motivated.

According to the situational model, there are four basic styles of leadership, (i.e., **telling**, **selling**, **participating** and **delegating**). Appropriate matches should be made between any one style and the maturity of the followers, given the specific task or function to be performed. Brief descriptions follow. While reading, remember that each style differs in terms of supportive and directive behaviour. Also, each has its own predominant communication pattern.

Situational Leadership Styles

1. **Telling (high task/low relationship behaviour)** This leadership style is essentially autocratic. People are told what to do, how to do it, when it should be done and where it's supposed to be done. Little relational support is provided. Directive behaviour is emphasized. The major focus is on providing specific instructions and supervising closely.

2. **Selling (high task/high relationship behaviour)** Leaders using this style display both directive and supportive behaviours. They explain decisions taken and provide opportunities for clarification. While this style involves issuing many directive instructions, significant support and reassurance are offered.

3. **Participating (low task/high relationship behaviour)** In this case, leaders provide much support, but show relatively little directive behaviour. Increasing maturity requires less direction. Using this style, leaders share ideas and facilitate decision making.

4. **Delegating (low task/low relationship)** Leaders who delegate show the least amount of directive and supportive behaviour. Since job maturity and psychological maturity are very high, followers can function independently with minimum supervision. All that is needed is to make them aware of the tasks and objectives for which they are responsible.

To help us decide on the most appropriate leadership style to use in a given situation, Hersey and Blanchard have combined a maturity scale with a leadership matrix that contains four quadrants, labelled according to the four types of leadership just described. (see Figure 11.3). First determine the maturity of the follower(s) in the situation. Mark this with an "X" on the continuum. Next, draw a vertical line upward from the "X" until it hits the bell-shaped curve. The line will meet the curve in one of the quadrants (either S1, S2, S3 or S4). The quadrant where line and curve meet indicates the most appropriate leadership style to use. If, for example, followers are high in maturity, then "delegating" becomes the style of choice. By contrast, if job and psychological maturity are low, then "telling" should become the predominate communication pattern for leadership behaviour.

telling
One of the situational leadership styles reflected by leaders who are essentially autocratic. The major focus is on providing specific instructions and supervising closely.

selling
One of the situational leadership styles reflected by leaders who display both directive and supportive behaviours. They explain decisions taken and provide opportunities for clarification. While this style involves issuing many instructions and directions, significant support and reassurance are offered.

participating
Situational leadership style assuming greater maturity on the part of subordinates.

delegating
One of the situational leadership styles reflected by leaders who show the least amount of directive and supportive behaviour.

Figure 11.3
Situational Leadership Model

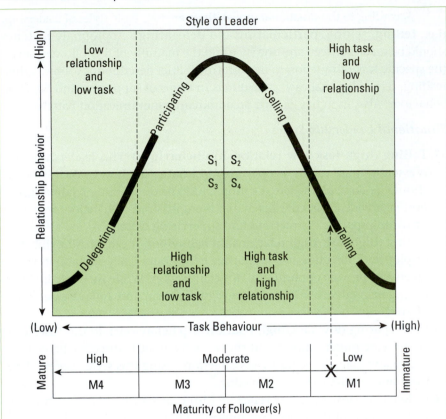

application exercise 11.3

(11.5)

Following the Leader at Camp Athabasca

Task: Given the information and details of the case study provided, your task is to analyze it using Hersey and Blanchard's model of situational leadership. Determine which leadership strategy is most appropriate. Explain why. This task may be completed individually or in groups.

Mary had been a leader at Camp Athabasca for the past three years. This particular year, and without any notice or job competition being posted, she was surprisingly selected by the owners of the camp to supervise all the other camp leaders. Mary was quite happy about her selection, but others were not. Some felt that they, not Mary, were more deserving of the supervisory position. They resented not having had a chance to apply for Mary's new position. As a consequence, they showed a reluctance to cooperate with her in any way. On top of this, Mary was asked by the owners of the camp to implement a whole new program of games and activities for the children who were about to attend the summer session at the lake. None of the camp leaders were familiar with these new games and activities. They seemed confused when trying to master the skills that they were supposed to teach the children soon to arrive. Necessary equipment and props required to do the new activities and games were constantly not put away, or else they were mishandled and often misplaced.

Question: If you were in Mary's situation, which leadership approach would be best to use in the process of training and supervising your staff? Explain why. What specifically would you do to reflect the application of your chosen approach?

Leadership by Temperament Style: Keirsey and Bates

The final leadership theory we will cover in this chapter has to do with the notion of **temperament**. This theory was developed by David Keirsey and Marilyn Bates. According to Keirsey and Bates (1984), temperament is a unifying principle of personality. It provides the overall colouration of someone's character. Temperament "is that which places a signature or thumbprint on each of one's actions, making it recognizably one's own" (Keirsey and Bates 1984: 27). Temperament can also be viewed as that which makes actions consistent—a consistency that can be observed from a very early age. While experience gives "content" to living, temperament is the "form" that gives experience its quality and texture.

temperament
In the assessment of leadership styles, temperament refers to observable patterns of behaviour, and describes the differences in people that have been witnessed and recorded by civilizations throughout history.

Keirsey and Bates (1984) maintain that leaders have stable temperaments, as do followers and subordinates. In any situation where you have people leading and following, there will necessarily be an interaction of temperament types. It is important to recognize this if effective leadership is to emerge. There is a human dimension to leadership that affects how well a person leads and to what extent people follow. We can become more effective leaders if we learn to work with temperamental differences.

Self Diagnostic 11.1 — Assessing Your Leadership Temperament

(11.6)

Background: This instrument will help you to start thinking about your personal leadership style, which is highly influenced by psychological temperament. The notion of temperament, as used here, refers to observable patterns of behaviour. It describes differences in people that have been witnessed and recorded by civilizations throughout history. There are four basic temperaments, which include the preferences of all 16 personality types identified by the Myers-Briggs Type Indicator (see Chapter 2). Reducing 16 personality types to four temperaments for purposes of analyzing leadership style simplifies matters. This instrument is a practical application based on the writing and research of Sandra Hirsh (1985: 13–16) and incorporates the insights of David Keirsey and Marilyn Bates (1984).

Instructions: In what follows you will find 11 incomplete statements. Your task is to look at the four possible ways of completing each statement and decide on your preference. Each option *must* be given a numerical value (i.e., 1 = 1st or most preferred choice, 2 = 2nd choice, 3 = 3rd choice, and 4 = 4th or least preferred choice). Note that there are no right or wrong answers. Please be accurate and honest with your replies. Answer in ways that indicate *your* true preferences, not others' expectations.

1. People occupying formal leadership roles should pay attention to
   ___ a. the immediate practical needs of the organization
   ___ b. the philosophy and systems of the organization
   ___ c. the organization's hierarchy
   ___ d. the future growth needs of the organization

2. As a leader, I am/would be best able to
   ___ a. use my charisma to facilitate participation and group decision making
   ___ b. build conceptual frameworks and develop models
   ___ c. respond immediately and realistically to problems in an open and flexible way
   ___ d. establish rules and policies while at the same time bringing projects to completion

3. As a leader of others, I am inclined to ask questions like
   ___ a. How will this affect people's morale? Who should be informed? What is most important to people?
   ___ b. What's the immediate need? Where is the problem? What are the risks and benefits? How soon can we get started to resolve the matter?
   ___ c. What's involved? Who possesses the power or authority? What's the system? What's the strategy?
   ___ d. What's my responsibility? What's the proper sequence? Why should we change? Can this be justified?

4. My personal belief is that leaders
   ___ a. should run an organization/group/institution to meet current needs
   ___ b. should run an organization using solid and reliable information
   ___ c. should help organizations and institutions to operate according to their missions
   ___ d. must use their followers' talents and potentials to maximize the strength of the group or organization

5. In functioning as a leader of people, I (would) value
   ___ a. co-operative effort and good interpersonal relations
   ___ b. an environment that encourages flexibility and risk taking
   ___ c. ability and intelligence, complexity and principles
   ___ d. caution, care and accuracy

6. At work, I (would) orient to
   ___ a. things that affect current needs
   ___ b. things that meet or don't meet standards
   ___ c. planned change for the future
   ___ d. motivating others to get the best from them

7. What I appreciate in myself as a (potential) leader is
   ___ a. my active nature, cleverness and great sense of timing
   ___ b. my high energy level, the unique contributions I can make, as well as my ability to value others
   ___ c. my sense of responsibility, loyalty and industry
   ___ d. my genius, thinking ability and idea production

8. As a leader, I need others to
   ___ a. respond to me
   ___ b. appreciate me as an individual
   ___ c. recognize my talents and abilities
   ___ d. approve of my efforts

9. I would be irritated at work
   ___ a. if people criticized me and treated me impersonally
   ___ b. by silly mistakes, stupidity, ill logic and unnecessary duplication
   ___ c. by ignored deadlines, rule violations and transgressions of standard operating procedures
   ___ d. by having limits imposed, being told what to do and having to do things conventionally

461

10. I irritate others by
   ___ a. lack of follow through, careless haste and ill preparation
   ___ b. my sarcasm, seriousness or by my critical, pessimistic attitudes
   ___ c. hurting their feelings, nitpicking, my skepticism and by taking others for granted
   ___ d. getting emotional, moralizing, overextending myself and creating dependencies

11. My liabilities as a leader arise from the fact that I
   ___ a. often ignore problems and sweep difficulties under the rug while playing favourites and trying to please
   ___ b. am impatient with human concerns, escalating standards and lack of personal execution after designing something
   ___ c. am impatient about project delays, I make hasty decisions, I am preoccupied with negative outcomes and I believe long and hard work is the way to succeed
   ___ d. am unpredictable, impatient with theoretical abstractions, tactless, and unconcerned with the past or its implications for the future

Scoring: Next to each lettered sentence completion above you indicated your preference for it. Now record those preferences below. Once all statement preferences have been recorded, add up the columns: SP, SJ, NT and NF.

Score Calculation

	Styles			
	SP	SJ	NT	NF
1. Attention	a. ___	b. ___	c. ___	d. ___
2. Abilities	c. ___	d. ___	b. ___	a. ___
3. Questions asked	b. ___	d. ___	c. ___	a. ___
4. Personal beliefs	a. ___	b. ___	c. ___	d. ___
5. Personal values	b. ___	d. ___	c. ___	a. ___
6. Orientation	a. ___	b. ___	c. ___	d. ___
7. Appreciates in self	a. ___	c. ___	d. ___	b. ___
8. Needs	a. ___	b. ___	c. ___	d. ___
9. Sources of irritation	d. ___	c. ___	b. ___	a ___
10. Irritates others by	a. ___	b. ___	c. ___	d. ___
11. Liabilities as leader	d. ___	c. ___	b. ___	a. ___
Totals	___	___	___	___

Preference Values

Strong Preference	11–17
Moderate Preference	18–26
Low Preference	27–35
Little or No Preference	35–44

Note: A low score means a high preference and a high score means a low preference. Your lowest score reflects your dominant **leadership style**; your second lowest score indicates your backup style; your third lowest score points to a leadership style you use only occasionally; your highest score points to your least preferred leadership style.

leadership style
One of the styles of leadership (i.e., troubleshooter, traditionalist, visionary, catalyst) preferred by individuals based on their temperaments, which, as used here, refers to one's observable patterns of behaviour.

Results Suggest the Following About My Leadership Style

	Dominant Style	Back-up Style	Supportive Style	Least Used Style
Style				
Score				

Leadership Styles

SP = The Troubleshooter

SJ = The Traditionalist

NT = The Visionary

NF = The Catalyst

Summary Descriptions of Leadership Styles

The Troubleshooter (SP)

As a **troubleshooter**, you see yourself as a negotiator or "fire fighter." When problems arise, you like finding clever solutions for dealing with them. You have a laid-back, flexible style with people. Your sensing orientation makes you realistic and clearly focused on the here and now. You enjoy teamwork and fraternity among your colleagues. Your flexibility contributes to your willingness to take risks.

troubleshooter
Leadership style exemplified by the negotiator or "firefighter."

The Traditionalist (SJ)

As a **traditionalist**, you are a stabilizing force. You enjoy working according to established policies and procedures. You pay close attention to detail and display caution and care in whatever you do. Working hard, showing loyalty and displaying responsibility are important for you. Such actions help you to consolidate your working environment.

traditionalist
Leadership style that acts as a stabilizing force.

463

visionary
Leadership style exemplified by the master builder or architect of systems.

catalyst
Leadership style that addresses an organization's growth needs.

The Visionary (NT)

As a **visionary**, you see yourself as the master builder or architect of systems. You love to develop prototypes, conceptual frameworks, models and plans. You place great importance on logic and ingenuity in what you do. You orient yourself toward the future. Your primary focus is on the mission and systems of the organization or institution in which you find yourself.

The Catalyst (NF)

As a **catalyst** of an organization, you address its growth needs. Your personal charismatic nature helps you to energize others into participating and group decision making. Your concern is with morale, people and what they need to know. You believe that effective leadership requires all workers, subordinates and followers to use their talents.

Character is fate.
~Heraclitus

The temperament approach to leadership is based on the assumption that we all are social creatures who wish to please (or displease) those who have authority over us. We cannot be indifferent. We may or may not wish to learn for our professor, win for the coach, or mature as responsible persons for our parents. Even highly independent people who function quite well apart from others desire a thank-you for their efforts. In short, "We all want appreciation, and we want it from the person in charge" (Keirsey and Bates, 1984: 129). People usually want the appreciation expressed to be proportional to their achievement. The greater the achievement, the greater the hunger for appreciation. Thus, if you're a high achiever, you probably have more appetite for appreciation than do low achievers. The importance of appreciation in leadership is nicely summarized by Keirsey and Bates (1984: 130) as follows:

> Since leadership is getting people to do what the leader wants them to because the leader wants them to, and since achievement creates a hunger for appreciation by the leader, then it follows that the primary job of the leader is appreciation. Other tasks the leader may have must be regarded as trivial in comparison to this. The leader has got to learn how to notice achievement and thereupon to thank the follower for his gift.

Source: Reprinted by permission of the Board of Prometheus Nemesis Book Co.

If we are to function as effective leaders, we must become aware of and sensitive to differing temperaments, both our own and those of our charges. If, as leaders, we are not self-conscious with regard to our own temperaments, we will be unconsciously predisposed to acknowledge only those things we personally value and remain oblivious to achievements valued by other temperaments. So even if we try to appreciate others who follow, we could botch things up by unwittingly imposing our own style onto subordinates. We may thank them for doing things they consider irrelevant or trivial.

Your preparatory task as a leader, then, is to learn more about your own temperament to see how it influences your perceptions, judgments and actions. It is also your task to develop an understanding of other temperament types so that you can learn to tailor your efforts to appreciate in ways that fit the values, priorities and preferences of subordinate others. Self-Diagnostic 11.1 allowed you to gain some preliminary insight into your leadership temperament. Let's now look at all temperament types in a little bit more detail.

Keirsey and Bates (1984) have identified four basic temperaments. Each is named after a Greek figure who, in myth, displays a distinctive style and spirit of character. The four are listed below.

Student employees are more likely to do a good job if they feel appreciated by their boss.
Courtesy of Bart Coenders/iStockphoto.

- The **Dionysian Temperament** (named after Dionysus, the god of wild nature and wine)
- The **Epimethean Temperament** (named after Epimetheus, who was loyal and long suffering)
- The **Promethean Temperament** (named after Prometheus, the Titan pioneer of civilization)
- 11.7 • The **Apollonian Temperament** (named after Apollo, god of manly beauty, poetry, music and wisdom of oracles)

These temperament types can be superimposed on the Myers-Briggs table of psychological types (see Table 11.1). SP types are Dionysian in temperament, SJs are Epimetheans, NFs are Apollonians and NTs are Prometheans.

The Dionysian Troubleshooter Leaders with a **Dionysian temperament** negotiate with great facility. Realists at heart, they love to deal with practical problems, relishing occasions when they can unsnarl messes. These troubleshooters display an attitude of sureness and a knack for gaining co-operation from others. Leadership strengths include practicality, adaptability and informed awareness. Rather than fight the system, troubleshooters use it to solve problems. The Dionysian temperament contributes to the leaders' ability to respond easily to others, if presented ideas are concrete. Their flexibility and patience makes them easy to get along with. The Dionysian leader will often encourage risk taking, not bothered much by the possibility of failure. Dionysians try not to judge others, but rather accept their behaviour as matters of fact. Approval and appreciation are easily and often expressed.

Dionysian temperament
One of the four basic temperaments identified by Keirsey and Bates. Realists at heart, individuals with this temperament love to deal with practical problems and to unsnarl messes. Their strengths include practicality, adaptability and informed awareness.

465

Table **11.1**

Keirsey-Bates Temperaments Superimposed on Myers-Briggs Personality Types

ISTJ EPIMETHEAN	ISFJ EPIMETHEAN	INFJ APOLLONIAN	INTJ PROMETHEAN
ISTP DIONYSIAN	ISFP DIONYSIAN	INFP APOLLONIAN	INTP PROMETHEAN
ESTP DIONYSIAN	ESFP DIONYSIAN	ENFP APOLLONIAN	ENTP PROMETHEAN
ESTJ EPIMETHEAN	ESFJ EPIMETHEAN	ENFJ APOLLONIAN	ENTJ PROMETHEAN

Psychological Type	Temperament Type	Leadership Style
SP	Dionysian	Troubleshooter
SJ	Epimethean	Traditionalist
NT	Promethean	Visionary
NF	Apollonian	Catalyst

On the downside, Dionysians may become impatient with abstract, theoretical ideas. They prefer to avoid the unfamiliar. A present-day orientation may occasionally interfere with past decisions and prior commitments.

How to Appreciate Dionysian Followers

- Recognize the clever fashion in which they do their work. Notice the *way* something is done, not just what is done. The SP individual is process oriented, not product oriented.
- Provide companionship for celebrating successful results.
- Offer encouragement and support when things don't work out.
- Applaud Dionysian boldness, stamina, cleverness, adaptability and timing.
- Allow freedom for how tasks can be done.
- If possible, try not to let standard operating procedures interfere with the SP individual's preferred ways of doing things.

11.7 *The Epimethean Traditionalist* Leaders displaying an **Epimethean temperament** could be called traditionalists, stabilizers or consolidators. These "company people" focus on the organization. SJ leaders' abilities are found in establishing policies, procedures, rules, schedules, routines, regulations and hierarchies. They are very capable when forming lines of communication and following through with actions. Loyal to the company, institution or organization in which they work, traditionalist Epimetheans conduct their affairs in an orderly fashion, and thereby bring stability with them. Epimetheans possess a strong sense of social responsibility. They seek to learn their duties and then get busy doing them. Epimetheans are industrious indeed. Decisiveness is a distinctive strength of SJ leaders. They enjoy the decision-making process. Once decisions are made, they will patiently and steadily work, persevering through any hardships. Thorough in approach, Epimetheans tend to run efficient meetings with well-ordered agendas.

The dark side of the Epimethean temperament reveals possible leadership weaknesses. Decisions may be made too quickly or prematurely. SJs' concern with tradition and stability may cause them to defend outdated and questionable rules and regulations. The traditionalist leader may also not be responsive enough to the changing needs of an organization—especially during times of great transition. SJs also tend to see worst-case scenarios first. They may expend significant energy worrying about things that never happen. When making evaluations, Epimetheans tend toward black-and-white thinking. Unfortunately, evaluations of actions as either good or bad sometimes get transferred onto people. When this occurs, Epimethean traditionalists cause tensions by their blaming and negativity.

How to Appreciate Epimethean Followers

- Since SJs are product oriented, comment on how outcomes conform to established standards.
- Reward their responsibility, loyalty and hard work.
- Show an abundance of appreciation, even if pleasure is not shown.
- Pay attention to the caution, carefulness and thoroughness displayed and valued by the Epimethean.

11.7 *The Promethean Visionary* In contrast to troubleshooters who enjoy putting out fires and traditionalists who like to set up rules and regulations, people who display the **Promethean temperament** need to conceptualize. They are intuitive-thinking visionaries who are designers by nature. They are inspired and energized when asked to build, engineer or serve as conceptual architects. Prometheans pride themselves on their technical knowledge. They enjoy using intellect to sort out complexities, develop models or respond to design challenges. Since visionaries tend to focus on the future, they typically function well as agents of change. Since they perceive things globally,

Epimethean temperament Characterizes leaders who can be described as traditionalists and stabilizers.

Promethean temperament Leaders with this temperament are inspired and energized when asked to build, engineer, or serve as conceptual architects.

467

they find it easy to fit parts into total systems. Interworkings of systems are appreciated in terms of their short- and long-term implications.

Just like other temperament types, Promethean visionaries also have their weaknesses. Focused on ideas, they are often unaware of others' feelings. They often fail to appreciate the joys and hurts of others. As a result, visionaries may present themselves as distant and cold. Others may not feel comfortable in their presence and find it difficult to carry on a casual conversation, which is not good for morale and team building. The intellectual probing nature of visionaries may also make them appear as terminal skeptics, hair-splitters of the worst kind. Failure to notice feelings and an inclination to take practical contributions for granted are not things that endear visionaries to others. Troubleshooters and traditionalists should not be ignored or offended. They are needed to execute and implement in practical terms those models and plans envisioned by the Promethean.

How to Appreciate Promethean Followers

- Acknowledge their ideas.
- Present yourself as an intelligent listener.
- Avoid comments of a personal nature; respond by recognizing capabilities.
- Don't offend NTs by complimenting them on routine tasks well done; they may become suspicious.
- Try not to let rules, traditions and standard operating procedures get in the way of maximizing the NT's productivity.
- Comment on good uses of logic, reasoning and principle.

(11.7)

Apollonian temperament
One of the four basic temperaments identified by Keirsey and Bates. People who focus on the growth needs of organizations, they are capable of drawing out the best in others. Their finest leadership ability is their talent for turning any liability into an asset. For these catalysts, problems always offer opportunities.

468

The Apollonian Catalyst Leaders with an **Apollonian temperament** are very personable. They are "people people." Focusing on the growth needs of organizations, they are capable of drawing out the best in others. What you'll find is that Apollonians can easily become committed to the progress of those around them. NF catalysts are sensitive to possibilities for people, both in terms of career development and personal growth. Catalysts have a way of bringing out latent potentials in those with whom they work.

Interest in, and sensitivity to, people makes catalysts natural democratic leaders who instinctively prefer participatory processes and co-operative ways of doing things. NF leaders are born appreciators, in fact, always searching for the best in others. Catalysts are good listeners and, when communicating, typically display excellent verbal fluency. Catalysts have the ability to act as enthusiastic spokespeople for their organizations. They are charismatic, "superbly empathic, and have a flair for dramatizing the mundane events of living into something special" (Keirsey and Bates, 1984: 149). Probably the finest leadership ability possessed by Apollonian catalysts is their talent for turning any liability into an asset. A positive and productive outlook greets any obstacle. For catalysts, problems always offer opportunities.

Negatively speaking, NFs may use up too much of their energy responding to others. Overly generous with their time, they may neglect obligations and necessary regenerating recreational time may be lost. Without time for self-renewal, energies can be drained to the point where catalysts find themselves immobilized and unproductive. Also, when NFs provide empathic sensitivity to opposing groups and individuals, commitments to help both sides may leave them torn apart. NFs may be so in tune with the feelings and emotions of others that they find themselves wanting to please all of the people all of the time—and we know this is impossible. Finally, concern for others and willingness to help may foster "dependency relationships." People may inappropriately lean for support on NFs when more responsible independent action is called for.

How to Appreciate Apollonian Followers

- Express your appreciation of NFs in personal terms. See them as unique individuals making unique contributions.

- Provide constant approval and positive feedback. Negative criticism is likely to discourage and immobilize the NF.

- Encourage personal growth and development. Allow for autonomy and individual expression.

- Try to understand both the feelings and the ideas of an NF.

- Avoid impersonal treatment.

In this chapter we've addressed the importance of leadership for mastering human relations. We've contrasted leadership with management and examined more closely the influence of temperament on leadership. With the aid of Self-Diagnostic 11.1, you started to reflect on your own leadership temperament style. An outline of Keirsey and Bates's work has helped you to see how, according to their theoretical model, there are four basic temperament styles in leadership, each having its own distinctive strengths and weaknesses. By now you've learned how to appreciate, according to temperament type, people under your management, authority or control.

If leadership really does depend on appreciating others, as Keirsey and Bates claim, we are now much better prepared to move forward in our professional lives. We know something about our own temperament, what we need to feel appreciated, what we tend to appreciate in others and, finally, what others need from us to feel appreciated. This knowledge will certainly further our efforts to achieve success and will no doubt help us in the future.

On that positive note, our journey to human relations mastery comes to an end. I hope you enjoyed the ride. I certainly enjoyed providing the transportation!

When subjects do not get what they want from their rulers, the rulers cannot get what they seek from their subjects either. What rulers and subjects give each other is motivated by reciprocity, for which subjects will exert themselves to the full and lay down their lives in the interests of their rulers, while rulers will grant honours for the benefit of their subjects.
~*Lesson from The Masters of Huainan*

Source: Reprinted by permission of Shambhala Publications, Inc.

Study Guide

Key Terms

leadership (446)
management (447)
planning (447)
organizing (448)
implementation (449)
communicate (449)
control (449)
evaluate (449)
managerial functions (449)
managerial skills (449)
trait leadership theory (450)
supervisory ability (451)
need for occupational achievement (451)
intelligence (451)
decisiveness (451)
self-assurance (451)
initiative (451)
behavioural leadership (451)

theory X (452)
theory Y (452)
traditional autocratic approach (452)
paternalistic attitude (452)
three-factor theory (454)
The Michigan Studies (455)
job-centred style (455)
employee-centred style (455)
task-oriented (455)
situational leadership (456)
maturity (456)
achievement motivation (456)
responsibility (456)
ability (456)
education and experience (456)

relationship building (456)
task directing (456)
telling (457)
selling (457)
participating (457)
delegating (457)
temperament (459)
leadership style (463)
troubleshooter (463)
traditionalist (463)
visionary (464)
catalyst (464)
Dionysian temperament (465)
Epimethean temperament (467)
Promethean temperament (467)
Apollonian temperament (468)

Progress Check 11.1

Fill-in-the-Blank Questions

Instructions: Fill in each blank with the appropriate word from the list below.

maturity
appreciation
trait theory
Dionysian
three-factor theory
work
theory X
Promethean

Epimethean
planning
leadership
theory Y
Apollonian
situational leadership theory
task-oriented
temperament

470

1. _____ is the ability to cause people to work toward common goals.

2. _____ is what puts a thumbprint on each of our actions, making it recognizably our own.

3. According to Keirsey and Bates, we are all social creatures who need _____.

4. Loyal and persevering workers probably possess a(n) _____ temperament.

5. One function of managers is short- and long-term _____.

6. According to _____, leaders are born, not made.

7. If you think that people essentially dislike work and therefore must be coerced into performing, then you probably buy into the _____ conception of behavioural leadership.

8. _____ takes the position that mental and physical work are as natural as play, given favourable conditions.

9. Tannenbaum and Schmidt's _____ identifies five points between the two extremes of boss-centred and subordinate-centred leadership.

10. Job-centred leaders can be generally described as _____.

11. _____ holds that the effectiveness of any particular leadership style depends on the situation.

12. According to Paul Hersey and Kenneth Blanchard, follower _____ largely determines which leadership style should be used.

13. Leaders who function as realistic troubleshooters possess a(n) _____ temperament.

14. Visionary leaders, who love to conceptualize systems, possess a(n) _____ temperament.

15. People-sensitive leaders, who serve organizations well as catalysts, display a(n) _____ temperament.

True/False Questions

Instructions: Circle the appropriate letter next to each statement.

T F   1. Most people will never become leaders.

T F   2. Leadership is something that comes automatically with managerial authority.

T F   3. Management and leadership are virtually identical.

T F   4. The Promethean temperament reflects the preferences of the NT (intuitive-thinking type).

T F   5. The Dionysian leader is a troubleshooter.

T F   6. Individuals with Apollonian temperaments serve well as catalysts, fostering growth and development for people and organizations.

471

T F 7. Managers don't have to learn how to communicate well with people because they mostly plan and organize.

T F 8. The idea that tall people should be the preferred leaders in any group or organization is consistent with trait leadership theory.

T F 9. Leadership based on theory X assumptions about people reflects the traditional autocratic approach.

T F 10. Leadership based on theory Y assumptions should be practised when followers' basic needs have not been met.

T F 11. Tannenbaum and Schmidt's three-factor theory identifies several styles of leadership that fall somewhere between theory X and theory Y.

T F 12. The Michigan studies suggest that employee-centred leadership is preferable to job-centred leadership, though no performance guarantees are possible.

T F 13. Hersey and Blanchard's notion of task-relevant "maturity" entails achievement motivation, responsibility, ability, education and experience.

T F 14. Edwin Ghiselli deemed the following traits to be important to leadership: supervisory ability, need for occupational achievement, intelligence, decisiveness and initiative.

T F 15. Theory Y leadership will always work better than a leadership style based on theory X assumptions.

Summary

1. What is leadership?
   - the ability to influence the actions of others
   - the ability to cause others to work toward common goals within social, institutional or organizational settings
   - a dynamic process
   - the ability to draw trust, acknowledgment, risk and loyalty from followers

2. How does leadership relate to management?
   - they are not equivalent
   - leadership is but one management function
   - leadership can be found outside formal managerial settings
   - it is possible to lead but not manage

3. What are some management functions?
    *   planning: short- and long-term
    *   organizing: listing priorities and establishing procedures and guidelines
    *   implementation: delegating tasks and issuing responsibilities
    *   communication: transmitting information, exchanging ideas
    *   evaluation and control: maintaining quality, achieving goals

4. What are some approaches to leadership?

Trait Leadership Theory
*   personal characteristics define an effective leader; leaders are born, not made; important traits include supervisory ability, need for occupational achievement, intelligence, decisiveness, self-assurance, initiative

Behavioural Leadership (Theory X and Theory Y)
*   leadership/management decisions based on fundamental assumptions about human nature and human behaviour; according to theory X, people dislike work and need to be directed; according to theory Y, work is as natural as play and people will exercise personal initiative and self-control with commitment

Three-Factor Theory (Tannenbaum and Schmidt)
*   a continuum model identifying five points between two extremes of boss-centred leadership (theory X) and subordinate-centred leadership (theory Y)

The Michigan Studies: Job-Centred Versus Employee-Centred Leadership
*   job-centred leadership is very task oriented and directive, and uses power as well as sanctions
*   employee-centred leadership is people oriented; there is concern for employees' welfare; there is much delegation; studies suggest employee-centred leadership is better

Situational Leadership (Paul Hersey and Kenneth Blanchard)
*   effective leadership must take into account the "maturity" of the followers (i.e., their achievement motivation, responsibility, ability, education and experience); followers cannot be ignored in the leadership equation; there are four styles of situational leadership: telling, selling, participating and delegating

Keirsey and Bates Temperament Style Approach
*   effective leaders work with temperamental differences; good leaders achieve goals by learning to appreciate the efforts of subordinates; temperaments identified are the Dionysian, Epimethean, Promethean and Apollonian

Related Readings

Fiedler, Fred A. (1967). *Theory of Leadership Effectiveness*. New York: McGraw-Hill.

Fitzgerald, Catherine and Linda Kirby, (editors) (1996). *Developing Leaders: Research and Applications in Psychological Type and Leadership Development*. Palo Alto, CA: Consulting Psychologists Press.

Gordon, Thomas (1989). *P.E.T.: Parent Effectiveness Training*. New York: New American Library.

———— (1980). *The Essentials of Situational Leadership: An Approach for Increasing Managerial Effectiveness*. Escondido, CA: Leadership Studies Productions Inc.

Hirsh, Sandra (1997). *Using the Myers-Briggs Type Indicator in Organizations:* A Resource Book. Palo Alto, CA: Consulting Psychologists Press, Inc.

Keirsey, David (1989) *Portraits of Temperament*, 2nd edition. Del Mar, Ca: Prometheus Nemesis Book Company.

Keirsey, David and Marilyn Bates (1984, 1998). *Please Understand Me II*. Del Mar, CA: Prometheus Nemesis Book Company.

Appendix
Progress Check Answers

Progress Check 1.1

Fill-in-the-Blank Questions

1. warm
2. emoticons
3. proximity
4. repeated exposure effect
5. smiling
6. interpretation
7. responsibility
8. stereotyping
9. selective
10. halo effect
11. attribution errors
12. self-concept
13. static
14. self-awareness
15. open self
16. self-disclosure
17. self-esteem
18. personal responsibility
19. social comparison
20. self-talk

True/False Questions

1. F
2. F
3. F
4. T
5. F
6. T
7. T
8. F
9. T
10. T
11. T
12. T
13. F
14. F
15. F
16. F
17. T
18. F
19. T
20. F

Progress Check 2.1

Fill-in-the-Blank Questions

1. others
2. your type
3. outer
4. inner
5. bipolar
6. analytical
7. processes
8. realists
9. innovators
10. now
11. future
12. thinking
13. feeling
14. decision making
15. life-orientation
16. judging
17. perceptive
18. intuitive-feeling
19. patterns
20. Jung

True/False Questions

1. T
2. F
3. F
4. F
5. T
6. T
7. F
8. F
9. F
10. T
11. F
12. F
13. F
14. F
15. T or F

Progress Check 3.1

Fill-in-the-Blank Questions

1. Heraclitus
2. choices
3. character development
4. cognitively egocentric
5. self-serving bias
6. objectivity
7. defensive
8. perfectionist

9. insincerity, deceit
10. histrionics
11. conformity
12. healthy skepticism
13. aggressively arrogant
14. principle of charity
15. respect for persons
16. ethical reciprocity principle
17. integrity
18. responsibility
19. fairness
20. moderation
21. courage
22. prudence
23. electronic multi-tasking
24. punctuality
25. gossip
26. sensitivity
27. appearance
28. bragging

True/False Questions

1. F
2. T
3. T
4. F
5. F
6. F
7. F
8. F
9. F
10. T
11. F
12. T
13. T
14. T

15. T
16. T
17. F
18. F
19. T
20. F
21. F
22. T
23. T
24. F
25. F

Progress Check 4.1

Fill-in-the-Blank Questions

1. reaction formation
2. repression
3. regression
4. displacement
5. projection
6. fantasy formation
7. denial
8. intellectualization/isolation
9. identification
10. rationalization
11. circular reasoning
12. straw man
13. *ad hominem*
14. two-wrongs
15. red herring

True/False Questions

1. F
2. F
3. T
4. T

5. F
6. T
7. F
8. F
9. T
10. F
11. T
12. T
13. T
14. F
15. F

Progress Check 5.1

Fill-in-the-Blank Questions

1. motivations
2. locus of control
3. nirvana principle
4. instinct
5. thanatos
6. healthy
7. desirous
8. hierarchy of human needs
9. prepotency
10. aesthetic needs
11. metamotivations
12. emotional intelligence
13. personal competencies
14. alexithymia
15. accurate self-assessment
16. moral components
17. empathy
18. other-centredness
19. thematic apperception test
20. basic needs

21. pictures
22. thermostat
23. total behaviour

True/False Questions

1. F
2. F
3. T
4. T
5. T
6. F
7. T
8. F
9. F
10. F
11. F
12. F
13. F
14. F
15. F
16. T
17. T
18. T
19. T
20. F

Progress Check 6.1

Fill-in-the-Blank Questions

1. stressors
2. occupational stressors
3. type A personality
4. conform
5. general adaptation syndrome
6. alarm reaction
7. eustress
8. interactionist
9. ineffective coping strategies
10. defence mechanisms
11. irrational beliefs
12. cognitive appraisal
13. thinking styles
14. reframe
15. meditation
16. mandala
17. endorphins
18. clinical biofeedback
19. fight-or-flight
20. control

True/False Questions

1. F
2. T
3. T
4. F
5. F
6. T
7. T
8. F
9. T
10. T
11. F
12. T
13. F
14. T
15. T
16. F
17. T
18. T
19. F
20. T

Progress Check 7.1

Fill-in-the-Blank Questions

1. enneagram
2. wing
3. triads
4. levels
5. disintegration
6. self-image
7. meaning
8. spiritual
9. mass neurosis
10. suffering
11. archetypal
12. delusions of insignificance
13. inner guides
14. gift
15. kingdom

True/False Questions

1. F
2. F
3. T
4. F
5. T
6. T
7. F
8. T
9. F
10. T
11. F
12. T
13. T
14. T
15. F

477

Progress Check 8.1

Fill-in-the-Blank Questions

1. transactional analysis
2. ego states
3. child
4. rational
5. adult
6. parent
7. transactions
8. crossed
9. ulterior
10. complementary
11. strokes
12. life position
13. marasmus
14. self-stroking
15. game-playing
16. victim
17. persecutor
18. crossed transactions
19. intimacy
20. unequal relationships

True/False Questions

1. F
2. F
3. T
4. T
5. F
6. F
7. T
8. T
9. F
10. T
11. F
12. T
13. T
14. T
15. T
16. F
17. T
18. T
19. F
20. T
21. T
22. T
23. F
24. F
25. F

Progress Check 9.1

Fill-in-the-Blank Questions

1. Lawrence Kohlberg
2. Carol Gilligan
3. Deborah Tannen
4. men, women
5. justice and fairness, care and relationship
6. acculturation
7. cultural context
8. ethnocentrism
9. empathy
10. jargon
11. nonverbal communication
12. paralanguage
13. ambiguous
14. Charles Darwin
15. articulation
16. artifactual
17. body-type
18. kinesics
19. neurolinguistic programmers
20. public distance

True/False Questions

1. T
2. T
3. F
4. F
5. F
6. F
7. T
8. T
9. F
10. T
11. T
12. T
13. F
14. T
15. T
16. F
17. F
18. T
19. F
20. F

Progress Check 10.1

Fill-in-the-Blank Questions

1. conflict
2. wrong
3. psychological
4. intragroup
5. approach-approach

6. dysfunctional

7. self-knowledge

8. conflict orientation

9. constructive

10. passive-defensive

11. aggressive-defensive

12. conflict management styles

13. competing shark

14. collaborating

15. win-win

True/False Questions

1. F
2. F
3. F
4. F
5. T
6. F
7. T
8. T
9. T
10. F

11. T
12. F
13. T
14. T
15. F

Progress Check 11.1

Fill-in-the-Blank Questions

1. leadership
2. temperament
3. appreciation
4. Epimethean
5. planning
6. trait theory
7. theory X
8. theory Y
9. three-factor theory
10. task-oriented
11. situational leadership theory

12. maturity
13. Dionysian
14. Promethean
15. Apollonian

True/False Questions

1. F
2. F
3. F
4. T
5. T
6. T
7. F
8. T
9. T
10. F
11. T
12. T
13. T
14. T
15. F

References

Adler, Ronald B. and George Rodman (1994, 2000). *Understanding Human Communication*. Forth Worth, TX: Harcourt Brace College Publishers.

Adler, Ronald B. and Neil Towne (1996). *Looking Out, Looking In*, 8th edition. Fort Worth, TX: Holt, Rinehart and Winston.

Andersen, Peter A. and Ken Leibowitz (1978). "The Development and Nature of the Construct Touch Avoidance." *Environmental Psychology and Nonverbal Behaviour* 3: 89–106.

Arkin, R.M., A. Appleman and J.M. Burger (1980). "Social Anxiety, Self-Presentation, and the Self-Serving Bias in Causal Attribution." *Journal of Personality and Social Psychology* 38: 23–35.

Asch, Solomon, (1946). "Forming Impressions of Personality." *Journal of Abnormal and Social Psychology* 41, 258–290.

Atwater, Eastwood (1983, 1996, 1999). *Psychology of Adjustment*. Upper Saddle River, NJ; Prentice Hall.

Bandura, Albert (1965). "Influence of Model's Reinforcement Contingencies on the Acquisition of Imitative Responses." *Journal of Personality and Social Psychology* 1: 589–596.

Bandura, Albert, D. Ross and S.A. Ross (1963). "Imitation of Film-Mediated Aggressive Models." *Journal of Abnormal and Social Psychology* 66: 3–11.

Barocas, Harvey, Walter Reichman and Andrew Schwebel (1983, 1990). *Personal Adjustment and Growth*. New York: Brown and Benchmark.

Baron, Renee and Elizabeth Wagele (1994). *The Enneagram Made Easy*. New York: Harper Collins San Francisco.

Barr, Lee and Norma Barr (1989). *The Leadership Equation*. Austin, TX: Eakin Press. Barry, Vincent (1996). *Philosophy: A Text with Readings*, 6th edition. Belmont, CA: Wadsworth.

Baumeister, Roy and Mark Leary (1995). "The Need to Belong: Desire for Interpersonal Attachment as a Fundamental Human Motivation." *Psychological Bulletin* 117, 495–527.

Beesing, Maria, Robert Nogosek and Patrick O'Leary (1984). *The Enneagram: A Journey of Self-Discovery*. Denville, NJ: Dimension Books.

Benton, Douglas and Jack Halloran (1991, 1997). *Applied Human Relations*. Englewood Cliffs, NJ: Prentice Hall.

Berne, Eric (1961). *Transactional Analysis in Psychotherapy*. New York: Ballantine Books.

_____ (1976). *Beyond Games and Scripts*. New York: Grove Press, Inc.

_____ (1964, 1996). *Games People Play*. New York: Ballantine Books.

Birdwhistle, R. (1970). *Kinesics and Context* (Chapter 9). Philadelphia: University of Pennsylvania Press.

Bornstein, R.F. (1989). "Exposure and Affect: Overview and Meta-Analysis of Research, 1968–1987." *Psychological Bulletin* 106, 265–289.

Brigham, J.C. (1980). "Limiting Conditions of the Physical Attractiveness Stereotype: Attribution about Divorce." *Journal of Research on Personality* 14: 365–375.

Brooks, William D. and Phillip Emmert (1976). *Interpersonal Communication*. Dubuque, IA: William C. Brown Co.

Burr, W.R. (1973). *Theory Construction and the Sociology of the Family*. New York: Wiley, p. 367.

Buss, D.M. (1985). "Human Mate Selection." *American Scientist* 73, 47–51.

Callahan, Robert E. and Patrick C. Fleenor (1988). *Managing Human Relations: Concepts and Practices*. Toronto: Merrill Publishing.

Carver, C. and M. Scheier (1988, 1996). *Perspectives on Personality.* Boston: Allyn & Bacon.

Cherrington, David (1989). *Organizational Behaviour: The Management of Individual and Organizational Performance.* Boston: Allyn & Bacon.

Chesney, M.A. and R.H. Rosenman, editors (1985). *Anger and Hostility in Cardio-Vascular and Behavioral Disorders.* Washington, DC: Hemisphere.

Chodorow, Nancy (1974). "Family Structure and Feminine Personality," in *Women, Culture and Society*, edited by M.Z. Rosaldo and L. Lamphere. Stanford, CN: Stanford University Press.

Cleary, Thomas (editor/translator) (1990). "Lesson from the Master of Huainan," in *The Tao of Politics: Lessons of the Masters of Huainan.* Boston, MA: Shambhala Publications Inc.

Coleman, James C. and Constance Hammen (1974). *Contemporary Psychology and Effective Behavior.* Glenview, IL: Scott Foresman and Company.

Colletti, Lorraine et al. (1984). *System for Creating Organizational and Personal Effectiveness: Leader's Manual.* Plymouth, MI: Human Synergistics.

Coon, Dennis (1997, 1999). *Essentials of Psychology: Exploration and Application.* St. Paul, MN: West Publishing Co.

Cozby, Paul (1973). "Self-Disclosure: A Literature Review." *Psychological Bulletin* 79: 73–91.

Davis, M., E. Eschelman and M. McKay (1988). *The Relaxation and Stress Reduction Workbook*, 3rd edition. Oakland, CA: New Harbinger Publications.

Delongis, A. et al. (1982). "Relationship of Daily Hassles, Uplifts, and Major Life Events to Health Status." *Health Psychology* 1 (January): 119–136.

DeVito, Joseph (1992, 1997). *The Interpersonal Communication Book.* New York: HarperCollins.

——— (1993, 1998). *Essentials of Human Communication*, 3rd edition. New York: HarperCollins.

Dusay, John and Katherine Dusay (2000). "Transactional Analysis," in *Current Psychotherapies*, 6th edition, edited by R.J. Corsini. Itasca, IL: F.E. Peacock.

Ellis, Albert (1973, 1974). *Humanistic Psychotherapy: The Rational-Emotive Approach.* New York: McGraw-Hill.

——— (1991). *Reason and Emotion in Psychotherapy.* New York: Carol Pub. Group. Engler, Barbara (1985, 1999). *Personality Traits: An Introduction.* Boston: Houghton Mifflin Company.

Ernst, Ken (1972). *Games Students Play.* Berkeley, CA: Celestial Arts.

Fehr, L. (1983). *Introduction to Personality.* New York: MacMillan Publishing Co.

Frager, Robert and James Fadiman (1984, 1997). *Personality and Growth.* New York: Harper & Row Publishers.

Frankl, Viktor (1963, 2000). *Man's Search for Meaning.* New York: Beacon Press.

——— (1973, 1986). *The Doctor and the Soul: From Psychotherapy to Logotherapy.* New York: Vintage Books.

Franzoi, S.I. and M.E. Herzog (1987). "Judging Physical Attractiveness: What Body Aspects Do We Use?" *Personality and Social Psychology Bulletin* 13, 19–33.

——— (1978, 1997). *The Unheard Cry for Meaning.* New York: Pocket Books.

Freed, Alvyn and Margaret Freed (1973). *T.A. for Kids.* Sacramento, CA: Jalmar Press.

Freedman, A.S. and S. Booth-Kewley (1987). "The Disease-Prone Personality." *American Psychologist* 43 (1): 2–14.

Freud, Sigmund (1915, 1924, 1953). "Repression." In *The Complete Works of Sigmund Freud*, Standard Edition, Volume 14. London: Hogarth Press.

——— (1930). *Civilization and Its Discontents.* In *The Complete Works of Sigmund Freud*, Standard Edition, Volume 22. London: Hogarth Press.

——— (1972). *The Ego and the Id.* Joan Riviere (trans.) and James Strachey (ed.). New York: W.W. Norton & Co.

——— (1973). *New Introductory Lectures on Psychoanalysis.* Middlesex, England: Pelican Books.

——— (1974). *Beyond the Pleasure Principle*. James Strachey (ed.). New York: W.W. Norton & Co.

Friedman, Howard, and Ronald Riggio (1981), "Effect of Individual Differences in Nonverbal Expressiveness on Transmission of Emotion." *Journal of Nonverbal Behaviour*, 6.

Friedman, Meyer and Ray Rosenman (1974). *Type A Behaviour and Your Heart*. New York: Random House Inc.

Friedman, M. et al. (1984). "Alteration of Type A Behaviour and Reduction in Cardiac Recurrence in Postmyocardial Infarction Patients." *American Heart Journal* 10 (2): 237–248.

Fuller, Rodney (1996). "Human-Computer-Human Interaction: How Computers Affect Interpersonal Communication," in *Computers, Communication and Mental Models*, edited by D.L. Day and D.K. Kovacs. London: Taylor & Francis.

Gardner, Howard (1985). *Frames of Mind: The Theory of Multiple Intelligence*. New York: Basic Books.

Ghiselli, Edwin E. (1971). *Exploration in Managerial Talent*. Santa Monica, CA: Goodyear Publishing.

Gibson, J., J. Ivancevich and J. Donnelly (1999). *Organizations: Behaviour-Structure-Processes*, 10th edition. Homewood, IL: Richard D. Irwin, Inc.

Gilbert, Shirley J. (1976). "Empirical and Theoretical Extensions of Self-Disclosure," in *Explorations in Interpersonal Communication,* edited by Gerald R. Miller. Newbury Park, CA: Sage Publications Inc.

Gilligan, Carol (1982, 1983). *In a Different Voice: Psychological Theory and Women's Development*. Cambridge, MA: Harvard University Press.

Gilliland, Burl, Richard James and James Bowman (1989, 1993, 1998). *Theories and Strategies in Counselling and Psychotherapy*. Englewood Cliffs, NJ: Prentice Hall.

Glasser, William (1975). *Schools without Failure*. New York: Harper & Row.

——— (1975). *The Identity Society*, revised edition. New York: Harper & Row.

——— (1975). *Reality Therapy: A New Approach to Psychiatry*. New York: Harper & Row.

——— (1976). *Positive Addiction*. New York: Harper & Row.

——— (1986). *Control Therapy-Reality Therapy Workbook*. Los Angeles: The Institute for Reality Therapy.

——— (1989). *Control Theory: A New Explanation of How We Control Our Lives*. New York: Harper & Row.

——— (1993). *The Quality School Teacher*. New York: Harper Perennial

——— (1995) *The Quality School: Managing Students without Coercion*, 3rd expanded edition. New York: HarperCollins.

Goleman, Daniel (1997). *Emotional Intelligence*. New York: Bantam Books.

Goleman, Daniel (2000). *Working with Emotional Intelligence*. New York: Bantam Books.

Good, Katherine C. and Lawrence R. Good (1973). "Attitude Similarity and Attraction to an Instructor." *Psychological Reports* 33 (August): 335–37.

Goulding, M. and R. Goulding (1979, 1997). *Changing Lives through Redecision Therapy*. New York: Brunner/Hazel.

Greenberg, Jerrold (1990, 1999). *Comprehensive Stress Management*. Dubuque, IA: Wm. C. Brown Publishers.

Gross, James, and Robert Levenson (1997), "Hiding Feelings: The Acute Effects of Inhibiting Negative and Positive Emotion." *Journal of Abnormal Psychology*.

Haas, John, and Christa Arnold (1995), "An Examination of the Role of Listening in Judgments of Communication Competence in Co-Workers." *The Journal of Business Communication*, April.

Hall, Calvin (1954, 1976). *A Primer of Freudian Psychology*. New York: New American Library.

Hall, Edward T. (1969). *The Hidden Dimension*. Garden City, NY: Doubleday and Co. Inc.

——— (1977). *The Silent Language*. Garden City, NY: Anchor Press/Doubleday.

Hamachek, Don E. (1997). *Encounters with Others: Interpersonal Relationships and You*. New York: Holt, Rinehart and Winston.

——— (1997). *Encounters with the Self*. New York: Holt, Rinehart and Winston.

Harris, A.B. and T.A. Harris (1985). *Staying OK*. New York: Harper & Row Publishers.

Harris, Thomas (1967, 1973). *I'm OK—You're OK*. New York: Avon Books.

Hergenhahn, B.R. (1990, 1998). *An Introduction to Theories of Personality*. Upper Saddle River, NJ: Prentice Hall.

Hersey, Paul and Kenneth Blanchard (1982, 1996). *Management of Organizational Behavior: Utilizing Human Resources*. Englewood Cliffs, NJ: Prentice Hall.

Herzberg, F., B. Mausner and B. Synderdman (1959). *The Motivation to Work*. New York: John Wiley & Sons.

Hiltz, S. R., and M. Turoff (1978). *The Network Nation: Human Communication via Computer*. Cambridge, MA: The MIT Press.

Hirsh, Sandra and Jean Kummerow (1989). *Lifetypes*. New York: Warner Books.

Hjelle, Larry and Daniel Ziegler (1981, 1992). *Personality Theories: Basic Assumptions, Research and Applications*. New York: McGraw-Hill Book Company.

Hokanson, J.E. and M. Burgess (1962). "The Effects of Three Types of Aggression on Vascular Processes." *Journal of Abnormal and Social Psychology* 64: 446–449.

Holmes, T.H. and R.H. Rahe (1967). "Social Readjustment Rating Scale." *Journal of Psychosomatic Research* 11: 216.

Horvath, T. (1981). "Physical Attractivness: The Influence of Selected Torso Parameters." *Archives of Sexual Behaviour* 10, 21–24.

Houston, Jean (1997). *The Search for the Beloved: Journeys in Sacred Psychology*. New York: The Putnam Pub. Group.

James, Muriel and Dorothy Jongeward (1971, 1978, 1996). *Born to Win*. New York: Signet.

——— (1975). *The People Book: Transactional Analysis for Students*. Don Mills, ON: Addison-Wesley Publishing Co.

Johnson, David W. (1990, 1999). *Reaching Out: Interpersonal Effectiveness and Self-Actualization*. Englewood Cliffs, NJ: Prentice Hall.

Johnson, R.H. and J.A. Blair (1994). *Logical Self-Defence*, 3rd edition. Toronto: McGraw-Hill Ryerson Ltd.

Jones, E.E. and R.E. Nisbett (1971). *The Actor and the Observer: Divergent Perceptions of the Causes of Behaviour*. Morristown, NJ: General Learning Press.

Jourard, Sydney M. (1971). *Self-Disclosure: An Experimental Analysis of the Transparent Self*. Toronto: John Wiley & Sons Inc.

——— (1971). *The Transparent Self*. New York: D. Van Nostrand Co.

Joy, L.A., M.M. Kimbal and M.C. Zabrack (1986). "Television and Aggressive Behaviour," in *The Impact of Television: A Natural Experiment Involving Three Towns*, edited by T.M. Williams. New York: Academic Press.

Keirsey, David and Marilyn Bates (1984, 1998). *Please Understand Me II*. Del Mar, CA: Prometheus Nemesis Book Company.

_____ (1993). *Type Talk at Work*. New York: Delacorte Press.

Kelley, Robert E. (1998), *How to Be a Star at Work*. New York: Times Books.

Keyes, Margaret Frings (1992). *Emotions and the Enneagram: Working through Your Shadow Lifescript*, revised edition. Muir Beach, CA: Molysdatur Publications.

Knapp, Mark L. and Judith A. Hall (1996). *Nonverbal Communication in Human Interaction*, 4th edition. Fort Worth, TX: Holt, Rinehart and Winston.

Kohlberg, Lawrence (1976). "Moral Stages and Moralization: The Cognitive-Developmental Approach," in *Moral Development and Behavior,* edited by T. Lickona. New York: Holt, Rinehart and Winston.

Kroeger, Otto and Karen Thuesen (1993). *Type Talk at Work*. New York: Delacorte Press.

Lafferty, Clayton and Ron Phillips (1990). *LSI Conflict: Self-Development Guide*. Plymouth, MI: Human Synergistics.

Lafferty, Clayton et al. (1984, 1988). *Stress Processing Report*. Plymouth, MI: Human Synergistics.

Lawrence, Gordon (1993, 1996, 1997). *People Types and Tiger Stripes: A Practical Guide to Learning Styles*. Gainesville, FL: Center for the Applications of Psychological Type, Inc.

Lazarus, R.S. (1981). "Little Hassles Can Be Dangerous to Health." *Psychology Today* 15 (July): 58–62.

Lazarus, R.S. and S. Folkman (1985). *Stress, Appraisal and Coping*. New York: Springer.

Lee, Royce and M.H. Bond (1996). *How Friendship Develops out of Personality and Values: A Study of Interpersonal Attraction in Chinese Culture*. Unpublished manuscript, Chinese University of Hong Kong, p.384.

Lefrancois, Guy R. (1999). *The Lifespan*, 6th edition. Belmont, CA: Wadsworth Publishing Co.

Levin, Pamela (1988). *Becoming the Way We Are: An Introduction to Personal Development in Recovery and in Life*. Deerfield Beach, FL: Health Communications Inc.

—— (1988). *Cycles of Power*. Deerfield Beach, FL: Health Communications Inc.

Levinger, G. (1986). "Editor's Page." *Journal of Social Issues* 42: 3.

Liebert, Robert and Michael Spiegler (1990). *Personality: Strategies and Issues*, 6th edition. Pacific Grove, CA: Brooks/Cole Publishing.

Likert, Rensis (1961). *New Patterns of Management*. New York: McGraw-Hill.

Loomis, Mary E. (1991). *Dancing the Wheel of Psychological Types*. Wilmette, IL: Chiron Publications.

Luft, Joseph (1970, 1984). *Group Process: An Introduction to Group Dynamics*. Palo Alto, CA: Mayfield Publishing Company.

Lussier, Robert N. (1990, 1995). *Human Relations in Organizations: A Skill Building Approach*. Homewood, IL: Irwin

Mack, D. and D. Rainey (1990). "Female applicants' grooming and personal selection." *Journal of Social Behaviour and Personality* 5, 399–407.

Maslow, Abraham (1977). *The Farther Reaches of Human Nature*. New York: Penguin Books.

—— (1987). *Motivation and Personality*, 3rd edition. New York: Harper & Row.

Masserman, J.H. (1961). *Principles of Dynamic Psychiatry*. Philadelphia: W.B. Saunders Company.

McClelland, David (1962). "Business Drive and National Achievement." *Harvard Business Review* (July–August): 99–112.

McCullough, J.L. and T.M. Ostrom (1974). "Repetition of Highly Similar Messages and Attitude Change." *Journal of Applied Psychology* 59, 395–397.

McGregor, Douglas (1960, 1985). *The Human Side of Enterprise*. New York: McGraw-Hill.

Montagu, Ashley (1971). *Touching: The Human Significance of the Skin*. San Francisco: Harper & Row.

Monte, Christopher (1987, 1995). *Beneath the Mask: An Introduction to Theories of Personality*. Fort Worth: Holt, Rinehart and Winston.

Monteiro, L.A. (1978). "College Women and Self-Esteem." *The New York Times*, December 10, p. 85.

Mulac, A. and M.J. Rudd (1977). "Effects of Selected American Regional Dialects upon Regional Audience Members." *Communication Monographs* 44: 184–195.

Murray, R. (1943). *Thematic Apperception Test Pictures and Manual*. Cambridge, MA: Harvard University Press.

Myers, David G., and Steven J. Spencer (2004). *Social Psychology*, 2nd edition. Toronto: McGraw-Hill.

Myers, Isabel Briggs and Mary H. McCaulley (1988). *Manual: A Guide to the Development and Use of the Myers-Briggs Type Indicator*. Palo Alto, CA: Consulting Psychologists Press.

Napoli, Vince, James M. Kilbride and Donald Tebbs (1992). *Adjustment and Growth in a Changing World*, 4th edition. St. Paul, MN: West Publishing.

Newcomb, T.M. (1961). *The Acquaintance Process*. New York: Holt, Rinehart and Winston, p. 367.

O'Connor, Joseph and John Seymour (1993). *Introducing Neuro-Linguistic Programming: The New Psychology of Personal Excellence*. London: Mandala.

Pearson, Carol (1991). *Awakening the Heroes Within: Twelve Archetypes to Help Us Find Ourselves and Transform Our World*. New York: Harper San Francisco.

———— (1993). *For Journey Guides: An Awakening the Heroes Within Handbook for Helping Professionals*. College Park, MD: A Meristem Project.

Pearson, Carol and Katherine Pope (1981). *The Female Hero in American and British Literature*. New York: R.R. Bowker Co.

Pearson, Carol and Sharon V. Seivert (1988). *Heroes at Work*. College Park, MD: A Meristem Project

Pearson, Carol, Donna L. Shavlik and Judith G. Touchton, editors (1989). *Educating the Majority: Women Challenge Tradition in Higher Education*. New York: MacMillan Publishing Co.

Pelletier, Kenneth (1992). *Mind as Healer, Mind as Slayer*. New York: Bantam Doubleday Dell Publishing Group Inc.

Pennebacker, James W. (1991). *Opening Up: The Healing Power of Confiding in Others*. New York: Morrow.

Peterson, Brent D. and Paul R. Timm. (1999). *People at Work: Human Behavior in Organizations*. West Publishing.

Rahim, M.A. (1983). "A Measure of Styles of Handling Interpersonal Conflict." *Academy of Management Journal* (June): 368–376.

Reece, Barry L. and Rhonda Brandt (2000). *Human Relations: Principles and Practices*, 4th edition. Boston: Houghton Mifflin Co.

Reis, H.T. et al. (1990). "What Is Smiling Is Beautiful and Good." *European Journal of Social Psychology*, 20, 259–267.

Riggio, R.E. and S.B. Woll (1984). "The Role of Nonverbal Cues and Physical Attractiveness in the Selection of Dating Partners." *Journal of Social and Personal Relationships* 1, 347–357.

Riso, Don Richard and Russ Hudson (1987, 1996). *Personality Types: Using the Enneagram for Self-Discovery*. Boston: Houghton Mifflin.

———— (1990, 2000). *Understanding the Enneagram: The Practical Guide to Personality Types*. Boston: Houghton Mifflin.

———— (1992, 1994). *Discovering Your Personality Type: The Enneagram Questionnaire*. Boston: Houghton Mifflin.

———— (1993). *Enneagram Transformations: Releases and Affirmations for Healing Your Personality Type*. Boston: Houghton Mifflin.

———— (1994, 1996). *The Riso-Hudson Enneagram Type Indicator* (Version 2.0). New York: Enneagram Personality Types Inc.

Robards, Martine J. and Steven Coats (1988). "Everything You Always Wanted to Know about Becoming a MBTI Wizard in Organizations." *Insight*, vol. 3. Edmonton, AB: Psychometrics Canada Ltd.

Robbins, Stephen P. (1993, 1998). *Organizational Behavior: Concepts, Controversies and Applications*. Englewood Cliffs, NJ: Prentice Hall.

Rohr, Richard and Andreas Ebert (1992). *Experiencing the Enneagram*. New York: Crossroads.

Rosenthal, Robert and L. Jacobson (1968). *Pygmalion in the Classroom*. New York: Holt, Rinehart and Winston.

Ryckman, Richard M. (2000). *Theories of Personality*, 5th edition. Pacific Grove, CA: Brooks/Cole Publishing.

Samovar, Larry A., Richard E. Porter and Nemi C. Jain (1990). "Intercultural Communication Problems and Guidelines," in *Bridges Not Walls*, edited by John Stewart. New York: McGraw-Hill.

Schultz, Duane (1977). *Growth Psychology: Models of the Healthy Personality*. New York: D. Van Nostrand Company.

Seligman, M.E.P. (1975). *Helplessness: On Depression, Development, and Death*. San Francisco: Freeman.

Selye, Hans (1974, 1975). *Stress without Distress*. Philadelphia: J.B. Lippincott Co.

———— (1976). *The Stress of Life*. New York: McGraw-Hill Book Co.

Sheppard, J.A. and A.J. Strathman (1989). "Attractiveness and Height: The Role of Stature in Dating Preference, Frequency of Dating and Perception of Attractiveness." *Personality and Social Psychology Bulletin* 15, 617–627.

Smith, Barry D. and Harold J. Vetter (1991). *Theories of Personality*, 2nd edition. Englewood Cliffs, NJ: Prentice Hall.

Spitz, R. (1945). "Hospitalism: Genesis of Psychiatric Conditions in Early Childhood." *Psychoanalytic Study of the Child* 1: 53–74.

Steele, Claude (1997), "A Threat in the Air: How Stereotypes Shape Intellectual Identity and Performance." *American Psychologist*, June.

Steiner, Claude (1977). *The Original Warm Fuzzy Tale*. Sacramento, CA: Jalmar Press.

Stewart, David and Gene Blocker (1996). *Fundamentals of Philosophy*. Pacific Grove, CA: Brooks/Cole Publishing Co.

Stewart, Greg L., and Kenneth P. Carson (1995), "Personality Dimensions and Domains of Service Performance: A Field Investigation." *Journal of Business Psychology,* 9.

Stewart, John and Gary D'Angelo (1997). *Together: Communicating Interpersonally*, 5th edition. Reading, MA: Addison-Wesley.

Tannen, Deborah (1990). *You Just Don't Understand: Women and Men in Conversation.* New York: Ballantine Books.

Tannenbaum, Robert and Warren Schmidt (1973). "How to Choose a Leadership Pattern." *Harvard Business Review*. May–June.

Thomas, Kenneth W. (1977). "Toward Multi-Dimensional Values in Teaching: The Example of Conflict Behaviors." *Academy of Management Review* 2: 487.

Vaillant, George. (1977). *Adaptation to Life*. Cambridge: Harvard University Press.

Wallace, Patricia (1999) *The Psychology of the Internet*. Cambridge, UK: Cambridge University Press.

Wasielewski, Patricia (1985). "The Emotional Basis of Charisma." *Symbolic Interaction*, 8.

Weaver, Richard (1993, 1996). *Understanding Interpersonal Communication*. New York: HarperCollins.

Weiten, Wayne (1988). "Pressure as a Form of Stress in Its Relationship to Psychological Symptomatology." *Journal of Social and Clinical Psychology* 61: 127–139.

Weiten, Wayne and J. Dixon (1984). "Measurement of Pressure as a Form of Stress." Paper presented at the meeting of the American Psychological Association, Toronto, Ontario.

Weiten, Wayne and Margaret A. Lloyd (1994, 2000). *Psychology Applied to Modern Life*. Pacific Grove CA: Brooks/Cole Publishing Co.

Weiten, Wayne, Margaret A. Lloyd and Robin L. Lashley (1991, 1999). *Psychology Applied to Modern Life: Adjustment in the 90s*. Pacific Grove, CA: Brooks/Cole Publishing Co.

Wells, Fran and B. Siegel (1961). "Stereotype Somatypes." *Psychological Reports* 8: 1175–1178.

Williams, K. and L. Zadro (2001). "Ostracisim: On Being Ignored, Excluded and Rejected," in *Interpersonal Rejection*, edited by M. Leary, p. 366. New York: Oxford University Press.

Witmer, D.F. and S.L. Katzman (1997 March). "On-Line Smiles: Does Gender Make a Difference in the Use of Graphic Accents?" *Journal of Computer-Mediated Communication* [online], 2 (4) Available: http://jcmc.indiana.edu/vol2/issue4/witmer1.html

Woodhouse, Mark B. (1997). *A Preface to Philosophy*, 6th edition. Belmont, CA: Wadsworth Publishing Co.

Wright, L. (1988). "The Type A Behaviour Pattern and Coronary Artery Disease: Quest for the Active Ingredients and the Elusive Mechanism." *American Psychologist* 43(1): 2–14.

Index

A

A-B-C model of psychological functioning, 249–251/251*f*
ability, 456
accent, 382, 384
accommodating, 425, 430–431
acculturation, 370
accurate self-assessment, 206
achievement drive, 211
achievement motivation, 456
actor-observer differences, 30
acts of kindness, 100–101
actualize, 184
ad hominem fallacy, 150–151, 151*f*
adaptability, 209–210
Adapted Child, 324–325
addition, 384
adrenalin junkies, 242
Adult ego state, 325
adult-world, 104
aesthetic needs, 187
aggrandize, 424
aggression, 181, 182*f*, 248
aggressive arrogance, 93–94
aggressive-defensive orientation, 424–425
alarm reaction, 236–239, 238*t*
alexithymia, 206
alienation, 298
angular ulterior transactions, 334, 335*f*
anima, 366
animus, 366
anxiety, 124
Apollonian temperament, 465, 468–469
appealing to authority, fallacy of, 156–158, 158*f*
appearance, physical, 112
appearance *vs.* reality, 30*f*–31*f*
application exercises
  appropriate conflict management style, 433
  be the star that you are, 13*t*
  boss-behaviour analysis, 453
  classroom chemistry, 71–73
  clothes talk, 389
  cognitive coping, 257
  Dad or Joe: who should go?, 362
  dealing with defensiveness, 147
  don't talk to me!, 381
  dream work, 127
  ego states and the effective memorandum, 316, 349
  events and ego-state reactions, 316, 350–351
  exploring your ego states, 329–330
  focused attention, 259
  following the leader at Camp Athabasca, 458–459
  identify the fallacy, 162–163
  may I have the first section, please?, 24
  my life story as a heroic myth, 307
  name the defence mechanism, 146–147
  personal experience of conflict, 426
  picture, picture in the book, 192–193
  self-expressions, 288
  take me to your leader, 448
  TBWA—Total Behaviour and Wants Analysis, 200–203
  TV types have different stripes, 73
  type tips for conflict resolutions, 437–439
approach-approach conflict, 418
approach-avoidance conflict, 418–419
archetypal psychology
  alienation, 298
  call to the quest, 300–301
  described, 271, 297–298
  diseases in the human kingdom, 298
  ego stage, 305
  existential vacuum, 298
  heroic journey concept, 298–300
  Heroic Myth Index, 302, 305
  journey stage, 302
  metaphysical blues, 298
  preparation stage, 302
  psychological archetypes, 301–309
  return stage, 302
  self stage, 305
  soul stage, 305
arguments, tips for, 162*t*
Aristotle, 91, 104
arrogance, aggressive, 93–94
articulation, 384
artifactual communication
  bodily adornment, 387–388
  clothing, 387
  colour, 386–387
  defined, 386
artistic creation, 182
assertiveness, self-quiz, 84
asymmetries, 367
attack, 150
attitude, 51
attitude adjustments, 86–95
attitudinal values, 296
attractiveness, 388
attribution errors
  actor-observer differences, 30
  defined, 30
  self-serving bias, 32
attributions, 30*f*
authentic self, 271
authoritarian control, 452
authoritative appeals, 156–158, 158*f*
authority, 425
autogenic training, 261
avoidance-avoidance conflict, 418
avoiders, 424
avoiding/withdrawing, 430
Awakening the Heroes Within: Twelve Archetypes to Help Us Find Ourselves and Transform Our World (Pearson), 297, 302

B

B-motivation, 189–190
B-values, 190*t*
bad faith, 270, 436
bandwagon effect, 92
Baron, Renee, 273
Barr, Lee, 447, 449
Barr, Norma, 447, 449
basic needs
  defined, 194
  need for freedom, 195
  need for fun, 195
  need for power, 195
  need to belong, 194–195
  need to survive and reproduce, 195
Bates, Marilyn, 459–469
begging the question, 153–154, 154*f*
behaviour, reasons for, 176
behavioural approaches to stress management, 254–262
behavioural leadership, 451–453
behavioural system
  behaviour as feedback loop, 199–200
  defined, 197
  total behaviour, 198–199
behaviours, 421
being motivation, 189–190
beliefs, 245, 421
belong, need to, 194–195
Berne, Eric, 318, 319, 340–341
"Best and Worst Leaders" (Lao-Tzu), 449
biofeedback, 260–261
Black, Arthur, 379
Black Elk, 98
Blanchard, Kenneth H., 456
Blemish, 342
blind ambition, 207
blind self, 6
bodily adornment, 387–388
bodily movement (kinesics)
  defined, 392
  eye movements, 392–393, 394*f*
  facial movements, 392–393
  physical gestures, 392
  posture, 392
body types, 390*t*, 391*f*
bond-builders, 219–221
Bonisteel, Roy, 293
Born to Win (James and Jongeward), 318
bragging, 112–113
Briggs, Katharine, 47, 50, 52
building bonds, 219–220

C

call to the quest, 300–301
catalyst, 464
catalysts, 468
Categorical Imperative, 96
categories, 22–23
catharsis, 181–182
causal connection, 156
cell phones, etiquette and, 107–108, 109

change catalyst, 219
character, 84–86
character development, 85, 96–106
charity, 94–95
Cherry, Don, 181
Chessman, Caryl, 339
Child ego state, 322–325, 322f
childhood orientations, 278
Chin, Jacqueline, 101
Chodorow, Nancy, 364
choice theory
    basic needs, 194–196
    behaviour as feedback loop,
        199–200
    behavioural system, 197–200
    defined, 194
    described, 199f
    need for freedom, 195
    need for fun, 195
    need for power, 195
    need to belong, 194–195
    need to survive and
        reproduce, 194
    pictures, and satisfaction of needs,
        196–197
    total behaviour, 198–199
chronemics, 398–399
circular reasoning, 153–154, 154f
Clemons, Michael (Pinball), 450
clinical biofeedback procedures,
    260–261
closing, 25–26
clothing, 387
coalition building, 215
cognitive appraisal, 244
cognitive egocentrism, 86
cognitive needs, 187
cognitive reframing, 253–254
cognitively egocentric, 435
cold impressions, 18–19
cold prickles, 337
collaborating/problem confronting,
    432, 434–436
collaboration, 220
collective neurosis, 292
collective thinking, 292
Colletti, Lorraine, 251
colour, 386–387
"Coming and Going" (Masten), 360
commitment, 211
common language, 375–377
communicate, 449
communication
    arguments, tips for, 162t
    and culture, 369–378
        see also intercultural
            communication
    defensiveness in. See psycho-logical
        defensiveness
    and economic
        interdependence, 369
    and ethnocentrism, 372
    gender communications, 361–368
    irrational thought processes, 122
    jargon, 376
    miscommunication, 148, 371
    morals and virtues for, 96–106
    nonverbal communication. See
        nonverbal communication
    precommunication attitudes, 375
    and self-esteem, 16t
    and social skills, 217
    unconscious influences, 122

communication process
    with cultural overlay, 371f
    noise, 112
communication tips
    for extraverts, 56
    feelers, 65
    for introverts, 55–56
    for intuitives, 60–61
    judgers, 66–68
    perceivers, 68–69
    for sensors, 59–60
    thinkers, 64–65
competing, 429–430
competition, 425
complement, 382
complementary transactions,
    331–332, 331f, 332f
Comprehensive Stress Management
    (Greenberg), 261
compromising, 431
computerese, 371
conciliatory, 423
conflict
    approach-approach conflict, 418
    approach-avoidance conflict,
        418–419
    avoidance-avoidance conflict, 418
    benefits of, 420–421
    defined, 414
    dysfunctional conflict, 421
    functional conflict, 421
    and goals, 427
    intergroup conflict, 417
    interpersonal conflict, 417
    intragroup conflict, 418
    intrapsychic conflict, 418
    "me or you versus them," 417
    nature of, 414
    psychological conflict, 417
    psychological orientations,
        421–425, 422f
    and relationships, 427
    social conflict, 417–418
    as stressor, 235
    types of, 417–420, 418f
conflict management
    constructive conflict resolution,
        collaborative style, 434–436
    and social skills, 217–218
    symptoms of inner peace, 437
    win-win conflict resolution, 433
conflict management styles
    accommodating/smoothing,
        430–431
    avoiding/withdrawing, 430
    collaborating/problem confronting,
        432, 434–436
    compromising, 431
    defined, 427
    described, 429f, 432t
    forcing/competing, 429–430
    self-diagnostic, 427
    type tips for, 437–439
conflict orientation
    aggressive-defensive orientation,
        424–425
    constructive orientation to conflict,
        422–423
    defined, 421
    described, 422f
    passive-defensive orientation, 424
"Conflict Resolutions for Life"
    (Keith), 419

conformity, 91–92, 235, 293
conscientiousness, 209
conscious, 125, 126f
conscious motivations, 176
consolidators, 467
constancy principle, 180
construction
    categories, 22–23
    defined, 21
    perceptual filtering, 23
    of personal and social reality,
        20–23
constructive orientation to conflict,
    422–423
contradict, 382
control
    authoritarian control, 452
    defined, 449
    external locus of control, 176–177
    of instincts, 182–183
    internal control index, 178–197
    internal locus of control, 176–177
    management and, 449
    over-control, 209
    self-control, 208–209
control theory. See choice theory
controllability, 245
Controlling Parent, 325
cooperation, 220
coping mechanism, 125
coping strategies
    A-B-C model of psychological
        functioning, 249–251, 251f
    aggression, 248
    autogenic training, 261
    clinical biofeedback procedures,
        260–261
    cognitive approaches, 249–254
    cognitive reframing, 253–254
    effective strategies, 249–262
    human synergistics,
        251–253, 252f
    with limited effectiveness,
        246–249
    meditation, 254–258
    path of disintegration,
        279–280, 280f
    physical and behavioural
        approaches, 254–262
    physical exercise, 260
    SCOPE (System for Creating
        Organizational and Personal
        Effectiveness), 251
    self-deception, 248–249
    stress processing report (SPR), 251,
        252–253
    thinking styles, 251–253
    WDEP method, 262
    withdrawal, 247–248
courage, 105–106
creating meaning in life, 293–294
Critical Parent, 325
crossed transactions, 333, 333f, 334f
culture
    see also intercultural
        communication
    acculturation, 370
    defined, 370
    described, 370–371
    economic interdependence, 369
    enculturation, 370
    and nonverbal
        communication, 381

politics,   369
and space communication,   393
and time,   398–399

D

daily hassles,   236
Darwin, Charles,   143
daydreams,   129
death instincts,   181
deceit,   90
decision making,   61–62, 63*t*
decisiveness,   451
deep relaxation,   254
defensive response patterns,   145*t*
defensiveness,   88–89
    see also psychological defensiveness
    as coping mechanism,   125
    defined,   88, 124
    excessive defensiveness, and
        neurosis,   128
    irrational defensiveness,   124–125
    unconscious defensiveness,
        124–125
deficiency motivation,   189
delegating,   457
delusions of insignificance,   300
denial,   143
depression,   137
Diagnostic and Statistical Manual of
    Mental Disorders,   273
"different voice of morality,"
    363–364
Dionysian temperament,   465–466
discriminatory attitudes,   94
diseases in the human kingdom,   298
displacement,   134–137, 135*f*
distortions of reality,   124
distress,   243, 252
diversion,   150
diversionary and intimidation
    tactics,   124
diversity, sensitivity to,   111–112
dominance,   36
dominator,   425
duplex ulterior transactions,
    334, 335*f*
dysfunctional conflict,   420

E

Early Adult,   322
Early Parent,   323
earned strokes,   336
Ebert, Roger,   392
economic interdependence,   369
education,   456
ego,   125, 128, 270
ego self,   270
ego stage,   305
ego state
    Adult ego state,   325
    Child ego state,   322–325, 322*f*
    defined,   318
    Parent ego state,   325–326
    self-diagnostic,   319–321
    strokes,   336
    structural and functional depictions
        of,   326*f*
    three ego states forming
        personality,   322–326, 322*f*
    typical behaviours,   326*t*
egocentrism,   86–88
egogram,   321*f*

electroencephalogram,   261
electromyogram,   261
electronic multi-tasking,   107
electronics, etiquette and,
    107–108, 109
Ellis, Albert,   249–250
email addresses,   19
emoticons,   18
emotional blind spots
    blind ambition,   207
    hunger for power,   207
    striving for perfection,   207
    unrealistic goals,   207
emotional competence framework
    defined,   204
    described,   205*f*
    empathy,   212–215
    motivation,   205, 210–212
    personal competencies,   205–212
    self-awareness,   205–208
    self-regulation,   205, 208–210
    social competencies,   212–221
    social skills,   215–221
emotional intelligence (EQ),   205
    see also emotional competence
        framework; social skills
emotions
    see also emotional competence
        framework
    alexithymia,   206
    catharsis,   181–182
empathy
    defined,   212
    described,   212
    developing others,   213
    and intercultural communication,
        375–376
    leveraging diversity,   214
    other-centredness,   213
    political awareness,   215
    service orientation,   213
    understanding others,   212–213
empiricists,   20
employee-centred style,   455
enculturation,   370
energy model,   180
energy sources,   52–55, 55*t*
enlarging,   25
enneagram
    childhood orientations,   278
    and contemporary psychology,   273
    defined,   271
    described,   272, 272*f*
    development of your type,
        273–278
    and Jungian, Myers-Briggs
        personality types,   274*f*
    levels of development,   279
    origins of,   273
    path of integration,   279–280, 280*f*
    personal growth through,
        270–272
    self-diagnostic,   275–277
    and traditional psychology,   273
    transformational/spiritual
        psychology,   272
    travel tips for life,   282–285, 290
    types, described,   278*f*
environment,   385–386
Epimethean temperament,   465, 467
Ernst, Ken,   345
eros,   180–181
escalates,   425

esteem needs,   186–187
ethical reciprocity principle,
    97–98, 99
ethno-centric,   94
ethnocentrism,   372
etiquette, electronics and,
    107–108, 109
eustress,   243
evaluate,   449
excessive self-confidence,   208
exhaustion stage,   239
existential frustration,   190, 292
existential vacuum,   298
experience,   456
experiential value,   296
external locus of control,   176–177
external orientation,   52
extraverts
    communication tips for,   56
    described,   54–55
eye movements,   392–393, 394*f*

F

facial movements,   392–393
failure,   235
fair,   423
fairness,   103–104
fallacies. *See* logical fallacies
fallacy of appealing to authority,
    156–158, 158*f*
fallacy of guilt by association,
    160–161, 161*f*
false consciousness,   270
false perception of difference,   373
false self,   270
familiarity,   245
fanaticism,   292, 293
fantasy formation,   141
fatalistic attitude,   292
fear,   88–89
Fechner, Gustav,   180
feelers
    communication tips for,   62–64
    described,   62
feelings,   206
fight-or-flight response,   237
finding meaning in life,   293–294
First Nations, and medicine wheel,
    288–289, 289*f*
focused attention,   259
force,   425
forcing/competing,   429–430
Fox,   431
*Frames of Mind: The Theory of Multiple
    Intelligences* (Gardner),   204
Frankl, Victor
    collective neurosis,   292
    existential frustration,   292
    finding and creating meaning in
        life,   293–294
    future orientation,   294
    love, as source of meaning,   296
    mission in life,   297
    noögenic neurosis,   292
    pursuit of happiness,   296
    roots of meaningless,   292–293
    self-transcendence,   271, 294
    the soul,   291–297
    suffering,   297
    suicide, and meaninglessness
        of life,   290
    three dimensions of life,   291

will-to-meaning, 291
work, as source of meaning, 295–296
Free Child, 324
freebie strokes, 336
freedom, need for, 195
Freud, Sigmund
    on consciousness, 125
    denial, 143
    energy model, 180
    human personality functioning, 47
    id, 134
    nirvana principle, 180
    pleasure principle, 180
    psychodynamics of enneagram personality types, 273
    repressed impulses, 129
    view of, 183
Freudian terms, 126f
Friedman, Howard, 216
frustration, 235
fun, need for, 195
functional conflict, 420
functional distance, 35
future orientation, 294

G
galvanic skin response (GSR), 261
games
    Blemish, 342
    breaking up psychological games, 347
    defined, 340
    described, 340
    High and Proud, 345–346
    If It Weren't for You (IFWY), 341
    persecutor, 347
    Rapo, 344
    rescuer, 347
    roles in, 346–347
    See What You Made Me Do (SWYMD), 344–345
    victim, 347
    "Why Don't You"-"Yes, But" (YDYB), 342–343, 344f
Games People Play (Berne), 318
Games Students Play (Ernst), 345–346
Gardner, Howard, 204
gender
    defined, 361
    identity formation, 364–365
    social morality, construction of, 361–365
gender communications
    asymmetries, 367
    eye movements, 393
    gossip talk, 368
    interpretation of responses, 361–363
    language usage, gender differences in, 366–368
    lecturing, 368
    listening, 368
    moral voice, 363–365
    private speaking, 367
    public speaking, 367–368
    rapport talk, 367–368
    report talk, 367–368
    self-aggrandizing information, 368
general adaptation syndrome (GAS)
    alarm reaction, 236–239, 238t
    defined, 236

described, 242f
    exhaustion stage, 239
    resistance phase, 239
"Getting the Job Done" (anonymous), 449
Ghiselli, Edwin, 451
Gibson, Dan, 259
Gilligan, Carol, 363
Glasser, William, 184–190, 252
goals, 427
Golden Mean, 104
Golden Rule, 97–98, 99
Goleman, Daniel, 204, 205, 216–217
    see also emotional competence framework
gossip, 110–111
gossip talk, 368
Gretzky, Wayne, 149
group synergy, 228
groupthink, 91–92, 93
guilty by association, fallacy of, 160–161, 161f
Gurdjieff, George Ivanovich, 273

H
Hall, Edward T., 395
halo effect
    defined, 29
    reverse halo effect, 29
Hamachek, Don, 328n
hand, non-dominant, 57
happiness, 296
haptics, 399–401, 401f, 402f
Harris, Thomas, 337–340
healthy skepticism, 92–93
height, 392–393
Heraclitus, 84
The Hero Within: Six Archetypes We Live By (Pearson), 297
heroic journey
    defined, 297
    described, 271
    as model for living, 298–300
Heroic Myth Index, 302, 305
hidden messages, 334
hidden self, 7
hierarchy of human needs
    actualize, 184
    aesthetic needs, 187
    cognitive needs, 187
    defined, 184
    described, 185f
    esteem needs, 186–187
    physiological needs, 185
    prepotency, 185
    safety and security needs, 185–186
    self-actualization needs, 188
    social needs for love and belonging, 186
High and Proud, 345–346
high sensation seekers, 242
histrionics, 90–91
homeostasis, 180
homepage construction, 19
honesty, 103
honourable intentions, 436
Horney, Karen, 273
Hudson, Russ, 273
human diversity, 51
human relations, morals, manners, and attitude, 82–113
The Human Side of Enterprise (McGregor), 451
human synergistics, 251–253, 252f

humanistic explanation of personality, 47
hunger for power, 207
hypo-stress, 242

I
I, 270
IBM, 420
Ichazo, Oscar, 273
id, 125, 134
ideal world, 197
identification, 137–139
identity formation, 364–365
If It Weren't for You (IFWY), 341
I'm Not OK-You're Not OK life position, 338
I'm Not OK-You're Ok life position, 338
I'm OK-You're Not OK life position, 338–339
I'm OK-You're OK (Harris), 318, 332
I'm OK-You're OK life position, 339–340
imminence, 246
implementation, 449
influence, 216
initiative, 211–212, 451
inner peace, 437
innovation, 209–210
insincerity, 90
instincts
    aggression, 181, 182f
    control of, 182–183
    death instincts, 181
    eros, 180–181
    and motivation, 180
    thanatos, 180–181
    types of, 180–181
Institute for Reality Therapy, 194
insulate, 424
integrity, 98, 100
intellectualization, 142–143
intelligence, 451
intentions, 421
interactionist model on stress
    beliefs, 245
    cognitive appraisal, 244
    controllability, 245
    described, 243–244, 247f
    familiarity, 245
    imminence, 246
    interests, 244
    personal wants, 244–245
    predictability, 246
    values, 244
interactionist perspective, 420
interactionist theory of knowledge, 20
intercultural communication
    common language, use of, 375–377
    defined, 370
    empathy, 374
    ethnocentrism, 372
    eye movements, 392–393
    false perception of difference, 364
    forms of, 370–371
    improvement of, 374–378
    jumping to conclusions, 377–378
    meanings attributed to words, 374
    miscommunication and, 361
    perception of difference, 373
    point of view, 378–379
    precommunication attitudes, 375

self-knowledge, 374–375
   and stereotype, 373
interests, 244
intergroup conflict, 417
internal control index, 178–197
internal locus of control, 176–177
internally centred, 423
interpersonal attraction
   defined, 35
   dominance, 36
   functional distance, 35
   physical attractiveness, 35–36
   proximity, 35
   repeated exposure effect, 35
   similarity, 36
interpersonal communication. *See*
   communication
interpersonal conflict, 417
interpreting, 26
intimate distance, 395–396
intimidation, 150
intragroup conflict, 418
intrapsychic conflict, 418
introverts
   communication tips, 55–56
   described, 52–54
intuitives
   communication tips, 59–61
   described, 58–59
irrational beliefs, 250
irrational defensiveness, 124–125
irrational thought processes, 122
isolation, 142–143

J
jargon, 376
job-centred style, 455
Joe dilemma, 361
The Johari Window, 8*f*, 10*f*
Johnson, David, 420, 433
Journal of Happiness, 101
journey stage, 302
judgers
   communication tips, 66–69
   described, 62–66
judgment function, 51
Jung, Carl, 47, 50, 51, 52, 54,
   273, 366

K
Kant, Immanuel, 96
Kaplan, Robert E., 207
karma, 100–101
Keirsey, David, 53, 459–469
Keith, Kent, 419
Kilbridie, James, 241*n*
kinesics. *See* bodily movement
   (kinesics)
Kohlberg, Lawrence, 361, 363, 365

L
Lafferty, J.C., 251, 255
Lao-Tzu, 449
Lawrence, Gordon, 47–48
leadership
   autocratic leadership, 452, 454
   behavioural leadership, 451–453
   catalyst, 464
   continuum of leadership
      tactics, 454*f*
   defined, 446
   delegating, 457
   emotional domain, 218

and empathy, 213
employee-centred style, 455
great Canadian leaders, examples
   of, 446
job-centred style, 455
and life, 446–450
maturity, 456–457
participating, 457
participative leadership,
   452–453, 454
relationship building, 456
self-diagnostic, 460–463
selling, 457
situational leadership,
   455–457, 458*f*
as social skill, 218–219
task directing, 456
telling, 457
temperament, 459–469
   see also temperament
theory X, 452
theory Y, 452–453
three-factor theory, 454
traditionalist, 463
trait leadership theory, 450–451
transformational leadership, 219
troubleshooter, 467
University of Michigan
   studies, 455
visionary, 464
vs. management, 446–450, 448*f*
leadership style, 463, 464
learned helplessness, 247
leveraging diversity, 214
libido, 180
life-event stressors, 231
life positions
   defined, 337
   I'm Not OK-You're Not OK, 338
   I'm Not OK-You're Ok, 338
   I'm OK-You're Not OK, 338–339
   I'm OK-You're OK, 339–340
   self-stroking, 339
   stroke deprivation, 339
   survivors, 339
lifestyle orientation, 62–64, 7*t*
Likert, Rensis, 455
linguistic softeners, 18–19
listening, 336, 368
Little Professor, 322
logical fallacies
   ad hominem fallacy, 150–151, 151*f*
   attack, 150
   begging the question,
      153–154, 154*f*
   circular reasoning, 153–154, 154*f*
   conscious motivations, 176
   defined, 148
   diversion, 150
   fallacy of appealing to authority,
      156–158, 158*f*
   fallacy of guilt by association,
      160–161, 161*f*
   as intimidation, 150
   red herring fallacy, 158–160, 160*f*
   slippery slope fallacy,
      155–156, 156*f*
   straw man fallacy, 152–153, 152*f*
   two-wrongs fallacy, 154–155, 155*f*
logotherapy, 291
Loomis, Mary E., 289
loss, 235
love, 296
low sensation seekers, 242

M
management
   communicate, 449
   control, 449
   defined, 447
   employee-centred style, 455
   evaluate, 449
   implementation, 449
   job-centred style, 455
   organizing, 448
   planning, 447–448
   vs. leadership, 446–450, 448*f*
manager factors, 454
managerial functions, 449–450
managerial skills, 449–450
mandala, 257–258, 258*f*
manners, 106–113
mantra, 257–258
marasmus, 336
Maslow, Abraham, 47, 183, 188, 189,
   189*n*, 190*n*
Maslow's humanistic theory of
   motivation, 183, 188
Masserman, Jules, 133
maturity, 456–457
McClelland, David, 193
McClung, Nellie, 446
McGregor, Douglas, 451
McLuhan, Marshall, 378
"me or you *versus* them," 417
meaning in life
   attitudinal values, 296–297
   collective neurosis, 292
   creating, 293–295
   existential frustration, 292
   finding, 293–294
   future orientation, 294
   logotherapy, 291
   love, as source of meaning, 296
   meaningless in modern
      society, 292
   mission, 297
   noögenic neurosis, 292
   pursuit of happiness, 296
   roots of meaningless, 292–293
   self-transcendence, 294
   spiritual emergency, 291
   suffering and, 297
   three dimensions of life, 291
   will-to-meaning, 291
   work, as source of meaning,
      295–296
meaningless
   defined, 293
   in modern society, 292
   roots of meaningless, 292–293
medicine wheel, 288–289, 289*f*
meditation, 254–258
metamotivation, 189–190
metaneeds, 190*t*
metapathology, 190, 190*t*
metaphysical blues, 298
Michigan studies, 455
Mind as Healer, Mind as Slayer
   (Pelletier), 261
mindless conformity, 92
mindless obedience, 293
miscommunication, 148, 371
mission, 297
moderation, 104–105
Mongrain, Myriam, 100–101
moral reasoning, 361–363
moral voice, 363–364
morality of care, 365

morality of impersonal justice, 365
morality of relationship, 365
morals, 96–106
motivation
  achievement drive, 211
  commitment, 211
  and conflict orientation, 421
  defined, 175
  external locus of control, 176–177
  initiative, 211–212
  internal locus of control, 176–177
  mysteries of, 174
  nature of, 175–177
  optimism, 211–212
  as personal competency, 205, 210–212
  reasons for behaving, 176
  theories of motivation. *See* motivation theories
  unconscious motivations, 176
  variance in, 175
Motivation and Personality (Maslow), 184
motivation theories
  being motivation, 189–190
  choice theory, 194–200
  energy model, 180
  eros, 180–181
  homeostasis, 180
  instincts, 180, 181
  Maslow's humanistic theory of motivation, 183, 188
  metamotivation, 189–190
  nirvana principle, 180
  pleasure principle, 180
  psychoanalytic theory, 177
  thanatos, 180–181
multicultural, 369
multi-tasking, electronics and, 107
Murray, R., 192
Myers, Isabel Briggs, 47, 50, 52
Myers-Briggs Type Indicator (MBTI), 465–466, 466t

N
name-dropping, 112–113
Napoli, Vince, 241n
Naranjo, Claudio, 273
Natural Child, 324
need for freedom, 195
need for fun, 195
need for occupational achievement, 451
need for power, 195
need to belong, 194–195
need to survive and reproduce, 194
needs. *See* basic needs; hierarchy of human needs
network, 215
neurosis, 128
Nietzsche, Friedrich, 143
nirvana principle, 180
noise, 122
non-dominant hand, 57
nonverbal communication
  accent of verbal message, 382
  artifactual communication, 386–388
  bodily movement (kinesics), 392–393
  body types, 390t, 391f
  classification of, 383–402

complement a verbal message, 382
contradict a verbal message, 382
and culture, 382
defined, 380
described, 380
environment, 385–386
eye movements, 392–393, 394f
facial movements, 392–393
multichannelled nature of, 381
nature of, 380–382
paralanguage, 380, 383–384
physical appearance, 388–392
physical gestures, 392
posture, 392
regulate, 382
repeat, 383
social function, 381
space communication (proxemics), 393–398
spatial distances, 395–396
time communication (chronemics), 398–399
touch communication (haptics), 399–401, 401f, 402f
and verbal communication, 382–383
noögenic neurosis, 292
Nurturing Parent, 325

O
objective perspective, 423
objectivity, 88
occupational stressors, 231–233
open self, 6
optimism, 211–212
organizing
  closing, 25–26
  defined, 25
  enlarging, 25
  management and, 448
  simplifying, 25
orientation, 421
orientation to outer world, 62–64, 63t
ostracism, 139
other-centredness, 213
over-control, 209
Owls, 432

P
paralanguage, 380, 383–384
Parent ego state, 325–326
participating, 457
passive-defensive orientation, 424
paternalistic attitude, 452
path of disintegration, 279–280, 280f
path of integration, 279–280, 280f
Pearson, Carol, 271
  see also archetypal psychology
peer pressure, 93
Penfield, Wilder Graves, 323, 324
The People Book (James and Jongeward), 347
perceivers
  communication tips, 66–69
  described, 66
perception
  construction of personal and social reality, 20–23
  defined, 20
  described, 20–21
  and interpersonal attraction, 34–36

interpreting, 26
organizing, 25
and psychological orientation, 411
reducing errors in, 33–34
responsibility for, 26–27
selecting, 24
perception of difference, 374
perceptual errors
  attribution errors, 30–32
  defined, 27
  halo effect, 29
  proximity, 32
  Pygmalion effect, 29
  role definition, 33
  self-fulfilling prophecy, 28–29
  stereotyping, 27–28
perceptual filtering, 23
perceptual mental processes, 51
perfection, 207
perfectionism, 89, 425
perfectionist, 89
persecutor, 347
personal competencies
  defined, 205
  motivation, 205, 210–212
  self-awareness, 205–208
  self-regulation, 205, 208–210
personal distance, 396
personal identity issues, 139
personal integrity, 209
personal liberation, 270
personal wants, 244–245
personality
  defined, 46
  energy model, 180
  humanistic explanation, 47
  Jung's analytical theory, 47
  Myer-Briggs Type Indicator (MBTI), 47
  psychoanalytic explanation, 47
  temperament, and leadership, 459–461
  theories of, 47
  Type A personalities, 233–234
  Type B personalities, 233–234
  understanding your personality, 46–47
personality types
  decision making, 61–62, 63t
  discrimination and, 76
  energy sources, 52–55, 55t
  and enneagram types, 280–282
  external orientation, 52
  extraverts, 54, 55
  feelers, 62
  guidelines for proper application, 74–76
  information gathering, 57–59, 59t
  introverts, 52–55
  intuitives, 58–59
  judgers, 63–65
  lifestyle orientation, 63–65, 67t
  Myers-Briggs Type Indicator, 50
  non-judgmental terms, 76
  perceivers, 66
  pigeon-holing and, 74
  preference scales, 52, 52t
  recognizable patterns of diversity, 51–52
  sensors, 57–58
  seriousness of, 74
  strong preference *vs.* ability, 75
  summary of, 70t

thinkers, 61–62
value of all types, 75
persons, respect for, 96–97
Phillips, Ronald, 251
phobias, 129
physical appearance, 112, 389–393
physical approaches to stress
    management, 254–262
physical attractiveness, 35
physical exercise, 260
physical gestures, 392
physiological needs, 185
Piaget, Jean, 86
pictures, 196–197
pigeon-holing, 74
pitch, 385
planlessness, 292
planning, 447–448
pleasure principle, 180
pluralistic, 369
Poehler, Amy, 108
"A Poison Tree" (Blake), 136
political awareness, 215
politics, 369
politeness, 109–111
posture, 392
power
    defined, 425
    and dominators, 425
    hunger for power, 207
    need for power, 195
Powers of the Four Directions, 289
"Practicing Compassion Increases
    Happiness and Self-Esteem" (Chin
    and Shapira), 101
pragmatic approach, 422
precommunication attitudes, 376
preconscious, 125, 126f
predictability, 246
predispositions, 421
preparation stage, 302
prepotency, 185
pressure, 234–235
pressure to conform, 235
pressure to perform, 235
principle of charity, 95
Principle of Moderation, 104
private speaking, 367
problem confronting, 432
projection, 88, 131–133, 132f
Promethean temperament, 465,
    467–468
proxemics. See space communication
    (proxemics)
proximity, 32, 35
prudence, 106
psychic energy, 134
psycho-babble, 371
psycho-logical defensiveness, 88–89
    see also defensiveness
    defence mechanisms. See
        psychological defence
        mechanisms
    defined, 88, 122
    and fallacies, 149–161
        see also logical fallacies
psychoanalysis, 125
psychoanalytic explanation of
    personality, 47
psychoanalytic theory, 177
psychological archetypes
    see also archetypal psychology
    archetypes and their stories, 308t
    defined, 301

described, 306t
ego stage, 305
journey stage, 302
preparation stage, 302
return stage, 302
self stage, 305
soul stage, 305
psychological attitude, 52
psychological conflict, 417
psychological defence mechanisms
    defensive response patterns, 145t
    defined, 128
    denial, 143
    displacement, 134–137, 135f
    fantasy formation, 141
    identification, 137–139
    innovation, attitude toward, 210
    intellectualization, 142–143
    isolation, 142–143
    projection, 131, 133, 132f
    rationalization, 129–131
    reaction formation, 133–134
    regression, 139–141
    repression, 128–129
    sublimation, 144
    summary of, 145
    unconscious level, 128
psychological games. See games
psychological orientations to conflict.
    See conflict orientation
psychological stressors
    conflict, 235
    defined, 233
    frustration, 235
    pressure, 234–235
    Type A personalities, 233–234
    Type B personalities, 233–234
psychological triads, 278f
psychological type, 47
    see also personality types
psychopathology of everyday
    life, 129
psychosexual disorders, 129
psychosomatic illnesses, 129
public distance, 396
public speaking, 367–368
punctuality, 109
pursuit of happiness, 296
Pygmalion effect, 29

Q
quality world, 197

R
Rapo, 344
rapport talk, 367–368
rate of speech, 383–384
rational-emotive behaviour therapy
    (REBT), 249
rational engagement, rule of, 95
rationalist thinkers, 20
rationalization, 129–131
Rawls, John, 88
reaction formation, 133–134, 248
realistic, 422
reality therapy, 262
Reason and Emotion in Psychotherapy
    (Ellis), 260
reasonable, 423
red herring fallacy, 158–160, 160f
regression, 139–141
regulate, 382–383
regulates, 424

relationship, 365, 427
relationship building, 456
The Relaxation and Stress Reduction
    Workbook (David, Eschelman and
    McKay), 261
religio-centric, 94
religions, Golden Rule and, 99
repeat, 383
repeated exposure effect, 35
report talk, 367–368
repression, 128–129
reproduction, need for, 194
requested strokes, 336
rescuer, 347
resistance phase, 239
respect for persons, 96–97
responsibility, 101–103, 456
return stage, 302
reverse halo effect, 29
Riggio, Ronald, 216
right speech, 109–111
Riso, Don Richard, 89, 273, 278
role definition, 33
roles, 33, 346–347
rule of rational engagement, 95

S
safety and security needs, 185–186
Salovey, Peter, 204
satori, 254
Saxe, John G., 415
scapegoating, 132
Schmidt, Warren, 454
Schultz, Johannes H., 261
SCOPE (System for Creating
    Organizational and Personal
    Effectiveness), 251
See What You Made Me Do (SWYMD),
    344–345
selecting, 24
selectivity, 28
self
    authentic self, 271
    defined, 4
    ego self, 270
    false self, 270
    self-awareness, 6–8
    self-concept, 4–5
    self-disclosure, 8–12
    self-esteem, 12–16
    self-presentation, 17–19
    and self-transcendence, 270–271
self-absorption, 294
self-actualization needs, 188
self-actualized individuals, 188–189
self-aggrandizing information, 368
self-assessment
    accurate self-assessment, 206
    and blind ambition, 207
    blind spots, 207–208
    and hunger for power, 207
    striving for perfection, 207
    and unrealistic goals, 207
self-assurance, 451
self-awareness
    accurate self-assessment, 206
    blind self, 6
    defined, 6, 205
    feelings, 206
    hidden self, 7
    increase self-awareness, 7–8
    lack of, 206
    open self, 6

self-confidence, 208
    unknown self, 7
self-centred, 87
self-concept
    defined, 4
self-confidence, 208
self-control, 208–209
self-deception, 248–249
self-deprecation, 137
self-diagnostics
    assessing your leadership
        temperament, 460–463
    conflict management style, 427
    current thinking, and stress,
        255–256
    defensiveness, 122–124
    ego state, 319–321
    enneagram type, 275–277
    Heroic Myth Index, adaptation of,
        302–305
    how tactile are you?, 403–404
    internal control index, 178–197
    personality preferences, 48
    reasonableness, 149
    self-concept, 5
    stress, 240–241
self-disclosure
    defined, 8
    described, 8–10
    guidelines, 10–12
    other's self-disclosures, responding
        to, 15t
self-empowered, 423
self-esteem
    defined, 12
    described, 12–16
    enhancement of, 16–17
    and interpersonal
        communication, 16t
self-fulfilling prophecy, 28–29
self-knowledge
    defined, 46
    and intercultural communication,
        376–377
    need for, 46–47
    and personality, 47
self-mutilation, 181
self-presentation
    cold impressions, 18–19
    described, 17
    email addresses, 19
    homepage construction, 19
    warm impressions, 18–19
self-regulation
    adaptability, 209–210
    conscientiousness, 209
    defined, 205
    innovation, 209–210
    self-control, 208–209
    trustworthiness, 209
self-serving bias, 32, 87
self stage, 305
self-stroking, 339
self-tests. See self-diagnostics
self-transcendence, 270–271, 294
self-transformation, 271
Seligman, Martin, 247
selling, 457
Selye, Hans, 236, 237, 251
    see also general adaptation
        syndrome (GAS)
sensors
    communication tips, 59–61
    described, 57–58
separation from others, 139

service orientation, 213
Shakespeare, 34, 90, 120, 139, 249,
    298, 390
Shapira, Leah, 101
Sharks, 429–430
similarity, 35
simplifying, 25
Siskel, Gene, 392
situation factors, 454
situational leadership, 455–457, 460f
"The Six Men of Indostan"
    (Saxe), 415
skepticism, 92–93
skin colour, 393
slippery slope fallacy, 155–156, 156f
slurring, 385
smoothing, 430–431
social competencies
    defined, 212
    empathy, 212–215
    social skills, 212, 215–221
social distance, 396
social morality, construction of,
    361–365
social needs for love and
    belonging, 186
social prejudice, 132
social readjustment rating scale, 232t
Social Sciences Research Council of
    Canada (SSHRC), 101
social skills
    building bonds, 219–220
    change catalyst, 219
    collaboration, 220
    communication, 217
    conflict management, 217–218
    cooperation, 220
    defined, 212
    described, 215
    influence, 216
    leadership, 218–219
    team capabilities, 220–221
socio-centric, 94
soul stage, 305
sour grapes rationalization, 130
space communication (proxemics)
    defined, 393
    described, 393–394
    intimate distance, 396
    personal distance, 396
    public distance, 396
    social distance, 396
    spatial distances, 395–396
    status and space, 397–398
    territoriality, 397
spatial distances, 395–396
speech, right, 109–111
spiritual emergency, 291
stabilizers, 467
Star Teams, 221
status
    and space, 397–398
    and time, 399
Steele, Claude, 214
stereotype, 375
stereotyping, 27–28
straw man fallacy, 152–153, 152f
stress
    and beliefs, 245
    cognitive appraisal, 244
    common sense S-R thinking
        about, 250f
    controllability, 245
    coping strategies. See coping
        strategies

defined, 231
distress, 242–243, 252
eustress, 242–243
and familiarity, 245
general adaptation syndrome (GAS),
    236–239
healthy human functioning,
    role in, 242
and high sensation seekers, 242
hypo-stress, 242
imminence, 246
as interaction, 243–246
and interests, 244
low sensation seekers, 242
and personal wants, 244–245
perspectives on, 230–231
predictability, 246
as response, 236–239
self-diagnostic, 240–241
and stressors, 231–236
and values, 244
stress management. See coping strategies
stress processing report (SPR), 241,
    242–243, 245–246, 246f
stressors
    classification of, 231
    daily hassles, 236
    defined, 231
    as explanation of stress, 230–231
    life-event stressors, 231
    occupational stressors, 231–233
    psychological stressors, 233–235
striving for perfection, 207
stroke deprivation, 339
strokes
    cold pricklies, 337
    defined, 335
    earned strokes, 336
    freebie strokes, 336
    listening, 336
    marasmus, 336
    need for, 336
    requested strokes, 336
    self-stroking, 339
    stroke deprivation, 339
    warm fuzzies, 337
sublimation, 144
subordinate factors, 454
substitution, 384
suicide, 181, 290
superego, 125
supervisory ability, 451
survival, need for, 194
survivors, 339
sweet lemon rationalization, 130
Swiftdeer, Harley, 289
symptoms of inner peace, 437

T
Tannen, Deborah, 367–368
Tannenbaum, Robert, 454
taped events, 323
task directing, 456
TBWA—Total Behaviour and Wants
    Analysis, 200–203
team achievement outlook, 220
team capabilities, 220–221
Tebbs, Donald, 241n
technology, etiquette and, 107–108, 109
Teddy Bears, 430–431
telling, 457
temperament
    Apollonian temperament, 465,
        468–469

defined,   459
Dionysian temperament,   465–466
Epimethean temperament,
   465, 467
and leadership,   459–469
Myers-Briggs Type Indicator (MBTI)
   and,   465, 466*t*
Promethean temperament,   465,
   467–468
territoriality,   397
thanatos,   180–181
Thematic Apperception Test
   (TAT),   192
theory X,   452
theory Y,   452–453
thinkers
   communication tips,   62–64
   described,   61
thinking
   and fallacies. *See* logical fallacies
   unsound conclusions,   149
thinking styles
   defined,   251
   and distress,   252
   domains of thought,   253*t*
   self-diagnostic,   255–256
   stress processing report (SPR),
      252–253
three dimensions of life,   291
three-factor theory,   454
time communication (chronemics),
   398–399
total behaviour,   198–199
touch communication (haptics),
   399–401, 401*f*, 402*f*
traditional autocratic approach,   452
traditionalist,   463, 467
trait leadership theory,   450–451
transactional analysis
   defined,   317
   ego states,   318–326
   game playing. *See* games
   life positions,   337–340

strokes,   335–337
types of transactions,   330–334
transactions
   complementary transactions,
      331–332, 331*f*, 332*f*
   crossed transactions,   333,
      333*f*, 334*f*
   defined,   330
   types of,   330–334
   ulterior transactions,   334, 335*f*
transformational leadership,   219
transformational/spiritual
   psychology,   272
transpersonal psychology,   271
   see also archetypal psychology
Trevelyan, Sir George,   86
troubleshooter,   463
Trudeau, Pierre Elliot,   446
Trudeau salute,   393
trustworthiness,   209
truthfulness,   103
turning against the self,   137
Turtles,   430
turtles,   242
two-wrongs fallacy,   154–155, 155*f*
type, also
   see personality types
Type 1 complementary
   transactions,   331*f*
Type 1 crossed transactions,   333*f*
Type 2 crossed transactions,   333*f*
Type 2 unequal complementary
   transactions,   332*f*
Type A personalities,   233–234
Type B personalities,   233–234

U
ulterior motives,   334
ulterior transactions,   334, 335*f*
unconscious,   125, 126*f*
unconscious defensiveness,   124–125
unconscious influences,   122

unconscious motivations,   176
The Unheard Cry for Meaning
   (Frankl),   290
University of Michigan leadership
   studies,   455
unknown self,   7
unrealistic goals,   207
unsound conclusions,   149

V
value questions,   157
values,   244
victim,   347
virtues,   96–106
visionary,   464

W
Wagele, Elizabeth,   273
warm fuzzies,   337
warm impressions,   18–19
WDEP method,   262
Weaver, Richard,   368
weight,   390–392
"Why Don't You"-"Yes, But" (YDYB),
   342–343, 344*f*
William Glasser Institute,   194
win-win conflict resolution,   433
withdrawal,   247–248, 430
women
   see also gender communications
   moral voice,   363–364
   private speaking,   367
   rapport talk,   367–368
work,   295–296
Working with Emotional Intelligence
   (Goleman),   216

Y
York University,   100–101
*You Just Don't Understand: Women and
   Men in Conversation* (Tannen),   367

Photo Credits